T0227491

Green IT Strategies and Applications

Using Environmental Intelligence

Advanced and Emerging Communications Technologies Series
Series Editor-in-Chief: Saba Zamir

Green IT Strategies and Applications

Using Environmental Intelligence

Bhuvan Unhelkar

CRC Press
Taylor & Francis Group
Boca Raton London New York

CRC Press is an imprint of the
Taylor & Francis Group, an **informa** business
AN AUERBACH BOOK

CRC Press
Taylor & Francis Group
6000 Broken Sound Parkway NW, Suite 300
Boca Raton, FL 33487-2742

© 2011 by Taylor & Francis Group, LLC
CRC Press is an imprint of Taylor & Francis Group, an Informa business

No claim to original U.S. Government works

ISBN 13: 978-1-4398-3780-1 (hbk)

This book contains information obtained from authentic and highly regarded sources. Reasonable efforts have been made to publish reliable data and information, but the author and publisher cannot assume responsibility for the validity of all materials or the consequences of their use. The authors and publishers have attempted to trace the copyright holders of all material reproduced in this publication and apologize to copyright holders if permission to publish in this form has not been obtained. If any copyright material has not been acknowledged please write and let us know so we may rectify in any future reprint.

Except as permitted under U.S. Copyright Law, no part of this book may be reprinted, reproduced, transmitted, or utilized in any form by any electronic, mechanical, or other means, now known or hereafter invented, including photocopying, microfilming, and recording, or in any information storage or retrieval system, without written permission from the publishers.

For permission to photocopy or use material electronically from this work, please access www.copyright.com (http://www.copyright.com/) or contact the Copyright Clearance Center, Inc. (CCC), 222 Rosewood Drive, Danvers, MA 01923, 978-750-8400. CCC is a not-for-profit organization that provides licenses and registration for a variety of users. For organizations that have been granted a photocopy license by the CCC, a separate system of payment has been arranged.

Trademark Notice: Product or corporate names may be trademarks or registered trademarks, and are used only for identification and explanation without intent to infringe.

Library of Congress Cataloging-in-Publication Data

Unhelkar, Bhuvan.
    Green IT strategies and applications : using environmental intelligence / Bhuvan Unhelkar.
       p. cm. -- (Advanced and emerging communications technologies series)
    Includes bibliographical references and index.
    ISBN 978-1-4398-3780-1 (hardcover : alk. paper)
    1. Data processing service centers--Environmental aspects. 2. Data processing service centers--Energy conservation. 3. Social
    responsibility of business. 4. Information technology--Environmental aspects. 5. Green technology. I. Title.

TJ163.5.O35U49 2011
658'.050286--dc23   2011024143

Visit the Taylor & Francis Web site at
http://www.taylorandfrancis.com

and the CRC Press Web site at
http://www.crcpress.com

Prabhavati

Contents

Foreword

Green IT means many things to many people, but most definitions boil down to two key aspects: internal and external. The first of these refers to the lowering of the energy consumption and carbon footprint of the IT process itself, and the second refers to the use of IT to lower the energy consumption and carbon footprint of the whole organization. This book examines both.

Not so long ago, sustainability was a fringe issue. Environmentalism was the preserve of "greenies" or "techies." Now these issues are mainstream.

Green IT is a natural result of the world's increasing interest in all things sustainable. The term did not exist 5 years ago—now it is an essential part of any discussion about the role of IT in the modern world. IT is pervasive in business and society, and it is closely linked with sustainability.

Sustainability is, ultimately, about ensuring that we take out no more than what we put into a closed system—an organization, a society, or a planet. How do we ensure this? We need to measure inputs and outputs. How do we measure them? Invariably, it is IT systems that provide the metering capabilities. IT is also used as the data repository and as the reporting tool. IT systems are intrinsic to the measurement and management of sustainability on both a local scale and a global scale.

Internal Green IT is becoming an important issue for many reasons. Data center power bills are soaring as electricity prices go up, and increased processing power means hotter processors, which means more cooling. At the same time, tough economic circumstances are putting a greater focus on running costs, and power consumption as a component of these costs is becoming more visible. Environmental reporting requirements are becoming more stringent, and there is an increased awareness across business and society of the unsustainability of many current consumption patterns.

Rising electricity costs mean that more and more IT departments are including power costs in their operating budgets as metering capabilities and measurement techniques improve. Power consumption will become a very significant component of the cost of enterprise computing in the next few years. Even if organizations are unable to directly measure their IT power consumption, they are often aware that it is too high and should be lowered if possible.

There are many well-documented ways of reducing IT's power consumption, such as server and storage virtualization and consolidation, "Green PCs," thin clients, and so on. Internal Green IT is important. By various measures, IT is responsible for 2%–3% of the world's carbon emissions, which puts it on par with the airline industry. In some IT-intensive industries, such as banking, it can constitute well over half of all electricity consumed. Lowering or reducing the growth rate of IT's energy consumption is a worthwhile activity. Thus, reduction in IT's energy consumption would have a significant effect on the big picture.

The disciplines, technologies, and methodologies of internal Green IT are reasonably well known, but not so widely discussed is IT's enabling effect—its ability to reduce an organization's carbon footprint by facilitating more efficient and less carbon-intensive work practices—teleconferencing instead of flying or commuting, improved supply chain management, the use of IT systems to replace carbon-intensive applications, IT-enabled energy reduction systems, smart metering, and so on. That is what we might call external Green IT.

IT has always been an enabling technology. Computers by themselves are nothing more than pieces of metal and plastic, and software nothing more than magnetized dust on a hard disk. IT systems exist to help individuals and organizations perform better—they are a means to an end. Just as IT can bring greater efficiencies to business processes, automate direct marketing campaigns, or improve the manufacturing efficiencies, so can it help reduce an organization's carbon footprint—both within and outside the IT department.

Technology, and especially IT, is the key to a more sustainable future. From smart metering in the home to international carbon trading systems, it is IT-based systems that make it all work. IT-based systems are used to design renewable energy platforms and run waste management facilities.

This book addresses all these issues. Unhelkar takes a holistic and pragmatic view of sustainability and Green IT, examining every aspect of Green IT and the way it can be implemented. This reflects the passion for and knowledge of these issues by the author. Unhelkar is particularly good at mixing the theoretical with the practical: discussing the ideas and demonstrating their use. That is this book's great strength.

This book also discusses the corporate responsibilities of organizations in a market-driven economy. Increase in profits, reduction in costs, application of innovations in business, adherence to governance standards, regulatory metrics and measurements, process management, environmental intelligence, and the sociocultural aspects of a business are all neatly intertwined with Green IT issues. Green IT is not treated as a separate silo of technology; this book shows Green IT as an integral part of reducing the environmental impact of all business activities. It looks at the facilities, processes, and people that can all be brought together to reduce the overall impact of business activities on the environment.

The bottom line in being more sustainable is greater efficiency. It is no coincidence that this is also the bottom line in success in business. The two go hand-in-hand. And more often than not, it is the effective use of IT that is the key to success. That is what this book will help you do.

Graeme Philipson
Wollongong, Australia

Graeme Philipson is one of the world's leading Green IT consultants. His company Connection Research developed the Green IT Framework, a system for identifying the different components of Green IT, and the Green IT Readiness Index, a benchmarking methodology for quantifying the maturity of Green IT within an organization. He was the founding editor of *MIS Magazine* and is a former research director with consultancy Gartner.

Preface

Profits versus carbon, customer services versus carbon, competition versus carbon, regulations versus carbon. For too long, the carbon reduction debate has pitched good environmental outcomes against good business outcomes. Yet the reality, however, is that best business practice delivers both good business outcomes and environmental benefits. Many CEOs are either looking to show leadership or leading in carbon reduction because it is good for their businesses.

The carbon reduction debate is changing. In the context of the environment, the questions revolve around what the strategies, policies, and objectives of a business should be. What are the green drivers a business should anticipate, and what are the motivational levers? CEOs are asking what they should measure and how they should report their attempts at green transformations to get the best business outcomes. How will enterprise architecture change when a Carbon Emissions Management Software (CEMS) tool is implemented? What are the risks a business will encounter as green strategies are developed and implemented? What are the risks to a business from a lack of environmental consciousness within the business?

These are some of the practical questions answered in this book. While respecting the contrary views within the carbon reduction debate, this book focuses pragmatically on the activities and tasks, roles and deliverables, and metrics and measurements that enable an organization to sensibly reduce its carbon footprint because of the business benefits achieved through good environmental outcomes.

The scope for carbon reduction is large. Therefore, Green IT, as discussed in this book, is not restricted to IT alone. Instead, Green IT (technology, communications, information, policies, procedures, governance, risk, audit, compliance, strategy, service levels, performance management, and more) is discussed in an all-encompassing manner covering a wide range of issues in environmental sustainability. Such an approach utilizes the resources available to a business in a unified (holistic) approach toward the environment to form a resulting environmental intelligence (EI) and keep business goals closely meshed with the environmental goals. This intelligence imbues the organization with a green value system that is highly relevant to the future carbon economy.

The discussion in this book is an opportunity to tap into this intelligence. It is a journey of transformation, expansion, and application of the resident business intelligence in a way that will benefit both the business and the environment. This is an invaluable discussion to have in today's business world, which is fraught with risks, regulations, and customer preferences—all impacted by environmental considerations.

The application of business intelligence to enhance the environmental credentials of a business can be formalized into the concept of EI. EI can be understood as the use of the organization's systems, applications, contents, processes, architectures, and designs to transform the organization.

This book also examines the areas of *Business Transformation* and associated aspects of *Change Management* in the context of the environment.

The ideas expressed in this book are a judicious combination of research (as a PhD project over the past three years), the practical experiences of the author as a consultant and trainer in the area of Green IT, and the scholarly and business insights of select colleagues who see the future profitability and sustainability of businesses aligned with environmental outcomes. Thus, you will find a substantial literature review, many statistical survey results, and insights gained within this book. This is a highly pragmatic and *practical* book that is written to demonstrate the role of EI within a business, particularly environmentally responsible business strategies (ERBS).

The practical aspect of this book comes from the fact that it demonstrates how ERBS can be implemented in an organization through modifications, upgrades, redeployment, and optimizations of existing systems and processes, together with systems and processes that are new to Green IT. This book discusses environmental issues from multiple and varied angles. These angles include the technologies that create carbon emissions, the technologies that can be used in reducing the organization's carbon footprint, the impact of carbon emissions on business, the existing and upcoming compliance requirements by business, and the role that business and society can play in utilizing IT in a green way. The sociopolitical challenges of environmentally responsible business are also discussed, together with strategies to ameliorate them.

This book aims to incorporate business intelligence, as used by business systems, technologies, and people, into environmental intelligence. This book also provides the roadmap for green business transformation using existing business intelligence. Finally, it also provides views on the future direction of Green IT.

Readers

Many types of readers interested in environmental issues from a business perspective will find this book interesting:

(a) *Decision makers:* Strategic decision makers in the industry who are involved in the process of improving their business operations and services to become environmentally responsible. This book includes advice on measurements to back their decisions and for transformation within and from outside the business.

(b) *Technologists:* The technical leaders of the organization, including IT managers, development managers, data center directors, and network managers. Such technologists will find the discussions in this book, especially Chapters 3, 4, and 6, highly relevant. Of focus is the application of various strategies and techniques to optimize the use of hardware and upgrade the *processes, measurements,* and *reporting* on the organization's environmental performance.

(c) *Developers:* Those involved in design, development, and testing of Carbon Emissions Management Software (CEMS). Chapter 7 in this book has detailed UML-based requirements and an initial design for such a system that is directly relevant to developers.

(d) *Trainers and Teachers:* This book is organized in a way that is highly conducive to industrial training and higher degree courses. The discussion points, action points, and case studies are highly relevant in this regard. The discussion topics can also be used for interactive discussions within a classroom environment.

(e) *Academics:* The rapidly increasing body of researchers and academics who are exploring various ways of incorporating environmental strategies in business. The chapters in this book are based on literature reviews that provide the scholarly background for the discussions in technologies and business intelligence for the environment. The social, cultural, political, and legal aspects of environmental compliance will also be of interest to non-IT researchers. For academic teachers, each chapter is organized with an introduction, detailed discussion, relevant summaries, and discussion topics.

Mapping to a Workshop

The book has material that can be divided into a two-day training course or workshop that can be delivered in public or as an in-house customized training, as shown in the following table.

Day	Session	Presentation and Discussion Workshop Topic	Relevant Chapters	Comments
		Mapping of the Chapters in This Book to a Two-Day Workshop		
1	8:30 a.m.–10:00 a.m.	Green IT strategies and policies	1, 2, 3	Covers drivers and dimensions of change; approach to policies, their deployment, and green metrics
	10:30 a.m.–12:00 a.m.	Green IT and data centers; devices; Green enterprise architecture	4, 6	Virtualization; smart meters; optimization; interfaces between existing systems (CRM, ERP) and new carbon systems
	1:30 p.m.–3:00 p.m	Green business process management	5	Process reengineering as applicable to Green IT
	3:30 p.m.–5:00 p.m.	A case study	12–14 (any one)	
2	8:30 a.m.–10:00 a.m.	Green enterprise transformation	9	In-depth business transformation process framework for Green IT
	10:30 a.m.–12:00 a.m.	Carbon Emissions Management Software (CEMS) design; Green HR	7, 8	UML-based models of a CEMS; rewards/motivation and structure of Green HR
	1:30 p.m.–3:00 p.m.	Green IT audits, laws, and standards	10	ISO 14001 and related standards. Audits
	3:30 p.m.–5:00 p.m.	Second case study	12–14 (any one)	

When used in an academic course, this book forms a 13-week teaching exercise for graduate-level study, with each chapter corresponding to a lecture topic, supported by practical group work based on the case studies.

Contents and Chapter Summaries

This book has 14 chapters. This first part of the book is made up of 11 chapters that discuss Green IT within a business a context, whereas the second part provides 3 supporting case studies. Each chapter in the first part is laid out in the following form: title, keypoints, main body of the chapter, summary, and discussion topics. Each chapter is interspersed with sidebars and concludes with action points that provide step-by-step guidance on implementing the discussions. Each chapter also includes detailed referencing, a comprehensive index, meanings of acronyms, and keywords, figures, tables, and appendices that are invaluable for practitioners. The following table provides a brief overview of each chapter.

Chapter	Description
Part A—Strategies and Applications	
Chapter 1	Green IT Fundamentals: Business, IT, and the Environment
Chapter 2	Green IT Strategies: Drivers, Dimensions, and Goals
Chapter 3	Environmentally Responsible Business: Policies, Practices, and Metrics
Chapter 4	Green Assets: Buildings, Data Centers, Networks, and Devices
Chapter 5	Green Business Process Management: Modeling, Optimization, and Collaboration
Chapter 6	Green Enterprise Architecture, Environmental Intelligence, and Green Supply Chains
Chapter 7	Green Information Systems: Design and Development Models
Chapter 8	Sociocultural Aspects of Green IT
Chapter 9	Green Enterprise Transformation Roadmap
Chapter 10	Green Compliance: Protocols, Standards, and Audits
Chapter 11	Emergent Carbon Issues: Technologies and Future

Chapter	Description
Part B—Case Studies	
Chapter 12	Case Study in Applying Green IT Strategies and Applications to a Hospital
Chapter 13	Case Study in Applying Green IT Strategies to the Packaging Industry
Chapter 14	Case Study in Applying Green IT Strategies and Applications to the Telecom Sector

The following appendices provide supporting information.

Appendix	Description
Appendix A	The Environmentally Responsible Business Strategies (ERBS) Research Project Survey
Appendix B	Case Study Scenarios for Trial Runs
Appendix C	Green IT Measurements from a CEMS

Language

The author firmly believes in gender-neutral language. However, in order to maintain the simplicity of reading *she* and *he* have been used freely. Terms like *user* and *manager* represent roles and not people. We may play more than one role at a given time—such as *consultant, academic,* and *analyst.* As a result, the semantics behind the theory and examples may change depending on the role you are playing, and should be kept in mind as you read this book. "*We*" throughout the text primarily refers to the reader and the author—you and me. Occasionally, *we* refers to the general business or the ICT community, depending on the context.

Critiques

Critiques of this work are welcome. The author will be grateful to you for your comments, feedback, and criticisms, as they surely will add to the overall knowledge available on mobility and mobile transitions. A very big *thank you* to all readers and critics in advance.

Bhuvan Unhelkar

Acknowledgments

Warren Adkins

Akshai Aggrawal

Prasanta K. Banerjea

Adriana Beal

Siddharth Bhargav

Dave Curtis

Julian Day

Yogesh Deshpande

William Ehmcke

Abbass Ghanbary

Tushar Hazra

R. Kinjal

Anand Kuppuswami

Amit Lingarchani

Mohammed Maharmeh

Girish Mamdapur

Javed Matin

Vikas Mehrunkar

San Murugesan

Dale Nott

Christopher Payne

Graeme Philipson

Amit Pradhan

B. Ramesh

Norbert Raymond

Prashant Risbud

Zahra Saeed

Manan Shah

Nawaz Sharif

Keith Sherringham

Vivek Shrinivasan

Chitra Subramanium

Louis Taborda

Amit Tiwary

Bharti Trivedi*

Sanjay Vij

Mindy Wu

Houman Younessi

In addition to the names above, the author is also extremely grateful to the students, colleagues, and friends at the University of Western Sydney, University of Technology Sydney, DD University (Nadiad India), Gujarat University (SVIT India), and Gujarat Technological University (GTU) for their valuable inputs, research opportunities, comments and criticisms, and practical experiences. My heartfelt thanks to all these wonderful people spread across the globe.

*Bharti Trivedi needs special mention for undertaking a noted PhD that provided an important backdrop to this book. Her assiduous research, meticulous reporting, and also some editorial help—all balanced with her family responsibilities—have been invaluable in the completion of this work.

My special thanks also to Graeme Philipson and William Ehmcke for their support. They are contributing to the field of Green IT and enterprises, particularly in the area of the Green IT readiness index and the Green enterprise transformation frameworks. Their permission to use some of their material is highly appreciated.

Finally, thanks to my family, Sonki, Keshav, and Asha, and extended family, Chinar, Girish, and Amit. This book is dedicated to a beloved person who came into my family before me and left quickly and softly, hardly making any footprints. Perhaps she loved the Earth too much to toddle (let alone tread) over it!

Endorsements (In Praise of *Green IT Strategies and Applications*)

The foremost reason I would buy this book is because it does not separate and thereby alienate business efficiency from carbon efficiency. That is an excellent approach to take toward carbon reduction in a market-driven economy.

Warren Adkins
Sydney, Australia

This book brings together the research on environmental sustainability with its practice in real life. The value of this book comes from this synergy of research and practice. The practical approaches in this book find support in the robustness associated with doctoral-level research.

Akshai Aggrawal
Vice Chancellor, Gujarat Technological University India;
and Associate Professor and Interim Director,
School of Computer Science
University of Windsor, Canada

Unhelkar has been on the panel of judges for the Consensus GreenTech Awards since their inception two years ago. He has also been a judge of the Consensus Software Awards for nine years. His passion for Green IT and environmental sustainability is well known—and is reflected in the pages of this book. This is a must-have book for anyone associated with efforts at reducing carbon emissions and understanding the key issues affecting the future of our planet.

Julian Day
MACS MAICD, Founder and CEO,
Consensus Group; Past Chair
QESP (Quantitative Enterprise Software Performance) Australia

The new economy is the green economy where cost and carbon savings are unified. My own experience in leading and promoting the development of an enterprise-class energy consumption monitoring and environmental impact analysis platform has convinced me that management of carbon footprint is an integral part of business—not an add on. Precisely the theme that comes out again and again through the chapters of this excellent book on Green IT strategies authored by Dr. Unhelkar.

Ramin Marzbani, AMSRS, FMA, EPTS
Director, Event Zero Pty Limited (Creators of Greentrac)

San Murugesan
Professor of Information Systems and IT Management
Multimedia University, Malaysia

For too long, the carbon emissions debate has pitched good environmental outcomes against good business outcomes when, in reality, the two are synonymous. It is refreshing to see a business-focused pragmatic and practical approach to delivering business outcomes through good environmental practice.

Keith Sherringham
Independent business consultant
Author of *Cookbook for Shareholder Value and Market Dominance*
Sydney, Australia

This book expresses very well the basic idea that carbon efficiency is not an isolated activity but, rather, implicit in running a lean and efficient business. The discussions on carbon efficiency of Green IT in this book span almost all the dimensions of an enterprise—strategies and policies, architecture and design, social [and] legal standards, and audits. A must read for any business embarking on the journey of Green enterprise transformation.

Aditya Ghose
Professor, Director of Decision Systems Lab
School of Computer Science and Software Engineering
University of Wollongong, Australia

Author

Dr. Bhuvan Unhelkar (BE, MDBA, MSc, PhD; FACS) has more than two decades of strategic as well as hands-on professional experience in the information and communication technologies (ICT) industry. As a founder of *MethodScience.com*, he has notable practical consulting and training expertise in business analysis (use cases, BPMN), software engineering (object modeling, Agile processes and quality), Green IT (environment), enterprise architecture (including SOA), project management, collaborative web services, and mobile business. His domain experience includes banking, financial, insurance, government, as well as telecommunication organizations, wherein he has created industry-specific process maps, quality strategies, and business transformation approaches. For the past few years, Dr. Unhelkar has been actively involved in researching Green IT and the environment—and its application in practice. He has supervised a PhD in the area of Environmentally Responsible Business Strategies (by B. Trivedi) and also set up and delivered a two-day training course approved by the Australian Computer Society titled "Green IT Design and Implementation" (delivered around Australia through Connection Research/Envirability). He is a winner of the Consensus IT professional award and the IT writer award under the "best author" category.

Apart from authoring this book, Dr. Unhelkar has published/presented the following in relation to Green IT:

Trivedi, B., and Unhelkar, B. (2009), Extending and Applying Web2.0 and beyond for environmental Intelligence, *Handbook in Research on Web 2.0, 3.0 and x.0: Technologies, Business and Social Applications* (Edited by San Murugesan), Published by Information Science Reference, USA, chapter no 43.

Trivedi, B., and Unhelkar, B. (2009), Semantic Integration of Environmental Web Services in an Organization, Selected in ICECS 2009 Conference held at Dubai 28th to 30th Dec 2009, to be published in *IEEE Computer Society Journal.*

Unhelkar, B., editor, the *Handbook of Research in Green ICT: Technological, Methodological and Social Perspectives,* IGI Global, Hershey, PA, USA. Edited. In press (close to 50 chapters contributed globally).

Unhelkar, B., Cutter Benchmark Review (CBR) (2009), Creating and Applying Green IT Metrics and Measurement in Practice, *Green IT Metrics and Measurement: The Complex Side of Environmental Responsibility,* 9(10): 10–17.

Unhelkar, B., and Trivedi, B. (2009) "Managing Environmental Compliance: A Techno-Business Perspective," *SCIT (Symbiosis Centre for Information Technology) Journal,* ISSN 0974–5076, Sep, 2009, paper ID: JSCIT09_015.

Unhelkar, B., and Trivedi, B. (2009) "Merging Web Services with 3G IP Multimedia systems for providing Solutions in Managing Environmental Compliance by Businesses," *Proceedings of the Third International Conference on Internet Technologies and Applications (Internet Technologies and Applications,* ITA 09), 8–11 Sep, 2009, Wrexham, North Wales, UK.

Unhelkar, B. and Trivedi, B. (2009), "Role of mobile technologies in an Environmentally Responsible Business Strategy," in *Handbook of Research in Mobile Business: Technical, Methodological and Social Perspectives,* 2nd Edition (Edited by B. Unhelkar), IGI Global Publication, Hershey, PA, USA.

Unhelkar, B., and Dickens, A. (2008), Lessons in implementing "Green" Business Strategies with ICT, *Cutter IT Journal,* Vol. 21, No. 2, February 2008, Cutter Consortium, USA.

Unhelkar, B., and Philipson, G. (2009), "Development and Application of a Green IT Maturity Index," ACOSM2009—The Australian Conference on Software Measurement (ACOSM), Nov. 2009.

Dr. Unhelkar earned his doctorate in the area of "object orientation" from the University of Technology, Sydney, in 1997. Subsequently, he designed and delivered course units such as Global Information Systems, Object Oriented Analysis and Design, Business Process Reengineering, and IT Project Management in the industry as well as across universities in Australia, China, and India. He led the Mobile Internet Research and Applications Group (MIRAG) at the University of Western Sydney, where he is also an adjunct associate professor. He has authored/edited 16 books in the areas of collaborative business, globalization, mobile business, software quality, business analysis, business processes and the UML and has extensively presented and published papers and case studies.

Apart from Green IT, many other industrial courses developed by Dr. Unhelkar have now been delivered to business executives and IT professionals globally (in Australia, USA, Canada, UK, China, India, Sri Lanka, New Zealand, and Singapore). Training courses delivered through MethodScience are consistently ranked highly by the participants.

Dr. Unhelkar is a sought-after orator, a fellow of the Australian Computer Society (elected to this prestigious membership grade in 2002 for his distinguished contribution to the field of information and communications technology), a life member of Computer Society of India, Rotarian at St. Ives (Paul Harris Fellow), Discovery volunteer at NSW parks and wildlife, and a previous TiE Mentor.

STRATEGIES AND APPLICATIONS

Chapter 1

Green IT Fundamentals: Business, IT, and the Environment

If you lose touch with nature you lose touch with humanity.

J. Krishnamurti's Journal, April 4, 1975

Key Points

- A strategy for Green IT forms part of and aligns to an overall business strategy.
- Astute business sees Green IT as organizational best practices that lowers costs, provides better customer service, and improves business operations.
- The practical discussions within this book on the alignment of business and environmental outcomes are underpinned by industrial research.

Introduction

An indisputably winning argument behind the implementation of Green IT* initiatives is based on business efficiency. This is the same reason why businesses strive to be lean, improve their quality, and reengineer their processes. Thus, while myriad reasons abound for why an organization should become green, the one reason that is beyond reproach is that "a green business is synonymous with an efficient business." When a reduction in carbon is allied with the economic drivers of a business, the search for justifying the costs to optimize business processes and virtualized

---

* The term IT implies information, technology, and communications domain. Occasionally, the term ICT is used—especially in emphasizing the communications aspect of IT.

data servers become relatively straightforward. A close synergy exists between a lean and a green business. In fact, in most cases, they are complimentary. This synergy between lean and green has immense potential to benefit both, the business and the environment. Add effectiveness to this compliment of lean and green and there begins a comprehensive journey toward environmental consciousness by business.

Green IT (also referred to as Green ICT or Green computing) has been defined or described by several sources including Murugesan (2008), Lamb (2009), Unhelkar (2010a and 2010c, 2011). Green IT definition appears in Wikipedia, 2010 as well. But it is the definition of Murugesan (2008) that is particularly comprehensive: "the study and practice of designing, manufacturing, using, and disposing of computers, servers, and associated subsystems (such as monitors, printers, storage devices, and networking and communications systems) efficiently and effectively with minimal or no impact on the environment." This definition can be interpreted as serving an organization's attempt to achieve economic viability and improve system performance and use, while abiding the social and ethical responsibilities. Lamb (2009) simplifies this definition: "Green IT is the study and practice of using computing resources efficiently." Thus, Green IT includes the dimensions of environmental sustainability, the economics of energy efficiency, and the total cost of ownership, which includes the cost of disposal and recycling.*

This opening chapter of this book on Green IT strategies and applications expands the aforementioned theme. Carbon efficiency has to be imbided in the overall efficiency and effectiveness of the organization. The equation of a market-driven economy is not eschewed in this philosophy but, rather, strengthened. Increasing the value and reducing the costs, the hallowed mantra of a lean organization, is investigated deeply only to discover that reduction in carbon, in so many ways, is closely aligned to reduction in costs. Seen from a better business perspective, carbon consciousness can be incorporated as an integral part of the mainstream business strategy, rather than as an "add on" to the core business. The time to explore, investigate, and experiment with the existing and future technologies and processes that can be used to dual advantage—business efficiency *and* carbon efficiency—has never been more appropriate.

The approach set in this chapter of alignment of business strategy and Green IT strategy permeates the chapters of this book. Subsequent chapters in this book delve into various areas of green business that includes management, processes, architecture, intelligence, and metrics—to name but a few. The basic philosophy adhered to throughout these discussions is that business goals need not be eschewed for the sake of carbon efficiency. The crucial connection between the business and carbon domain is expounded here through the dimensions of technologies, processes, people, and economy. Long-lasting environmental strategies are not treated in isolation from the corresponding business considerations. Through the discussions of strategies, policies, practices, and metrics, these discussions strive for an enduring impact of carbon considerations on the individual, organization, industry sectors, and even governments. This is so because starting right with an individual's attitude and working life style, Green IT is shown to affect the way the business is organized, its underlying infrastructure, and the formulations of its regulatory policies. Government rules and regulations, carbon offsets and carbon trading underpin both legal and economic requirements, which, in turn, are shaping the businesses of now and the future.

The market-driven philosophy of businesses, thus far, has worked *against* the environment. This is obvious because the free market economies started with the basic premise of profit,

---

* For more definitions of Green IT see: Cameron (2009), Chen and Boudreau (2008), Dedrick (2009), Fuchs (2008), Murugesan (2007, 2008), Poniatowski (2010), and Velte, Velte, and Elsenpeter (2008).

which, perhaps, got translated into profit *at any cost*. Besides that, reflecting different views, a strong consensus is currently missing and has led to formation of camps along political and economic lines. Therefore, those aspects of society and life that belonged to the "common good" suffered. The environment did not belong to a particular organization, a particular profit making entity. The sanctification of profits lead to dilution of attention to everything that was outside the organizational boundary—and the environment was indeed outside the organizational boundary. Major effort in the environment domain, in the last decade, has been to shake this erroneous yet unflinching belief that anything that happens outside of *my* organization is none of my concern. Not only is the environment with the seemingly unending pumping of emissions of great concern for corporate social responsibility, but studied closely, it also offers hitherto unknown opportunities. Creative ways of looking at the environmental challenge opens up opportunities to examine processes for collaboration, take stock of the inventory and infrastructure for optimization, and explore the possibilities of new business streams. Needless to say, multiple disciplines, skills, and imaginative capabilities need to synergize to explore this unknown. As Yousif (2009) in his keynote *Towards Green IT,* says, "serious collaboration between technologists, developers, researchers, consumers and politicians is needed to achieve green and sustainable ICT."

With a focus on the business and the environmental domain working *together*, the need to debate on *real* cause of climate change also starts fading. There is less pressure to ascertain the exact cause of climate change and more freedom to start merging sensible business strategies with the environmental strategies. Abstaining from the philosophical debate on the occurrence of climate change (not that such debate is not important; but my focus here is purely business-technology nexus and environmental value to business), frees up precious business time and energy to focus on environmentally responsible business strategies (ERBS) around a very practical viewpoint: *"an efficient business, by default, is also a environmentally-efficient business."*

Thus, what starts becoming prominent is the age-old quest of businesses to improve their efficiencies and effectiveness. An efficient business will, in most cases, emit less carbon in the environment. For example, an efficient data center will not only reduce the operational expenses of an organization's IT department, but will also be environmentally responsible. Another example would be that of an efficient airline management process. Checking-in passengers quickly and accurately, or sidestepping certain "bureaucratic" steps within ticketing, will invariably reduce the carbon generated by these processes. This can be the result of highly optimized data entry using mobile devices, obviating the need for any printing in the process or simply automated, digital authorization. Apart from the operational efficiencies that also eliminate the carbon wastage points, similar arguments also apply for the organization's long-term strategic assets and infrastructures including building and facilities, furniture and equipments, vehicular fleets, inventories, supply chains, human resources, and the overall administration of the business.

Standards, processes, governances, intelligences, business solutions, applications, data warehouses, and myriad of other technology and business elements are brought to bear on business efficiency. The ensuing discussions not only demonstrate the need to and the approach for such collaboration amongst these various business elements but also demonstrate the results from that effort through the use of metrics and measurement. Moving beyond the technology focus of Green IT, this book explores the many dimensions of business that lie beyond Green IT and that affect its carbon footprint in a substantial manner. The end result is a discussion of issues that affect the overall environmental performance of an organization to achieve a Green Enterprise that meets the needs of the various stakeholders.

The Environment Today

As mentioned earlier, whether human activity is the cause of change in the environment or not becomes a background conversation to improving business and achieving environmental outcomes in the process. It is this business-driven collaborative path that opens opportunity for corporate action.

While the cause for climate change can be investigated Pachauri, R.K. and Reisinger, that cause in itself need not be the deciding factor in undertaking Green IT initiatives. For example, if only the facts are considered (and not necessarily the philosophical discussion as to who is creating this climate change), then it is plain and obvious that the Earth as it stands (or revolves) now *will* run out of coal and oil. This also implies that the source for plastics and related chemicals will dry up; but the pollution and wastage generated from these plastics will remain with us. Thus, in a way, the closing scene of this play is known. What is required is astute business innovation to see that when the curtain falls the actors and the audience still have food, air, and water.

Figure 1.1 shows that the information technology (IT) affects business, which, in turn, influences the society and the overall environment in which the business exists.

For example, IT in business makes use of massive computing and networking technologies that require large and dedicated data centers. The location of these data centers and the people who work in them are all socially affected by this use of IT by business. Furthermore, as the social fabric gets disturbed, it in turn affects the overall environment in which the society exists. Finally, there is also a direct influence of IT on the society and environment—independent of its influence on business.

This direct influence of IT is seen in the massive proliferation of household gadgets, use of computers in schools and hospitals, the popularity of social networking, and the high level of communications technology (such as a GPS) in vehicles.

Despite this huge popularity of IT, it appears as if the corresponding environmental considerations of the impact of IT's usage have lagged behind substantially within business strategies. Events, such as the global financial crises (GFC, 2009) Shah, A. (2010), British Petroleum's oil leak in the Gulf of Mexico, and the Icelandic volcanic ash have further exacerbated this lack of

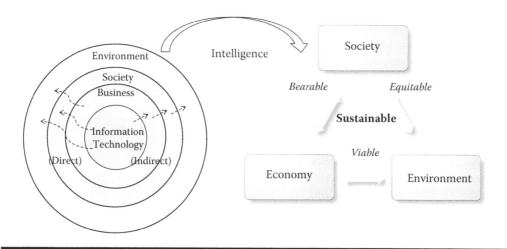

Figure 1.1 Information technology influences business, society, and environment—lead up to the sustainable triangle.

environmental considerations in business strategies. On the one hand, the CEO strapped for cash is asking about the environmental initiatives: "why?" or "what is in it for me?," and on the other hand, these global events are screaming for incorporation of environmental consideration as a part of normal enterprise risk management. For example, if carbon emission is considered holistically by business, then even the risks associated with the aforementioned disasters could have been ameliorated through forward planning, risk mitigation strategies, and effective governance.

The answer to the question of "why?" (should I undertake carbon reduction strategies if they are going to cost me in the short term) lies in observing how closely the risks associated with a business is tied to its carbon generation. Businesses that generate carbon and pollute the atmosphere are unlikely to be sustainable in the long run, whereas green businesses that use IT intelligently add substantially to their risk management repertoire and are most likely to be successful businesses both now and in the future.

This viewpoint is depicted on the right side in Figure 1.1, wherein the sustainable triangle of an organization is shown to be made up of a balance between society–economy (how much can the society bear?), economy–environment (is the environmental initiative viable?), and society–environment (is the environmental consideration equitable?). The quest for the answers to these questions forms the basis of *this* Green IT initiative—and its fundamental principle is to have the economic, social, and environmental factors in balance.

This holistic, balanced approach to the business *and* the environment is strongly repeated through the thought processes of various consulting practitioners and researching academics (Unhelkar, 2011). The varied viewpoints in that handbook range from the need to optimize supply chain processes, switching off computers when not in use, and designing low-carbon emitting microprocessor chips to creating long-term awareness about the environmental protocols and standards, incorporating carefully construed carbon metrics and measurements, and changing attitudes of users and employees through education and training.

A comprehensive Green IT strategy fully utilizes technology resources, reengineers processes, and uses the positive attitude of people in bringing about environmental consciousness in the daily activities of the business. The Green IT metrics and measurements support the justification of all the green enterprise transformation actions (Bell and Morse, 2008). Due consideration is also given in this holistic approach to the "soft" factors relating to people, their attitudes, and the sociocultural influence of Green IT. The transformation process also includes a model of the current objectives and strategy of the organization as well as a model of the future state of an organization from an environmental perspective. Eventually, the transformation process leads the organization to change systematically its state from where it is to the future state.

The strategy, policy, and practice relating to Green IT are concepts that change at varying levels within an organization. For example, the formation of the initial Green IT strategy will be a collaborative, dynamic effort that will stabilize and provide sound basis for formulation of Green IT policies. These policies, in turn, are practiced within the organization with various levels of intensity and attitude. Thus, the dynamicity of Green IT strategy, policy, and practice imply an ongoing learning and coordination of various faculties of the organization to come up with eco-innovations within and across the organization. Nidumolu, Prahalad, and Rangaswami (2009) have in fact equated sustainability with innovation stating that such eco-innovative approach will lay the groundwork for these organizations to stay ahead in the next economic upturn (at the end of this recession). This is the intelligence aspect of the environmental initiative. For example, a dynamic Green IT strategy would ensure that the tacit knowledge within the organization's people is connected with the explicit knowledge within the data warehouse to produce intelligence that is used in environmental management of the organization (Unhelkar and Tiwary, 2010). Hercheui (2011) has further outlined the role played by knowledge management tools in fostering Green ICT related change in organization.

This learning and its dissipation includes efficient ways of organizing production and consumption, improved design of products to reduce their carbon emissions, creative and optimized supply chains, optimized inventory processes, and excellence in customer service from an environmental perspective.

Thus, a specific green knowledge management domain emerges within the organization that supports the entire organization in its Green IT initiatives and, eventually, becomes an integral part of the organization.

As Jonathan Lash and Fred Wellington advise businesses in their *Harvard Business Review* article (2007), "Companies that manage and mitigate their exposure to climate-change risks, while seeking new opportunities for profit, will generate a competitive advantage over rivals in a carbon-constrained future." The effect of environmental issues on businesses is not just limited to "feeling good" or handling regulatory compliance; instead, this effect is reflected directly in the share prices of companies on the stock exchange. Similarly, when making purchasing, leasing, or outsourcing decisions, many customers have begun to take into consideration the company's current environmental records and initiatives, and their future plans (Ambec and Lanoie, 2008; Brown, 2008).

Developing a comprehensive approach to an environmental strategy is not limited to the formulation of the strategy and corresponding policies for Green IT. A roadmap and plan for formal transition from the current state of an enterprise to a green enterprise through a staged transition process is also required (such a roadmap and its enactment is detailed in Chapter 9). The green enterprise transition results in a long-term, sustainable business that is a "lean" business with energy efficiency and optimized processes. This transitioning to a green enterprise needs to be further validated and justified through supporting return on investment (ROI) metrics and related carbon measures (discussed in detail in Chapter 3). The results of these green measurements should be part of a company's annual report that makes it obligatory to report the carbon performance of the organization to its stakeholders and shareholders. The end result of such a unified approach is that the environmental strategy finds support across an organization, addressing technology, processes, architecture, and metrics. Thus, a carefully construed strategy for Green IT is a crucial enabler for an organization's overall transition toward an environmentally sustainable business.

The following are some of the specific ways in which a comprehensive Green IT strategy is beneficial to an organization:

- Incorporates environmental issues within the business strategies in way that is complimentary to each other.
- Demonstrates the importance of environmental issues as one of the "core" business issues rather than merely "good to have" add on.
- Explores the possibilities of enhanced green performance to discover and develop new business opportunities.
- Expands the technologies of Business Intelligence for the purpose of reducing the organization's carbon footprint—leading into what is called *Environmental Intelligence* (EI) (Unhelkar and Trivedi, 2009; Wrexham and Cutter, 2009; Unhelkar and Tiwary, 2010).
- Applies the concepts of carbon efficiency to business processes leading up to Green business process management (Green-BPM) and Green business process reengineering (GPR).

- Develops the idea of the carbon footprint of collaborative business processes (Unhelkar, Ghanbary, and Younessi, 2009) that cut across multiple organizations and approaches to improve that collective carbon footprint.
- Proposes a Green enterprise architecture (GEA) that builds on the technologies of Web Services/Service Oriented Architecture and Cloud computing.
- Discusses the importance of people, their attitude, and approaches to Green IT that would bring about a positive change without condemnation.
- Expands on the role on Green HR including the training and positioning of roles and responsibilities in the green space.
- Expands on the vital role of business leadership in bringing about positive green change across the organization.
- Presents the legal and political aspects the international protocols on greenhouse gases (GHGs).
- Argues for the use of ISO 14001 family of standard for the environment within the organization.
- Discusses metrics and measurements related to carbon data with an aim of understanding and mitigating the sources of carbon generation within and outside the organization.
- Incorporates the use of mobile technologies and smart metering for real-time measurements and use of carbon data.
- Discusses and advises on the use of Carbon Emissions Management Software (CEMS) in the context of carbon metrics, measurements, and reporting.
- Outlines the approach to Green IT audits for reporting and compliance.
- Explores the futuristic issues impacting environmental performance of an organization.

An environmentally responsible business strategy (ERBS) is a judicious combination of business and environmental goals of the organization. The synergy among business, technology, and environment can be achieved by viewing the organization holistically as an environmentally conscious organization. This is quite a different approach as compared with the piecemeal approach to Green IT, or the one that focuses on the "quick runs" that result in some immediate impact on reducing the carbon footprint of an organization, but does not provide long-term green value to the organization.

As is seen by the above list, a Green IT strategy offers a lot more value to the organization that goes beyond the confines of IT per se. The offerings of Green IT strategies and policies, together with an approach to implementing them in practice, are studied, modeled, explored, and reported under the umbrella of green business strategies. Thus, a green business strategy can also be called an ERBS (Unhelkar, ERBS, Cutter Report, 2010c).

Information Technology and Environment

As mentioned earlier, IT is an inseparable, integral part of modern business. In fact, IT is so closely intertwined with business processes that it is difficult to imagine any modern core business process sans IT. In addition to being an integral support to business processes, IT particularly with communications technologies, is a creative cause for many new and wide-ranging business interactions. The maxim "Business *is* IT" is even more relevant in today's heavily analyzed, networked, and interconnected world of business. It is impossible to imagine a typical banking, insurance, and hospital or airline process without IT. The synergy between business and IT implies that growth in business also implies corresponding growth in IT. This, in turn, also implies greater IT-based carbon generation.

Jain (2011) mentions studies that show the effects of IT usage on the environment (Erdmann and Hilty, 2004; Plepys, 2002). These studies specifically indicate the various levels at which IT affects the environment. An initial level of impact is associated with production, use, and disposal of IT hardware that affects the environment directly. The subsequent level of impact is caused by the effect of IT on the changes in structure and behavior. Plepys (2002) describes a rebound effect that is the result of widely available and plentiful IT resources used in excessive quantities in lieu of other resources. This IT effect on carbon footprints can be seen in global trade transcending organizational and regional boundaries. For example, the decree by European Union (EU) is binding to all organizations operating within the Union to comply with their carbon benchmarks. This, in turn, implies that the service providers from other regions need to be carbon compliant in order to trade with organizations in the EU.

Verticals such as financials, travel, and hospitals are all affected fundamentally by IT and its emissions. While these industries are themselves not IT, still there is hardly any transaction in them that can be conducted without IT being an integral part of it. The process of getting a quote for an insurance cover, the process of buying an airline ticket, and the process of checking the availability of a doctor all have information and communications technology at their base. Each process requires an underlying database (or data warehouse), a means of communication (the Internet together with all its add-ons), user interfaces, data and transaction security, and the overall user experience considerations. Therefore, modeling, examining, and optimizing any of these processes requires due considerations of all IT elements. Changes to the technical systems and database aspects of these processes impact the business aspect of those processes. In fact, it is increasingly becoming difficult to segregate the IT aspect from the pure business aspect of these processes. Therefore, many a thinkers believe that the IT industry has a significant role to play in reducing GHG emissions (Tang, 2008). Philipson (2010) has recently published a whitepaper that categorically discusses the role of IT industry in the overall environmental performance of businesses. As argued in that report, the technology to bring about reduction in IT's carbon emissions is already there. "The other necessary ingredients are political will and appropriate economic initiatives—which can in many cases be facilitated by appropriate government policy."

To start with, this indicates that a reduction in overall carbon footprint of the organization can be effectuated by specifically tackling IT-based emissions. Reduction in IT-based emissions—such as the data center and the end-user monitors—will have an immediate and positive impact on the overall carbon footprint of the organization. More importantly though, as is envisaged by Unhelkar and Philipson (2009), Murugesan (2008), Unhelkar (2010a and 2010c), and others, IT in systems and processes can be positive enablers, across the entire organization—providing opportunities for improving the carbon footprint of both the IT and the non-IT aspects of an organization.

Thus, in discussions on business efficiency and effectiveness, IT considerations are integral and mandatory. It thus follows that these IT-led business interactions are directly correlated with the production of carbon and related GHGs. The greater the interactions between IT and business, the more are the amount of carbon pumped in the environment. Therefore, it follows that investigation and amelioration of IT related processes leading to GHGs will lead to reduction in the overall carbon footprint. Similarly, improving the efficiencies of business interactions supported by IT will also reduce the carbon content emanating from the business.

Figure 1.2 attempts to depict this ongoing interplay between the business and the environment.

The IT sheath that encompasses the business is shown on the left in Figure 1.2. Any business activity that involves IT—and most does—impacts the environment. The carbon impact is shown by an arrow from left to right. This impact of business activities through IT on the environment has to be understood in three ways: from the length of time, the depth of activity, and the breadth

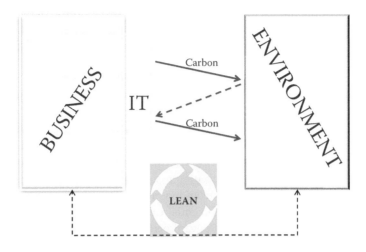

Figure 1.2 Interplay of business and environment through information technology.

of coverage of the carbon effect. The greater the intensity of business activities, the higher is the carbon generation. The awareness of environmental issues, in turn, influence the way in which IT is structured and operated (as is attempted here). This effect, in turn, would lead to an improved IT sheath that would be optimized and efficient. The *lean* approach to business is thus easily applicable to the Green IT strategies; as a lean business would also have a corresponding lean IT—opening up the idea that *lean is green.*

Developing an understanding of the intertwining of business and IT, together with the concepts of lean business in the background, helps in ascertaining the areas of business that are particularly carbon intensive. Consider, for example, a simple web-enabled process for paying insurance premiums. The manual process of payment was by posting a cheque (check), whereas payment can now be performed using BPAY or credit card either online or on the phone. This electronic process will generate carbon that is direct result of use of IT in the process. The more this insurance business grows and expands across regions, the greater will be the number of transactions and, in turn, the intensity and breadth of coverage of IT in their processing. Greater the BPAY transactions, more will the use of IT systems and their associated hardware, software, networks, and communications. While IT provides the necessary fuel for conducting and expanding the existing and new business processes, it also forms the basis for increasing carbon emissions. Growth and expansion of a business, such as the aforementioned insurance business, will require further investments in IT. The environmental angle to those IT investments now starts coming into play. The databases, the business rules, the user interfaces, the security and privacy, and the overall customer experience envisaged by the business has to now consider the carbon costs. While costs themselves were earlier justified if they provided enhanced customer experience, they can now no longer be justified as independent of their carbon contents. In fact, an erudite customer base may not accept a good customer experience if it is highly carbon intense. The attempt of an organization to apply lean principles gets translated and applied here to become lean-green principles. The process elements that support lean ensure that this is not achieved at the cost of the green credentials.

Following are the specific areas of IT systems, processes, architecture, and people that impact the carbon footprint of an organization. These respective IT areas have a dual influence: the increase in business activities through these packages increases the carbon footprint of the organization, but the optimization of the business processes and backend IT servers and networks has the potential to reduce the carbon footprint of the organization. These IT areas are discussed as follows:

- Software Applications and Packages: These are the existing ERP/CRM/SCM applications within the organization that need to undergo a major revamp to incorporate green factors. These applications will be modified to enable incorporation of real-time carbon data from within and without the organization. These data, measured through various means such as smart meters, are inputted directly by users or updated through interfaces from other systems (such as power usage calculating systems). Carbon usage data are then fed into the *financial-type* calculators of the organization to ascertain the corresponding carbon calculations. This area of IT is discussed in detail in Chapter 4.
- Carbon Trading Applications: With potential carbon trading on the cards, these organizational applications will also be geared toward performing analytics on the real-time (mobile) data that will enable the organization to figure out trends in its own carbon performance as well as that of the market. Carbon reporting tools will play equally significant role in the carbon economy. This area is discussed in detail in Chapter 6 and also alluded to in Chapter 10.
- Green Enterprise Architectures: This is the ground-up building of new enterprise architectures that take a fresh look at the enterprise applications from a green perspective. This area of IT finds detailed discussion in Chapter 6.
- Green Infrastructures: This is an area of IT that deals with the buildings, data centers, vehicles, and other nonmovable and movable assets of the organization. The design, development, operations, and decommissioning of these IT and non-IT infrastructure assets of the organization needs to be investigated. For example, most data center buildings that are more than a quarter century old, are just buildings that house servers. These buildings present the challenges to the green aspirant organization of either increasingly improving their operational efficiencies or completely replacing them with purpose-built data centers. Efforts toward improving operational efficiencies include virtualization, aisle reorganization, and improved attitude through training and similar initiatives. Additional processes and provisioning of new services forces the data center directors to seek techniques and technologies to improve their data center performances. For example, organizations like HP, VMware, and IBM (e.g., blade servers) are offering hardware technologies that are a combination of improved performance and comparative carbon efficiency. This area of IT is explored in Chapter 4.
- Governance standards (such as ITIL and CoBIT) need to be revisited to ensure significant Green strategies are reflected in the use of these governance standards. The way in which the governance standards are implemented is also reflective of the organization's carbon initiative.
- People: Social networks as well as employee/worker socialization tools are IT products and services that have a corresponding green angle. The attitude of the end-users and the extent to which they are trained and educated in the efficient use of resources, and the feedback provided to them on their carbon usage is vital in the creation of a Green IT culture within and around the organization. This area of IT is discussed in Chapter 8 in detail.
- Dynamic Social Groups: the creation of social groups that reflect their usage and consumption patterns can lead to not only directed marketing and sales but also help the organization in its green credentials. Customers and employees, as well as suppliers and other stakeholders in the business come together in melee of dynamic groups whose common interest, trust, direction, and dissolution provide immense sociocultural significance to a Green enterprise. This area is also discussed in Chapter 8.

■ Wired and Wireless Communication: The way in which various communications technologies are exploding has connotations from Green IT. The Quad functionality of the Internet (Video, Audio, Data, and TV) will bring further fuzziness to the boundary between TV and the Internet. As Vince Kellen prognosticates (2010): "On the Internet, TV can be very easily viewed live or later, thus providing wider access to specific content. As high-definition technology advances and associated edge devices grow in number, high-definition streaming will explode." Thus, the way in which these wired and wireless networks are configured and deployed will impact the carbon footprint of the organization. Advances in networking technologies—such as self-correcting networks, cognitive networks with energy-conscious nodes that switch performance based on the load—will provide basis for reduction, as well as auto-calculation and reporting of carbon data associated with them.

■ Emerging Cloud Technologies. Computing is becoming increasingly decentralized and having a dedicated data center is no longer the privilege that it used to be. The nebulous Cloud, comprising myriad different technologies including networks, storages, and services, enable organizations to tap into the storage and computer power of the world. The resultant synergy has correlation with the carbon generation of the users of the cloud. A cloud essentially enables sharing of large-scale storage of data, corresponding computation, and analysis and reduces overall carbon. Chapters 6 and 10 elucidate why this emergent trend of Cloud computing has a positive potential to impact the environmental performance of a growing and expanding organization.

■ Green Peripherals: This is the area of printers, copiers, shredders, and similar office equipments that are associated with IT and that contribute to the overall carbon of the organization. While individually, a unitary item may not produce substantial visible emission, collectively, these peripherals have a substantial impact on the carbon footprint of a growing organization see ACS 2007.

■ Renewable Energies: These include alternate sources of clean and green energies such as solar, wind, and nuclear. These energies will be treated separately in terms of their costs, and in terms of calculating their carbon contributions. Therefore, they will impact a growing organization through its IT consumption substantially.

■ Development of Efficiency Solutions Based on IT Systems. These solutions would include measurement, monitoring, and reporting on energy performance. These solutions would further monitor and control resource usage and energy consumption.

■ Design, Development, and Use of Power Efficiency in IT and Non-IT Hardware: This would include not only power efficiency in electronic chip designs, but also expansion into green power grids and management of equipment through software and operating systems.

■ Adherence to Regulations and Standardization: Includes active participation in creation of new standards, agreements, and consortium-based protocols. These protocols and standards are discussed in Chapter 3 on policies and Chapter 10 on the ISO 14001 family of standards.

■ Recycling and Disposal of IT Hardware: This will impact the procurement as well as disposal aspect of IT that is associated with efficient design of equipment, as well as ethical disposal of the same when their use is consummated.

Information technology influencing the carbon emissions of business includes end-user devices (typically the large number of computers, laptops, and mobile devices), the large data servers residing in the data centers of the organization, the networks and communications equipments (such as switch gears, routers), and the buildings and related infrastructure (such as the data center building). These various elements of IT pose the risk to business through their emissions. A comprehensive metrics and measurement framework is required as an integral part of this IT-business relationship in the context of Green IT.

Table 1.1 summarizes the major IT areas that influence the environment through their incorporation in the business.

Table 1.1 Major IT Area Influencing Environment

IT Areas	Major Environmental Influence
End-user devices (desktops, laptops, mobiles)	Large numbers of these devices, together with their rapid obsolescence that depends on factors other than their usefulness. Aim to reduce the number of devices and the emission per devices.
Data center servers	Growth of business associated with greater transactions invariably requires greater number of servers. Together with their backups, security, and mirroring requirements, these servers substantially impact the carbon generation. Techniques of optimization and virtualization need to be incorporated in data server management.
Communications equipment (switches, networks)	These equipments, usually part of the data centers, increase in numbers and usage with growth in transactions. New networking technologies, self-healing networks, and use of mobile networks over wired ones can be part of the Green IT strategy here.
Infrastructure (buildings, towers)	Greater the number of servers and office machines, more is the office space required. This increase in physical facilities and infrastructures have their own carbon impact that contributes to the carbon footprint. Building architecture and design, policies and practices for its operation, and maximum use of space as well as location are of importance here.
Metrics and measurements	Inclusion of new KPIs for carbon-related performance in the measures.
Risk management	Includes risks associated with not controlling emissions. Also includes the risks that may come due to green enterprise transformation.

Business and Environment

As established earlier in this chapter, the business and the environment interact with each other primarily through IT. IT has served businesses well by enabling them to expand their capacities, providing them with global customer reach, and enhancing their customers' experience. IT has also enabled businesses to optimize their internal processes such as inventory management and HR management and cut their operational costs through process automation. The provisioning of IT resources, in particular, is not just limited to the databases or the application servers. Instead, IT is integrally embedded in business processes* making them cost efficient and/or enabling businesses to grow and expand. Care in the use of IT to ensure minimal carbon footprint is now becoming a priority for both business and IT. Global initiatives, such as the Copenhagen summit, on GHGs, focus more on the political and legal aspect of carbon emissions. The sensible and sensitive use of technologies within business is usually relegated to a second position—behind the sociopolitical issues associated with these challenges.

---

* See www.business-ecology.org

Technological advances, particularly in the information and communication domain, are seen in terms of the value they add to business. Consider, for example, recent developments in IT (e.g., high-end data servers, sophisticated desktop computers with their low-power using monitors and myriad varieties of laptops), telecommunications (e.g., broadband Internet, mobile devices, transmission towers, switch gears), and associated technologies (such as the ever improving gadgetry of the ubiquitous photocopiers and shredders). These technologies have been used by businesses but an argument can now be made for those businesses to pay attention to the use of these same technologies to reduce their overall contributions toward GHG emissions. Sir Nicholas Stern in his now well-known *Stern Report* (2007) correctly identified and underscored the correlation between the environment and the economic (financial) stability and prosperity of business organizations. This correlation has immense value as it paves the path for accepting "business sense" to embark on strategies and programs that will reduce GHG emissions—particularly those emanating from the use of IT.

The key to creating Green IT strategies for business is to treat the entire organization holistically. While the practical implementation of those strategies will mostly be based on different levels of sophistication within departments and user groups, still a unified strategy will enable the consolidation of organization wide effort. Therefore, the starting point for a green business is the organization itself. Indeed, during the execution of the green enterprise transformation program, the organization will be divided into many smaller, departmental level manageable chunks; the Green IT strategy itself cannot be for a single unit of the business. Instead, unified strategy will apply to the entire organization as an entity. This unified approach provides valuable checks and balances in the Green IT efforts of the organization. An individual, or a single department, can always attempt to become green by applying its own procedures and practices so long as the effects of these changes is not to increase in carbon and costs elsewhere. The significance of having an ERBS (whose creation is discussed in detail in Chapter 2) is that it moves the organization away from a one-off or ad hoc implementation of procedures and instead outlines a long-term approach to the greening of the enterprise that encompasses all its business dimensions. The increasing impact of legislation also implies that the directors and leaders of the organization would become responsible for the carbon emissions of the organization. This responsibility of the directors is akin to the responsibility of the directors for the financial performance, governance, and reporting of the company's financial data. Anticipating a Sarbanes-Oxley (discussed by Raisinghani and Unhelkar, 2007) type legislation that impacts carbon performance and reporting would not be out of place; a legislation that places personal responsibilities of the emissions on the directors.

Green Enterprise Characteristics

The discussion thus far stresses the various levels and ways in which IT affects the carbon footprint of an organization. At times, IT is the cause of carbon emissions—therefore, switching off computers when not in use produces immediate effect in terms of reducing those emissions. At other times, however, IT is a key enabler of many business processes; therefore, in those cases, IT has to be used in a creative way to bring about reduction in the overall business processes of the organization, such as supply chains and inventory management.

A Green enterprise encompasses various facets of IT as well as non-IT carbon reduction. Switching off monitors and recycling laptops focuses on an important yet small part of an organization. A holistically green enterprise can be achieved by reducing IT's emission, as well as creatively using IT to reduce the emissions of the rest of the organization. Eventually, the communication capabilities of IT—particularly web services—can lead to collaborative environmental intelligence, which goes beyond a single organization.

Figure 1.3 shows these various levels at which IT affect an enterprise. Envisioning the enterprise is a consolidated and green enterprise with different areas of IT directly responsible for emissions, and other areas that go beyond just the IT aspect of an organization's carbon footprint.

Figure 1.3 shows four encompassing layers of a comprehensive Green IT vision of an enterprise, as follows:

- *IT as a Producer:* This very first attempt by an organization at Green IT is to handle the emissions produced by the IT gadgets themselves. This, as shown in Figure 1.3, aims to reduce IT's own emissions that is based on the end-user computer emissions as well as those from the data centers housing the servers and communications equipments.
- *IT as an Enabler:* This area of IT includes its use to enable reduction of emissions across all areas of an enterprise. Thus, IT systems, supply chains, contents, and metrics together with specific CEMS play a role at this level of a green organization. IT governance also plays a role in controlling the procurement and the disposal of IT equipments.
- *Green Enterprise:* This is the level of an organization that is holistically applying environmental strategies to all aspects of its business—irrespective of IT. While IT remains a vital part of this initiative, a green enterprise also deals with infrastructure and buildings, people and attitude, legal and standards, and marketing and sales—areas that may not be directly IT but are supported by IT.
- *Green Collaboration:* Going beyond a single enterprise, this is a collaboration of green enterprises that may come together due to their belonging to a common vertical market, or providing collaborative services using web services on a global scale. These collaborative

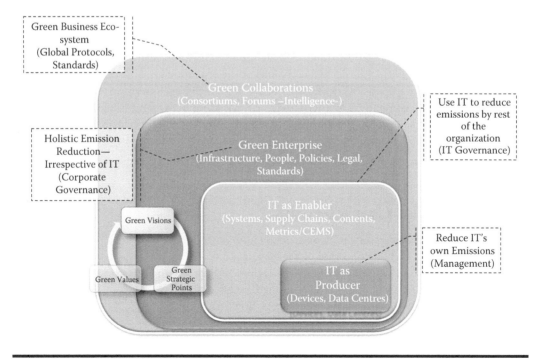

Figure 1.3 Envisioning green enterprises—beyond Green IT.

organizations are consortium-based approaches to green enterprises that aim to reduce carbon emissions across multiple organizations. While they are the most challenging and complex Green IT effort, they have a far more long-lasting effect than that of a single organization.

Green enterprises exhibit characteristics that show their awareness in terms of their carbon emissions that covers all dimensions and all departments of the enterprise. Furthermore, green enterprises also show clear business strategies and policies that are integrated with their carbon reduction effect. Astute and visionary corporate leadership and enhanced preparedness in risk management that identifies and deals with the strategic pressure points (such as those highlighted by Haas (2004) and Melnick (2005) and further developed by Hercheui (2011)) of the organization can also be seen in these green enterprises. The Green enterprise and the Green collaborations are the end result of effort that is long term and strategic. While the so-called low hanging fruits of small-time effort are not shunned, they are also not the main focus of this approach. Green enterprise characteristics are evident in their individual employees' attitude, in the end-user gadgets, in the way the data centers are organized, the changes to their supply chain systems and the use of CEMS for data collection and reporting. Green enterprises are not only managing and optimizing their emissions, but are showing preparedness for the eventual carbon trade that is likely to dominate the coming decade.

The approach to understanding the core characteristics of an organization and bringing about a change in it has been tried in areas such as globalization and process reengineering. For example, according to Bartlett and Ghoshal (1998); also discussed by Lan and Unhelkar (2005), enterprises are encouraged to review and improve their core organization characteristics that would enable them to succeed in their globalization effort. These approaches are also applicable to a green organizational effort. Moran and Riesenberger (1996) have expanded these elements into a number of core organization characteristics that can be called the vision, strategic points, and values. These core organization characteristics translate to green vision, green strategic points, and green values as summarized in Figure 1.3 and discussed in detail next in the context of a green organization.

Green Vision

Green vision is the development of a suitable global strategic vision for an enterprise. This vision, based on the arguments thus far in this chapter, has to be necessarily holistic. A sectional or fragmentary approach to the vision will not lead to a green organization which benefits from the carbon reduction effort in the long term. It is expected that the CEO, together with the board, will understand and analyze the trend of environment factors and review the positioning of the enterprise as well as the industry in the context of these trends.

Presentation and discussion with the employees and the incorporation of their viewpoints also needs to be incorporated in this green vision. This green vision can encompass the future of the organization in the carbon economy. Therefore, this vision can include not only what a carbon-efficient organization will be, but also new avenues of business in the new green markets. The green strategic vision will need acceptance and support across the organization.

Furthermore, customers and business partners who will be invariably affected by the future changes need to be taken in confidence in the development of a green vision. These external stakeholders can also provide valuable input to this vision, especially if they have themselves experienced change due to their own green enterprise transformation.

Green Strategic Points

The operational behavior of an organization cannot be plotted as a flat or a linear graph. Operationally, an organization's performance can be viewed like a seismograph that will show ups and downs at many different spatial-temporal points within the organization. These up and down points are the ones at which an organization feels stressed—in terms of its carbon performance as relating to this discussion. These are thus the strategic points of an organization that impact the structural and dynamic aspects of the organization. The organizational structures—especially in the global organizational context—have challenges, pressure points, and obstacles that are spread across the entire organization. For example, the human resource (HR) department has the challenge, in a large organization, to maintain hierarchies and levels of staff; but the continuously changing business processes subsume the effort of maintaining the hierarchies. These changes result in an unsettled workforce that may not have the right attitude or the desire to gain a positive attitude relating to carbon emissions. At other times, the dynamic, process aspect of an organization creates pressure by having wasteful processes with slack in them, requiring action by management. Temporally, the organization may do well at one time in one area of business but not so well at others.

Thus, the organizational structures and dynamics are continuously vying against each other, creating pressure points. If these pressure points can be identified, then those are also the precise points for action when it comes to green enterprises. The development of a green strategy, green policies and practices, and eventually a complete transformation, can all be based on these strategic points. Particularly in the context of this discussion on Green IT, these organizational pressure points can be understood as the green strategic points. Examples of green strategic points include the need for enterprise architectural stability versus the need to provide dynamic process models, or the need for manufacturing division to increase the throughput versus the need for HR division to enforce procedures. These green strategic points put pressure on the decision makers in the IT departments. Examples of decision making includes, say, consolidation of servers versus their virtualization, or as another example, reducing carbon versus undertaking major marketing that would require new servers dedicated to electronic marking.

The organization feels the pressure when forces pull the organization in different direction: static versus dynamic, structural versus process oriented, high throughput versus efficiency, and low costs versus low carbon. These challenges are business challenges, but in the context of Green IT, these challenges need to be seen afresh, keeping the carbon perspective in mind. Therefore, the techniques and procedures used by organizations to create and implement their business strategies can now be reapplied for the development of a green strategic plan. A green strategic plan is the core business plan of the organization but now produced with respect to the green pressure points of the organization.

Green Value

Green enterprises need work on the premise that the effort in transforming into a green enterprise has to create and maintain lasting value for the organization. The creation of green strategies and their implementation is eventually meant to produce this long-lasting green value for the organization. This value is a combination of tangible and intangible benefits to its employees, customers, and shareholders. As mentioned earlier, overbearing and visible motivation for businesses to undertake green initiatives is business efficiency and effectiveness. While this can be a wide-ranging area of work, the fact that the business derives value out of green initiatives is of immediate importance in this work. This importance of green value to business has to be measured through appropriate ROIs and promoted within an outside of the organization. Metrics for ROI on green investments are discussed in Chapter 3. It is, however, also worth mentioning that some aspects of the green value may not be directly measurable—and may produce returns to the organization that may be intangible.

Green IT Opportunity

The strategic approach to Green IT views the carbon challenge as actually a green opportunity. Environmental issues have a long-term and strategic impact on the overall business decision-making process on the organization (Garnaut, 2008; Stern, 2007). This also implies that the search for Green IT opportunities should also be at the strategic levels, rather than merely at the operational levels. Business opportunities that include sensitivity and response to market conditions, legislative needs, reengineering of business processes, a realignment of information exchange, integration of unified communication, and, above all, changing the business model to align with evolving business trends and market opportunities are the ones that will provide maximum green value to the business (based on Sherringham, 2011). This, of course, leads to the direct involvement of business decision makers in the Green IT initiatives of the organization.

Green IT is a challenge and an opportunity. The initial attempt by the industry at Green IT was through the so-called low hanging fruits (e.g., acquiring low-carbon emitting monitors and switching off computers in periods of inactivity). These actions still remain important but are by no means strategic. Strategic Green IT views the challenge of reducing carbon emission as an opportunity to optimize the business, make it lean, and capitalize on that effort through new markets, different sales approaches, and collaborating with partners.

Initial involvement of this business leadership in the Green IT initiative can encounter a fundamental challenge that emanates from a possible viewpoint of the leadership that carbon efficiency and cost efficiency are vying against each other. There is also a justifiable uncertainty around the future of the carbon economic, including carbon offsets and carbon trading. This Uncertainty was evident at the recently concluded Copenhagen summit, wherein even the global melee of "non-conclusions" was hailed as "one small step for mankind." Effective use of green metrics and the resultant ROI indeed take a small step, but in the right direction, to demonstrate that costs and carbon efficiency are indeed aligned along many dimensions of the business. However, effective green metrics are achieved only with increasing level of maturity of the organization and effective use of CEMS. This can take time and effort that, in themselves, require upfront justification. For example, the purchase of a CEMS or upgrading the data center of the organization will help it ascend the green maturity ladder, but these precise actions need investments that need upfront justification. In order to reduce the pressure on the strategic points of an organization with respect to its green challenges, it is recommended that the intersection between the business priorities and the environment priorities be studied right at the beginning of the initiative. The areas where the two overlap should clearly be the areas where the initial attempt at Green IT initiatives is focused. As shown in Figure 1.4, these intersecting area are where the primary opportunity for Green IT success lies.

This challenge is also akin to the classic CAPEX (Capital Expenditure) versus OPEX (Operational Expenditure) issue. Green IT's strategic approach requires CAPEX but in order to do so, this initiative has to start demonstrating savings from OPEX (Sherringham and Unhelkar, 2011). Strategically, once the organization moves into the overlapping areas shown in Figure 1.4, the challenges it faces from its Green IT initiatives start becoming more manageable as they are

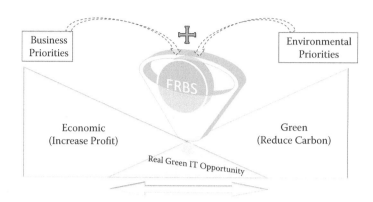

Figure 1.4 **The real Green IT opportunity exists where the environmental and business priorities are complimentary to each other.**

also better understood by the entire organization. These overlapping areas shift the focus of IT to being a utility infrastructure that is used and applied as an assembly line for knowledge workers (based on Sherringham, 2005). For businesses to significantly change their environmental footprint, all of the issues around incumbency (e.g., time, scale, integration, cost, expectation) need to be addressed, while supporting both existing and future requirements of IT and business.

The aforementioned overlapping areas of business and IT encompass many significant activities of an organization. For example, an environmental initiative by a business can include reduction in use of paper and electricity, improved use of buildings and facilities, revised data center management, efficient end-user computing, supply chain optimization, up-skilling and training of people (including dealing with their attitude, concerns, and reporting structures), dealing positively with trade unions, complying with legislations and other regulatory elements, and handling public opinion. In almost all of these areas of activities of a business there is an element of IT that is integrally embedded. The areas where IT and the rest of the business intersect are the areas that offer maximum opportunity for initial success in a Green IT initiative by business. Thus, the intersection between the economic and the green priorities in Figure 1.4 is the area of strategic points for Green IT transformation.

This viewpoint as a basis for creation of an ERBS can also be justified by interpreting an audit by the Australian Computer Society (2007) on the amount of carbon dioxide generated by Australian businesses in their use of IT. This survey indicated that IT as an industry is responsible for 1.52% of the total carbon dioxide emissions, as compared with road transport—12.6%, metal production—2.3%, and the cement industry—1%. These figures indicated that it is the combination of IT and the non-IT aspects of a business that is together responsible for creating the carbon footprint. These figures and the discussion in the aforementioned report also underscore the need to handle environmental issues by creating an organization-specific environmental strategy rather than an IT focused one. While the emissions that can be attributed directly to the IT gadgetry such as the monitors, laptops, and data servers can be reduced by switching them off, the true value of a Green IT strategy will emerge only when IT is considered as a Green IT enabler across the entire organization.

Such a strategic and long-term approach focuses on the architecture, processes, people, and technologies to bring about substantial reduction in carbon emissions over a number of years.

A comprehensive ERBS would judiciously exploit the entire IT domain including its use of software applications and systems, modeling and modification to its business processes and changing the attitude and working style of its people. Experiences of implementing such an initiative within a large IT organization have been discussed in the past (Unhelkar and Dickens, 2008).

In addition to these discussions, one of the easiest and vital approaches to understanding and ameliorating the negative effects of IT usage by business on the environment has been discussed by Murugesan (2007). There are also efforts to outline the approach to Green IT strategy creation as published in an Australian Computer Society report. A summary of all these approaches can be listed as follows:

■ Engagement of key stakeholders is considered as a vital first step
■ Conducting Green IT audits to ascertain the current state of the organization
■ Setting of internal and external targets that describe the "to be" position of the organization
■ Developing and implementing Green IT strategies and ensuing policies in a holistic manner
■ Participation and encouragement of the organization's workforce in the Green IT initiative and indexing their own rewards and growth to the initiative
■ Use of a sophisticated metering and recording system for regular monitoring of carbon emissions
■ Publicizing and promoting the green initiatives—both internal and external to the organization through a range of channels
■ Maintenance of ethical standards in promotion of green achievements
■ Formation of consensus within the organization on the Green IT initiative
■ Creation of a comprehensive green enterprise transformation programmed optimization of IT resource usage based on positive changes in attitude and underlying shift in the use of technologies
■ Virtualization of servers and workstations to enable consolidation of hardware and its power usage
■ Introduction of ISO 14000 family of green enterprise standards within the organization
■ Focus on integrating networks and communications, including internet telephony that will consolidate power requirements within and outside the organization. Detailed consideration of renewable energy sources and making the choice of using energy precisely from those sources despite potential increase in energy costs

These aforementioned considerations can be seen to include green issues integrally in the business strategies. These considerations are based on an understanding that opportunities for Green IT and those for an organization's growth go hand-in-hand. These Green IT considerations and approaches end up providing the organization with opportunities for overall sustainability and growth. A similar holistic, unified approach to business transformation has also been discussed by Unhelkar (2010a and 2010c) in detail in terms of mobile technologies.

The greening of an enterprise can thus be considered almost as a benchmark of the wisdom of the enterprise. The wiser the enterprise, the greater are the chances that it will use its available resources in the most optimum way possible. IT can be put to great use in order to improve the capacity of the organization to produce goods or enhance services and in the process maximize the environmental value.

Thus, improving the production capacity and making it efficient not only reduces costs, but also has a positive impact on the environment. For example, using mobility to enhance the supply chain management system of a pharmaceutical company results not only in time and cost savings, but also benefits the environment. This is so because, the Mobile Supply Chain Management (M-SCM) with its mobile-enabled business processes reduces wastages, particularly in terms of packaging and distribution of information between stakeholders (discussed in detail in Chapter 5).

Similarly, a business dealing with distribution of goods and materials using a mobile Enterprise Resource Planning (M-ERP) solution finds that the ensuing optimum routing of transport facilities not only reduces costs and enhances customer value, but also provides a positive value to the environment by reducing unnecessary goods and people movement. These various environmental advantages need to be kept in mind in production, distribution, recycling, design, process, and service related activities of an organization when it incorporates mobile technologies in its business processes.

Challenges of a Carbon Economy

The environmental science *per se* is a field in which most knowledge depends on the efficient overlapping of what we know generically with what might be a specific carbon issue in an organization. In practice, the carbon reduction action taken within the context of certain department or process feeds back to the more generic sustainability knowledge. Knowledge management systems facilitate a continuous loop between the localized, subjective knowledge and the stored, explicit knowledge in the systems.

Thus far, the entire Green IT effort of an organization primarily emanates today from the inevitable obligatory nature of the upcoming carbon economy. This implies a mandatory need to produce and implement a comprehensive program for the greening of the enterprise. In addition, in handling the regulatory compliance requirements, a carefully crafted green enterprise program will view the challenge of carbon compliance as an opportunity for optimizing business processes and exploring business growth. Such well-crafted programs not only produce immediate results in reducing power consumption, but include the approach to handling challenges of sustainability of the supply chain, strategic planning around sustainability, and incorporating sustainability requirements throughout processes, applications, operations, and infrastructure of an enterprise.

The carbon economy revolves around rising energy prices, concerns about energy sustainability in the long run, and the ensuing pressure from society to reduce GHG emissions related to fossil fuels (Unhelkar and Dickens, 2008). Kahn has pointed out that the market mechanism fails to allocate resources efficiently when private costs are not equal to social costs or when private benefits are not equal to social benefits. This situation can be balanced by environmental legislations at the government level and environmental policies at the organizational level.

Carbon economies in the developing countries, however, are unlikely to respond to the carbon reduction challenge only through legislations or negotiations. In those economies, direct enforcement of regulation by polluters, an approach disdained by most economists, has been the most widely used method of pollution control (de Steiguer, 2006). The challenges of carbon protocols and agreements in the context of developing economies are outlined in Chapter 10.

A program for the greening of the enterprise is about business transformation and organizational change. Changing the mindset of people, bringing about changes in their practices, and demonstrating the value of the greening effort are all crucial ingredients of this change. Understanding what the green transition entails, its goals, and the transformation process itself (discussed in detail in Chapter 9) require leadership and support that needs to come from the top echelons of the organization. As Rosen et al. (2011) report, when enterprises, such as SAP, DuPont, Google, and Georgia-Pacific, create the position of Chief Sustainability Officer (CSO), they signal their commitment to implement sustainability throughout the business. The role of a

CSO (or, as discussed in Chapter 3, that of a Chief Green Office, CGO) signals and establishes a high-level commitment from an organization—as this role works closely with that of the CEO to foster holistic green movement external to and surrounding the organization. The CSO/CGO aspires for a strategic rather than tactical change—coming up with business strategies incorporating Green IT, setting up of sustainability policies and practices throughout the organization and fostering the formation of working groups to discuss the challenges, and bring about a consensus in adherence to standards and protocols relating to green initiatives of the organization. The CSO has the necessary authority, influence, and expertise to bring about organizational change.

Elements of this change require project and program management, HR, and marketing and communications. An interesting view expressed by Rosen et al. is that the enterprise architecture (EA) of an organization also provides an excellent mechanism for handling the challenges of sustainability (Ross, Weill, and Robertson, 2006, further developed by Rosen et al.). This is so because the skills, frameworks, and practices required for EA have been proven in other transformative initiatives and, therefore, lend themselves to a green enterprise transformation as well. An architectural approach provides a conceptual framework that divides the problem space into smaller, more manageable pieces. The EA provides an understanding of both the breadth and the depth of the enterprise. Thus, the use of EA in a Green IT initiative can be considered as a very good technical option that enables handling of the many architectural challenges and constraints that remain embedded in the overall challenges of green transformation.

Apart from the technical challenges, there are also social challenges associated with the green initiatives. The basic challenge in this social context is the acceptance of the green initiative across the entire organization. In practice, some sections of the user groups are convinced of the effort, others are skeptics, and then there are some who may actively work *against* the effort. The reasons for this variation in Green IT support could be that the terms Green IT and sustainability are themselves susceptible to varying interpretations. Added to that is the fact that the level of interest in sustainability by each individual varies depending on a combination of personal and professional goals of that stakeholder. For example, a business analyst in the customer service department has different concern of sustainability than that of a manager in the data center. The former wants fast, fail-safe retrieval of information to ensure the business's financial viability. Yet the latter wants to reduce redundant systems to decrease power consumption for both the financial viability and the environmental responsibility of the business. Both the analyst and the manager may be concerned about sustainability, but their views of what is necessary to sustain are different based on their own perspectives.

Thus, this challenge associated with the subjective nature of Green IT, which has to deal with both individual and collective attitude of the organization, requires significant effort in education and training, internal promotion of the initiative, and creating and sustaining an ongoing atmosphere of environmental responsibility. Inculcating and supporting environmental responsibility and sustainability into all the processes and practices of the organization and promoting them internally is a part of handling this challenge. Identifying and operating a suitable rewarding structure for effort toward the environment is another one.

The complex, subjective nature of Green IT requires further attention to the organizational context. While some generalization is acceptable, there is still usually a specific issue and a specific challenge that depends on the people, processes, and technologies within the departments of an organization where it is being applied. The contextual nature of Green IT and its metrics is discussed in greater detail in Chapter 3.

Thus, the individual sustainability requirements need to be considered in the context of other requirements of the business and the entire approach needs to be holistic. The infrastructure and operations of the business also need to be aligned with the overall green goals of the organization (this is discussed in greater detail in Chapter 2). Eventually, the entire context in which the green initiative is applied in an organization becomes a multidimensional green enterprise transformation program (see Chapter 9 for greater details).

An interesting challenge that traverses both technical and social dimensions is that of the terminologies within the environmental domain. For example, in this chapter itself, terms such as environmental responsibility, Green IT, sustainability, and green enterprise have been used. A separate section in this book attempts to describe and, in turn, clarify the meanings. However, being a nascent domain, the work in this environmental space is likely to be challenging in terms of these terms. Despite all the definitions, one may find that there are terms whose meaning is not clearly defined or well understood. For example, the term Green IT itself, as discussed in this chapter and this book, has different meanings and interpretations. The need for a common set of terms and definitions could not have been higher, requiring an international initiative from ISO and consortiums (Kamani, 2011).

Later, as discussed in Chapter 3, the carbon metrics and their measurements is also not very clear. Governments, scientific bodies, organizations, and individuals are all uncertain about how to measure carbon. Carbon calculations, in some approaches, require assumptions that create further uncertainty in arriving at the carbon footprint of an organization. This uncertainty impacts Green IT strategy and policy formation especially as the rules and regulations surrounding the green domain are vague and open to interpretation.

Environmental sustainability requires definition of parameters for measuring the carbon footprints. Maturity levels and benchmarks of best practices in environmental management are also required. Lack of such benchmarks and best practices create obstacles in bringing about green enterprise transitions. Convincing the users of the utility of their effort through robust measures is as important as convincing the CEO of an organization of the same effort.

Following is a list of challenges faced by organizations in their endeavor to be ready for the carbon economy:

- Contextual nature of the environmental sustainability initiative
- Subjective nature of Green IT that depends on the context and also on the personal motivation of the individual
- Lack of robust metrics and measurements associated with Green IT
- Lack of understanding of drivers for the environmental sustainability initiative
- Likely confusion due to number of motivators and drivers for a green initiative
- Lack of robust metrics and measurements across all dimensions of an organization
- Lack of availability of substantial "winning stories" and corresponding supporting metrics
- Uncertainty in terms of rules and regulations that can be applied and adhered to with confidence
- Uncertainty in terms of the scopes of the emissions to be included in the calculations (e.g., measurements of the scope 3 emissions; scopes are discussed in Chapter 3)
- Technologies such as virtualization, thin clients, and Cloud computing are implemented in organizations, but not for improving its environmental performance
- Lack of justification (ROI) for investing in the environmental sustainability solutions
- Nonrecognition of inefficient businesses processes and lack of corresponding business process management
- Uncertainty in terms of trying out new products and services that may be eco-friendly as they may disturb the existing processes

- Overall shortage of consulting and in-house skills in the area of EI
- Facilities like data centers cannot be replaced as quickly as the servers inside them due to high infrastructure costs—leading to a mismatch between the hardware and the facilities that house them
- Skepticism from various sections of an organization including, occasionally, some part of the leadership
- The uncoordinated emergence of macroeconomic levers (such as carbon taxes and carbon trading) that are also not uniform across regions
- Disagreements amongst nations—especially divided amongst the developed versus developing economies—to ratify and implement
- Stringent environmentally sustainable legislative and regulatory frameworks
- Lack of accountability on the part of staff for their own carbon emissions—perhaps due to lack of feedback metrics
- Smart/auto meters not sufficiently integrated with the CEMS
- Lack of choice in terms of strategies for cultural change
- Emerging information and communications technologies and corresponding innovations make early attempts at reducing redundant carbon emissions
- Lack of overall industry experience in business transformation programs that are specifically aimed at Green IT
- Highly complex supply chain systems that include collaboration amongst multiple organizations—making it extremely challenging to implement environmental initiatives across the entire supply chain
- Operational requirements usually taking precedence over strategic approach to the environment

Environmental Intelligence

The discussion thus far has been on the strategic, holistic approach to environmental sustainability that is based on making the best use of the IT resources available to the organization. Examples of this usage of IT resources include optimization at the end-user level, virtualization at the server level, and reengineering of processes. Procuring and installing a CEMS is also a part of this utilization of IT resources—but from a systems and applications viewpoint. An interesting part of this extension and use of IT resources comes from the extension and application of the concepts and technologies of business intelligence to the environmental initiative of the organization. This is discussed in detail next.

Intelligence, in fact, is an interesting concept. Attempts are being made on a regular basis to incorporate intelligence in computing (e.g., through Artificial Intelligence). Progressively complex use of data and information, creation of dynamic and varied business processes, and use of knowledge management systems are all attempts in this direction. For example, attempts are made to enable vast data warehouses to communicate through service-oriented technologies and expand to include analytics and correlations amongst otherwise unrelated information to produce actionable knowledge. Intelligence, in business, has been a summation of all these technologies and processes—and some more.

Business Intelligence

Business intelligence derives knowledge, or insights, by analyzing an organization's information. This information can be of many different types including carbon data, financial data, environmental parameters, human relations data, and organizational strategy data. These data and information about the organization can potentially reside in silos that may not easily interface with each other. The challenge for the organization is to correlate these varied pieces of information—and their subsequence analysis—in a way that provides opportunities for it to create actionable steps, including those that enable it to undertake a green enterprise transformation. For example, an operational support system in a telecommunication company will have a need to correlate its switch maintenance information to the billing support system. This correlation will help the organization understand and prioritize its switch upgrades based on the clusters of customers and their bill payment patterns. Similarly, an Electronic Patient Record (EPR) system needs to correlate with an accounting or HR system in a hospital to be able to glean valuable knowledge on planning and organizing patient services. The ability to correlate such information silos has potential application in the domain of environmental sustainability.

In the earlier examples, the telecom company can take action on continuing with the existing switch gears or upgrading them. Similarly, the EPR together with the HR system can help in scheduling the right staff for the patients on an almost real-time basis. These organizational processes have greater value when they are based on business intelligence as through the BI tools, information and knowledge is provided at a time and place where it is needed. For example, instead of providing a monthly or a daily report, BI provides that same information through interactive graphics on varied mobile devices to the decision makers. The data itself can be sourced from places beyond the organizational boundary.

Thus, increasingly, through the potential offered by BI tools, practitioners are considering BI as a suite of technologies that are well positioned to be used with regards to the environmental initiatives of the organization (Unhelkar and Tiwary, 2011). Such use of BI for the environment would combine people together with the aforementioned technologies and processes (Unhelkar and Tiwary, 2010). The systems and applications for BI include CRM packages, Supply Chain systems, Wikis and Blogs and Executive Dashboards. These technologies make use of Cloud computing, Software-as-a-Service (SaaS) and Web X.0. Needless to say, this intelligence garnered by the business also has immense potential to improve its environmental credentials. This is so because, BI brings together an organization's existing as well as new carbon data and provides insights that can be used in timely decision making. BI offers an excellent opportunity to make use of both these categories of data and information, as is explained next.

Application in Environmental Domain

The potential for use of BI in the environmental domain is on the rise. Extending and using BI to progress environmental goals of the organization will benefit both the environment and the business as well. This is so because combining BI with the environmental factors results in an approach that is not based on treating carbon reduction only as a cost to business. Instead, the EI approach brings together the tools and techniques of BI to achieve the dual purpose of business and environmental efficiency. EI garners all available resources at the disposal of the organization—both within and outside of the organizational boundary—and applies it to reduce the organization's carbon emissions without sacrificing its core business goals. EI also enables an organization to gain insights into its carbon performance as well as opportunities for carbon ameliorating behavior. This is a sensible, long-term approach to sustainability in business.

While the focus of BI is primarily on business efficiency, EI extends and applies BI for environmental efficiency. EI can thus be considered as a superset that encompasses BI. EI rests on the principle that if a business is honestly made lean and efficient, than in most cases it will be a carbon-efficient business. A business leadership that subscribes to such intelligence will imbue its people, processes, and technologies in organizations with a unique value system that easily correlates business efficiency to the environment. As a result, every decision associated with every work-package in the organization will be affected by carbon consciousness; this includes procurement of new technologies, up-skilling of staff, reengineering of processes and organization of resources (Sharif, 2010).

EI thus goes beyond only installing and using a new CEMS. Instead, service-oriented interfaces that enable the creation of a Green IT portal that uses internal and external information on the environment is the result of EI. EI requires an understanding of the current business processes; the way people use those processes, the current product/service portfolio, and the underlying technologies that support the business. Furthermore, the organization needs to gain or import substantial practical application in converting, expanding, and applying EI in a way that does not reduce the existing Key Performance Indicators (KPIs) of the organization.

For example, business processes can be improved and optimized to reduce their carbon contribution through collaboration with other business processes—both within and outside of the organization. Implementations of comprehensive software systems riding on the Internet communications can be updated and fine tuned to record and report on carbon emissions based on the assets and inventories data sourced from the ERP systems of the organization. Upgrading the skills of the people that would eventually reflect the changes in their attitude will require coordination and collaboration with the HR system as well as part of CEMS that record attitude and behavior surveys. Furthermore, Emerging technologies such as Cloud computing, Mobile technologies as well as the existing ERP and CRM systems in the organizations, are reined in, modified, and deployed within the organizations to help them discharge their environmental responsibilities. Thus, all significant aspects of business intelligence get extended and applied toward the environmental responsibility. Table 1.2 summarizes this BI to EI impact across the technical process, social and economic dimensions of an organization.

Figure 1.5 shows the creation of EI based on the existing systems and data warehouse of the organization. The CRM, ERP, and SCM systems will all undergo modifications and update as the organization moves toward EI. These modifications will primarily deal with making provision for calculation and storage of carbon data associated with the assets and processes of the organization. The addition of new carbon-related data as well as the quality of existing data will come under scrutiny in this process of moving toward EI.

BI tools, usually playing a major role in the accounting departments, tend to be focused on monitoring inventory, costs, down times, and customer service. These same tools, with appropriate modifications can now, within EI, also forecast carbon impacts, revenue growth or losses associated with carbon performance, and, eventually, get the organization ready for carbon trading in the future.

Technologies, sociocultural aspects, business processes, and economic calculations provide the four dimensions or areas along which environmental intelligence can be applied. These are the four areas of a business that are impacted when any change takes place. In the context of the environment, technologies create, and are used to reduce, emissions; attitude is changed through training and education; business processes require modeling, optimization, and governance; and the ROI metrics for a green transformation project provides the financial basis for initiating the change.

EI will encounter opportunities to provide carbon performance executive dashboards that can analyze data across multiple systems to present the carbon-picture of the organization. The CEMS will have its own database that will focus entirely on carbon data and associated analysis; however, this will be achieved by its interfaces with the other organizational systems such as CRM, ERP, and SCM—as shown in Figure 1.5.

Table 1.2 Business to Environmental Intelligence Impact across the Technical Process, Social and Economic Dimensions of an Organization

Organizational Dimensions	BI to EI Impact
Technologies	Use of Smart meters; implementation of CEMS; modification to existing software systems and packages to incorporate carbon data
Processes	Equipment and infrastructure lifecycle to change—now including carbon factors in all activities and tasks. Green business process management
People	Attitude change brought about by training and education. Indexing personal growth to carbon reduction. Green HR
Economic	Reimagination of financial growth through carbon. Incorporating carbon calculations in micro- and macroeconomic functioning of the organization

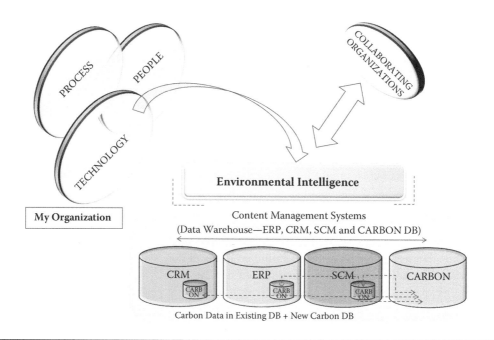

Figure 1.5 Environmental intelligence intersects people, process, and technologies, and creates new correlations in the organizational data warehouses.

EI would not only deal with the existing structured data relating to carbon and noncarbon headings, but will also explore the unstructured aspects of the organization: email exchanges amongst group of employees, collaborative information exchanges with external parties of the organization, analysis of meeting minutes, and corporate events to name a few. All these data can be correlated with each other through BI tools such as mashups, IMS, Web 2.0, Cloud computing, and mobile technologies, to analyze, forecast, collaborate, and figure out how the organization is performing now, and what can be intelligently undertaken in the future, to reduce its carbon footprint.

A sensible and carefully created environmental strategy will not only handle the immediate environmental impact but will also include carbon performance as a part of its risk management approach. The products, services, and infrastructure of the organization is investigated and optimized to create green value—not just reduce their carbon emission. The environmentally conscious practices of such an organization are not just restricted to its IT equipment and processes; instead, this becomes an all-encompassing adventure by the organization that also includes consideration for its use of natural resources such as water, air, and sunlight. The organization endeavors to reduce emissions across its entire value chain, including its suppliers, its operators, and eventually its disposal policies and practices.

Envisioning the Green Future

The future economy is the carbon economy. Bradfield-Moody and Nogrady (2010) have described this phenomena very well as the "sixth wave." Trust in a green future is a combination of skills, processes, leadership, technologies, and sound financial modeling for the future to keep the green credentials of the organization and its collaborating partners in mind. The futuristic technologies and business models associated with Green IT are discussed further in Chapter 11. Certainly, the generation that is studying in schools today will be different to the Gen-X or Gen-Y or any such generation; it will be most likely a Gen-G (for Green). These customers of the future are most likely to be a green consumer and will expect the organizations of the future to be prepared for green consumers.

The anticipated impact of emerging technologies is also not necessarily carbon negative. The design, development, production, and distribution of new generation of computer monitors, laptops, servers, and associated processes will all be impacted by the incessant pressure to produce carbon-efficient architectures, designs, and development. The businesses of the future will be ready to handle the influx of not just new carbon generation equipments but the high-end, well-designed, and low-power emitting equipment that will require a different approach in their usage.

Businesses preparing for carbon trading that, while in some ways being similar to the current stock exchange, will have additional variations due to assignment of different values to such trades. For example, the unit of carbon (as discussed later in Chapter 3) is likely to have its "exchange rate" with corresponding cash currencies, equities, and options.

The "temporal windows" within which the emissions of an organization, an industry, or a nation is measured and views is itself a very fluid concept. The future of green/carbon industry remains fuzzy because of this uncertainty of "how long back" one should go to ascertain the total cost of carbon production—by an organization, industry, or nation? Time will be a crucial factor, as a unit, in the mix of futuristic macro- and microeconomic levers that the governing bodies will use to regulate the future emissions of business organizations. The total free market economy where the only index is "cash" will have to give way to "cash-and-carbon."

Renewable energy sources are subjected to significant exploration. Organizations have to reimagine themselves in the light of new renewable energy sources. Chapter 11 explores the possibilities further.

Discussion Points

- What do we mean by Green IT?
- How does IT relate to business? What is the impact of this close relationship between IT and business on the environment?
- What would be a good, astute approach to environmental leadership?
- What are the major factors that contribute to carbon emissions in an organization?
- What role do people play in improving the Green IT performance?
- What are the local and global standards for green organizations?
- What are the major internal organizational considerations in an environmentally conscious approach (e.g., Employee buy-in management commitment)?
- What are the major external considerations in an environmental initiative (e.g., media, activities, consumer)?
- What are the likely repercussions of an EI approach to carbon reduction? Are there mechanisms to automatically record and use carbon-related data (such as interfaces to accounting systems that maintain records of the power bill)?
- Are there opportunities for executive dashboards on carbon performance (alongside) financial performance of the organization (using tools and techniques of Business Intelligence)?
- What are the opportunities to use mobile technologies and devices in the carbon mitigation strategies?
- Where do you see the maximum buy-in at the start of a carbon mitigation initiative—the directors in the boardroom, the middle management, and administrators or the operational staff on the ground?
- Where are the opportunities for real-time carbon data analysis and trend plotting within your IT systems?
- What is the impact of the Global Financial Crises (GFC) on existing or potential green initiatives?
- What is the impact of networking and social technologies (such as blogs, wikis, interactive media, etc.) on green initiatives?
- Where is Green initiative/movement likely to go in the next 1, 3, 5, and 8 years?

References

ACS. (2007). Cover Story: "ICT Gets Its Green House in Order" (Information Age—publication of the Australian Computer Society including the ACS policy, 2007), October/November 2007. Available from: http://www.infoage.idg.com.au/.

Ambec, S. and Lanoie, P. (2008). Does it pay to be green? A systematic overview. *The Academy of Management Perspectives*, 22(4): 45–62.

Bartlett, C. A. and Ghoshal, S. (1998). *Managing Across Borders: The Transnational Solution*, 2nd ed. Harvard Business School Press, MA.

Bell, S. and Morse, S. (2008). *Sustainability Indicators: Measuring the Immeasurable?*, 2nd ed. Earthscan, London.

Bradfield-Moody and Nogrady. (2010). *The Sixth Wave*, Random House Australia—Published: 1/Apr/*2010* - ISBN: 9781741668896

British Petroleum's Oil Leaks in the Gulf of Mexico and the Icelandic Volcanic Ash (2010). Achieving business benefits by implementing enterprise risk management. *Cutter Executive Report*, 7(3), July 1, 2010, Enterprise Risk Management & Governance Service (coauthored with Sherringham, K.).

Brown, D. (2008). Environmentally friendly credentials are influencing business outsourcing decisions. Strategic outsourcing. *International Journal* (Toronto, Ontario), 1(1): 87–95.

Cameron, K. W. (May 2009). The Road to Greener IT pastures. *Computer*, 42(5): 87–89.

Chen, A. and Boudreau, M. (2008). Information systems and ecological sustainability. *Journal of Systems and Information Technology*, 10(3): 186–201.

de Steiguer, J. E. (2006). *The Origins of Modern Environmental Thought.* The University of Arizona Press, Tucson, USA.

Dedrick, J. (2009). Green IT. *Proceedings of AMCIS*, Paper 717. Fifteenth Americas Conference on Information Systems San Francisco, California August 6–9, 2009

Erdmann, L. and Hilty, L. (2004). *The Future Impact of ICTs on Environmental Sustainability.* Institute for Prospective Technology Studies & European Commission Joint Research Center.

Fuchs, C. (2008). The implications of new information and communication technologies for sustainability. *Environment, Development and Sustainability*, 10(3): 291–309.

Garnaut, R. (2008). *Garnaut Climate Change Review.* Cambridge University Press, Cambridge, UK, Available from: http://www.garnautreview.org.au, Accessed October 2010.

GFC (2009). Global Financial Crisis. http://www.reuters.com/article/pressRelease/idUS193520+27-Feb-2009+BW20090227

Haas, P. M., Kanie, N., and Murphy, C. N. (2004). Conclusion: Institutional design and institutional reform for sustainable development. In N. Kanie and P. M. Haas (eds.), *Emerging Forces in Environmental Governance*, pp. 263–281. United Nations University Press, Tokyo, New York, NY, Paris.

Hercheui, M. (2011). Using knowledge management tools in fostering Green ICT related behavior change. In *Handbook of Research in Green ICT: Technical, Business and Social Perspectives*, pp. 290–299. IGI Global, Hershey, PA, USA.

Information Age publication of the Australian Computer Society, Available from: www.acs.org.au.

Jain, H. (2011). Green ICT organizational implementations and workplace relationships. In B. Unhelkar (ed.), *Handbook of Research in Green ICT: Technical, Business and Social Perspectives*, pp. 146–168. IGI Global, Hershey, PA, USA.

Kamani, K., Kathiriya, D., Virparia, P., and Parsania, P. (2011). Digitl Green ICT. In B. Unhelkar (ed.), *Handbook of Research in Green ICT: Technical, Methodological and Social Perspectives*, pp. 283–289. IGI Global, Hershey, PA, USA.

Kellen, V. (2010). Trends and Anti-Trends for 2010, Senior Consultant, Cutter Consortium, December 12, 2008, Cutter Blog, Available from: http://blog.cutter.com/2008/12/12/it-trends-and-antitrends-for-2009/.

Lamb, J. (2009). *The Greening of IT: How Companies Can Make a Difference for the Environment.* IBM Press, Lebanob, IN.

Lan, Y. and Unhelkar, B. (2005). *Global Enterprise Transitions.* IDEAS Group Publishing, Hershey, PA, USA.

Lash, J. and Wellington, F. (2007). Competitive advantage on a warming planet. *Harvard Business Review*, March, 95–102.

Moran, R. T. and Riesenberger, J. R. (1996). *The Global Challenge: Building the New Worldwide Enterprise.* McGraw-Hill, UK.

Murugesan, S. (August 2007). Going green with IT: Your responsibility toward environmental sustainability. *Cutter Consortium Business-IT Strategies Executive Report*, 10(8).

Murugesan, S. (2008). Harnessing Green IT: Principles and practices. *IT Professional*, 10(1): 24–33.

Nidumolu, R., Prahalad, C. K., and Rangaswami, M. R. (2009). Why sustainability is now the key driver of innovation. *Harvard Business Review*, September 1, 2009.

Orsato, R. J. (2009). *Sustainability Strategies: When does it Pay to be Green?*, Palgrave Macmillan, UK.

Pachauri, R. K. and Reisinger, A. (eds.) (2008). *Climate Change 2007: Synthesis Report. Contribution of Working Groups I, II and III to the Fourth Assessment.* Report of the Intergovernmental Panel on Climate Change. IPCC, Geneva, Switzerland.

Philipson, G. (2010). A report for the Australian Computer Society (ACS) by Connection Research, "Carbon and Computers: The Energy Consumption and Carbon Footprint of ICT Usage in Australia in 2010," http://www.acs.org.au/attachments/ICFACSV4100412.pdf – 2010.

Plepys, A. (2002). The grey side of ICT. *Environmental Impact Assessment Review*, 22: 509–523.

Poniatowski, M. (2010). *Foundations of Green IT: Consolidation, Virtualization, Efficiency, and ROI in the Data Center*. Prentice Hall, Indianapolis.

Raisinghani, M. and Unhelkar, B. (2007). Complying with sarbanes-oxley: Addressing the IT issues and risks. *Cutter IT Journal; Enterprise Risk Management & Governance*, 20(1): 23–28.

Rosen, M., Krichevsky, T., and Sharma, H. (2011). Strategies for a sustainable enterprise. In B. Unhelkar (ed.), *Handbook of Research in Green ICT: Technical, Business and Social Perspectives*, pp. 1–28. IGI Global, Hershey, PA, USA.

Ross, J. W., Weill, P., and Robertson, D. C. (2006). *Enterprise Architecture as Strategy: Creating Business Foundation for Business Execution*. Harvard Business School Press, Boston, MA.

Shah, A (2010). Available at http://www.globalissues.org/article/768/global-financial-crisis, accessed October 2010.

Sharif, N. (2010). Based on a carefully construed model of work packages entitled THIO—Technoware, Humanware, Inforware and OrgoWare.

Sherringham, K. (2005). *Cookbook for Market Dominance and Shareholder Value: Standardising the Roles of Knowledge Workers*. Athena Press, London.

Sherringham, K. and Unhelkar, B. (2011). Strategic business trends in the context of green ICT. In B. Unhelkar (ed.), *Handbook of Research in Green ICT: Technical, Business and Social Perspectives*, pp. 65–82. IGI Global, Hershey, PA, USA.

Stern, N. (2007). *Stern Review on the Economics of Climate Change*. Cambridge University Press, Cambridge, UK.

Tang, M. (2008). Smart 2020 Enabling the low carbon economy in the information age, A report by the Climate group on behalf of the Global e-sustainability Initiative (GeSI), Published by the Climate Group, © Creative Commons.

Unhelkar, B. (2010a). Creating and applying green IT metrics and measurement in practice. *Cutter Benchmark Review: Green IT Metrics and Measurement. The Complex Side of Environmental Responsibility*, 9(10): 10–17.

Unhelkar, B. (2010b). *Mobile Enterprise Transition and Management*. Taylor & Francis Group (Auerbach Publications), Boca Raton, FL, USA.

Unhelkar, B. (February 2010c). Cutter Executive Report on ERBS. *Environmentally Responsible Business Strategies for a Green Enterprise Transformation*, 13(2), February 2010, Business-IT strategies resource centre, Cutter Executive Report.

Unhelkar, B. (Ed.) (2011). *Handbook of Research in Green ICT: Technical, Business and Social Perspectives*. IGI Global, Hershey, PA, USA.

Unhelkar, B. and Dickens, A. (2008). Lessons in implementing "Green" business strategies with ict. *Cutter IT Journal, Special Issue on "Can IT Go Green?"*, S. Murugesan (ed.), 21(2): 32–39.

Unhelkar, B. and Philipson, G. (2009). The development and application of a Green IT maturity index. *ACOSM2009—Proceedings of the Australian Conference on Software Measurements*, November 2009, Sydney.

Unhelkar, B. and Trivedi, B. (2009). Merging web services with 3G IP multimedia systems for providing solutions in managing environmental compliance by businesses. In B. Unhelkar, *Proceedings of the 3rd International Conference on Internet Technologies and Applications (Internet Technologies and Applications, ITA 09)*, September 8–11, 2009. Wrexham, North Wales, UK.

Unhelkar, B. and Tiwary, A. (2010). Business Intelligence 2010: Delivering the Goods or Standing Us Up? D. Higgins (ed.). *Cutter IT Journals*, 23(6).

Unhelkar, B. and Tiwary, A. (2011). Extending and applying business intelligence and customer strategies for green ICT. In B. Unhelkar (ed.), *Handbook of Research in Green ICT: Technical, Business and Social Perspectives*, pp. 83–97. IGI Global, Hershey, PA, USA.

Unhelkar, B., Ghanbary, A., and Younessi, H. (2009). *Collaborative Business Process Engineering and Global Organizations: Frameworks for Service Integration*. IGI Global, Hershey, PA, USA.

Velte, T., Velte, A., and Elsenpeter, R. (2008). *Green IT: Reduce your Information System's Environmental Impact While Adding to the Bottom Line*. McGraw-Hill Companies, New York.

Unhelkar, B. and Trivedi, B. (2009a). "Merging Web Services with 3G IP Multimedia systems for providing Solutions in Managing Environmental Compliance by Businesses," *Proceedings of the 3rd International Conference on Internet Technologies and Applications (Internet Technologies and Applications, ITA 09)*, Sep. 8–11, 2009, Wrexham, North Wales, UK.

Yousif, M. (2009). Keynote "Towards Green ICT" ERCIM—*European Research Consortium for Informatics and Mathematics*—news; 79, 3–4, Available from: www.ercim.org.

Chapter 2

Green IT Strategies: Drivers, Dimensions, and Goals

Some experiences are so intense while they are happening that time seems to stop altogether.

Al Gore, An Inconvenient Truth

Key Points

- Presents Green IT strategies as encompassing and Environmentally Responsible Business Strategies (ERBS).
- Outlines the approach to developing specific organizational Green IT strategies.
- Presents the four dimensions of business transformation (economy, technology, processes, and people) along which green business transformations can take place.
- Presents approaches to managing the challenges in establishing green strategies in an enterprise.
- Outlines the factors that drive and influence an organization's green business strategies.
- Outlines the environmental legislations and regulations, and proposes an approach for compliance.
- Discusses the steps involved in the implementation of an ERBS.
- Presents some key performance indicators (KPI) for reduction of energy consumptions in an organization.

Introducing Green Strategies

Green strategies outline a long-term and unified approach of an organization toward environmental responsibility. Green strategies include Green IT, but as argued in the opening chapter, this consolidated approach to Green IT implies due consideration to all aspects of an organization from the environmental viewpoint. Individuals and business areas within the organization move at different speeds and have varying and occasionally conflicting priorities. A unified approach would accommodate these variations and, at the same time, not restrict the organization on the basis of immediate visibility of its return on green investment. The green strategic approach considers both internal and external organizational characteristics, including its structure, dynamics, macroeconomic incentives, compliance constraints, and the need to align corporate social responsibility with mainstream corporate business. Realignment of existing business strategies to a new set of environmental objectives requires the organization to reimagine itself. Such reimagination and green transformation is the mainstay of the approach described here.

Thus, the crux of the discussion in this chapter is a new, unified organization that treats carbon issues and performance integrally. In addition to this aligned, unified approach to alignment lean, green business, the rapidly advancing carbon economy is also likely to offer opportunities for many new business ventures that are specifically in the green domain. Diversification, mergers and acquisitions, expansions and creation of new business streams are all highly likely scenarios in the carbon economy—and a strategic approach is invariably required to prepare organizations for these opportunities. Green strategies have wide ramifications, not only on the way the business interacts with external and internal entities, but also with its internal organizational structure, attitudes, policies, and practices.

Esty and Winston (2006) discuss some of these business strategies for building an eco-advantage that revolve around the eco-friendly approach to business. Ghose (2011) has also expanded on the approaches to Green IT strategies that consider holistic approach to environmental consciousness based on micro- and macroeconomic factors. This holistic approach exploits IT to its fullest, but is not restricted to IT. For example, such comprehensive green strategy would also cover the organization's supply chain, reusable designs, production processes, recycling approaches, attitude of its people, and the risks associated with changes. For example, incorporating RFID tags in the supply chain will not only help the organization manage its inventories better, but will also open up opportunities to reduce its carbon footprint due to reduced material wastage. Thus, a Green IT strategy, as discussed here, includes wide and varied dimensions of a business that are not just restricted to computing per se. The hallmark of such green business strategies is that they provide a much more robust foundation for sustainability to the organization than, say, focusing on IT alone would provide. Thus, business optimization processes (e.g., Lean or Six-Sigma), whether IT focused or not, become important to the greening of an organization. Consider the use of Lean. Lean as a method, aims to eliminate the wastages in the organization's processes. The same method can be interpreted as one providing opportunities to ameliorate carbon emissions too. Optimization and/or elimination of activities within business processes drive not only business efficiency but also carbon efficiency. Gartner (2009) identified business process improvement as the top most priorities for CIOs in making a difference to their organization. Thus, green business strategies are combination of extending existing business strategies as well as coming up with new strategies that have a specific environmental focus.

Care needs to be taken to ensure that the new elements of a Green IT strategy are not too far removed from the core business strategies of an organization. Instead of coming up with a brand new green strategy that does not align with the core business of the organization, it is worthwhile considering the overall strategic approach to the environment as a business approach—environmentally responsible *business* strategies (ERBS, 2010; Unhelkar, 2008)—that are the business strategies.

The alignment of business strategies with the environmental consciousness of the organization can be best viewed as an intersection between business and carbon interests of the organization (as was discussed in Chapter 1 and depicted in Figure 1.4). As a result, effective Green IT strategies need to continuously demonstrate their value to business. The discussion in this chapter focuses on creating and implementing strategies that would enable an organization to survive and thrive in an increasingly carbon-dominated future by encompassing its people, processes, and technologies in the strategies.

ERBS is a conceptual framework that has evolved from earlier works by Unhelkar and Dickens (2008) and further refined through research by Unhelkar and Trivedi (2009). The ERBS as a framework has been further developed, extended, and published as a Cutter Executive Report by Unhelkar (2010). This model is being refined on an ongoing basis and is finding support in various business transformation and business intelligence domains—being called green enterprise transformation (GET) and environmental intelligence respectively.

In addition to the ERBS, there are several other frameworks and models that can be considered as a basis for ERBS. Researchers and practitioners in the field of Green IT have developed their thinking further in this domain and abstracted it as frameworks. For example, Philipson (2009) has developed further an original RMIT (Molla, 2009) framework for Green IT into a fairly comprehensive Green IT framework that can be used in practice to model an enterprise from an environmental perspective. This model is discussed later in the book (Chapter 9, Figure 9.5) as an excellent option to be considered during GET also see Connection Research, 2010. In addition to these, there are other Green IT frameworks such as the GITAM (Molla, 2009), Worthington (2009), and Procedural Model toward Sustainable Information Systems Management (Schmidt et al., 2009). These models or frameworks for Green IT provide valuable input into the development of an ERBS.

This chapter initially discusses the various drivers that provide a major fillip to a business in its considerations to undertake green business strategies. The drivers that motivate an organization to formulate an approach to a sustainable future need to be considered in the context of a particular enterprise and the industry sector. The type, size, and location of a business, all influence the way in which the business would interpret and use these drivers and motivators to undertake GETs. These drivers shape the response of an organization and its leaders in overcoming incumbency to make investments in Green IT and organizational transformation. The discussion on what motivates an organization needs to be followed by a discussion on the lines or dimensions along which an organization needs to transform itself. This chapter develops the four dimensions for Business Transformation (BT) outlined earlier by Unhelkar (2008). These four dimensions of economy, technology, processes, and people provide the foundation for creation of a roadmap, or a project plan, for GET. While the detailed description of the GET process is available in Chapter 9, this chapter outlines and describes these four dimensions in the context of Green IT, followed by a description of what exactly constitutes a green business strategy and the steps involved in the creation of green business strategy.

Green Strategic Mindset

Effective green strategies result from an approach that cuts across all the tiers and silos of an organization. Such strategies come from individual understanding, leadership, vision, knowledge about the structure and dynamics of the organization, awareness of the operational nuances of the organization, and the attitude of people (stakeholders) to utilize change. Such individuals would be reading, training, rewarding, promoting, educating, sharing, and encouraging everyone around them to develop further that green strategic mindset. A major benefit of developing an organization's green mindset is that it helps the organization manage the long-term implementation issues whilst achieving returns from the "low hanging fruits" of Green IT to show progress and what can be achieved. Indeed, it is important to immediately start switching off of monitors when they are not in use and immediately stop the wastage of printing paper; but those advantages are not considered

A green strategic mindset makes use of the available environmental intelligence (EI) tools and techniques within the organization. The strategic approach is based on a comprehensive use of technologies and systems that are based on extending business intelligence and applying it to the environment domain. Enterprise Risk Management (ERM)* can benefit the application of business intelligence toward environmental intelligence. While the traditional ERM is based on the risks associated with profits and cash flow, the Green strategies can incorporate carbon-specific risks, their sources, creation of carbon risk management frameworks as well as approach to risk mitigation. Green ERM also includes strategies for minimization of carbon impact through effective governance, creation and compliance with standards, and all the associated tools and technologies. Sherringham (2010) has advised that this strategic approach to ERM is based on incorporation of risks into routine business operations as a norm rather than an exception.

strategic and nor is the organization gratified by simply achieving some of them. The green strategic mindset acknowledges these vital initial efforts especially for the visibility they add to the initial effort, but does not remain entangled only with these initial efforts. Instead, a long-term, integral, all encompassing effort is undertaken by the green strategic mindset of the organization.

Green IT strategies translate into policies that deal with energy reduction across all areas of an organization. For example, strategies indicate policy formation on energy consumption in data centers or optimizing equipment procurement and lifecycle processes. Eventually, policies translate into practice (as discussed in Chapter 3) that requires accurate collection and reporting of carbon data and ensuring immediate compliance with the legal requirements.

Strategic use of carbon data involves not only collection and reporting of data, but also identification of risks and opportunities associated with the green domain as also plotting of trends and patterns in terms of internal carbon savings and external carbon credits and trading. Green IT strategies, thus, expand into the areas of capacity planning for the organization, resourcing and skills (HR) strategies, technology acquisitions, and risk management and governances.

An important aspect of the risk in undertaking a strategic approach is that its value accrues over a longer period of time. This, in turn, may entice the decision makers to dismiss the strategic approach in favor of visible, tactical approaches to Green IT.† To add to the challenges of undertaking strategic approach to Green IT, even the current return on investment (ROI) calculations in the Green IT domain are easier to compute, compare, and present when they are based on the immediate, tactical approaches as compared with the strategic one. Therefore, one of the most crucial considerations for the organization's decision makers is to engender a change of *mindset* from a tactical one to a strategic one. This is an inherently challenging situation in a market-driven economy, where all the micro- and macroeconomic levers are pulled by the organization to boost its share prices. Therefore, a positive way of looking at the development of the green strategies is the fact that they encompass not only carbon mitigation today, but also work to transform an organization so that it is ready for the carbon economy of tomorrow. Carbon trading in the future is inevitable and the carbon factor will play a crucial role in the stock exchange of the future. Thus, the organization as a whole has to ask the questions: Are the people involved in the green initiative having a positive mindset? Have they been educated and trained in the long-term sustainability approaches that the organization is planning to undertake? Is reduction in power consumption only as a result of switching off monitors (as, say, discussed by Forge, 2007), or are there some fundamental changes being brought about in the company processes? Are there mechanisms to be put in place that also measure this long-term environmental sustainability approach of the organization?

The answers to these and similar questions are not easy. In fact, we may have not yet fully answered the questions pertaining to strategic approaches itself. Therefore, a green strategic approach is certainly fraught with many challenges. These green challenges were alluded to earlier in Chapter 1. Following is a further list of such challenges (in no particular order of importance)

---

* A risk is something that has the potential to impact the achieving of an outcome. An issue is a realization of a risk and is something that is now impacting upon achieving an outcome.
† For details, see *Harvard Business Review on Green Business Strategy*.

that an organization is likely to face in its effort to cultivate a green strategic mindset and subsequently a comprehensive green strategy.

- There is still a substantial amount of subjectivity, skepticism, and doubt about the entire green enterprise. This is a personal, individual attitude challenge that is difficult to quantify through contemporary metrics and measurements.
- Quantifying the economic returns of a green project remains uncertain especially when it is considered strategically. However, it is the strategic approach to Green IT that has tremendous significance in terms of green value and meaningful returns.
- Organizations tend to take a hurried and, as a result, fragmented approach to environmental initiatives. Instead, a holistic, unified approach is required.
- There is no single packaged solution that can work as an application to transform the organization to a green one; instead, painstakingly, a collaborative effort that brings together and integrates existing packages as also the carbon emissions management software (CEMS) is required.
- The attractiveness of immediately switching off physical carbon emitting hardware (e.g., monitors, data servers) and the ensuing feeling of smugness at having achieved something for the environment.
- Fuzzy cost-benefit analysis and equally fuzzy metrics associated with green projects. The uncertainty in the payback on the environmental initiatives can discourage an organization-wide initiative.
- Potential risks associated with the use of technology-based initiatives such as Cloud computing, business intelligence, and knowledge management in the area of green initiatives. The inherent risks and challenges associated with these technologies also translate into risks for green initiatives.
- Design, development, and production of goods, as well as appropriate services keeping the carbon costs in mind may initially require greater effort than the status-quo or business as usual scenario. Furthermore, products and services will have to be reconfigured in a manner that produces long-term advantage from a green perspective. For example, the existing CRM, SCM, and HR applications can and will undergo modifications and enhancements to cater to the green consciousness of the organization.

Philosophical Considerations in Green IT Strategy

The impacts of technology in business and upon society have been discussed extensively by Toffler (1980). In the context of the environment, however, it is worth starting with a thought by Pearce (1989) who, more than two decades ago, presented two separate yet interrelated viewpoints that gave an insight into businesses, their wealth generating activities, and the environment: (1) leave future generations with at least as much capital wealth as we inherited and (2) future generations must not inherit less environmental capital than we inherited.

These two viewpoints need to be treated together. One is not exclusive to the other, although both, in their own right, provide a major insight into the market-driven economies that most of the

Green IT strategic planning includes due considerations to the business goals of the organization, its demographic characteristics, its existing approach in the context of Green IT as also its maturity in terms of Green IT. Earlier approaches to strategic planning were based on the principles and models based on Porter (2008; e.g., the Five Forces model and the Value Chain models). SWOT and PEST analysis also provide a good starting point for strategic planning, as these techniques ascertain the position of the enterprise in terms of where it stands and how it can approach the transformation. Unhelkar (2009b) and Atkins and

Ali (2009) have extended and applied these techniques to mobile business transformation. Here, these techniques provide the basis for strategic planning for Green IT.

The philosophy behind a green strategy can be risk, associated with growth; social, nonprofit; careless, without any strategy; and the lean-intelligent, balanced one.

world is now used to. If only the first of the two viewpoints is considered, then it will lead to generation of wealth capital at the cost of the environmental capital. The ensuing environmental losses cannot be compensated by generation of corresponding wealth. The second viewpoint underscores the need for intelligent utilization of environmental capital in a way that will result in production of wealth capital. Note that the second viewpoint does not eschew creation of wealth. However, such development and growth of an organization has to be synergistic. Further, Pearce's viewpoint (1989) that "it is possible to have economic growth (more gross national product—GNP) and to use up fewer resources" also needs to be considered and fully developed for a practical, successful ERBS. These aforementioned viewpoints lead to the philosophy for a green strategy itself. The green strategic mindset, especially at the decision-making level, is functioning at its best when the business and carbon interests of an organization continue to overlap each other visibly. Figure 2.1 shows, simplistically, the philosophy of a green strategy mix. This green philosophy is exhibited by organizations when it comes to their carbon versus cost priorities. The philosophy of the green strategic mindset can vary from the obvious one—gaining both carbon and cost advantages—to a complete lack of strategy or a dysfunctional view of Green IT. This is shown in Figure 2.1 as four quadrangles. Following are the ways in which each tab of the quadrangle can be viewed:

■ *Risky, Growing*: Strategies that directly improve the economic performance of the organization but also add to the carbon contents. Expansion of the products and services portfolio by an organization will increase its turnover, but at the same time, there is a very high possibility that its corresponding carbon contents will also go up. This may happen due to increased production activities in the organization. For example, an airline expanding its services to new regions would expect to increase the carbon it produces as it flies to these new geographical regions but with new fuel-efficient aircraft, the increases can be minimized. Organizational growth, which is usually associated with increase in operational costs relating to manufacturing and distribution (supply chains), can be reasonably expected to increase its carbon costs as well.

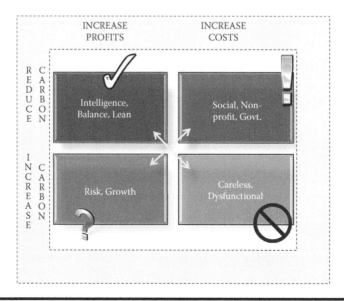

Figure 2.1   Strategy matrix—carbon versus profit.

■ *Social, Government, Nonprofit:* Strategies that improve the carbon performance of the organization but hurt the bottom line. For example, optimized insurance services by an insurance organization may imply shifting some aspects of such service to less powerful servers. Such strategies may reduce the carbon generation by those business processes but may also reduce the customer service. Such strategies can hurt the revenues and/or increase the costs.

■ *Careless, No Strategy:* These are the less well-managed and even dysfunctional organizations whose activities hurt both their economic and carbon performance. For example, careless increase in the number of servers within a data center without proper estimation of their workload may laden the organization with unnecessary servers. The data servers would not add any discernable gain in terms of economic returns, nor would they provide any business value. The carbon footprint of such an organization would also increase due to additional GHG generation. In most cases, though, such an organization may not be even aware of its carbon impacts as the necessary metrics and measurements are often missing.

■ *Lean, Intelligent, Balanced:* Strategies that improve both the economic and carbon performance. This is the core winning philosophy of an ideal Green IT strategy. This is an approach that applies the principles of lean business to evolve into a green business. This is the philosophy that invites and expands the technologies of business intelligence to move toward environmental intelligence. This is an approach that is highly balanced—ensuring that the goals of the business are in balance and in sync with its environmental goals. For example, the same airline mentioned earlier, in its expansion strategy, would consider procurement of new, low-carbon-emitting aircrafts with less fuel consumption. Furthermore, the airline might encourage its passengers to opt for carbon offsets—the proceeds from which can be used in that business's effort to reduce carbon elsewhere. These strategies will be intelligent, lean, and in balance—providing the much needed economic growth as well as reduction in carbon for the business.

Using the right philosophy behind the creation and implementation of the strategy is vital. While the last of the four quadrants discussed earlier is the most ideal, and in most cases the only philosophical option to use, still there may be occasional reasons for an organization going for increasing costs to reduce carbon, or taking the risk of increasing the carbon in order to grow the business. These four quadrants provide a simple yet fundamental basis for the philosophy of becoming green, and, sticking to the lean, intelligent, and balanced approach to developing and implementing green strategies is the winning philosophy.

Green IT Strategies: Range of Impact

Figure 2.2 shows the range of impact of Green IT strategies on the organization. This is primarily a temporal view of the effect of the Green IT strategies. Figure 2.2 also throws light on the various time-based impacts on the execution of the strategy within and across the organization. Also shown in Figure 2.2 are the various roles that are affected by and involved in these Green IT strategies. Following is a brief discussion of the time-based impact on Green IT strategies:

Strategic approach to Green IT is a long-term approach that includes business and environmental factors. Starting with the immediate or tactical actions, such as switching off monitors, the strategic approach goes into long-term planning, typically 3–5 years, that will include environmental issues integrally in the business. Eventually, the think tanks need to envision the future for not only one organization but also a collaborative group of organizations that may be geographically spread into different regions.

■ **Today** [Operational]. This is the typical, immediate action taken by an organization with respect to Green IT. For

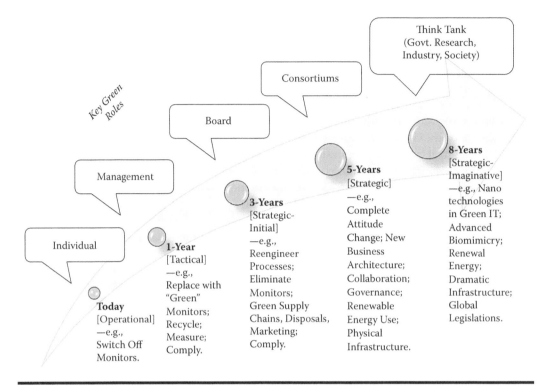

Figure 2.2   Range of impact of Green IT strategies.

example, switching off the computer monitors when not in use, or not printing on paper whenever possible are the immediate actions, the "low hanging fruits." While these are most visible actions, they do not require what is considered as a strategic approach. Simply inform the users that they need to switch off computers when not in use; or, implement an internal method to charge the users (i.e., their cost center) for the use of paper. Feedback in terms of carbon usage per action, developing a consensus amongst a group of users, and initial training is helpful in getting these operational Green IT initiatives off the ground. Many early adopters of Green IT have done precisely this. The caveat, as mentioned earlier, is to constantly remember that this is not a strategic action. The impact may be visible, may also provide the basis for shaping the culture of the organization to a green one, but the effect may not be long lasting and the actions may not lead to a strong organization that is ready for the carbon economy. Individual employees and stakeholders within the organization can effectuate these changes immediately—as these changes primarily deal with their own habits in terms of computer usage.

■ **1-Year** [Tactical]. An organization cannot do everything at once. Therefore, even at a tactical level, it has to build up its ability to reduce its carbon emissions over some time. A 1-year time period is ideal for some aspects of the Green IT strategies that enable action that is manageable. These tactical actions, for example, include the replacement of existing computer monitors within the organization with green, flat-screen monitors. Similarly, small-time gadgets and equipments can be replaced within a year by agreements within the middle management and administrative staff. Similarly, recycling programs can be put together by the managers for their respective departments that will encourage staff to have processes for recycling of paper and reduction in printing. This is still a tactical approach but the one with benefits of some measurements and metrics in place that can start showing ROI on the effort. This effort certainly makes moves in the right direction for organizational compliance to carbon regulatory requirements.

■ **3-Years** [Strategic-Initial]. The 3-year timeframe for the impact of Green IT initiatives is certainly based on strategic initiatives as promoted in this discussion. These initiatives would include the senior leadership of the organization including a dedicated "C" level role (such as that of a Chief Sustainability Office or a Chief Green Officer—mentioned in Chapter 1). These Green IT strategies are formulated and approved by the board, have substantial budgetary backing, and require a holistic approach by the organization. Thus, this strategic approach will include Reengineering of Business Processes that may result in not only upgrades to low-carbon emitting devices but also elimination of some of these devices due to the reengineering effort. Other areas of the organization such as its data centers, buildings, supply chains, disposal strategies, and even sales and marketing are affected through these strategies. The organization is able to comply with the regulations and is able to move forward strongly in the new carbon economy.

■ **5-Years** [Strategic]. This Green IT strategy is a further extension of the aforementioned 3-year strategy but has greater depth and breadth of coverage. For example, in addition to the reengineering effort over the 3-year period, this strategy would also bring about a complete attitude change in people at all levels, reorganize the business architecture, and implement substantial governance mechanisms for the board. The physical infrastructure, such as buildings and data centers will also undergo a major revamp in this period. Furthermore, the organization will be influenced by and, in turn, will influence other partnering organizations through a collaborative effort. Renewable energy sources are explored and consumed with fully automated, systems-based measurement, reporting, and monetizing. The CEO, board of directors of the organization, *and* those of its collaborating partners, are involved in this long-term strategic approach.

■ **8-Years** [Strategic-Imaginative]. A Green IT strategy that is stretched over this long a time period would include elements of controlled imagination. Considerations of environmental issues over a long time period may not produce immediate results, and yet, they are important, especially for large and global organizations as well as government bodies. Large, global organizations have a need and an opportunity, through their think tanks, to consider the implications of futuristic technologies on Green IT. For example, such organizations will have the resources to create prototypes and measure the impacts of, say, Nano technologies and Biomimicry on their carbon emissions. Over this period, the expectation is that the carbon economy will be a truly mainstream economy and organizations will be dealing with carbon in all aspects of their business. The imaginations here should be all encompassing—including aspects of technologies as well as economy (e.g., carbon trading on the stock exchange).

Although the above discussion covers a period close to a decade, the Green IT strategic approach is ideally poised to impact the organization in the next 3–5-year period. This is based on the initial literature review and the environmental survey conducted by Trivedi and Unhelkar (2010). The study asked the participants to rate their views on the factors that are likely to influence an organization's strategies, particularly in the next 3–5 years. The results from that survey are shown in Figure 2.3. These results can also be interpreted as follows:

■ More than 51% of the participants agreed and close to 8% strongly agreed to the use of IT in minimizing the organization's environmental footprints, indicating the importance of IT felt by participants in the role it can play in reducing carbon impact.

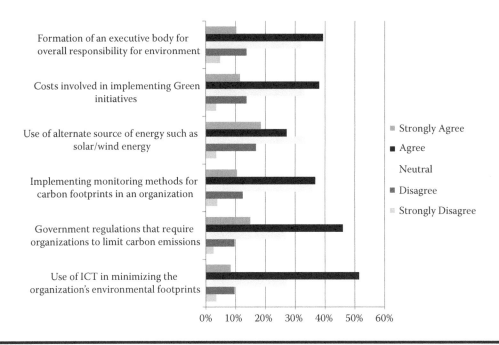

Figure 2.3 Environmental factors influencing organization's business strategies over next 3–5 years.

■ Forty-six percent agreed and 15% strongly agreed that government regulations that require organizations to limit carbon emissions are a substantial factor in the organization's formulation of Green IT strategies affecting them over next 3–5 years. Thus, the strategists of an organization are likely to keep a strong eye on the policy makers of the government to see what legal, financial, and social implications those policies will have on the business in terms of Green IT.

■ Forty-eight percent of the responses agreed-to-strongly agreed on the need to implement monitoring methods for carbon footprints in an organization; and the same percentage, 48% agreed-to-strongly agreed on the need to include alternate source of energy such as solar/wind energy in the organization's Green IT strategies. While some of these alternative sources of energy, such as solar, will take more than 3 years to be fully effective, nonetheless, they are a vital consideration in the current Green IT strategies of the organization.

■ Exactly 50% respondents thought that the costs involved in implementing Green initiatives have a major impact on the Green IT strategies of the organization. These are the costs associated with the changes to the hardware, software, people, and processes. Almost all aspects of an organization's structure and dynamics change when it undertakes Green IT. The investment in those changes is not going to be readily visible—unless it is coupled with the business efficiency view.

■ Finally, only 19% disagreed-to-strongly disagreed on the formation of an executive body for overall responsibility for environment for the organization. The rest of the participants seem to support the view that a dedicated executive body with powers to bring about change, and budget to support the powers, needs to be formed. The formation of such an entity is akin to almost all previous major revolutions in business transformations—such as process reengineering, lean and quality initiatives.

Keeping the 3–5-year period as a strategic period with maximum advantage for the organization, the environmental survey (Trivedi and Unhelkar, 2010) further asked the participants about their organization's strategic plans to achieve Green targets for that time period. The results from that survey are shown in Figure 2.4. Some of these results can be simplistically interpreted as follows:

- Fifty-four percent of the participants agreed and close to 4% strongly agreed to the use of a methodology to undertake suitable and defensive power consumption. This indicates the need for a strategic initiative rather than a tactical or operational plan to achieve Green targets. Such strategy initiative would result in even greater savings in energy bills than the already significant estimates of 20%–30% made by the Carbon Trust (see carbontrust.co.uk). While there was no need to ascertain a specific methodology in the survey, examples of methodologies for Green IT framework and transformation are presented in Chapters 4, 6, and 9.
- Fifty percent of the participants agreed and close to 4% strongly agreed to the creation of power management polices to reduce energy consumptions. These power management policies, based on the strategic decision taken by the management, can cover a wide gamut of decisions such as use of smart switches for reducing power consumption, off-peak use of power, seeking renewable sources of power if available (e.g., wind or solar), or even refurbishing buildings and facilities of the organization (e.g., installing solar panels on the roof or providing cross ventilation for factory floors). In this regard, note the discussion by Przybyla and Pegah (2007), which highlights the carbon challenges in managing the cooling of data centre infrastructures.
- Forty-four percent of the participants agreed and close to 7% strongly agreed to the need for training plans and budgets to help employees understand Green issues and achieve Green

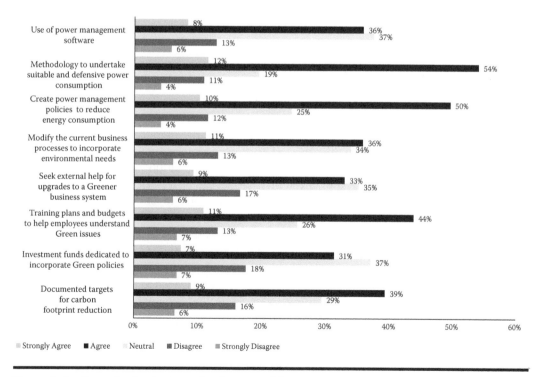

Figure 2.4 **Organization's strategic plans to achieve green targets over next 3–5 years. (Based on Trivedi and Unhelkar, 2010.)**

targets. This response is also anticipated, and is in line with almost all business change experiences. The importance of sociocultural and HR issues is dealt with in Chapter 8.

■ About 45% of the participants agreed-to-strongly agreed to the need for a use of power management software that will automate the process of tactical/operational reduction of carbon in the first instance. However, this kind of power management software can also include the operating systems that can be used for desktop virtualization and optimizations.

■ Similarly, about 46% agreed-to-strongly agreed for the modification of the current business processes to incorporate environmental needs. The entire domain of Green BPM finds discussion in Chapter 5.

■ Thirty-three percent agreed and 9% strongly agreed to seek external help for upgrades to a Greener business system.

■ Thirty-one percent agreed and 7% strongly agreed to an investment fund by the organization that would be dedicated to incorporate Green policies in the organization.

■ Finally, 48% agreed-to-strongly agreed on the need for an organization to have documented targets for carbon footprint reduction—indicating a strong desire on the part of the participants to see the creation of a strategy and a plan that is supported by metrics and measurements.

These aforementioned figures indicate not only the support for a strategic plan for Green IT, but also help develop an understanding of the timeframe where they will be all applicable. For example, the figures mentioned earlier indicate the support for policies, use of software and application of metrics that will provide tremendous value to a green enterprise transformation—and that value will itself be maximized by keeping a 3–5-year timeframe for implementing those strategies and plans.

Green Strategic Alignment

Green IT strategies can be roughly divided into two types—the ones that are reacting to the carbon challenge, and the ones that are based on positive action to meet the challenge now and in the future. With the inevitable carbon economy of the future, a combination of both reactivity and proactivity is required in the development of Green IT strategies.

Green IT strategies, especially in the 3–5-year impact range, are well poised to provide continuous alignment of the organization's business and carbon goals. Significant work has been done in this aspect of developing a conceptual framework for strategic alignment by Wang and Ghose (2006). Alignment in the context of Green IT strategies can be seen as transforming the firm's resource base in a way to cater to both goals—business and green—of the organization simultaneously. While the framework of Wang and Ghose views alignment as a binary relationship between two strategies, in this discussion it can be understood as the application of that conceptual tool kit to synergize between Green IT and the core business strategy of the organization. As further developed and reported by Wang and Ghose (2011), Green IT strategic alignment is basically viewed as a resource allocation decision that, when deployed correctly, bring about action that brings the business and carbon goals close to each other. Commonalities from existing strategic work within the organization can be identified and applied to the Green IT domain. For example, the prerequisites of a strategy are the conditions that should be met before such strategy translates into policies and practice. These conditions, in the instance of a Green IT strategy, would be the availability of funds and the decision by the board to proceed with the initiative. Similarly, the precondition of a resource base for a strategy is handled through the formation of a green transformation board, a green transformation program, and the nomination of a Chief Green Officer to lead that change. Finally, the execution of a strategy should be done in a manner that keeps the business and carbon goals aligned.

Proactive Green Strategies

Extending the earlier discussion on green strategic alignment leads also to an understanding of the general "bent" of strategies. Green strategies can encourage the organization to bring about significant organizational change. These changes are based on an understanding of the various Green IT drivers by the organization's leadership. These strategies, that are not enforced on the organization but are based on *anticipation* by the leadership of the organization, can be considered as the proactive green strategies. The organization's own understanding is translated into a Green IT initiative and is supported by most layers of the organization. The solution is also coordinated and integrated in a holistic way (see paper by Raghavendra et al., 2008). In case of such proactive strategies, the organizations take the initiative in identifying, determining, and enlisting the factors that will influence the transformation of the organization to a green organization. For example, proactive strategies will identify the opportunities for new business streams in the green domain, or completely new business models. Globalization, multinational business market, and the economies of scale in terms of greening an enterprise can be part of these proactive strategies. Proactive strategies also affect the infrastructure, equipments, and people of the organization by bringing about radical change in them that is based on a combination of organizational and personal initiatives.

Reactive Green Strategies

In addition to undertaking green transformation on its own volition, there are also significant elements of reaction by an organization to the external green influences on it. For example, the impact of government rules and regulations relating to carbon provide a major impetus for the organization to undertake green strategy formulations. When the organization has to put together an immediate response to an external change in legislation, it results in reactive strategies that are short-term strategies (less than 3 years on the scale outlined earlier in Figure 2.2). External competition, outsourcing, globalization, and customer demands can all put the organization in reactive mode resulting in reactive Green IT strategies.

Major drivers for Green IT strategies and their impact on formulation of the strategies are discussed later in this chapter. It should be noted that all Green IT strategies will have elements of both proactive and reactive within them. The next section describes the overall mix of various elements within the Green IT strategy formulation by an organization.

Green IT Strategies Mix

Table 2.1 summarizes the various elements of an ERBS. These elements are grouped in four categories:

- Drivers—these are the motivating factors for an organization to put together a Green IT strategy and undertake transformation. Six such drivers have been identified in the Green IT strategy formulation discussed here, and listed in the first column in Table 2.1.

According to the Global CEO study (www. 935.ibm.com), chief executives believe that energy and environmental activities can help differentiate their brands and promote the reputation of their products and services. Enhanced green brand image can deliver enhanced market penetration and facilitate customer loyalty—especially from the new generation customers that are demanding carbon-conscious products and services.

Table 2.1   Elements of an ERBS Forming the Green Strategies Mix

Drivers	*Dimensions*	*Business*	*Systems*
• Costs and revenues • Sociocultural and political • Regulatory and legal • Enlightened self-interest • Responsible Business ecosystem • New market opportunities	• Economic • People • Process • Technology	• Policies, practices, and procedures • Systems and support • Legal compliance • Architecture • Environmental Metrics • Maintenance	• Data • Information • Process • Knowledge • Environmental intelligence • (EI implementation includes Green ICT)

■ Dimensions—these are the various areas along which an organization undertakes transformation. There are four such dimensions identified and listed in Table 2.1 in the second column. The corporate ERBS needs to consider all four significant components of any strategy: economy, people, processes, and technologies.

■ Business—this is the domain of policies, practices, and procedures undertaken by the organization along each of the four dimensions.

■ Intelligence—this is the systems, information technology, and contents aspect of Green IT. This is the further evolution of the concept of business intelligence into what is considered here as environmental intelligence.

This table also highlights the fact the Green IT strategy (also interchangeably known as an ERBS) is incorporated into and made an integral part of the overall business strategy of an organization. Since each of these elements influences the way in which the organization operates, it has specific bearings on its green credentials.

Green IT Drivers

The drivers that impact the underlying motivations of a business for its environmental responsibility are, Figure 2.5, where six separate yet interrelated areas are seen. Figure 2.5 also shows a mapping between the drivers and the corresponding Green IT framework. The strategies, policies, design, implementation, and practice of Green IT are primarily driven by one or more combination of these drivers. These six groups of business drivers for environmental responsibility, as shown on the left in Figure 2.5 are the costs (including energy costs, operational costs); regulatory and legal; sociocultural and political; new market opportunities; enlightened self-interest; and responsible business ecosystem. The recognition of these drivers for Green IT lead to a further investigation by Trivedi and Unhelkar (2010) who reported the results surveys relating to these drivers as presented in Figure 2.6.

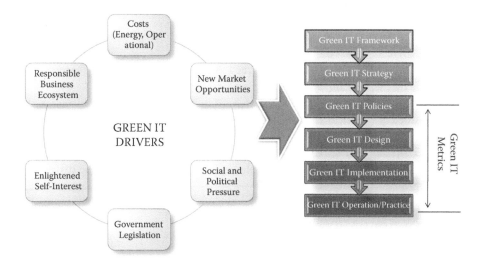

Figure 2.5   Drivers for environmental responsibility of business.

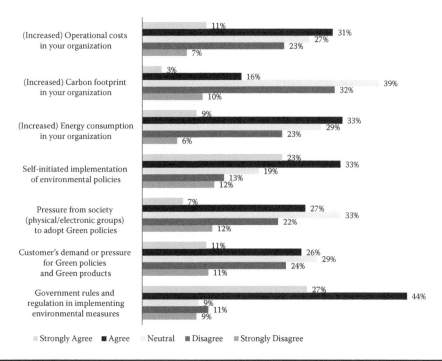

Figure 2.6   Drivers for carbon reduction. (Based on Trivedi and Unhelkar, 2010.)

The results from Figure 2.6 can be interpreted as follows:

■ Forty-four percent of the participants agreed and close to 27% strongly agreed on that government rules and regulation in implementing environmental measures is the major driver for carbon reduction.

◼ Thirty-three percent of the participants agreed and close to 15% strongly agreed that self-initiated implementation of environmental policies and energy consumption by organization is the drivers for carbon reduction.

◼ Thirty-one percent of the participants agreed and close to 11% strongly agreed that operational costs by their organization is the driver for carbon reduction.

◼ Twenty-seven percent of the participants agreed and close to 7% strongly agreed that pressure from society (physical/electronic groups) to adopt Green policies as the driver for carbon reduction.

◼ Twenty-six percent of the participants agreed and close to 11% strongly agreed that customer's demand or pressure for Green policies and Green products is the driver for carbon reduction.

◼ Sixteen percent of the participants agreed and close to 3% strongly agreed that carbon footprint in their organization is the driver for carbon reduction.

◼ About 25% disagreed-to-strongly disagreed on these as drivers for carbon reduction in their organizations.

These drivers and how they encourage organizations in the formulation of an ERBS are explained in greater detail next.

Costs (Energy, Operational)

As discussed in the previous chapter, the positive impact of Green IT on the bottom line of the business is part of what organizational leadership is trying to achieve. A good sustainable approach by an organization includes opportunities to optimize its processes, consolidate its technologies, and thereby reduce its costs. Thus, costs provide an excellent driver for the organization to come up with a comprehensive Green IT strategy. Examples of cost reduction include reduction in the use of raw materials and equipment, recycling of equipment, and optimization of storage and inventory as a result of the green initiative. While effort to reduce costs can provide an impetus for reduction in carbon emissions, the organizations undertaking green transformations need to be aware of the spending that they have to incur as a result of the greening effort. For example, optimizing a business process can eliminate the need for a desktop machine but, instead, there may be a need to replace that desktop with a mobile device. At the organizational level, costs associated with the green enterprise transformation program need to be factored in along with the anticipated reduction in costs due to the transformation.

Regulatory and Legal

Environmental legislations put together by governing bodies have a greater enforcing power than the aforementioned social opinions. (These regulations are discussed in greater detail later in Chapters 8 and 10.) For example, in Australia, it is now legally binding for an organization emitting more than 150 kT (kilo tonne) of carbon to calculate and report it to the government on an annual basis.* These regulatory and legal requirements now make it mandatory for organizations to comply with carbon emission requirements. This, in turn, forces a company to implement environmental measures within its business operations. Formation of a comprehensive environmentally responsible strategy is then undertaken to ensure that the organization is compliant with the legal requirements.

---

* NGERS website—www.climatechange.gov.au.

Figure 2.8 indicates that the government rules and regulations are a major driver for many green enterprise transformation programs. The relative importance given to this regulatory factor, as compared with the other factors such as organization self-initiation, customers demand, and the pressure from society are the highest—70% as shown in Figure 2.8.

Regulatory acts such as NGERS and CPRS (www.climatechange.gov.au) require organizations to mandatorily report their carbon emissions once they reach a certain level. Regulatory bodies also provide some basic calculators (e.g., OSCAR) to enable calculations of greenhouse gases. These calculators are used to arrive at the total carbon emissions of the organization that can be used to decide whether the organization falls under a mandatory reporting requirement. In addition to the basic calculators, green information systems also source external regulatory data (such as permissible emission figures), store, analyze, and broadcast the results that enable monitoring and improvement of performance of the organization. These organizational specific green information systems need to be much more sophisticated than the basic calculators provided by the regulatory bodies (Unhelkar and Philipson, 2009).

An example of such mandatory reporting requirements is the Australian government regulation. On October 31, 2009, approximately 1000 Australian businesses fell under the mandatory reporting requirements for carbon emitters above 150 kT per annum (National Greenhouse and Energy Reporting Act, 2007). Another example is of the American Clean Energy and Security Act that was passed to reduce emissions by 17% in year 2020 (compared with 2005 levels) and around 80% by 2050 (this legislation is yet to reach a vote in the Senate). The EU also has a mandatory target of a 20% reduction in greenhouse gases by 2020 (compared with 1990)—with particular emphasis on the cap-and-trade EU Emissions Trading Scheme (EU ETS), that covers major emitters of CO_2. Finally, the U.K. government has also passed legislation in November 2008 that aims to achieve emissions reduction of at least 26% by 2020 and 80% by 2050, against a 1990 baseline.

As early as 1992, the United Nations Conference on Environment and Development "placed the issue of sustainable development at the heart of the international agenda" (Boutros-Ghali, 1995). Agenda 21, as it is called, provides the background for eventual agreements and legislations by individual countries relating to sustainable development. Agreements in the Rio conference also resulted in declaration of rights and responsibilities of nations forming the basis for two legally binding conventions: climate change and biodiversity, signed by 150 countries.

In addition to the controlling of carbon emissions on operational basis, there are also stringent regulatory requirements in many industries that deal with the physical procurement, handling, and disposal of goods and equipments. For example, the EU's Waste Electrical and Electronic Equipment (WEEE) Directive requires manufacturers of electrical and electronic equipment to assume responsibility for the collection and disposal of their manufactured products (European Commission, 2009). Thus, for other non-EU countries to do business with EU requires them to comply with these WEEE requirements. The vendors of materials and equipments from, say, China or Japan, have to provide a recycling program that would also accept the return of expended equipments such as printers and copiers. This legislative requirement is a major driver for vending organizations to revamp their architectures and designs that would enable easier recycling and reduce the issues associated with electronic waste that is generated at the end of the life of a equipment rather than the carbon generated during its operation.

The appropriateness and application of the legal, compliance requirements relating to the environment will change depending on the industry. For example, as described by Godbole (2011), within the healthcare sector, hospitals have significant challenges with disposal of hazardous waste, while insurance companies are more concerned with reducing paper utilization or decreasing power consumption in their data centers (see Przybyla and Pegah, 2007, for greater details).

Eventually, legislative changes can drive markets and influence the strategic directions of organization. For example, as mentioned in the EU discussion earlier, legislative demands require vending organizations to restructure their offerings. Legislation changes the bar for competition and requires creation of new business streams and business formats. Another example is the incoming legislations allowing trading of carbon on the stock exchange—that will result in significant changes in the business models of organizations as the value of the organization will depend on its carbon credits.

An HBR Spotlight article, "Why Sustainability Is Now the Key Driver of Innovation" argues that sustainability offers immense opportunities for organizational and technological innovations that yield both top-line and bottom-line returns. The sustainability journey of organizations, according to Nidumolu, Prahalad, and Rangaswami, is based on five distinct stages of change: (1) viewing compliance as opportunity; (2) making value chains sustainable; (3) designing sustainable products and services; (4) developing new business models; and (5) creating next-practice platforms.

On the manufacturing front, carbon tariff and carbon-related tax breaks would change the way, say, cars or toasters are produced. Even operationally, in the coming few years, one would expect a gauge next to the mileage odometer, showing the total carbon emitted by that auto; and legislations that would be binding to the way that vehicle is manufactured and operated.

Sociocultural and Political

This driver comes mainly into play when the society in which an organization resides accepts the environment as of significance in its value system. Such acceptance of the importance of the environment by the society brings pressure on the organization to change. For example, the increasing popularity of the *Earth Hour* (last Saturday of March), wherein almost all large edifices around the world switch off their electrical power for an hour, or *Earth Day* (April 22 in the Unites States and March 20 by UN) has a corresponding bearing on many large businesses' sustainability strategies. This groundswell of opinions also leads to corresponding shifts in political viewpoint. As a result, the organization is forced to seriously reconsider its business priorities and processes in light of the environment. For example, pressure of social opinion is felt by the marketing department of an organization—by way of its needs to differentiate the products or services; another example is of the school education system that inculcates green values in the upcoming generation that then brings to bear political pressure in the form of an emancipated electorate. Such sociopolitical pressure may, however, not be always legally binding. This is the reason, perhaps, for the 34% importance given to it in Figure 2.7 (Trivedi and Unhelkar, 2010). The power in the ability of a collective opinion to enforce good corporate citizenship cannot be underestimated. This effect of the social opinion is seen in the formation of corporate social responsibility (CSR, 2010) as a part of an organization's portfolio of activities. CSR, also known as corporate responsibility, corporate citizenship, responsible business, and sustainable business, integrates self-regulation into a business model. The formulation of a CSR policy, that functions as a built-in, self-regulating mechanism, monitors the organization's behavior, its adherence to law, ethical standards, and international norms. This same CSR extends to embrace responsibility for the impact of the organization's activities on the environment, consumers, employees, communities, stakeholders, and members of the public. The scale and nature of the benefits of CSR for an organization can vary depending on the nature of the enterprise, and are difficult to quantify (Garito, 2011). However, the importance of the same cannot be discounted.

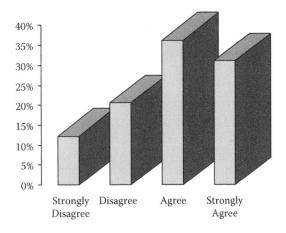

Figure 2.7 Green policies are taken up to increase revenue in an organization. (Based on Trivedi and Unhelkar, 2010.)

Enlightened Self-Interest

This driver comes into play when an organization, on its own accord, realizes the need to be environmentally responsible, and creates or adopts a green strategy. This driver can include a range of interests including the desire of an organization to undertake genuine *common* good, the need of the business leadership to achieve personal satisfaction, or simply the understanding of the decision makers that costs can be reduced and customers can be more satisfied with a self-interest approach that also helps the environment. The desire to have a brand recognition based around environmental sustainability or an understanding of its impact on business continuity also forms part of these drivers for an ERBS (Cartland, 2005). As seen in Figure 2.8, the survey results indicate that a substantial 56% respondents believe that self-initiation is a driver for undertaking green transformation. This figure indicates that self-motivation has the potential to be an effective green driver for businesses. A variation of this driver known as incentive-driven compliance (IDC) incorporates innovation and self-motivation within its environmental approach for better carbon compliance. Enlightened self-interest, as a driver, is in between the good behavior for financial gains and avoidance of bad, carbon-intensive behavior due to fear of penalties.

Enlightened self-interest can translate into green *Essential value* (discussed in detail in Chapter 3) that goads the firm to operate not only within environmental constraints but also social, ethical, cultural, and legal ones. There are number of incentives for organizations to align their business interests with enlightened interests for the environment. For example, US $78 billion from the American Recovery and Reinvestment Act funds are allocated for energy efficiency and green transportation initiatives (U.S. Government, 2009); CAD $1 billion dedicated by the Canadian government to support environmental improvements for the Canadian pulp and paper industry (Natural Resources Canada, 2009); and Green Building Fund (Grants ranging from AUD $50,000 to $500,000 are available for up to 50% of project costs, $90 million over four years) from the Australian Government to go toward reducing energy consumed in the operation of existing commercial office buildings.

Self-interest can itself depend on varying factors such as the size, sector, methods of production, climate, location, and even management decisions of the firm in question. Although a firm may not be entirely driven by self-interest, the fact that it is pursuing a honest abidance of local environmental laws and regulations without finding methods to bypass them, in itself is a good demonstration of enlightened approach to ERBS. Such a firm will be under no pressure from the government to fit environmental regulations—it would have already found a way to meet them.

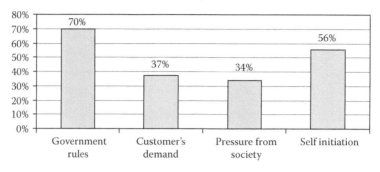

Factors influencing your organization to adopt Green policies

Figure 2.8   Drivers influencing ERBS. (Based on Trivedi and Unhelkar, 2010.)

Responsible Business Ecosystem

As reported by Rosen et al., in the San Francisco Bay area, if a company tracks its resource usage and its waste generation, it can be certified by the Bay Area Green Business Program. This gives the business a higher profile in an environmentally sensitive community and may translate into customer and brand loyalty.

Hewlett-Packard is also known to have been a pioneer in the domain of environmental sustainability (Velte, Velte and Elsenpeter, 2008; Unhelkar and Dickens, 2008). As far back as 1970s, HP had created an internal program of recycling printouts and punch cards that has eventually blossomed into a full take-back program of its electronic goods. Once returned, these electronic goods can then be safely and responsibly disposed off. Interestingly, HP capitalizes on its large size and goes beyond its organizational boundaries to leverage its experience and reputation to help suppliers and others improve along the environmental responsibility dimension.

This driver is based on the simple fact that if a large organization that has myriad different associations with its many collaborating smaller sized organizations changes its direction and priorities, then those collaborating organizations have to change their priorities accordingly. Figure 2.9 shows this green business ecosystem. A large global green organization in Figure 2.9 has three major areas through which it can influence: Green Processes, Green Data Center, and Green Consortiums. When such a large, global organization changes to environmentally sustainability, an entire ecosystem made up of the business partners, suppliers, and customers and internal users organizations, together with the industry and the corresponding business consortiums in which the organization exists are all affected. These various stakeholders and associations are invariably pushed into implementing environmentally responsible initiatives and strategies. This happens by virtue of the multiple interactions—by physical and electronic—that are undertaken in the course of daily business activities. For example, if a large organization insists on dealing with many small organizations only if their product or service is within a certain self-ascertained or permissible carbon emission range, then the smaller organizations are automatically geared toward carbon compliance. This scenario is demonstrated by HP, wherein not only are the environmental impacts monitored and managed by the organization, but also by virtue of its own management and active involvement with the members of its supply chain, the overall carbon impact of the activities of the suppliers to HP is also reduced (based on Velte, Velte, and Elsenpeter, 2008).

The impact of business ecosystem can also be felt in the reverse. Thus, for example, if a large group of collaborating organizations form a consortium and start moving together toward ERBS, then that will force even a large organization to follow suit as, otherwise, it would be left behind. The end result is an environmentally responsible business "ecosystem" that also encourages and

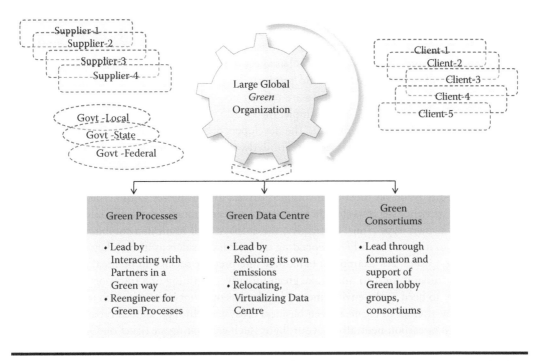

Figure 2.9 Green business ecosystem of a group of organizations—a large green organization, in its wake, influences its partners, customers, and even regulatory bodies.

enjoins these smaller partnering organizations to implement environmentally responsible business practices and initiatives.

In addition to the impact of collaborating organizations in a business ecosystem, there are also considerations of superimposition of long-term trends upon short-term markets (Goel et al., 2011). Such superimpositions bring about major business changes and restructuring of ideas that are environmentally friendly.

This is particularly true with long-term suppliers who continue to influence the organizations they supply to, and are, in turn, influenced by them. A business ecosystem is not just made up of physical relationships between customers and suppliers; such an ecosystem would be made up of electronic collaborations on the web—driven by web services and service oriented architecture (see Chapter 6 for more details). Electronic collaborations offer opportunities to reduce total carbon within a collaborative process through integration of systems. This integration also leads to an opportunity to facilitate electronic sharing of information and sharing common operational platforms relating to Green ICT.

Impact of changes to government legislation is also felt by a collaborative suite of businesses. Legislative changes impact areas of governance, audit, reporting, and compliance across a group of organizations in an industry. Given the timeframes involved around the implementation for and compliance with legislation, business is often faced with the need to implement tactical solutions to meet immediate needs, which may then become the incumbent or are replaced by longer-term solutions (Sherringham and Unhelkar, 2011). Green ICT can be used to deliver both tactical solutions for businesses to meet legislative needs as well as enable longer-term solutions across a group of organizations that form a green business ecosystem.

New Market Opportunities

As mentioned in earlier discussion, global environmental awareness, corresponding legislations, and the sociocultural and political pressure on businesses has resulted in a new market that was not visible a decade ago. This new market is based on the suite of opportunities that have opened up for creating and providing services and products that *assist* other organizations in achieving their green initiatives and goals. Thus, we are talking not only about "businesses that are green" but "green as a business offering." For example, the CEMS is a new breed of software applications that are suddenly available in the market. The developers of these new software applications have discovered a market that did not exist earlier. Similarly, smart meters to measure carbon emissions, opportunities to apply new standards for optimization of emissions, and new architecture and design of low-carbon gadgets is a market that is likely to grow in the carbon economy.

Despite the discussion on the aforementioned drivers for businesses to undertake green initiatives, practical experience suggests that these drivers of a green strategy are usually interpreted by the organization in its own ways. Thus, in practice, these drivers will result in a combination of drivers for the business to initiate Green IT—depending on what it considers as its own key environmental as well as business issues. For example, a bank may interpret the social and political pressure as the most important initiator for it to undertake green initiative; a mining or a transport company may find it important to heed to the environmental legislations up-front in its approach to ERBS; or, an organization may attempt to create a green business ecosystem through a green broadband (such as done by Iprimus) or carbon-neutralizing your flight (such as booking air ticket on Qantas.com.au). Thus, in the development of a Green IT strategy, not only do these drivers need independent analysis, but they also need to be studied together to see their overall impact on the organization.

Green IT Business Dimensions (Factors)

Economy, people, processes, and technology provide the four core dimensions of an organization along which it can change. These are not independent dimensions, but are dependent on each other as the organization undertakes green enterprise transformation. However, usually, one or two dimensions may lead the transformation depending on the type, size, and current green maturity of the organization.

Once the drivers that provide the impetus to the business for its green initiatives are identified and documented, they lead to the discussion on the areas of business that are likely to be affected by the changes. The changes resulting from the Green IT initiatives transform the organization. An organization changes or transforms along four different lines, or dimensions. These business transformation dimensions have been studied and published by Unhelkar (2010) and are applicable to any kind of transformation. Figure 2.10 shows these four dimensions of an organization in the context of ERBS.

These dimensions can also be understood as the factors that will change as the organization changes. Figure 2.10 highlights how each of these four dimensions comes into a play when an organization considers environmental responsibilities within its business strategies. These four dimensions/factors are: economy, people, processes, and technology (Unhelkar, 2009a, 2010). Next four sections describe these four dimensions of change for a greening organization.

Economy

Economic considerations are one of the key factors in an organization's decision to implement environmental policies and systems. These considerations that deal with the costs associated with green transformations and the return on those costs, are the first ones to appear in the minds of

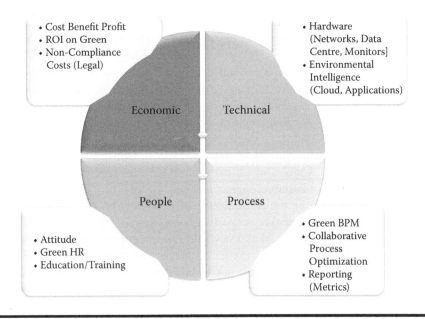

Figure 2.10   Economy, people, processes, and technology dimensions in an ERBS.

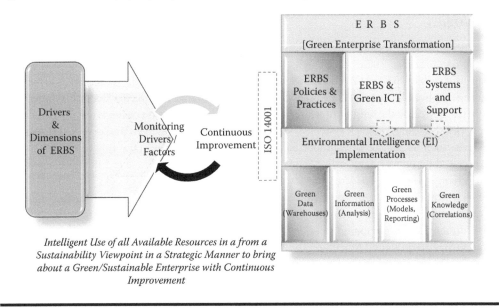

*Intelligent Use of all Available Resources in a from a
Sustainability Viewpoint in a Strategic Manner to bring
about a Green/Sustainable Enterprise with Continuous
Improvement*

Figure 2.11   Drivers and Factors lead to an ERBS.

the leaders and those in charge of the green transformation. Therefore, this is a primary dimension along which green transformation occurs in an organization. These include the cost-benefit
analysis, as well as financial ROI metrics—as depicted earlier in Figure 2.7. Figure 2.7 further
highlights the stark reality of environmental approaches by an organization. When asked in the
Trivedi and Unhelkar (2010) survey as to whether green policies are taken up by organizations in
order to increase their financial bottom line, close to 35% "Agreed" and 30% "Strongly Agreed" (a

total of 65% above the neutral line). These data underscore the arguments throughout this book—that unless environmental initiatives are coupled with economic performance, the motivation to undertake ERBS is much reduced.

Economic growth in the current economy is usually associated with increase in carbon emissions. This is particularly true of the developing economies, where all the industries are on the rise—leading to increase in emissions across the board and not just restricted to a particular organization. For example, this economic dimensions brings friction between the "developed" and the "developing" worlds—as was evident in the Copenhagen summit completed in December 2009. The dichotomy between the developed world's consumption of resources and their demand for the BRIC nations (Brazil, Russia, India, and China) to undertake their share toward conserving the environment for the future can lead to economic and legal quagmire.

This is particularly so because the consumption of resources and corresponding GHG generation does not appear to be equitable across the globe. Should a uniform regulation on carbon emissions reduction be applied globally, it would take away resources and growth potential from the aforementioned developing economies. However, not reducing carbon emissions will harm the future generations globally and is not sustainable. Thus, the economic dimension for green business transformation is fraught with challenges for the single organization, a consortium within an industry, and with entire nations. Additional discussion on this dimension appears in Chapter 3—especially on the economic impact of policies and vice versa.

Technologies

Technologies primarily include the hardware, network infrastructure, software, and applications within the organization. These technologies are summarized in Figure 2.12. This is also the more "popular" and visible aspect of Green IT. Switching off monitors, virtualization of servers, and eschewing printing on physical paper are the initial, visible aspect of change that occurs along this dimension. This is then followed by the long-term strategic change in the way the data center is organized (including its physical building, the rack system, and the actual servers themselves) and operated. Emerging technologies, such as Service orientation, SaaS, and Cloud computing take this dimension to the next level—leading up to what is called "Environmental Intelligence." These technological aspects of Green IT changes are discussed later (particularly Chapters 4 and 6) in this book.

The technical dimension presents challenges in terms of the size and position of the organization. For example, small and medium enterprises (SMEs) tend to have a different approach to the technical dimensions as compared to large multinational technology producing vendors and conglomerates (Marmaridis and Unhelkar, 2011). What in the SME space is heralded as technologically innovative and new may actually have been around at the enterprise space for years. For example, virtualization, which is considered a "given" for most large organization, may have just appeared in a small business—perhaps only as a desktop virtualization. Thus, in the technical dimension, large enterprises can make significant inroads toward their Green IT accomplishments through server consolidation and energy-efficient data center technologies, whilst smaller businesses may not able to achieve the same rate of change because they do not use that many servers or rely on data center's for their hosting. In such cases, SaaS-based solutions that are now rapidly emerging may provide excellent opportunities for small businesses to shift their hardware/operating costs and carbon generation over to the SaaS vendors. SaaS-based information technology solutions will make information readily accessible while leveraging data center cooling and power consumption efficiencies and do away with up-front capital costs for purchasing hardware servers to run from their premises. There is also a direct correlation between turning away from desktop computers to using laptops

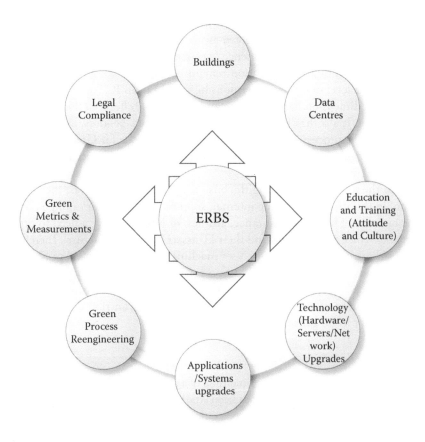

Figure 2.12   Various areas of influence of a ERBS.

and other mobile or portable devices and moving closer to Green IT. This dimension of Green IT transformation is thus affected by more than one of the drivers discussed previously—particularly rules and regulations and responsible ecosystem. The introduction of eco-friendly technologies and technical management practices sees the organization comply with rules and regulations measuring power consumption. On the other hand, lowering the organization's carbon footprint through intelligent application of technology and greener infrastructure helps the organization further comply in the context of responsible business within its ecosystem of operation.

Processes

The process dimension of an organization deals with "how" things are done within an organization. Figure 2.10 lists Green BPM, Collaborative business process optimization and reporting (with metrics) as some of the key elements of process aspect of an environmental strategy. Green BPM (discussed in detail in Chapter 5) is made up of process management as well as process reengineering. Business process reengineering is the fundamental rethinking and radical redesign of business processes to achieve dramatic improvements in critical, contemporary measures of performance such as cost, quality, service, and speed (Hammer and Champy, 1993). The need to reengineer the business operations, process, and services according to the environmental parameters has also been highlighted by Murugesan (2008). Herein, an organization model studies and optimizes its processes in order to improve its green credentials. This work is made up of optimizing existing processes and that of introducing new green-aware processes that will not only reduce carbon emissions but also enhance customer experience (e.g., Aronson, 2008).

The process dimension of an organization remains as perhaps the most visible one and it is often used to judge the level of ecological responsibility for Green ICT of the organization. This is because the process dimension has immediate and measurable effects to the carbon footprint of the business operation. It also has far-reaching effects on clients, vendors, and business partners in the collaboration. The process carbon footprint and compliance for Green ICT operations by other business partners can serve as a good proxy for measuring the effectiveness of Green ICT initiatives within the organization.

In addition to the need for optimizing the business processes themselves, there is also a need to pay attention, in this dimension to the internal, support processes. For example, organizations that are in the business of banking, insurance, airlines, or hospitals have a need to organize their support and maintenance processes around their IT assets and infrastructure. Therefore, support processes such as those called upon when a user machine breaks down, need to be considered in light of their overheads and corresponding carbon generation within the organization. Proactive maintenance of devices and systems, outsourcing of noncore service function, precautionary actions such as installation of antiviruses and antispam, can all contribute to optimized support processes and reduced carbon generation.

People

This is the most difficult and most complex dimension of a green enterprise transformation. While the people aspect of an organization's behavior has been studied to in great depths, in this discussion the focus is on the attitudes of individuals and the sociocultural setup in which they operate in the context of the environment. The same sociocultural driver that drives the organization toward Green IT also provides the challenge when the organization actually undertakes that transformation. In addition to the individual employee and, also, the customer at the grassroot level, there is a significant challenge in this people dimension when it comes to business leadership for Green IT transformation.

An enterprise-wide green strategy is best driven from the top of the organization in order to ensure its success. Leadership within this people aspect, such as that by senior directors and CxOs, plays a decider in an environmental initiative. The involvement of senior management in bringing about a change in this people dimension is vital—and it has to be done at an early stage of a green initiative. Making the key stakeholders fully aware of the importance of the green initiative for the organization and, through them, promoting the initiative to bring about fundamental change in the attitudes is the key to work in this dimension. While such involvement from the senior leadership requires substantial commitment in terms of time, money, and other resources (as discussed earlier in the economic dimension), still the attitude and the subjective viewpoints of people play an equally major role in the success of a Green IT project.

People thus become a major differentiator between two organizations with similar drivers for sustainability. Organization of teams for the Green IT project and further effect of the CGO's mindset on the project are discussed in Chapters 3 and 8. Finally, people also need to be considered by large organizations in terms of attracting new talents. It is not uncommon for the bright MBA graduate to select and choose to work for an organization that boasts high green credentials than only a good workplace. Thus far, the discussion in this chapter has been on the drivers and the dimensions for Green IT transformation. These drivers and the dimensions under which the transformation takes place are discussed from the viewpoint of their core characteristics.

Finally, in this discussion, it is worth reiterating that there is no single driver, dimensions, or Green IT strategy that will fit all organizations. Figure 2.11 shows a comprehensive view of the drivers and dimensions leading to a comprehensive ERBS. The policies, systems and support providing basis for what is called Environmental Intelligence (EI) (Trivedi and Unhelkar, 2009). The data, information, process and knowledge aspect of Green IT are also integral to the ERBS as shown in Figure 2.11. Although the earlier discussion has distilled the commonalities in these aspects of a strategy, still organizations need to identify, develop, and implement their own specific short- and long-term green strategies. Thus, these various aforementioned aspects of Green IT drivers and dimensions vary depending on the industry sector and the size (small or large) and type (product or service) of the organization. These aspects of Green IT drivers are applied in different combination and with varying emphasis. The case studies, later in this book, attempt to highlight these differences in the way the drivers and dimensions are interpreted and applied to Green IT. Table 2.2 lists the major Green IT considerations for different organization types—with examples of corresponding industry sectors in which these organizations exist.

Table 2.3 lists some of the nuances of Green IT strategies when it comes to specific industry verticals. Each industry sector listed in Table 2.3 has its own variation to Green IT depending on whether it is a product, service, or infrastructure organizations. Similarly, size and location of organizations bring variations in their Green IT strategies.

Developing an ERBS

An ERBS is the result of the strategic vision of the organization's leadership. In the context of this discussion, this ERBS aims for strategies that will be relevant in a 3–5-year time period. Developing such a strategic vision refers to what the leaders of the enterprise would expect it to look like in the future (Lan and Unhelkar, 2005). In the context of green strategies, this ideal image, made up of expectations and goals of the organization,

Wills (2009) has applied the lean approach to the greening approach under the aegis of what is called Green-Stream Mapping (Wills, 2009). Those environmental considerations include seven areas of focus that are derived from the International Standard of Sustainability Reporting: Energy, Water, Materials, Garbage, Travel/Transportation Emissions and Effluents, and Biodiversity.

Table 2.2 Organizations Consideration of Green IT Strategies

Type of Organization	Major Green IT Consideration
Product (retailers, electronic goods vendors, vendors of consumables, packaging)	Operational carbon (as they don't have production infrastructure and overheads). The unit of carbon-producing device or product is, however, easier to calculate. Therefore, economy and technology dimensions may be more handy to start with. Furthermore, inventory, supply chains, and distribution processes may assume significance in the Green IT effort.
Service (banks, insurance, education/healthcare)	People and their attitudes play a crucial role in service-based organizations. Therefore, process and people dimension of transformation become highly significant. Efficiency in processes can have a dramatic impact on the carbon footprint of service-based organizations.
Infrastructure (buildings, telecom)	Architecture and design at the start of the project is a vital consideration. Furthermore, with telecom, improvement and efficiency in communication around the world can be another major contributor to reduction in carbon footprint.

Table 2.3   Industry Verticals and Green IT

Industry Verticals and Green IT Nuances
Education—A service industry in which processes are important. Green IT can be used in collecting as well as promoting educational material globally. Online education mechanisms, sharing of online classrooms, and tutorials can provide significant advantage in terms of reduced infrastructure and, therefore, reduced carbon.
Hospital/Medicine—In addition to the processes and people relating to Green IT, attention should also be paid to the fact that major IT revolutions have resulted in high-end medical equipments, which, while saving lives, also contribute to the carbon footprint of the hospitals. These medical equipments, together with the IT systems and support, make up a substantial amount of carbon emissions.
Entertainment—has significant infrastructure as well as operational carbon-costs. For example, most high-carbon emitting equipments such as televisions, cable TV, movies, theaters, and gaming are studded with carbon-generating gadgets. There is a need to calculate the carbon footprint by separating the procurement/ installation, operation, and disposal of equipments.
Finance—Information technologies and systems are heavily used in the financial world, right from providing prices for stocks through to completion of trades. The entire global wealth generation and growth depends on these high-end servers and equally high-end communication equipments that have direct carbon connotations.
Security—In a different, security-conscious new world, the security vertical is replete with electronic gadgets that produce significant carbon. Furthermore, with security gadgets, it is almost mandatory that they operate all 24x7 duration. Therefore, gadgets such as alarm systems in homes, vehicles, business premises, and the associated TV monitoring, recording, and analysis have a tremendous carbon-cost in addition to the actual costs of having and operating these devices.
Telecom—Clearly an infrastructure type of organization, with challenges in terms of procurement and installation of large (and many a times public) infrastructures. The carbon footprints of the installations are much higher than those of the operations. End-user devices and applications supporting telecom business (such as the billing and operational support) also need to be studied from their procurement and operational emissions viewpoint.
Bank—Although a financial services industry, the IT infrastructure and applications used in the banking sector are staggering. Banking vertical is one of the very high emitter of carbon emissions and, as such, requires strategies that span both services and infrastructure aspects of Green IT.
Packaging—A unique product-based industry that is involved in producing and delivering packaging materials in myriad different forms. Reusability and recycling of packaging materials as well as innovative ways of creating packaging is likely to impact environmental sustainability in a major way in this vertical. Green IT can be used as a support mechanism to facilitate optimized production of packaging.

provide the primary input for the development of those strategies. This input into the initial envisioning process of a green organization is provided by the drivers and dimensions of Green IT. A simple and direct vision, based on the drivers and dimensions translates into the strategic plan. The strategic vision and the ensuing strategic plan should be an actionable plan. Leadership and senior management need to be directly involved in the development of the green strategic vision for their enterprise. This requires them to carefully evaluate the enterprise from its carbon perspective and the trends of the entire future business environment in which the enterprise exists.

While a 3–5-year time period is a good starting point in terms of the impact of the strategic plan, still this period can vary from industry to industry. For instance, the oil industry may have a 10+ year strategic plan, whereas a dress manufacturer in the fashion industry may have only a strategic plan for Green IT that would be current for no more than a couple of years as the contents and expressions in that business sector changes rapidly.

Green IT strategies require due consideration to the resources, knowledge, and skills that are required in the green transformation, as also the current resource utilization in development, production, services, markets, and sales. Perhaps some indication of what the competitors are doing in the green space may also be of importance, as it may indicate the urgency and importance of action.

Wide-Ranging Considerations in ERBS

Development of an ERBS requires due consideration to wide-ranging organizational factors as shown in Figure 2.12. Many of these considerations also appear in the development and implementation of a Lean IT strategy and framework.

Figure 2.12 lists the specific considerations in development of an ERBS. They are as follows:

- Buildings and associated infrastructures need to be considered from their initial design and construction viewpoint. There is opportunity for substantial reduction in the emissions of an infrastructure if attention is paid to its initial design and construction from a carbon reduction viewpoint.
- Data centers, which are specialized buildings to house data and computing servers as well as network equipments of the organization, require major strategic attention from a carbon perspective as the impact of such decision in the early stages of a data center are long lasting.
- Education and training (attitude and culture) of the staff is of primary concern in developing an ERBS. This would require not only paying attention to the current attitude and understanding the path for change, but also considering green HR that provides support and encouragement for changes to the attitude.
- Technology (hardware/servers/network) upgrades that will invariably occur as the organization prepares strategies for a green transformation. This consideration includes reuse and recycling of existing hardware as well as strategies for replacing it with new, more carbon-efficient hardware.
- Applications/systems upgrades need to be considered in two major areas—first, the upgrade of the existing applications and systems to enable incorporation of carbon data within them and, second, to strategize for the new carbon emissions management software that is dedicated to collecting, storing, analyzing and reporting only on carbon data.

- Green process reengineering also includes green business process management (as discussed in Chapter 5). The reengineering strategies need to appear in the overall ERBS in terms of the approach to their identification, modeling, and optimization.
- Green metrics and measurements that form part of identifying the "as is" and modeling the "to be" state of the organization (in-depth discussion in Chapter 3).
- Legal compliance has to be an integral part of Green IT strategies. Legal requirements can vary from local and state legislations through to carbon legislations at the national level. There are also international consortiums and summits that dictate the legal requirements and need to be incorporated in the ERBS.

The above discussion indicates that a business striving to be green needs to create a comprehensive strategy that should include these wide-ranging considerations in it. In fact, depending on the type, size, location, and industrial vertical, many more factors will have to be considered in the development of a Green IT strategy.

Rosen et al. (2011) have also suggested factors that need to be considered in developing economic viability of green initiatives. These include waste management, toxin measurements, water quality, resource usage, recycling and reuse, and product lifecycle impact.

ERBS also requires detailed consideration to environmental intelligence across all factors within it. Thus, the existing business intelligence systems, processes, and contents are extended and refined to handle EI when it comes to implementing ERBS.

Steps in Developing an ERBS

After giving due consideration to the wide-ranging factors influencing ERBS, the focus should be on the steps in developing that strategic document. Figure 2.13 shows, at an abstracted level, what are the major phases (steps) in the development of an ERBS.

- As mentioned earlier, though, the development of an ERBS requires active participation from the business leadership—including the CEO and the CGO (Chief Green Officer—discussed in Chapter 3). Murugesan (2008) has also highlighted the need to engage with the

Figure 2.13 Steps in developing an ERBS.

key stakeholders and create awareness of environmental issues in the green strategies for the enterprise. The drivers, dimensions, length and breadth, metrics, and measurements are all required to be embedded in the ERBS.

These major phases in the development of policies and practices (discussed in Chapter 3) and the Green IT transformation roadmap (Chapter 9) are further expanded in the ensuing sections. However, these phases are worth discussing here in terms of what they entail and what resources are required by organizations to undertake these steps.

Green Business Objectives

The green business objectives are the core objectives for a business undertaking green transformation. Following are some of the points that can be used to formulate specific green objectives in the development of ERBS:

■ Ensuring a synergy between the core business objectives and the accompanying green objectives
■ Length of time for potential application—3–5 years being ideal
■ Key drivers and dimensions that are impacting the organization
■ Identify the growth potential and means for returns on green investment
■ Attention to collaborative opportunities especially at a global level identification of markets and regions for green products and services globally
■ Finding the niche where the competitive advantage for the organization lies
■ Identifying the areas for formal Green IT audits to ascertain the green maturity of the organization
■ Development of Green HR as a part of the strategy
■ Optimization and integration of supply chain systems
■ Incorporation of government rules and regulations

A SWOT (Strength, Weakness, Opportunity, Threat) analysis can be carried out to further fin-tune the green business objectives. In this regard, the environmental survey (Trivedi and Unhelkar, 2010) quizzed the participants about the current state of their organizations with respect to its green credentials. This current state would give a good indication of the green preparedness of the organization and also an indication of the areas in which efforts need to be focused. The results from that survey are shown in Figure 2.14.

These results can also be interpreted as follows:

■ Forty-three percent of the participants agreed and close to 26% strongly agreed on the fact that their organizations are aware of the importance of Green metrics. This indicates that there is a significant awareness of the need for specific green metrics when the green business objectives are specified and developed within the ERBS.
■ Thirty-five percent of the participants agreed and close to 8% strongly agreed on assuming responsibility for its carbon footprints within their organizations. These results also indicate that there are a significant number of respondents who do not believe that their organizations are taking responsibility for its carbon footprint—leading to a primary consideration of responsibility in developing ERBS.

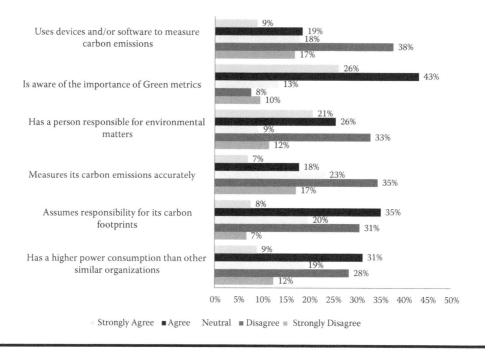

Figure 2.14 Current state of organization with respect to its green credentials.

- Thirty-one percent of the participants agreed and close to 9% strongly agreed on the fact that their organization has a higher power consumption than other similar organizations.
- Twenty-six percent of the participants agreed and close to 21% strongly agreed to the fact that they have a person responsible for environmental matters at their organizations.
- Nineteen percent of the participants agreed and close to 9% strongly agreed to the fact that they are using devices and/or software to measure carbon emissions in their organizations.
- Eighteen percent of the participants agreed and close to 7% strongly agreed on the fact that their organizations are measuring its carbon emissions accurately.
- Sixteen percent of the participants agreed and close to 3% strongly agreed to the fact that carbon footprint in their organization is the driver for carbon reduction.
- About 29% disagreed-to-strongly disagreed on using or having these green credential in their organizations.

Strategy Descriptions

Strategy descriptions include specifications of the products and services affected by Green IT, current and anticipated market conditions and customer behavior and supplier behavior, spelling out the necessary and required expertise, knowledge, skills and goals/objectives.

Figure 2.13 shows strategy descriptions as second phase in the development of an ERBS. Describing the green strategy should be done in clear terms and with goals and KPIs that are measurable. Strategy descriptions include analysis of current business process, consideration to organizational values, and description of underlying IT systems and hardware. For a 3–5-year strategic

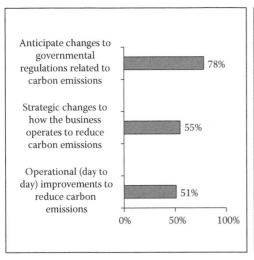

Figure 2.15 Green strategies are formulated to handle the seven organizational (business) factors.

plan, it is not uncommon for the organization to spend anywhere between 3 and 6 months developing a comprehensive strategy description. Strategy descriptions lead to green enterprise transformation projects that influence the organization for between 3 and 5 years. This also requires an understanding of the current strategic plan if it exists.

In the environmental survey (Trivedi and Unhelkar, 2010), the participants have been asked about the green strategies that are formulated to handle these factors at their organizations. The results from that survey are shown in Figure 2.15.

These results can be understood as follows:

■ Seventy-eight percent of the participants agreed that their organizations anticipated changes to governmental regulations related to carbon emissions.
■ Fifty-seven percent of the participants agreed that their organizations enhanced the human resource management through green strategies.
■ Fifty-five percent of the participants agreed that their organizations conducted strategic changes to how the business operates to reduce carbon emissions.
■ Fifty-two percent of the participants agreed that their organizations elevate corporate reputation by adopting green strategies.
■ Forty-six percent of the participants agreed that their organizations are identifying new market opportunities through adoption of green strategies.

Policy-Based Conditions

Develop and implement a Green IT policy that aims to achieve higher utilization of your IT systems while reducing energy use and lessening your other environmental impact. You don't have to do all at once—adopt a phased approach.

The Green IT policies of an organization are derived from its strategic descriptions. Chapter 3 discusses the development of policies and their practices in great detail. The impact of policies, however, is not just in their manual practices. Instead, policy-based conditions for Green IT can be embedded in the organization's service-oriented architecture and protocols. Thus, the policy-based conditions have the opportunity to influence the automation of Green IT implementation. This is an excellent and profitable opportunity for an electronic organization to embed policies within its services, applications, and packages and thereby take lead in Green IT implementations.

Physical development of policies, as discussed in Chapter 3, can be based on the SMART (http://www.smart2020.org/_assets/files/02_Smart2020Report.pdf—accessed March 16, 2011) approach to green enterprise transformation. In terms of green policies, they need to be SMART—specific, measurable, attainable, realistic, and timely. SMART can be further understood as follows:

- Standardize (S) how energy consumption and emissions information can be traced across different processes.
- Monitor (M) energy consumption and emissions across the economy in real time, providing the data needed to optimize for energy efficiency.
- Accountability (A) with the help of tools and systems.
- Redesign (R) based on systems and technologies—that will impact the equipments, materials, processes, and attitudes.
- Transform (T) the way we work and play and will do so in a low-carbon economy. This will be based on a green enterprise transformation plan.

Resource Requirements

A green strategic plan has to have a suite of resources that are required to undertake and maintain green transformation. Resources include people, processes, and technologies that engender the green transformation as well as those that are affected by the transformation.

Transformation Plan/Timelines

Development of a green enterprise transformation plan is the final and important step in the development of an ERBS. This transformation plan is a project plan that contains tasks, roles, and deliverables together with the timeline for delivery. Chapter 9 discusses in detail the creation of such a transformation plan. Usually, this transformation project plan provides the roadmap for transformation. This plan can be divided into two parts—a high-level roadmap that identifies major areas of work, deliverables, and timelines. This can then be followed by a detailed, task-by-task project plan that makes use of all know project and program management techniques.

Iterations and Risks

Figure 2.13 also indicates that the development of an ERBS should not be a unidirectional process. Instead, it should be developed as an iterative process—going through the drivers, dimensions, risks, and metrics more than once. Ideally, there should be three iterations to arrive at the final and comprehensive actionable Green IT plan. These iterations, over a period of 3–6 months, would also include observing the industry trends and new developments with respect to Green IT. The green policies have to be revised based on these trends.

These iterations also indicate the approach to implementation of the policies—that should also be based on iterations. Iterative refinements of the policies are expected during practice. However, the concepts of continuous improvements in processes, people, and technologies that provide impetus to a lean business initiative also apply here.

KPIs in Green Strategies

Key performance indicator (KPI) provides information on an organization's performance against defined and measurable criteria. KPIs can provide help in measuring the progress of an organization in the area of environmental sustainability and Green IT. Since the progress of a green initiative must be measured against the stated goals, the KPIs provide an opportunity to ascertain whether the strategic goals have been achieved or not. The KPIs not only measure the progress but also provide indication of what needs to change during the course.

Since the drivers, discussed earlier, provide the necessary impetus for the environmental approach in an organization, they provide valuable input in creating KPIs. However, the four dimensions are along which an organization transforms itself—therefore, the four dimensions of a green enterprise transformation, namely the economy, people, process, and technologies, provide an excellent basis for the formulation of the KPIs.

These environmental KPIs can vary depending on the business and the specific goals of the business. For example, an airline may decide to base its KPI on the "carbon produced per passenger kilometer" whereas a hospital may have "carbon emission from IT instruments per patient" as its criteria to measure its carbon performance. Measurable targets for each KPI need to be set as the strategies evolve. These performance areas are then measured to ascertain success or otherwise of the environmental strategies of the organization. KPIs in the Green ICT domain will reflect the organization's environmental goals and provide the basis for measuring the factors that are crucial to the organization's success.

The KPIs lead to an indication of the Green IT metrics that need to be collected. Standards, metrics, and monitoring the progress of sustainability are closely associated with KPIs evaluated for adoption. Standards allow the enterprise not only to measure success in a standard way, but also to compare itself against industry benchmarks and other organizations.

Having identified KPIs and metrics, the processes and systems to collect the metrics need to be in place. For example, if reduction in paper consumption is a KPI, then the measurement of paper consumption needs to be planned across departments, processes, and then the company. There will be a need to know different usages of paper (e.g., mailing, reports, copy machines, employee printing, forms), and a means of measuring consumption across these different usage categories. After collecting this data on the KPI, there is a need to store the results and analyze them for their sustainability knowledge.

Following are some typical KPI that is required to be embedded in an organization that is undertaking green strategies.

The KPI groups, listed in Table 2.4 can be further expanded along the four dimensions. However, each dimension has its own nuances when it comes to Green KPIs. For example, a KPI that is entirely focused on carbon reduction irrespective of cost considerations may not be acceptable in the economic dimension of the organization. Alternatively, a technologically advanced energy-efficient cooler might use less energy and hence lower operational cost; but the capital expenses toward such a cooler will be part of the economic dimension. Thus, KPIs should regularly tie business efficiency with carbon efficiency. Savings in carbon related to various aspects of the organization such as production, sales and marketing, research and development, and administration—all need to be related to savings in costs.

Table 2.4 Green KPIs in Four Groups

Primary Dimensions	*Example Goals/KPIs (Timelines, Lengths, and Depths) My Organization Will Experience the Following:*
Economic	Reduction in energy consumption by 10% of its current level per year for 3 years.
	Increase in green services (addition of one detailed service dedicated to green).
Technical	Use virtualized data servers for all its data warehouse; use smart meters to record, repost, and control emissions.
Process	Optimize SCM to reduce emissions by re-engineering individual processes.
People	Train people for Green IT at all levels.
	Telecommute once a week to reduce emissions.

Further, when KPIs are discussed, there is a need to keep in mind the metrics and measurements that are required to support such KPIs. Setting KPI targets is the easier part; measuring and reporting on the actual emissions is the greater challenge. Therefore, setting a measurement program using smart meters that feed the data into the system that can collate and analyze the resultant data is an important aspect of KPIs. Formulation of KPIs also requires referencing to the local, national, and international standards and practices—feasible. Finally, each KPI needs to be considered in the context of the organizational conditions, requiring some premonition of the caveats that should be adhered to in the use of those KPIs.

EXAMPLES OF GREEN KPIs

Example KPI-1: My organization will reduce 10% over its last year's energy bill. This reduction is aimed over next 3 years, at the end of which, we will review all factors associated with this reduction.

Caveat: Without reducing business activities.
Explanation: Enhancement in business sustainability through not only reduction in energy consumption but also through efficiency in overall business processes. ERBS provides organizations with a mechanism to consider energy-efficient measures, monitor, assess, and manage their carbon emissions.

Example KPI-2: My organization will eliminate the use of paper in all communications in the next 3 years.

Caveat: Except where it is legally binding to produce paper-based documentation.
Explanation: Elimination of paper, especially in banks, insurance, and legal firms, is not going to happen immediately. Due consideration to the legal requirements of paper-based documentation is required.

Example KPI-3: My organization will reduce production machines operation hours by 20% via intense focus on idling times of the machines over the next 3 years. At the end of the 3-year period, all factors impacting operation and production costs will be reviewed against their carbon costs.

Caveat: This 20% reduction over 3 years will require training for the staff, as well as use of power-saving gadgets (including software) that can help detect idling times of various machineries and equipments in the organization and switch them off.

Explanation: The cost of training of personnel and the costs associated with procurement of power-saving gadgetry are important aspects of this KPI. Therefore, they need to be included in the calculations of ROI on the carbon reduction initiative.

Example KPI-4: My organization will promote the creation and implementation of Green IT strategies and the subsequent carbon savings by adhering to standards and guidelines and proper labeling of green compliance in products.

Caveat: Standards associated with labelling of Green products are continuously changing; they are also different from region to region. Costs and effort are required to ensure formal labelling.

Explanation: All products and services need to disclose their carbon contents. This would usually result in enhancement of public image and thereby increase the marketability. A 2009 study by Forrester Research, Inc., "The Rise of the Green Enterprise: A Primer for IT Leadership's Involvement," notes that in the "Economist Intelligence Unit's February 2008 survey of more than 1,200 business executives, companies that rated their Green efforts most highly over the past three years saw annual average profit increases of 16 percent and share price growth of 45 percent" (Carotenuto, 2009).

Example KPI-5: My organization will ensure its carbon emissions are within 150 kT as stipulated by the government regulations in the year 2010–2011.

Caveat: The government regulations will change. Keep in mind this changing nature of the regulations and caps when committing to staying within stipulated limits.

Explanation: An ERBS can help an organization start complying with the governmental regulations. For example, an ERBS implementation contains environmental web services that increase the access to the information about the carbon status of the organization. Functional capabilities of the enterprise can be updated to ensure carbon compliance. However, such compliance is based on a dynamic figure that will keep changing as new regulations are brought in place.

Example KPI-6: My organization will provide easy access to information about carbon emission status.

Caveat: Privacy of information should be of immense importance, as increasing carbon performance of an organization will be as important as its profit performance.

Explanation: Access to carbon performance of the organization can be part of good corporate citizenry. This carbon data presents the personality of the organization to the consumer and the general public. Therefore, making this data available is going to help the organization and the consumers in understanding its direction. This is similar to the requirements to disclose the company's financials to the stock market within limits and legal requirements. However, similar to financial data, there is a need to limit what gets presented to the public to ensure that the company is not disadvantaged in its market dealings.

Example KPI-7: My organization will compare its green efforts against industry standard benchmarks in order to improve its carbon performance. This rating comparison will occur over next 5 years, at the end of which, we will review the impact of rating on organization revenues, profit increase, and share price growth.

Caveat: The benchmarks and standards are themselves likely to change over the period of 3–5 years.

Explanation: None of the standards and benchmarks associated with carbon performance of organizations are steady. As this gets written, the prime minister of Australia, Ms. Julian Gillard has met with President B. Obama - and the meeting has reflected a new direction associated with carbon taxing for the Australian government. Similar vacillating policies relating to carbon emission control can be seen elsewhere in the world resulting in uncertain standards and benchmarks.

Example KPI-8: My organization will establish a suite of green alliances across various business lines. The alliances are aimed over the next 3 years, at the end of which we will review the impact of these alliances on organization business growth.

Caveat: Trust and security of alliances is a factor that should be considered upfront.

Explanation: ERBS promotes organizations to collaborate with each other, resulting in a suite of green alliances across various lines of business. Organizations can assist each other through formation of common standards and subscribing to them, sharing carbon data and information through collaborative web services, and share experiences in terms of successes and risks associated with their green initiatives. Eventually, the monetizing of carbon processes will require greater alignment by multiple businesses—as is envisaged by ERBS.

Additional KPI Examples

- My organization will reduce the energy consumption of its IT systems by 20%, 15%, and 10% every financial year over the next 3 years which will results in total cost savings over the current operation of 50%.
- My organization will reduce the rest of its energy consumption (non-IT, such as smart lighting, air conditioning, car fleet) by 10% per year over previous year for the next 3 years.
- My organization will introduce reuse of materials and equipment by making conscious attempt in training, educating, and equipping personnel. Such reuse includes responsible recycling of e-waste (inc toners, unused IT/mobile phones; see Unhelkar (2009b) for detailed discussion).
- My organization is committed to buying Green IT products.
- My organization is committed to use of renewable/green energy wherever possible. All business processes in the organization will be modeled and subjected to Green IT audit.
- Forty percent of all work that requires physical meetings will be conducted using teleworking facilities such as video conferencing and social media networks.
- My organization will achieve Green IT maturity of Level 3 in the next 3 years.
- All employees will be provided 2 days of training per quarter in developing an understanding and use of Green IT.

Discussion Points

- What is a green strategy mix? Consider examples of organizations that you know of that would fit within the strategy mix.
- What are Green IT strategies? How would you develop Green IT strategies for an organization looking 3–5 years ahead in time?
- Discuss the importance of consortiums in an 8+ year Green IT strategy.

- Explain how costs and profit margins play a role in driving an organization toward ERBS? (hint—refer to Figure 2.7 in your discussion)
- Compare enlightened self-interest with the sociopolitical pressure as Green IT drivers.
- How does a green business ecosystem influence many small organizations? How does it influence a large organization?
- What are the four dimensions along which an organization can transform to a green organization?
- Show how you would incorporate data centers, metrics, education and training, and green process reengineering within an ERBS.
- Argue for the need for iterations in following the steps for ERBS.

Action Points

- Identify the most important ERBS driver that will impact your organization in the short term (within an year, e.g., regulatory and legal—identify the specific regulation that you may be required to comply with).
- List that driver specifically against the current business goals of your organization (e.g., customer experience enhancement and regulation).
- List the potential conflict between the two goals—environmental and business (e.g., need to comply with lower carbon emission requirement may lead to reduced customer experience).
- Identify areas of business where ERBS can cause substantial and measurable impact.
- Discuss a strategy to ameliorate the above situation (e.g., by highlighting to the customer the reduction in carbon through a slightly slower process of providing service).
- Update the above strategy with an approach that can do both—enhance the customer experience *and* reduce carbon (e.g., through the use of an upgraded device, or reengineering of the process to provide service that makes it more efficient).
- Measure the driver for which the approach or initiative is taken. For example, measure customer experience through customer survey or find it out by customer uptake.
- Discuss all the above steps, but now in the context of a driver for ERBS that will affect your organization in the long term (3–5 years).
- List the potential Green KPIs in four groups corresponding to the four dimensions for your organization.
- Revise the list of Green KPIs after discussions with your green strategy team.

References

Arveson, P. (1998). Background And History Of Measurement-Based Management. Accessed 3rd April, 2011, from http://www.balancedscorecard.org/bkgd/bkgd.html

Aronson, J. (2008). Making IT a positive force in environmental change. *IT Professional*, *10*(1), 43–45. doi:10.1109/MITP.2008.13.

Atkins, T. and Ali, H. J. (2009). Mobile strategy of strategic E-business solution by Dr. Tony Atkins and Hairul, A. K., Nizam, P. G., Ali, H. J., chapter 3 in *Handbook of Research in Mobile Business: Technical, Methodological and Social Perspectives*, 2nd ed., ed. B. Unhelkar. IGI Global, Hershey, PA, VSA.

Boutros-Ghali, B. (1995). *Agenda for Peace*. Paper presented United Nations Conference on Environment and Development, Rio.

Carotenuto, D. (2009). *Propelling Green initiatives with BI, Business Intelligence.* Available at http://www. ebizq.net/topics/bi/features/11624.html, accessed October 12, 2009.

Cartland, S. (2005). Business continuity challenges in global supply chains. In Y. Lan and B. Unhelkar, eds., *Global Integrated Supply Chain Systems.* IDEAS Group Publishing, Hershey, PA, USA.

Connection Research. (2010). Connection Research Website. Available at http://www.connectionresearch. com.au/, accessed October 2010.

CSR. (2010). Mallen Baker in "Corporate Social Responsibility—what does it mean?" Available at http:// www.mallenbaker.net/csr/CSRfiles/definition.html, accessed October 2010.

Esty, D. C. and Winston, A. S. (2006). *Green to Gold: How Smart Companies Use Environmental Strategy to Innovate, Create Value, and Build Competitive Advantage.* John Wiley and Sons, NJ, USA.

European Commission, 2009

Forge, S. (2007). Powering down: remedies for unsustainable ICT. *Foresight-Cambridge,* 9(4): 3–21. doi:10.1108/14636680710773795

Garito, M. (2011). Balancing green ICT business development with corporate social responsibility (CSR). In B. Unhelkar, ed., *Handbook of Research in Green ICT: Technical, Business and Social Perspectives,* pp. 607–620. IGI Global, Hershey, PA, USA.

Gartner (2009). Gartner EXP Worldwide Survey of 1,500 CIOs Shows 85 Percent of CIOs Expect Significant Change Over Next Three Years. Available at http://www.gartner.com/it/page.jsp?id=587309, accessed October 4, 2009.

Ghose, A. (2011). In B. Unhelkar, ed., *Handbook of Research in Green ICT: Technical, Business and Social Perspectives* IGI Global, Hershey, PA, USA. and Billiau, G., "Chapter 12 The Optimizing Web: A Green ICT Research Perspective." pp. 184-196.

Godbole, N. (2011). In B. Unhelkar, ed., *Handbook of Research in Green ICT: Technical, Business and Social Perspectives* IGI Global, Hershey, PA, USA.Chapter 34 Green Health: The Green IT Implications for Healthcare and Related Businesses pp. 470-479

Amit Goel, A., Tiwary, A. and Schmidt,H. Chapter 11 Approaches and Initiatives to Green IT Strategy in Business pp. 169-183 (2011). In B. Unhelkar, ed., *Handbook of Research in Green ICT: Technical, Business and Social Perspectives* IGI Global, Hershey, PA, USA.

Hammer, M. and Champy, J. (1993). *Reengineering the Corporation: A Manifesto for Business Revolution,* Harper Collins, London.

Hendrik, G. and Volk, C. (2008). *Green ICT. Pink Elephants or Real Return?* (pp. 1–140). West LB, Germany.

Lan, Y. and Unhelkar, B. (2005). *Global Enterprise Transitions.* IDEAS Group Publishing.

Marmaridis, I. and Unhelkar, B. (2011). Collaboration as a key enabler for small and medium enterprises (SME) implementing green ICT. In B. Unhelkar, ed., *Handbook of Research in Green ICT: Technical, Business and Social Perspectives,* pp. 256–264. IGI Global, Hershey, PA, USA.

Molla, A. (2009). An exploration of green IT adoption, drivers and inhibitors. *Annual Conference on Information Science and Technology Management (CISTM 2009),* July 13–15, 2009.

Murugesan, S. (2008). Can IT go Green—Introduction. *Cutter IT Journal,* Cutter Consortium, 2008, Vol 21, No. 2, February 2008, Cutter Consortium, USA.

Murugesan, S. (2008). Harnessing Green IT: Principles and Practices. IEEE. *IT Professional,* (January–February): 24–33.

National Greenhouse and Energy Reporting Act 2007 (NGER). http://www.climatechange.gov.au/reporting accessed March 17, 2011.

Patterson, M., Pratt, A., and Kumar, P. (2006). *From UPS to Silicon, an End-to-End Evaluation of Data Center Efficiency.* Paper presented at the Proceedings of the EPA Event: Enterprise Servers and Data Centers: Opportunities for Energy Savings. Hershey, PA, USA.

Pearce, D. (1989). *An Economic Perspective on Sustainable Development.* Environmental Economics Centre, London.

Philipson, G. (2009). Green IT and Sustainability in Australia, Report by Connection Research, http://connectionresearch04.goodbarry.com/GreenIT09.htm, accessed April 3, 2011

Przybyla, D. and Pegah, M. (2007). *Dealing with the veiled devil: Eco-responsible computing strategy.* Paper presented at the Proceedings of the 35th annual ACM SIGUCCS Conference on User services, Orlando, Florida, USA.

Raghavendra, R., Ranganathan, P., Talwar, V., Wang, Z., and Zhu, X. (2008). *No "power" struggles: Coordinated multi-level power management for the data center.* Enterprise Systems and Software Laboratory HP Laboratories Palo Alto HPL-2007-194 December 20, 2007* http://www.hpl.hp.com/techreports/2007/HPL-2007-194.pdf

Rosen, M., Krichevsky, T., and Sharma, H. (2011). Strategies for a sustainable enterprise. In B. Unhelkar, ed., *Handbook of Research in Green ICT: Technical, Business and Social Perspectives*, pp. 1–28. IGI Global, Hershey, PA, USA.

Schmidt, N.-H., Erek, K., Kolbe, L. M., and Zarnekow, R. (2009). Towards a procedural model for sustainable information systems management. *42nd Hawaii International Conference on System Sciences—2009, IEEE.*

Sherringham, K. (2010). Pragmatic Business Takeaways from the Icelandic Volcanic Ash Events. Available at http://contingencyplanning.com/articles/2010/05/05/pragmatic-business-takeaways-from-the-icelandic-volcanic-ash-events.aspx, accessed February 02, 2011.

Sherringham, K. and Unhelkar, B. (2011). Strategic business trends in the context of green ICT. In B. Unhelkar, ed., *Handbook of Research in Green ICT: Technical, Business and Social Perspectives*, pp. 65–82. IGI Global, Hershey, PA, USA.

Swallow, L. (2009). Creating your sustainability plan. In L. Swallow, ed., *Green Business Practices for Dummies*, pp. 51–80. Wiley publishing, Hoboken, NJ, USA.

Trivedi, B. and Unhelkar, B. (2010). PhD research, conducted at DDU University, Nadiad, Gujarat, India in 2010. Data appearing in the PhD thesis due for Submission.

Carbon Trust. See www.carbontrust.co.uk The Business of energy efficiency - a paper from Carbon trust Advisory Services http://www.carbontrust.co.uk/cut-carbon-reduce-costs/reduce/large-organisation/Documents/energy-efficiency-report-2010.pdf, accessed March 17, 2011.

The climate group (2008–2011). see http://www.theclimategroup.org/publications/

Toffler, A. (1980). *The Third Wave.* Bantam, New York.

Unhelkar, B. (2008). Mobile enterprise architecture. *Cutter Executive Report.* Boston, USA, April 2008, 11(3).

Unhelkar, B. (2009a). *Business Transformations: Framework and Process*, (16,000 words), Cutter Executive Report, Nov, 2009, USA. Vol. 12, No. 10, *Business-IT Strategies practice.*

Unhelkar, B. (2009b). *Mobile Enterprise Transition and Management.* Taylor & Francis Group (Auerbach Publications), Boca Raton, FL, USA.

Unhelkar, B. (2010). *Environmentally Responsible Business Strategies for a Green Enterprise Transformation*, Vol. 13, No. 2, Feb 2010, Business-IT strategies resource centre, Cutter Executive Report.

Unhelkar, B. and Dickens, A. (2008). Lessons in Implementing "Green" Business Strategies with ICT. *Cutter IT Journal, Special issue on "Can IT Go Green?"*, Ed. S. Murugesan, 21(2): 32–39.

Unhelkar, B. and Philipson, G. (2009). The development and application of a green IT maturityindex. *ACOSM2009—Proceedings of the Australian Conference on Software Measurements*, November 2009, Sydney.

Unhelkar, B. and Trivedi, B. (2009). Merging web services with 3G IP Multimedia systems for providing solutions in managing environmental compliance by businesses. *Proceedings of the 3rd International Conference on Internet Technologies and Applications (Internet Technologies and Applications, ITA 09)*, September 8–11, 2009, Wrexham, North Wales, UK.

Velte, T., Velte, A., and Elsenpeter, R. (2008). *Green IT: Reduce your Information System's Environmental Impact While Adding to the Bottom Line.* McGraw-Hill Companies, New York.

Wang, H.-L. and Ghose, A. (2006). On the foundations of strategic alignment. *The Proceedings of the 2006 Australia and New Zealand Academy of Management Conference.* Dunedin, New Zealand, December 2006.

Wang, H.-L. and Ghose, A. (2011). Green strategic alignment: Aligning business strategies with sustainability objectives.In B. Unhelkar, ed., *Handbook of Research in Green ICT: Technical, Business and Social Perspectives*, pp. 29–41. IGI Global, Hershey, PA, USA.

Wills, B. (July 2009). *Wills, Brett, Green Intentions: Creating a Green Value Stream to Compete and Win.* Productivity Press. Taylor & Francis Group 270 Madison Ave NY 10116. USA.

Worthington, T. (2009). Green Technology Strategies. Available at http://www.tomw.net.au/green/

Chapter 3

Environmentally Responsible Business: Policies, Practices, and Metrics

"Nature shrinks as capital grows. The growth of the market cannot solve the very crisis it creates."

Vandana Shiva (Soil Not Oil: Environmental Justice in an Age of Climate Crisis)*

Key Points

- An overview of what makes an environmentally responsible business is presented.
- The translation of Green IT strategies into actionable policies is addressed.
- Understanding and insights from survey data are used to shape environmental policies of a business.
- Discusses and analyzes the goals that need to be defined by an organization in order to adopt green policies.
- Addresses the importance of renewable energy sources in practicing Green IT.
- Creates an understanding of Green metrics and the applicability of the 5Ms (Measure, Monitor, Manage, Mitigate, and Monetize) of audit.
- Discusses greenhouse gas emission types and their analysis.
- Provides a framework for Green IT metrics and their practical relevance to an organization.

---

* Dr. Vandana Shiva has been described as an eco-feminist and antiglobalization campaigner. She won the Sydney Peace Prize in 2010.

■ Discusses company policies on usage of nonrenewable resources consumed in the company premises.
■ Defines guidelines for providing recycle facilities for biodegradable materials.

Introduction

This chapter discusses the policies, practices, and metrics that result from the development of the Green enterprise strategies. Such policies, practice, and metrics are an important and integral part of an overall Green initiative of an enterprise. Development of green policies equips an organization to handle the inevitable resulting challenges when changing the way it currently operates. While both the Kyoto and Copenhagen summits on climate change did not produce globally binding legislations, these summits have had a direct bearing on the green drivers, dimensions, and subsequent green policy formulations of organizations. The use of macro- and microeconomic levers are also brought to bear in this chapter to show their role in the organizational decision making because as highlighted by Ghose and Billau (2011), the current thinking on climate change emphasizes the use of economic levers and the associated monetizing to alter energy consumption behavior. The organization responds to this demand for behavioral change through business strategies that set the direction of the organization, as discussed in the previous chapter. Development and validation of strategies is a significant step by an organization in its green transformational effort. For a fundamental discussion of these Green IT strategies see Murugesan (2007). Such strategies, however, need to be brought down to the level where the organization can act on them, that is, monetizing. The strategic discussion of Chapter 2 is translated into policies and practices on carbon control for an organization. Developing, defining, and refining policies relating to carbon emissions is also an ideal way for the organization to prepare for legislation, binding standards, and corresponding protocols that are likely to result from upcoming global summits and consensuses on global carbon control.

Green business policies and corresponding practices, as discussed in this chapter are also related to a lean business because green policies align themselves with the lean business principles and practices. For example, an organization can change its practices to reduce the slack in its business processes in response to a lean business initiative aimed at reducing waste. Such lean initiative would not only reduce waste due to reengineered activities but also reduce the organization's carbon footprint. Alternatively, an organization might decide to improve its product design in response to the changes in customer preferences in terms of green products and services. This redesign of product will also help to reduce the emissions as there will be operational efficiency embedded in the product as also enhanced customer satisfaction with the use of the product. Thus, green policies as discussed here are closely associated with the business itself and are an integral part of the business.

One word to describe the future of the business world is "Lean." Therefore, the focus of corporate governance has to shift to include the lean-green nexus. The policies and practices of a lean organization will also help it become green. This lean-green status is achieved primarily through process efficiencies. However, all five principles of lean business (see www.lean.org) can be formally applied in a green initiative.

As shown in Figure 3.1, organizations address their green initiatives by defining sustainability policies and goals that align with the corporate objectives. These policies are then prioritized and applied in practice and their effectiveness measured against a base line. These metrics are developed to measure and report the carbon emissions resulting from various sources within the organization such as computers used by individuals, data servers, networks, and the business processes that use these devices.

Figure 3.1 further shows the shift in the values and use of corporate governance in the last decade. With increasing carbon

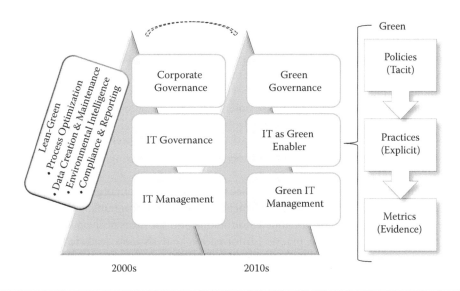

Figure 3.1   Green corporations based on green policies, practices, and metrics (shifting of IT function).

footprints organizations are adding "green" aspects to their corporate governance resulting in "Green Governance." Green governance allows companies to set policies and practices to assess their current energy consumption as well as the environmental impact of business practices of the company. As also seen in Figure 3.1, IT governance is shifting focus toward use of IT as an enabler of green initiatives across the organization. IT initiatives in optimizing the business services and business practices as well as use of virtualizing technologies (Murugesan, 2007) that enable energy efficiency result in a wide impact on the organization. Figure 3.1 illustrates these shifting perspectives that extend the corporate governance to green governance, IT governance to incorporate the role of IT as a green enabler, and routine IT management to Green IT management. Green Governance includes controls, policies, and practices that are supported by Environmental Intelligence (EI) (Unhelkar and Trivedi, 2009b). EI was introduced in Chapter 1 as an intelligent use of business tools and technologies that can lead an enterprise to being a green enterprise.

Therefore, Green Governance combines EI with lean process optimizations for data creation and maintenance. The green policies are expressed either as high-level or abstract policies that are worded by the corporate board, or are electronically embedded in the web services protocols of an e-organization. Policies are implemented through practices adopted by the green organization (see Murugesan 2008a and Murugesan 2008b for examples of some of these practices). Practices, however, result from a combination of good policies as well as training, education, and the overall attitude of the individuals working in the organization.

Thus, practices are the greater challenge than the formulation of green policies. Eventually, the success (or otherwise) of practices is judged based on metrics. Green metrics can measure not only the reduction in the carbon emissions per process but also the lean-ness of the business processes as a result of process optimization. These metrics and measurements are carried out in practice with the help of carbon emissions management software that uses smart metering.

In the context of green policies and practices, it is worth mentioning a significant modern management insight into business sustainability. As discussed by Younessi (2009), development of business strategies and corresponding actionable policies need not be based only in terms of profits but, instead, need to incorporate the time factor. A business whose strategies and policies are focused only on a single dimension, that of "making money" in the short term is likely to lose sight of the bigger picture in terms of long-term profitability and sustainability. Long-term profitability and sustainability can be achieved through policies that facilitate an organization to exploit technologies together with environmental considerations. For example, technologies such as mobile (Unhelkar, 2009a), offers immense potential to reduce people and material movements and radically optimize the business processes from an environmental viewpoint. Green policies need to be developed through a combination of profitability and environmental sustainability. Every new innovation, approach and lean business initiative is increasingly judged on sustainability and environmental responsibility.

In addition to affecting the way IT governance is implemented in an organization, the practice of Green IT also results in creation and implementation of green programs within the organization. These green programs can be developed around one or more areas of the overall policies, and work toward implementing them in practice. Information analysis tools, knowledge management techniques, and environmental intelligence are all utilized when green programs are launched as a result of policy implementations.

The practice of Green IT within these green programs requires leadership and resources to implement the programs. Implementation at a technical systems level requires creation and diffusion of data, information, knowledge, and intelligence. The wording and promotion of policies is subjective (tacit), whereas their implementation in practice is objective (explicit). Together, green policies and their practice affect an organization's core culture and belief system in both tacit and explicit ways.

Green programs and projects result from the commitment of an organization to fulfill its policies. Figure 3.2 shows the correlation between policies and practice. While the policies are tacit, their implementation is explicit. Also depicted in Figure 3.2 is the positioning of metrics in implementation of the policies in practice. Existing approaches to policy development and implementation in an organization can be used here, with some caveats. For example, the carbon

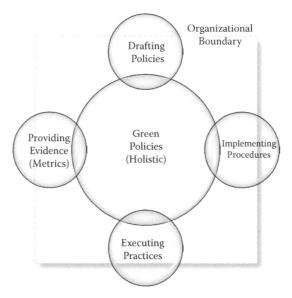

Figure 3.2 Green policies are implemented through practices, and proved through metrics.

factor is now brought into the policy wordings along with the cost factor. Metrics are the means to ascertaining whether a green program has actually fulfilled a policy goal. Studying the results of the metrics would result in modification, updates, or occasional cancellation and re-initiation of green programs. Attempts of converting policies into practices through the green programs may also result in occasional modification of the policies themselves. This should be anticipated and provisioned for in any good policy development schedule.

Policies and Practices in ERBS

In practical terms, a policy can be a high-level document that spells out what the organization will (and will not do) when it comes to business decision making. Green policies ensure that the decision making in the organization has carbon reduction as its integral component. The green policies are created with significant input from the senior management of the organization and are embedded into the business strategy of the company. While the policies state, through detailed statements what is implied in the ERBS, the green practices are the implementation of the policies (see Pratt 2009 for related discussion). Together these policies and practices drive the environmentally responsible activities of the organization. For example, these policies and practices help in ascertaining both internal and external decisions made by the organization. Therefore, these policies and practices need to be carefully drafted, validated, and embedded within the strategy of the organization. The policies and practices are based on a number of sources from within and outside of the organization. For example, a Green IT strategy based on technical dimension will result in policies on server procurement and choice of data center building and acceptable risks by the data center directors.

There are various types of environmentally responsible business policies. Some of these policies and their relative importance are shown in Figure 3.3. Following is a discussion of those environmentally responsible business policies which should be taken into consideration for devising organizational policies. The insights gleaned from the survey around the importance of these environmental policies is also discussed below.

- *Purchasing Green equipments/services and turning existing services into green services.* This policy requires the organization to devise standards around procuring new equipments or buying new services from external parties. Figure 3.3 shows that 40% people "agree" with formation of such a policy whereas 15% people "strongly agree" to incorporating such policies for green equipments/services. Such environmentally responsible purchasing for IT products is being incorporated into purchasing programs of many private and public sectors. For example, the EPEAT and Energy Star standards have been widely adopted for government purchases at the Federal, State, and Local government levels (Manuel and Halchin, 2010). These environmental objectives form part of the objectives within government procurement programs
- *Disposal of used materials and equipments.* Disposal of hazardous and harmful waste particularly out of computing equipment requires careful policy consideration. In Figure 3.3, almost equal number of people "agree" (34%) as and "strongly agree" (32%) to having a policy around disposal of waste material. This policy will also ensure that the waste management is performed in accordance with the legislative requirements. This policy should also accompany promotion of environmental awareness that will also encourage change in attitude toward waste minimization, reuse, and recycle. The amount of waste generated from any organization is directly proportional to the business activities. Therefore, this policy will be closely associated with the lean policy on waste reduction.

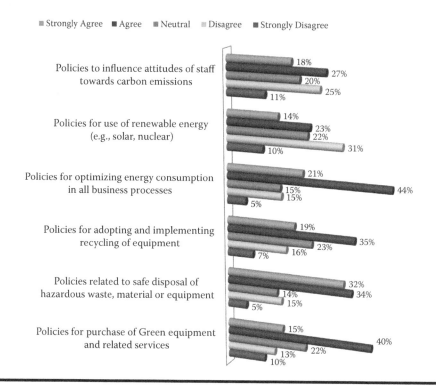

Figure 3.3   Environmentally responsible business policies.

■ *Equipment recycle and use.* This policy reduces the disposal of equipments which may still be functioning. Figure 3.3 shows that 35% people "agree" that it is good to have policies for implementing recycling of equipments whereas nearly half of them (19%) "strongly" recommend the formulation and implementation of such policies. This survey response also indicates that if waste cannot be prevented then as many of the materials as possible should be recovered through recycling. Policy for adopting and implementing recycling of equipments will recover usable materials and components, postpone replacement of working equipment, and increase reuse awareness.

■ *Environmentally responsible business policies.* Business processes can vary from utilizing low level resources such as paper to highly required resources such as electricity. In carrying out business processes, a lot of energy is wasted and that energy cannot be recycled at many times. Hence, policies to optimize energy consumption in business processes should be incorporated in business strategy. The survey tells that about 44% people would like to have such a policy as their organizations are viewing their energy resources as a path to strategic competitive advantage. Twenty-one percent respondents suggested implementing such policies strictly.

■ *Use of renewable energy sources.* Different sources of renewable energy such as solar power grids, nuclear plants, and wind farms are increasingly coming into play. The survey in Figure 3.3 shows that only 23% "agree" and 14% "strongly agree" to the creation of policies for use of renewable energy sources. Issues around the solar cells, their life, and sunlight were cited by organizations using solar energy. In the case of wind power, consistency of wind for continuous power generation was raised as an issue and for geothermal energy, the management of pollutants was cited. Further analysis of the survey data indicates that decision makers and quality managers strongly believe in alternative, or renewable energy sources, but cost appears to be a big constraint in the use of alternate source of energy. As this gets written, Japan's east coast suffered the tragedies of a massive earthquake followed by a Tsunami that destroyed the cooling systems of its Fukushima nuclear plant. The resulting leakages from the near meltdown is having worldwide impact in terms of use of nucelar technology for renewable energy. Thus, it is worth noting that 41% respondents disagreed (including strongly) to the policy for the use of renewable energy sources in business processes.

■ *Awareness and positive attitude.* Awareness and positive attitude amongst the employees and users within the organization about carbon emissions can bring about substantial changes in the way the organization operates. This awareness need to be inculcated within an organization's culture. Twenty-seven percent of the respondents "agree" and (18%) "strongly agree" to having policies that raise awareness of green issues among people. These policies that influence the staff requires training plans and budget as well as support from human resource (see discussion on Green HR in Chapter 8).

Lean Impact on Green

Environmental returns can be gained by rethinking and redesigning the existing paradigm and processes. An organization can achieve the sustainability goals through eco-efficient and eco-innovative policies. Policies for reduction, reuse, and recycling leverage the reduction of carbon footprints of an organization and the survey results depicts that most organizations are committed to adopting policies for environmental compliance. The first requirement of such commitment is the support from and involvement of the leadership of the organization. The decision makers bring the green strategic concepts to the green policies. Other sources for green policies and practices include data of industry specific climate change and corresponding analysis with respect to greenhouse gases. Allocation of resources in an optimized manner as undertaken in a lean business also impact Green IT initiatives.*

Application of lean principles in IT can be easily extended, understood, and applied for Green IT. For example, understanding the product from the standpoint of the customer will ensure that the product is easily accepted by the customer with minimal or no rework. This efficiency in product development translates into carbon reduction due to immediate acceptance of the product (or service). When process optimization occurs in a lean effort by business, steps that do not add direct value to the production process are eliminated. This concept is discussed in the context of Green IT in great detail in Chapter 5. However, modeling of processes, critical examination of its steps, elimination and/or merger of steps—all of these activities that form the basis of lean business principles, also reduce carbon emissions due to efficiency and effectiveness of the development, production, or supply process of the organization.

Thus, lean processes continuously strives to eliminate wastage and slack within the business. Such lean initiatives also equip employees with systems level support to help them in reducing the carbon generated through their routine work. The government rules and regulations relating to carbon emissions should also be made known within the organization. This awareness of the regulatory requirements can encourage the employees to participate in and perfect their processes under the lean-green initiatives to enable them and their organization to comply with the emission limits set for their products and processes. External entities such as customers, business partners, and support center staff also provide a significant input into what is expected of a Green IT policy from an organization. Customers, in particular, are encouraged to play an active role in a lean business initiative. This same effort can be handy in the lean-green initiative, wherein customers

---

* For example, www.eia.doe.gov.

are consulted for their needs, wants, preferences, and timings. The proper, formal, and successful implementation of environmental policies of an organization that successfully capitalize on its "lean" effort can be summarized as follows:

- *Lean-green goal identification.* These goals extend the business goals to incorporate carbon efficiency and reduced wastage. To identify the correct lean goals, all stakeholders need to be taken in confidence by the leadership. Thus, customers, employees, and owners need to participate in the lean-green goal identification.
- *Product differentiation.* The practice of price and product differentiation in business can be applied in green business; in both the short and long term (Younessi, 2011). In the long term, a shift from the traditional economic models of business to new lean and green business models is evident. From the consumer's perspective, the perceived differences in value results in costumers comparing a green product with a traditional product, or comparing the same green product from one organization as against another one.
- *Alignment with green enterprise goals.* Ensuring that the green policies and practices are aligned with the lean principles being applied in the organization. It is important to optimize the lean-green practices of the organization with respect to the business strategies and goals. Such alignment of green policies and practices will result in value creation that also occurs in a lean business.
- *Lean-green measurements.* Lean measures would provide an organization with an indication of the effort and costs saved through the optimization of processes. Lean-green measurements provide basis for not only ascertaining the reduction in costs but also reduction in carbon. Furthermore, green measures (such as discussed later in this chapter) also provide an understanding of potential increase in carbon due to cost reduction effort. For example, extending the life of an old equipment may be a cost-effective decision but not necessarily a carbon-effective decision as the old equipment design may not be based on carbon efficiency. Therefore, all lean-green decisions and actions, relating to green business processes must be based on a set of measurable actions. Green metrics provide assessment of Green readiness, and goal setting. Setting arbitrary goals of becoming carbon-neutral without respect to the industry within which the organization operates can be potentially detrimental to the organization. For example, the goals for carbon reduction that may be achievable in a service or technology firm may not, in practice, provide the same challenge that a manufacturing or mining firm may face. Each industry sector needs to have its own benchmarks and achievable goals.
- *Lean-green structures and interactions.* Organizational structures define the way in which people and processes are put together. These structures include the hierarchies within the organization, their interactions, and the corresponding system support. Lean-green enterprises must be viewed in terms of their structures, their processes, and functions. Detailed models of all the structure and interactions of a lean-green organization are essential for comprehensive understanding of how sustainability might be incorporated along with lean in such an enterprise. For example, an organization's HR structure that has multiple, unwanted layers of hierarchies between the workers and the managers will neither be lean, nor green. Merger of a deep, hierarchical structure that would result in a flatter management structure will obviate the challenge and result in a lean-green value.
- *System support for lean initiatives.* Multilayered systems used for optimizing organization processes need to focus—at each layer—on the support required to reduce carbon impact. For example, Trivedi and Unhelkar (2009) have described four layers—Business layer, Carbon Emission Monitoring layer, Service layer, and IT-infrastructure layer. Each layer

defined in this business strategy system focuses on the mitigation and management of the environmental impacts of the process, services, and products of an organization that also make the organization a lean organization.

- ▪ *Lean-green marketing.* Marketing efforts of green technologies in an organization need to align with its lean effort. Thus, using green technologies should be shown to enhance or upgrade the level of productivity. For example, value of carbon reduction afforded by the use of Green IT technologies can be realized in lean marketing approach.

- ▪ *Lean-green process quality and process improvements.* Engendering process changes with respect to green initiatives have a parallel in the corresponding changes during a lean business initiative. Specifically the impact of decisions in production, service, and marketing to reduce wastages and tighten the slack in a process also reduces the carbon contents of the process. However, in employing Green IT technologies in process optimization, care should be taken to ensure the technology integrates throughout with the business layers. Keeping the process separate from the technology will not produce the desired carbon reduction as technology, on its own, may not serve a specific business goal and, instead, simply produce carbon for no discernable value.

- ▪ *Lean-green business framework.* Enabling technologies such as Green IT might be identified, justified, and implemented through the development of a lean business framework. Green technologies can be used to: (1) assess and measure the extent of a concept (e.g., effectiveness of Green IT introduction project) within a specific level of an organization or a particular process or project; (2) do a gap analysis based on a comparison between status quo as determined through an assessment and an optimal scenario, which often times can be logically defined; and (3) set policies and strategies of an organization with respect to the environmental challenges at all levels of the business framework.

Lean organizational policies tacitly include carbon efficiencies in them. However, they have to be made explicit in practice by combining them with green procedure and metrics. Thus, the metrics that measure the lean-ness of an organization need to be updated to also reflect its green-ness. These measures are context sensitive and depend on the nature and type of the organization.

Environmental Areas Covered

Policies and their practices can be viewed from three different angles—the breadth of coverage, the depth at which they operate, and the length of time they are influential within the organization. Figure 3.4 shows these three areas of consideration in the development of green policies. These areas are also summarized in Table 3.1 and discussed in the following sections.

Breadth of Environmental Policies (Areas Covered)

As shown in Figure 3.4, one axis shows the breadth of environmental policies that cover the various areas of an organization, including its various departments, subsidiaries, and partners. For example, the green policies in an organization may affect its inventories and its production activities. This may be a relatively "narrow" effect of the green policies on the organization as reduction in inventories itself may not immediately and necessarily affect the supply chain of the organization.

However, alternatively, the breadth of Green IT policies may cover not only the production of goods within the organization, but also its building, infrastructure, and operative environment. This will be a much broader impact of the green policies on goods and inventory. The broader the impact of the policies, the closer the organization is to implementing a holistic approach to Green IT.

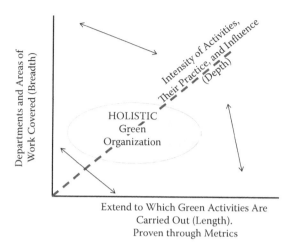

Figure 3.4 Green IT policies impact in three ways (length, breadth, depth).

Table 3.1 Policies, Practices, and Metrics

	Policies	*Practices*	*Metrics*	*Tools*
Breadth	Departments and activities covered; collaborative partners	Number of activities; people and partners practicing them	Green activities per departments	Leadership techniques; administration
Depth	Described intensity of activities	Reach—influence of each activity; honesty and seriousness	Carbon amount per activity;	Smart meters; CEMS implementations.
Length	Period of green policy implementation	Sustained period of practice by individuals and departments	Daily, yearly; other time units; staggered implementation periods	Duration on meters; time calculators; KPIs.

Thus, what is highlighted is the need to consider the overall organization and its entire breadth in terms of Green IT policy development and implementation. Such consideration will result in appropriate creation of green programs, corresponding use of analyzing, modeling, and simulation tools for the study of environmental risk management and improved accuracy of measurements. The broader is the coverage of green policies, the better are the organization's chances at success.

However, this breadth of coverage also increases the risks associated with the green transformation and, therefore, requires greater coordination amongst the four dimensions of change and additional upfront resources. The policies, practices, metrics, and corresponding tools (techniques) that are relevant in considering the breadth of a green organization are shown in Table 3.1.

Depth of Environmental Policies (Intensity of Coverage)

As shown in Figure 3.4, another axis represents the depth of environmental responsibilities of an organization. This depth is an indicator of the intensity with which the policies are implemented and practiced by the organization. For example, if reduction in inventory is correlated with reduction in wastages and therefore reduction in carbon production, then the participation, coordination, and use of systems and tools to achieve that inventory reduction will be concentrated to provide the necessary depth of coverage.

A deep practice of policies in large organizations is usually well supported by tools for eco-management, operating on dedicated systems platforms resulting in not only support but also measurements and reporting of carbon performance for single and collective business processes. The depth of coverage for each process includes detailed description, mapping, responsibilities, and execution of roles, deliverables, activities, and tasks within the organization. The depth of coverage of green policies also facilitates audits and feedback to the same process in greater detail.

EI and corresponding environmental knowledge management systems, sharing of environmental knowledge through common platforms, and collaborative environments for decision support are also enabled in deep coverage of green policies and corresponding practices. Similarly, development of environmental ontologies and their availability on environmental portals for the organization (see Chapter 6 for greater details) are also facilitated when an organization goes deeper into the Green IT coverage.

The policies, practices, metrics, and corresponding tools (techniques) that are relevant in considering the depth of a green organization are shown in Table 3.1.

Length of Environmental Policies (Duration of Coverage)

Figure 3.4 also shows that length of time in terms of Green IT polices formation and practice is another vital consideration. Sustainable policies are the policies that, interpreted simply, enable a business to sustain itself for a long period of time. The longer a business stays "in business," the better are its chances of success including economic success. Therefore, a correlation between environmental sustainability and economics can be established through time. The relationship between success and time has the potential for driving green business advantage depending on the understanding and emancipation of the policy makers. The polices and practice can be analyzed in a three dimensional axis: breadth of coverage, depth of operation, length of time. Breadth indicates the number of department/people participating. Depth indicates the intensity of the "Green" activities undertaken. Length measures the time duration for which the policy was implemented. These axes translate to coverage, duration, and intensity in measuring the carbon footprint of an organization.

makers. The policies, practices, metrics, and corresponding tools (techniques) that are relevant in considering the length of a green organization are shown in Table 3.1.

Green policy formulations require the policy makers to have the ability to look at the future strategies that make predictions regarding the future of the firm. When incorporating time in policies, it becomes important to consider the longevity of the firm itself, together with the longevity of the Green IT initiative. A Green IT can transform the organization, but maintaining that transformed green state over a period of time is only given due importance when the "length" is considered. Ideally, such length should be the length of the organization itself, and are therefore an integral part of its sustainability drive. Implementation of policies, however, require them to be further broken down and applied with varying timings to ensure they are gently and successfully introduced with the organization.

Figure 3.5 shows that eventually, the carbon footprint of an organization is made up of the coverage, duration, and intensity across all its functions. Carbon footprints are directly proportionate to the work area of an organization and the type of business sector. For example, a chemical industry which is manufacturing dyes and fertilizers will emit more emissions than the education sector.

Office practices such as use of computers, printers, space heating and cooling, lighting, paper, employee travel, and communication, all contribute to carbon footprints of an organization. Emission reduction can be achieved through efficient use of resources. Efficiency with respect to carbon footprints is measured as an "intensity." Intensities can be useful metrics and must be interpreted to attain information. Intensities can be good indicators of the emission trends. For example in service oriented sectors, intensities may be defined as emissions per employee, or per unit of office space. In the manufacturing industry, emissions intensity is invariably defined in terms of pollution per unit of electricity produced (e.g., CO_2-e/kWh or some variation of these units), trends can be interpreted at the industry-level because large firms may own numerous facilities using different types of fuel. Their holdings may change from year to year, leading to dramatically different ratios of emissions to output.

The measurement of this footprint is a combination of reduction in carbon due to successful Green IT initiatives across length-breadth-depth or the organization. This measurement, as listed in Table 3.1, enables the organization to fully understand and reduce its energy costs, streamlined IT processes, increase collaboration, and have a more efficient interaction with suppliers and customers.

Thus, a unified length-breadth-depth backdrop can result in a lean, agile business which can be measured to demonstrate its carbon reduction. Such corporate commitment to environmental awareness not only reduces emissions but also enhances brand value significantly.

Specific IT initiatives may involve end-user working practices, energy-efficient office environments, or reducing back office and data center energy consumption. Efficiencies are also being derived by taking a unified view of the procurement and supply chain management process that includes material choice, acquisition, packaging, delivery, and disposal. Taking these potential benefits into consideration, CIOs are thus in a position to play a key role in enhancing brand value and competitiveness as well as meeting compliance requirements.

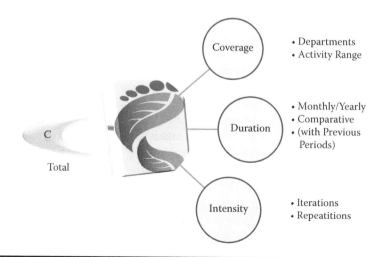

Figure 3.5 Carbon footprint of an organization is based on coverage, duration, and intensity.

Green Values in Practice

Converting policies to practice becomes an immediate action on the part of the organization that can be seen within a short timeframe. Therefore, even if the strategies and policies are formulated for the long-term change in the organization, their effect in practice can be seen immediately. The approach to converting the green policies into practice is through a combination of training, usage, incentives, and possible introduction of penalty risks.

Younessi (2011) has developed a matrix of various Green values that can be considered in the development of green policies. These are the utility, exchange, essential, and longevity values. Table 3.2 lists and expands them in the context of Green IT. Also listed in this table are the premise on which that value is based, the factors that influence the green values, and a mention of the techniques to achieve these values in green policy development.

The short-term operational strategies discussed in Chapter 2 are easy to implement in practice. For example, shutting down unused computers or reducing the amount of paper being printed (e.g, discussion by Pratt, 2009). Tactical, 1-year time framed strategies have the potential to translate into immediate actions such as implementing efficient power management, use of energy-efficient lighting, reduction in paper usage, and maintenance of optimal room temperature (further discussed in detail by Murugesan, 2007, 2008a, 2008b). These basic practices, however, only have a short-term, visible impact on the overall green transformation.

Examples of converting short-term policies into practice are as follows:

■ *Computing power management.* Upgrades to the operating systems of computers—especially desktops—can be undertaken to enable automatic shut down or "sleep" mode when not in use.

Table 3.2 Various Green Values Derived by Organizations

Type of Green Value	Premise of That Value	Factors Influencing the Green Value	Technique to Achieving the Green Value
Green utility value	Based on the demand for green initiative	Quality; differentiation; marketing and relevance of the green initiatives	Trend analysis and forecasting of green data and information; optimization of green processes for quality
Green exchange value	Based on the green market and their structure	Elasticity; demand and supply market structure; as impact green products and services	Forecasting, estimating, and optimization of green markets
Green essential value	Based on social values of the organization and its partners	Economic and social environment that promotes (or demotes) sustainability	Forecasting, estimating and analysis of carbon data for trends in the context of green economy and society
Green longevity value	Based on sustainable time duration—future	Integration and innovation or green products, services, and systems	Forecasting, optimization, and trend data analysis from Green IT systems perspective

For example, all machines that are inactive for over 30 minutes can be forced into sleep mode centrally, and the ones not in use for 2 hours or more can be centrally shutdown. This subsequent reduction in power consumption occurs without reduction in performance. According to an estimate by the US Environmental Protection Agency (EPA), having "sleep mode" on desktops can save energy use by 60%–70%. This is estimated to provide savings in electricity of up to US $2 billion, and reduce carbon dioxide emissions by the equivalent of 5 million cars (CEC 2005).

■ *Use a blank screen saver.* Use of a blank screen saver without the moving images can reduce electricity consumption. This is due to minimal power consumption by the monitor and also its reduced interaction with the machine's CPU. This still results in some carbon emission as compared with the sleep mode.

■ *Limited printing.* Capping the number of pages printed per employee, per day, is one tactical way of reducing emissions as well as wastage. Similarly, double-sided printing, draft printing as a default option, and stringent recycling can directly impact wastage reduction. Printing paper and ink eventually end up as a waste. Furthermore, the power consumed in the printing process contributes to the emissions. An online report on the use of printing pages by employees, also provided to the line managers, is helpful in implementing this practice. Alternatively, a centralized helpdesk service to print documents can also be considered.

■ *Reuse and recycling of equipment.* While this is not an immediate tactical practice, still it can be applied for all ICT equipments from the very first day of the organization's commitment to Green IT. A balance between length (longevity) of the equipment and its ongoing power consumption needs to be achieved. Reuse of equipment—even outside the organizational boundary—can reduce the overall emissions, and therefore should be enshrined in the policies and their practice. Equipments that simply cannot be used, reused, or donated need to be disposed in an environmentally responsible manner.

■ *Environmentally conscious procurement.* Any new procurement must be based on its energy efficiency. This energy efficiency needs to be validated and be compliant with local and international standards. Thus, sourcing of equipments should be based on costs together with energy efficiency. All new procurements should be Energy Star compliant or EPEAT certified and be approved by the Green IT program committee.

■ *Single machine.* An employee is provided with either a laptop or a desktop but not both. However, a set of common desktop machines are available using shared desk principles. While such practice would require regular monitoring to ensure they don't result in loss of business efficiency and effectiveness, they are still worth considering even though they may appear radical in the first instance.

Green Practice: A Balancing Act

A green sustainable policy is defined as a policy that incorporates a "Green" factor and helps business to sustain over a longer period of time. Utility value, exchange value, essential value, and longevity values are a few factors that need to be considered for developing such a policy.

The green utility, exchange, and essential values discussed in Table 3.2 provide an understanding of the need to balance the green policies and their practice in an organization. Figure 3.6 depicts this balancing between the external and the internal pressures on the developers of the green policies for the organization. The green values and the green costs (that is the costs associated with developing and implementing green policies) may occasionally vie against each other. Therefore, there is a need to reflect their balance as the policies are drafted.

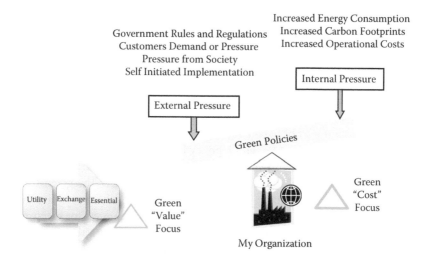

Figure 3.6 Development of green policies is a balancing act.

The internal pressure on the development of these Green IT policies and their practices comes from the need to reduce both energy consumption and costs. The internal focus and concern, therefore, can be rightfully also on the increased costs associated with green initiatives. Implementation of Green IT policies in practice may bring about, internally, substantial changes to the underlying IT infrastructure of the organization such as its buildings, or its networks and data servers. Implementation of these changes should, therefore, be in a phased approach. Known and standard project management as well as risk management techniques can be brought in use here.

The balancing act, in practice, also requires consideration of the IT versus non-IT assets of the organization. In developing the green policies and eventually practicing green in a holistic way, the organization needs to consider Green IT from both IT and non-IT viewpoint. While the overall influence of IT on the greening effort will vary depending on the type and size of the organization, still understanding this mix of IT and non-IT assets is important for both policy development and eventual practice.

For example, in a manufacturing organization, the plant and equipment involved in the manufacturing activity may not be IT related; whereas a service-based organization, such as a bank or an insurance company, may have more IT equipment. Both types of equipments, together with their users, play a role in green policies and practices.

The value-based approach, discussed earlier, applies to the way the changes in the organization are prioritized. For example, combination of utility, exchange, and essential values indicate which of the Green IT practices should be prioritized (e.g., operational reduction in energy consumption, or refurbishing/renewal of computing equipment, or upgrading the networks).

For example, the consolidation and virtualization of computer systems and servers will require modeling and understanding of business processes and enterprise architecture EA. Similarly, implementing new policies on procurement, operation, and disposal of computing resources would require sep-by-step changes to the SCM. Factors such as branding, image creation, and marketing are also going to come in the mix of this balanced act.

A balanced policy for Green IT also accepts that profit and costs remain prime necessity for business. Therefore, profit-costs form part of this balancing act. However, as argued by Younessi

(2011), the value-based approach is not entirely based on the profit-cost difference. Freeman et al. (2007–2008) and Figge and Hahn (2005) have outlined and expanded on the various values that need to be considered by firms in their measurement of return on investment (ROI). They are the utility value, (assessed subjectively by customers and related to the concept of product quality), exchange value (realized in the form of revenue), and essential value (realized in the fundamental improvement of the societal condition). These values, as shown in Figure 3.6, directly affect the "delta" green value—that is from the current green value of the organization to its future green value and form an important part of balancing act.

The length, depth, and breadth of Green IT policy implementation come into play in expanding and enhancing the "delta" for both costs and values of the firm in terms of its sustainability effort. Consider, for example, the "utility" value of green technology. The green transformation can provide an effective marketing strategy which presents the organization as a market leader in green technology. This creates a perceived value on the part of consumers for green products and services from the organization. This practice then translates into utility value through brand recognition based on an honest organization with a commitment to true green values.

This practice eventually also translates into product and service differentiation within the industry vertical and its market. Such practice will serve to buffer the shocks of moving to green production, as well as providing the firm with a business model that is dynamic and responsive to the needs and wants of the market for green products.

Sherringham (HRG) has also discussed and expanded on the concept of value, applying it to Green IT business beyond its normal or essential value. While the reengineering of business processes and implementation of green practices may provide essential value, it maybe the marketing opportunities of being green that are realized first. The need for balanced consideration comes from the costs, effort, and time for returns. Businesses looking for a market differentiator and a customer engager are increasingly likely to canvass their green credentials. The ability of a business to say "it has Green IT," "it uses Green IT to do good," or "it is returning value to customer's vested interest through the use of Green IT" are all powerful tools that apply to development, production as well as marketing. From charging a premium price to have an environmental footprint reduced through to making donations to community and environmental organizations, the marketing, and business opportunities are almost limitless (Sherringham, 2011, HRG).

Thus, the exchange value of a reduced emission identifies the "worth" of the goods and services in the open markets. Practices across the length-breadth-depth of the organization (optimized and carbon-conscious design, development, storage, and distribution), leads to higher exchange value for the product or service. Eventually, this higher exchange value at a single product level translates into higher exchange value for the entire organization on the stock exchange.

Mobility and Environment

The application and implementation of a Green policy is a fine balancing act. This requires careful understanding of the business process and enterprise architecture. ROI also needs to be considered for expanding a green policy. Factors like energy consumed, emissions, efficiency, and reputation also should be considered. Even though renewable energy sources offer an alternate solution, it is still in its infancy to be considered as an alternate path.

This discussion on development of policies and their implementation in practice requires due consideration to mobile technologies. Mobility has a significant role to play in the reduction of carbon emissions as it has the potential to offer location independence, that is, reduce the need to travel, to most business processes. Some of the advantages and challenges in the use of mobile technologies in business from the point of view of environmental sustainability are noted in this discussion.

Advantages to Environment

Mobility offers location independence and personalization (Unhelkar, 2009a), both of which are characteristics that can be used to optimize business processes and reduce carbon. Therefore, mobile technologies—including devices, networks, and contents—have a significant role to play in the global carbon reduction effort. For example, mobility influences the way in which people access information on their location which in turn reduces people-movement and, therefore, influences the environment. Another example, is that of a small sized mobile phone (although this device may need to use batteries) which still has a much lesser need for energy than a larger desktop device.

Similarly, there are influences on processes through optimization of supply chains, customer relationships, and financial systems; changes to the social networking styles of employees and their unions; technical changes to the architecture and design of software and enterprise systems to reflect the environmental responsibility, and even the way in which corporate sponsorships change due to the need for environmental considerations. These various influences of mobility on the environment have been discussed in detail in *mobile enterprise transition and management* (Unhelkar, 2009a).

Mobile technologies can also aid the sustainability effort of organizations through redesign and recycling of products and optimization of processes. Mobility, of course, has to be incorporated strategically in the approach, and implemented through policies and practice. As mentioned earlier, examples of activities resulting from such green use of mobility are incorporation of mobile processes that reduce physical movement of men and materials, collaborative use of mobility in recycling of products (including their design), and making the physical wired networks within the organization redundant. Furthermore, both technical and process dimensions of green transformation encourage consolidation of mobile data centers as well as the use of virtualization through mobility, wherever possible. The resultant environmentally responsible business has less need for physical movements and activities, reduced power consumption, lowered carbon emissions, and savings in time and space resulting from an overall wireless operation of business.

Challenges to Environment

Despite its seemingly obvious advantage, there are some interesting and unique challenges of mobility when it deals with the environment. Consider, for example, how mobility enables virtual collaborations between business and individuals. These virtual collaborations, especially between businesses, can introduce management challenges in implementing environmentally responsible strategies. This is so because virtual collaborations bring together multiple stakeholders with diverse vested interests. While these stakeholders collaborate to provide unified services to customers, the collaborations themselves become very complex and dynamic. In such collaborations, enabled by mobile technologies, it is difficult to identify the precise contributors to the greenhouse gas emissions and pollutions.

Mobile users also present challenges from an environmental viewpoint. This is so because these mobile users are difficult to track due to their location independence, which results in challenges in tracking their environmental activities and calculating the pollutions that may have been generated.

Furthermore mobile networks, mobile computers, and corresponding mobile devices consume significant amounts of electrical energy. While the devices themselves are small, their numbers are growing by the millions, especially in the earlier mentioned BRIC nations. This increasing use places a heavy burden on the electric grid that, in turn, contributes to greenhouse gas emissions, resulting in an imbalance in the environmental equilibrium. This imbalance can be potentially further exacerbated with large number of mobile networks and servers. Therefore, when incorporating mobile technologies in business, it is vital to keep the environmental impact of the transition in mind.

In addition to the technological balance, there is also a need for careful "engineering" of business processes of an organization from an eco-friendly viewpoint. This careful engineering of business processes can be achieved through excellence in modeling the way in which its people and technologies are employed to achieve the process goals. Modeling of mobile business processes can be based on the goals to be achieved by the users with minimal impact on the environment, reduced waste, and increased productivity. Process modeling can play a very creative role in the environmental performance of the organization by simply helping the users of the organization to do things differently. However, experience suggests that creation of such eco-friendly business processes can succeed only when they are part of the overall environmentally responsible business strategy.

Relating Environmental Business Policies to Goals

The importance of policies and their practice is that they enable an organization to achieve its environmental goals. Therefore, policies need to reflect the green strategies of the organization in this regards. Policies, in practice, also need to provide help and guidance in terms of prioritizing the actions to be undertaken by the organization.

Figure 3.7 shows results from the survey on how these green policies enable an organization to prioritize its environmental goals. These results are discussed further in details as follows:

- Energy Consumption—Energy gets consumed as various processes are executed within the organization. Reducing energy consumption has to be incorporated within policy development as a business goal. Many opportunities exist, especially at the corporate governance level, to make changes to policies and practices that do not cost much but produce carbon savings. For example, the carbon trust (www.carbontrust.co.uk) estimates that most business in the service sector can cut their energy bill by 20%–30%, while those in industry can make saving from 5% to 10% by simply changing user behavior and processes. Encouraging people to change behavior can lead to substantial carbon savings. However, the energy management activities comprise analysis, improvement, control, and monitoring. User attitudes can be surveyed, analyzed, and presented to the decision makers of the organization as recommendations. Energy consumption can be reduced across the entire lifecycle of an equipment or product starting right from design and specification, production, quality control, installation, commissioning, and ongoing energy monitoring. The survey results shown in Figure 3.7 shows that about 25% of respondents don't believe that there is any reduction in energy consumption in their organization. Whereas about 38% agree and 26% strongly agree to the need for and effort in incorporating reduced energy consumption as a goal within their policies.
- Energy Efficiency—The key of business sustainability is energy efficiency and the reduction of emissions. Organizations devising carbon abatement strategy, consider energy efficient measures, monitor, assess, and manage their carbon emissions. Carbon footprints need to be

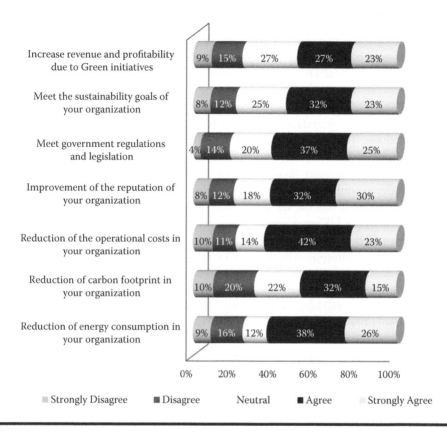

Figure 3.7 Green organizational goals to be achieved through policy development.

reduced by implementing policies that change business processes. About 10% people in the survey results shown in Figure 3.7 believe their organizations have no such policies to reduce carbon footprints whereas 15% people strongly agree for incorporation of such policy. In contrast, 22% of respondents were not able to express their view clearly for or against existence and development of such green policies and their practice.

▪ Operational Costs—These are significant in all major business activities. These operating costs include sales and marketing, research and development, and administrative costs associated with business. Reduction in these operational costs is closely associated with the policies and practices of reducing carbon emissions. The survey results seen in Figure 3.7 indicate that most of the respondents (about 65%) are in favor of policy implementations that would reduce the costs together with carbon reduction, whereas about 21% were disagreed to strongly disagreed that reduction of operational costs will reduce carbon emission.

▪ Organizational Reputation—Improvement in the reputation of the organization as a goal associated with carbon reduction is a valid and important goal to have. The green initiative can provide a much needed brand name in a competitive market. Implementing green policies offer organizations many benefits, including enhancement of public image, increase in marketability, reduction of operation costs, and improvement in employee morale. Thus, apart from being environmentally responsible, there are opportunities for business in a green initiative. Energy efficiency and environmental activities can help differentiate products and services and engender customer loyalty. In Figure 3.7, 18% respondents emerged as "neutral" toward incorporation of the policies that improve organization reputation. On other side, about 62% respondents believe (agree to strongly agree) in formulation of such policies whereas 20% clearly don't agree with the value of such green policies in brand creation.

■ Environmental Performance—Improved environmental performance as an international business standard and foundation for competitiveness is increasingly a mandatory requirement for business. The compliance of IT with existing and new legislations leads to a heightened environmental performance by business itself. For example, when an organization complies with the European "Eco design for energy Using Products" (EUP) directive, it is enabling itself to compete beyond emissions and also on costs and other performance indicators. Another example is of the UK government's carbon neutrality target by 2012. There are further targets by the UK government to reduce Greenhouse gases by 26% or more by 2020 and by at least 60% by 2050. Compliance with these legislative requirements results in lower power consumption, improved business efficiency, and better competitiveness. Emissions are reduced by implementing the lean business practices such as optimized business processes, lean working practices, and stringent outsourced services contracts. The survey shows that very high percentage (62%) of respondents believe in setting goals that enable compliance with the regulatory standards of the specific countries or regions in which the business operates. Interestingly, about 20% of the respondents were not sure (neutral) in terms of the relevance of legislative compliance as goals associated with carbon reduction.

■ Green Sustainability—Such goals need to be incorporated in the overall organizational policies and their practice. SSA & Company, a global operations consulting firm, found that businesses were able to improve their performance by an average of 30%–40% in areas such as energy consumption, recycling, and waste reduction, saving those companies tens of millions of dollars annually by adopting Green policies in their business. About 65% of the respondents "agreed" to "strongly agreed" with the need to develop green policies and practice them in achieving the sustainability goals of the organization; whereas about 20% did "not agree" that such green policies can indeed help an organization achieve its sustainability goals.

■ Increased Revenues—Green initiatives could help in increasing overall revenues which in turn can help to provide good incentives to employees. Companies today are considering every resource available to adopt more Green standards in an effort to not only reduce their carbon footprint, but also to increase revenue. About 50% respondents agree with such policy implementation, whereas a quarter of them (about 24%) did not agree with the possibility that green initiatives can increase the organizational revenues.

Renewable Energy Resources

Apart from discussing the policies and practices associated with the organization in its current state, it is also worth considering the impact of totally different types of energy as is currently consumed within an organization. For example, if instead of oil or gas, the energy was generated from coal—will that make a difference in the way the organizational policies are developed? As another example, should the organizational policies relating to carbon emissions reflect the fact that the power consumed in the organization is generated from brown coal instead of black coal (the former being more polluting than the latter)?

These considerations lead to a discussion on renewable energy, its sources, and its usage. While renewable energy is a carbon-efficient way to run a business, not all renewable technologies may be appropriate in all situations or locations. Furthermore, renewable energy itself may not be cheap (as discussed in this chapter in the previous section). Therefore, the use of renewable energies will require the government and the regulatory bodies to play a vital role in encouraging its use by changing market levers through legislations and use of carbon offsets.

European countries, in particular, are foremost in the trials and use of green/renewable power sources. In Germany and Spain, for example, up to 40% of power is now green—Germany using a large amount of hydroelectric power and Spain using wind and solar. Companies, such as the Spanish power conglomerate *Iberdrola*, are leading the way in switching to green power sources (Russell, 2009; Sanford, 2009). While the consumers themselves may not be aware of the fact that the power sources are renewable, business customers in particular show sensitivity and concerns in pushing for greater use of green technology through a commitment to purchase only renewable green power.

Figure 3.8 shows some of the popular renewable energy sources. Different types of energy sources such as nuclear, thermal, solar, water, wind, and biomass can be used as core enabler of green environment. This is so because, instead of focusing only on reducing the power consumption within the organizations, these alternative energy sources provide an opportunity to reduce emissions based from the source itself—in generation of the energy. Thus, these renewable energy sources are set to play an important role in the formulation of the green policies of an organization. These renewable energy sources should be incorporated in the core business strategies of the organization as an enabler of green initiatives. Using renewable energy is one way that businesses can minimize their greenhouse gases. Consumers, businesses, and organizations may use renewable energy to reduce the environmental impacts of conventional electricity generation. Renewable energy certificates are one way for organizations to support green energy. Impact of renewable sources of energies is usually felt through Government regulatory standards. Government devises regulatory standards which controls and support the energy providers. Energy providers implement those standards and as a result, organizations have the opportunity to source from one or more energy providers.

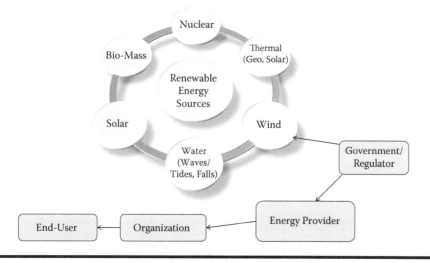

Figure 3.8 Renewable energy sources need to be increasingly incorporated in green policies.

Mind Map for the Role of a Chief Green Officer (CGO)

Chief Green Officer (CGO) or the Chief Sustainability Officer (CSO) is the most senior person in the organization responsible for green strategies. He/she is responsible for the development and maintenance for the green policies. The green policy should have the ability to justify the Return of Investment (ROI).

Formulation of environment policies is in itself a complex affair. Converting them into practice is often as equally as complex. This results in a green enterprise transformation program discussed in detail in Chapter 9. The success of green transformation and practice depends on a linchpin role that deserves discussion here. The Chief Green Office (CGO), also called the Chief Sustainability Officer (CSO), is the most senior person in the organization, working at the board level, responsible for green strategies, green policies, and green governance. The CGO, together with the corporate board, is responsible for development and maintenance of green policies that are integral to the overall business policies. The CGO, in the first instance, is also the person responsible for undertaking green transformation (see Chapter 9). Makower and Pike (2009) have highlighted the CEO's needs for becoming green *without* going into what the CIO has to offer in terms of existing intelligence in the business. The role of a CGO fits in between the CEO and the CIO; although, in many instances, the CIO may be asked to perform the CGO role.

Figure 3.9 shows the mind map of a CGO. The drivers and the four dimensions remain uppermost in the mind of a CGO. These green drivers and dimensions push for green strategies that, in turn, translate into policies. Green IT policies are developed in consultation with various departments as also external parties like customers and suppliers. Green metrics provide the ability to justify the ROI. Technically, the CGO would coordinate with the CIO to exploit the potential offered by Environmental Intelligence. Metrics can also be used in official reporting on the carbon performance of the organization, and its legal compliance.

An understanding of this mind map of a CGO can be helpful in setting and directing the green enterprise transformation of an organization. This mind map, however, needs to be created specifically for each organization and elements that are specific to the organization need to be

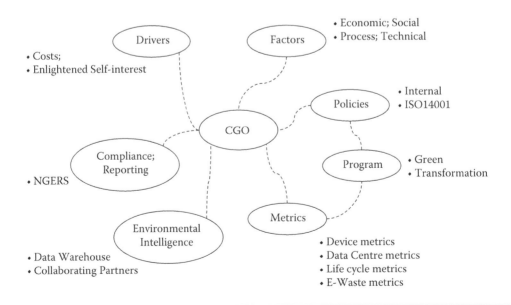

Figure 3.9 Mind map for the role of a CGO.

listed in this mind map. This figure is a dynamic figure, so the importance of the elements can keep changing depending on the way the transformation of an organization takes place.

Environmental Practices

The CGO takes the responsibilities for green enterprise transformation as well as ongoing practice after the transformation is successfully achieved. Figure 3.10 shows the many environmental practices that can be used by a green organization. The survey was used to ascertain the extent to and ease with which these environmental practices can be incorporated in a green organization. Following are the results and discussion on the responses:

■ *Operational improvements to reduce carbon emission:* Usual business activities and processes are carried out as part of operations of any organization. Improvements in operational practices should be conducted to make a green organization. Employing the correct level of change to the operational program to attain environmental goals will improve service level performance without placing undue burden on the operational staff. The survey shows about 50% respondents agree with this practice whereas about 24% are in disagreement.

■ *Strategic changes to how the business operates to reduce carbon emission:* Changing the way business operates help in providing an enhanced background for green organization. The business strategy should be changed in order to change the business operations. About 45% respondents agree to make strategic changes to change business operations, whereas 31% don't agree and 24% have neutral view on this.

■ *Anticipate changes to governmental regulations related to carbon emission:* Government standards should be changed in order to implement carbon emission regulations so that they are implemented by every organization. Fifty-four percent respondents look forward toward changes in government standards. In contrast, only 21% respondents disagree to look toward the changes in government standards.

■ *Influence governmental regulations related to carbon emission*: Governmental regulations should be incorporated throughout the chain mentioned in Figure 3.8. The influence of governmental regulations related to carbon emissions is thought to be an important practice by about 41% respondents in the survey whereas 25% disagree with the influence of the governmental standards toward green organization.

■ *Access new sources:* One of the important green practices involves accessing new sources of capital, energy, and raw material as part of procurement process. This would help in providing green structure for an organization. About 44% respondents agree with this practice whereas 25% disagree with it.

■ *Improve risk management:* Risk management is very important to incorporate any policy. Changes to risk management structure are needed according to the environment changes. More than half respondents (about 54%) agree with the practice to change risk structure according to environmental changes whereas 22% disagree.

■ *Elevate corporate reputation:* Adoption of green strategies will elevate the corporate identity. Organizations around the world are taking initiatives to reduce pollution and waste generation through reduce, reuse, and recycle methods. Apart from helping environment, these organizations are also gaining a green corporate image in the market. Fifty-four percent respondents agree that green practices, conservations, and reuse should be incorporated as part of business strategy. According to these respondents, green business strategies are

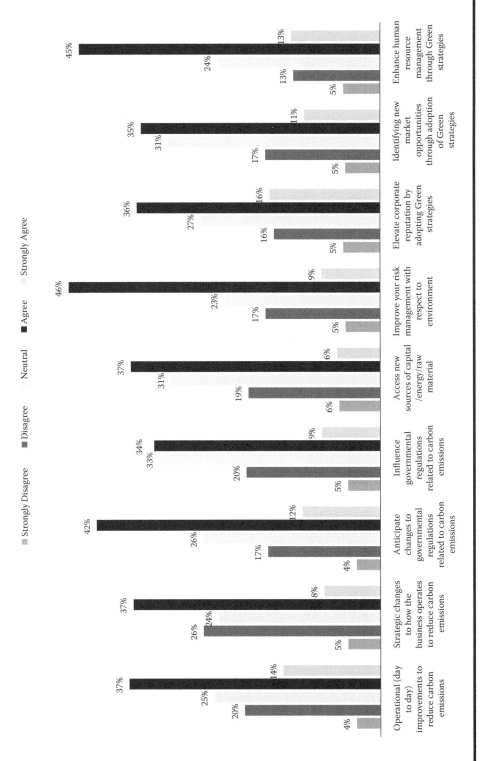

Figure 3.10 Incorporating environmental practices in green organization.

catalyst for innovation, new market products, and eco-services, whereas 21% disagree with its implementation.

■ *Identify new market opportunities:* Adopting green strategies can lead to development of another new market segment in a competitive market. Businesses are capitalizing on growing consumer desire for sustainable business by "greening" their practices to make them environmentally friendly. Businesses are viewing a new market opportunity for green products and services. Today, green business is an extremely profitable branch of the business world, and it hosts a range of companies, from prestigious multinational companies to small, locally based companies. About 46% respondents believe in adoption of this practice, whereas about half of them (about 23%) disagree with this practice.

■ *Enhance human resource management:* Green strategies and their practice require enhanced human resources management. This has been discussed in detail in Chapter 8. Employees and contractors following green practices and contributing toward reducing carbon emissions need to be provided with formal incentives. Guang (2008) argues for a green labor-management relations in which environmental protection is made integral to green labor management and associated negotiations. About 58% respondents agree with this potential practice of embedded environmental issues in green labor management, whereas 18% disagreed with it.

Green IT Metrics and Measurements

Measurement is an implicit requirement of management. Therefore, for an effective Green IT strategy to be implemented in practice, robust measures are required. These measures should clearly identify reduction targets and measures in such areas as achieving energy savings, reducing carbon emissions, and improving recycling efforts.

Green IT initiatives can be fraught with dispersed collection of individual and subjective opinions, vacillating policy documents, personal recommendations, and varied interpretations of experiments—all reported differently and across a variety of media. They need to be classified properly, recorded, managed,

Mobility technologies can play a significant role in the carbon reduction process. Location-requirement independence and personalization of mobile devices can optimize business process and reduce carbon emission. Mobile technologies also help in virtual collaborations. In spite of all the advantages offered, it does introduce few challenges. The mobile devices though small, but with large number in operation, increases the cumulative emissions. Also with new collaborative working, it becomes difficult to identify the precise contributor.

and made available for use within the organization in many different formats that suit the need of the user and the situation. The need for a comprehensive Green IT metrics and measurement program could not have been higher. Metrics provide a sound basis for Green IT implementation that includes all stakeholders, employees as well as management, all coming from different perspectives and concerns and from sources both inside and outside the organization. While many aspects of Green IT are generally applicable, metrics help in making them specific to the organizations.

The measurement resulting from carefully construed metrics provide excellent support to a green transformation program. Such metrics provide individual, organizational measurements, and, in addition, also provide vital benchmarks at industry levels and equally vital comparisons amongst industries and industrial verticals. Green IT metrics support the fundamental requirements of an organization—and that is to provide justification to the business leadership to invest in green transformation.

Thus, Green IT metrics become a major area, on their own, in the overall green movement—especially as these same metrics are also used by the organizations to demonstrate their compliance with the regulatory requirements. A Green IT framework (a specific example of such a framework is discussed later in Chapter 9) as part of the green transformation process, thus becomes a tool, or a mechanism, to not only enable organizations to rapidly implement their Green IT strategies but also enables comparison, demonstration of ROI, and the all important compliance requirements. These comparisons pave the path for reporting and imminent carbon trading.

The CEO of an organization is easier to convince and, in turn, is able to convince his/her board to undertake carbon initiatives, provided the business case is supported by measurable data. The acute need for carbon emissions data to be calculated in detail, regularly, accurately, and then analyzed, reported, and used for optimization purposes, cannot be overstated. Such data analysis can be used to ascertain the Green IT readiness and maturity of an organization, its corresponding industry, and at a global level (Unhelkar and Philipson, 2009). These reasons propel the business to start measuring carbon data and then using it in a compelling fashion to bring about green investment and green initiatives. Green IT metrics provide data that can be used in support of a formal business case for green transformations.

However, in order to use such data, it is important to measure such data on a regular and accurate basis, as also record, calculate, analyze, report, and use it for optimization purposes. Such green measurements/data and its analysis can be used to ascertain the Green IT readiness and maturity of an organization, its corresponding industry and at a global level (Unhelkar and Philipson, 2009). Philipson (2010) together with the earlier work done by Molla (2009) has outlined attitude, policies, practices, and technologies are areas that need to be understood and used in measuring the carbon footprints of an organization. Governance and enablement of Green IT has also been discussed, based on the potential for accurately measuring emissions. This need of businesses to have reliable carbon data, however, does not appear to be served well with the existing carbon metrics and measurements. The level of maturity of environmental metrics today is perhaps akin to the maturity of measures in the early industrial revolution—wherein new metrics and measurements had to be invented rapidly and be standardized across the industry. As is true with most nascent approaches, the dearth of concrete carbon measures prevents proper comparison, justification, and optimization of an organization's green credentials. This lacuna is addressed in this discussion. Creation and validation of Green IT metrics is important in a green enterprise transformation. First, these Green IT metrics provide that robust ROI that enables the business leadership to justify its investment. Second, increasingly, the performance of an organization will not be only measured by its financial books. Instead, organizations will have to report their carbon performance as much as they have to report their financial performance. The increasing relevance of carbon performance of an organization and the way it gets integrated in understanding the overall performance of an organization implies that carbon measurement is no longer a "nice to have" feature within an organization. Customers can easily demand to see, in their invoices, not only the monetary figure but also an associated "Carbon" figure that indicates the amount of carbon generated in the production of a particular product or service.

Following are the specific ways in which Green IT metrics are relevant to an organization (Unhelkar, 2009b):

- Helps in measuring the carbon footprint of a product or service in an organization, thereby enabling a unit-level measurement of the product or service which can then be totaled to arrive at the overall carbon emission
- Understanding of the extent of carbon generated and, therefore, providing a benchmark for current as well as reduction in the future of the carbon contents
- Provide an ability to compare the carbon performance of one organization against another organization, within same or dispersed geographical regions

■ Enable marketing of products and services not only for lower costs and higher quality, but also for reduced carbon generated in the development and distribution of that particular product or service
■ Ability to comply with the regulatory requirements through mandatory measurement and reporting of carbon generation
■ Potential to trade carbon by measuring and storing the credits generated by optimized carbon performance
■ Opportunity to mature the green processes in an organization thereby enabling increasing optimization on the green CMM scale

Carbon Metrics Coverage

Figure 3.11 shows the various activities that are covered by carbon metrics. These activities including measuring, monitoring, managing, mitigating, and eventually monetizing the carbon emissions associated with the organization. These five "M"s of carbon metrics determine the current and future state of a green organization as also the degree of success in terms of reaching that state. These are described as follows:

Measurement is a key for the implementation of any policy. Green policy, we need clear techniques to measure energy savings, reduction in carbon emissions. These measurements will eventually provide benchmark at industry levels and vital comparison statistics. Green IT framework provides the required tool and techniques.

■ **Measure:** This is the primary application of metrics—which is to measure the emissions. This measurement is achieved through a range of emission sensors, measurement platforms, monitoring and inventory systems, and inference methods. Systems associated with

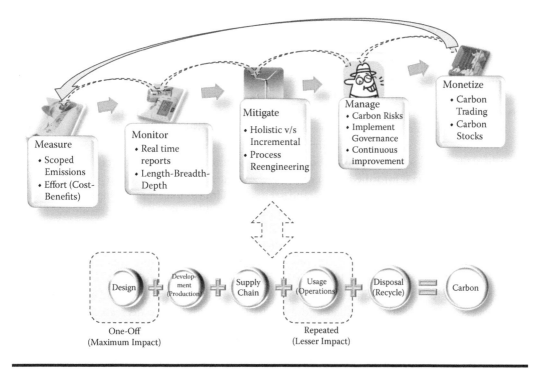

Figure 3.11   Coverage of carbon metrics.

the measurement are required to establish baselines and measure carbon storage and emissions changes on various scales from individual machines to large processes of the business. Improved measurement and monitoring technologies and capabilities can help to identify and guide future opportunities for technology development. Measurements can only succeed if these metrics are created and tested for their validity. Currently, in the Green IT domain, very few metrics exist that are robust enough to be applied across the organization. Furthermore, units for these metrics are also not available in a unified and well-accepted manner.

■ **Monitor:** ICT's crucial role in economic recovery is the key to unlocking the opportunity of Green growth and standardized metrics are required for the net CO_2 reductions. Once the metrics are developed, they are used to monitor the performance of the organization from a carbon perspective. This monitoring also implies continuous measurement using smart metering devices as well as ability to ascertain improvement. Standards to monitor and verify carbon emissions with reference to a baseline need to be defined in advance. Use of a reporting dashboard (Environmental Sustainability Dashboard) assists with the task of monitoring emissions and taking appropriate actions. Software systems need to be designed to ensure that environmental data collection is considered as a normal part of the business and that regular and frequent feedback is provided to the users.

■ **Manage:** Taking the results of the measurement and monitoring process and determining from that data what should be done to improve the process. Managing emissions involves commitment to reduce business impact on climate change, auditing the emissions, making the target plan. The plan must be integrated in the business policies by reviewing the performance and encouraging carbon reducing policies.

■ **Mitigate:** Mitigation (Molina et al., 2009) is the action taken to reduce greenhouse gas emissions. This can be achieved by reducing their origin through the places from where they are sourced or by improving the ability of the organization to dissipate or sink the emissions. Mitigation strives for improvement in the process so as to result in permanent reduction in the emissions. Thus, after measuring carbon footprints using intelligent data collection and modeling technology, carbon emissions are mitigated through performance tracking of reduction targets and improved energy efficiency.

■ **Monetize:** Deals with converting the improvement of the organization over its carbon performance into monetary value such as through its marketing effort or on the stock exchange or through carbon trading. Developing strategies for energy use, combined with the widespread misconceptions about the energy system. Human resource of an organization essentially be informed and educated about energy. Such education also helps create support for energy-related policies and strategies. Continuous monitoring of automation and behavior change of the business can help to establish new standards and legal precedents to further mitigate the causes and effects of the greenhouse gas emissions from that business. This will also help to develop alternatives to high carbon activities in that business. The standards and the alterations in the processes must ensure conformance to environmental standards such as ISO 14001. Understanding the organization's carbon liability and managing carbon reduction investments, renewable energy credits, and energy-efficient processes with clarity (Unhelkar and Trivedi, 2009a) will help to decrease the intensity of carbon footprints.

The variation in importance given to these measures is evident in the response to our surveys—and is depicted in Figures 3.12 and 3.13. Figure 3.12 shows the percentage importance of emissions

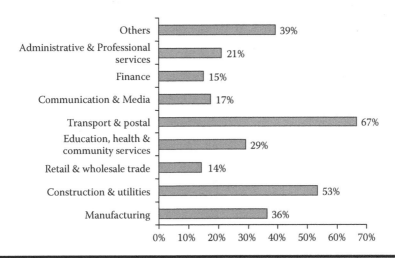

Figure 3.12   **Emissions monitoring by different industry sectors.**

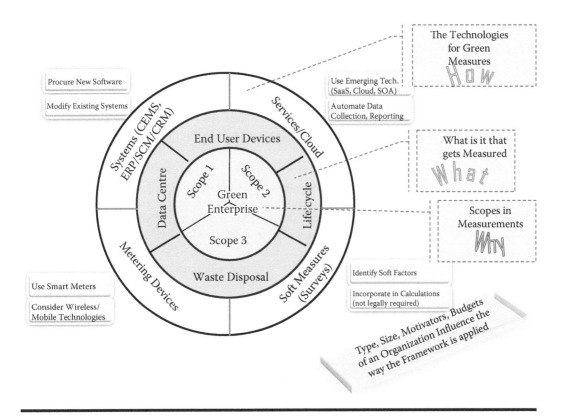

Figure 3.13   **Framework for Green IT metrics.**

measurement for different industry sectors which, as can be seen, is different for mining, oil gas, and so on. Further notice how, in terms of percentage importance to emissions monitoring, the transport industry gives very high importance (67%) to the measurement of carbon emissions, whereas financial services provide the least importance (15%) in terms of carbon measurements. This relative importance placed by the industry sectors is interestingly reflected in the actual results in terms of the emissions.

The way in which these Green IT metrics get customized and implemented in an organization depend on the original goals of the organization, its drivers, and also the challenges in obtaining these measures depending on the context. The context-sensitive nature of these measures and how this can be represented and managed is the primary discussion in this section. Furthermore, the opportunities for deploying these measures are also discussed here, for example, in IS design and management or green BPM or other IT-mediated design/monitoring settings.

Green IT Measurement Challenges

Five "M"s of carbon metrics determine the current and the future state of the organization. Measure: this is the core "M" for the green policy. This provides the metrics for capturing the statistics. Monitor: after measurement, we need to monitor the system for refining the policy. Manage: we need to manage the measured and monitored information to improve the process. Mitigate: reduce greenhouse gases by reducing the sources or increasing sink. Monetize: convert the improvement into monetary values for the organization.

Having discussed the Green IT metrics and measurements, it is also important to identify and deal with the challenges organizations are likely to face in implementing them in practice. Following are the specific challenges and issues relating to the use of Green IT metrics and measurements within organizations:

■ Lack of formal metrics and associated measurements related to carbon performance of an organization, particularly at the end-user and the data center level. For example, carbon emission calculations cover many different factors such as power, cooling, floor space, carbon offsets or emissions, ROI, TCO, TCCO, and other calculations relating to an IT data center. Each of these calculations can vary for different organizations and even departments within the organization.

■ Lack of availability of real-time data and corresponding defined metrics to calculate carbon performance. There is high complexity and difficulty of information gathering as well as deficiency of reliable primary and secondary sources of data.

■ Lack of robust cost-benefit calculations that would demonstrate to the corporate governance board and the shareholders the ROI on green initiatives. Actual investment cost of implementation of green business strategies has many aspects which are still undiscovered.

■ Lack of experience and necessary expertise within the organization to put together a measurement and optimization program. Most organizations currently lack both the methodology and metrics to undertake defensive and suitable power consumption and carbon footprint measurement programs.

■ Lack of standards and agreements amongst a group of organizations belonging to an industry group as to what should and should not be included within carbon emissions calculations (in spite of the ISO 14001 standard, the Scope 1, 2, and 3—as categories of carbon emissions—is still not standardized, and does not include electronic waste disposal calculations).

■ Confusing rules and regulations and their inadequacies in addressing the complete and comprehensive carbon footprint of an organization (as against measuring only the operational emissions). There is no agreed baseline to measure carbon emissions; government support is insufficient and quite absurd literature regarding environmentally responsible business strategies.

■ Lack of proper motivation, especially at the top-end of the business leadership, to initiate and implement carbon control programs. Top management of organization is not aware. There is a lack of support, awareness, and willingness. Commitment to cause is also lacking in organizations.

■ Unknown and/or unclear value proposition for business through its green initiatives both internally and externally, and the information is not properly available anywhere in the open source libraries.

■ Unclear understanding of how to incorporate attitude and viewpoints of participating employees and management in measuring the green credentials of an organization. Confusing carbon calculations resulting from increased global collaborations amongst businesses. For example, outsourced projects and global work can result in duplicated or missed carbon calculations spread across partners.

■ Differences in calculations of carbon emissions based on electricity consumed from different sources (Deshpande and Unhelkar, 2011). For example, power generated from fossil-fuel fired power stations needs to be calculated differently to the ones from gas stations or renewable energy generators. This adds significant complexity to the challenge of calculating emissions. In this regards, it is worth mentioning that popular models to compute power consumption of electronic equipment tend to be simplistic. Some metrics do not even allow for variations in usage or variability in consumption depending on the state of the equipment (busy or idle).

■ Assumptions. Monitoring the actual power consumption of large number of electronic equipments can be a logistical nightmare. Green policies in practice require assumptions in terms of the number of equipments and their usage patterns. These assumptions need to be validated periodically. Furthermore, these assumptions need to be carefully generalized across industries and even regions. Scientific sampling, statistical techniques for extrapolation, and also sophisticated metering and measurements are part of the Green IT metrics challenge.

Framework for Green IT Metrics

When it comes to measuring the carbon emissions, especially across medium to large businesses, there is urgency to measure and report carbon data. As argued earlier, two important things related to carbon emissions stand out: the need to comprehend how much of carbon is being generated by the business activities and, even more importantly, the lack of standardized and detailed measurements necessary. Furthermore, IT systems support for these calculations is also limited. For example, at the time of this writing, an official site (OSCAR) providing information on calculating carbon emissions provides an excel spreadsheet—and that too, with a disclaimer! Similarly, at an individual level, we have a much lesser feel for the carbon emissions occurring through their activities than we have for our power or water usage. For example, an average home PC user is occasionally surprised to note that his/her computer emits anywhere between 0.4 Tonne to 1.6 Tonne of carbon in a year (depending on how it is being used).

Green IT measurement has a few specific challenges. Lack of issues like formal metrics and associated measurement, robust cost-benefits calculations, experience and expertise, standards and agreements, and proper motivation. Also unclear value proposition and confusing rules aggravate the challenges.

Detailed metrics and measurement program for carbon emissions requires a framework. Figure 3.13 shows such an overall framework for measuring carbon emissions. In the center of this framework are the three scopes (discussed next) of carbon emissions. These emissions falling into the three scopes are measured across four areas of the organization: the end-user devices, the data center, the lifecycle, and the waste disposal. These areas for carbon emissions indicate what gets measured. On the outside of the framework are the means, the "how to" of carbon emission measurement—achieved through systems, services, metering devices, and surveys. Effective carbon emission measurement program is best provided through the framework presented in Figure 3.13.

Figure 3.14 details the scopes as well as the various elements appearing in carbon emission measurements. The CO_2e provides the basic unit of GHG Measurement and the resultant output is measured in Tonnes (and kilo tonnes = kT). The corresponding energy consumption from which the emissions are calculated is calculated using terajoules (TJ). Costs are usually available in the organization's ERP systems that correspond to the energy consumption and/or the carbon emissions—summarized in Figure 3.14.

Formal approaches to measuring Greenhouse Gases (GHG) starts with an understanding of the six major types of GHGs—Carbon Dioxide (CO_2), Methane (CH_4), Nitrous Oxide (N_2O), Perfluorocarbons (PFC), Hydrofluorocarbons (HFC), and Sulphur Hexafluoride (SF_6). GHGs are measured in Tonnes (and kilo tonnes = kT). The energy consumed in producing those GHGs is calculated in Joules/Terra Joules (TJ). When it comes to calculating the total emissions for an organization, these six greenhouse gases emitted by the use of materials and equipment, and execution of various processes by the organization need to be calculated and converted to CO_2e (Carbon dioxide equivalent). While CO_2e comprises only 0.05% of the atmosphere, it is the one that has tremendous detrimental effect and is, therefore, the focus of carbon metrics.

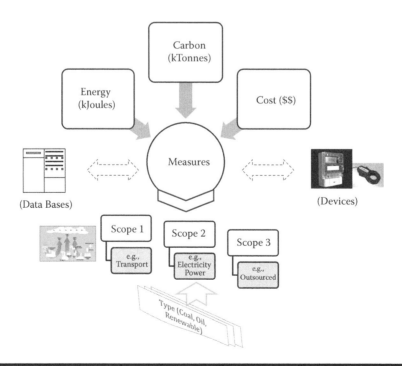

Figure 3.14   Elements and scopes of Green IT metrics.

The CO_2e calculations, based on the National Greenhouse and Energy Reporting System (NGERS), are required to be divided into three different categories, or scopes. These scopes of emissions facilitate their calculations and reporting. These emissions are distinguished under Scope 1, 2, and 3 emissions depending on their characteristics.

- *Scope 1 emissions* are those caused by direct emissions of carbon dioxide and other greenhouse gases into the atmosphere, for example, vehicle exhausts, manufacturing emissions, and so on. These are the emissions resulting from manufacturing activities, physical movement of people and materials, chemical emissions, and so on.
- *Scope 2 emissions* are those caused indirectly through the usage of energy that causes GHG emissions in its generation. By far the most common Scope 2 emission is the usage of electricity from the power grid.
- *Scope 3 emissions* are those caused by the organization's supply chain, that is, the embedded carbon used in the manufacture of products it buys or services it uses.

Currently, NGERS requires reporting only on Scope 1 and 2 emissions. Therefore, most carbon emissions metric become important only for these two scoped emissions.

Each area of the organization such as manufacturing, logistics, energy management, and waste management produces measurable GHG emissions. Carbon emissions data regarding the carbon footprints is collected and stored in database for further retrieval, reports, summary, and manipulation.

Eventually, carbon metrics have to measure and report on the TCCO (Total Carbon Cost of Ownership) measures for various groups of emissions (as shown in Figure 3.13) and eventually add them up for the organization.

Measuring the Carbon Footprint of Your Organization

Figure 3.15 shows the practical aspect of arriving at the carbon footprint of the organization. The measures of carbon emissions of an organization, in Figure 3.15, are divided into two major categories: the static measures and the dynamic ones. In a typical Green IT metrics and measurement exercise, only the dynamic measures get considered in detail. However, this figure argues for the need to include both static and dynamic measures of an organization's environmental performance in order to arrive at a comprehensive carbon footprint of the organization. The overall footprint of an organization is represented by a "C" notation in Figure 3.15.

The dynamic measures shown in Figure 3.15 are the measures of energy consumed during the day-to-day operation of the organization. Thus, the dynamic measures change on a daily basis, and are made up of the emissions of the organization in its production line, service processes, and also include the impact of attitude and behavior of the people working within the organization. The dynamic measure is an ongoing measure that needs to be computed over a specific period of time (e.g., one month, one year) to ascertain the emissions of the organization. The scope of emissions measured in the dynamic aspects is usually Scope 2 and Scope 1. Scope 2 is more prevalent and easy to measure as it is usually based on the power bills of the organization.

The static measures are a group of measures that are ascertained based on the procurement, design, and also the disposal aspect of materials and equipments in the organization. Furthermore, these measures also include the buildings, infrastructures, and all such procurements that are one-off, usually undertaken at the start of a project within the organization and do not change during the course of the usage. For example, the carbon emissions associated with the construction of a data center form occur only once at the start of the data center. These emissions result from the

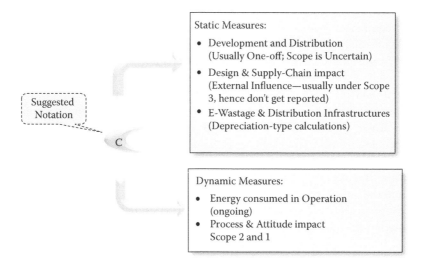

Figure 3.15 Measuring CO₂e.

building, its materials, installation of air conditioning, and so on. These are the static, upfront emissions that need to be calculated and added to the overall emissions of the data center.

Eventually, the total static carbon emission measures will be apportioned over the life of an infrastructure or equipment to arrive at the Total Carbon Cost of Ownership (TCCO).

Measuring Operational Costs in Your Organization

The dynamic measures referred to in the previous section are mainly the operational measures of carbon emission in the organization. This is so because these dynamic measures encompass the carbon produced when an equipment (such as a computer monitor, a data server, or a network router) is operational or in use. Since the way in which an equipment is used is likely to change on a daily basis, these operational carbon calculations vary from day to day and from equipment to equipment.

The calculation of CO_2e for an organization would be made up of operational carbon produced by its business units (or departments) as shown in Figure 3.16. As this is the operational carbon calculation, it is made up of not only the equipment itself, but also time duration for which it is in use. For example, in Figure 3.16, the total departmental usage of PCs is calculated per month to add up to the yearly emission. Each departmental usage and corresponding carbon calculation is itself made up of PC usage by each individual user, per day, in the department or business unit. Thus, operational carbon emission calculation will be a combination of the equipments in use and the various time durations for that use.

Green Balanced Scorecard

Green IT metrics and measurements need to consider yet another popular option of measuring organizational performance, that of the "balanced scorecard." Applying the concept of a balanced

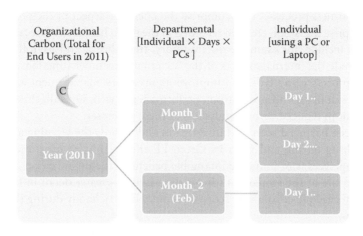

Figure 3.16   Typical breakdown in measuring carbon emissions (example of end-user devices).

scorecard (Arveson, 1998) to Green IT can help organizations in creating and implementing *balanced* Green IT strategies and their policies. A green balanced scorecard can provide the necessary measure and benchmark for the balanced approach to Green IT discussed earlier (see Figure 3.6). The concept of the balanced scorecard is valuable in Green IT as it builds on four perspectives: financial, internal business processes, customer, and learning/growth. The balance in these four perspectives is achieved based on the core vision and strategy of the organization. This core business vision would deal with the core business itself and which remains at the center of the balanced scorecard. The four perspectives of the balanced financial scorecard with respect of Green IT can be understood as follows:

The financial perspective in a balanced scorecard is used to assess the business activities and financial standing of the organization that assists in identifying the strengths and weaknesses of the organization. Therefore, in a way, this perspective of the balanced scorecard is similar to a cost benefit analysis for the green initiative. The financial perspective of the balanced scorecard investigates the financial performance record of the organization. This investigation includes a measure of the transitioning organization's business activities, its green objectives, and the method of measuring those green objectives. Senior management can undertake this activity at the start of a Green IT initiative, formulate a project, discuss, and comment on the overall green approach that an organization need to take in adopting Green IT. The Green IT metrics associated with this Green IT initiative of the organization provide the feedback on the success (or otherwise) of the transition. The need for additional Green IT business processes over and above the greening of existing processes is also in this section of the balanced scorecard. An understanding of the financial perspective helps a business measure its performance in the economic dimension of a green enterprise transition.

The financial perspective of the balanced scorecard is followed by the profiling and understanding of the demographics of the customer. This profiling of the customer is primarily an understanding of the objectives of the customer in dealing with the business. The manner and extent to which the customer uses the business indicates the influence of the customer on the business. Details of the customer, his or her green preferences, and the desire and ability to specify those preferences in consuming services or purchasing products from the organization are important measures in this aspect of the green balanced scorecard.

The internal business processes that comprise the operative aspect of the organization undertaking green enterprise transition are then recorded in the green balanced scorecard. These internal business processes include, for example, the inventory, time sheets, and payroll functions. These processes also include the internal aspects of the "external" customer functions. For example, an internal business process using RFID to improve its inventory management and stock location processes would result in an improved carbon performance as well. Overall, these internal process optimizations result in reduced carbon emissions of these processes.

Finally, the green balanced scorecard investigates and records the learning and growth of the organization resulting during and from its Green IT effort. This learning and experience that occurs with its employees is of immense intangible benefit to the organization as it improves the quality of working life of the employees (this is discussed in greater detail in Chapter 8). Thus, this management technique of balanced scorecard comes in very handy during the formulation of Green IT strategies.

Table 3.3 summarizes the four aspects of a green balanced scorecard.

Table 3.3   Measures for Green Balanced Score Card

Green Balanced Scorecard Aspect	*Elements of Scorecard That Affect the Green IT Metrics Measurements*
Financial Measures	Risks associated with environmental fines and penalties
	Operational energy costs and corresponding emission calculations
	Investments in equipments and infrastructures that (a) are currently emitting carbon and (b) are required to ameliorate the effect/emission of carbon
	Costs associated with reuse and disposal
Customer Measures	Green product preferences and resultant increase/decrease in sales as a result of green-specific actions by the organization
	Marketing and sales of green products based on the demands of the customer. Varying the way in which products are promoted, requires understanding of varying customer preferences
	Pre- and postsales services associated with green products and services
Internal Business Processes	Power consumption of internal processes
	Use of technologies (e.g., RFID) in reducing internal power consumption and optimizing processes
	Supply chain processes (e.g., procurement of materials) that are optimized and that enable conformation to set carbon limits
	Recycling, reuse, and disposal of materials and equipments
Learning and Growth	Training and education of employees and other users (e.g., customers using the Internet-based services of a bank)
	Ascertaining attitude through survey questionnaires. Also, ascertaining changes in that attitude due to the green initiatives
	Green HR and its support (e.g., for Telework, videoconferencing)

Green IT Readiness and CMM

Yet another function of Green IT metrics and measurements is to ascertain the preparedness of an organization with respect to the environment. Metrics open up opportunities to measure the emissions of the organization in the "as is" and the "to be" state. Green IT metrics also create a comparative index that enables an understanding of the level at which an organization is in comparison with other organizations within the industry sector.

A significant development in enabling such comparison is the Green IT Readiness Index (Connection Research, 2009). Connection Research (also known as EnvirAbility), an Australian market research and consultancy company, together with RMIT (Molla, 2009), has devised this index that provides a simple yet effective measure of the green preparedness and maturity of an organization. Based on the CMM (Capability Maturity Model) (Humphrey, 1988), the Green IT readiness of an organization is measured across four aspects: attitude, policy, practice, and technology.

Connection Research determines the Green IT maturity levels through a survey quizzing the participants on the aforementioned four (and metrics) aspects. Answers enabled a rating on a CMM scale from 0 to 5. Level 0, an additional level, indicated absolutely no readiness or awareness of Green IT on part of the firm. Level 1 indicates some awareness of Green IT but ad hoc implementation. Level 2 is the level where a firm is able to make formal attempt at Green IT which it is able to replicate in time. Level 3 is where the Green IT processes, roles, and deliverables are fully defined. Level 4 is a comprehensive Green IT metrics level, and Level 5 is where the results from the metrics are used to optimize the green performance of the organization. This is the "Best practice" level of an organization.

The relevant answers to questions in each of the four aspects of Green IT were aggregated and weighted by Connection Research and used to create a score (out of 100). Based on responses from over 300 organizations (Philipson, 2010), this survey provides a sufficiently large base to develop average ratings for industry sectors and different sizes of organization. Averaging the response across each Green IT aspect of the organization has resulted in a Green IT maturity or "readiness" by industry sector and by size of organization, as shown in Figure 3.18. Figure 3.18 further reveals that the transport sector was by far the best sector in terms of carbon emissions control, whereas the banking and finance did not fare that well. Use of this readiness index has the potential to enable an individual organization to easily determine whether it is above or below average in its Green IT maturity in each area. Further analysis of the responses to

The Green IT readiness of an organization can be ascertained by comparing it with a benchmark. Connection Research-RMIT has developed such a benchmark, which is based on CMM. Alternative ways of measuring the Green IT readiness include measurements for financial, customer, internal business process and learning and growth. For example, ROI calculations on the green initiative is a financial measure, measuring eco-efficiency of product or service related to the customer, measuring electricity consumed can be an internal business process, and imparting employee training on Green IT is measured to ascertain learning and growth. Organizations measured along these aforementioned areas can then be indexed and categorized as follows:

- *Watchers:* These are the organizations that prefer to wait and see what happens in terms of regulations, competition, and the overall impact of the drivers. These organizations are not interested in taking the green initiative and do not have the green ROI in place.
- *Minimalists:* These organizations only take the minimum action required to ensure they maintain the legal and other regulatory compliance. While compliant, these organizations are unlikely to be leaders in the green economy. They miss out on the potential advantages of developing green products and services for the future.
- *Transformationals:* These organizations are keen to significantly undertake transformation. They have specific goals, budgets, and transformation teams in place to undertake green enterprise transformation program. The CGO is a revered role in these organizations and they are changing to achieve leadership positions in the green economy.
- *Leaders:* These organizations lead a group of collaborative organizations by example, and also by using their own green standards in interacting with other partnering organizations. This leads to leadership in consortium-based Green IT initiatives.

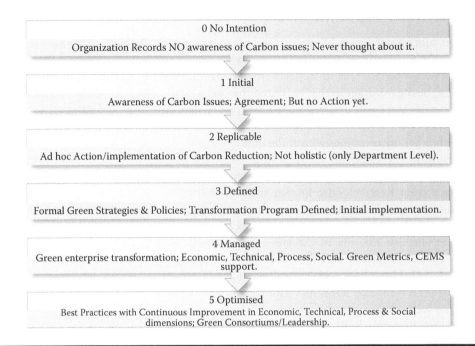

Figure 3.17 Green Capability Maturity Model. (Based on Philipson, G., www.connection research.com, 2009, accessed 15 October 2010.)

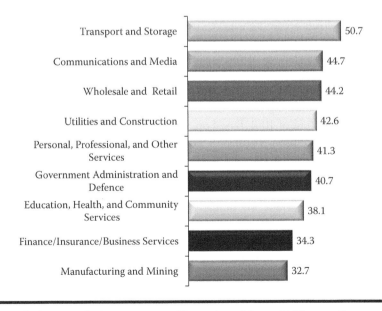

Figure 3.18 Emissions per industry sector. (Reproduced from Philipson, G., www.connection research.com, 2009, accessed 15 October 2010. With permission.)

individual questions in the survey can then identify specific policies or technologies that might be implemented to improve the organization's Green IT maturity in that area.

Context Sensitivity and Automation in Green IT Measures

In this concluding section of this chapter, the importance of automation in Green IT measures and the context-sensitive nature of these measurements are discussed. Automation assists in measuring and monitoring of emissions in real time. This is usually accomplished by means of smart meters at the data collection end of the Carbon Emissions Management Software (CEMS). Smart meters record and report on the carbon emissions from equipments and operations. The carbon emissions data from these meters are used by CEMS to analyze, plot trends, and provide alerts to the workers and the leaders in terms of emission and potential actions. In addition, web services from regulatory bodies, SaaS (software as a service), and mobile technologies also play a positive role in the automation of carbon measurements as they enable integration of systems and services that measure and monitor emissions. For example, mobile devices can be used to collect carbon data from remote and mobile locations; mobile user devices can provide instantaneous feedback to users in terms of their carbon ratings; and web services pick up changes to regulations on an instantaneous basis. A well designed CEMS can also be subjected to audits and certification. This will enable cross-organizational comparisons on carbon performance, as also pave way for carbon credits and their trading. The resultant environmentally responsible business "ecosystem" can have a snowball effect on many other business partners.

One of the challenges of current carbon measurements arise from the context-sensitive nature of these measures. This context sensitivity extends from the specific nuances of an organization, its size, its physical location, and also its industrial sector (NGERS). For example, the transport sector would be focused on the combustion of fuel and its direct carbon generation, whereas a peripheral manufacturer will be equally keen to ascertain the e-waste disposal metrics. Industries such as agriculture and mining have their own unique criteria which need to be incorporated in the metrics.

The following tables provide summaries of various carbon metrics. These measures suggested in these tables also cater to the context-sensitive nature of carbon metrics. Table 3.4 lists the Green IT metrics, their suggested unit, and their context from the perspective of the management. Table 3.5 does the same from the data center viewpoint, Table 3.6 from the organizational and equipment lifecycle view, and Table 3.7 from the social and attitude viewpoint. Note that these tables provide the starting point for Green IT measures that are likely to change depending on the context or the situation in which they are measured, analyzed, and reported.

Table 3.4   Management and Cost-Benefit Metrics for Green Enterprise

Metrics	Unit	Context
Cost of Green IT transformation for the enterprise (Replacement costs of devices—primarily of IT domain) (Systems upgrades, people costs—training and consulting)	$ (or equi)	Derived by close work with existing financial and inventory management systems.
Costs associated with change in business (possible loss of customers Rewriting of SLAs; this will be usually outside of IT; need to calculate NPV of the carbon initiative for next 3–5 years)	$	Green IT may reduce the quality of service for some customers. Corporate customers may enforce rewrite of SLAs.
Savings resulting from the Green IT transformation Reduction in operational expenses (Scope 1) Reduction in energy expenses (Scope 2)	$	These savings need to be included in the budgets for greening of the organization. Carbon and cost are both reduced.
Potential penalty costs (likely to change dramatically as the legislations mature)	$	Green IT projects need to be budgeted keeping these potential penalty costs in mind.
Green IT strategy within business strategy (can be measured in terms of the total number of elements within a strategic business approach, and the numbers within them that are related to Green IT/carbon emissions)	%	Derived from the existing elements of strategic measures (a financial/time measure in percentage).

Table 3.5   Enterprise Data Center Metrics

Metrics	Unit	Context
Carbon emission per megabyte of data stored on the servers	CO_2e	Relates the carbon emissions to the total electronic storage occupying the servers
Carbon emission per MIE (million instructions executed—time, or speed of execution, can be incorporated later after this metric is refined)	CO_2e	Relates the carbon emissions to the *speed* with which the data center is operating
Carbon emission of the data center per user (this needs to be divided into internal users/employees versus external customers)	CO_2e	Relates the carbon emissions to the total users being served by the data center
Power usage effectiveness (PUE) (existing) versus PUE of outsourced data center (potential—the outsourcing vendors will have to provide this) (PUE or DCiE)	% or ratio	Well-known measure that provides a ratio of effectiveness of power consumption for data storage purposes

Table 3.6 Organizational Behavior and Lifecycle Metrics

Metrics	Unit	Context
Green supply chain index (total green-specific or green-rated materials/total materials); similarly, extended for equipments	CO_2e	Carbon calculation for the lifecycle of equipment/material. Carbon generated during the production of the equipment, then its transport and installation.
Green recycling index = [(number of days or years beyond the official life of an equipment x carbon emission)/(corresponding emissions from new equipment) + carbon generated in production and transportation of the new equipment)]	Ratio	This measure should provide a benchmark for the extent of recycling.
Carbon generated in disposing existing equipment	CO_2e	This carbon is calculated toward the end of the equipment, after it has been decommissioned and being disposed off.
Landfill	Tonne	Total landfill generated by disposal of equipments and/or materials by the organization.

Table 3.7 Attitude and Other "Soft" Metrics

Metrics	Unit	Context
Level of positivity of employee attitude toward Green	Level 1 through 5	Ascertained through a survey at the start and completion of a Green IT transformation program.
Level of positivity of senior management attitude toward Green	Level 1 through 5	As above
Separate level of positivity of data center manager/director attitude toward Green	Level 1 through 5	As above
Level of positivity of customers toward Green	Level 1 through 5	As above

Discussion Points

■ What are the differences in focus between organizations a decade ago, in terms of their governance focus?

■ How does a Lean organization correlate to a Green organization?

■ How would you go about drafting green policies from the strategies discussed in the previous chapter? How would you convert those green policies in practice?

■ Discuss the coverage, duration, and intensity of CO_2e measures.

■ Why formulation and application of Green IT policies are required to be in balance? What are the factors that vie against each other are required to be in balance ?

■ Discuss the various renewable sources of energy. How do these different energy sources impact the carbon emission calculations?

■ List and discuss any three elements in the mind map of a Chief Green Officer.

■ Discuss two environmental practices that can be incorporated in a green organization. Identify the challenges one would face in implementing these environmental practices.

■ What are the five purposes of Green IT metrics?

■ List, with examples, the "Why, What, and How" of a Green IT metrics framework.

■ Separate the static and dynamic Green IT measures and then show how the two can be used together (through apportionment).

Action Points

■ Identify existing policies in your organization that deal with the environment.

■ Identify the limitations and challenges of those policies that your organization faces to implement environmentally responsible policies and strategies.

■ Create a list of new environmental policies that would be appropriate for your organization. These policies should be based on the strategies developed in the previous chapter. Update your business strategies on the basis of green policies that can be put in practice. (Note: the actual process of policy formulation will take a few weeks, and will be accomplished after internal discussions.)

■ List the challenges your organization is likely to face in measuring carbon emission data. This list should be based on various departments, their user devices, the data center, and the supply chain processes.

■ Extend and apply the Green IT metrics framework (Figure 3.13) to your organization.

■ Study the how, what, and why of carbon measurements in your organization. List them for a specific "pilot" department.

■ List the current "as is" Scope 1 and Scope 2 emissions of your organization.

■ List the desired "to be" state of your organization through the management, technology, process, and social metrics.

■ Apply the Green IT readiness index to ascertain the current Green IT maturity of your organization. Introduce relevant measures to help improve the green readiness for the organization.

References

CEC (Colorado Environmental Center). (2005). *Energy Conservation: Past & Present Projects: Green Computing Guide*. University of Colorado, Boulder, Colorado, USA (available at http://ecenter.colorado.edu/energy/ projects/green_computing.html).

Deshpande, Y. and Unhelkar, B. (2011). Information systems for a Green organisation. In B. Unhelkar, ed., *Handbook of Research in Green ICT: Technical, Methodological and Social Perspectives*, pp. 116–130. IGI Global, Hershey, PA, USA.

Figge, F. and Hahn, T. (2005). The Cost of Sustainability Capital and the Creation of Sustainable Value by Companies. *Journal of Industrial Ecology*, 9(4). doi:10.1162/108819805775247936.

Freeman, R., Hart, S., and Wheeler, D. (series editors) (2007–2008). *Business Value Creation and Society.* Cambridge, UK: Cambridge University Press.

Greenfield, A. (2006). E*veryware: The Dawning Age of Ubiquitous Computing. New Riders.* Indianapolis, IN: New Riders.

Ghose, A. and Billau, G. (2011). The optimizing web: A Green ICT research perspective. In B. Unhelkar, ed., *Handbook of Research in Green ICT: Technical, Methodological and Social Perspectives,* pp. 184–196. IGI Global, Hershey, PA, USA.

Guang, Y. (2008). Green labor management relations: a guarantee of enhancing green quality of products and competitive power of the company. *IEEE Xplore,* 3.

Humphrey, W. (1988). Characterizing the Software Process: A Maturity Framework [New York: IEEE.]. *IEEE Software* (March): 1988.

Makower, J. and Pike, C. (2009). *Strategies for the Green Economy: Opportunities and Challenges in the New World of Business.* McGraw Hill Publishers, New York.

Manuel, K. and Halchin, L. (2010). Environmental considerations in federal procurement: an overview of legal authorities and their implementation. Congressional Research Service. Available at http://government-policy.blogspot.com/2011/01/environmental-considerations-in-federal.html, accessed January 25, 2011.

Molina, M., Zaelke, D., Sarmac, K. M., Andersen, S. O., Ramanathane, V., and Kaniaruf, D. (2009). Tipping elements in earth systems special feature: reducing abrupt climate change risk using the Montreal Protocol and other regulatory actions to complement cuts in CO_2 emissions. *Proceedings of the National Academy of Sciences,* 106: 20616.

Molla, A. (2009). An exploration of green IT adoption, drivers and inhibitors. *Annual Conference on Information Science and Technology Management (CISTM 2009),* July 13–15, Abstract.

Murugesan, S. (2007). Going green with IT: Your responsibility towards environmental sustainability. *Cutter Executive Report,* 10(8).

Murugesan, S. (2008a). Harnessing green IT: Principles and practices. *IEEE IT Professional,* January–February, 24–33.

Murugesan, S. (Ed.). (2008b). Can IT go green. Special Issue, *Cutter IT Journal,* 21(2): 3–5.

Murugesan, S. (2011). Chapter 4, Strategies for greening enterprise IT: Creating business value and contributing to environmental sustainability. In B. Unhelkar, ed., *Handbook of Research in Green ICT,* pp. 51–64. IGI Global, Hershey, PA, USA.

NGERS. (2007) Available at http://www.climatechange.gov.au/government/initiatives/national-greenhouse-energy-reporting.aspx, accessed February 1, 2011. Department of Climate Change and Energy Efficiency, Australian Government.

OSCAR. (2008) Available at https://www.oscar.gov.au/Deh.Oscar.Extension.Web/Content/NgerThreshold Calculator/ Default.aspx; also see www.climatechange.gov.au/reporting, accessed February 1, 2011. Department of Climate Change and Energy Efficiency, Australian Government.

Pratt, M. K. (2009). How to get your Green IT crates. *Information Age,* December 2009/January 2010, 57–59.

Russell, Pam. (2009). "Iberdrola wins state approval to build 306-MW wind project in South Dakota," *Global Power Report,* 15(3).

Sanford. (2009). "Renewable Energy—Towering Achievement," Modern Power System, 12(7).

Sherringham, K. and Unhelkar, B. (2011). Strategic business trends in the context of green ICT. In B. Unhelkar, ed., *Handbook of Research in Green ICT: Technical, Business and Social Perspectives,* pp. 65–82. IGI Global, Hershey, PA, USA.

Trivedi, B. and Unhelkar, B. (2009). Semantic integration of environmental web services in an organization. *Proceedings of the 2nd International Conference on Environmental and Computer Science,* 284–288. Published by IEEE Computer Society, ISBN 978-0-7695-3937-9.

Unhelkar, B. (2009a). *Mobile Enterprise Transition and Management.* Taylor & Francis Group (CRC Press), USA.

Unhelkar, B. (2009b). Cutter Benchmark Review (CBR*):* Creating and applying Green IT metrics and measurement in practice. In G. Piccoli, ed., *Green IT Metrics and Measurement: The Complex Side of Environmental Responsibility, Cutter IT Journal,* Boston, USA, 9(10): 10–17.

Unhelkar, B. and Philipson, G. (2009). The development and application of a green IT maturity index. *Proceedings of the Australian Conference on Software Measurements, ACOSM2009,* November 2009.

Unhelkar, B. and Trivedi, B. (2009a). Managing environmental compliance: A techno-business perspective. *SCIT Journal,* IX, August 2009.

Unhelkar, B. and Trivedi, B. (2009b). Merging web services with 3G IP Multimedia systems for providing solutions in managing environmental compliance by business, *Proceedings of ITA09 Conference,* Wrexham, UK, September 8–11, 2009.

Younessi, D. (2011). Sustainable business value. In B. Unhelkar, ed., *Handbook of Research in Green ICT: Technical, Methodological and Social Perspectives,* pp. 98–115. IGI Global, Hershey, PA, USA.

Younessi, H. (2009). Strategic view on creating business value through mobile technologies. In B. Unhelkar, ed., *Handbook of Research in Mobile Business: Technical, Methodological and Social Perspectives,* 2nd Ed., Chapter 1. IGI Global, Hershey, PA, USA.

Chapter 4

Green Assets: Buildings, Data Centers, Networks, and Devices

When the soil disappears, the soul disappears.

Ymber Delecto

Key Points

- Describes the various assets (buildings, data centers, and devices) of an organization from their carbon generation perspective.
- Investigates the importance of carbon-efficient buildings and in particular the green data centers.
- Creates a relationship between the "bit, watt, and cost" that further relates data, data servers, and the corresponding data centers in which they are housed.
- Presents various data center strategies for carbon reduction such as server virtualization, device optimization, and hot–cold aisle arrangements.
- Describes networking and communications assets of an organization, usually in the data centers, from their carbon generation perspective.
- Discusses mobile technologies in the way they contribute to e-waste as also the opportunities they offer for carbon reduction.
- Discusses the smart metering technologies for measurements that invariably come into play when green metrics and strategies are automated.

Introduction

This chapter focuses on the assets of an organization from the point of view of their impact on the overall carbon contribution of the organization. While these assets have been grouped from an accounting perspective in tangible and intangible assets, it is worth grouping them into two groups from a carbon perspective: the static, infrastructural assets (e.g., the data center) and the nonstatic assets (which are mobile, such as a laptop computer) of the organization. These assets impact the carbon footprint of the organization right from their procurement and installation through to their disposal. Eventually, astute carbon management of these assets results in reduced carbon footprints that can be exchanged, traded, and used to increase the value of the organization, its products, and services. This chapter outlines the approaches to management of assets that would ameliorate the impact of carbon through environmental-consciousness such as maintenance and replacement of assests, computer virtualization, and ethically correct electronic waste disposal.

The static, infrastructural aspect of an organization requires separate, special attention. The long-term strategies of the business in terms of ownership, design, procurement, operation, and disposal of these infrastructure assets all affect its carbon footprint. This is so because the infrastructure has a one-off decision-making point at the time such as when it is procured and/or constructed. After that initial decision-making process is consummated and an asset has been procured, the only way its carbon impact can be reduced is through optimized operation. However, the upfront decisions, when a static, structural asset is being procured or constructed, have a much longer and strategic impact on the overall carbon footprint of the organization than when that asset is in operation. Therefore, the practices of procurement and construction gain immediate importance in the discussions on Green IT.

Similarly, special attention is required when an asset is disposed off. This is so because when it gets removed from the asset register of an organization, it may not generate the carbon emission it used to generate during operation. This may create a false impression that the asset is no longer the organization's responsibility. However, has that electronic (typically computer) asset been ethically disposed off? Or is the lead or cadmium from a desktop box or laptop battery leaking into the water supplies of a community? How are its parts being dismantled? Ethical disposal of electronic waste can cost multiple times (some estimates range from 10 to 20 times) in a fully developed country than in a developing nation—primarily due to availability of cheap labor and not so stringent legislations. These costs need to be factored in the overall green strategies of the organization. This chapter delves deeper into these organizational practices associated with the assets and infrastructure of the organization.

In the context of these electronic assets, the strategies and policies of a green organization discussed in the previous two chapters need to be translated into practice of the way it procures, uses, and then disposes these various assets. This chapter expands on how those practices can be developed and implemented. For example, this chapter develops further the ideas relating to the green data center strategies and their implementation. In practice, these strategies translate to not only the servers and their positioning within the physical data center, but also correlating the impact of one extra bit of storage on the overall planning and operation of the data center. Mapping a bit to the overheads it produces in the data center, and educating and training employees as it relates to their use of databases, is a part of this practice. Subsequently, in this chapter, there is also a discussion on mobile devices and smart meters that play a crucial role in measuring and monitoring the overall carbon emissions. The calculations and reporting of the organization's carbon performance can be simplified and automated through the use of smart carbon measuring devices. Finally, this chapter also underscores the importance of networks and related gadgets in sustainability.

Consider the Figure 4.1 which is based on the Trivedi and Unhelkar (2010) survey. This figure shows the relative importance of various organizational practices primarily relating to its assets as adopted across the entire organization. While these practices were also discussed in the previous chapter, this chapter lays particular emphasis on the green practices relating to the static as well as mobile assets of the organization. As shown in Figure 4.1, these practices range from reducing the use of peripherals and their consumables such as paper, ink, or toners through to the practices associated with procurement and operation of high power consuming equipments, typically the data servers, housed in the organization's data centers. Figure 4.1 is

The carbon footprint of an organization comprises lot more than its carbon emissions. Apart from the emissions during the operation of its assets, an organizational carbon footprint is also directly affected by the procurement and disposal strategies and practices relating to its assets. Fifty-three percent of the survey participants (40% agreed and 13% strongly agreed) were in favor of the need for a full lifecycle assessment of energy-consuming assets. Without such assessment and inventory list, it will be very challenging to start implementing Green IT.

consistently ranking high on "agree" option (40%–45%) for most of these assets and hardware related factors contributing to carbon emissions. Encouraging product innovation and environmentally conscious design, assessing the lifecycle assessment of energy-consuming equipments and optimizing the overall operations of the assets are all high on "agree" to "strongly agree" ratings by most respondents. Similarly, efficient operation of equipments through training, lifecycle assessments, and good maintenance have a combined score of more than 75% for "agree" and "strongly agree" in Figure 4.1.

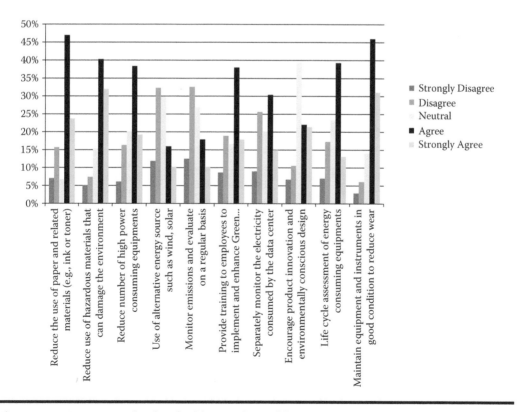

Figure 4.1　Green organizational-wide practices with emphasis on assets.

Green Assets

The green assets and infrastructure comprise substantial part of that long-term approach (discussed in Chapter 2) to managing the carbon performance of the organization. Figure 4.2 depicts examples of these enterprise infrastructure assets (both movable and nonmovable) on the left. On the right side, in Figure 4.2, the three major phases or activities associated with the lifecycle of these assets is depicted: the way they are established or procured, the manner in which they are operated or run, and eventually the strategies for their disposal or demolishment. These assets made up of building, data center, devices, and vehicles are also summarized in Table 4.1. Each of these three major activities relating to the infrastructure assets has the following carbon repercussions:

- *Establish (Procure)* deals with the green credentials of the asset in terms of its design and development. This is a one-off decision-making process that decides on the carbon efficiency of that assets design. For example, the original design of a car engine or a mobile phone that make it carbon efficient. This is a one-off factor when an organization is procuring the asset. Similarly, in case of buildings, the one-off factor that comes into play has to do with its architecture and design, as also highlighted in Table 4.1.
- *Operate (Run):* The manner of operation of the asset has a bearing on the total carbon contribution of the organization. Length of operation of the asset, such as operating a vehicle for 10 years or a mobile phone for 2 years will impact the overall emissions of that asset over its lifetime. The user of the asset is responsible for operating (using) it in such a way as to reduce its carbon impact. Thus, this is an ongoing, daily decision-making process.
- *Dispose (Demolish):* This is the eventual phase of an asset and it also impacts the overall carbon footprint of an organization. This impact is through the organization's approach to disposing or demolishing the asset. This is also a one time decision-making process with long-term effect on the environment. For example, ethical disposal or desktop and laptops are a major domain for discussion and action—especially within medium to large organizations, wherein policies might dictate the end of use of an asset rather than its actual

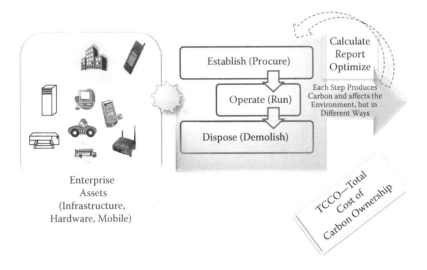

Figure 4.2   Green assets need to be organized in an efficient way throughout their lifecycle.

Table 4.1 Types of Assets (Categories) and Their Impact on the Environment

Type of Assets	Impact on Environment
Buildings and Facilities (e.g., offices, meeting rooms, training centers, social rooms, sports facilities)	Long-term impact as major environmental considerations should be during architecture and construction. Purpose of buildings, people movements, geographical locations (weather), and durability of the building impact their overall carbon contribution. Examples of one-off decision making in design include the materials used in the construction, the extent to which the building is facing the sun, the wind directions, and the way in which these natural light and natural cooling are put together to reduce energy consumption.
Data Center (as separate, dedicated buildings to house servers)	This is a special purpose building to house data servers. In addition to the standard building considerations, the ratio between power usage by the servers versus the rest of the power is a popular environmental consideration. CRAC (Computer Room Air Conditioning) is a discipline in its own right that separates the cooling of the servers from the air conditioning required in rest of the building. Thus, building technologies together with data server technologies are put to use here to reduce carbon.
Devices (e.g., laptop, mobiles)	Design, development, procurement, operation, and usage of devices is considered here. Example of this includes low-power consuming design for laptops and mobile devices, efficient batteries for them, carbon-conscious electronic chip design, biodegradability of materials used, and so on. Apart from the operational carbon generated by these devices, their disposal itself is an important issue.
Vehicles (e.g., cars, trucks, corporate vans, and buses)	Direct fuel emissions, pollution level of the type of fuel, design of the engines, and so on. Procurement, operations and disposal activities apply to vehicles used by the organization. These vehicles produce the Scope 1 emissions. Fleet maintenance systems need to be updated with carbon calculations. The kind of vehicle, its design, how long it will be operated, and the method of its disposal has to be considered. Vehicle emission consideration is vital when considering the entire organization. This table lists vehicles as an important reminder. However, detailed discussion on vehicle emissions is out of scope for this chapter.

disfunctionality. Therefore, policies for recycling of assets that are beyond the "use by" date for the organization need to be studied and revised to ensure that the assets are disposed ethically and with least impact on the environment. Such revision of policies will also open up opportunities for reuse and recycling, before the eventual disposal is effectuated.

This is the Green Procurement-Operation-Disposal (P-O-D) lifecycle of an assets. Figure 4.2 also highlights the fact that each step of P-O-D produces carbon that affects the Total Carbon Cost of Ownership (TCCO) of that asset—albeit is different ways. Thus, assets need to be considered in the context of not just their current costs, but their TCCO. The concept of Total Cost of Ownership (TCO) for ICT equipment was made popular by research consultancy Gartner (as reported by Kirwin, 1987). TCO, as its name suggests, is based on the full cost of equipment over its entire life, not just the purchase price. It takes into account running costs, maintenance, upgrades, and so on. For computing equipments, it is reasonable to expect their TCO to exceed the original purchase price by a factor of three or more. Therefore, counting the total carbon costs over the lifetime of an asset including its carbon content in production, the carbon generated during its operation over its lifetime and the carbon produced in its disposal, is vital.

Until recently many TCO computations have not taken into account the costs of the power to run the ICT equipment. This is so, because power costs have been comparatively low, and because ICT departments and users are rarely billed separately for the electricity they consume and have no visibility of it (Philipson, 2010). However, when the TCCO calculations are made, it becomes important to incorporate the carbon that is generated along with the calculations of costs associated with equipments. TCCO can be improved with smart metering capabilities, carbon calculations throughout the life of the equipment and its disposal. Since the power consumption of data centers is rising, so is the heat generated by data center processors. TCCO has to also include the power involved in the effort for cooling (Philipson, 2010).

Subsequent sections of this chapter develops this Green P-O-D lifecycle further and applies it to buildings, data centers, and other electronic assets of an organization.

Building and Facility Management

Building and facilities impact the long-term strategic approach to carbon reduction. Consider, for example, the activities of Wal-Mart in this context, as reported on Wal-Mart (2009). The roofs of most of its warehouses are painted white to reduce the heat generated from direct sunlight. The expense in painting the roof is compensated by reduction in the cooling expenses along with reduction in corresponding carbon generation. Another example by the same organization is to install LED lights instead of normal lights in its freezer facilities to reduce both its costs and carbon emissions (Wal-Mart, 2009). In 2007, the company also reached out to its customers with an in-store education program to encourage replacement of incandescent light bulbs with compact florescent bulbs (Sanders, 2008).

Similarly, Google too is reported to have solar panels installed in its office campus in the United States. These solar panels, installed over the rooftops of eight buildings, together with two solar carports produced 5,327 kilowatt/hours of electricity from the sun in 1 day. Google's offices in Darling Park, in Sydney, Australia also boast the highest 6-star ratings in terms of their environmental credentials. These infrastructure projects are a combination of one-off strategies relating to architecture and design of the buildings together with operational strategies relating to the use of the buildings and facilities.

The physical buildings and facilities belonging to the organization form the crux of its nonmovable assets. Buildings, while usually not a part of IT directly, are still a major contributor to the organization's carbon footprint. This carbon generation from buildings, as described briefly in Table 4.1 depends on the material of the building itself, its air conditioning, and related operational features such as lighting and ventilation. The architecture and design of the buildings used by businesses impact the long-term carbon generated by them. While most contemporary focus of Green IT has been on the operational aspect of these facilities, the architecture and design of offices, factories, and also related facilities (such as, a sporting complex or a community room) have a strategic role to play in the organization's carbon footprint. The need and demand to consider the carbon issues upfront, during initial procurement and/or construction of buildings and facilities and subsequently focusing on its optimized operations is crucial to the holistic approach to a green enterprise. This forces the construction industry to handle issues such as the type of insulation used, facilities to recycle water, and the use of natural light in determining the TCCO for that building. These factors would affect indirectly or directly on every previous step taken into consideration. For example, the location of an operational room, where staff is ideally located, should have natural and sufficient sunlight during day time that would reduce electricity usage. Use of translucent materials for dividers, focus on solar charging, and use of solar equipments and cells are all examples of strategic aspects of environmental asset management. When applied specifically to buildings, these considerations fall under the category of green facilities management that has capabilities to show significant savings on a long-term basis.

The NABERS (the National Australian Built Environment Rating System, http://www.nabers.com.au/) legislation specifically focuses on the carbon footprint of buildings and facilities. Table 4.2 summarizes the location, architecture and design, construction, livability, and promotional aspects of green building and facilities that eventually contribute to the carbon footprint of the organization.

In addition to the office buildings and relevant manufacturing facilities, when it comes to buildings that house the data centers of large organizations, the entire perspective on their carbon productions shifts to being IT specific. Therefore, the data center aspect of Green IT relates to both building management and IT management. Due to its importance and its impact on the overall green credentials of the organization, the management of data centers needs to be discussed separately—as has been done later in this chapter.

Green IT Hardware

The hardware aspect of Green IT deals with the architecture and design of IT hardware, the manner in which it is procured and operated. While operational energy consumption is increasingly an important issue for computer manufacturers, what is even more interesting is the impact a good, energy optimum design can have on the overall energy consumed by a piece of hardware over

Table 4.2 Rating Building Features to Environmental Factors

Building Features	Environmental Relevance	Comments and Actions
Location	Use of geographically specific natural resources such as cool weather, natural sunlight.	Locating a data center in Iceland can reduce the cooling costs, effort and corresponding carbon.
Architecture and design	To maximize the use of available natural resources for the building.	Windows facing sunlight; cross-ventilation; air and water cooling of data centers.
Construction	Use of material (concrete, carpets, terracotta) to compliment the location and design to ensure that the material reduces wastage and maximizes natural resources.	Use terracotta roof instead of concrete.
Livability (occupancy)	People friendliness of the building/facility that has health as well as aesthetic benefits.	Optimizes the way in which people use the facilities. A naturally lit, cheerful building will need less power.
Visibility	Promoting the physical building as a place of attraction adds marketing value, as also improved asset value.	Ivy's climbing on the walls. Terrace gardens.

its entire life. A purpose-built computer chip, or an efficient laptop battery design has potentially greater impact in reducing carbon emissions over its lifetime than its operation would have.

Figure 4.3 summarizes a range of Green IT hardware that would be of interest to an organization in the context of its Green P-O-D. These Green IT hardware elements, listed in Figure 4.3, are affected by their P-O-D in different ways as was also alluded to in Table 4.1. Following is a more detailed description of these IT hardware assets of an organization:

- Data servers—deals with the physical machines and the specific buildings in which they are housed. These servers also have both wired and wireless networks and corresponding communications equipment associated with them that are directly emitting carbon. The discussion on data centers is undertaken in the next section, and forms substantial part of the rest of this chapter.
- End-user computers—laptops, desktops, their capacities, operational efficiencies, and their disposal (especially as the lifecycle of a computer is getting shorter by the day) need to be discussed from their P-O-D viewpoint. While the efficient design and manufacturing of these end-user devices remains the perceiver of the hardware manufacturers, the efficient operation and disposal is with the user organization.
- Mobile devices—the mobile devices and associated hardware (e.g., extension leads), their batteries including the recharging mechanism and disposal of the batteries and the policies and actions when the devices become outdated (quickly). The mobile devices P-O-D is affected heavily by the corresponding attitude of their users. For example, a perfectly working mobile phone may be discarded by a young user if it goes out of fashion. Thus, a sociocultural issue is an important contributor to the carbon behavior of these devices.

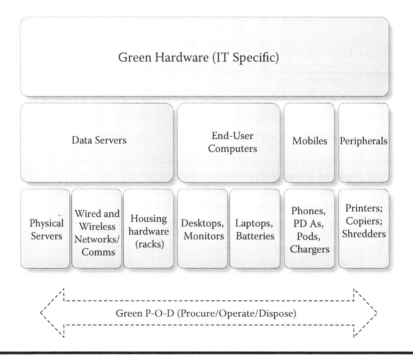

Figure 4.3 Range of Green IT hardware generating carbon.

■ Peripherals—printers, photocopiers, shredders, and so on. These electronic gadgets are of immense interest in Green IT due to their large numbers, their potentially unnecessary overuse, the operational waste that is generated as a result (such as paper, ribbons, and ink), and the carbon associated with the eventual disposal of these "fast moving" items.

The carbon emissions from each of these Green IT hardware group mentioned above is affected by its procurement, operations, and disposal (Green P-O-D) phases in its lifecycle. Procurement focuses on well-designed, low-carbon emitting data servers or monitors, buying it from a green supplier and using the most efficient means of packaging and transporting the equipment. For example, the energy efficiency incorporated in the design of blade servers would be a one-off factor influencing the carbon emission of that server over its lifetime. Operation is the ongoing use of hardware in an efficient and effective manner. Attitude of the end-user, affected usually by visible metrics, plays a significant part here. And finally, disposal of IT equipment requires due considerations as well. The IT department similar to the building and facilities management department can focus on recycling, reuse, and "buy-back" policies to improve its disposal function.

The Green P-O-D phases are practiced based on the policies of the organization. The development of these Green IT policies was discussed earlier, in Chapter 3. Figure 4.4 shows the output of the survey on these organizational policies and practices, particularly as it relates to the Green IT hardware. While considerations to energy saving capabilities of new hardware was uppermost in the mind of most respondents (43% agree, 18% strongly agree), it is interesting to note that the counting and monitoring of ICT devices from their carbon emission perspective was not happening in many organizations (almost 35% disagreed and 13% strongly

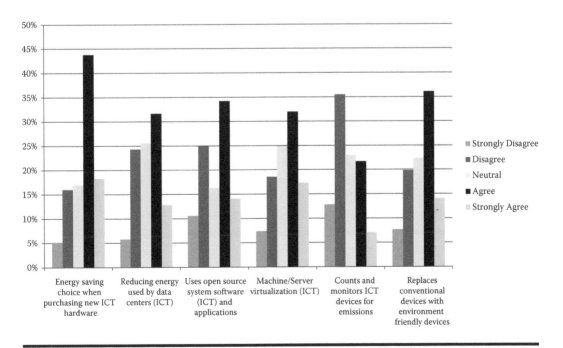

Figure 4.4   Organizational policies and practices relating to Green IT hardware.

disagree when queried on such use—as seen in the second right set of bars in Figure 4.4). This response indicates an urgent need for the green conscious organization to adopt smart metering (also discussed later in this chapter) and also modify their existing ERP systems to incorporate carbon calculations against their IT assets. Other responses, such as those to questions relating to reduction in energy consumption by data centers, use of open source software, server virtualization, and replacing conventional devices with environmentally friendly devices were as expected. That is, respondent agreed-to-strongly agreed around 60%–70% mark with these Green IT practices indicating a strong desire of these professionals to move toward carbon-efficient computing.

Green Data Centers

The demand for data center capacity worldwide has been on the rise. This has also lead to a steady increase in carbon emissions. For example, by year 2020, the world will be using 122 million servers up from 18 million or so in 2008–2009 (IBM, 2008; Chuba, 2008). In addition to the annual increase of approximately 9% in server numbers, one can also anticipate a change in the type of these server machines. This is so because servers will not only handle greater volume but will also require greater processing.

As mentioned earlier, data centers form the major chunk in the overall Green IT hardware assets of an organization. They house a suit of large computers and associated networks of the organization, forming the "heart" of most businesses. They hold the data and information residing in the organization's data warehouses that are residing within these data servers, which in turn, are placed in the data centers. Data servers, in practical terms, can be seen as powerful computers that have the capacity to store as well as process vast amount of multiformatted data. Therefore, these data centers are, understandably, the major power guzzler for an organization. This growth in demand for vast amount of data storage coupled with corresponding demand for increasingly fast processing resulting in carbon emissions. As Cloud computing makes rapid strides, data, in its myriad multimedia format will have to be stored and instantly made available upon request. Apart from the business users who need to store data in perpetuity—at times justifiably as it enables them to comply with legislations (such as the Sarbanes–Oxley accounting data legislation)—consumers of these data also range from school students doing their projects, doctors exchanging new techniques in treating patients, and social users loading and watching video clips on YouTube. The demand of storing and processing of data is unabating. Therefore, businesses that particularly deal with contents (e.g., entertainment, news) have to improve the energy efficiency of their data centers through innovative strategies in data management. This means finding efficiency even in complexity. The data management solutions need to be agile so as to cater to rapidly changing data needs. Dynamic and agile data management implies ability to modify, update, backup, and mirror data even as the organizational needs of the data keep changing. Innovation, together with disciplined operational management of the data center is required. Costs and carbon emissions are also closely tied together in case of data centers. Green data centers include the architecture, design, construction, operation, and decommissioning of buildings specifically used for housing servers. Green data centers also include the architecture, design, development, production, procurement, installation, operation, and disposal of the data server machines and their associated paraphernalia—such as monitors, printers, storage devices, and networking and communications systems.

Figure 4.5 summarizes the specific areas of a data center that needs to be considered in detail when discussing Green IT. These areas are expanded based on the earlier discussion on green buildings and facilities of an organization and need to be supported by organizational

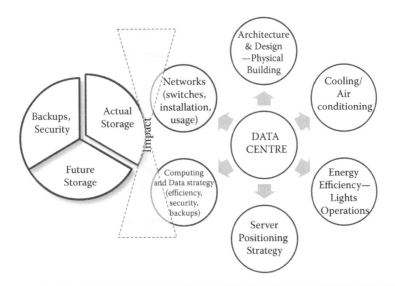

Figure 4.5 Green data center influencing factors.

as well as industrial metrics relating to carbon emissions from buildings, racks of servers, and individual machines. Specific areas for Green IT with respect to data centers shown in Figure 4.5 are discussed as follows:

■ *Data center design, layout, and location*—Physical building in which the data center resides. This can be one building, or multiple buildings that house the machines but are themselves spread across geographical regions. Architecture and design of the building (physical shape, naturally cooling and ventilation, natural light, ease of access etc.), geographical region (e.g., locating a data center in Iceland), and the material used in construction of the building (Terracotta for roofing; painting the roofs white) are all valid considerations here. The size and design of rooms in which servers are housed and also the location of the server rooms within the data center can play a role in carbon reduction. For example, if the room to house the server exactly fits the server size, cooling effect will be maximized. These purpose-built data center buildings are a major influence in an organization's green endeavor.

■ *Cooling, air conditioning, power source and power consumption.* This includes the cooling strategies of the servers; and the air conditioning relating to the actual building. CRAC, as a specialist discipline, plays a role here. Also wherever choice permits, this also includes use of green energy sources (such as wind or solar). Furthermore, the impact of the physical location of the rooms to be cooled, that are housing the servers.

■ *Power management*—*lights and operational aspect.* Number of people working, opening and closing of doors. This would include procurement and installation of green products (such as LED light bulbs) and use of green services. The source of renewable energy mentioned in the previous factor also plays a role in power management.

■ *Servers*—*their numbers, their positioning and corresponding energy-efficient computing*—Physical location of the racks, their positioning (hot isle/cold isle). Architecture and the physical rooms in which they are placed. Design of each server—water cooled, air cooled, and other efficiencies are also to be considered.

■ *Data strategy—including security and backup.* Virtualization within each server, and combined virtualization. Organization of a cluster of servers—private cloud. Space storage and usage strategy. Virtualization aims to pool resources together to deliver data center services by pooling resources that may be otherwise underutilized. Adopting virtualization strategies and creating ground-up virtualization architectures will enable data center energy efficiencies. Virtualization software such as VMware and SWsoft, coupled with consolidation analysis software such as CiRBA, can enable people to maximize server production while providing the same reliability and functionality (Ryan, 2008). There are new server management tools for better control and visibility into the capacity usage (Yi and Thomas, 2007).

■ *Networks and communications equipment*, made up of land-based as well as wireless communications such as switchgears, routers, and modems. The numbers and capacities of these equipments in the data center contribute to its carbon footprint.

These aforementioned data center factors need to be discussed alongside their financial impact, their attitude impact, and the Total Cost of Carbon Ownership (TCCO). The usual linear relationship between cost and energy may not be sufficient to bring about behavioral change.

For example, although the cost of energy is high, companies are not often organized so that the person paying for the IT equipment is also paying for the energy consumption of that equipment. Costs and carbon need appropriate distribution between business and IT. Data centers need to lead a significant consolidation trend that can also help in dealing with the impact of existing or legacy data center. Furthermore, by focusing on the TCCO, as against only initial procurement costs or only operational efficiencies, it is possible to ascertain and lower the overall carbon emissions from equipments.

The correlation between data and data servers is as important as that between servers and the data centers. Thus, data center carbon costs need to match its data storage and data usage. As has been indicated on the left in Figure 4.5, the actual data storage requirements are usually coupled with additional backup storage as well as future storage requirements. Thus, for every new byte stored by the data center, there are additional overheads associated with backup storage, and provision for future storage, that adds to otherwise nonproductive demand on the data center. In subsequent sections, various aspects of these green data center influencing factors are further developed.

Data Center Building—Design, Layout, and Location

The data center buildings are specialized buildings to hold the large computing and communications equipments of the organization. Table 4.2 earlier, listed building features and their corresponding environmental relevance. Each of those factors affecting the long-term carbon generation needs to be considered in the content of the data center.

The challenges in handling data centers from carbon perspectives arises from the fact that the data center buildings themselves are based on a ROI over 15–20 years, whereas the internal equipment, the data servers and other computing equipments themselves are usually upgraded every 3–5 years. Therefore, the data center building, together with the data center's non-ICT infrastructure, can quite easily (and most often does) consume more power than the ICT equipment within it. This can be because of the legacy architecture and design of the infrastructure and facilities that may not have kept up with the server technologies themselves.

According to Gartner, "Traditionally, the power required for non-IT equipment in the data center (such as that for cooling, fans, pumps and UPS systems) represented on average about 60% of total annual energy consumption. In fact, in many cases, the newest data centers of most organizations are seven or more years old whereas the oldest servers in the same data centres are less than five years old." As a result there is a mismatch between the operational efficiency of the data center over its lifetime as compared with the cooling strategies of the data server. The older data centers may thus not be equipped to power and cool the newer IT equipment (servers) in an energy-efficient manner. There will usually be a need to upgrade the data center building in order to handle its carbon efficiency requirements. Alternatively, the data center may have to be shifted to a building that is dedicated to handling the needs of the servers. These mismatches between the building and the servers it houses, requires a study of its design and layout, as well as its time in use. With the backdrop of Table 4.2, following are the specific design, layout, and location consideration for data centers.

- Physical (geographical) location of the building. This includes the weather patterns of the geographical region (such as warm or cold), proximity of the data center building to water and air (for cooling) and the ease of access to the staff.
- The building that houses the data center. This may be a dedicated stand-alone facility, or it may be purpose-built within a larger facility, or it may be retrofitted into existing premises. Whatever the case, there are a number of aspects of the built environment that will have an effect on power consumption, such as insulation.
- The power supply. Data centers usually have dedicated power supplies, and very often more than one. Their efficiency varies enormously. Data centers can also generate their own power, and backup power supplies are common for business continuity.
- Cooling and lighting. Modern ICT equipment typically demands significant amounts of cooling, either air cooling or water cooling. There are many design and implementation issues that affect power consumption. Lighting is also a factor that maintains ambient temperature.
- Server and storage virtualization. While this technology is meant to reduce power consumption as it reduces the overall number of devices; however, in practice the power consumption of data centers can rise as the virtualized servers may be more powerful and may use greater electricity.
- Facilitation of new and emerging technologies. The building of the data center should be conducive to wireless communication, Cloud computing-related communication, and such best practices.

Data Center ICT Equipment—Server Strategies

They are housed within the green data center and require specific strategies for positioning, cooling, and usage.

Servers are powerful computers that form a significant part of the IT assets of an organization. Increasingly these powerful servers provide the organization with the ability to access, provide, analyze, and store data, information, knowledge, and intelligence in myriad different ways. As argued earlier, there is ever increasing demand for more powerful servers with increased storage and processing facilities. With more powerful processors and proliferating number of servers the power consumption continues to climb rapidly (Koomey, 2007).

The average power consumption of a rack of servers has increased fivefold over the last ten years (Gantz, 2009) when cooling requirements are taken into account. Storage usage not only increases exponentially as prices drop, but that usage also tends to become increasingly inefficient. Furthermore, each instance of the use of the server requires strategies for uninterrupted power, security, and storage, and that has repercussions on the carbon footprint of the organization. While desktops are predominantly individual machines, servers belong to the data center manager who is responsible for providing a service to the rest of the organization rather than using it directly themselves. This philosophical difference between a desktop and a server requires different server-side strategies for carbon control. This is particularly so because the users of the data application are usually removed from the physical data center. Following are a list of green server strategy considerations that need to be expanded in detail in practice:

- Online, real-time list of server inventory that enables location and uses of the servers.
- Power consumption bill in real time—mapped to carbon generation, that provides operational feedback to the entire organization.
- Bit to carbon ration as part of comprehensive—data strategy—that provides metrics on not only the used "bits" but also the carbon generated by the provisioned bits.
- Pue, DCiE—these popular metrics providing comparative data over a length of time, as also across the industry.
- Mirroring backup strategies that are balanced by the "acceptable risks" of the data center director.
- Data capacity forecasting. Server capacities need to be estimated on a continuous basis as the business changes. The correlation between business change and growth, and corresponding data center capacity, is ascertained based on statistical analysis, trend spotting, and estimating the impact of technological innovativeness.
- Carbon-cost visibility. Lack of visibility of server costs and particularly its mapping to individual or departmental use of space.
- Efficient decommissioning. Once the purpose of a server is consummated, there is a need for a formal yet quick way of decommissioning the server. Manual processes for decommissioning and lack of confidence of the data center director/manager can lead to servers lying around and consuming power for no apparent purpose.
- Incorporation right redundancy. Earlier discussion on bit-watt indicates the crucial need for optimum redundancy.
- Enhanced server distribution. Need to distribute, through proper assignment, the use of the data space across and between various departments/users. This would also enable server sharing between operational development and test environments.
- Incorporate server switching. Data servers should be capable of being switched from one type of usage to another (e.g., from test usage to production). This also enhance capacity sharing and peak load performance.
- Incorporate Cloud computing and server virtualization.

Data Strategy and the Carbon Emitting Bit

Closely associated with the data server strategy is the data strategy itself. This data strategy encompasses the use, storage, mirroring, security, backups, clean ups, and architectures for data. It covers both external and internal approaches to data management. Data efficiency in relational database management systems includes use of techniques such as data normalization and incremental storage. Such practices enable creation of nonredundant and flexible data structures which tend to save data storage space when multiplied on a large scale. Using the correct data type would also affect the amount of data space that is being used in every "bit" of data.

The strategy relating to emails and email storage directly reflects on the size and numbers of servers required. According to a study, nearly one-third of emails contain attachments and 95% of the information that flows through email systems in the typical organization is attachments (http://www.biscomdeliveryserver.com/collateral/wp/BDS-wp-osterman-200901.pdf). Emails themselves, and the corresponding attachments can not only create poor delivery performance, but also increase the storage requirements and corresponding backup requirements of the data strategy.

Figure 4.6 shows the impact of a single bit on the corresponding increase in the use of storage space in the data center. Every "bit" adds to the carbon generation from the data center. The end-user is usually privy to only that one bit. However, one additional "bit" of data is not just that a bit. There are many entities associated with the data that add to the carbon and data challenge of the data center. Following are the ramifications of one extra bit in a data center on the green performance of the organization:

- *Additional free space provisioning.* For example, for every used bit, there is an additional 0.7 bit (70%) is required to be kept aside as an "unused" space that might be required immediately for use in future.
- *Speed and density.* Each additional bit of data comes with an implicit demand for computing capacity. Thus, increase in storage of data is not mere increase in space use, but also increased demand on computing power. Furthermore, higher computing speeds demand greater computing power.
- *Backup.* Every bit needs another bit or more of space used for backing up the data. This backup not only occupies digital space but also communication mechanism as usually this data has to be stored elsewhere from the main data center.

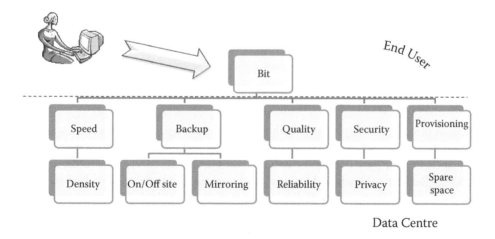

Figure 4.6   A carbon-emitting bit—repercussions on overall carbon emissions.

- *Mirroring.* A bit may require another bit that is a live copy (and that is more than a backup). This live mirror copy would be required for mission critical systems with security and safety risks. In such systems, every data bit added has significantly higher overheads than the bits in noncritical systems.
- *Quality and reliability.* Every additional bit of data adds to the effort required to keep the data clean. Such data cleansing effort are also carbon intensive. Therefore, increase in quality and reliability of data can improve the carbon performance of the organization.
- *Security.* With every additional bit, there is a need to provide security of access. The effort needed in checking and validating the security access and security levels can be carbon intensive and needs to be factored in when data size is increasing.
- *Provisioning.* Each bit requires provisioning for spare capacity, with corresponding need for spare room space, people and infrastructure.

[1 bit + m bit (additional) *leads to* $\rightarrow$ 1.m bit $\times$ n watts (direct energy need) $\rightarrow$ *leads to* nxp watts (support energy-infrastructure) *influences* $\rightarrow$ People (attitude)]

The above equation attempts to summarize the impact of 1 additional bit on the overall energy consumption by the organization. As shown in the equation, each bit requires an additional m fraction of additional bit as part of provisioning. For mission critical, security or defense related applications, this m fraction may be greater than 1.0. In turn, every bit has corresponding need for power coupled together with demand for supporting infrastructure. Eventually, the bit continues to influence and is influenced by the attitude of people (resulting in the need for training and education).

In addition to the data server strategies discussed thus far, there is also a need to compliment those strategies with astute IT governances that ensure incremental improvements to the data center performance. IT governance with additional focus on data centers help to manage the overall number of servers, their lifecycle and the underlying server virtualization strategies. Thus, the governance frameworks such as COBIT, ITIL, CMMI, and Six Sigma could be applied to optimize the performance of the servers. Consider, for example, the application of ITIL. Organizations governed by stringent ITIL standard (typically a government department) have a long lead time for procurement of hardware. To obviate these challenges, data center directors may provision, procure and install servers. These servers would be all ready, with necessary configuration and operating systems ready to go in anticipation. This can lead to unnecessary and wasteful server uptime and corresponding carbon generation. Conversely, if ITIL implementation is made to adhere to carbon control requirements, then use of ITIL can reduce the occurrences of such anticipatory behavior.

Data Servers Optimization

Optimization of servers deals primarily with the numbers, usage, and collaborations amongst the servers. This data server optimization can be improved through better organization of the databases including their design, provisioning for redundancy, and improved capacity forecasting, following RDBMS (Relational Database Management Systems) standards such as data normalization and usage of proper data types within database as and when required. Optimization also includes consolidation of various physical servers that would reduce their total numbers. Standardization of equipment also reduces the overall capacity needed for backups and mirroring of databases. Improved technologies of the servers themselves (e.g., Blade) also help in the optimization process.

It is worth noting that the cost associated with cooling of servers is much more than the initial cost of procurement and installation of the hardware. Furthermore, power consumption of the servers themselves is rapidly increasing. Therefore, the costs associated with the cooling of the servers are equally on the rise.

There is a discrepancy between the advanced technologies used in the servers, the supporting rack level infrastructure of the data center, and the lagging air conditioning and building infrastructure of the data center. Data centers are also heavily occupied and are stretched for their cooling capacity as these buildings are catering for far more sophisticated servers than they originally are designed for.

More techniques that could be considered by an organization for server optimization are described as follows:

■ Undertake intense and iterative capacity planning for the data center. This will involve management, anticipation, and optimization of storage capacities of the data center.
■ Undertake in-depth optimization through identification of unused capacity of servers and storage disks within them.
■ Implement full storage virtualization that will enable hosting of multiple data warehouses on the same server. This will include conversion of existing physical servers to "virtual servers"—partition servers that can operate in parallel without any interference.
■ Efficient server operations. For example, a server that is on but idle would consume half the power it needs when being used fully. Therefore, instead of operating multiple servers, some of which may be idling, optimization and management of servers will enable running of servers as closer to their maximum capacities.
■ Efficient management of air-conditioning and cooling equipments that require, at times, even more power to cool the servers than required to operate them.
■ Decommissioning servers once their service level agreement has expired.
■ Applying virtualization during architecture and design of the servers, corresponding operating systems, and even applications. Enabling virtual servers easily will enable efficient capacity management and reduced hardware maintenance costs.
■ Making use of infrastructural and hardware economies of scale. This can be achieved by implementing Cloud computing and making use of services or software services from an already existing repository. This will significantly reduce the amount of resources being used in order to provide a software solution or a result.
■ Increasing B2B relation for a more common and efficient solution service. Outsourcing services help organizations reduce their man power and energy utilization in order to complete a particular task.

Data Servers Virtualization

Of the many approaches and options discussed in terms of efficient data server management, virtualization can be considered as the most important one. Data server virtualization, as a key strategy, includes creation of many virtual servers from one physical server. Virtualization has been popular as an efficient hardware resource utilization; however, it also has significant impact on reducing carbon emissions.

Through virtualization, data centers can consolidate their physical server infrastructure as multiple virtual servers are hosted on lesser number of servers. This result in reduced power consumption, reduced number of servers, and also reduced

IBM has a U.S. $1 billion per year investment program which capitalizes on virtualization to double the energy efficiency of its computer data centers and those of its corporate customers (IBM, 2007). This data center specific program aims to improve energy monitoring, advanced 3-D power management and thermal modeling capabilities, better design techniques, cutting-edge virtualization technologies, enhanced power management systems, and new energy-efficient liquid cooling infrastructures. These initiatives can not only improve building (floor space) use, data server use (computing), but also reduce carbon emissions by almost 7,500 tons a year (IBM, 2007).

demand on the data center infrastructure. For example, virtualization reduces the demand on the data center floor space, which, in turn, reduces building size, number of people required to run the center, and reduced number of support tasks. Virtualization has to be supported by the operating system that would separate the underlying hardware from corresponding application software. This is shown in Figure 4.7. As also shown in Figure 4.7, virtualization software is mainly focused on creating multiple views of the same underlying hardware and operating system. Sometimes, the operating system is itself equipped with virtualization capabilities. There are various ways and at various levels at which virtualization can be implemented. These include presentation virtualization (wherein users get a feel for owning the presentation of an application, whereas it is actually shared), application virtualization (enables multiple users to use the same application), desktop virtualization (applies the virtualization techniques of the servers at a local, desktop level), storage virtualization (applied to databases), and network virtualization (relates to the communications and networking equipments of the data center). These various virtualization techniques are not independent of each other. For example, presentation virtualization, which gives users the opportunity to access the presentation layer in a shared way, is actually closely connected with the application virtualization. Application virtualization is where an application is delivered to the end-user in a virtualized environment separated from the underlying operating system (see Figure 4.7). Multiple application versions can be executed in this way also where there are compatibility issues between an application and the operating system.

Desktop virtualization would separate the environment of the user from the hardware. Operating systems may also enable session virtualization (that use technologies like Citrix) to enable separate execution of sessions on the same instance of application and hardware.

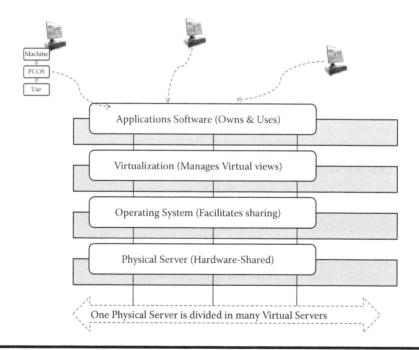

Figure 4.7   Data server virtualization.

Physical Data Server Organization and Cooling

The physical arrangements of data servers, their aisle organization, and the manner in which the floor space and racks are physically organized also impacts the overall carbon emission from that data center. Figure 4.8 shows a popular physical arrangement of servers to reduce the power required to cool them. This is called the hot-aisle–cold-aisle arrangement. Figure 4.8a shows a typical server machine. Figure 4.8b shows the aforementioned arrangement.

The physical cooling of the data center is one of the most important approaches to reducing the carbon footprint of an organization. These strategies start with architecture, design, and construction of the data center building, location of the center itself, positioning of the servers. and strategies for using air, water and other means for cooling the servers.

According to the EPA, we can expect a global consumption of 100 million kWh energy for cooling data centres that should cost approximately $7.4 billion. This is mainly because there is rapid increase in sophistication of data server technologies demanding greater power but the corresponding cooling technologies have not kept pace. Therefore, physical organization of the data servers, their operational effectiveness and cooling strategies all play a crucial role in the overall reduction in carbon footprint.

Based on http://googledatacenters. blogspot.com/2009/11/data-center-cooling. html accessed March 23, 2011.

As discussed by Philipson (2011), data centers use a number of different techniques to cool their servers. Water cooling has been popular to handle the heat dissipation issues (Cronin, 2008). In addition to water cooling, air cooling of servers using the concepts of hot-aisle and cold-aisle (i.e., making the servers face different directions to maximize cooling) is also popular—as shown in Figure 4.8.

These techniques are becoming far more important because they not only reduce the carbon footprint of the organization but, at the same time, improve its economic performance by reducing running costs of power consumption. Furthermore, reporting requirements are becoming increasingly stringent and there is an increased awareness across business and society of the unsustainability of many current consumption patterns (Philipson et al., 2009).

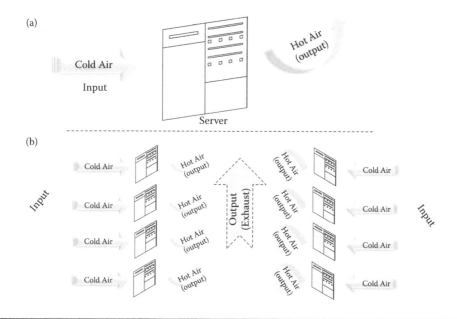

Figure 4.8   Physical server organization to reduce cooling effort.

Physical arrangements of servers require the following careful considerations:

■ *Server optimization.* While physical data servers usually reside in the data center, there are still numerous opportunities in a large organization for some of these servers to appear in offices. Eventually, this "server hoarding" can result in unmanaged, unaccounted servers that keep consuming power without the benefit of virtualization. This can also happen in particular with test servers which, although not hidden, may proliferate within the data center itself. Multiple servers may be used for different test scenarios. After the testing is completed, the servers may remain unused and unaccounted.

■ *Disk identification.* In addition to the servers, identify the disks and other memory mechanisms used in the servers. Optimized use of storage devices in the data center is vital to reducing the overall power need of the data center. Storage devices that are operational and running but not providing any services should be formally accounted for and decommissioned.

■ *Implement a multitiered storage solution.* Provide hot access to used data and less speedy access to data that is there as a backup or legal requirement. A large amount of data that is ready to be used on storage devices is not accessed frequently.

■ Specify low-power consumption, low voltage servers together with high-efficiency Power Supply Units that have a conversion of 80% or more.

■ Equipment Reuse. Ensure reuse of equipment that is no longer required but is still serviceable. Energy is required to manufacture, distribute, and recycle equipment as well as to use it. Extending its use or seeking its reuse elsewhere will save energy as well as purchase and disposal costs.

■ Re-engineer Layout. Data center auditing identifies mismatches between the current physical layout and the layout that would maximize the effectiveness of cooling from air conditioning units. Up to a 20% reduction in cooling could be achieved by doing this.

Employ cooling strategies that are applicable at various levels within the data center—such as room-based, rack-based, and component-based cooling. These cooling strategies are interspersed with water-based and air-based cooling for example.

Cloud Computing and Data Centers

The offerings of Cloud computing have a role to play in carbon reduction. However, it has to be a highly balanced act. The cloud can take the responsibility of carbon emissions of a business outside its boundaries. But that is not necessarily an overall reduction in carbon emissions by the IT industry. A cloud, as a offering of computing services on the Internet, provides "a new consumption and delivery model for information technology (IT)" (Mell and Grance, 2009). Consolidation and optimization of services on a Cloud, resulting from on-demand self service, ubiquitous network access, location independent resource pooling, rapid elasticity and provisioning, and pay-per-use—all go toward reducing carbon footprint of the IT industry.

Cloud computing (Murugesan, 2011) provides substantial opportunities for organizations to consolidate their hardware and corresponding data space requirements. Cloud computing offers the potential for economies of scale that go beyond a single data center and a single enterprise. This is so because with Cloud computing there is opportunity to not only consolidate the costs of services but also shift the carbon generation to a relatively centralized place where it can be better controlled and optimized. Alford and Morton (2009) estimated that the use of Cloud computing costs an organization two-thirds less than running the same workload on a private nonvirtualized data center. The concept of Cloud computing is also applied within the organizational boundaries, especially for large, multinational organizations. This results in consolidation of applications, data warehouses, and hardware

within the organization, resulting in what is called a private cloud (discussed by Velte et al., 2009). The "software as a service" (SaaS) business model emanating from Cloud computing allows companies to access key enterprise applications such as customer relationship management (CRM) and supply chain management (SCM) through the Internet. As a result, the cloud obviates the need to host these applications in a proprietary data center. The opportunities to reduce carbon emissions increase with consolidation of both hardware and software applications. Furthermore, the payment models for SaaS-based applications is usually based on its usage—akin to the typical monthly bill received for utilities such as gas or electricity. The typical data center planning that makes provision for eventualities can be sidestepped for an overall planning by the cloud service provider. Therefore, future business growth (including mergers and acquisitions) can be planned without producing excessive and, eventually, unusable data center capacity. The resulting carbon savings from not having a private data center can be phenomenal.

Networking and Communications Infrastructure

The discussion thus far has been on data centers and the physical servers housed in them. However, the data centers also usually hold the communication equipments and related assets of the organization. These communications infrastructure support the internal and external networks of an organization and play a significant role in its carbon footprint. This "C" for communications in ICT that contributes to the carbon generation includes the switches, routers, the LAN, WAN, and associated mobile transmission devices. Monitoring of networks, their interoperability, their uptimes and full-times, are also factors contributing to the carbon footprint.

Well-integrated and optimized networks that also incorporate combination of centralized and decentralized approaches and plug-in sensors which can increasingly play a major role in reducing carbon effects.

Networking strategies that are part of information architecture can not only help reduce traffic but also improve carbon performance. For example, having a thick-client architecture, which enables substantial processing at the client end, can reduce the processing traffic. Reduction of communication traffic eventually reduces the server load minimizing memory and processing time on the server. However, this is also a balancing act that requires careful attention to the overall performance of an application. If server-side traffic is reduced, then the thick-client will require installation and configuration of a large part of the application. This can result in increased infrastructure at the client end. The approach has to be a unified one, balancing the network traffic reduction with the potential increase in overheads at the client side. Following are the categories of networks that need attention of the network manager in terms of their carbon connotation.

Local Area Networks (LAN). These are the local networks of the organization that are made up of the physical connections amongst the machines and primarily the data center. Usually, these may be a collection of cables that may have "grown" as the organization grew; lack of planning and architecture for LANs is a major factor in consuming substantial power and thereby adding to the cooling requirements. A well-architected and efficient LAN will imply lower power consumption and therefore lower emissions.

Wide Area Networks (WAN). Going beyond a local region, the wide area networks of an organization enables communication amongst its desktop and laptop machines with and beyond its data center. Typically, the WAN comprises use of communication lines that make up the virtual private network (VPN) of the organization. Such VPN is made up of leased communications lines which reduce the extent of influence an organization has over its power consumption and carbon generation.

Mobile Networks. Unhelkar (2008) has discussed in detail the various mobile network technologies and mobile enterprise architecture that can also provide the backdrop for carbon reduction. The mobile communications infrastructure stack is made up of TCP/IP at the base, followed by the WAP, personal area networking (PAN), and, depending on the needs of the applications, metropolitan area networks (MAN). These network communications technologies further include the IEEE 802.1x group of standards and Infrared, Bluetooth, RFID, WiMax, and Wireless VoIP. Using a good MEA enables calculations of carbon across this entire stack of networks together with its links or programmable interfaces for Infrared, Bluetooth, and the cellular networks. As discussed by Jamalipour, and also by Ghanbary, the upgrading of the current mobile network architectures is inevitable—as the future demands from the mobile Internet are likely to be dramatically different (e.g., the imaginative 4G and 5G).

Wireless LAN/WAN. The paraphernalia associated with wireless communication becomes a major source of carbon generation and needs to be considered in comparison with the wired communications. While wireless communication may give the impression of reduced hardware and infrastructure (due to lack of physical wiring), it may still be inefficient and result in substantial carbon if not properly architected during installation and not monitored during operation. For example, if wireless transmitters and receivers are left on when they are not being used (full-time), they would produce more carbon than their wired counterparts. For example, short-range mobile networks such as those used in offices, homes, and local "hotspots" (such as a coffee shop or an airport) tend to have an unplanned usage pattern.

WiMax is another mobile standard for point-to-point communication that is based on radio-frequency standardized technology (IEEE 802.16) that tends to guzzle power, especially when it is on but not in use. WiMax, made up of transceivers to base antennas, need standards to ensure these networks are switched on-and-off depending on their usage pattern. The need to develop these standards is urgent, especially as the newer (IEEE 802.20) standards for mobile broadband communications technology providing further high-speed wireless, IP-based connectivity to mobile devices like cell phones, PDAs, and laptops comes into play. The end-users, however, can play a role in the use of these communications technologies as they are short-range communications that can be controlled partially by the end-user.

The long-range communications networks, primarily made up of the cellular networks (defined through their generations (G)), require a much more organized and consortium-based

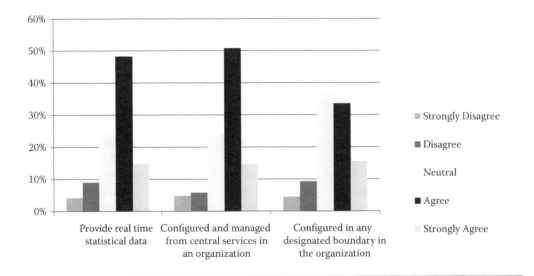

Figure 4.9 ICT devices as green enablers.

approach for controlling their carbon emissions. In particular, transcending to the 3G networks demands significant improvement in the quality-of-service (QoS) to enable provision of all the services that the vendors want to provide. The carbon contribution to improve the QoS has not been considered thus far. Now, it is vital to balance the provisioning of 3G with its carbon coefficient.

End-User Devices

End-user devices and gadgets including the peripherals that are employed by the users were depicted in Figure 4.3. These gadgets and devices are part of the movable assets of the organization. These devices need to be considered from their carbon contribution viewpoint, typically in the initial tactical or operational approach to Green IT by the organization. This is the typical 3–5 years strategy (as described in the Figure 2.2). For example, HP lab tests have found that configuring PCs with the optional 80% efficient power supplies along with the other ENERGY STAR 4.0 hardware requirements can reduce total system power consumption as much as 52%, translating into an average annual cost savings ranging from $6 to $58 per PC

As per the climate group (2008) the number of PCs are expected to increase globally from 592 million in 2002 to more than 4 billion in 2020 (Garito, 2011). An important development in this regards is that the desktop PCs that dominate today's market (84%) will be largely replaced by laptops. Year 2020 may see 74% of all computers in use as laptops. The remaining will have fully used the low energy alternatives, such as liquid crystal display (LCD) screens. Research areas such as quantum and optical computing could also have a substantial impact on the hardware assets.

(Palo Alto, 2007). On the infrastructure front, broadband networks and cyber-infrastructure can go a long way in helping reduce the U.S. carbon footprint. Estimates of 15%–20% overall reduction of CO_2 are possible through virtualization and dematerialization using broadband networks (Hatch, 2009).

Devices need to be inspected and formally audited to ensure they are serviceable. Proper maintenance of equipments will ensure their longer operating life and eventually their reuse. Nonreusable equipments should be recycled. Eventually, if they can not be formally recycled, equipments should be ethically disposed. This disposal implies decomposing the equipment (typically a PC) into its plastics, metals, and other basic materials which can then be reused in future. A "green" disposal like this would ensure necessary safety as well as security procedures are carried out prior to reuse, recycling, or disposal.

Following Table 4.3 (Kamani et al., 2011) lists the initial or tactical approach to devices in Green IT that is based on the Green P-O-D. This table reflects the fact that a substantial amount of carbon can be saved by paying attention to the manufacture, delivery, and disposal of computing equipments.

Smart Meters in Real Time

Smart meters are meters that not only measure the power consumption automatically, but also provide feedback to the users in real time. Thus, these smart meters give businesses an opportunity to monitor and take immediate actions to mitigate their power consumptions. By adding price information and by providing trends and patterns, households and businesses can be encouraged to monitor and reduce their use of power consumption.

In addition to gathering real-time information from devices in use (such as computers and monitors at work and microwaves and dryers in households), smart meters can also transmit this

Table 4.3   Polices and Practice of Green P-O-D in the Context of Devices and Peripherals

Tactical Green IT Activities	*Comments and Reasoning*
Eliminate the use of active screen savers	The amount of energy used by a monitor with an active screen saver is almost the same as the one doing useful work. Therefore, active screen savers should be eliminated.
Implement active power management	Operating systems of end-user devices should be controlling the switching-off of the devices when not in use. Hibernate feature is much more useful than standby in this case. Furthermore, standby, hibernation, and switch-off features for end-user devices should be automatically configurable—enabling their shutdown without user intervention, at given times, and reducing the overall energy consumption.
Central management of machines	Many large office environments (such as banks and insurance organizations) have thousands of computer machines that can be managed centrally. At certain times, such as at night, these end-user machines need not be even on standby power. Even if a fraction of these machines are left on standby or running, they consume power. Central management of these machines will enable much better handling of their on- and off-times.
Specify low-power consumption CPUs and high-efficiency power supply units (80% conversion or better)	System specifications should be optimum. Over specifications with rich functionality on a device draws more power even if the features are not all used. Similarly, power supply units with corresponding power surge protection need to be specified for the power requirements at hand. Efficient power supply units can go a long way in reducing energy consumption.
Consider thick versus thin client carefully	Ensure right balance between a thick- and a thin-client architecture. While a thin client is less complex than a PC and contains fewer components. However, additional energy is required to support the greater bandwidth necessary for connection to its server as well as to run the server and its supporting air-conditioning equipment.
Use timer switches to gadgets (e.g., printers)	Peripheral devices, such as fax machines, printers, and copiers consume power even when on standby. Improved switch-off mechanisms including timer switches can reduce their overall carbon footprint. The use of timer switches to turn off such equipment automatically has to be a mandatory feature of these devices.
Printer setup	Setting the printer, centrally, to a default feature of draft, duplex, and grey scale can reduce the amount of ink and paper used by printers. Other procedural features such as providing only a limited number of common printers (rather than one per desktop), counting and providing real-time feedback to users on their paper usage, and reducing the printing to only legal and formal documents can produce significant carbon savings.

Table 4.3   Polices and Practice of Green P-O-D in the Context of Devices and Peripherals (continued)

Tactical Green IT Activities	*Comments and Reasoning*
Device consolidation and sharing	Consolidating the total number of electronic devices such as PCs and printers is a part of tactical/operational strategy. Such consolidation and reduction in numbers will reduce not only the energy consumed by the devices but also their support and maintenance effort. For example, shifting from a PC to laptop, using the same laptop in the office and at home and using integrated mobile phones can all reduce emissions.
Green P-O-D and the Polices and Standards on Peripherals	
Open source system software (ICT) and applications	Open source systems are much better positioned to support an agile organization. Changes to business processes can be handled easily by the underlying applications as they are not restricted to a proprietary environment. Cloud computing is likely to further add to the opportunities for open source systems. Therefore, the relationship between open source and carbon reduction is a positive one and should be explored in the organizational policies on Green IT.
Device replacement approach.	Polices on device replacement should incorporate replacing conventional devices with environment-friendly devices. This replacement, however, should not be undertaken in one go—but should be phased to coincide with the end of working life of an equipment.
Attitude and practice	Procurement, operation, and disposal of user devices are influenced by the attitude and practices of individuals. Therefore, provide training to staff and support the practice of Green IT.
Encourage product innovation and environmentally conscious design	This is an important consideration for manufacturers of end-user devices. A carbon-efficient product design has tremendous opportunity to influence overall carbon reduction over the life of the device.
Lifecycle maintenance and assessment	Put together a maintenance program that also includes preventative maintenance. Apply metrics to measure the emissions of a device over its entire lifecycle. This includes calculations of the TCCO. Thus, a device that is produced with less carbon emissions should also be measured for the emissions it generates over its lifetime— and during disposal.
Maintain current device inventory	Device inventories provide an understanding of not only the carbon-emitting devices that are in use, but also the ones that are on standby or in the stores and not yet being used. An improved understanding of the devices and their usage can lead to a reduced inventory and corresponding reduced carbon footprint.

(continued)

Table 4.3   Polices and Practice of Green P-O-D in the Context of Devices and Peripherals (continued)

Tactical Green IT Activities	Comments and Reasoning
Green IT technical standards	Apply standards such as the ISO 14001 family of standards to reduce emissions.
Supporting ICT infrastructure	For every device within the organization, there are supporting infrastructure requirements. These include external cables, routers, and repeaters. External to the organization are the fiber optic networks, transmission towers, and related communications infrastructures. Correlate the devices to these external requirements. Reduction in the number of devices can also reduce the infrastructure requirements.

data for further analysis. Smart meters can thus be the front end of environmental intelligence (EI) applications. By computing the carbon data in real time, and correlating it to other information such as weather patterns, production planning, and HR, EI applications can provide actionable information to the users.

The transmission of carbon data also occurs to the utility organization that is providing the energy or, simply locally, to the business or householder. Smart meters can further enable automatic management of a device or group of devices. For example, apart from providing the power consumption data in real time, a smart meter can also be configured to shut the device when a certain level of power has been consumed.

Smart meters thus require a supporting infrastructure that includes the installation, configuration, and communications with the meters. This infrastructure facilitates changes to the meter configuration, its activation and reading, and its reporting mechanisms. For example, currently, smart meters can be configured to generate hourly, half-hourly, or quarter-hourly readings. Increasing the frequency of carbon data collection can improve its monitoring and potential mitigation—but will increase the infrastructure associated with the meters themselves.

Managing Devices for Central Green Services

Most large organizations (e.g., banks, airlines, hospitals) will have thousands of end-user devices such as computers and printers. Strategic Green IT will not leave the management of these devices to the individual users. Instead, increasingly, it is making sense to manage these myriad devices through centralized green services. See Figure 4.9 for the ways in which devices are used for green services. For example, all the desktops or laptops in a large bank or insurance organization can be configured according to the Green IT policies of an organization. This can include specific use of tools (e.g., BigFix's power management, http://www.bigfix.com/content/green-it) that would enable management of thousands of PCs with a single server that would consolidate and automate the management of their operating system, upgrades, and security management tasks. Centralized management of large number of machines for an organization is set to play a significant role in an organization's attempt to reduce its carbon footprint as it enables consistency across all the machines in terms of power management software, low-level power settings, lower energy configurations, and also consolidated green procurement and disposal.

Centralized services for managing computers can make use of environmental sensors and intelligent controls to monitor and manage a cluster of computers remotely. For example, a wireless smart meter can generate an alert in response to the occurrence of an event. Centralized device management can take appropriate action as a combination of automated response and manual intervention—to reduce the effect of the event.

Smaller-sized, smart, mobile devices can also play a major role in reducing emissions. This is so because mobile devices are now able to support and handle asset management, marketing, outsourcing, security and information distribution, and other business collaborative activities location independently. This can ensure performance and availability of the corporate system by real-time access of the enterprise and, at the same time, enable easier management of these smaller-sized devices as compared to desktop computers. Mobile devices can also reduce unnecessary movement of people and materials. However, mobile devices may produce electronic waste due to shorter lifespan of their batteries and the devices themselves. Therefore, they should be introduced and used in the organization in a balanced way.

Devices and Organizational Boundaries for Measurements

Devices in the Green IT discussion play two roles: those that emit carbon and others that are used to measure, monitor, and mitigate carbon. The previously mentioned smart meters that automatically measure and report on carbon emission are part of the tools and techniques that are used in measuring and mitigating carbon emissions. It is important to take care in the use of such metering devices as they themselves may be carbon emitters. The devices should meet standards, operating with minimum energy requirements and be tested for quality before installation and usage. This should ensure that the device itself would not act as an energy consumer which would although reduce the process' emission but would itself consume energy. They are also very effective tools in measuring and monitoring emissions.

Adding to the complexity in the use of devices is the fuzzy nature of organizational boundaries. Collaborative businesses and web services make it challenging to calculate an organization's carbon footprint. While devices that belong to the organization are relatively easy to account for, these same devices when outside the physical boundary of the organization may still contribute to the carbon emissions. For example, a laptop belonging to an organization, being used by an employee who is on an overseas trip, is getting charged at an overseas destination belonging to another. Energy consumed in such charging may not get calculated in the power bills of the organization.

Figure 4.10 shows the importance given by the survey participants to the various tools and techniques in carbon measurement.

- Dashboard displays attached to the devices to display emissions: 5% strongly agreed, 20% agreed whereas 47% disagreed-to-strongly disagreed when asked whether such device displays were in use in their organization. This could be due to the lack of availability of such devices or, more importantly, lack of supporting infrastructure based on wireless communication that would enable collection and reporting of carbon data on dashboards.
- Mobile gadgets attached to devices for measuring emissions: 20% agreed-to-strongly agreed to the use of such gadgets currently occurring in their organization. Forty-two percent felt that such use was not occurring—indicating a need for further investigations into promoting the use of mobile gadgets in carbon measurements.

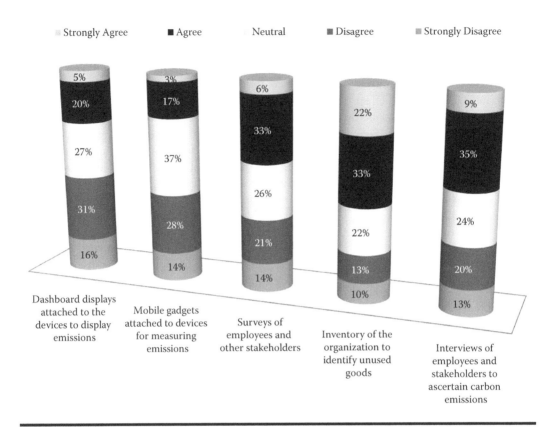

Figure 4.10 Tools used for measuring carbon emissions in your organization.

■ Surveys of employees and other stakeholders: 39% on the favorable side whereas 35% viewing such a tool unfavorably in its current format. However, this survey technique will be required for measuring the subjective factors such as attitude.
■ Inventory of the organization to identify unused goods: 22% strongly agreed and 33% agreed (total of 55%) that such inventories are available in their organizations and that these inventories of unused goods plays an important role in their carbon management strategy.
■ Interviews of employees and stakeholders to ascertain carbon emissions: 9% strongly agreed and 35% agreed to the use of this technique in their organization. 33% did not agree with the suggestion that such technique was used in measuring carbon emission.

Mobile Devices and Sustainability

Mobile technologies including mobile networks and mobile devices have a substantial role to play in the sustainability effort of an organization. Unhelkar (2008) has discussed in detail the impact of mobility on business sustenance and the physical environment in which the business exists. That discussion also extended to the discussion on responsibility of mobility toward people and society from an environmental perspective. Mobile users are increasingly concerned with the cost of energy and the energy consumption of their devices. This leads to discussions specifically focusing on improving energy and reducing the environmental impacts associated with mobile usage by business.

The demonstration of the importance of the environment in mobile technology deployment is considered as an essential factor to this rapidly emerging technology. This is so because, mobile technologies and devices, through their permeation in the fabric of our society, influence the physical environment as well as social attitudes as never before. Mobile technology around the world has made mobility a unique environmental challenge, requiring attention toward what is called Green Mobile. Figure 4.11 summarizes the concept of Green Mobile. Green mobile can be considered as effective adoption of mobility by business in environmental consideration. Thus, green mobile affect economic viability, business process optimization, social responsibility, and technological capabilities, which form the four dimensions in a green enterprise transformation. Figure 4.12 indicates the percentage use of mobile technologies across various industrial sector. This figure highlights the corresponding opportunities for carbon reduction with the use of mobile technologies.

Green mobiles encompass carbon-sensitive business strategies, optimized and collaborative business processes based on environmental intelligence approach,

Mobile devices, in particular, impact the carbon footprint of an organization by consuming operational power, generating electronic waste as the devices and their batteries become redundant, and, on the positive side, offering opportunities to reduce carbon by being incorporated in the green processes of the organization. Thus, mobile technologies, like the data centers, are both—the cause for carbon generation and the potential help in ameliorating that carbon.

According to the Environmental Impact Assessment Review (July 2005), between 1994 and 2003, PC disposal resulted in 718,000 tons of lead, 287 tons of mercury, and 1,363 tons of cadmium being placed in landfills. As PC penetration continues to increase worldwide, the e-waste problem will only get worse. Fortunately, the mobile devices are smaller, lighter, and contain far fewer electronic parts compared to a PC. In fact, mobile gadgets reduce e-waste by 98% because they weigh less than a typical PC. (www.hardwarezone.com)

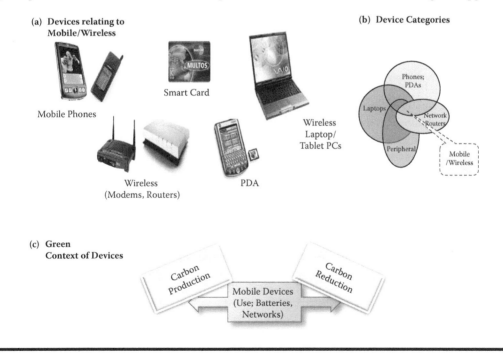

Figure 4.11   Mobile devices and Green P-O-D (outside of data center). The devices shown in (a) are grouped in (b). Each group of devices have their own uniqueness in terms of carbon emissions. For example, phones and laptops have lesser infrastructure but greater operational impact, whereas its the otherway round with networks and routers. Figure 4.11 (c) further highlights the need to consider the carbon production and reduction in both design and operation of these devices.

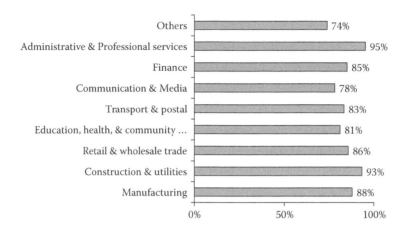

Figure 4.12 Use of handheld devices across industrial sectors.

mobile networks, incorporation of the RFID tags, mobile transmissions, improved design of the devices and their batteries, and also their ethical disposal.

Examples of green mobile includes policies for reuse rather than upgrade of mobile phone, introduction of mobile smart meters, improved analysis and reporting on environmental data (EI), and biodegradable material usage in the devices themselves (e.g., Biodegradable "Sunflower Phone" that has a built-in seed that will grow once the phone is planted in the ground; or Nokia— 3110 "bio-cover," the casing is composed of 50% recycled material and packaging made from 60% recycled material).

The use of laptops in the business processes also have an interesting aside in their use as compared with the desktops and servers on the business side. The desktop computers are heavy in size, need more power to run, and contains more amount of toxic materials such as lead, cadmium, and zinc. Mobile laptops such as notebooks, sub-notebooks, PDAs, and palmtops require low weight, low-power consumption, and good interactive performance (Douglis et al., 1994). They also tend to consume less power than the corresponding desktop machines.

"Mobile enterprise transitions," as discussed by Unhelkar (2008), presents a comprehensive framework that has greater details on how to approach these environmental issues in a holistic and responsible manner. For example, in addition to recycling the phone itself, the mobile transformation framework also focuses on the place of the mobile device in the overall business process—and investigates the need to use that device in the process. This may be the use of a wireless PDA for an insurance agent that will reduce people movement. Reengineering the process with sustainability in mind can further lead to potentially eliminating the mobile phone as a device and, perhaps, replacing it with a messaging system combined together with a laptop or a tablet PC. This responsible approach toward mobility is in sync with the thoughts on sustainability by business experts working in this area. For example, Cartland (2005) writes about the significance of studying and optimizing supply chains with regards to sustainability in business. Unhelkar and Dickens (2008) and Unhelkar and Trivedi (2009) have also argued for the importance of Green ICT and environmentally responsible business strategies (ERBS) and have explored various ways in which mobility can help the environment and sustain the business.

Discussion Points

■ What is the impact of the data center aspect of Green IT strategies on carbon reduction?
■ Describe how organization's Green IT strategies could be translated into practices in terms of procurement and disposes of assets that leads to reduction in carbon emission?
■ How an efficient use of Green assets could lead to reduction in energy consumption?
■ Describe how the building location, design, and architecture has a direct impact on the overall carbon generated by the organization?
■ List, with examples, the factors influencing Green data centers.
■ What is just one extra "bit" for an end-user evolves into a significant overhead for the organization. Discuss the various ways in which one bit influences the overall carbon footprint of the organization.
■ What is virtualization? What are the advantages and risks associated with virtualization?
■ How can Cloud computing help reduce carbon emissions?
■ What is the role of smart meters in Environmental Intelligence?
■ Discuss in detail the role of green mobile.

Action Points

■ Identify the various Green assets for an organization.
■ Does your organization have a data center? Identify two important factors that are affecting the carbon emissions of your data center.
■ Update your Green IT strategy with approaches to improving data center building based on the discussion in this chapter.
■ Apply data center strategies for carbon reduction such as server virtualization and device optimization.
■ Identify the impact of asset management procedures on carbon reduction such as procurement of assets and asset disposal.
■ Incorporate smart meters in your EI implementation.
■ Incorporate green mobile in your EI implementation.

References

Alford and Morton. (2009). http://www.techrepublic.com/whitepapers/cloud-cube-model-selecting-cloud-formations-for-secure-collaboration/2311549

Chuba, M. (2008). *Gartner Survey Suggests Extensive Data Center Expansion Plans Are on the Horizon*. Stamford, CT: Gartner.

Cronin, D. (2008). *Using Water Cooling in the Data Center Brings Challenges*, Facilitiesnet, Feb. 2008. Retrieved December 12, 2008 from www.facilitiesnet.com/datacenters/article/Using-Water-Cooling-in-the-Data-Center-Brings-Challenges--8227

Fred, D., Ramón, C., Frans, K. M., Krishnan, P., Kai, L., Brian, M., Joshua, T. (1994). *Storage Alternatives for Mobile Computers*: Operating Systems Design and Implementation.

Gantz, J. (2009). *The Diverse and Expanding Digital Universe*. Framingham, MA: IDC. http://www.dcgtasia.com/ index.php/dcgtasia/Sydney

Ghanbary, Abbass. (2006). Evaluation of Mobile Technologies in the Context of their Applications, Limitations and Transformation. In *Handbook of Research in Mobile Business*. Edited by Bhuvan Unhelkar. IGI Global, Hershey, PA, USA.

Hatch, D. (2009). "Green IT/broadband and cyber infrastructure." *Telecommunications*, May 2009.

IBM GBS. (April 2008). *The Green Data Center: Cutting Energy Costs for a Powerful Competitive Advantage*, pp. 1–16.

IBM. (2007). *IBM Unveils Plan to Combat Data Center Energy Crisis; Allocates $1 Billion to Advance "Green" Technology and Services*. Press release, 10 May (www03.ibm.com/press/us/en/pressrelease/21524.wss).

Jamalipour, Abbas. (2003). *The Wireless Mobile Internet: Architectures, Protocols, and Services*. Wiley. See also A. Ghanbary's subsequent research conducted at the Mobile Internet Research and Applications Group at the University of Western Sydney and published in a PhD thesis by the researcher (2008).

Kamani, K., Kathiriya, D., Virparia, P., and Parsania, P. (2011). Chapter 19, Digital Green ICT: Enabling eco-efficiency and eco-innovation. In B. Unhelkar, ed., *Handbook of Research in Green ICT*, pp. 282–289. IGI Global, Hershey, PA, USA.

Koomey, J. G. (2007). *Estimating Total Power Consumption by Servers in the U.S. and the World*. Stanford, CA, USA. Retrieved January 13, 2010 from http://enterprise.amd.com/Downloads/svrpwruescompletefinal.pdf

Murugesan, S. (2011). *Cloud Computing*. Chapman-Hall, USA.

Palo Alto, Calif., March 12, 2007. HP Delivers Industry's First PCs to Meet ENERGY STAR 4.0 hardware requirements. Available at http://www.hp.com/hpinfo/newsroom/press/2007/070312b.html, accessed October 2010.

Philipson. (2010). *ICT's Role in the Low Carbon Economy*. Australian Information Industry Association (AIIA), September 2010, Scott Evans and Josh Milln.

Ryan, E. J. (February 2008). Building sustainable IT. *Cutter IT Journal*, 21(2): 6–12.

Sanders, T. (2008). *Saving the World at Work*. New York: Doubleday.

Unhelkar, B. (2008). *Mobile Enterprise Transition & Management*. Auerbach, NY: Taylor & Francis Group.

Unhelkar, B. (2008). Mobile enterprise architecture. *Cutter Executive Report*, Boston, USA, April 2008, 11(3), Enterprise Architecture Practice.

Velte, T., Velte, A., and Elsenpeter, R. (2008). *Green IT: Reduce Your Information System's Environmental Impact While Adding to the Bottom Line*. New York: McGraw-Hill Companies.

Wal-mart. (2009). *Sustainable Buildings*. Retrieved March 23, 2011, from Walmart.com: http://walmart-stores.com/Sustainability/ Trivedi and Unhelkar. (2010). PhD research, conducted at DDU University, Nadiad, Gujarat, India in 2010. Data appearing in the PhD thesis due for Submission.

Yi, L. and Thomas, H. R. (August 2007). A review of research on the environment impact of e-business and ICT. *Environment International*, 33(6): 841–849.

Chapter 5

Green Business Process Management: Modeling, Optimization, and Collaboration

Just understand the natural way of things, and do not go against nature, because going against nature creates all sorts of problems.

Master Osho

Key Points

- Develops the concept of business process management (BPM) further to a Green BPM, that of a lean business process to a lean-green business process, and that of business process reengineering (BPR) to a Green BPR.
- Green BPM applied from the individual, organization, and collaborative perspective to ensure proper understanding of the levels of green processes.
- Green governance aligned to corporate governance and standards makes it part of routine business.
- Use of green standards aligned with other corporate standards to improve and enhance green best practices because of the business benefits achieved.
- Green business policies and business rules are discussed as necessary part of green business processes.
- Green BPM affects people, facilities, transport, development, production, and information and communication of an organization.
- Green business analysis applies efficiency, effectiveness, and agility to organization's business processes.

■ Green business processes are best handled by keeping in mind their incremental complexities: broadcast–informative–transactive–operative–collaborative.
■ Mobile technologies support environmental initiatives in technical, economical process and social dimension.

Introduction

Green business process management (Green BPM) deals with the overall management of all internal and external processes of an organization from a green perspective. BPM is a well-established industry practice encompassing process modeling, reengineering, and optimization of processes, and the measuring, merging, and elimination of business processes. Chapter 2 previously highlighted the four dimensions of green transformation (technology, people, processes, and economic aspects of the organization) and this chapter extends and focuses on the process aspects of an organization to outline ways in which transformation can occur. The discussion in this chapter uses the premise that considerable carbon savings can be made if an organization changes *the way* it does things because it is good for business. Such a premise does not discount the carbon savings through the other aforementioned dimensions. Synonymous with the *Lean* approach to business optimization, a greening effort is heavily dependent on activities, tasks, their sequencing, and their utility to business goals.

Green business processes can be understood as environmentally conscious business processes that are necessary, efficient, effective, agile, and measureable in the context of an organization. Process characteristics that are significant to making a green process are summarized in Table 5.1.

Processes and their aforementioned characteristics are investigated in greater detail in this chapter. In order to undertake this investigation and follow it with green process transformation, a process needs to be defined and understood. In the context of this discussion, a process can be understood as the "manner in which" things are carried out within and by an organization. Processes are thus the "how" aspect of an organization's functions. The manner of operating a machine, the manner of serving a customer, the manner of administering the human relations, and the manner of sales and marketing activities by an organization are all examples of these processes. Other examples of this "how" of an organization, include: how does a customer withdraws cash in a bank; how does a passenger buys an airline ticket; and how is a patient admitted in a hospital? These are common examples of business processes that, in reality, are highly complex and intertwined with other processes as well as technologies and people. Therefore, modeling and investigating them in detail reveal invaluable opportunities to cut the overall carbon generation by the organization. In the green process optimization exercise, processes are challenged for their necessity in the first place, others are optimized for efficiency, some others are made more effective and agile, and all are measured in order to ascertain their carbon contribution. The exploration of processes in this manner leads to many opportunities to improve and optimize them during a green enterprise transformation.

It is worth nothing that the focus of carbon reduction from a process viewpoint implies that in some ways, this effort would be independent of the corresponding changes to the hardware and applications of the organization. While changes to technologies and people are inevitable in a comprehensive green enterprise transformation, it is important to note that significant advantages can be gained simply by changing the way things are being done in the organization.

Table 5.1 Basic Process Characteristics and Corresponding Green Connotation

Process Characteristic	Description (Lean Business)	Green Business Connotations
Necessary	Challenges the need for the process in the first place. There is no point in making a process efficient and effective if it is not creating business value.	Eliminating an unnecessary process (not involving in value creation) will also eliminate its carbon contribution.
Efficient	Models the process to study its various activities/tasks. Challenges, automates, and merges activities to ensure they are performed with the best tools, technologies, and people.	Aims to reduce the carbon generation within the process by optimizing and/or eliminating the activities/tasks within the process. Technology is used by being embedded in the process.
Effective	Ensures that the process is actually achieving the goals it is meant to achieve. A process that is otherwise efficient and agile, but does not achieve business goals is not considered as effective.	Substantial wasteful carbon is generated by a process that is not effective—as it does not achieve business goals. Also, a process that is repeated more than once in order to produce the desired effect is a carbon-*inefficient* process.
Agile	Deals with the ability of the process to change itself in response to (or in anticipation of) external and internal changes affecting the organization. Deals with the dynamicity of the process.	An agile process will change easily and effortlessly in response to changing external situation. The agile virtue also renders the process green, as it can change with minimum carbon generation.
Measurable	Enables monitoring, control, and ascertaining the success of its optimization. Ongoing management of process performance is also supported.	In addition to the standard process measures, such as cost, time, and quality, now the "carbon content" of a process is measured. This helps in identifying the slack and optimizing it.

For example, in the cash withdrawal process by a customer, efficiency from a carbon perspective can be achieved by, say, not printing a physical receipt; or reducing the time in the queue for a physical cash withdrawal by applying the principles of operations research. While process reengineering and corresponding process management has been a part of business strategies for more than two decades, in this chapter, that knowledge and experience is applied to the organizational processes from a green perspective. This chapter develops the concept of BPM further to a Green BPM, that of a lean business process to a lean-green business process and that of BPR to a Green BPR.

Green Business Process Management

Green business process transition is based on resource optimization. These resources include computers, contents, systems, and communication platforms that are part of the business processes. Green ICT includes tools for process modeling and many of the process-enabling technologies such as business rules, policies, and metrics. Examples of tools in Green BPM include *Abnoba* and *Lombardi*. Green BPM thus becomes an extension and sophistication of the process management domain that utilizes the concepts of process efficiencies and effectiveness and applies it for carbon reduction. The earlier BPR advantages such as reduced expense, faster processing time, concurrency/multiple access ability, efficiency, and effectiveness can be identified and mapped to reduction in carbon contents.

Green BPM is an overall approach to modeling, optimizing, consolidating, and executing business processes of an organization from a carbon perspective. Application of Green BPM results in improving the ways in which an organization (users and business areas within an organization) undertake operations. BPM can be understood as a discipline of modeling, realizing, executing, monitoring, and optimizing business processes (ACS, 2010). Each of these aspects of BPM can be applied toward a green enterprise. Silver (2006) has also described various flavors of BPM such as enterprise application integration (EAI), workflow, content management, and enterprise-wide human and system process automation that can be applied toward Green BPM. Thus Green BPM, as discussed in this chapter, has opportunity to capitalize on the BPM approach in an organization and can be considered as a set of management and technology disciplines focused primarily on workflow and process automation that drives the implementation of optimized and sustainable business processes.

Such optimization of processes covers many aspects of the performance. Processes can be optimized to ensure efficient utilization of resources. Alternatively, processes can be reengineered to creatively eliminate the use of some redundant or duplicate resources. For example, a home loan (mortgage) process that requires application by a broker, credit check validation, and risk assessment through three separate agencies can be electronically consolidated as one. Such reengineering of processes has been a hallmark of business efficiency over past few decades.

Reengineering has been described as the fundamental rethinking and radical redesign of business processes to achieve dramatic improvements in critical, contemporary measures of performance such as cost, quality, service, and speed (Hammer and Champy, 1994). Davenport and Short (business process redesign, 1990) developed the ideas of reengineering further toward holistic redesign of the organization based on processes. BPR aimed at a complete and radical change to the entire organization as against a piecemeal change per department. BPR also creates organization-wide, holistic opportunities for carbon reduction as discussed in Chapter 2 on green strategies. Furthermore, Green BPR brings about dynamic changes to the business—implying, thereby, that not only are the processes changing but also the fact that those are continuous changes.

Green process management has a lot to gain from "Lean" and "Lean IT." The popularity of these "Lean" approaches to business and IT can be attributed to their focus on reducing and/or eliminating wastages within the organization processes. The relevance of lean to green policy formulations (lean-green) is discussed earlier in Chapter 3. These methods or approaches are initially applied by large and global organizations in order to produce process optimizations because such large enterprises are ideally suited to apply and capitalize through lean processes. Unlike smaller business, large organizations have greater strategic resources available to them and stand to gain more. Activities of large organizations, especially mining, agriculture, and airlines, have a much greater impact on the environment than smaller organizations. Therefore, reengineering of processes and application of the lean principles has a major role to play in Green BPM using an environmental parameter. Thus, lean-green can be viewed as a change to business practices together with changes to business models and methods. However, in addition to making use of the lean approach toward greening an organization, enterprises, government, and society have to also get together on a common platform in order to improve environmental processes and practices that go beyond immediate business motivation.

Thus, it is not only the changes to the processes or "how" an organization operates that is important, but also the underlying business models, technologies, and social aspects of that business. For example, business processes need not be only supported by technology resources, common infrastructure, or application platform, but also through a transparent business methodology (see www.business-ecology.org) and business models. IT plays a substantial role in providing a utility or a service to the business that can then be used by the business in its models and methods, such as lean, to become green.

Green Reengineering

As mentioned earlier, Green BPM includes reengineering of business processes to optimize their emissions. Reengineering of processes to green processes will incorporate reevaluation of processes and also an understanding and modeling of their supporting hardware, software, and people in order to cut down the carbon generated through them. Similar to original Business Process Re-engineering (BPR) exercise by Hammer and Champy (1994), the success of Green process reengineering (GPR) depends heavily on undertaking a model-based, performance-driven approach that is applied to the entire organization.

Figure 5.1 illustrates the concept of process reengineering in a simple way from a green perspective. The simple distribution process on the left in Figure 5.1 shows a manual distribution

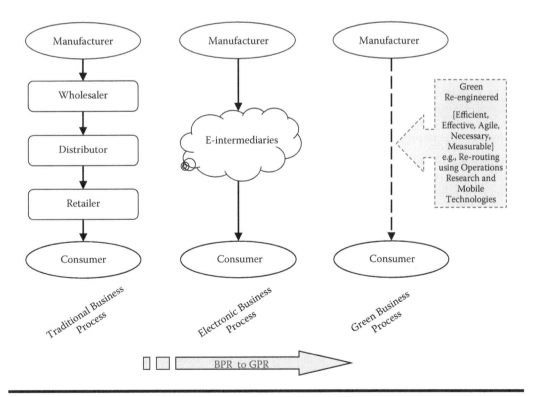

Figure 5.1   Core concept of GPR—a distribution example.

process, with steps leading from the manufacturer through to the warehouse, retailer, and the end-user. A reengineering exercise will lead to the formulation of the process shown in the middle of the Figure 5.1. This is an electronically enabled process that will provide business efficiencies and effectiveness in terms of the distribution network. Such efficiencies are typically achieved by displaying the product on an organization's web site and enabling the consumer to order it directly from the web site. With such reengineering, the steps associated with the wholesaler and the retailer can both be avoided—although the intermediaries can be the technology service providers and content managers (Unhelkar and Ginige, 2010).

However, the third process model, shown on the right in Figure 5.1, is aiming for yet another alternative. This reengineered process is efficient and effective from a cost and time viewpoint, and also from a carbon viewpoint. For example, the third process model will aim to completely eliminate the E-intermediaries. Customer driven reengineering will optimize collaborative business processes to eliminate steps that were required only because of lack of alternative technologies (Unhelkar et al., 2009). Location-sensitive mobile technologies can improve the carbon performance by eliminating intermediary steps that result in carbon. The premise here is that if the same process goal is achieved with fewer steps, the end result would be a carbon-efficient process.

Green metrics help in understanding the effects of reengineering. For example, green reengineered process can be measured for the total carbon content of the production process, the carbon generated by customer searches, and the overall carbon produced in ordering, packaging, and distribution to the consumer. The closeness of efficiency and effectiveness with carbon reduction has equal impact on cost reduction. The resultant quality, end-user experience, and carbon reduction would all come under the umbrella of BPM. As Nott (2010) succinctly mentions, increasing awareness of the environment by businesses has also opened up the opportunities for businesses to use the BPM approach to model, measure, analyze, and mitigate the carbon impact of business activities.

Green BPM includes fundamental changes to the processes and their ongoing management. The change to the processes is that Green BPR aims for a dramatic drop in the carbon emissions by a combination of process changes and systems (technology) support. For such Green BPR initiatives, carbon can be used as an important performance measure, together with contemporary measures of performance, such as cost, quality, service, and speed. Measures that support carbon-related performance provide required justification as well as proof of success for process optimizations. BPM can thus be considered as a vital key to the overall green business strategy and specific player in the process dimension of green enterprise transformation.

BPR initiatives lead to customer-focused processes whose end-goal is to achieve customer satisfaction rather than create hierarchical reorganization. Serving a customer efficiently and providing an enhanced customer experience reduces waste and therefore reduces carbon. An efficient and optimized supply chain will also reduce the organization's carbon footprint.

In addition to lean and reengineering, it is also worth considering TQM (total quality management) and its impact on the green process dimension of an organization. TQM brought about significant changes to the way an organization operated—imposing discipline and quality consciousness to the organizational processes. The resultant improvement in quality leads to reduction in rework. This reduced rework can be directly correlated with reduction in carbon. A process that achieves its goal by a single attempt for each process cycle is, by implication, going to generate less carbon as compared with the same process attempted more than once for a particular cycle. In other words, a process cycle which needs to go back and forth to achieve its business goals through additional reworks will not be very efficient and will generate more carbon. A high-quality process that gets the work done right in first attempt will reduce its carbon content and increase the user satisfaction.

Green Processes: Individual, Organizational, and Collaborative

Figure 5.2 shows the various levels of processes within an organization and their corresponding key factors. These are the individual, organizational, and collaborative processes that need to be considered in detail during GPR. Changes made can be either tactical (bearing immediate results) or strategic (long-term results). In general, individual processes tend to be tactical and tend to provide quick-wins, such as individuals switching-off their computers when not in use. Changes to collaborative processes tend to deliver longer-term results. Modeling and optimization of the collaborative processes requires more time and effort and include more players and multiple systems.

Reengineering of business process to reduce their carbon contents has to happen at three levels: individual, organizational, and collaborative. These levels tend to be increasingly strategic, taking longer time and greater effort as the business moves from individual processes through to departmental- and organizational-level processes. Collaborative processes cut across multiple organizations and systems—making them even more challenging to be reengineered in the context of carbon reduction.

There is a need to understand and relate the core processes as well as peripheral activities of the organization to the corresponding carbon contents. Modeling and optimizing core processes from a carbon perspective has higher risks than peripheral. For example, a hospital has its core competency of treating patients. A hospital is often associated with pharmacies for dispersal of medications and pathology laboratories for conducting a suite of tests on patients. These pharmacy and pathology processes are closely supporting the core processes dealing with treatment of patients. The core and the peripheral or supporting processes need to be modeled, measured, and optimized from their carbon perspective. For example, a hospital cannot afford to modify its patient-related core processes even if they are carbon-intensive if they increase the risks to the patient. Therefore, each step within the process has to be studied before it is changed or eliminated.

Table 5.2 summarizes these types of processes and also lists the key factors (shown in Figure 5.2) that are important in handling the carbon aspect of these processes. Processes can vary widely

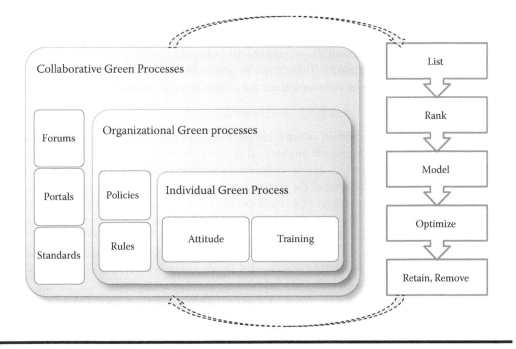

Figure 5.2 Individual, organizational, and collaborative green processes and their reengineering.

Table 5.2 Green Process Categories and Their Carbon Impact

Green Process Categories	Key Factors That Influence Carbon	Comments
Individual	Attitude, Training	Personalized processes are influenced by attitude and training. Motivation of the individual may be based on personal value system, personal reward, and growth.
Organizational	Policies, Rules, KPIs	Dynamic creation and management of business rules that optimize processes. Metrics are crucial to demonstrate the ROI on investment for green enterprise.
Collaborative	Portals, Forums, Standards	Collaborative processes transcending organizational boundaries. Portals containing green knowledge, regulations across regions.

depending on their importance, their technology support and the end-goals they achieve for the organization. Ideally, processes need to be identified and modeled from end-to-end. In reality, especially for large businesses, there will be layers within processes leading to the idea of composite processes—that is processes containing subprocesses and subprocesses containing activities. Furthermore, the business rules embedded within the business processes also need to be addressed in Green BPR. For example, existing business rules associated with, say, a cash withdrawal process that requires two forms of identification will have to be adhered to irrespective of its carbon content. The manner in which the rule is implemented (e.g., matching of signatures with stored electronic signatures, or validation of pin-codes) can be optimized by modeling, studying, and changing the activities of the process.

During a Green BPR exercise, careful evaluation of all these business processes at individual, organizational, and collaborative levels within the organization needs to be undertaken. During this evaluation, these processes are listed, ranked (prioritized), modeled, optimized, and eventually, either retained or eliminated. These steps, as applicable collectively to all processes in the organization, are shown on the right in Figure 5.2. These steps, in terms of Green BPR, can be further described as follows:

- *Listing*—of all processes within an organization. This is an initial list, which will be refined as this green transformation exercise proceeds. This list can be created based on the value creation of the organization and which can be categorized into primary, secondary, or supporting processes based on major functions of the organization such as production, inventory, supply chain, customer relations, finance, and HR. Each group of processes can again have levels, such as end-to-end processes, subprocesses, activities, and tasks. Each process within the list can have a description of what it provides or which goal of the organization is served by the process.
- *Ranking*—of the processes within the process list can be undertaken based on the carbon-criteria. Thus, while normal BPM exercises list the processes with criteria such as their costs and effectiveness, in Green BPM, these processes are also ranked based on the amount of estimated carbon they produce. While this estimation can be uncertain in the first instance, still as the organization proceeds with its Green BPM exercise, it can easily reevaluate its carbon estimates. This ranking is meant to provide an understanding of which particular processes should be given highest priority in terms of green reengineering.

- *Modeling*—process reengineering requires accurate modeling of those processes. If an organization has already undertaken a BPM exercise, process models for all major processes should be available. If not, the green transformation project can start by modeling the processes that are ranked high in the previous step. Process modeling in itself is a vast topic; however, here it has been discussed within the narrow context of Green BPR. The (Unified Modeling Language) UML (particularly its use cases and activity graphs), user stories, BPMN (business process modeling notation), and (Integration Definition) IDEF are all well-known techniques for process modeling. Any of these techniques, or their combination, can be used for modeling of processes.

- *Optimizing*—this step is the study of the processes that are modeled from their carbon impact. Thus, each activity within the process model can be studied and the carbon generated within that activity ascertained. Then, that activity can be modified to reduce its carbon, supported by technologies and systems to again reduce its carbon, or eliminated if found to be unnecessary. The optimization of processes is a substantial part of the Green BPM exercise and has to be taken in coordination with other dimensions of the organization (for greater details, see Chapter 9 on green business transformation).

- *Retaining*—processes that are modeled and optimized will reduce their carbon contribution. These are the processes that can be retained and placed in a continuously optimized mode. These processes will also be the core business processes of the organization that have to be maintained in the best possible way. Therefore, for processes that have to be retained, the rankings will be high and the optimization process will be iterated two to three times.

- *Removing*—the BPM exercise will also identify processes that are either redundant/duplicated or are so excessively carbon inefficient that they have to be replaced. These are the processes that will be removed from the suite of business processes. The impact of their removal has to be studied across all other dimensions before processes are removed. In practice, it is also discovered that some processes, typically manual processes, that were being undertaken without total awareness on the part of the rest of the organization, will get eliminated. The informal processes, however, are the most difficult to eliminate as they don't have proper process models and supporting technologies.

Green BPM and Standards

Green BPM can be carried out in a number of ways, and using different tools and techniques. Innovation in BPR is a synergy of business process thinking and corresponding tools and techniques. Ken Orr (2007) has described the concepts and strategies involved in business process innovation including the major threads of business process thinking. This discussion also includes technical approaches, such as service oriented architecture (SOA) that are closely intertwined with BPM. The relationship between SOA and BPM becomes more important in the green enterprise space as changes to processes to make them green cannot be brought about independent of the information and enterprise architecture. Michael K. Guttman and John H. Parodi have also outlined in their Cutter article the potential convergence of the BPM, SOA, and MDA paradigms. This convergence leads to efficiency and effectiveness, but also business

BPR involved use of technologies to reorganize the business along process-lines that would enhance the business performance multiple times. Green BPR uses the same principles of BPR to explore the possibility of reduce carbon contents of the organization in multiples. This multiple reduction in carbon is to be achieved not merely by optimizing the existing processes but also by creating a new business architecture that may not need all of the existing processes. Review of business rules, use of systems and applications, and encouraging customers to be a part of this initiative, GPR can make substantially effective and efficient use of organizational resources. For example, with Internet-based processes, not only can queuing times in a line can be reduced but the queues themselves can be given up, thereby reducing the overall carbon content of the processes and the footprint of the organization.

agility. Since each of these characteristics are important from a green perspective (as highlighted in Table 5.1), they provide the reasons for Green BPM/Green SOA. Green SOA is discussed in greater detail in Chapter 6.

Green BPM remains a superset of Green BPR. Excellence in Green BPM is based on understanding and application of the reengineering and process management concepts to the organization but with the focus on carbon reduction together with cost reduction.

Viewing the organization as a whole including its people, processes, and technologies is the key to applying Green BPM in practice. Figure 5.3 shows various aspects or layers of an organization that also have their own processes. The end-user is shown accessing the device, which in turn is linked to a presentation process. This is then supported by the business or system level processes. The business processes are supported by applications, corresponding data warehouses, and eventually the technical infrastructure such as data servers and communications networks. Each of these technologies and people within the processes are affected during Green BPM effort. This is so because a comprehensive Green BPM is a combination of technology-enabled but business-driven process management. Figure 5.3 also shows another important aspect of Green BPM—that of application and use of standards for process improvement, governance, and even project management. Following are the important aspects of the use of these standards in Green BPM:

■ TQM, Kaizen, and Six Sigma provide standards and techniques to optimize and improve business processes. This will result in improvement in quality of product and, thereby,

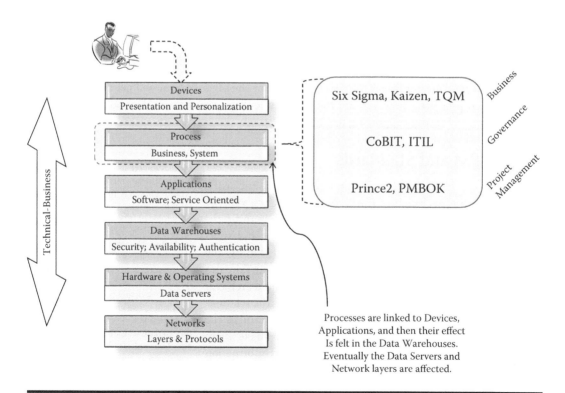

Figure 5.3 Applying business, governance, and project management standards to green business processes.

improve organizational performance. The business efficiency techniques arising from these quality management approaches can also be used to improve the carbon credentials of the organization.

■ Efficient business processes may also create opportunity to produce greater quantity of goods resulting from improved production capacity. However, care has to be taken to ensure that improvement in production does not dent the green credentials of the process.

■ Customization and personalization of products to suit the demands of customers is the result of process reengineering. Once again, care has to be taken to ensure that personalization does not lead to addition of carbon in the process.

■ Reengineering of processes also results in optimizing the internal organizational structure. This includes rearranging and repositioning people.

■ Communications, together with IT, has lead to the customer being able to effectively create his/her own product and service that is tailored to the specific need; dynamic creation of products and services is the result of the Internet-based communications that has to be factored in the Green BPM.

■ Knowledge management enables keeping track of customer preferences; and now it can be used to manage green preferences of the customer and the green performance of the processes.

■ Integration of processes is facilitated by integration of underlying applications and systems. Integrated processes offer tremendous opportunities for customers to fulfill their specific needs. At the same time, such integration also creates opportunities for overall carbon reduction.

■ Outsourced processes are another example of the opportunity to reduce overall carbon emissions. Processes of the outsourcing vendor are usually optimized for a specific purpose (Unhelkar, 2008), resulting in carbon efficiency.

■ Knowledge about the customer, suppliers, and the manufacturing process can be used to strategically organize the manufacturing, call center support, and other assets of the organization in order to derive maximum green potential.

Green BPM creates opportunities to allow user-driven processes to influence the overall carbon footprint of the organization. This influence is based on inputs and comments made from the customers regarding the business processes. Given an opportunity, customers are keen to provide input into the business processes which would help the organization improve its green credentials. Therefore, during green reengineering of business processes toward green processes, customers should not be considered as "external parties" but, instead, invited to participate in the modeling, optimization, and management of the processes. Some of the important considerations in customer-driven reengineering from a green perspective are as follows:

■ Setting up of regular communications with the customers in terms of their precise needs. Such identification of the needs of the customers upfront enables their provision in an efficient and effective way, reducing the carbon overheads associated with unplanned provisioning of customer requirements.

■ Creating and engaging customer groups that can then participate in the green strategic planning sessions as well as green policy formulation. This can be done both face to face and electronically. An asynchronous discussion group resulting from an online collaboration can provide valuable input in to the green demands of current and future customers.

■ Inputs from select customers can result in creation of training packages that facilitate ease of use of those processes by customers. Customer education and training can also result in effective use of green business processes that makes use of technologies and positive attitudes in reducing the carbon contents of those business processes. This education and training can result in effective use of organizational processes.

■ Measurement and feedback on customer service. Use of real-time metrics in terms of carbon associated with a business process (such as with smart meters) can result in a immediate impact on customer behavior.

Information and communications technologies—especially applications and systems—can aid and support Green BPR. For example, this help occurs when a particular step in the process is automated by using a software service or a network gadget. Such use of technology in GPR requires careful consideration because even though the introduction of a network and communications technology will optimize the process, there are corresponding carbon overheads in the network and computing infrastructures. Whenever reengineering effort requires technical support, the potential of increased carbon generation exists and should be given due consideration.

Reengineering of processes also leads to changes in existing organizational processes that demand a clear understanding of the potential disruptions resulting from those changes. These changes include the way the organization relates to the customers, the organization of the internal business, and the potential changes to the operating platforms. Green BPR can involve use of virtualization technologies or, alternatively, incorporation of a new technology in the process with the intention of reducing its carbon footprint. However, in the absence of good modeling and study of processes, the likelihood of increased carbon exists as most practical business processes are highly complex and have associated infrastructure. Consider, for example, the way in which organizational services are modeled and provided. Due to Green BPR effort, the total services offered may be reduced. Alternatively, new green services might be introduced with corresponding infrastructure and support requirements. Therefore, even with the use of virtualization, risks associated with increase in carbon exist. Similarly, there are risks associated with customer satisfaction if only carbon performance is kept in mind during Green BPR.

Careful weighing of every green process optimization needs to be made to consider the technology-process nexus. Performance of ICT applications need to be studied by business process modelers in the context of its satisfaction rating from the customers. Addressing the risks associated with the GPR is vital in its success.

Green Business Analysis

During any discussion of green business processes, one needs to consider the role of business analysis activity, including the gathering of business requirements, understanding and modeling processes, process analysis and optimization, and testing prior to deployment. The green business process modeling and the role of a Green business analyst (BA) has been discussed succinctly by Beal (2011). This role of a Green BA can provide analytical help and support for green business process modeling. BA is the role that owns and models the requirements of the project. This is particularly so in a software development or maintenance project. Green BA is involved in understanding and documenting the use cases (for examples of use cases, see Chapter 7). The BA is also responsible for working with the key business executives and users to determine the goal and expectation of the business process. These expectations are documented by the BA with reference to the technical capabilities of the IT solution. Therefore, the BA is in an excellent position to start incorporating green business goals in the modeling of business processes. A green-conscious participation of a BA in the system requirements lifecycle can result in new business processes that are optimized right from the beginning. A Green BA can play a dual role: First, modeling requirements for a Green IT project and, second, modeling existing processes for their optimization from a green perspective. BAs can ensure alignment of a Green IT technical solution (e.g., CEMS) with environmentally responsible business strategies. The Green BA involvement in a project promotes an understanding that even if certain business requirements are important to a stakeholder, they may not be still necessarily desirable in a solution if they are not aligned with the need to generate least carbon. For example, if a Green IT project facilitates the generation of ad-hoc reports, then the daily report generation can be excluded from the solution as that will save potential wastage of paper or wastage of system resources.

A Green BA will also aim to create flexible green processes. Similar to any normal business processes, the green business processes should also be flexible and continuously evolving (Hercheui, 2011): This flexibility allows the processes to be adaptable to different contexts in which they are being used. Changes to green business requirements are rapid and should be incorporated immediately in the green business processes.

Furthermore, this flexibility also caters for the users who have varying levels of knowledge about sustainability depending on their own personal context. Considering the urgency of environmental issues and the need of finding solutions that foster sustainable development, Green IT should be adaptable for the use of as many people as possible (Hercheui, 2011). Green BAs cater for the modeling and implementation of these varying requirements of green business processes.

Green BAs also facilitate the diffusion of knowledge on sustainability. Later, in Chapter 8, there is a discussion on the importance of the use of IT tools and technologies for creating and promoting green awareness across wide cross-section of society. Green BAs incorporate channels within the processes to foster creation of green groups and spread corresponding green knowledge amongst them.

Green Requirements Modeling

One of the major responsibilities of a Green BA is to undertake modeling of requirements for a green process or system. This requirements modeling can be considered as a subdiscipline of systems engineering that is concerned with the behavior, quality attributes, and also technical constraints. Requirements modeling is widely recognized as both a challenging aspect of software development, as well as a crucial one, because it lays the foundation for all the subsequent project work (Wiegers, 2006). Examples of functional requirements of Green IT systems are provided in Chapter 7. While they are in the form of use cases, Green BA can work to model requirements using other approaches such as user stories, scenarios, and simple flowcharts.

Green practices can affect requirements related to hardware, software, and business processes. A requirement may establish, for example, a solution that must not only fulfill business goals, but also measure and report energy improvement over previous generations. Approaches such as server consolidation and virtualization, storage virtualization, Cloud computing, and power management, among other green-related technologies, can help ICT solutions become more efficient, flexible, resilient, and environmentally friendly while economical to operate (Murugesan, 2008).

Green requirements modeling keeps these technologies in the background as it pursues green business goals. BAs working for corporations implementing green practices become responsible for defining requirements and validating solutions that take advantage of these aforementioned advancements in technologies. Green requirements modeling can be divided in two major parts— functional and nonfunctional (or operational).

Functional requirements, the most well-known type of software requirements, describe the behavior that the software will have and the information the solution will manage. Functional requirements are associated with the required behaviors and operations of a system, defining its capabilities in terms of actions and responses. Functional requirements are frequently captured in the form of use cases (Unhelkar, 2005). Green IT frequently impacts functional requirements as a consequence of new procedures or business rules emerging from corporate environmental policies and industry standards.

Consider a corporate guideline issued to help reduce paper reports by encouraging online reporting. While defining the requirements for a new application with reporting functionality, the BA must spend time investigating the capabilities needed in the system to convince users (system users and indirect users, such as managers and customers who do not work directly with the system, but need access to its outputs) to stop printing, and read from their computer screens instead. In order to achieve this objective, functional requirements may be added to the software specification, to facilitate tasks related to reading and distributing online reports to their intended audiences.

There are requirements, however, that go beyond system behavior. These requirements describe the properties and attributes of the solution and are referred to as *nonfunctional requirements*. Examples of such requirements include availability, performance, usability, portability, robustness, etc., and they provide the design constraints for the project (e.g., technology or regulatory limitation). Green IT policies typically add nonfunctional requirements to software projects, imposing new demands in terms of quality attributes that become necessary or desirable, and also establishing new constraints.

Take, for example, a company adopting a mechanism to control all monitors and computers, so they can be placed into a low-power consumption mode (such as shutdown, hibernation, or standby) when they are not being used. Imagine that this company is also building an application that a few users will access via their PCs to update the state of alerts affecting a core business service. The BA in charge of capturing the requirements for the alert system would have to investigate the potential impact of a delay caused by the need to recover the computer from its energy-saving state before the application could be used to update the status of an alert. The BA would also be responsible for discussing with the stakeholders the expected system behavior under these circumstances. A decision could be made stating that a user returning to her desk after taking care of an event that triggered an alert should be able to access the application within 5 seconds or less, to post an update. As a consequence, a nonfunctional requirement could be created establishing that "once an alert is issued, and until it is resolved, the application will prevent the workstation from going into any energy-saving state that requires more than 5 seconds to reverse."

Corporate environmental practices, sustainability policies, regulations, and contractual obligations to meet environmental standards may impact both functional and nonfunctional requirements of ICT applications. Green BA tasks relates to enterprise analysis, requirements elicitation and analysis, and solution assessment and validation in determining the green optimal solution to fulfill the business needs. As such green policies have to deal with procurement, operations, application design, and/or disposal of computing resources, and establish the necessary foundation for defining the scope and requirements of ICT projects.

Green IT Governance

Green process management matures as proper business governance which align with performance governance, project governance, change governance, and IT governance and control is applied to it. An ideal way to do this is to incorporate green aspects within the existing governance structure within the organization. This can take shape of modifying the business process architecture, balance score card, and business policies for governance. Chapter 3 discussed the creation of green business policies out of the organizational strategies for carbon reduction. These policies, when translated in practice, dictate organizational compliance toward a green outcome. This brings in the opportunity to update the corporate and IT governance standards and use them for green compliance,

ITIL, as a best practice framework describing an end-to-end service management environment can provide a significant input into the business rules and policies related to Green IT. For example, green business rules can be embedded within ITIL's service management. This would result in efficient and effective management of IT services, application of green metrics to the services, and their internal and external reporting in terms of carbon contents. ITIL can help in mapping IT, business, and green strategies by bringing together the service goals policies, rules, and practices from each of them.

see Figure 5.3. Governance standards bring together legislation, regulation, industry standards, contract agreements, and internal rules together in a synergy. These standards also provide the framework for BA to capture and define requirements from varying sources within and outside the organization, on an ongoing basis that handle the compliance needs both at the enterprise and project levels.

Green organizational policies require business rules. These business rules are either embedded electronically or followed manually. Thus, these business rules have a wide-ranging influence on both the manual processes used by individuals within the organization, and the software systems and applications with business embedded business rules. Whether business rules are embedded within the application software or not, such business rules still have a bearing on the requirements. Therefore, there is a need to correlate policies to rules to requirements. Table 5.3 provides an example of some green business policies that are part of the updated IT governance, which translate into business rules and requirements.

Table 5.3 indicates how a governance standard is translated into policies and practices through business rules. These business rules also apply to external business processes, thereby ensuring that the external and, particularly, collaborative business processes are also carbon compliant. When it comes to buildings, data centers, communications, and networks infrastructure (as were discussed in Chapter 4), the most commonly used governance standard is the Information Technology Infrastructure Library (ITIL) also known as Infrastructure Management Service (IMS). The five core publications of ITIL (ITIL, 2009) are briefly discussed below in the context of Green IT process and management.

Service Strategy—provides guidance on explanation and prioritization of service provider and their customers' investments in services (Addy, 2007). The service strategy should have some "Green" factor embedded into them and this can influence the way in which an organizations IT services are provided, with green factor introduced, this is even more influential. This service strategy influences the service providers as well as service consumers. Green business processes, in this context, can be modeled through use cases or user stories to dictate the rules to be followed in the execution of those processes. For example, green business priorities and technical estimations can be combined to ascertain the level and scope of services. As mentioned earlier in the context of interrelated standards, the service strategy of an organization can also be based on SOA and incorporate web services—which would, in turn, have embedded rules during service collaboration (Unhelkar, Ghanbary, and Younessi, 2009).

Table 5.3 Business Policies, Rules, and Process Requirements

Green Business Policy	Corresponding Business Rule Description	Green Business Purpose
Carbon content of solutions cannot exceed current levels	All deployments must be preceded by the evaluate alternatives for reducing the solution's total power consumption.	Ensures that the green solutions themselves are not carbon intensive. Servers and data center infrastructures should not add to the carbon footprint that exists.
Apply automation in all power management	Power management systems to be used in all organizational environments.	Prevent waste of energy by shutting off, hibernating, or putting systems on standby. Centralized device management is of immense value here.
Reduce data center carbon	Make extensive use of Cloud computing to shift the data center activities and resources.	Effective reduction in emissions due to consolidation of data center resources on the Cloud.
Increase carbon awareness in products and services	EPEAT style labeling of products and services resulting from the organization.	Carbon value calculations appearing on products and services can assist the customers in choosing products that are low in carbon.
Business processes to be carbon responsible	Introduce KPI for all major activities and processes in the organization; apply metrics to measure process outcome for carbon.	Assists in understanding, benchmarking, and improving green performance for each iteration of activities and processes.
Reuse and recycle	Reuse equipments through their entire lifecycle, then recycle.	Reduces not only emissions during the life of the equipment, but also reduces electronic wastage toward the end of useful life.

Service Design—provides guidance on design of new or modified IT services through a catalogue. The design of each service can be based on the Green IT policies and practices, thereby ensuring that the systems and applications consuming these services have an implicit green angle to them. Customer input can be used in these service designs to ensure that they cater for the ever increasing demands of the customer for green services. Furthermore, green service designs will ensure that meeting the level of service expected is not counterproductive from a carbon perspective. Functional as well as nonfunctional (or operational) areas of services are handled here to reduce their carbon impact.

Service Transition—facilitates transition of a service to the operational area of the business with environmental considerations inbuilt into them. This requires proper planning and controlled changes to the services. This is a unit-level change to the overall changes in business processes of the organization with a delta change toward "Green." Thus, a service transition to a green service is made up of changes to the activities that make use of technical web services to reach the process goals. Formal service transition based on ITIL will now also bring in green business rules that will improve the overall carbon performance. These measures can additionally be used in tracking and maintaining services.

Service Operation—is when the service has become operational and can be called "Green Service" when the environmental considerations are taken into effect. These are typically the web services based activities of a business process and, therefore, have to be measured for their carbon impact during operation. The ITIL guidance in monitoring the service during operation including recording faults during operation can be extended to calculate its carbon impact. Identifying and fixing service failures during operation and quickly restoring service operation to a user are a part of ITIL and, therefore, can be used to measure, understand, and improve the carbon emissions resulting from those services.

Continual Service Improvement—provides guidance on the things that need to be controlled and measured for improving service quality, particularly from a green business perspective. Continual Service Improvement in ITIL deals with engaging IT and business management in an ongoing dialog. Such dialog would also provide measurements for service availability, reliability, and performance and reporting. This ongoing improvement and maintenance of services can produce highly optimized services with the bare minimum carbon footprint. Service orientation should enable developers to produce ongoing improvements by isolating and updating services on a "need" basis so as to have minimum carbon losses.

Green Business Processes—Incremental Complexity

Figure 5.4 shows how the four dimensions of green business transformation (economic, technical, social, and process) influence the formulation of green business strategies and policies. These policies and their corresponding rules are then brought to bear on the processes of the organization. Earlier in this chapter, these processes were categorized as individual, organizational, and collaborative. This categorization of processes is based on original work on processes by Unhelkar (2003) and later by Unhelkar and Murugesan (2010), wherein a finer categorization is attempted. Figure 5.4 hints at the increasingly complexities of these processes and also indicates that at the operational and collaborative levels, the application of lean and agile principles will support business sustainability.

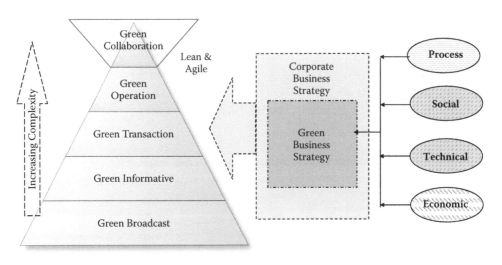

Figure 5.4   Green business strategy drives incrementally complex GPR.

Figure 5.5 further specifies the increasing complexity of these green processes. These processes are also discussed again, later in this chapter, in the context of mobile green processes.

■ Broadcast processes—These are easiest processes to understand, model, and optimize when they are the one-way broadcast processes typically used by the organization to promote and advertise their products. Ideal way to reduce the green contents of these broadcast processes is by reducing the "bells and whistles" around the actual contents, need-based broadcast, and keeping the contents direct and short.

■ Informative processes—The green aspect of this informative category comes from the fact that the receiver of the output of this informative process is known to the organization. These informative processes provide data on carbon emissions per day, per asset, and so on. Such a receiver can also contribute, albeit in a small way, to the reduction in carbon by only seeking the bare minimum and necessary information.

■ Transactive processes—Typically called the electronic commerce processes requiring a 3-way interaction between the vendor, the customer, and the payment facility (such as PayPal or Visa credit). The carbon content of a transactive process is higher than the previous two processes because multiple parties are involved and the transaction is stored electronically in a secured and also mirrored format because of its higher value (including the corresponding legal obligations). This increases the number of "bits" to be stored on the servers and, therefore, the overall load on the data servers of the organization.

■ Operative processes—These processes are of more complexity and deal with the internal, operational aspect of the organization. Therefore, they include processes such as HR, inventories, and time keeping. These processes also include the supply chains, the procurement,

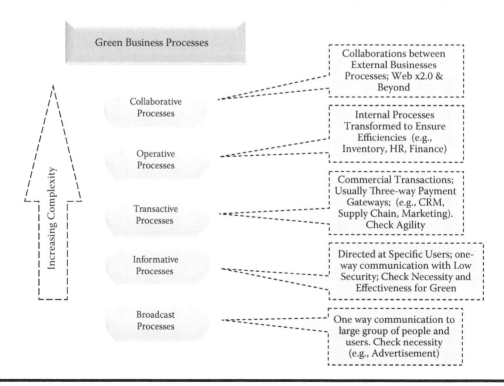

Figure 5.5 Increasing complexity of green processes.

and eventually, the disposal processes of the organization. The carbon content associated with these operational processes can be significant, as the organizational inventory of equipment and materials comes under these processes. Rules-based modeling and optimization is the only way to improve the carbon performance of the operative processes.

■ Collaborative processes—When multiple organizations interact with each other through collaborative web-based processes, the carbon generation is not only significant, but also increasingly challenging to trace because the organizational boundaries of these processes is extremely fuzzy. When collaborative business processes occur electronically through web services (Unhelkar, Ghanbary, and Younessi, 2009), the complexity is so phenomenal that it would be impossible to ascertain the true carbon content that can be attributed to single, participating organizations. This is particularly true in ascertaining Scope-3 emissions, as in collaborative processes organizational boundaries are fuzzy. So, it becomes difficult to ascertain whether the Scope-3 emission of one organization is actually a Scope-1 emission of another organization. In spite of these challenges, however, collaborative processes offer a unique perspective in carbon savings. This is so because, as discussed by Unhelkar and Tiwary (2010), collaborative processes have the potential for saving carbon, as they prevent reinvention of the basic business functions. For example, name and address can be sourced as a service from a third-party provider, thereby preventing the need to create the software to manage name and addresses in the systems of every participant organization in that collaboration. This is an area of further investigations and research, although collaborative processes are also mentioned again, later in this chapter, in the context of mobile green.

Green Business Applications

Figure 5.3, earlier in this chapter, depicted a mapping, or relationship of processes to devices and applications. Most green business processes will have to be supported by corresponding green systems and applications. Understanding this relationship between processes and applications is important as, during the BPM exercises, changes to the processes will require corresponding changes to those systems and applications that support the processes. Figure 5.6 shows this relationship and impact of green business processes on corresponding organizational level systems and applications. For example, Figure 5.6 shows how the broadcast, informative, transactive, operative, and collaborative processes impact business applications such as—financial management information systems (FMIS), enterprise resource planning (ERP), supply chain management (SCM), and customer relationship management (CRM). In addition to these applications, there are many more specialized and in-house developed custom applications that are industry specific, and that are affected by GPR.

Modeling Green Business Processes (UML, BPMN)

The modeling of processes is a crucial step in process optimization. There are few different ways of approaching process modeling. However, if modeling of processes is based around constraints, then it needs to start from the business processes architectural view of the enterprise architecture—that itself could be based on the value chain concept. In the case of Green BPM, the value at the end of the process is not independent of

Green business applications require due consideration of modeling, quality of service (QoS) and documenting the goals. QoS is, in particular, important as it can not only enhance customer experience but, in many cases, legally binding. Most importantly, though, higher the QoS, lower would be the need to repeat the process, translating directly in reduction in carbon.

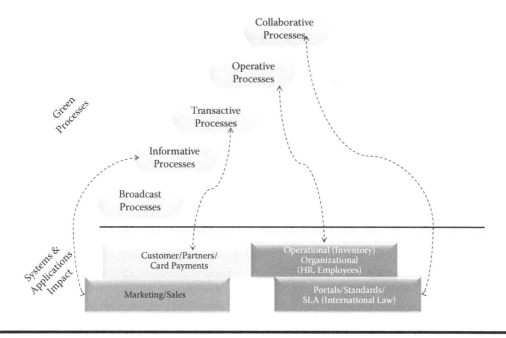

Figure 5.6 Relating green business processes to systems and applications.

the carbon generated. Therefore, all process modeling has to include carbon consideration at each step and for each process. Thus, each process needs to be modeled in an optimized way, with minimum activities and tasks that relate to each other and that achieve the process goals with reduced carbon footprint.

This modeling of processes can be undertaken with the help of process modeling standards such as the UML or the process-specific notations of the BPMN. The modeling notations are made available through process modeling tools (Unhelkar, 2003) and can be used in a team structure wherein a group of BAs could be working in unison to produce and optimize process models. Examples of such intense business process modeling activities are provided in greater detail in Chapter 7.

Quality of Service (QoS) and Green Business Processes

While process models play a crucial role in Green BPM, they have to be also validated and verified for their quality and their impact on the quality of services offered by the organization. The process models depict the flow, or functionality of a particular process or service. The activities within the process are then optimized for their carbon content. However, an ever greater impact of these processes on the carbon footprint of the organization is through the expectations of the quality of service (QoS) of these processes. Apart from the functional accuracy of the processes, this QoS is usually the result of the nonfunctional or operational demands on the business processes. Organizations are generally involved in enhancing their QoS through varied efforts at various levels within the organization. This can include effort at optimizing processes through use of communications as well as knowledge management technologies.

In a Green BPM, however, QoS is not enhanced entirely for the sake of customer satisfaction. In fact, the carbon content of enhancing a customer experience and, thereby, improving the QoS is also demonstrated to the customer. Therefore, QoS, in a Green BPM, is now balanced with quantity of carbon (QoC) within the process. Finally, in the context of this discussion, it is worth mentioning that an assumption that enhancing the QoS will result in increased carbon content may not be correct. This is so because an enhanced QoS will result in less repetition and therefore less wastage. In fact, enhancement in QoS has a high potential for reduction in QoC over the entire life of the interaction of the customer with the organization.

Documenting Process Goals

Processes can be measured for their efficiency and effectiveness as described by Unhelkar (2003). When applied in the green context, each process has to be measured for its carbon content. For example, the business process dealing with "cash withdrawal from a bank counter" has a certain carbon content that is based on the activities, the people undertaking those activities and the deliverables produced. Similarly, processes in airlines, hospital, and insurance organizations have their corresponding carbon contents that need to be measure. Later, in Chapter 7, use cases and activity graphs are discussed as a means of modeling business processes. The UML diagrams are also relevant in measuring the carbon generation when they are executed.

Achieving Green BPM

Figure 5.7 shows the entire breadth of factors that need to be considered in the Green BPM. These are as follows:

Green BPM covers people, facilities, transport, development, production, information, and communication within and across an organization from a green perspective. These areas of Green BPM form a matrix with the individual, organizational, and collaborative type of processes.

- People know processes and execute processes. They need to know the purpose and the passion to perform processes in such a way to achieve Green BPM goals. So it depends on how much people knows about green concepts and how they want to approach the environment that results in the success of Green BPM goals.
- Transport is a substantial contributor to the greenhouse gases. The Green BPM should essentially reduce the need of transports while doing jobs. Although transportations is necessary for business, the success of Green BPM depends on how the business processes are re-engineered to reduce transportation.
- Facilities are essential for any business and these facilities should be rearranged to suit green business goals. The Green BPM should facilitate to have any facility which could produce less carbon footprint during the business operation and in idle time.
- Development of product or service in any business is one of the core components of the value chain of the business. The development processes should be carefully modeled so that the carbon footprint for the development of any product or service could satisfy the Green BPM goals.
- Production is a continuous work done in businesses which also add carbon footprint to the outputs. The production processes needs much attentions in modeling and optimizing in terms of carbon contents so that the outputs will lead to lesser carbon footprint.
- Information is the most important part of any process. The way of managing information is the key to achieve the Green BPM goals in any business. Information modeling, capturing,

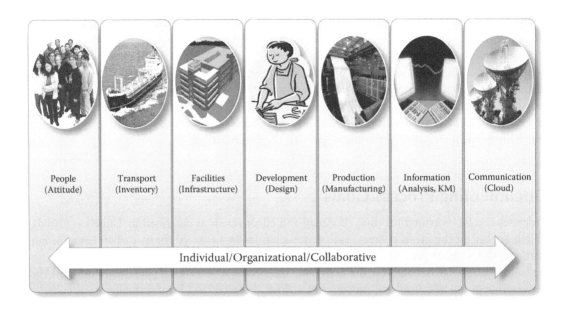

| People (Attitude) | Transport (Inventory) | Facilities (Infrastructure) | Development (Design) | Production (Manufacturing) | Information (Analysis, KM) | Communication (Cloud) |

Individual/Organizational/Collaborative

Figure 5.7   The Green BPM factors.

presenting, and analyzing would impact on carbon content as well as it can provide the knowledge of green status of the processes.

■ Communication is one of the most important enabler for Green BPM. Effective communication will pave the way to achieve Green BPM goals quicker and it can also reduce the effect of carbon footprint. So the Green BPM requires the use of communication factor effectively and efficiently to achieve Green BPM goals.

Organization-wide GPR needs to consider processes in groups. Figure 5.8 shows an example of how business processes can be grouped as internal and external. This enables creation of commonly applicable green criteria to these processes. The external group is made up of processes that require cooperation and coordination with business partners of the organization. Therefore, this may be a more challenging group to apply green practices to. The second group, shown on the right in Figure 5.8, is internal process group. This group can benefit by support from the employees and unions within the organization. These are example groups—and in practice processes can be grouped in multiple ways to produce manageable chunks for green transformations.

Green Mobile Business Processes

Mobile technologies can be incorporated in business processes to improve their carbon efficiencies through location-independence and personalization. This incorporation of mobility has to be in the manner of increasing complexity of those mobile processes—from mobile-broadcast to mobile-collaborative.

Unhelkar (2009, METM) has discussed the approach to incorporating mobile technologies in the business processes of an organization that is undertaking green enterprise transformation. This green mobile business was described in the context of the four dimensions discussed earlier in Chapter 2 (economic, technical, process, and social factors) from their environmental-responsibility viewpoint. These four dimensions, which form

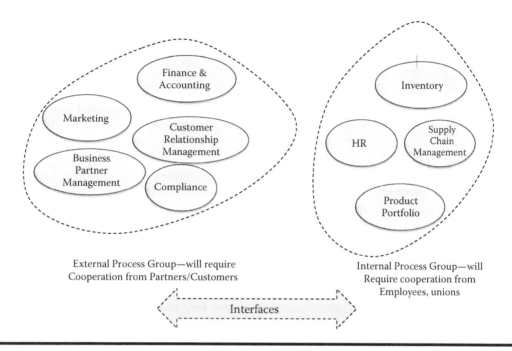

Figure 5.8 Grouping of "business processes" for green reengineering.

the part of any enterprise transformation, are also incorporated in the ERBS (Unhelkar and Dickens, 2008). In this section, the discussion is on the effect of each of these dimensions on green mobile business processes. These four dimensions work together in the environmentally conscious approach of an organization and, hence, not a separate and isolated addition to the business. The way in which mobile green processes are enacted by incorporation of mobility in to the business processes is also based on the increasing complexities of the processes as was discussed earlier. These are the broadcast, information, transactive, operative, and collaborative business processes. An understanding of this increasing complexity also provides opportunity, through the use of mobile technologies, to reduce corresponding carbon contents of these processes. Increasing complexity of transactions also implies an opportunity to reducing that complexity and, thereby, reducing carbon emissions in those processes.

■ Mobile-Broadcast—use of mobile technologies enables sending of one-way information to a large group of people who may or may not be registered as users. Such broadcast use of mobility, for example, is seen in providing traffic flow information to a group of mobile devices in a particular area. The opportunity to redirect traffic during a congested period has significant carbon connotations (as discussed by Bhalla and Chaudhary, 2011).
■ Mobile-Informative—use of mobility provides the organization with the ability to provide environment-related information to the various stakeholders within the business. There is a potential to collect contents on carbon emissions, temperature levels, and so on, from the organization's activities, and disburse them using mobile gadgets. Informative usage of mobility facilitates real-time update of the benchmarks set by the regulatory bodies on acceptable levels of carbon emissions for specific industries.

■ Mobile-Transactive—usage includes collection, collation, and reporting of environmental data with the use of handheld mobile as well as stationary but wireless devices. For example, the measurement of the temperature of a furnace or an engine can be conducted using wireless devices. This information is then further analyzed and used in order to manage, monitor, and control the corresponding system. Transactive capabilities of mobile or wireless devices can thus be put to good use to measure and monitor carbon emissions and report on those emissions to internal management and external regulatory bodies. Thus, transactive use of mobility has a greater opportunity to influence the environment positively, than the informative use of mobility.

■ Mobile-Operative—usage provides opportunities for the organization to model and optimize its internal processes that will produce environmentally friendly results. Examples of such initiatives include management of people in a way that reduces their unnecessary movement, virtualization of teams to enable dispersed team members to get together without travel, and enabling internal inventory management processes in a way that reduces the burden on the environment and reporting and optimization of these internal processes. Mobile telecommuting is a serious consideration for mobile-operative use by business, wherein workers need not be physically present at the premises of the company. The employees have an access to the environmentally intelligent systems which can help them carry out their day-to-day activities in an eco-friendly way.

■ Mobile-Collaborative—where organizations are influenced by their business partner's policies and strategies toward green environment. This influence results in a cluster or group of companies to have environmentally responsible policies that are not limited to the boundaries of a single organization. Instead, the mobile collaboration influences the entire "ecosystem" of companies that are together, dealing with each other using mobility. Collaborative environmental intelligence is also a futuristic topic that is discussed in Chapter 11.

Having thus discussed the gradually increasing complexity and influence of mobility on the environment, in this section, the four dimensions are also discussed from the environmental-mobile context.

Environmental–Economic Mobile Use

The economic influence of mobility needs to be considered here in terms of its relevance to the environment. For example, the economic reasons for transitioning to mobile business can be extended and discussed in terms of the economic reasons for transitioning to and managing a sustainable mobile business. The important economic factors of costs and competition for mobile transitions have a correlation with the environmental issues as well. Focusing on the environmental issues in the short term tend to occasionally give an impression that they will incur costs (such as costs of recycling gadgets or costs associated with modifying the mobile business processes). In the sustainable and long-term timeframe, however, these costs translates to goodwill and hence customer retention and growth. At an individual level too, economic attitude translate into environmental attitude (such as, for example, not throwing away old, out-of-date, and fashion mobile devices but reusing those mobile devices or their parts).

Apart from the mobile gadgets, there are also costs associated with creating and implementing environmental strategies and costs associated with maintaining them through environmental programs within the organization. Furthermore, economic considerations need be brought in with collaborating mobile businesses—in terms of their own budgets and willingness to spend money on environmental issues. Organizations are keen to promote their "green awareness" by providing part of their proceeds toward green activities. For example, the *Green broadband* from iPrimus, is a green initiative that, based on less than a dollar per month extra, encourages the customers and the service provider companies to participate in tree plantation activities that can compensate for the greenhouse emissions (www.iprimus.com.au).

Environmental–Technical Mobile Use

Millions of new mobile phones are bought each year worldwide under various reasons including the social reasons for the adolescent market (Unhelkar, 2009, METM). Mobile gadgets are environmental challenges both during manufacture and at disposal (Unhelkar and Dickens, 2008). Mobile gadget manufacturers can play a major role in reducing the environmental impact of mobile products by ensuring their products are free of hazardous materials such as brominated flame retardants (BFRs), PVCs, and heavy metals like lead, cadmium, and mercury. Beginning with their design, manufacturers can improve reuse and recycling of their mobile products, including the use of effective and responsible take-back and recycling that can be put to good use by the users. Mobile phones that can be recycled more effectively at end of life are more environmentally friendly than the ones that cannot be recycled. Regulatory approaches for product reuse and recycling can also be used.

Environmentally responsible mobile businesses apply the concept of reuse to the design and distribution of mobile gadgets as well. Technical designers seek to create mobile gadgets which will have minimum impact on the environment. This environmentally responsible design of mobile phone can reduce the amount of the materials used, reducing the impact of those materials and thereby increasing the efficiency of the use of the mobile phones with the customers. Nokia has released a model called "3110 Evolve" which is claimed to use "bio-cover"—the casing of the phone, which is composed of 50% recycled material and packaging made from 60% recycled material (http://www.compareindia.com). Furthermore, according to the specifications of the phone, this Nokia phone model also has a high-efficiency charger, as well as an eco-friendly user interface. Other attempts include the "Sunflower Phone" by Green Mobiles introduced in the United Kingdom that claims to be biodegradable as it has a built-in plant seed which will grow once the phone is planted in the ground.

In addition to the mobile devices, there is also a need to consider environmental issues through optimized use of other mobile hardware such as base stations, transmitters, and computer servers that support mobile applications. For example, an environmentally responsible mobile infrastructure will include appropriate location of mobile transmission towers to ensure minimal environmental impact on people and forests. The inherently complex issues of mobile infrastructure planning need further considerations due to challenges of environmental considerations.

Thus, mobility infrastructure planning becomes a crucial technical aspect of environmental planning for a mobile organization. Such infrastructure planning goes beyond a single organization and becomes an important part of the governmental initiatives, or that of the regulatory bodies. A major issue in the setting up of systems and architectures is to take into account the impacts of the mobility system on environmental and social quality (Borri et al., 2005).

Environmental–Process Mobile Use

As discussed earlier in this chapter, the way in which businesses operate can have a tremendous impact on the environment. The modeling, study, and optimization of business processes need to be undertaken from a mobile perspective. The potential of mobile devices to reduce people movement is obvious; this potential needs to be woven in the green business processes of an organization. A mobile worker who can access the information he needs at the location where he is, reduces physical and vehicle movement—making the business processes progress one successful step in going green.

Business intelligence (BI) processes can also make use of the wireless capabilities to implement, maintain, and sustain the environmentally intelligent business systems. IT has been thrust into limelight as a key element in advancing strategic business objectives and certainly mobile BI plays a major role in achieving these objectives. Therefore, IT must have its own set of mobile BI capabilities to maintain and sustain the overall environment (Imhoff, 2005).

Enterprises are looking to use mobility to extend the BI solutions that coordinate office, field, and home decision making. This extension of BI and its application to green business is termed environmental intelligence (EI) and has been discussed in detail in Chapter 6. Mobility equips users with real-time access to critical business applications, analytical application, decision-making systems, queries on performances, and customer data. Therefore, enterprises are looking to mobility solutions to extend their BI solutions to involve and coordinate office, field, and home decision making resulting in potentials for the communities. These improvements enable organizations to gain environmental advantage by optimizing mobile field and workforce.

The BI users (executives, analysts, financial planners, strategists, and field workforce) who are equipped with mobility are able to utilize their time and location free connectivity to reduce movements. Companies with a high number of mobile sales and service personnel in industries like retail, financial institutions like banks, healthcare, and manufacturing are using mobile technologies and EI in order to improve access of data and information to mobile workers.

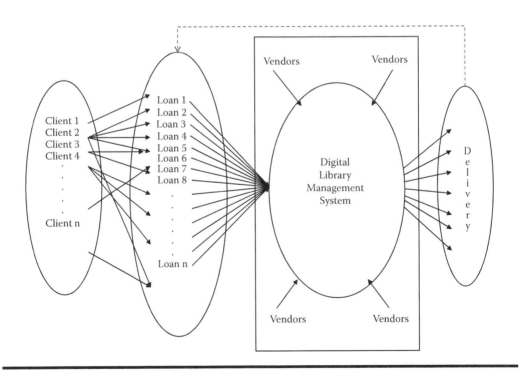

Figure 5.9 Example existing digital library—core business processes.

Environmental–Social Mobile Use

The social dimension of mobile technologies—particularly the devices and the social networks—relate to the environment in many ways. For example, the ability of personalized transmission of messages can be utilized in raising environmental awareness amongst specific users. Mobile businesses can also take additional social responsibilities by investing in communities that can be helped to learn, work, and thrive in a "green" environment. Mobile businesses can also facilitate mobile networking amongst interested groups of users on the issues of environment. For example, all transitioning organizations can setup green blogs that form an important part of the green initiatives of an organization. Blogs, wikis, and discussion groups can be an attractive way of creating and spreading social awareness of environmental issues. The free exchange of information amongst the participants between the readers can become an important part of public dialog on environmental matters (Dicum, 2006). According to Alex Steffen, founder of one of the most widely read green blogs, "Climate change has become a big issue. A lot of people are interested in green building, green fashion and green product design." Mobile businesses need to encourage and support these social networking opportunities, enabling users and customers to express their views and share innovative ways to go green.

Example—Digital Library GPR

Consider, for example, the reengineering of the processes of a digital library. The overall architecture of this digital library is shown in Figure 5.9. The clients approach the library through the loans processes, and the vendors update the offerings of the library. Figure 5.10 shows a detailed process flow of a digital library. The process can be divided into internal and external domain. Demand estimation, purchasing, catalog management, storage management, delivery management, disposal are some of system comprising the internal business process. Web search, physical search, loan service, return management, delivery management are some of the systems present in the external process. Apart from these, the reservation management and the circulation management overlaps between both the processes. On detailed analysis, some of these components can either be eliminated or consolidated.

For example, the physical search on the external process can be eliminated and replaced by an overall search system. Storage, reservation, and loan processing are closely coupled systems with numerous overlapping components. With intelligent reengineering applied, these could be designed as one central system to manage all these processes. The centralized system could either be maintained in-house or can be outsourced to external agencies or can be deployed into the Cloud environment. As a result of these various computing equipments can be disposed and for the remaining equipments, a high-end energy conservation panel could be applied, which can lead lower-carbon emissions. Also when deployed to external agency or to Cloud environment, the services could be offered to other digital libraries. This could reduce the number of systems which individual libraries have and reduce the overall carbon emissions cumulatively.

> Process reengineering in practice is based around three important elements: the roles, the activities performed by the roles, and the technologies that support the activities. For example, roles can include the client, supplier, and owner of the organizational processes that are all concerned with carbon. Activities include the check-in and check-out of items that are provided directly to clients. These are the steps that are merged or eliminated as part of Green BPR. Eventually, the supporting technology can move from the local data warehouse to, say, Cloud computing.

Finally, this chapter of green business processes concludes with a simple yet popular example of a digital library that loans or vends digital media for entertainment or informative purposes. The purpose of these examples is to show how the change in process can reduce carbon contents of that entire business.

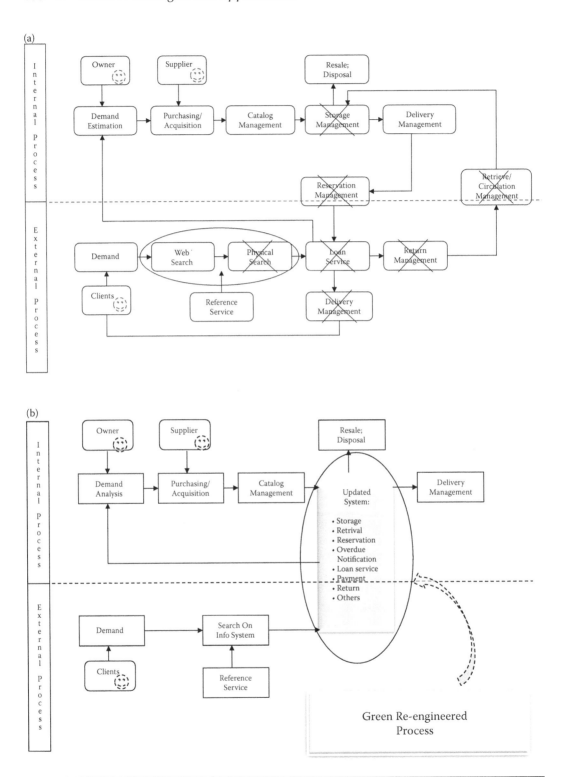

Figure 5.10   (a) Digital library GPR. (b) Digital library GPR—results.

The core processes of existing digital library deal with content vendors and clients. Content vendors supply digital contents and the library manage the catalog and digital content storages to serve clients. In this case, our focus point is the digital library itself for the Green BPR. The digital library has to acquire digital contents, manage inventories, manage delivery, and manage loan services. Some of these are in manual and physical form in the existing processes. The first stage in GPR is to model existing processes so that the holistic view of the digital library is presented. These flows of core processes are shown in Figure 5.10a, where manual activities and ineffective green processes are identified. This model is analyzed and relevant business rules are documented before starting to optimize those processes under the GPR effort.

The green business policies will help in rewriting the business rules related to digital library processes. Once the policies and rules are documented and necessary performance indicators are established, the core process can be re-engineered. These reengineered core processes are shown in Figure 5.10b. This figure shows extensive automation of processes and reduced number of manual processes. All these processes should be monitored through KPIs that are defined together with green business KPIs. These KPIs results will enable the business to gain more knowledge on the carbon footprint generation throughout the processes and helps to improve the digital library and make it green.

These green core processes for digital library could be mapped to the Green BPM factors which were shown in Figure 5.7. For example, carbon footprint by the storage facilities can be reduced by adopting a smart inventory management system. Enabling online search and lending services will reduce transport and thereby help to reduce the carbon generation. Adaptation of Cloud computing by the digital library can also help to reduce carbon generated down for the information storage and processing. This Green BPR will also enable people (clients, vender, and society) to adopt and comply with green business.

Conclusion

The business processes management is a vital component for an organization's operation. Reengineering the business process can help identify various aspects that can improve the overall efficiency of the organization. Infusing the "Green" component to the BPM can have tremendous impact on the environment. Eliminating redundant steps and consolidating various components into a centralized system can have myriad advantages. The money invested in the business process reduces as a result of eliminated and consolidated systems. Also with outsourcing, the maintenance cost for the organization is eliminated. Furthermore introduction of mobile devices for remote computing can offer various advantages. With careful strategic planning, this could be used for better process management and offer improvements to carbon emission levels.

Discussion Points

- What is Green BPM? Discuss the role Green BPM plays in the reduction of an organizational carbon footprint.
- What are the characteristics of a process and how do they apply to a green process?
- Explain how you understand individual, organizational, and collaborative processes. Discuss why individual green processes are short-term strategies, whereas collaborative green processes are long-term strategies.

- Discuss how "Green" BPR can improve organization's efficiency and aid in achieving better carbon efficiency.
- What is the relevance of process modeling in Green BPR? What techniques you would use to undertake green process modeling?
- Take any one phase of ITIL. Discuss how it is applied in the context of a green initiative.
- Discuss how to employ mobile technologies to reduce paper-based work and how to reduce the carbon footprint with careful planning.
- What are the advantages of Cloud computing in the context of Green IT? What are the challenges and risks associated with Cloud computing in the same context?

Action Points

- List the existing processes in your organization. Divide the list into individual/single user processes, departmental-organizational processes, and the ones that go beyond an organization and into the collaborative space where multiple organizations are involved.
- Apply a "rough" Green IT metric to ascertain the amount of carbon each of these processes are generating.
- Focus initially on the departmental-organizational processes as that is where the maximum carbon value will be derived.
- Rank the processes based on their carbon generation—highest carbon generators being listed on the top.
- Categorize them as broadcast, informative, transactive, operative, and collaborative processes.
- Undertake process modeling of the top five "transactive" business processes using BPMN, use cases or any other appropriate mechanism.
- Step through each activity/task of the process. Reengineer the processes to optimize them by combining activities.
- Eliminate activities that do not add value to the goals—or replace them with system supported services.
- Identify the individual processes (such as ones carried out by staff members) that are carbon intensive. These may also be categorized as operative processes that deal with the operations of the business.
- Model and optimize them by studying each activity, task, and deliverable within the process.
- Collaborative processes are the most challenging of all. In the initial attempt at Green BPR, collaborative processes should only be modeled as far as possible. Once collaborating partner organizations are on board, collaborative BPR can be applied to these processes from a carbon reduction/elimination viewpoint.

References

Addy, R. (2007). *Effective IT Service Management to ITIL and Beyond.* Berlin Heidelberg, Springer, pp. 89.

Beal, A. (2011). Role of business analysis in Green ICT. In B. Unhelkar, ed., *Handbook of Research in Green ICT*, pp. 42–50. IGI Global, Hershey, PA, USA.

Bhalla, I. and Chaudhary, K. (2011). Applying service oriented architecture and cloud computing for a greener traffic management. In B. Unhelkar, ed., *Handbook of Research in Green ICT*, pp. 332–347. IGI Global, Hershey, PA, USA.

Borri, D., Camarda, D., and Liddo. (2005). A De, Mobility in Environmental Planning: An Integrated Multi-Agent Approach. *Cooperative Design, Visualization, and Engineering published by Springer Berlin/ Heidelberg, Volume 3675/2005*, retrieved March 24, 2010, from http://www.springerlink.com/content/8r09mvbfq42glv26/

Hammer, M. and Champy, J. (1994). *Reengineering the Corporation: A Manifesto for Business Revolution.* HarperBusiness, Business Process Re-engineering (BPR) exercise by Hammer and Champy.

Hercheui, M. D. (2011). Using knowledge management tools in fostering Green ICT related behavior change. In Unhelkar, B., ed., *Handbook of Research in Green ICT*, pp. 290–300. IGI Global, Hershey, PA, USA.

ITIL (2009). What is ITIL?, APM Group Ltd. Available at http://www.itil-officialsite.com/AboutITIL/WhatisITIL.asp, accessed July 16, 2009.

Imhoff, C. (July 12, 2005). Business Intelligence Environments: The Need for Mobility, *Business intelligence networkTM*. Retrieved March 24, 2010 from http://www.b-eye-network.in/view- articles/1128

Murugesan, S. (2008). Harnessing Green IT: Principles and Practices. *IT Professional*, 10, (1), 24–33, Jan./Feb. IEEE.

Nott, D. (April 2010). Sustainability & Agility. Available at www.Alinement.net, accessed February 2, 2011.

Orr, K. (July 2007). Business process modeling fundamentals. *Cutter Executive Report* 10(7), Cutter, Boston, USA.

Philipson, G. (2010). ACS Report, "Carbon and Computers in Australia." Available at http://www.aiia.com.au/docs/AIIA%20and%20the%20ICT%20Industry/Green/ACS%20Carbon%20and%20Computers%20Energy%20Consumption%20and%20Carbon%20Report%200510.pdf

Silver, B. (2006). The ABCs of BPM. *Information Age* April 2006, http://www.infoworld.com/d/applications/abcs-bpm-807

Unhelkar, B. (2003). *Process QA for UML-based Projects*. Addison-Wesley, Boston, USA.

Unhelkar, B. (2003). "Understanding Collaborations and Clusters in the e-Business World," *We-B Conference* (HYPERLINK "http://www.we-bcentre.com" www.we-bcentre.com; with Edith Cowan University), Perth, Nov. 24–25, 2003.

Unhelkar, B. (2005). "Practical Object Oriented Analysis," *Thomson Publishing*, Australia, March, 2005. Pages 221; ISBN 0-17-012298-0 (Foreword by Prof. Houman Younessi, Rensselaer Institute of Polytechnic, Hartford, USA).

Unhelkar, B. (2008). Sourcing methods. *Cutter IT Executive Report*, 9(3).

Unhelkar, B. (2009). *Mobile Enterprise Transition and Management.* Taylor & Francis Group (Auerbach Publications), Boca Raton, FL, USA. 393 pages, ISBN: 978-1-4200-7827-5 (Foreword by Ed Yourdon, USA).

Unhelkar, B. and Dickens, Annukka. (2008). Lessons in implementing "Green" Business Strategies with ICT. In S. Murugesan, ed., *Cutter IT Journal, Special issue on "Can IT Go Green?"*, Vol. 21, No. 2, February 2008, pp. 32–39.

Unhelkar, B. and Ginige, A. (2010). A framework to derive holistic business transformation processes," Paper 44, *Proceedings of International Conference on E-Business*, 2010. Greece

Unhelkar, B. and Murugesan, S. (2010). "The Enterprise Mobile Applications Development Framework," Computer.org/ITpro, IEEE Computer Society publication, May/June 2010, pp. 33–39.

Unhelkar, B. and Tiwary, A. (2010). "Collaborative Intelligence" in *Cutter IT Journal* edited by Dave Higgins' Business Intelligence 2010: Delivering the Goods or Standing Us Up?- Vol. 23, No. 6, June 2010.

Unhelkar, B., Ghanbary, A., and Younessi, H. (2009). *Collaborative Business Process Engineering and Global Organizations: Frameworks for Service Integration.* IGI Global, Hershey, PA, USA, ISBN: 978-1-60566-689-1; 323 pp; (c) 2010.

Wiegers, K. E. (2006). *More about Software Requirements: Thorny Issues and Practical Advice.* Microsoft Press.

Chapter 6

Green Enterprise Architecture, Environmental Intelligence, and Green Supply Chains

I, Cyrus, the Emperor of Persia, say... Who keeps the earth cleansed, Appreciates rain, Respects Mother Nature and her kindness...

Cyrus the Great; circa 600 BC, first Zoroastrian Persian emperor

Key Points

- Enterprise architecture (EA) of the organization is extended with due consideration to the environment, resulting in a Green enterprise architecture (GEA).
- Importance and relevance of a GEA in an organization's transformation to a green organization. Various types of architectures within the enterprise, such as information architecture and solutions architecture, are discussed and their role in Green information systems (GIS) highlighted.
- Fundamentals of a Green solutions architecture (GSA)—the data, service, and interface tiers—are discussed.
- Discusses evolution of GSA to incorporate a collaborative green process model.
- Discusses the vital role of supply chain management (SCM) systems in the GEA and their evolution to a Green SCM.
- Equips Green SCM with mobile technologies to reduce carbon emissions in the supply chain process.
- Maps green contents to corresponding green functions and Green web services (GWS).
- Discusses green systems integration using service oriented architecture (SOA) using data, application, services, processes, and messaging.

■ Discusses systems integration amongst Green CRM, Green ERP/SCM, CEMS, and the Green regulatory portal.
■ Expands on the elements of a green information portal and describes the role of agencies, technologies, ontologies, and stakeholders in these green portals.
■ Develops in detail the concept of environmental intelligence (EI) including its evolving complexities—from data, information, and processes to knowledge and intelligence.
■ Relates EI architecture's implementation with Cloud computing/web services.
■ Relates mobile technologies to the overall GEA and presents the path to EI with mobile technologies.

Introduction

This chapter discusses enterprise architecture (EA) in the context of the green initiatives of an organization. The EA can be seen as an umbrella for all other architectures that form a part of the organization. These architectures together are meant to provide the business with stability and agility. These architectures also play an integral part in enabling the business to meet its specific goals. Therefore, despite many generic EA frameworks, most practical EA are organization specific. The EA defines relationships between the specific domain architectures and how the different architectures relate to each other and contribute to the overall enterprise (Rosen et al., 2011, HRG). When these architectural relationships are further investigated and developed from the point of view of their underlying carbon impacts, the end result is a Green enterprise architecture (GEA). A GEA is thus an EA that provides sound basis for the organization to transform its systems, applications, and processes that would eventually support a green organization. The enterprise-level architectural concepts are extended in GEA to provide long-term, strategic basis for updating the existing systems, procuring future systems, and integrating them into the day-to-day activities of the green organization. A GEA is also instrumental in providing technical constraints within which the organization must operate. In the absence of such constraints, the existing organizational systems and processes will encounter challenges, especially when they have to be integrated with the new Green information systems (GIS). These challenges are discussed in depth in this chapter.

With the help of an EA-based approach, the organization can define, assess, measure, analyze, report, and monitor the systems and processes that specifically deal with Green IT. In addition to providing constraints, this architectural approach to Green IT also results in the development of common terminologies that bring clarity, understanding, and consistency to the green enterprise initiative (based on Weill and Ross, 2004). Thus, using an architectural approach within the Green IT paradigm can facilitate the adoption of sustainability in an integrated way throughout an enterprise. Rosen et al. (HRG, 2011) have also described in detail such positive value and impact of EA on sustainable initiatives of an organization. Extending an EA to a GEA, and then using that GEA as a basis for transforming the systems, applications, and processes of an organization to a green one provide the following advantages:

■ An understanding of the existing systems, applications, and processes of the organization and its current technological capabilities and constraints
■ The relationship of the systems within the current EA to the new Green IT systems and applications (their development discussed in Chapter 7)

■ Alignment of existing and new infrastructure, operations, systems, and applications with each other and with the environmentally responsible business strategies (ERBS) of the organization in a synergetic manner (discussed in Chapter 2)

■ Creation and description of commonly used terminologies, semantics, and business rules relating to the organization as well as to its green initiative

■ Creation of specific Green IT frameworks, that are based on known architectural frameworks, are developed or ground up, specific to the organization (also discussed in Chapter 9—on transformation)

■ Holistic decision support by providing inputs from multiple dimensions of the organization's carbon performance and bringing together of otherwise disparate information together in a knowledge base—leading up to environmental intelligence (EI)

■ Provide basis for changes to the large applications supporting the organization—such as the CRM, SCM, HR, and financial applications—with particular emphasis on SCM

■ Reduce the risks associated with incorporating new carbon contents (such as carbon emissions and regulatory benchmarks) within the organization

■ Facilitate incorporation of service orientation architecture (SOA) and web services (WS) in green systems

■ Explore the possibilities of Cloud computing in Green IT that will not only improve the carbon footprint but also source and provide carbon contents from beyond the organization's systems

■ Enable the creation of GIS portals with corresponding models for green content providers and consumers

■ Evolution of business intelligence (BI) toward EI using data, information, processes, and knowledge associated with the organizational systems

■ Evolving the green contents and processes to collaborative green processes that go beyond organizational boundaries, through architectural models

■ Enhancing existing knowledge of the enterprise and using emerging technologies (such as Cloud, SaaS, SOA, and Web 2.0)

■ Incorporating mobile technologies with the evolving EI

An "enterprise" is a high-level, strategic view of the organization and an "architecture" implies a structured framework for the analysis, planning, and development of resources. SOA is a conceptual business architecture where business functionality or application logic is made available to SOA users or consumers as shared, reusable services on an IT network. An EA-based approach to Green IT helps reduce the risks in both technological and process dimensions. This is so because a GEA helps the organization visualize the impact of new carbon data, processes, and services on the existing systems. A GEA provides sound basis for development of GIS and portals.

Green Enterprise Architecture

The aim of a GEA is to develop an understanding of different viewpoints of business, technology, and the environment in which the business exists. This understanding also reduces the risks associated with the green transformation. Developing such an EA would imply an understanding and modeling of the business as well as technology space of the organization. For example, an EA would include a model of the way in which information is used by the business. This model can be a process flow or, at an abstract level, even a simple block diagram. Similarly, the solution architecture would model the technology space in the organization. This solution model would incorporate the Green resources, networks, their speeds and bandwidths, and the contents and applications. The GEA superimposes organizational and technical constraints on the information and solutions architecture. EA frameworks such as Zachman and TOGAF provide practical means of bringing technology and business together and providing a comprehensive way of modeling of an enterprise. For example, the Zachman framework provides a neatly laid 6 rows by 6 columns view of an enterprise. This view can be used in order to understand the business that is undergoing transformation. TOGAF also provides a technical architectural framework that can be used in green transformation.

The GEA can thus be made up of well-defined and reusable business and technical components that are put together to handle rapidly changing external business. GEA-based approach to Green IT is particularly helpful in understanding and integrating heterogeneous enterprise applications (that include internal legacy code and/or new software components that could be sourced as services and collaborative applications from business partners). This results in data integration, process integration across multiple systems, collaboration amongst internal and external business applications, and extension to real-time information using mobile technologies and systems. The end result is a unified view of the business that can be updated and tuned for a green enterprise. A GEA also incorporates interfaces to the organization's customers, suppliers, and other trading partners.

These interfaces include the technical interfaces (Green web services) as well as people-to-people interactions (between business leaders, and also workers). Suppliers and partners of the organization need to comply with all environmental laws and regulations as much as the organization itself. However, sometimes it can become challenging for an organization to enforce compliance on its suppliers. A GEA can be used as a basis for technical assistance (e.g., training, CEMS implementation, policy interpretation) that can help suppliers to conform with the regulations and standards. Similarly, a good GEA also helps the customers by providing them with the necessary Green web service interfaces, promoting the organization to them and assisting the corporate customers to setup their own GEA.

GEA is also crucial in providing technical basis for development and implementation of a GIS. The development of GIS (also called Carbon Emissions Management Software, CEMS), are discussed in greater detail in the next chapter. These GIS provide the organization with software system level support in measuring, monitoring, and reporting carbon data. However, in most cases—especially with large organizations—GIS are a combination of implementing a new software system, together with significant upgrade of and integration with existing systems. Thus, typically, the following activities are undertaken, with help and support of a GEA when it comes to GIS in an organization:

- Integration of new systems with existing organizational systems (typically ERP packages, CRM) using SOA-WS interfaces
- Modification of existing data structures to accommodate new carbon data elements and related contents associated with a Green IT hardware and other carbon-emitting assets
- Conversion of existing organizational data in a new format that will enable use of that data in calculating carbon emissions after the organization has transformed
- Populating parts of data and systems with external carbon data (such as regulatory requirements/standards/benchmarks)
- Evolution of existing decision support and knowledge management systems toward environmentally intelligent systems
- Creation of a suite of green services using SOA and WS
- Applying mobile technologies to provide location-independence and personalization to GIS interfaces with green information portals that facilitate collaboration
- Quality assurance and testing of Green info systems

Views of Green Enterprise Architecture

A comprehensive GEA encompasses an understanding of the various views of the organization and its interrelationships. Figure 6.1 shows these various architectural views together with the key functionality and the roles that hold primary responsibility within those views. The Green information architecture (GIA), shown in upper half of Figure 6.1, primarily deals with the models of information capture and information provisioning to both external and internal parties in the business space. The information architect and the business analyst work in this space identifying and modeling the information requirements. The GIA describes the enterprise from a business perspective. This architecture is developed based on the business requirements in the "problem space" and takes into account the strategies and policies of the organization (Unhelkar, 2003). The GIA identifies the basic functional requirements that are modeled in the context of the Green IT strategies, processes, applications, and IT governance of the enterprise. This would result in a prioritized suite of functional and operational requirements that become part of the green transformation program. Green solution architecture appearing in the lower half of the architectural spaces, deals with the design and development of systems from a technical perspective. This solutions architecture primarily handles models and implementation of contents, networks, applications, their testing, and deployment.

The solution architect predominantly works in this space supported by the systems analysts and developers. Finally, the all encompassing GEA, depicted in the background in Figure 6.1, provides the constraints across all the systems and applications. The GEA also influences both the information and solution architecture models. These three form the basic enterprise architectural views of the organization. There are many other additional architectural views of the organization. Rosen et al. (2011, HRG) have described different architectural domains such as the business

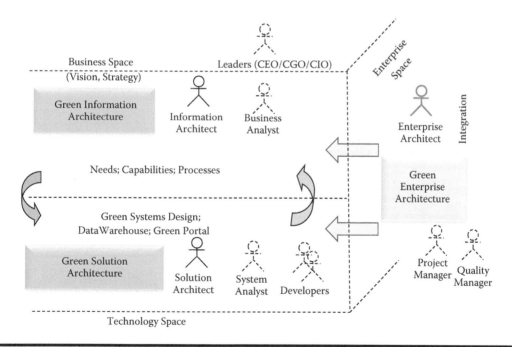

Figure 6.1 Various views of a comprehensive Green enterprise architecture: Business, technology, and enterprise spaces.

architecture, information architecture, application architecture, technology architecture, and operational architecture. They have also added performance architecture, which has been added for the sake of accountability and continual improvement to the enterprise and is meant to cut across all other domain architectures. The overall GEA encompasses all of these architectures and provides constraints, limitations, and requirements for each of these architectural domains. For example, in Figure 6.1, the GIA domain deals with the needs and capabilities of the organization, the technical-solution space with the implementation of green portals and data warehouses, and the background-enterprise space with the integration and constraint models that are also super-imposed on the information and solution architecture. The project manager and quality manager support the architectural work by helping in formulating and scoping Green IT projects and using appropriate and matured standards and processes.

Green Enterprise Architecture—Categories of Requirements

The GEA is not an independent entity per se. While a GEA deals with constraints, compliance, integration performance, and security issues, it also influences both—the GIA in the business space and the GSA in the technology space. Thus, the activities with GEA span the problem, solution, and background space.

Figure 6.2 expands and groups the various activities that form part of the overall green architecture of the enterprise. The activities that deal with the business and information aspect of the organization are primarily the requirements; the ones that are in the solution space are related to the data and applications; and the overall GEA that provides the constraints and is in the background space. It should be stressed, however, that the GEA shown in the background in Figure 6.2 is not a separate entity.

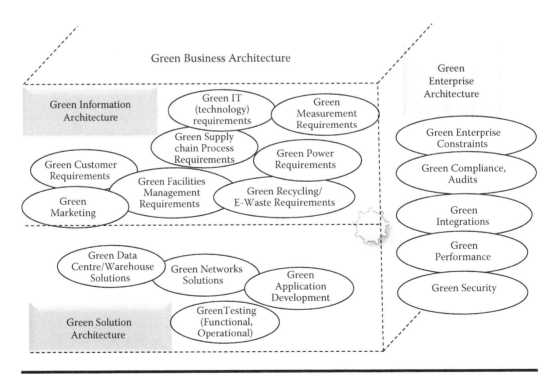

Figure 6.2 Categories of requirements in the various green architectural spaces.

The GEA in the background is influencing and influenced by the GIA as well as the GSA from the problem and the solution space respectively.

The GIA provides the basis for using enterprise applications, processes, and contents. The semantics for the master data including the green data are defined and the operational and analytical information is modeled in this architectural space. The requirements that influence the information architecture come from the business, information, and enterprise domains. This information architecture provides the context for facilitating integration across various applications. The information architecture also outlines the processes for capturing and modeling requirements. The information architecture also contains a repository of overall applications and their interrelationships. A good understanding of this interrelationship can help eliminate redundancy and eventually also contribute to the reduction of resources.

- Green customer requirements that are based on the demands of the customer for green products and services.
- Green marketing requirements that promote the organizations green products and services.
- Green supply chain process requirements that interface with the suppliers systems.
- Green technical requirements that are specifying the technologies that are needed to handle the Green IT initiative.
- Green facilities management requirements that describe the building and facilities infrastructure and the approach for measuring and reducing their carbon. The design and construction of facilities (Chapter 4) are important here.
- Green metrics and measurement requirements that specify the elements to measure and report.
- Green recycling and e-waste management requirements that deal with the one-off disposal of assets.

The GSA includes the models of technologies and infrastructure required to support applications, operations, and reporting requirements in the information space. These solutions architecture needs to cater for distribution, scalability, reliability, device support, security, and application integration (Rosen et al., 2011). The infrastructure is also a primary contributor to carbon emissions. Thus, this is a two pronged approach is the solution space use of IT to reduce emissions and reduce the IT domain's emissions.

- Green data center design and solutions relates to the building and facility requirements that are IT specific.
- Green content strategies that are influenced by the backup, mirroring, and so on.
- Green networks and architecture solutions that provide the communication hardware.
- GIS programming solutions that relate to green information and solution.

The background space architecture deals with constraints, compliances, integration, performance, and security. This provides a consistent mechanism to define, collect, analyze, and report on metrics (e.g., KPIs at the business level, paper utilization at the application level, and server and power utilization at the technology level).

- Green enterprise-level constraints that span across both information and solution
- Green compliance requirements that are dictated by the regulatory portals
- Green systems integrations (SOA based)

- Green performance (KPI that are related to all dimensions—discussed in Chapter 3)
- Green security deals with carbon data, storage, transmission, and its interfaces with other data

Green IT and Organizational Systems

A GEA provides various views of the organization and its systems. These views reflect the effect of changes in one area of the organization on the other areas and systems. This view enables an overall understanding of the impacts of the charges and thereby reduces the risks associated with changes to the systems and operations of the organization as a result of the green initiatives.

In the previous chapter, Figure 5.5 provided a mapping of the organization's systems to its business processes. Figure 6.3 further expands on those impacts, and shows the significant areas of organization systems affected by changes due to Green IT processes. Figure 6.3 also summarizes this impact of Green IT transformation on the infrastructures and portals of the organization. On the left, in Figure 6.3, are the typical IT systems that are affected by the change. These include the existing systems that need to change, and also the changes associated with the new GIS's implementation.

A good GEA is a mechanism to incorporate the changes associated with Green IT transformation on the right in Figure 6.3 into the systems and processes on the left. The changes to the systems are as follows:

Organizational Systems

These are the core systems that are primarily internal to the organization. For example the typical CRM, SCM, and Payroll applications that need to be updated with the new carbon data and that also need to be integrated with the GIS/CEMS. SOA provides basis for these integration.

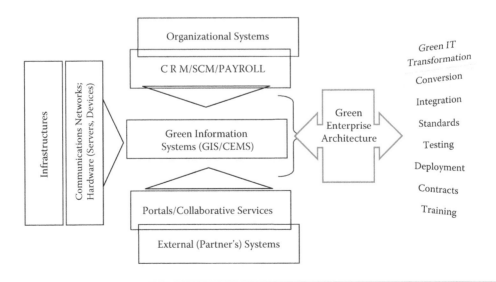

Figure 6.3 Green enterprise architecture helps in handling the impact of Green IT transformation on the rest of the organizational systems.

External Systems

These are not just systems external to the organization, but also external interfaces of the organizational systems. These external systems and interfaces belong to the green organizational portals that relate with the regulatory portals, and also the collaborative services offered and consumed by the organization.

Infrastructure

These are the communication Networks and Servers (discussed in Chapter 4).

These are the IT-specific infrastructures of the organization as against building and facilities. They change to replace existing carbon-intense equipments and also provide basis for GIS/CEMS communication and integration.

On the right, in Figure 6.3, are the various IT areas that need to be handled when an organization embraces Green IT. These are as follows:

- *Conversion* of some of the existing data that will ensure it works well with the new carbon data. Some applications and interfaces may also require conversion to a potential new format (e.g., XML interfaces that have to now deal with carbon data exchange with other data).
- *Integration* of data with applications, as well as across applications that are both existing business applications as well as new carbon-specific applications.
- *Standards* dealing with web service interfaces at technical level and ISO standards applies to the systems at organization level. The technical standards assist in the conversion of data and interfaces, whereas the business standards enable streamlining of business processes.
- *Testing* of new applications and their interfaces—requiring a suite of carbon test data to test the functionality and operational aspects of the systems and their integration.
- *Deployment* of new applications—especially as the CEMS are most likely to be SaaS-based deployments using Cloud computing.
- *Contracts* that implement policies in SOA and SLAs. Electronic contracts becoming prominent when green organizational portals deal with other external portals of partnering organizations and regulators.
- *Training* of users as well as support personnel for the new green applications, in terms of how to use their metering capabilities, recording, and analysis of carbon data and identifying the trends in carbon emissions.

Green Solutions Architecture

The transformation of the organization to a green enterprise entails changes to its systems. These systems and applications are part of the solution space.

Each of the groups of systems shown in Figure 6.3 will undergo change in their three basic areas—data, services, and interfaces. These basic areas are the same as those of a fundamental 3-tiered architecture in an IT system. They are discussed here with consideration to green-specific issues.

Figure 6.4 highlights these basic considerations in a GSA. These are the data, services, and interfaces that are affected as follows:

- Data: changes here deal with creation of new carbon data and modification of existing enterprise data. For example, the SCM will change its list of inventory to include carbon

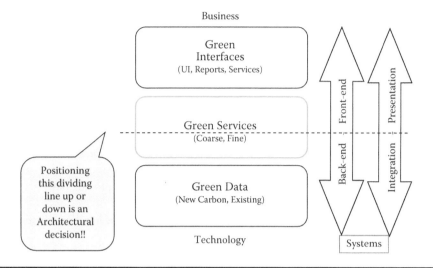

Figure 6.4 Fundamental considerations of a Green solutions architecture.

emission record for a particular asset. This new data element will have to be read and used by the reporting modules. These green carbon data reside in the back-end of the GSA, and present the challenge of integration. This would involve building interfaces or wrappers around legacy systems to include green data in the reporting modules.

◾ Services: These include the functions, applications, and their use in analyzing green data. Services plot trends, estimate emissions, enable reporting, and create opportunities for collaboration. Services can be coarse or fine, depending on their reuse requirements. The coarse or fine level of modeling and amount of services that need to be exposed externally is a solutions architect's decision. This decision is shown as dotted line across green services in Figure 6.4.

◾ Interfaces: These are primarily the display mechanism of the services and applications. Figure 6.4 shows three interfaces as graphic user interfaces (GUI), the reporting and related physical interfaces, and the web service interfaces. They form the front-end of the GSA and enable personalization of services.

Figure 6.4 further highlights the solutions architect's views of the data, services, and interfaces. This view predominantly handles integration challenges at back-end of the system, and presentation challenges at the front-end.

For example, the organizational data residing in its existing ERP systems has to be modified to accommodate carbon calculations and, at the same time, this data has to be integrated with new suite of CEMS data. Occasionally, an entire new version of ERP software, fully equipped with carbon data and calculations can be procured to replace existing systems. Design and development of GIS/CEMS that promotes compatibility with existing ERP systems can provide significant advantages in implementing GIS. Analyzing how market leaders for ERP software store and manage data would help CEMS/GIS to take advantage of the already existing ERP data and minimize data transformation changes during integration.

Figure 6.5 reflects the viewpoints of the respondents in the survey corresponding to the use of ERP software for environmental purposes in the organization. Participants were asked to rate

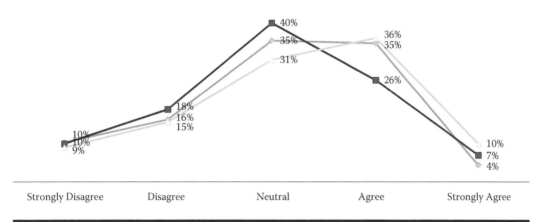

Figure 6.5   ERP software—organizational action.

their views on modifying existing ERP software versus buying a new and external ERP package that will handle all environmental needs of the organization. As seen in Figure 6.5, 36% (agree) and 10% (strongly agree) went for modification of existing ERP packages, as against 26% (agree) and 7% (strongly agree) for buying external packages. This response indicates that participants felt that greater effort would be required in implementing new ERP packages that can handle the environmental issues as against modification of existing packages. This effort can include conversion, integration, and deployment issues. There was also some support for external help in implementing a Green ERP as against carrying out the implementation in-house.

The green transformation board (discussed in Chapter 9), lead by the CGO (discussed in Chapter 3), will have to use this information to decide the green strategy. Usually, the final organizational action will be a combination of the various options shown in Figure 6.5.

Evolving Green Systems Architecture

Figure 6.6 shows how basic systems architecture evolves into a more complex and a collaborative green process-based architecture. The basic architecture, discussed earlier in Figure 6.4 is shown in Figure 6.6 as evolving to a suite of linear green process, which eventually becomes a suite of collaborative green processes that make use of the concepts of SOA and WS.

A GEA has evolved from a basic base 3-tiered architecture, to a collaborative green process architectures. The data, services, interfaces, and security apply to existing and new green processes in a collaborative manner.

The linear green processes would be the typical business processes such as customer, supplier, and accounting. Linear processes also include totally new green processes within the organization such as counting carbon PPM. These are, however, all organization-specific linear processes—and were discussed in detail in Chapter 5. The collaborative processes on the right will include the data, services, interfaces, and security that encompass all the aforementioned processes that are

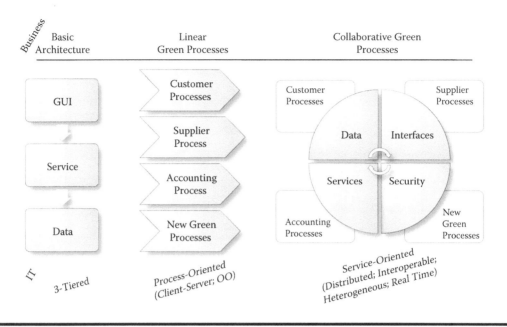

Figure 6.6 Evolving Green systems architecture: Basic to linear process and then collaborative process-based architecture.

now interconnected through WS. These collaborative processes are both internal and external to the organization. For example, the customer processes are modified internally, through their data models, to reflect the carbon in a particular sale of product or service. When that customer process is exposed as a WS, the modifications are to the interfaces of the CRM—an external impact. Similarly, the service offering of a supplier may include the guarantee of a certain carbon emission during the operation of an equipment supplied (e.g., a green monitor). That carbon emission limit, supplied by the WS of the supplier, is internalized for comparison against actual emission. When a complete green enterprise transformation takes place, collaboration of the organization with suppliers and customers is inevitable. Therefore, apart from being a technical issue, this relationship with business partners also becomes a social issue. The green initiatives and enthusiasm shown by the organization needs to be shared by its suppliers and customers to achieve the overall objective of the transformation.

Aspects of Green Solutions Architecture

The GSA brings about a synergy of technologies that can enable efficient use of IT resources. Thus, the resources are themselves used efficiently and, in turn, these IT resources provide the basis to enhance the efficiency of the rest of the equipments and processes in the organization. While Chapter 4 focused primarily on the user devices, this discussion is all encompassing in terms of the solutions technologies that can be used in the solutions space.

Sherringham (HRG, 2011) has discussed in detail the impact of Green IT solutions on the green enterprise. The Green IT solutions deal with internal carbon recording, reporting of carbon externally, implementation of SaaS-based solutions, collaborative green services and also

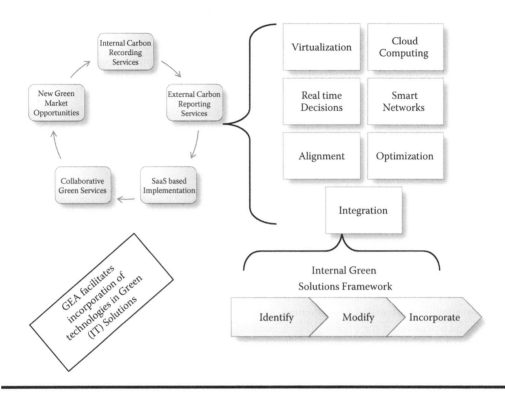

Figure 6.7   Various aspects of a Green solutions architecture.

technology-based opportunities for new green services. These are shown on the left in Figure 6.7. In order to deal with the aforementioned impact, the solution space of the enterprise uses many technologies. GEA facilitates incorporation of technologies in the Green IT solutions by providing the right interfaces and models. Figure 6.7, on the right shows these technologies as virtualization, Cloud computing, real-time decision making, smart network management, self healing, alignment, integration, and optimization (extending Sherringham, HRG, 2011). The solutions space has its own internal Green IT framework that encourages the solutions architects and the systems analysts to continuously identify new and emerging technologies, model them to examine their repercussions, and eventually incorporate in the overall architecture of the organization. The solution space technologies are all affected by the identify-modify-incorporate phases. These technologies are further expanded below:

Cloud Computing

The Cloud, as mentioned in Chapter 4, is a significant technology in the solution space. Cloud computing is already in use and, yet, there are many emergent aspects of it (they are discussed in Chapter 11). Identification and incorporation of Cloud-based solutions bring about immediate change in the carbon emissions of large data centers. This is so because, through the use of the Cloud, data and applications that were stored and executed within the data servers now transcend the organizational boundaries. The organizational data together with the new and updated green solutions data is stored and executed externally. Cloud computing in the solution space leaves the organization to deal only with the remaining end-user computing devices and therefore limited carbon responsibility. However, this arrangement does shift the infrastructure outside the organization—so the *overall* emissions, calculated collectively between the Cloud and the organization, may still be substantial. It is important, therefore, in a Cloud computing scenario, to explicitly discuss and document in the service contract the sharing of carbon emissions resulting from this shift in the infrastructure. It is only when the carbon responsibility is shared appropriately amongst the users and providers of Cloud computing that the overall reduction in carbon can be ascertained. However, since the Cloud merges the infrastructure across many organizations, it results in assured delivery of service and the sharing of risks—eventually leading to an overall green advantage.

Virtualization

This solution space technology was also discussed in detail in Chapter 4. As a part of the solutions architecture, however, virtualization provides the basis for consolidation of the data center's hardware that reduces the overall carbon emissions of the organization. Virtualization, as its name suggests, creates multiple operating views on the same physical machine resulting in much reduced use of hardware than if the servers were all physical. Carbon performance requirements from virtualization should be identified, documented, and measured in accordance with the overall green strategies and objectives of the organization (discussed in Chapter 2). A green solution architecture will ensure, though, that the specific virtualization technologies are able to operate along with the new, SaaS-based implementations of the new systems.

Smart Networks

Smart networks and their management make use of automated devices, sophisticated switch management, optimized network operations and real time reporting of the network performance. Efficient network operations assure delivery at lower cost and improved environmental footprint. Further interesting developments in both the wired and wireless network architecture is the ability of these networks and communications devices to self diagnose. As a result, these networks are able to make corrections to their links and thereby provide uninterrupted operations. Sherringham (2011, HRG) highlights how upgrading the organization's communication networks can not only assure service delivery, lower operational costs, but also create a smaller environmental footprint. Incorporating the self-healing capabilities of the networks in the green solutions space creates opportunities for network efficiencies in operations and thereby, reduces the overall carbon emissions of the organization.

Real-Time Decision Making

Real-time decision making in the solution space is based on availability and delivery of information precisely and in the context of the need of the user. Such real-time delivery of information is primarily achieved through mobile technologies, devices, and applications (Unhelkar, 2009). Incorporation of mobile computing capabilities in the GSA provides two distinct yet interrelated advantages: (a) augments the real-time aspect of decision making. Such decision making also frees up staff to spend more time on value-added services. Travel times are reduced with associated environmental impact; and (b) improved ability to understand and interpret carbon data and information that can be used to fine-tune the performance of the organization in real time to reduce the carbon emissions.

Alignment

Alignment of data, processes, and interfaces is an architectural issue in the solution space that focuses on reducing the friction within and amongst the systems. Ideal Green IT solutions, therefore, can be understood as absence of contradictions amongst data, processes, and interfaces. Ghose and Biliau (2011, HRG) have further developed these ideas of alignment by highlighting how an optimization architecture can help an organization align with its carbon footprint minimization. They have further described the need to understand how to measure (or monetize) the trade-offs between the local objectives of an optimizing factor and the global (carbon mitigation) objective of the organization. This factor focuses the attention on modeling and investigating the impact of changes in data, processes, and interfaces in one aspect of the systems on the rest of the systems and the organizational functioning. Green IT systems need to be aligned with the existing organizational systems in order to have the desired positive impact of carbon reduction. If Green IT systems are themselves not aligned, they will create the friction mentioned above—resulting in waste of organizational energy.

Optimization

Optimization is closely associated with alignment and deals with the alignment of the solution technologies such as the servers, applications, and databases. Optimization, in the GSA, is the choice amongst possible alternative solutions that are aligned with the carbon footprint minimization objective of the organization. Thus optimization includes mechanisms to incentivize an agent to adopt behavior that is potentially suboptimal relative to its own objectives, in the interests of the global objective (Ghose and Billau, HRG, 2011).

Integration

This is a major activity in the green solutions space that works across two technological areas: (a) integration of carbon data with green services and interfaces within an application; and (b) integration amongst the different applications themselves. Integration in the GSA is a detailed activity that requires independent discussion as undertaken next.

Contents and Integration with Service-Oriented Architecture

An important challenge in the solution space relating to green technologies is the rapidity and complexity of carbon-specific changes. These changes primarily relate to carbon contents that comprise the data in terms of emissions and regulatory benchmarks, as well as strategic information on what a collaborative group of companies are doing and performing in terms of their carbon credentials. These carbon data are going to be a mix of existing data that is modified as well as new carbon data. Similar to the challenge of exposing the legacy of COBOL and ISAM data to the Internet-based user, this challenge of green data management also requires substantial interfaces and integration. The technology of WS together with the concept of SOA needs to be discussed in this context. Services are self-contained (and usually

Integration is a major challenge in implementing new GIS. Service orientation with WS is the answer. The SOA approach breaks down large software applications and systems into sets and subsets of smaller, manageable components called services. These services then provide the building blocks of many different kinds of business applications and business processes. They can thus be used for creation of Green IT services and applications.

object-oriented) software components that have well-defined interfaces. Information systems based on the concept of offering and consuming of services are considered service oriented in nature. Therefore, a software architecture that comprises many self-contained services and which process data and information through the interfaces of these services is known as SOA. SOA enables most software applications to easily offer and publish, as well as locate and consume services.

SOA, in the solution space, utilizes web services (WS) to provide the basis for information systems architecture that assimilates software contents and corresponding software components. The core content and their wrapping by the functions are shown in Figure 6.8. The contents, however, are sourced from myriad places including internal and external contributors such as employees, customers, and users as well as the various regulatory governmental bodies. WS take these functions further and expose them over the Internet. As a result, green solution architectures that incorporate WS-based applications open up opportunities for the contents to be received and exported globally through collaborative WS. These collaborative WS interfaces are dynamically created, consumed, and dispersed. This exchange of green contents includes exchange of core data types belonging to the GIS, message formats, and communication protocols. WS-based interfaces enable exchange of information irrespective of the specific platform or vendor specifications. This enhanced ability of information systems to connect and communicate with each other leads to a collaborative opportunity for green enterprises. This is based on the fact that all green-specific software entities are now able to interact with each other over the Internet irrespective of their underlying platforms.

Services lend themselves to reuse and integration in many different ways. The characteristics of these services with respect to a collaborative business model are (a) self-contained so that they are able to process data and information within themselves, (b) having a well-defined interface with the intention that inputs to and outputs from these services can be easily understood, and (c) available for communication—that is they are Internet enabled.

The ability of executable services being made available across different communication channels enhances collaboration. This services-based approach also results in overall less software code, lower cost of developing and deploying software solutions, and increased standardization

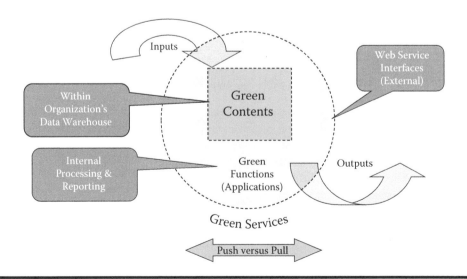

Figure 6.8   Sourcing and dissemination of green contents through functions and services.

(Hazra, 2007). Such SOA approach together with the use of Web as more than mere communication tool (i.e., Web 2.0) facilitates communicating, connecting, collaborating, and expressing information in new ways.

SOA provides opportunities for integration of various business applications at the enterprise level. An example of the practical application of SOA in green integration is shown in Figure 6.9. This figure shows four major groups of applications that are benefitted by a service-oriented approach to the GEA.

- CEMS—has to deal with new green (carbon) data, as well as modeling and implementation of new green services. The data and information are then processed and are available to other services that are calling them.
- Green CRM—primarily deals with modification of data models that will accommodate the elements of carbon emissions in them. Mostly external.
- Green SCM/ERP—also has to deal with modification of data models that will enable inventories and other operational information to be expanded to include carbon data.
- Regulatory—deals with the legal and other compliance aspects that are provided by the relevant authorities through a regulatory portal through a web service.

SOA potentially frees up the organizational resources to focus on optimizing its carbon performance rather than the underlying technologies and systems. Each service has three basic features (Hazra, 2010) of a service: modularity, granularity, and loose coupling. Modularity enables carbon data to be properly encapsulated and then exchanged with other data and systems; granularity of a service deals with the level of abstraction incorporated in a service; and, finally, loose coupling

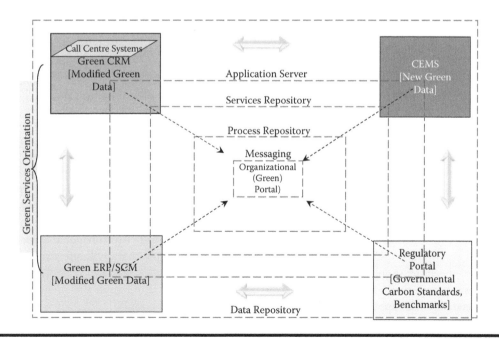

Figure 6.9 Detailed Green-SOA (this figure is a 3-dimensionsal top view with the center part of the figure indicating height).

separates services from each other, thereby enabling implementation of GIS without disturbing the existing services that support the business flows. Enabling easy sharing and exposure of information, SOA allows well-defined message formats to exchange data. Figure 6.9 further shows these various layers of repositories in a SOA:

■ Data repository is made up of data that belong to each of the four groups of systems. The data repository integration should be kept to minimum, as existing data will require substantial effort.
■ Application server that enables data to be analyzed.
■ Services repository that provides storage, consumption, and exposure of WS. Services, thus, encapsulate application logic with a defined set of interfaces and make these interfaces publicly available.
■ Process repository that creates processes based on services.
■ Messages that eventually provide the integration amongst the various layers of a SOA. These messages form the building block of support for collaboration and coupling of remote resources.

Green Supply Chain Management

Green supply chain systems, especially with mobile technologies incorporated in them, are a major component of GEA. They reduce inventories, costs, and carbon. However they require contract negotiations. SCM have evolved rapidly to automate and optimize the lifecycle of material procurement. Similarly, SCM are also integral to procurement and use of equipments and corresponding infrastructure. (Lan and Unhelkar 2005) Integration with supply chains has also been studied resulting in integrated SCM (ISCM). Unhelkar and Lan (2011) have extended the concept of ISCM to incorporate environmental considerations within them resulting in Green integrated supply chain management (GISCM) that brings together various stakeholders in the supply chain within and outside the organization.

Supply chain management (SCM) systems are an integral part of organization's systems, as was shown earlier in Figure 6.3. Therefore, they deserve specific attention when the GEA is discussed. Figure 6.10 highlights the results from the Trivedi and Unhelkar (2010) survey that depicts this importance of various aspects of a supplier relationship and their environmental responsibility. The need to bring together the suppliers, customers, employees, and senior management in order to produce an integrated and efficient supply chain that will reduce carbon emissions cannot be overstated. The SCM of an organization needs to be analyzed, planned, and optimized for sourcing and deliveries in an environmentally conscious manner. All modern-day supply chain systems are web-based. Undoubtedly, these electronic (Internet-based) systems deliver the enterprises with a competitive advantage by opening up opportunities to streamline processes, reduce costs, increase customer patronage, and enable thorough planning abilities. SCM thus includes geographical, relational, environmental considerations between buyer and supplier. Green issues require further attentions as different legislations apply to the integrated supply chain management (ISCM) across regional boundaries. Cross-borders logistics, culture, language, and economic and regulatory climate are additional considerations which can affect the integration of business processes between regional offices and external organizations. One ill-performing participant in the supply chain will affect the performance of the entire supply chain (Strausl, 2001).

These characteristics of a good ISCM now need to be converted to handle the environmental issues related to the supply chain. Following are the advantages of GISCM:

■ Reduction in unwanted inventory through accurate identification of material requirements within the integrated process leads to reduced storage space and less materials resulting in corresponding carbon savings.

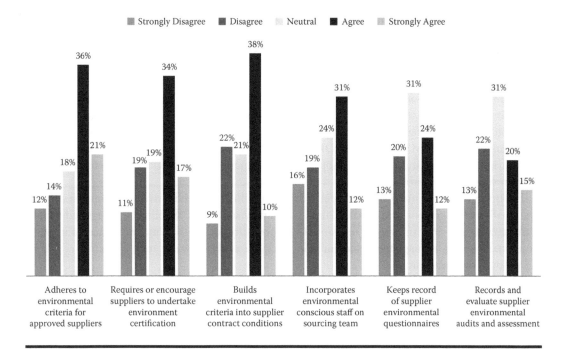

Figure 6.10   Organization's supply chain and procurement management.

- Improved usage of infrastructure/equipment through sharing of resources reduces number of equipments and infrastructure needed.
- Reduction in carbon overhead relating to material transfer and storage.
- Optimize the number of people that need to handle material on their way to the end customer, thereby reducing the carbon content of that process.
- Eliminate business processes that do not add direct value to the most optimum movement of goods, thereby reducing carbon.
- "Buy-in" from customers by enabling them to provide input into the design and manufacturing of the goals or services that can be based on green initiatives.
- Real-time integration and improved logistics of distribution centers reduces carbon.
- Planning the demand and supply, management of infrastructure planning, and planning the production includes environmental consciousness and metrics.
- Sourcing of materials, services, maintenance of catalogs, collaborative supply management of electronic payments are integrated and measured to ensure reduction in carbon.
- Integration in supply chain enables optimum product lifecycle management, demand planning, production management, and event management. These activities are improved with reduced carbon as they are all integrated together with the production, quality assurance, packaging, and distribution.
- Disposal of electronic waste and consumed products is handled much better with integrated supply chains and systems.
- Improved and effective handling of returns from customers, especially as the organization that provides the material in the supply chain is in the best position to also accept returns from customers.

Mobility in Green Supply Chain Management

Mobile technologies in SCM enables business transactions to be location independent, reduces unnecessary inventory and transportation of material (Unhelkar, 2009). Thus, a mobile not only adds value to the businesses but also opens up opportunity that enable the organization to handle environmental issues. For example, the mobile flow of information can create greater sourcing opportunities for raw materials and their locations—resulting in long-term effects such as reduction in stocks and holding costs (see Borri et al., 2005 for an interesting early discussion on mobile and green). The WS (XML, SOAP, UDDI, and WSDL) standards on mobile gadgets can simplify information exchange and optimize supply chain business processes within the enterprise and between supply chain partners.

Environmentally sound processes together with mobility can be effective in vendor assessment, total quality management, lean and collaborative supply strategies. Mobility in integrated supply chains enable real-time analysis of relevant consumer attitudes, legislation, and concepts in environmentally sound management that includes lifecycle analysis, waste management, recycling, and product procurement.

Mobile supply chain management (MSCM) can bring together, dynamically, factors such as number, location, and size of warehouses; corresponding distribution centers and facilities; and relationships with distributors and customers. MSCM bring together technology infrastructure, demand planning, forecasting, sourcing, production, logistics, scheduling, inventory, and transportation that are also supported by mobile devices.

MSCM can also use radio frequency identification devices (RFIDs) to improve material handling in distribution logistics. At individual customer levels, shipping, receiving, and store deliveries are also improved through mobility resulting in optimized business processes and reduced carbon emissions.

There are numerous applications of mobility in SCM that can help an organization in its carbon reduction effort. For example, in case of the organization's transport and fleet logistics, mobile technologies help improve and optimize processes such as mobile rerouting, mobile order tracking, mobile package tracking, instant messaging, exception alerts, vehicle tracking, mobile reporting, fuel tax calculations, GPS, route, and vehicle information and integration to various data collection devices. The resultant improvement in efficiency and accuracy in logistics and material handling would all also reduce the carbon contents of these processes.

Mobility solutions and services in the SCM ensure that supply chain information and statistics will be accessible to the organization on an anywhere, anytime basis. This results in reduction in carbon together with an increase in productivity, customer satisfaction, and employee satisfaction.

Building Environmental Criteria into Supplier Contract Conditions

GISCM can include environmental criteria within its contracts. These contracts can be at multiple levels. For example, a supplier agrees to sign a contract that requires it to produce and supply a gadget that has a specified, low-carbon emission. This would be a one-off action. However, then the contract at the next distribution level, may apply to an environmentally conscious delivery of supplies every time.

Table 6.1 lists some criteria that need attention during negotiating a contract.

The discussion thus far has outlined the side of GEA, its relevance in reducing the risks in implementing Green IT, the organizational systems affected by Green IT, the extension of

Table 6.1 Supplier Contract Conditions in the Context of Environmental Intelligence

Supplier Contract Condition	*Comments from EI Perspective*
Certification	Proves the green credentials of the supplier. Ensures compliance. This would apply to all dealings with the supplier, externally auditable.
Maturity	Shows the ability of the supplier to repeat carbon-efficient processes in providing materials and services. This criteria is applied to all iterations of the process.
Supplier's supplier	Enforceability of collaboration amongst a suite of suppliers.
Attitude	Indicates the sociocultural factor of the organization. This is the least measurable of all in a supplier contract.
Reactivity and Responsiveness	Ability of the suppliers to respond to increases in carbon outputs along the supply chain.

a basic three-tired architecture to a collaborative Green architecture, alignments and optimizations, integration, and the GSCM. The subsequent discussion brings all of this together into green portals.

Green Portals in Green Enterprise Architecture

This section discusses the creation and use of Green ICT portals and the consequent use of information. The discussion on contents, described earlier in Figure 6.8, forms the basis for these Green ICT portals. Deshpande and Unhelkar (HRG, 2011) have discussed several aspects of collecting data and information relating to green portals. The first one is the possible sources of green information. The second aspect is the scale of this green information that is available at any given time. The third aspect combines reliability and relevance of the available information to the organization in question. After gathering the relevant information, it has to be analyzed and made available to management, employees, and customers, keeping in view their separate perspectives.

A portal is an electronic means for an organization to interact with the external world. A green portal will be specifically focused on carbon data and information. Portals provide the organizations with what they want to know collaboratively—across other organizations, government agencies, and standard bodies (that are entrusted with benchmarking and regulating the carbon emissions).

Green ICT portals can collect (source) and provide (disseminate) information in various ways. Outsourcing, in-sourcing and "crowd-sourcing" are applications of distributed problem solving and production models.

Figure 6.11 depicts the external and internal aspect of these data collections and dissemination strategies for an organization. A Green ICT information portal would have external agencies, technologies, and ontological elements supporting its data collection strategy—external to the organization. The internal stakeholders, solution space technologies (such as SOA and WS discussed earlier) and access media will form part of the internal strategy for carbon data for the portal.

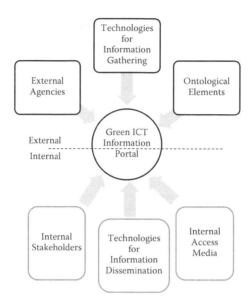

Figure 6.11 Elements of a Green ICT information portal. (Based on Deshpande, Y. and Unhelkar, B., Information systems for a Green organization. In B. Unhelkar, ed., *Handbook of Research in Green ICT: Technical, Methodological and Social Perspectives*, pp. 116–130. IGI Global, Hershey, PA, USA, 2010.)

Figure 6.12 shows a combination of these strategies that evolve into the Green ICT information portal. This portal is shown at the center, with sources and destinations of information on either side of the portal. The left side of the portal in Figure 6.12 corresponds to information coming from external sources. These are the content providers for the portal. The right of the portal, in Figure 6.12, corresponds to the internal sources and destinations for information. These are the content consumers who, in turn, provide internal information. The arrows show the direction of the flow of information into and out of the portal.

The green contents are rapidly changing dynamic contents that are usually diffused amongst various agencies and media within and external to the organization. Examples of such agencies include ICT organizations, governments, industry, research organizations, and standard bodies. For example, companies, such as Intel, IBM, Microsoft, Oracle, and Google, as well as professional organizations such as ACM, BCS, and IEEE form part of agencies providing and using carbon data. "Government" sources could be local, state, or national. "Research centers" include research institutes in general with specific projects in Green ICT or specialized research institutions concentrating on Green ICT like GreenGrid or more general ones, like IPCC. "Standards bodies" cover standards as well as legislations dealing with carbon data for the Green IT portals.

Business Intelligence and Green IT

Business intelligence (BI) was discussed in the very first chapter as a basis for EI. Therefore, BI is an important consideration on a GEA. There is a phenomenal amount of intelligence that exists in business. This intelligence, which is more than mere analysis of data and information, is gleaned from the various systems of the organization (such as ERP, CRM, HR, and SCM), corresponding

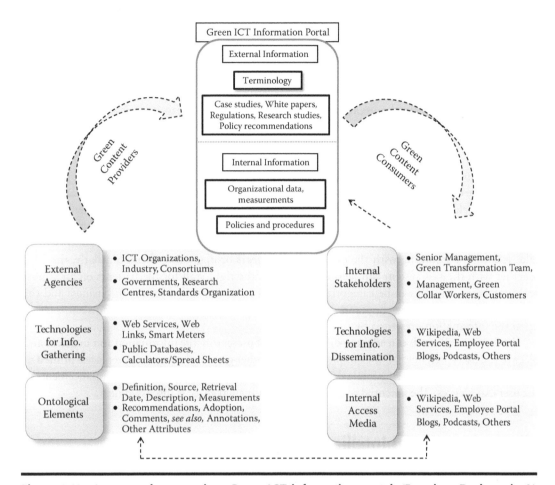

Figure 6.12 Inputs and outputs in a Green ICT information portal. (Based on Deshpande, Y. and Unhelkar, B., Information systems for a Green organization. In B. Unhelkar, ed., *Handbook of Research in Green ICT: Technical, Methodological and Social Perspectives*, pp. 116–130. IGI Global, Hershey, PA, USA, 2011.)

processes and vast amount of underlying data in multiple formats. BI can be thought of as a rich matrix of applications that access, collect, store, process, and analyze data within and outside the organization to produce new bodies of knowledge. Decision support system (DSS), online analytical processing (OLAP), statistical analysis, forecasting, and data mining are examples of BI tools (see Bryla and Merchant, 2009, for BI tools) that need to be revisited from EI perspective, wherein they help to reduce the number of data services and, thereby data centers.

This intelligence garnered by the business also has immense potential to improve its environmental credentials.

These various elements of an organization's intelligence that are embedded in its systems and data emerge as invaluable decision-making tools when they all work together. This systems-level collaboration and correlation results in ongoing improvement in customer service and optimization of business activities. The creation of this collaboration and correlation is BI (see Bryla and Merchant, 2009). BI is the process of using collective information within the organization to optimize its business performance, enhance its customer service, and provide it with overall competitive advantage and sustainability (Unhelkar and Tiwary, 2010).

BI primarily works to exchange and analyze information that resides in information silos. The challenge for the organization is to correlate these varied pieces of information—and their subsequence analysis—in a cohesive whole so as to assist the organization with its environmental efforts. For example, an operational support system (OSS) in a telecommunication company will have a need to correlate its switch maintenance information to the billing support system (BSS). This correlation will help the organization understand and prioritize its switch upgrades based on the clusters of customers and their bill payment patterns. A further correlation between these data entities and their carbon emissions data can also be made. Another example can be from the health domain. An electronic patient record (EPR) system needs to correlate with an accounting or HR system in a hospital to be able to glean knowledge on planning and organizing patient services. Effort can be made to extend these new bodies of knowledge to see their relationship with, say, the electronic wastage from hospital information systems, or the ratio of patients to data center emissions. BI tools are helpful in correlating a myriad (and at times seemingly unrelated pieces of) information into actionable insights. In the earlier examples, the telecom company can take action on continuing with the existing switch gears or upgrading them. Similarly, the EPR together with the HR system can help in scheduling the right staff for the patients on an almost real-time basis. This BI can be categorized according to domains and sectors in business and the portal could help in setting the standards and benchmarks specific to domains and sectors based upon the information presented by BI.

Furthermore, BI tools can adapt to different ways of presenting the information and in a time and place of the users preference. For example, videos and other graphical means may replace a printed or tabled daily or weekly report. Mobile devices used in BI systems can make further enhancements to the user experiences. The potential of BI in the environmental space is discussed next.

The Environmental Intelligence Domain

BI can be considered as a technology that enables users to not only access historical and current data but to also create new correlations. These new correlations between data items produce insights that are used in business—to optimize processes, enhance customer experience, and reduce inventories. BI systems typically include online analysis, reporting, data mining, provision of consolidated dash boards, and enabling business performance management. Combining people together with the aforementioned technologies and processes further enhances the capabilities of BI.

EI combines tools, architecture, databases, data warehouses, business performance methodologies, and quality initiatives in order to produce environmentally responsible decisions and action. EI is further enhanced by the availability and application of mobility that enhances decision support system (DSS), executive information system (EIS), and knowledge management system (KMS).

Business intelligence has tremendous potential for application in the modern-day environmentally conscious business world. In fact, the business environment today mandates a highly intelligent approach that would make optimal use of all resources available to an organization. The environmental issues of a business are not too far removed from the issues of business efficiency and customer service. However, care needs to be taken to ensure that the environmental considerations of business do not embroil the business in expensive and, occasionally expansive, projects emanating out of its greening effort. For example, an organization embarking on environmental consciousness should not add to the already existing complexities of data warehouses and business systems in the organization. Another simpler example would be that a reduction in paper usage by the organization should not result in greater use of server space. An environmentally astute approach would make use of existing intelligence, without overloading it, to enable the organization to achieve its environmental objectives. EI has been discussed by Unhelkar and Trivedi (2009a, 2009b, 2009c) in various ways. Their approach focuses on extending and applying BI toward EI.

This discussion extends BI to the EI domain. The evolving nature of EI systems implies usage of incremental data, information, processes, and knowledge toward intelligence. EI system will be implemented with WS and Cloud computing. The ICT systems and the corresponding processes also contain significant checks and balances in order to ensure the implementation of the strategy. For example, a system supporting recycling effort of the organization ensures that the benchmarks set for recycling effort are met by the organization. A system calculating and estimating the movement of "field engineers" provides a count on the reduction in overall miles traveled by those staff members as a result of the green initiative by the organization. The checks and balances provided by the ICT system for EI becomes a "core" rather than a peripheral responsibility of businesses and, therefore, provides ongoing input into the core business decision making.

EI systems consist of the tools, technologies, and processes that turn environmental data into information and knowledge that optimizes decision making. EI processes ensure effective and efficient use of green enterprise resource as well as compliance of the enterprise with its green policies and procedures.

EI systems bring together information, knowledge, and intelligence related to all business activities with other members (organization/business) of the value chain. Similarly companies can utilize WS and mobile technologies for collaborative EI on mobile Internet. EIS allows companies to benefit from well-coordinated effort of mobile devices, wireless networks, mobile Internet, and mobile WS.

Thus EI can be considered as an excellent enabler of environmental initiatives through the use of an organization's existing BI capabilities. EI aims to expand and update the existing applications to now handle the environmental aspect of the business operation. Figure 6.13 depicts an overall view of the EI domain.

According to a Gartner survey of CIOs, EI projects were the most important technology priority for companies in 2007. EI has been defined in many different ways in the literature with different context and meanings. EI can be considered as an umbrella term that encompasses integrated suite of tools, architecture, databases, data warehouses, performance management, and methodologies. The EI can also refer to processes, techniques, or tools to support faster and better decision making for environmentally responsible strategies.

Incorporation of mobile and communication technologies in collaborative business ecosystem can add EI to the current BI. The increasing awareness of the adverse effect of current business activities on the environment will force the corporate sector to add EI with mobility to help our earth go green.

Externally, this domain is made up of systems and interfaces that deal with regulatory portals, design portals (aimed at green product design), interfaces to various business partners (as a part of business ecosystem), systems for environmental strategies (futuristic scenarios), and normal measurement and reporting systems (CEMS). These systems and interfaces, as also shown in Figure 6.13, are based on people (HR), suppliers, marketing, customers, and asset management systems. These systems exist in the organization and are upgraded to provide help and support to the external interfaces. The fundamental basis of these systems and interfaces, however, is the data-information-process-knowledge base that is shown in the inner circle in Figure 6.13. This EI base is further expanded based on its evolving complexity.

Environmental Intelligence Systems' Evolving Complexity

Figure 6.14 shows the evolving complexities of EI systems. These evolving complexities are of data-information-process-knowledge, eventually leading to highly collaborative and complex EI that is a combination of myriad data, systems, and insights. This evolving EI complexity is understood as follows:

(a) *Data*: Identification of carbon data related to equipments (gadgets) across the company that generates greenhouse gases; Provisioning the step-by-step collection and collation of the

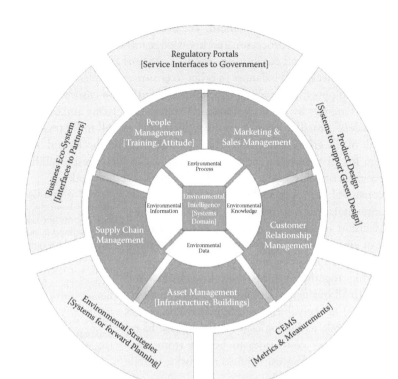

Figure 6.13 The environmental intelligence. (Systems Doamin—Based on Unhelkar, B. and Tiwary, A., Collaborative intelligence, Cutter IT Journal. In Dave Higgins, ed., *Business Intelligence 2010: Delivering the Goods or Standing Us Up?* Vol. 23, No. 6, 2010.)

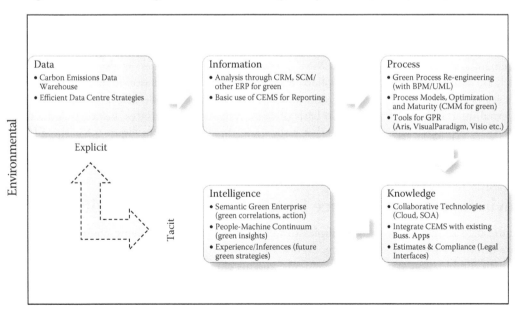

Figure 6.14 Evolving complexities in environmental intelligence systems.

carbon-related data within the organization. Incorporating mobile technologies in business processes to measure and report on carbon data. Adding indirect carbon data (such as by other partners). Storing of carbon data in data warehouse with a provision of enabling interfaces with other data. Security of reporting data.

(b) *Information*: Analysis and processing of the data in order to provide information to all parties concerned regarding the carbon-position of the organization. Environmental transactions are recorded and processed here in order to produce valuable information. Setting up interfaces with the urban development and planning systems and services provided by local governmental bodies (such as councils)—again through service-oriented technologies and the Cloud. Providing detailed and timely feedback to the decision makers/strategists through a systematic program of green metrics and measurements.

(c) *Process*: Optimizing procedures and controls within the organization using the concepts of business process modeling (BPM) to ensure efficiency; developing an understanding of process maturity in the context of green processes. Influencing business partners to change their business processes to reflect environmental awareness—as part of the business ecosystem that has evolved around WS-based communication.

(d) *Knowledge*: Incorporation of external climate change data such as those provided by governmental bodies or other third-parties, into the internal systems of the company by using WS and Cloud computing fundamentals (discussed in detail later in this chapter). Forming basis for new insights that can be acted upon. The intelligence aspect of these systems comes into play when stakeholders such as employees, customers, and partners are enticed to pay attention to the environmental issues through their actions and use of the systems.

(e) *Intelligence*: This is the semantic green enterprise. This is where the systems embrace people-machine continuum. EI system requires two major activities from an organization: upgrading existing BI systems to incorporate environmental data, information, processes, and knowledge; and, analyzing, designing, developing, and deploying systems that are specific to the environmental needs of the organization. The new Green ICT systems may integrate with existing applications through interfaces. EI system bring together data and information from existing databases containing organization-specific information, through interfaces with systems outside the organizational boundaries (e.g., partner organization's systems or an SCM) as well as with government and related regulatory databases and standards. According to Azvine et al. (2006), EI comprises technologies like data warehouses, analytical tools, and reporting tools. Thus intelligence is a combination of ground-up Green IT systems, existing BI systems, and organizational processes that combine them with the tacit knowledge carried by people.

Communication Channels in Environmental Intelligence

Environmental intelligence, as mentioned earlier, combines not only myriad systems through correlations, but also synergistically brings in people. Figure 6.15 shows the various ways in which the EI systems interface with people. This is important in a GEA that has to incorporate systems intelligence (shown on the right in Figure 6.15) with the human intelligence (shown on the left). The iterative influence of systems on stakeholders, and vice versa, is through the various communication channels shown in the center in Figure 6.15.

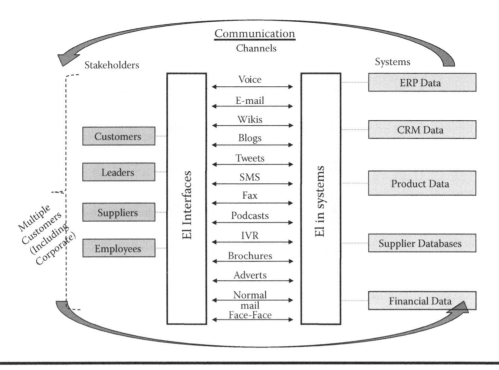

Figure 6.15 **Environmental intelligence—people to system interactions.**

Environmental Intelligence Implementation with Web Services

IBM's Green Sigma process can be considered here in the context of SOA. That is a five-step process which starts with the definition of the emission, establishing a baseline for measurement and metering, deploying a carbon monitoring dashboard console, process optimization, and finally management/compliance (Dzubeck, 2008). Carbon emission monitoring is a dynamic real-time concept that makes use of SOA-WS to measure, control, and optimize carbon emissions. Furthermore, SOA-based EI can be employed to track and account for carbon credits and eventually trade them.

Figure 6.16 shows an EI implementation using Cloud computing and WS. Typically, this would be either a CEMS or an existing ERP system that is specifically upgraded to deal with data, information, and processes environmentally. Trivedi and Unhelkar (2009) have emphasized that WS form an excellent basis for collaborating with multiple organizations and regulatory bodies for environmental action. WS can be used to create and modify environmental services that would integrate carbon information silos by connecting them, and providing real-time reporting features to decision makers. This would result in an EI implementation using SOA.

Figure 6.16 elaborates how WS can be used in the business environment to measure, monitor, and finally help for the process optimization with respect to the environmental factors. With the help of the tools such as Green web services (GWS), business can begin to develop EI systems, implement them in the business, monitor, measure, and mitigate the emissions and monetize the process (Trivedi and Unhelkar, 2009). Process improvements not only improve the compliance and performance but also decrease the business cost. GWS will facilitate service interoperability across platforms, applications, and programming languages through the use of standards refinement and integration into profiles. Using GWS presents an organization an opportunity to take advantage of environmental services offered by other organizations and third parties, as well as government rules and regulations.

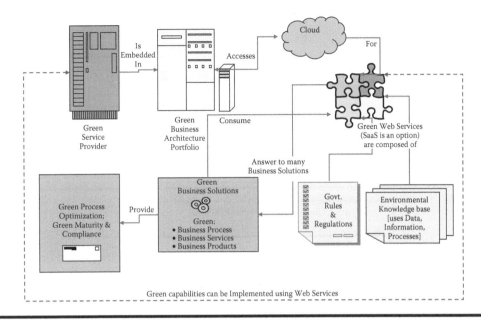

Figure 6.16 EI implementation using Cloud/web services (From Unhelkar, B. and Trivedi, B., Chapter XI, Role of mobile technologies in an environmentally responsible business strategy. In B. Unhelkar, ed., *Handbook of Research in Mobile Business: Technical, Methodological and Social Perspectives*, 2nd ed., pp. 214–232. IGI Global, Hershey, PA, USA, 2009; and Unhelkar, B. and Trivedi, B., Merging web services with 3G IP multimedia systems for providing solutions in managing environmental compliance by businesse. In *Proceedings of the Third International Conference on Internet Technologies and Applications (Internet Technologies and Applications, ITA 09)*, Sep. 8–11, 2009, Wrexham, North Wales, UK, 2009a. With permission.)

Environmental Intelligence with Mobility

Mobility has the potential to further enhance the data sharing among the EI application. This is so because mobility enables location independent data sharing. Mobility reduces access times, optimizes entering of data, and offers location-based insights. Mobile Internet can provide the platform for accessing data using mobile devices, database as well as WS. Mobile networks (discussed in Chapter 3) can optimize search techniques, provide location-specific data, and make that data available anywhere, anytime.

Mobility can play a vital role for the sustainability of a business, and sustainable businesses provide impetus for economic growth as well. Thus, mobility has a role to play in the environmentally responsible business strategies that make an organization sustainable which, in turn, makes it a long-lasting and profitable organization. Mobility can be said to help the business be EI. Mobility enables virtual collaboration between business and individuals. Reengineering the business processes with mobility provides enormous opportunities for virtualization. The more virtual a business is, the less physical resources it will consume—therefore, well-modeled mobile processes greatly assist in creation of environment friendly businesses.

The EI results from an increasing analysis and correlations between silos of information, as shown earlier in Figure 6.14. Enterprises are looking at the effects and use of mobility to extend the EI solutions. EI systems involve and employ mobility solutions to coordinate office, field, and home decision making. Figure 6.17 extends the EI concept with mobility. The correlation of environment-related information and utilizing that information in a knowledge management system can lead to environmental intelligence systems (EIS). Mobility is a key player in EIS. Figure 6.17 shows how, starting with subjective (tacit) observations, and recording them (and

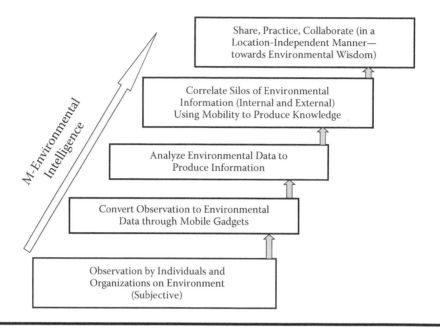

Figure 6.17   Path to environmental intelligence with mobility.

making them explicit), the organization can move up toward knowledge and wisdom related to the environment. Mobility is a significant factor on the quality of life of individuals and society as a whole (Unhelkar, 2005, 2009, METM). Application of mobility to BI results in mobile EI that combine enterprise information access with mobile devices like mobile phones, PDAs, smart phone, the BlackBerry, and other handheld wireless devices (based on Turban et al., 2006). Such combination can enable the production of carbon-specific BI reports, key performance indicators (KPI), and business analytics.

EI can interface with many existing enterprise systems such as the decision support systems, executive information systems and knowledge management systems, as discussed by (Clark et al., 2007; Watson and Wixom, 2007). Mobile EI is the successful collection, evaluation, and application of information by the business leaders and users using mobile gadgets, networks, and processes.

EI with mobility has four technical areas: data warehouse, business analytics, business performance management, and a user interface. EI data warehouse sources data from organizational systems (e.g., CRM, ERP) to support decision making. The data warehouse can then be subjected to online analytical processing (OLAP) wherein data is drilled-down and rolled-up for analysis (based on Kimball et al., 1998).

EI can take advantage of mobile data and information on potentially wasteful use of materials, energy, space, and labor. This data can then be converted into intelligence. Information on labor usage, physical work space, process flow, set up times, and management concepts such as *lean* systems and *kaizen* can all be used, in real time, through mobile technologies, for carbon reduction. For example, kaizen is a mindset that aims to improve the efficiency of any organization by primarily discouraging any idle inventory. Through mobile SCM (discussed earlier) kaizen can dramatically reduce emissions. [*kaizen* aims to meet the demands of the customers to have deliveries on time, shorten the development cycle time, and be able to forecast the demand for the products and services with minimum margin of error.] These operational business processes of an organization can be optimized substantially by the real-time mobile usage. Mobility improves the decision-making processes of the organization that can also result in environmental advantage for the enterprise and, in turn, the society. For example, producing higher quality of products and services has a positive correlation with the environment. A high-quality product that lasts an additional year is an environmentally good product. This correlation is created, maintained, and utilized by bringing together data and information using the mobile platform. EI-based software tools are able to provide visual reports, historical and emerging carbon data and interfaces with external regulatory data.

An Example of Green Enterprise Architecture

Figure 6.18 presents an example of GEA. This is an example architecture that encompasses the business, technology, process, and people dimensions of an organization discussed in detail in Chapter 2. The business layer is made up of the drivers and the transformation dimensions for Green IT. The legal requirements relating to carbon emissions directly affecting the business layer are shown on the left. This architecture further shows business decision making, environmental data collection and processing, the impact on systems, supply chains and people, and the emissions monitoring layers in Figure 6.18. The elements of a GEA are supported by the WS and infrastructure layers, as seen in Figure 6.18. The policies, practices, and procedures continue to influence these technical layers.

This example architecture covers adoption of environmental principles and practices, development of environmental competencies and protocols, and facilitates novel application opportunities for CEMS. Such GEA makes provisions for business rules within business processes that are environmentally conscious. The various layers of such architecture are depicted in Figure 6.18 and discussed in detail by Unhelkar and Trivedi (2009).

ICT has a key role in creating systems/technologies which systematically and continuously regulate the energy consumption; inform the business about the energy consumption, and enforce eco-sensitive consumption. This is evident in Figure 6.18 through the input-analysis-output activities, which are technically supported by the emissions monitoring layer (CEMS).

In Figure 6.18, the smart metering devices shown on top of the left side are usually mobile devices. These smart meters (also discussed in Chapter 4) need to be attached to the equipment whose emissions are required to be measured and monitored on a regular basis. Smart meters provide the basis for lifecycle assessment of an equipment and bring about positive changes to the usage of that equipment from a carbon perspective.

Finally, the GEA also enables relating the infrastructure issues in businesses to EI. Thus, the hardware, networks, public infrastructure, third-party owned infrastructure are all identified, understood, and positioned in a way to make them most carbon and cost effective with the help of a GEA. Occasionally, these infrastructure elements may be outside the organizational boundary and therefore not easily changeable. Furthermore, a GEA also provides input and guidance for quality assurance and quality control (testing) of EI data, services, and interfaces. This is so because, based on the architecture, a strategy for incorporating changes, testing those changes, and working out the deployment can be achieved. A GEA also assists in comparative investigation of differences between EIS-specific applications and the rest of the business applications. As of today, however, EI applications are not as common place as other business applications, thereby hindering their comparison and audits (more details on audit in Chapter 10).

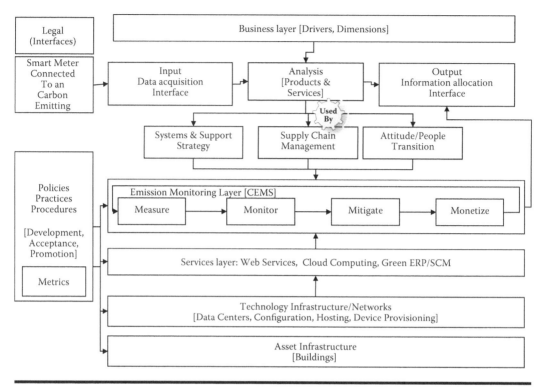

Figure 6.18   An example of ERBS architecture. (Based on Unhelkar, B. and Trivedi, B., Merging web services with 3G IP multimedia systems for providing solutions in managing environmental compliance by businesse. In *Proceedings of the Third International Conference on Internet Technologies and Applications (Internet Technologies and Applications, ITA 09)*, Sep. 8–11, 2009, Wrexham, North Wales, UK, 2009a).

Discussion Points

- Explain the various types of Green architectures within the enterprise, such as information architecture and solutions architecture.
- Describe the importance of GEA in an organization transformation to a green organization.
- Explain how a Green systems architecture evolves from a basic to a linear and eventually a collaborative process-based architecture.
- What comprises green contents? What are the sources and the users of green contents?
- What is a Green ICT information portal? Discuss the important elements of the inputs and outputs of a green portal.
- Discuss the role of EI together with Cloud computing. What are the various people to system interactions facilitated by EI?
- Explain the role of SCM systems in the GEA.
- Describe how carbon emissions could be reduced by extending SCM with mobile technology.
- Discusses your current organizational portal. What challenges you expect to face when you add sources and provisioning of carbon data to this portal?

Action Points

- Organize a workshop to review your existing EA.
- Create/cross-check inventory of your BI system suite.
- Plan to modify/update existing data within BI suite to incorporate carbon calculations (this will be more than just a database update). New applications/modules may get added to your existing systems.
- Create the outline of a green information portal. Identify the elements specific to the portal for your organization.
- Create a strategy for integrating your SCM system.
- Identify areas to modify in existing data structures to accommodate new carbon data elements.
- Convert existing organizational data to accommodate external carbon data such as regulatory requirements and standards.
- Create a suite of green services using SOA and WS.
- Prepare a quality assurance policy for testing of Green Info Systems.

References

Azvine, B., Cui, Z., Nauck, D. D., and Majeed, B. (2006). Real time business intelligence for the adaptive enterprise." Paper presented at the *E-Commerce Technology, 2006, The 8th IEEE International Conference on and Enterprise Computing, E-Commerce, and E-Services*, San Francisco, CA, USA.

Borri, D., Camarda, D., and De Liddo, A. (December 2005). Mobility in environmental ICT gets its green house in order. Information Staff, *Information Age,* Publication of the Australian Computer Society.

Bryla, M. and Merchant, D. (2009). *Business Intelligence and Performance Management from IBM Cognos*, p. 11. Australian Computer Society. Available at http://www.acs.org.au/nsw/sigs/bi/IBM_BI.pdf, accessed August 4, 2010.

Clark, T. D. J., Jones, M. C., and Armstrong, C. P. (2007). The dynamic structure of management support systems: theory development, research focus, and direction. *MIS Quarterly*, 31(3): 579–615.

Deshpande, Y. and Unhelkar, B. (2011). Information systems for a Green organisation. In B. Unhelkar, ed., *Handbook of Research in Green ICT: Technical, Methodological and Social Perspectives*, pp. 116–130. IGI Global, Hershey, PA, USA.

Dzubeck, F. (2008). *Are You Ready for Green SOA, Network World*. Business InfoWorld. April 2008. Available at http://www.infoworld.com/t/business/are-you-ready-Green-soa-440?page=0,1

Ghose, A. and Billiau, G. (2011). Chapter 12, The optimizing web: A Green ICT research perspective. In B. Unhelkar, ed., *Handbook of Research in Green ICT*, pp. 184–196. IGI Global, Hershey, PA, USA.

Hazra. T. (2007). Doing SOA Right Today. Available at http://cutter.com/

Hazra, T. (2010). SOA: Understanding the Practice 2010—Creating Business-Driven Services. *Cutter Executive Report*, Boston, USA, November 2009, 12(11).

Kimball, R., Reeves, L., Thornthwaite, W., and Ross, M. (1998). *The Data Warehouse Lifecycle Toolkit: Expert Methods for Designing, Developing and Deploying Data*. John Wiley & Sons, Inc. New York, NY, USA.

Rosan, M., Krichevsky, T., and Sharma, H. (2011). Strategies for a Sustainable Enterprise. In B. Unhelkar, ed., *Handbook of Research in Green ICT*: Technical, Methodological and Social Perspectives, pp. 1–28. IGI Global, Hershey, PA, USA.

Sherringham, K. and Unhelkar, B. (2011). Strategic business trends in the context of green ICT. In B. Unhelkar, ed., *Handbook of Research in Green ICT: Technical, Business and Social Perspectives*, pp. 65–82. IGI Global, Hershey, PA, USA.

Strausl, D. (2001). Four stages to building an effective supply chain network. *EBN*, Feb. 26, p. 43.

Trivedi, B. and Unhelkar, B. (2009a). Semantic Integration of Environmental Web Services in an organization. Selected in ICECS 2009 Conference to be held at Dubai, Dec. 28–30, 2009, to be published in IEEE *Computer Society* Journal.

Trivedi, B. and Unhelkar, B. Chapter 15, Role of Mobile Technologies in an Environmentally Responsible Business Strategy. In B. Unhelkar, ed., *Handbook of Research in Green ICT: Technical, Business and Social Perspectives,* pp. 233–242, IGI Global, Hershey, PA, USA.

Turban, E., Lee, J., King, D., and Chung, H. M. (2006). *Electronic Commerce 2006: A Managerial Perspective.* Pearson, Prentice Hall.

Unhelkar, B. (2003). "Understanding Collaborations and Clusters in the e-Business World," *We-B Conference,* (*"http://www.we-bcentre.com" www.we-bcentre.com; with Edith Cowan University*), Perth, Nov. 24–25, 2003.

Unhelkar, B. (2005). Transitioning to a mobile enterprise: a three-dimensional framework. *Cutter IT Journal,* special issue on "Mobile Computing," Ed. S. Murugesan, 18(8): 5–11.

Unhelkar, B. (2009). *Mobile Enterprise Transition and Management.* Boca Raton, FL: Taylor & Francis Group (Auerbach Publications).

Unhelkar, B. and Lan, Y. (2011). Chapter 38, Integrating Green ICT in a supply chain management system. In B. Unhelkar, ed., *Handbook of Research in Green ICT,* pp. 523–534. IGI Global, Hershey, PA, USA.

Unhelkar, B. and Tiwary, A. (2010). "Collaborative Intelligence" in *Cutter IT Journal* edited by Dave Higgins' Business Intelligence 2010: Delivering the Goods or Standing Us Up?- Vol. 23, No. 6, June 2010.

Unhelkar, B. and Trivedi, B. (2009). Chapter XI, Role of mobile technologies in an environmentally responsible business strategy. In B. Unhelkar, ed., *Handbook of Research in Mobile Business: Technical, Methodological and Social Perspectives,* 2nd ed., 2008, pp. 214–232. IGI Global, Hershey, PA, USA.

Unhelkar, B. and Trivedi, B. (2009a). "Merging Web Services with 3G IP Multimedia systems for providing Solutions in Managing Environmental Compliance by Businesses," *Proceedings of the 3rd International Conference on Internet Technologies and Applications (Internet Technologies and Applications, ITA 09),* Sep. 8–11, 2009, Wrexham, North Wales, UK.

Weill, P. and Ross, J. W. (2004). IT Governance: How Top Performers Manage *IT Decision Rights for Superior Results.* Boston, MA: Harvard Business School Press.

Chapter 7

Green Information Systems: Design and Development Models

In all affairs it's a healthy thing now and then to hang a question mark on the things you have long taken for granted.

Bertrand Russell*

Key Points

- Applies the discussions on processes (Chapter 5) and architecture (Chapter 6) to the development of a Green information system (GIS)
- Presents the functional requirements of a GIS with use cases and activity graphs of the unified modeling language (UML)
- Analyses the stated requirements of GIS in order to identify its key design entities
- Presents class diagrams as the static structural models of a GIS
- Presents sequence diagrams to highlight the architectural and design decisions relevant to the dynamic aspect of a GIS
- Presents the models of various states for green objects—using state machine diagrams

Introduction

This chapter describes a generic Green information system (GIS). A GIS is a system that is dedicated to management of carbon data. Therefore, a GIS forms the basis for measuring, monitoring, and reporting on the carbon data of the organization. As such, this system is integral to environmental strategies of an organization. This chapter focuses on the design and development aspect

---

* http://www.brainyquote.com/quotes/authors/b/bertrand_russell_3.html.

of such a GIS. To separate this discussion on the software design and development aspect of green systems from their overall list, the system here is specifically referred to as GIS (rather than Carbon Emission Management Software [CEMS]) in this chapter.

The requirements of an overall system for environmental management have been outlined in the ISO 14001 standard (described later in Chapter 10).

GIS can be of different sophistication and can operate at varying levels. Most GIS have web services-based implementations and are deployed as SaaS. Philipson has done a substantial work in studying, collating, analyzing, and listing close to 60 vendors offering over 100 GIS products.* These CEMS products have been grouped on CEMSUS ranging from spreadsheets and free online calculators through to large vendors and consulting organizations providing comprehensive green ERP solutions.

Describing a GIS

A GIS (or a CEMS or EIS) is a software system that provides support to the business to implement its environment responsible business strategies (ERBS). Thus, this system has to cover the length, breadth, and depth of various structural and dynamic aspects of the business. Some aspects of this system are similar to any other software system—it has underlying carbon emissions data that is gleaned from the devices that emit that carbon, it has processes and applications that help analyze that data, identify the trends, and, eventually, it has interfaces that present, report, and interact (and collaborate) with other external sources of carbon services and data.

A generic GIS should be architected and designed in a way that enables it to be configured and used in all industry sectors. Furthermore, a good GIS must be able to cater for product service and infrastructure industries.

The development of a GIS has to also cater to the interfaces with existing software packages (such as the existing ERP packages, including those that provide customer relationship, CRM, and supply chain management [SCM]). The development of a GIS has to provide a strategic purpose—especially as it is designed from ground up. The technologies to be used will include an underlying content management system, an object-oriented approach to design, an object-relational database, support for mobile devices and interfaces, and implementation in an object-oriented language (say, Java). The deployment of almost all new GIS is expected to be SaaS-based. Therefore, the system should be aware of SaaS and Cloud computing.

GIS system is the software with the functions for measuring, monitoring, and performance checking of the various emissions generated by devices employed in the business activities. Organizational emissions values are computed by the system. These values are then compared to the standards set by the regulatory bodies.

Phases in a GIS Development and Deployment

Figure 7.1 depicts the major phases of any typical software development lifecycle. In terms of GIS, they apply as follows:

Develop—GIS needs to be developed by following agile practices and considering the important phases of a SDLC starting from requirements, analysis, design, and code to testing. Development has to consider issues of deployment, integration, and operations. Analysis and

---

* www.cemsus.com

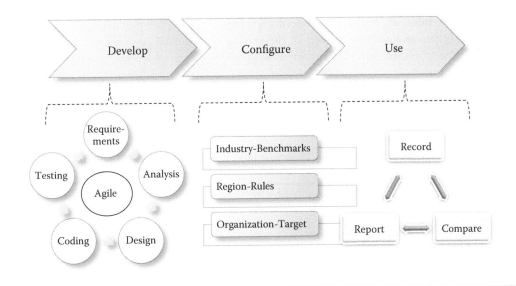

Figure 7.1 Major phases in GIS: development, configuration, and use.

design of the system is undertaken using the unified modeling language (UML) diagrams that helps in modeling the problem space and develop a solution in design space (model of solution space). CAMS provides this overall methodological approach.

Configure—Configuring GIS according to benchmarks and rules of organization. This would be an activity specific to each organization within each industry sector.

Use—Use of GIS will lead to ongoing recording of carbon data creation of reports as well as comparisons.

Features of GIS

GIS are required to have all relevant features for supporting the organization in its green initiative. These include support for the routine, operations, and also strategic trends. GIS also includes enhancement of the business systems with green capabilities. This would enable the organization to make use of its existing data and processes and extend them for carbon control.

GIS implementation needs to consider the integration issues—particularly as organizations have many existing ERP applications that will continue to be used irrespective of the environmental initiatives. Integration projects within ERBS will immensely benefit by the earlier discussion on technologies and EI. The earlier mentioned metrics and the three scopes in carbon emissions are all implemented through GIS.

The features of a GIS that play a significant role in enhancing this ability of business to coordinate its environmentally responsible approaches can be listed as follows:

- Collecting environment-related data in real time. The GIS has to be geared to collect data such as number of devices in use and on standby. Mobility further enhances this data capture ability and makes it real time. GIS has to also relate this data to other business applications.

■ Providing querying tools, key performance indicators (KPIs), and business analytics to field workers and decision makers in the area of EI. Availability of querying mechanisms can provide information that enables closing down of unused servers, desktops, and other equipments.

■ Enhancing the decision-making capabilities of senior management by collating and computing up-to-date information from varied external sources (e.g., government regulatory bodies and weather information) and feeding that into GIS. As a result, knowledge management in the green domain of the organization is enhanced. This service-oriented approach in GIS and the resultant real-time analytics goes a long way in enhancing the organization's green credentials.

■ GIS substantiates the green effort of the organization through the metrics, thereby providing positive feedback and impact on the employees' job satisfaction.

■ GIS can continuously identify and upgrade business processes and business practices in manufacturing, sales, and field support operations in order to make them environmentally responsible. GIS can help in optimizing the business processes (as was discussed in Chapter 5).

■ GIS also provides feedback to customers and other external users of the business on its environmental performance—potentially resulting in increased customer service and satisfaction—especially for the environmentally sensitive and responsible customers.

■ Aligning office and home activities through GIS can be a tremendous boost to the organizational effort in improving its green credentials. This is so because GIS can identify the areas of work that are overlapping with each other due to their location-specific nature and make them location-independent as far as possible.

■ GIS extends the tools and techniques of business management (such as KPIs, business analytics, and reporting) and applies them to the environmental aspect of business. Mobility further enhances the application of these management tools and techniques.

■ GIS provides the business with the ability to sustain itself for a long time. An environmentally responsible business and a sustainable business are complimentary. GIS can bring together technologies and processes for environmental sustainability.

■ GIS enables collaboration amongst businesses for the purpose of achieving environmental responsibilities. This collaboration is achieved through the use of service orientation architecture (SOA) as discussed in Chapter 6.

Modeling and Architecting GIS—Requirements, Design, Implementation, and Testing

The UML has been used in presenting the models of the GIS. The modeling constructs of the UML that are used in this chapter are as follows:

Package diagrams—Used to create and model subsystems/Green information portals. Packages can also be used to create increments and sprints in an agile development approach.

Use cases—Used to show functionalities and business processes from a user's point of view. This is the expected behavior of the system documented as interactions.

Use case diagrams—Provides a model describing all the related business processes/functionalities of a particular package. These diagrams also provide the scope of the system.

Activity graphs—Provides a detailed view of every step of a business process. They provide the flow within a use case or a package of GIS.

Class diagrams—Provides a static model of GIS based on its key business entities. This diagrams can also be used to model underlying carbon data warehouse.

Sequence diagrams—Provides a model for the interactions between objects and also rules for these interactions that are architectural decisions.

State Machine diagrams—Provides a view in which a particular entity passes through different states as a business process is executed.

Component diagrams—Used to show the interaction of every component with each other.

Deployment diagrams—Used to show the way application will be deployed including hardware and related infrastructure.

While these diagrams are used to show the various aspects of a GIS, they are highlighting these important aspects of the system. A large ERP application will require substantially more effort and will involve more complexity than the GIS models depict.

GIS Requirements

The Green ICT is developed to measure only energy consumption and environmental parameters such as carbon emissions, chemical wastes, and other office and industrial wastes. The Department of Environment, a government agency, is responsible for monitoring the carbon footprint of all the companies. This document will concentrate on process of gathering requirements, the resources needed to build the standards module of the project, and monitoring the progress of the project through a Gantt chart.

Green ICT system analysis and design is performed using the UML. UML diagrams such as use case, class, sequence, activity, state machine, package component, and deployment diagram are used in modeling the problem space and in designing of the system. As mentioned earlier, these diagrams help in modeling the operations and interactions at the business level and also in system design thorough classes, packages, components, and deployment diagrams. A typical GIS would involve two subsystems:

- Green organizational portal (GOP)
- Regulatory standards portal (RSP)

Regulatory portal provides the standard emission value determined by the regulatory body for each emission type based on the industry and company.

Organizational portal focuses on the capture of emission data and its comparison with the emission standards. These standards, set by regulators are made available through the RSP. Interaction between different users and operations performed by individual users are modeled as part of designing the system. Access to the system needs to be provided though an authentication mechanism to ensure the confidentiality and integrity of data.

Green Organizational Portal

The GOP is made up of organizational data on its "green" performance. These data are updated by the organizational representatives on an ongoing basis. These data record the organization's pollutant performance such as (a) heat generated by the desktop machines, data centers and network equipments within the organization, (b) carbon emissions in the petrol/diesel consumed by the organization, and (c) hazardous materials produced by the organization's activities such as lead in batteries and mobile phones.

The organizational portal should be fully customizable. This means, it should be usable in many different industries. Therefore, it should have the ability to create and record various categories of pollutant data. The organizational portal should have the ability to record the energy ratings of all the devices used within the organization (such as computers, vehicles, air-conditioners, and fridges). However, this GIS will not store the details of the organization's inventory, but only its carbon emissions. Therefore, the GIS's organizational portal will have to have an interface with the existing inventory management system, supply chain system and the customer relationship management system. The system is not meant to immediately measure the scope 3 emissions. However, it should have the provision to do so later, when scope 3 emissions become mandatory and need to be included in the system.

Regulatory Standards Portal

RSP is a large portal that will be maintained by the government agency responsible for emission control within a country or region. The RSP will have to have detailed and continuously updated information on the pollutant categories that are producing the carbon emissions. There are a large number of pollutant categories, which are also growing as new pollutants of the environment get

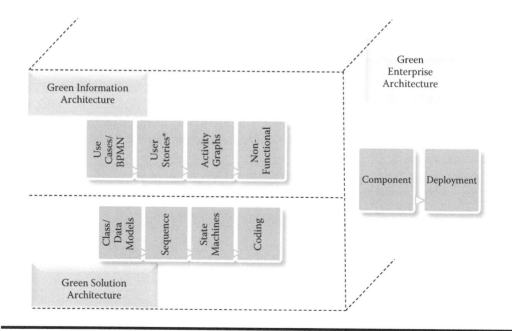

Figure 7.2 Categories of requirements in the various green architectural spaces. *User stories are popular with the advent of Agile methods; they may replace the formal use cases.

recognized and added to the list. RSP is made up of thousands of units of data, examples of which are as follows:

(a) Various types of pollutants that may not be directly related to IT such as petrol fumes from vehicles.
(b) Pollutants that are related to IT equipment and consumables—such as monitors, printer ink, and lead batteries.
(c) The approved standard for each of the pollutants—for example, 0.03 mg carbon per liter of petrol, and 0.05 mg of carbon per cartridge of printer ink.
(d) The variations to the pollutants depending on the type of industry. Currently, RSP supports hundreds of industries such as airline, hotel, car rental, packaging, computer manufacturers, restaurants, farms, and so on.
(e) The standards also vary depending on the size and location of the organization. For example, in developed regions, organizations with less than 20 employees are categorized as small, 20–100 as medium, and more than 100 employees as large organizations. The same pollutants are allowed in different levels for different size of organizations. For example, if a small restaurant is permitted 0.03 mg of carbon per liter of petrol use in its commuting activities, a large airline is only allowed 0.025 mg of carbon per liter of petrol in its activities.

Stakeholders/Actors

There are number of actors (also called stakeholders) in the GIS system. These actors are typically the people who are directly responsible for measurements, monitoring, and mitigation of emissions. In addition, these people/roles also include employees directly responsible for production or services within an organization. Thus, for example, in an airline or a hotel industry, for example, there will be an "Environmental Manager" who will be responsible for the implementation of the strategies for reducing greenhouse gases. In addition, the check-in manager (airline) or the duty manager (hotel) will have some responsibilities toward carbon management as well, which need to be supported by the GIS.

There will be numerous additional roles in this system, such as the workers responsible for entering the environmental data, the government representatives responsible for entering the standards or acceptable benchmarks, and also the senior management of the organization, who will be interested in having a bird's eye view of the "green" performance of their organization.

Furthermore, it is expected that the "general public" will also be interested in finding out the performance of the organization in relation to its green-ness.

In addition to the abovementioned end-users, there are also administrators of the system, both within the organization and external to the organization, who will be maintaining the data, information, and the applications.

Finally, these users can be individual users and there can be organizational users (who have individual nominees) who can use this system.

There will be several types of users of the system. Each of those users will have specific access to system functions so that they can view specific information such as average carbon emissions registered for a specific company, what pollutants an organization produces, and so on. Some users will be in-charge of entering the environmental data for a specific organization (data entry officer).

Senior managers of the organizations will be able to have a glance on the green performance of their organizations. Government representatives will have access to other parts of the system in order to set up the benchmarks for all the organizations. It is also expected that the general public will have access to the system to find out information regarding the green performance of any organization registered in the system. User administrators are expected in the system and they will be in-charge of setting up access and creating user-id for each of those different users of the system.

These users at both a personal and organizational level need to interact with GIS in various ways. Thus, some users will be keen to login on the organizational web site in order to access GICT, whereas others will be coming in through a handheld device. There is a need for the system to handle interactions from users who are "in the field" and not in front of a desktop. Furthermore, each interaction, which can include a query, an update, a retrieval of data, a check for control total on the green performance, and so on, needs to be stored securely. The privacy of the individuals making those enquiries and updates need to be secured—especially as this system has the potential to be politically sensitive.

Databases

The back-end, underlying carbon data needs to be stored in a database that can handle multimedia contents. The basic carbon data relating to emissions and compliance can be modeled and stored in relational structures. However, there will be a need to interact with the many other data elements in the existing CRM/SCM/HR systems. Furthermore, carbon data is likely to be multimedia data, demanding provision for storing video posts and webinars that can also be used for carbon dashboards. Following are specific requirements of a Green IT system's database:

- Ability to identify polluting equipments, materials, and other assets of the organization
- Ability to store the relationship between assets and corresponding pollutions
- Storage of various types of GHG emissions on a time-period basis
- Ability to configure and create various dashboards and pollutant performance reports from within data available for pollutants
- Creation of various pollutant types and storing them in a reference table
- Storing energy rating of all assets (devices)
- Storing of benchmarks/standards for each polluting asset
- Ability to search for different assets, polluting gases, and across various time periods
- Storing of trends for pollutants, assets, and time periods
- Storage and management of user accounts

Package Diagrams and System Scope

The system should cover all the functionalities required to record, calculate, analyze, and report on carbon emissions.

GOP and RSP functions like emission details management and comparing them with standards are done based on the company size and location.

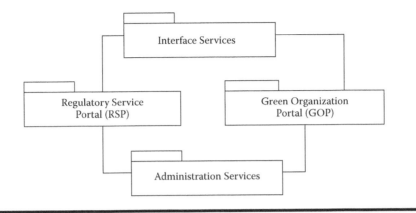

Figure 7.3   GIS major packages (subsystems).

The GIS system is meant to support any organization in varying industry verticals—and map their performance against the standards set by the regulatory agency.

Emission performance check done by environmental manager in the organizational portal. Emission Standard's value are managed through create, update, and delete performed by the government administrator. User ID and password authentication to access the system and also permissions to any user are managed by the administrator in the two portals. Management of inventories and assets that keeps track of the devices and the automated service-based reporting by different portals is part of the subsequent iteration.

Based on this scope, Figure 7.3 shows the core packages or subsystems of the GIS. The GOP and RSP are shown as two packages that also interface with the interface and administration services. While the GOP will have multiple instances across various organizations, the RSP will have a single instance. Both portals will be deployed using SaaS.

Use Case Diagram for GOP

Figure 7.4 shows the use case diagram for GOP. It shows actors, use cases, and their relationships. Some of the use cases shown in this diagram are documented in subsequent sections in this chapter.

Figure 7.5 depicts use case diagram for ROP. It shows actors, use cases, and their relationships for creating, updating, and maintaining emission benchmarks.

Figure 7.6 depicts use case diagram for ROP. It shows the model for the process by which the regulatory authority establishes emission standards. Use cases corresponding to this diagram are not currently documented.

Figure 7.7 depicts the activity diagram for the use case "Calculate Emissions." Worker specifies emissions and pollutants in device. Device provides the values and then worker calculates the emission on basis of those values.

Figure 7.8 depicts activity diagram for use case "Maintaining Emission Standards." Government administrator logs in portal and provides device details as well as create/update standard on basis of emission and pollutant specifications provided by portal. After creating/updating those standards, government administrator sets standards in the system and stores them.

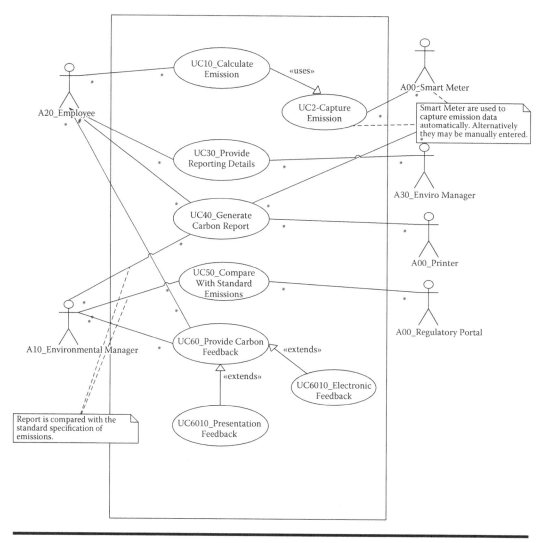

Figure 7.4   Use case diagram for "green organizational portal."

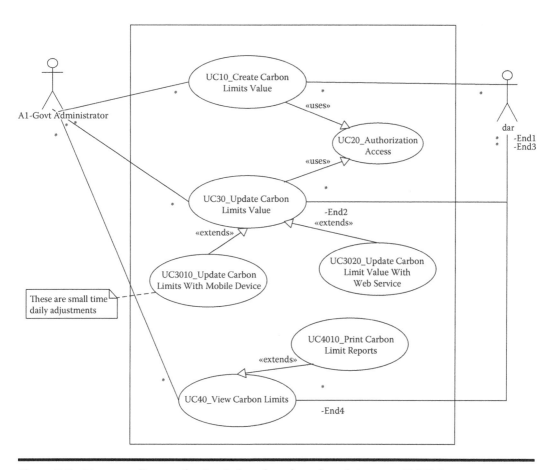

Figure 7.5   Use case diagram for "emissions benchmark maintenance (ROP)."

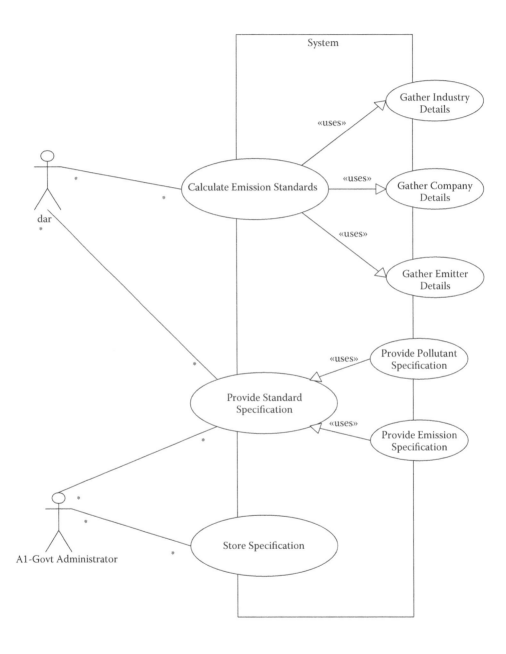

Figure 7.6   Use case diagram for "establishing emission standards (ROP)."

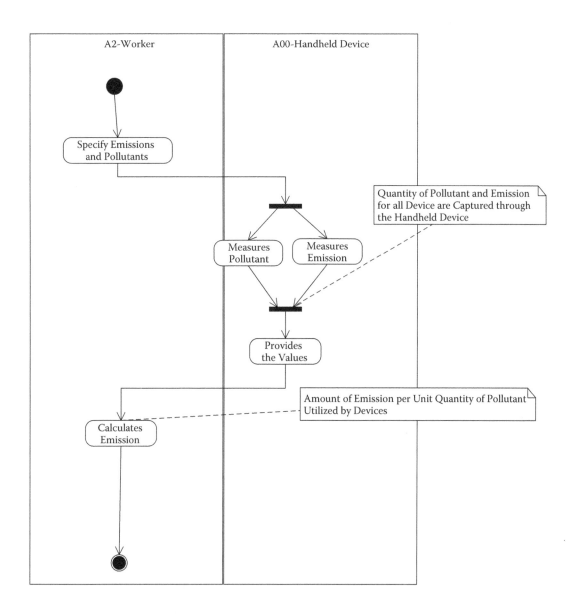

Figure 7.7   Activity diagram for "UC1_calculate emissions."

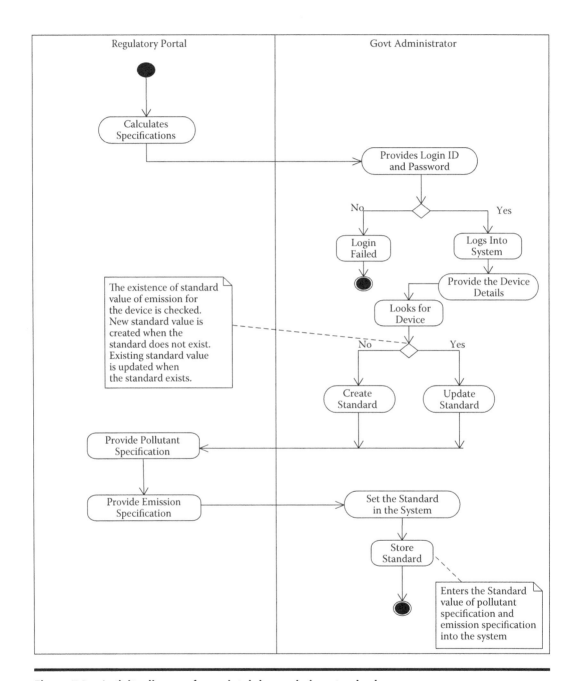

Figure 7.8 Activity diagram for maintaining emission standards.

Use Cases for "Green Organizational Portal"

Use Case	UC10-Calculate Emission
Actors	A20-Employee, A00-Smart meter
Description	The employee calculates the amount of emission of one or more assets by capturing carbon data through handheld device or a smart meter (or handheld device)
Precondition	Employee is authenticated Employee is authorized to access the smart meter data
Postcondition	Emission value is successfully calculated
Complexity	Medium
Normal Course of Events	1. The employee prepares a list of assets for which emissions are to be calculated. System validates the list (through asset management) 1.1 <<include>> UC20-Capture emission 2. Employee initiates recording of emissions 3. The value of carbon emission from each smart meter is provided (A1) 4. System validates value of carbon emissions 5. The employee requires total amount of emission to be calculated (per dept per day) 6. System calculates and reports on total emissions
Alternate Course of Events	A1-The emission values could not be provided by the meter, manual collections of data will be required
References	Government document outlining pollutants per assets, their categories, and their emission limits. This data is available electronically as a web service from the government portal

Use Case	UC20-Capture Emission
Actors	A20-Employee; A00-Smart meter
Description	The employee uses the smart meter or other device to capture the emissions from organizational assets corresponding to various pollutants
Precondition	The employee is authorized to capture the emission Smart meters have been installed
Postcondition	The smart meter successfully transmits the emission
Complexity	Simple

Normal Course of Events	1. The smart meter device is electronically switched on
	2. The smart meter registers itself to the system
	3. The system validates the smart meter (A1)
	4. Smart meter is assigned to an asset pollutant (A2)
	5. Smart meters monitors and captures emission data
	6. Smart meter transmits data to the system
Alternate Course of Events	A1-Invalid smart meter
	Switch to alternative handheld device to capture the emission value
	A2-Smart meter is not directly assigned. Create a manual mapping for the assignment of the meter to the pollutant
References	Smart meter operating procedures

Use Case	**UC30-Provide Reporting Details**
Actors	A20-Employee,
	A30-Environmental manager
Description	The employee reports on the emission values. Environmental manager collates them and creates physical reports
Precondition	Emission values have been successfully transmitted to the system
Postcondition	Emission value are reported by environmental manager
Complexity	Simple
Normal Course of Events	1. The employee indicates to the environmental manager that the emission details are ready for storage
	2. Environmental manager accepts the request and asks for the details (A1)
	3. Employee provides the details such as the asset, the category of pollutant, and the emissions generated in units
	4. The environmental manager receives and stores the details in system provided by the worker
	5. Environmental manager provides required search criteria in system
	6. System generates appropriate report clearly mentioning emission values for each pollutant in units
Alternate Course of Events	A1-Environmental manager will electronically accept data
References	The emission feedback use case diagram in organizational portal

Use Case	**UC40-Generate Carbon Report**
Actors	A30-Environmental manager
	A00-Printer
Description	The employee generates a report providing amount of emission released from each device

Precondition	The employee provides the emission data to the administrator and it is stored in the system
Postcondition	The employee successfully generates the report to be viewed by the environmental manager
Complexity	Simple
Normal Course of Events	1. The employee performs analysis of emission values for each of the device 2. The employee prepares the report by specifying the emission value for different category of pollutants utilized by each device 3. The report is generated (A1) 4. The employee sends the report to the environmental manager 5. Environmental manager receives the report
Alternate Course of Events	A1-Report is submitted electronically
References	Green organizational portal

Use Case	**UC50-Compare with Standard Emissions**
Actors	A10-Environmental manager; A00-Regulatory portal
Description	Environmental manager analyses the report generated by the worker and checks if they are within the standard specifications which is provided by the regulatory portal
Precondition	The environmental manager received the report from the worker
Postcondition	The report confirms with the standard specifications
Type	Complex
Normal Course of Events	1. The environmental manager analyses the report 2. The regulatory portal is accessed 3. The environmental manager compares emission values in the report with the standard emission values for each device type from the regulatory portal 4. Report confirms to the standard specification (A1) 5. Report is approved and filed
Alternate Course of Events	A1-Report does not confirm the specification and should be enquired
References	Organizational portal

Use Case	UC60-Provide Carbon Feedback
Actors	A30-Environmental manager; A20-Employee
Description	The environmental manager provides a feedback depending upon the confirmation of the standard specifications
Precondition	Report for emission is compared with the standards by the environmental manager
Postcondition	Feedback is submitted by the environmental manager
Type	
Normal Course of Events	1. Environmental manager verifies actual emissions against standards specified 2. Feedback is prepared based on the conformance to the standards 3. Environmental manager sends the feedback to the worker
Alternate Course of Events	N/A
References	Organizational portal

Use Cases for "Emissions Benchmark Maintenance Use Case Diagram"

Use Case	UC10-Create Carbon Limits Value
Actors	A10-Government administrator
Description	The government administrator creates new carbon limits value for the nonexisting emission value after receiving value from the government representative
Precondition	The carbon limits value is already calculated by government representative
Postcondition	The administrator successfully creates the carbon limits value
Type	Medium
Normal Course of Events	1. The government administrator requests for creating carbon limits value 2. The system requests for the authentication 2.1 <<include>> UC2-Login 3. The system authenticates and asks for the new standard value (A1) 4. The government representative provides the standard value to government administrator 5. The government administrator enters the value 6. The system accepts and stores the value

Alternate Course of Events	A1-The system does not authenticate for creating standard value due to invalid login
References	Regulatory portal—Standard value maintenance use case diagram

Use Case	**UC20-Authorization Access**
Actors	A1-government administrator
Description	To access the standard value, the government administrator has to login into the system. The login ID and password are checked and if correct, provided authentication
Precondition	N/A
Postcondition	Government administrator successfully logs in to system
Type	Simple
Normal Course of Events	1. The system asks for the Login ID 2. Government administrator provides with the Login ID 3. The system asks for the Login password 4. Government administrator provides Login password 5. The system verifies and provides authentication (A1) 6. The government administrator successfully access the standard value and operations
Alternate Course of Events	A1-The system does not provide authentication due to wrong Login ID or Login password
References	Regulatory portal—Standard value maintenance use case diagram

Use Case	**UC3-Update Carbon Limits Value**
Actors	A1-Government administrator—Primary; A2-Government representative—Secondary
Description	The government administrator will update the standard values which is provided by the government representative in the system
Precondition	Standard value for the device must exist
Postcondition	Standard value successfully updated
Type	Medium
Normal Course of Events	1. The government administrator requests for updating standard value 2. The system requests for the authentication 2.1 <<include>> UC2-Login 3. The system authenticates and provides access for updating the standard value

	4. The government representative provides the standard value to government administrator
	5. The government administrator may change the standard value or delete the standard value based on the values provided by government representative
	6. The system accepts and updates the value
Alternate Course of Events	
References	Regulatory portal—Carbon limits value maintenance use case diagram

Use Case	UC4-View Carbon Limits Value
Actors	A1-Government administrator—Primary; A2-Government representative—Primary
Description	The government administrator and government representative view the standard values
Precondition	
Postcondition	The actors successfully view the standard value
Type	Simple
Normal Course of Events	1. The government administrator/government representative requests for the standard emission values for a particular emitter 2. The system asks the emitter details 3. The actor provides the emitter details like type, name, and so on 4. The system successfully displays the standard values
Alternate Course of Events	N/A
References	Regulatory portal—Standard value maintenance use case diagram

Class Diagram for GOP

Figure 7.9 shows an example of a class diagram for a GOP. This diagram shows the key entities in the portal and their interrelationships. These entities are derived from the "Use Case Analysis." This class diagram will be expanded in detail in practice. This object-oriented structure will also have to be configurable in practice—for each company, depending on different industry sector.

"User" and "Organizational User" are the primary actors of the system. Environmental manager and worker are major organizational users of system. User works in a department of a company which is dedicated to specific industry. In addition to above users, there are some external devices such as smart meters which are used to calculate emission of a pollutant. Different types of reports such as emission-specific reports are created by user.

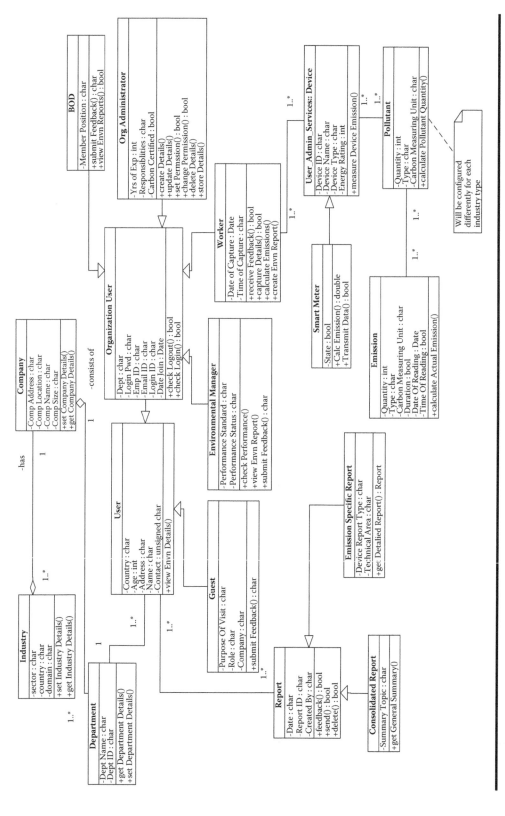

Figure 7.9 Class diagram (static model) within "Green Organizational Portal."

Sequence Diagram for "Emissions Check"

Figure 7.10 shows an example of a sequence within the GOP that deals with emissions check.

Environmental manager calculates emissions and they are sent to an employee who captures the details and creates them in system under administrator's access. Administrator generates report out of system and sends the reports back to environmental manager. In addition to it, feedback on each pollutant and related emission values is sent to environmental manager.

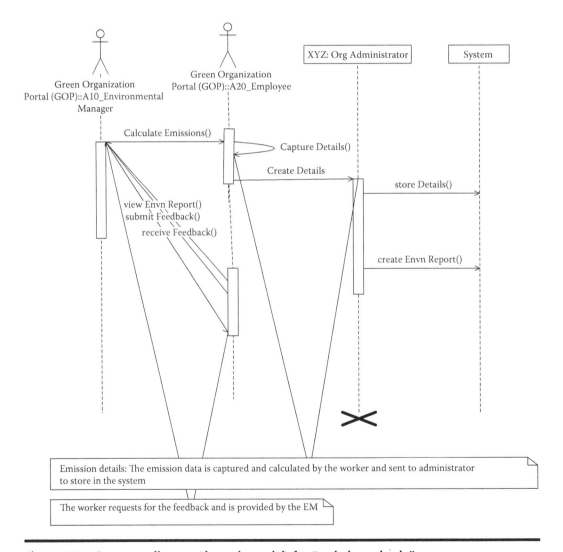

Figure 7.10 Sequence diagram (dynamic model) for "emissions check."

Class Diagram for RSP

Figure 7.11 shows a regulatory service portal. This service is provided by regulatory and compliance department of the government authority. The key business entities are government user, industry, company, device, pollutant categories, and standard emission values.

The key relationships are inheritance, aggregation, and association. Government administrator is inheriting government user characteristics. Industry has different types of companies which show aggregation. Every pollutant category has standard emissions which show association relationship.

Sequence Diagram for "Setting Standard Emissions Value"

Figure 7.12 shows an example of a sequence diagram for setting standard emissions values within a Regulatory Server Portal.

Regulatory Server Portal sets standards that are created by government administrator. Government administrator collects industry details, company details, and emitter details. On basis of those details, government administrator calculates emission standards, pollutant specifications, and emitter specifications.

State Machine Diagrams for "Emission Report" and "Emission Standard Value" Objects

Figure 7.13 shows state machine diagram for an emission report. It shows all the states starting from creation of an emission report till it gets filed.

Emission report is created initially by worker. It is analyzed on the basis of existing standards by environmental manager. Environmental manager checks whether the report is above permissible limit. If yes, then the report is enquired, appropriate steps are suggested and it is then filed, but if the report is okay, then it is approved and filed.

Figure 7.14 shows state machine diagram for an emission standard value. It shows all the states starting from providing emission standard values till it gets stored.

Government representative provides standard values for emissions and checks for the standard values. If the values are existing and need updates, then the values are updated and stored successfully, but if the values are new, then they are created and stored in the database.

Implementation Diagrams for GIS

Figure 7.15 depicts the component diagram for complete GIS including all the important components like ROP and GOP.

Organizational portal and regulatory (government) portal are two major components of the system. They are connected with major interfaces for create, update, remove, and view functionalities.

Figure 7.16 depicts the deployment diagram of the complete GIS including all the external actors connected to major components of the application.

Two high-end servers are connected to each other. GOP and RSP sits on each server. Standard emissions are provided by RSP and they are provided to be compared for each pollutant. GOP creates report and sends for enquiry. Handheld device is useful in creating reports and tracking emission values in units.

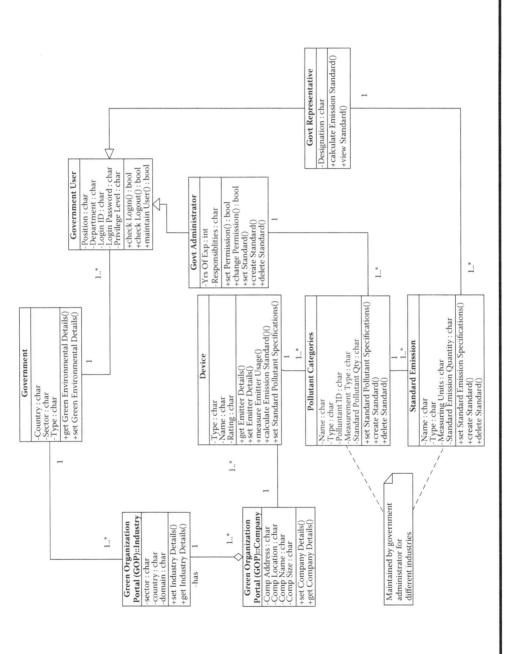

Figure 7.11   Class model (static model) within "regulatory portal."

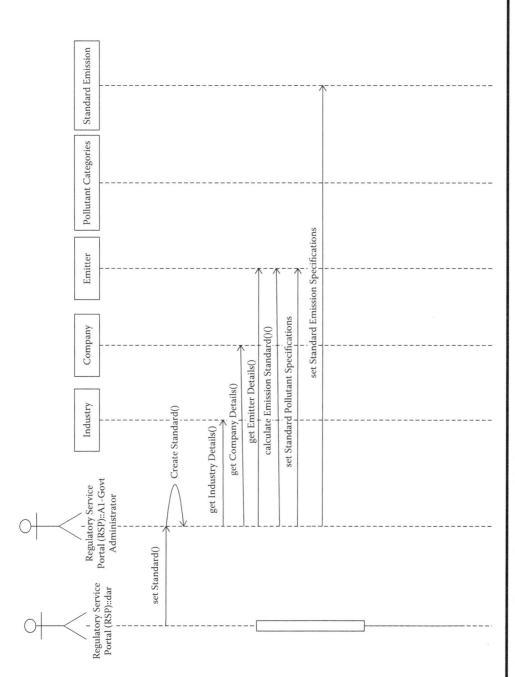

Figure 7.12 Sequence diagram (dynamic model) for "setting standard emissions value."

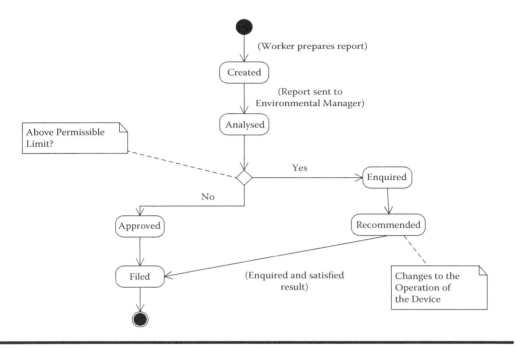

Figure 7.13   State machine diagram for class—emission report.

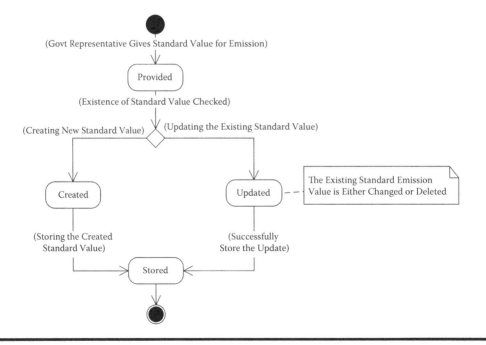

Figure 7.14   State machine diagram for class—emission standard value.

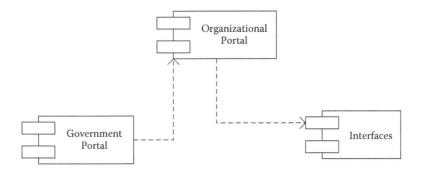

Figure 7.15   Component diagram for GIS.

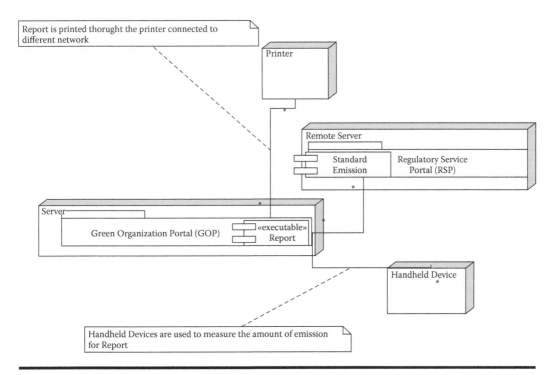

Figure 7.16   Deployment diagram for GIS.

GIS—Technical Requirements

In addition to functional requirements, GIS also has operational technical requirements. They are listed as follows:

- ■ GIS should be able to run in a wide variety of platforms such as Windows, Unix, Linux, and so on. Some components of the software application will be installed in mobile devices. Those mobile devices run several operative systems such as Windows mobile, Symbian, I-phone OS.

- GIS should be able to operate on a variety of hardware including PC, laptop, and mobile devices.
- The data should be stored in a server located in a secure environment. However, network connectivity with the applications should be on a 24×7 basis.
- GIS will be deployed as SaaS via internet. The system will allow users to connect from different locations via Internet service providers.
- GIS user access should be based on a secured identification and password. Users will have levels of authorization and access. Those access levels will be administered by system administrators. Carbon data information should be available to regular users (e.g., staff), casual users (e.g., members of the public), strategic users (e.g., CGO), and regulators. Informative users need not sign-up.
- The GIS should have a sophisticated firewall that would block unwanted connections from outside the organizational boundary.
- GIS should incorporate encryption. Public key encryption is a preferred mode although secret key encryption can be considered for the sake of speed.
- A virtual private network (VPN) would be established to ensure private communication between collaborating organizations using the same GIS.

Discussion Points

- What are the major areas of a GIS (refer to package diagram)?
- How would you separate functional from nonfunctional requirements of a GIS?
- Create a use case diagram for the major aspect of a GIS relevant to your organization.
- Study the two class diagrams provided in this chapter as a starting point for discussion on key business entities. Expand a few classes with all attributes and operations you can think of.
- List the operational requirements for the GIS from your organization's viewpoint.

Action Points

- Study www.cemsus.com and identify two most appropriate GIS for your organization. Compare their cost-benefits.
- Compare the cost-benefits of developing an in-house GIS as against procuring a ready-made GIS. Consider the importance of SaaS-based deployment of the GIS selected.
- Discuss the key functional requirements for a GIS for your organization.
- Discuss the key nonfunctional or operational requirements for your organization.
- List the challenges in configuring, testing, and deploying GIS in your organization.

Chapter 8

Sociocultural Aspects
of Green IT

To condemn is stupid and easy, but to understand is arduous, requiring pliability and intelligence ... Condemnation or identification is a barrier to understanding.

J. Krishnamurti*

Key Points

- Discusses social dimension of green enterprise transformation that is based on people and their attitude.
- Discusses the impact of Green information technology (IT) on society and vice versa.
- Highlights the subjectivity of individuals in understanding, interpreting, and applying Green IT.
- Discusses the importance of corporate social responsibility (CSR) as embraced by businesses.
- Discusses the social impact of Green IT initiatives (such as telecommuting, teleconferencing) or individual working lifestyle and the corresponding support required by an organization's HR.
- Presents Green IT in the context of the social communication networks and how these social networks help green initiatives; encourages reaching out to communities and social groups to foster diffusion of the Green IT-related information and knowledge.
- Discusses the human resource (HR) and changing organizational structure due to Green IT. New roles, their definition, and positioning within the enterprise are discussed.
- Maps the increasingly popular professional competency skills set of SFIA (skills framework for information age) to Green IT.

---

* *From The Collected Works of J. Krishnamurti, Published by the J. Krishnamurti Foundation*, see http://www.jkrishnamurti.org/index.php, Vol. IV—143.

- Social impact (travel, health, education, etc.—see the case study chapters) of Green IT and the role of HR in understanding this social impact.
- Describes the ethics and a code of conduct for Green IT as norms for professional behavior in this rapidly developing domain.
- Discourages green washing by ensuring honesty in calculations and reporting of carbon emissions both internal and external to the organization that will be subject to audits.
- Highlights the importance of privacy and security of green data and information that combines technical and social issue, and is addressed by the data center, the legal experts as well as the HR department of the organization.
- Safety issues in Green IT—ensuring that critical and safety systems of the organization are not jeopardized due to the green initiative.

Introduction

This chapter discusses the importance of the sociocultural aspect of Green IT as it comprises the important and subjective element of the green enterprise transformation. This discussion is vital in undertaking a holistic approach to transformation and therefore, is not limited to technologies and processes of an organization. Earlier, in Chapter 2, the social dimension of Green IT was discussed as one of the four dimensions or channels along which an organization can undertake green enterprise transformation. This chapter discusses this social dimension of Green IT and the changes that affect an organization in the sociocultural context. Apart from the employees, business partners, and senior management of the organization, this sociocultural impact of Green IT is also felt by people in the society that may not be a part of the organization. The transition to a green enterprise affects a range of stakeholders in different ways and an understanding of the impacts assists in preparing an organization for the transition.

Sociocultural and political issues are one of the six crucial drivers of Green IT. As the organization transforms itself into a green organization, the social dynamics of the organization changes to match the green working lifestyle and a green attitude. These social dynamics also influence individuals beyond their workplace and go into their associated personal/family lifestyles. Green initiatives in an organization have corresponding wide-ranging impact on the working lifestyles of the employees that goes beyond their immediate place of work. For example, when an organization embarks on carbon reduction through a telework/telecommuting program, the commuting styles of employees are affected. This, in turn, has an effect on their family lives. A comprehensive green enterprise transformation program will require cooperation and input from the organization's human relations (HR) department. Green IT social implications are often subjective because different individuals are impacted differently by the green transformation of the enterprise. For example, those employees with families and who need to travel significant physical distances in peak hour traffic may make extensive use of remote access and mobile computing to work from home. HR will enable separation and definition of these roles based on the familiarity of individuals with this mode of work as well as identification of roles within the organization that are non-customer facing.

The social dimension of Green enterprise transformation is a subjective affair that needs to bring together the tacit knowledge and viewpoints of individuals including the explicit knowledge stored in database.

Adding to the complexity of this social dimension of Green IT is the fact that the multiple stakeholders have different interests, are operating at different levels, and progress at varying speeds. Socially, the rate of change in terms of Green IT for these stakeholders is a subjective element of the transformation.

As shown in Figure 8.1, the society, government, industry sector, and the organization are all involved in and affected by the changes resulting from Green IT at different levels and at varying speeds. The department or business unit within the organization is more agile as compared with the organization itself as shown in Figure 8.1. Finally, the individual employees within those business units can change almost immediately if they decide to do so. However, the attitudes and preferences of individuals come into play at this level. While personal preferences can change for each individual quickly, they also provide a major challenge due to their subjective nature and, at times, due to vested interests taking preference over carbon reduction. Therefore, development of Green IT policies with consensus and their practice right from the leadership of the organization down to departmental heads and team leads becomes important. Effectiveness of green transformation changes depend on this leadership changes. There is a significant amount of subjectivity in the decisions and practice of Green IT by the leadership. Furthermore, the leaders of the organization represent that organization in consortiums. Thus, at an industrial level, the leaders and decision makers of the organization play an important role in discussing, debating, and arriving at consensus on policies and practices that can be adopted by consortium of green organizations.

Green transformation of an entire society involves green ethics, morals, value systems, and attitude across multiple layers of people. This makes environmental changes for the society even more complicated than organizational and governmental changes. Thus, while a government can bring about changes through ratification of agreements and converting them into law, the changes in the society are based on protocols and understanding that is "in grown." The social dimension

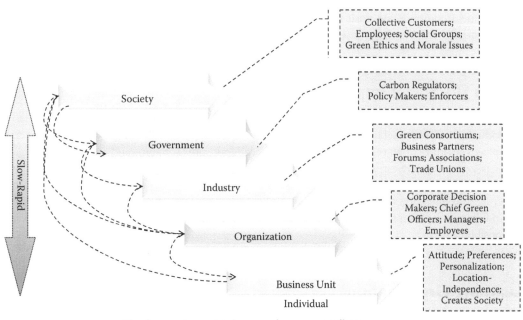

The slow moving society has a much more compelling
influence on the greening of the organization; society influences governments;
governments in turn, influence industry and the organization;
organization undertake or are "forced" to undergo
green enterprise transformation. Ultimately the individual is affected.

Figure 8.1 Relative speed of change in green enterprise transformation.

of Green IT thus requires discussion of these wide-ranging considerations. The success of a green enterprise transformation depends on not treating any one dimension in isolation but, instead focusing on each of the dimensions with due consideration to the others.

Initial efforts at green transformation by business units present the social challenge of resistance to change. The inbuilt resistance to change that has been discussed in most management literature is also applicable to green transformations. In addition to overcoming this resistance, there is also a need to consider the variations in the way in which this resistance to green transformation appears in various industry sectors. For example, the way in which policies, protocols, and practices of Green IT are interpreted in the banking domain are likely to be different to those in the mining sector. Individuals in banks may focus on optimizing the processes relating to financial transactions, whereas individuals in a mine would focus on the way in which it drills and extracts metal or oil. Similarly, staff in a hospital will interpret the green initiative with due consideration to patient care and biowastage, as compared with, say, the education sector where the focus will be on laptops and networks used in schoolwork. Government is also involved in these activities and interpretations with various industry sectors: supporting common outcomes, providing incentives, agreeing of commonly accepted penalties, and facilitating transition arrangements. While the industry sectors and the market can determine the best solutions, government help and support can influence the subjective aspect of those solutions in a positive way.

Training and awareness associated with the Green IT issues can play a key role in handling the subjective nature of green transformation. This is particularly so if the message is clear, consistent, and based on consensus. Eventually, social values change and green consciousness gets "inbuilt" in the new generation of individuals. Such sociocultural transformation takes time to achieve and needs to be accommodated with the economic levers and any market-driven setup that may be implemented.

Green IT's Social Impact

Discussions of the social aspects of Green IT involve individuals, government, and society. Individuals, however, operate in several roles, as the individual, as member of a family or social group, as a member of an organization (business, academic, government), and as decision makers. There is a growing interest by individuals to understand the organizations they are associated, its values and its performance in terms of the environment. Environmental responsibility affects the structure and operation of the organizations and the society in which it exists. As mentioned earlier in Chapter 2, this interest leads a business to have what is popularly known as corporate social responsibility (CSR).

Learning Organization

One of the ways an organization can successfully discharge its CSR is by incorporating Green IT in both the tacit (subjective) and explicit domains of the organization. Thus, to be environmentally and socially responsible, an organization requires regular and unified systems for knowledge management that lead it to be a learning organization [based on the original concept of Senge (1990)]. This is so because an organization has to learn how to develop the necessary capacities and capabilities in discharging its CSR. Management for sustainability demands a multidisciplinary approach that range from the generic to the contextual and from the scientific to subjective levels.

Hercheui (2011) has further developed the concepts of knowledge management as important in bringing about behavioral change within the organizations relating to sustainability. Hercheui's arguments extend original studies by (Haas, Kanie, and Murphy, 2004) which point to the need for creating knowledge management frameworks which diffuse best sustainability practices within the organization.

The knowledge management aspects of Green IT comes into play in the social dimensions of the organizations when data and information within the data warehouses of the organization are continuously updated by the tacit knowledge of people working within and outside the organization. Green information systems need to ensure that what is subjectively understood and used by people at work also gets captured and coded in the green data warehouses.

Such knowledge synchronization results in a learning organization highlighted by Unhelkar et al. (2009) in business collaborations. As the enterprise evolves to a green enterprise, there are changes associated with attitude, leadership and management styles, interpretation of technology, and the business environment. These subjective change require the organization to implement green knowledge management (as a part of its environmental intelligence as discussed in Chapter 6). Extending an earlier definition of knowledge management by Laudon and Laudon (2002, 2008), and applying it here, a green knowledge management can be understood as "the process of systematically and actively managing and leveraging the stores of carbon-related knowledge in the organization."

These green knowledge management systems involve synchronization of the tacit and explicit bodies of knowledge carried by its stakeholders. For example, the department head carries the knowledge of changes to production schedule as well as likely unavailability of two key personnel in the production run. This knowledge needs to be made explicit and shared across multiple departments to not only optimize the production but also reduce the corresponding carbon content. A knowledge management system will enable the department head to update the information in both formal, explicit form (such as updating a relational database) and also in a descriptive form (such as alternatives or backups to the key personnel for the production run). This knowledge synchronization aspect of Green IT becomes more challenging in global, multinational organizations, whose business units and subsidiaries are often spread across geographical regions, exhibiting their quite distinct cultural attitudes and characteristics. Stakeholders in such global organizations need to particularly consider cross-cultural interactions in their green initiatives.

Green Social Stakeholders

One of the important ways to handle cross-cultural issues in long-scale green transformation is by increasing and enhancing the opportunities for physical (face-to-face) communications amongst the diverse stakeholders. While increasingly challenging, physical communications can help handle cross-cultural issues, especially when the transformation plan is implemented. Information flow between various groups of employees in different regions supported by the organizational change management is required for successful transition to a green organization.

The issues relating to collaborative groups of people and organizations need to be considered in global green effort. These issues include their individual preferences, corporate policies, government regulations, social norms and practices, and ethical codes of conduct. In fact, even different age groups, their preferences as customers, employees, and regulations, and their sociocultural background influence the Green IT initiative. The greening of an enterprise thus continues to demonstrate substantial subjective element to it. Successful transformations acknowledge and incorporate that subjective element within the transformation program. Age groups, professions, cultural upbringing, special needs, and education are some of the criteria that seem to dictate these personal viewpoints. Table 8.1 lists these potentially subjective viewpoints on environmental issues for some of these categories of people. Table 8.1 also lists the typical activities undertaken by each of these categories of people and the corresponding green implications. These views can be spread out over the various levels of social changes that were shown in Figure 8.1.

Table 8.1 highlights the differing viewpoints and impacts of some of the roles in the society. These same roles with their potentially different viewpoint also influence the roles within the organization.

Table 8.1 Views of Various Cross-Sections of Society (Children, Elderly, Tax Payers, Households, Sports People, Defense, etc.) on Environmental Initiatives

Categories	Activities (Typical)	Green Viewpoint (Typical Examples)
Children	Playing games Being entertained Being monitored	Carbon emission due to use of electronic gadgets, TV, and computers Usage not controlled and financed by actual users
Adolescents	Games Entertainment message Exchange (IM, Email)	Carbon emissions resulting from gaming gadgets Increased electronic storage and use of Internet-based communications for group games
	Study activities (education)	Reduced outdoor activities Reduced activities with paper and pen Reduced readings from books and journals (and therefore, less visits to the library, for example) Desirous of faster results
Adults	Social networks Email/communications Learning Banking/finance Work related Search engines	Concerns about the environment from futuristic viewpoint (what will happen to my children and their children?) Reduction in travel through—telecommuting Capable of influencing policies and regulations
Elders	Increase in social networks Health	Skepticism and inhibition in using IT
People with special needs	Online facilities Communication Search engines	Ease of movements Hiring of experience

Table 8.1   Views of Various Cross-Sections of Society (Children, Elderly, Tax Payers, Households, Sports People, Defense, etc.) on Environmental Initiatives (Continued)

Categories	Activities (Typical)	Green Viewpoint (Typical Examples)
Patients in hospital	Social networks	EPR storage, improved health, increased carbon
	Email/news finance	
Sports people	Search engines	Enhanced competitive performance
	Social networks	Training
Defense personnel	Information	Increased storage of data
	Communication	More data servers
	Protection/security	Communication equipment
		Improved security and surveillance but also increase in carbon

Role-Based View of Green IT

Green IT initiatives and their subjective interpretations are based on various roles. Typical roles within the society in general were discussed in the previous section and highlighted in Table 8.1. When it comes to organizational stakeholders, these roles within an organization require detailed study. The reason for this role-based study is to understand the subjectivity as well as the personal interests these roles would have in undertaking and supporting green transformations.

The subjectivity of Green IT is seen in the various roles within an organization. For example, the decision maker is primarily interested in the ROI on the green initiatives, where an engineer is interested in improvement of design and production process.

Figure 8.2 shows the various roles that participated in and were studied as a part of the Trivedi and Unhelkar (2009) survey. While these demographic data are of immense interest from a pure research and statistical viewpoint, it is also worth having a look at the roles of the survey participants. Twenty percent of respondents were decision makers in the industry, who would be taking that strategic decision, based on available ROI metrics, to undertake a green enterprise transformation. It is also worth noting that only about 2% respondents were in the role of an environmental regulator. The survey was spread out over the various roles and has provided the basis for further in-depth research by Trivedi (2011). Table 8.2 shows the Green IT subjective views or areas of interest corresponding to these roles.

The survey further explored various industry sectors and the viewpoints of the roles described in Table 8.2. It is observed that the viewpoints on Green IT change depending on the industry sectors.

Green IT initiatives thus continue to have a wide-ranging subjective impact on the individuals and roles they play at work. This, in turn, also affects the way people are organized and operate within organizations. Formation of attitude toward carbon emissions and its impact on the workplace provides a significant challenge to the transformation of the society to a carbon-conscious society (Godbole, 2009). Technologies, such as mobile communications technologies, also impact the formation of attitude as they can completely change the way in which work is carried out. Therefore, this use of mobility has to be studied in this social dimension of Green IT.

Figure 8.3 shows the impact of Green IT on working lifestyles of individuals. The gap between the place of work and that of residence is bridged through various means in Figure 8.3. There is physical commuting (the normal, standard way of working) followed by land-based or wired means of communications and, eventually, totally location-independent mobile communications. The use of these varied communication mechanisms have direct bearing on the carbon contents

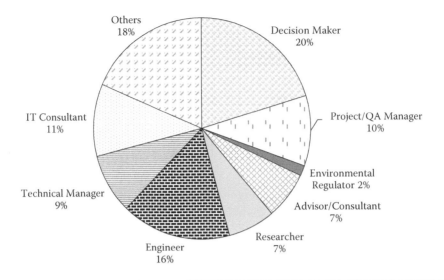

Figure 8.2   Role-based view of Green IT.

Table 8.2   Roles within Organization and Their Subjective Viewpoint

Role	Green IT Subjective Viewpoint
Decision maker (20%)	Major interest in the ROI, as that justifies their actions. Legal, compliance requirements, however, change the balance of their ROI metrics. Green IT strategy formulation, policies. Participation in consortiums.
Project manager/quality assurance manager (10%)	Interested in the implementation of the green program, the steps to be taken for that implementation, and the successful review at the end of the project. Aims to complete the project with minimum time and budget.
Environmental regulator (2%)	Creation of regulatory benchmarks. Compliance metrics, their measurements, reporting of that carbon data. Interested in issues arising out of noncompliance. Participation in standard creation.
Advisor (management consultant) (7%)	Analyses of the organization business processes in order to introduce green environment. How to reduce risks in implementing Green IT. Lean process. Participation in standards compliance.
IT consultant (including Green IT) (11% + 7%)	Model processes, optimize, smart networks, green enterprise architecture (ISO standards).
Engineer (manufacturing/production) (16%)	Optimize production, improve design.
Technical manager (9%)	Focus on technologies for carbon reduction (as against economy and services).
Researcher (7%)	Undertaking Green IT investigation, pure and applied research. In any or all four dimensions of Green IT.

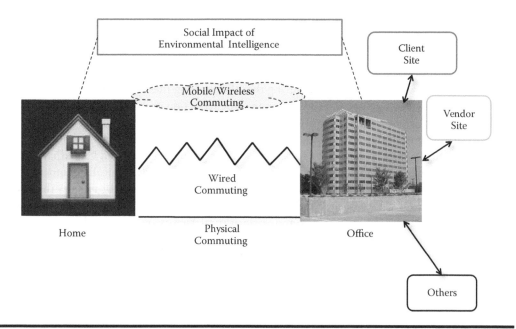

Figure 8.3 Green IT influencing working lifestyle.

of the processes followed by these employees. For example, mobility enables the office itself to be location-independent; therefore, it is not uncommon to have an employee working out of a client site, a vendor site, or any other location that is not a fixed office location. In particular, knowledge workers (e.g., consultants) or service providers (e.g., telecom engineers or insurance agents making site visits) can easily work through a "mobile office." Such a mobile office, which is also a virtual office, can provide immense carbon benefits coupled with social benefits.

The energy saved from reduced commuting to and from work or by completing a sales transaction on the spot using a mobile device also needs to be calculated and accounted for. The opportunity to access back-end databases instantaneously, meeting business partners in a dynamic mode by making instantaneous changes to negotiating stances are all excellent business benefits that are always pursued by businesses; however, these same advantages also have the carbon saving advantage due to reduced movement of people and optimized processes through mobile computing devices.

The effort, from an organizational perspective, are the need to change business models and management (see green enterprise transformation work areas discussed in Chapter 9), incorporating the use of collaborative technologies (e.g., desktop sharing, image sharing as also facilitate social networking tools such as blogs, Wikis, Twitter, and Facebook). Virtual desktop, which was mentioned in Chapter 4 in discussing virtualization, facilitates collaborative use of resources to enable sharing of work amongst people. Such collaborative tools enable sharing of tasks, quicker time to completion, and, as a result, less carbon.

The use of abovementioned technologies results in a collaborative workplace that changes the carbon footprint of the organization. Collaboration also changes the social dynamics within and outside of the organization. This change include corresponding changes to workplace relationships, elements of HR policies and practices, as well as legal and ethical responsibilities of both the organization and the workers.

The social dimension of Green IT is instrumental in engendering these aforementioned changes enhancing corresponding capabilities of the organization. The Green IT transformation framework is also effective in ensuring that the changes are proved through the Green IT metrics (Trivedi and Unhelkar, 2009). For example, the reduction in commuting as a result of these initiatives, and the corresponding reduction in infrastructure and building facilities translate into major carbon savings for the organization that have to be factored in those metrics. The HR department of an organization will be involved in ensuring that the working lifestyle of an individual worker is not adversely affected by these Green IT changes. The reduction in travel and potential increase in job satisfaction can be considered as the spin off benefits of carbon reduction.

The underlying technologies and systems relating to environmental intelligence have also been used to reorganize processes that have a social impact. For example, Bhalla and Chaudhary (2011) have discussed clever use of environmental intelligence systems that dynamically compute travel times and traffic congestion and, subsequently, advise motorists in a way that reduces that travel times, idling times for their vehicles, and improves traffic flows. Gala and Unhelkar (2009) have also reported on the impact of attitude and sociocultural factors on mobile phone usage that potentially impact Green IT. These are activities within the Green IT space that have a direct impact on a large cross-section of society in general, and working lifestyle of people in particular.

Green User Practices

Videoconferencing, telecommuting, and use of mobile technology in work—all have substantial, positive impact on the organization's carbon footprint. All these green users' practices also affect the social aspects of the users.

Figure 8.4, based on the Trivedi and Unhelkar (2010) survey, highlights three of the many major areas of changes to working lifestyles that are involved in a green enterprise transformation. Survey participants were quizzed in terms of the importance they gave to the ICT practices that they felt would impact the carbon footprint of their organization. These practices included videoconferencing, telecommuting/teleworking, fleet and field force management, web, and use of collaboration tools such as emails and mobile phones/PDAs. Figure 8.4 shows these practices in terms of their importance to carbon reduction. The percentage respondents who "agreed" and "strongly agreed" to the use of the approaches shown in Figure 8.4 in reducing the carbon footprint of the organizations itself proves their tremendous importance in the green initiative.

A total of 57% of the respondents "agreed" to "strongly agreed" that videoconferencing will improve the carbon footprint of their organization. Similarly, a large 79% of respondents "agreed" to "strongly agreed," when asked about the positive impact of telecommuting/teleworking on the carbon credentials of their organization. Finally, almost all of the entire respondents (close to 90%) felt that the use of mobile technologies will reduce commuting and thereby reduce carbon footprint.

Videoconferencing is increasingly on the use, especially as the costs associated with it are dropping rapidly. This technology can thus be used to better communicate with a group that may be geographically dispersed. Care should be taken, however, to balance the carbon savings due to the use of videoconferencing (such as fuel costs associated with vehicles or airplanes) versus the carbon generated as a result of videoconferencing itself.

Another important user practice with respect to Green IT is the reengineering of business processes of an organization based on virtual team. The changes resulting from formation and operation of virtual teams require corresponding changes to the processes that describe the way in which business is carried out. For example, an insurance claim process that requires coordination between the accounting, the legal, and the business portfolio processes could all be coordinating virtually rather than physically to settle a claim. This would change the description of the claims

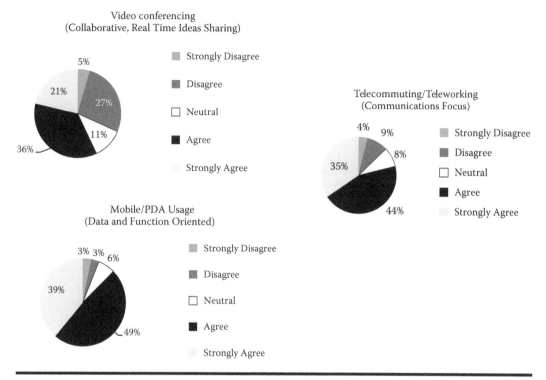

Figure 8.4 Green user practices that have social impact.

process, the deliverables, and documentation associated with it and the organizational roles. In terms of project-based work, virtual teams can be project specific, with teams being put together through the communication technologies to achieve an outcome, and then being disbanded. These virtual teams will often be collaborating globally across the time zones, with colleagues from diverse areas of business at various levels all drawn together to deliver outcomes.

Attitude and Subjectivity in Green IT

Subjectivity of Green IT was mentioned at the start of this chapter and summarized, from a sociocultural perspective in Table 8.1 and role-based perspectives in Table 8.2. The green enterprise transformational work in the social dimension is based on bringing together the viewpoints of roles within and also outside the organization. Harding (2002), in his preface to the book *Environmental Decision-Making*, puts it rather succinctly: "Given the critical state of the world's environment, it is crucial to employ all of the beneficial knowledge, technology and tools that scientists, engineers and other professionals can offer." Thus even the most sophisticated scientific and technological knowledge is by itself inadequate. The need for an all inclusive commitment to applying the principle of environmental consciousness during their work and personal lives is vital.

Figure 8.5 highlights the source of this subjectivity from an employee's viewpoint. The business priorities, the environmental priorities, and the personal priorities of individuals are many times at odds with each other. For example, an employee has a business priority to provide excellent service to a customer, but the environmental priority requires that the service be provided with

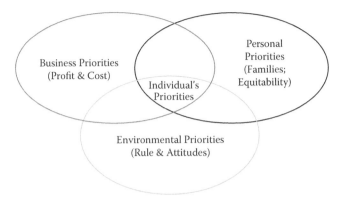

Figure 8.5 Subjectivity in Green IT arises from differencing priorities of the same individual.

a shorter time period and with minimal opportunity for a social interaction. These two priorities can not only be at odds with each other but can also be at odds with the personal priority that includes family time, personal interests, and the desire to be treated equitably. For example, one employee should not be disadvantaged due to additional, carbon producing, activities of other employees. The area of intersection of these three priorities needs to be studied under the social aspect of Green IT. The organizational (HR) policies and practices then have to work on expanding that intersection of the three priorities as shown in Figure 8.5.

This is particularly important because, as argued by Hercheui (2011), the domain of sustainability is not only complex and uncertain but is also highly dependent on the context (Kanie and Haas, 2004; Pachauri and Reisinger, 2008). Furthermore, the application and practice of sustainability requires knowledge that is specific to the context. This context is the situation and role played by the person. The environmental science *per se* is a field in which most knowledge depends on the efficient overlapping of what we know generically and what is known locally (Hercheui, 2011). Individuals change their attitude and behavior when the objective on carbon emission relates to them, personally. Thus, the data and information related to carbon emission is likely to be interpreted in accordance with the personal needs, existing attitudes, and interests of individuals. The social, economical, and political contexts provide the background for the change. However, attitude change in individuals is a subjective matter that occurs only when the personal interests of the individual are also catered for in the Green IT initiative of the organization.

Whenever approached with a new system, processes, and corresponding changes in the approach to work, users tend to be extremely sensitive. Figure 8.6 shows how the individuals in an organization, on its path to green transformation, are likely to personalize the entire initiative. The success or failure of the entire green enterprise transformation program, from a social perspective, rests on the perceived ease, perceive usefulness, and perceived relevance of the initiative. Technology adoption, in this case, is the adoption of the Green IT systems to help, support, measure, and report on the activities and tasks of individual users. The effect of the green system on the career, future growth, and rewarding structure are issues of concern for the individual users. Starting right from the "personal" aspects of the drivers that drive this Green IT transformation and the dimensions or channels along which the transformation actually takes place, this personalization remains at the center of the attitude of the users and their personal "buy-in." Figure 8.6 further shows the tiers of influence—social, followed by organizational and eventually personalized—of the green enterprise transformation.

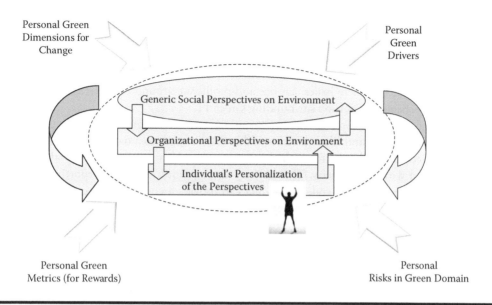

Figure 8.6 Personalization of the green context by end-users leads to change in attitude.

Deshpande and Unhelkar (2011) have discussed the need for management, ICT, and other professionals within the organizations to collaborate in using the emerging technologies as a means to effect changes in their environmental behavior. This collaboration, according to Deshpande (and Unhelkar (2011), also requires employee and customer participation. Thus, it is essential that the strategies for acquisition and management of information as well as for proper implementation include all the employees in order to influence their practices, secure their participation, and thus ensure success of the overall campaign.

Green IT Ethics and Code of Conduct

Ethics and professional codes of conduct have been discussed, formulated, and promoted by the IT profession through its various associations.* These codes set the expectations of professional behavior from those who adhere to the code. While IT itself is a nascent profession as compared with, say, medicine or construction, Green IT is even more new. Therefore, having an ethical base will enable Green IT to have a common view, a common set of behavior, and understanding that is shaped by the experiences of practitioners, sharing of case studies, and relating of work experiences. Green IT ethics are meant to provide guidelines through which an interpretation of what is commonly believed to be right or wrong can be made. These ethical code need to expand on seven areas of information criteria, that is, effectiveness, efficiency, confidentiality, integrity, availability, compliance, and reliability (based on ACM) as they apply to Green IT.

Green IT needs a code of conduct. Extending the current IT professional codes of conduct, and adding green-specific requirements to them, produces a list of code that individuals and organizations can strive to follow. Having such a code of conduct is vital, especially as Green IT is a nascent profession as compared with, say, medicine or construction. Having an ethical base enables Green IT to have a common view, a common set of behavior and understanding that is shaped by the experiences of practitioners, sharing of case studies, and relating of work experiences. Green IT ethics are meant to provide guidelines through which an interpretation of what is commonly believed to be right or wrong can be made. Similar to the IT ethical code, the Green IT code of ethics also needs to delve into the seven areas of Information Criteria, that is, effectiveness, efficiency, confidentiality, integrity, availability, compliance, and reliability (based on ACM).

* The associations are IEEE, ACM, and ACS.

In discussing the social aspect of Green IT, it is worth delving into these ethical codes of conduct as they apply to Green IT. A Green IT code of conduct can augment and support the expectations and behaviors of individuals operating as employees and consulting professionals as well as the organizations that subscribe to that code of conduct. This is particularly helpful in a new domain such as that of Green IT, where issues can rise and proliferate around the validity of carbon data and mechanisms of communication surrounding Green IT.

The tiers of audience for Green IT communications are wide ranging—from the general public, school going children, and likes (listed in Table 8.1) through to a data center director. What is being discussed, debated, and researched in terms of a clean energy economy also needs to be communicated with authenticity. This honesty in communication and reporting is another area wherein a Green IT ethical code of conduct can provide a good starting point. The need to understand the terminologies such as energy efficiency, renewable energy, and carbon neutral and explain them in layman's terms is vital. Similarly, the need to isolate vested interest groups who may launch into a potential misinformation campaign is also vital. Ethics and code of conduct for Green IT can control such activities and bring in clarity and positive focus—resulting in reliability and trust in green data, information, and knowledge.

From the ethical point of view, Green IT needs to ensure that the transformation of the organization to a green organization contributes to society and human well-being. Furthermore, such a code of conduct provides the organization that subscribes to it with guidelines and direction to remain compliant. Green transformation process must ensure ongoing compliance while evaluation of IT systems, analysis of possible risks, and their impacts are considered.

While the code of conduct for Green IT only expands and builds on the existing professional codes, it is important to foster trust amongst the Green IT professionals, users, and consumers of the Green IT initiatives and the society at large. McDermid (2008, p. 33) describes "ethics involves being reasonable and having good reasons to support the choices we make." A publicized code of conduct for Green IT can go a long way in establishing and maintain a high ethical bar within this relatively nascent domain.

Following are the statements and potential advantages of having a Green IT code of conduct. *Organization following the Green IT code of conduct will:*

- Agree to a fundamental obligation of businesses to reduce carbon emissions in all their activities.
- Conform to total honesty in recording, analyzing, and reporting of carbon data—both manually and through IT systems.
- Ensure that the effort to reduce carbon is undertaken in a socially responsible way and with no harm to people involved in the reduction attempt (this is particularly important in the hospital sector).
- Ensure ongoing effort at all levels of IT—architecture, design, development, testing, deployment, and maintenance—of hardware, software, and networks—to reduce their carbon emission (this code goes beyond the operation and maintenance and also focuses on the design aspects of IT hardware and systems).
- Ensure ongoing effort to reduce carbon in procurement, operation, and disposal.
- Promote confidentiality and integrity within the organization and the IT profession (this will nurture public trust and confidence).
- Maintain security and confidentiality of carbon data and information (within the organization and the way this data interfaced with the regulatory and compliance portals).
- Make the carbon data available publically.

- Avoid green washing or incorrect promotion of the organization's carbon reduction effort.
- Contribute toward development of Green IT standards worldwide and their application in practice.
- Ensure participation in industry and research surveys including workshops to increase the overall body of knowledge.
- Attempt to use all emerging technologies to reduce existing carbon emissions and prevent increase in carbon emissions due to future business activities.
- Endeavor to maintain validity of carbon data by subjecting itself to regular reviews and audits.
- Maintain the security and privacy of carbon data.
- Honor contracts, responsibilities, protocols, and agreements associated with Green IT and carbon trading.
- Promote public understanding of the issues related to carbon emissions particularly in the context of the industry sector in which the individual/organization operates.
- Prioritize all business activities based on their ability to reduce carbon emissions.
- Adhere to these ethics and endeavor to create values that are based on the new green order of things.
- Ensure high level of competency in all carbon-related activities of the organization such as measurement and reporting of carbon data.
- Honestly represent "skills, knowledge, service and product" relating to carbon.
- Endeavor to interact with other disciplines within the organization to reduce the overall carbon footprint.

Privacy and Security of Green Information

The transformation of an organization to green enterprise also needs to consider the privacy and confidentiality of the information that is generated in the process. The increasingly sensitive nature of the carbon data requires careful control, secured storage, and relevant reporting. Management has to take responsibility in protecting this data as the firm undergoes green transformation and later, as the data gets stored in the organizational systems. This security of data, however, has to be balanced with the need for greater access to green information. This balancing act will become challenging especially if carbon trading becomes the norm rather than an exception because previously confidential information is now public and has the potential of influencing the future of the organization.

Carbon data can include the emissions data pertaining to an individual, a department, or an organization. This data can include time span—such as for a day, a week, or a year. Furthermore, through web services, the organization is likely to compare its carbon performance against the permissible government regulatory limits in a real-time basis. This comparative information may get distributed intentionally or unintentionally. A small organization may be able to protect the privacy and security of this data in a relatively easy manner. For a larger organization, especially with multiple geographical regions, maintenance of carbon data can be more challenging. Elements of enterprise data architecture, principles of backup and security of data, and risks associated with maintenance of data need to be applied to carbon data as stringently as it is applied to cash-flow data. Furthermore, when smart metering is used for automatic recording and analysis, stricter security measures are required to protect data. For example, carbon usage by the employee has the possible side effect of decreasing the trust between managers and employees. Therefore, security policies of an organization must specifically include sections to protect carbon data.

Green Washing

Claiming something that is not entirely accurate in terms of carbon emissions and the overall carbon footprint of the company is "green washing" (made up of "green" and "whitewash"). Green washing results from overzealous desire to capitalize on an organization's environmental and sustainability initiative. For example, green washing is said to have occurred with terminologies such as carbon neutral, energy efficient, fuel efficient, low carbon, and environmentally friendly have been used carelessly and without due consideration to the underlying standards and definitions. Adherence to Green IT's professional code of ethics requires organizations to refrain from green washing.

The complexity of terminologies and lack of commonly accepted standards for those terms is a contributor to the phenomena of green washing. This phenomena result in public mistrust and suspicion of any claims by organizations in reducing their carbon footprint.

Green products, green processes, and green infrastructure need to be sustained by valid measures and authenticated by independent audits. Energy star ratings, green CMM, and similar ratings can go a long way in reducing green washing.

Communications in Green Transformation Projects

Effective organizational communication, from a green viewpoint, focuses on creating and understanding of the technologies and processes that are explicit and the green attitude that are implicit. The technologies and processes are relatively easier to communicate, but communication to change the attitudes is not. The subjectivity of attitude toward Green IT requires communication at multiple levels and various forms. The purpose, content, channel, frequency, entities involved, feedback, and interactivity are all part of the Green IT communication.

Green transformation also involves interactions amongst people, departments, organizations, and governing bodies. Communication is required between internal departments of organizations to relate corporate philosophies, encourage teamwork, and develop strong relationships within and outside of an organization.

The internal communication of the organizations includes instruction in the development and maintenance of transformed green process. Enhancements to the processes and the green knowledge management systems also need to be communicated. Good communication will socialize and support employees and customers in understanding the reality of Green IT within the organization. Effective organizational communication, from a green viewpoint, focuses on creating an understanding of the technologies and process that are explicit and the green attitude that are implicit.

There are two major important areas of communication:

■ Within the organization—between managers and employees.
■ Outside of the organization—with the customers, partners, and regulators.

Communication within the organization can be directed by the management. These communications include standard documents, emails, verbal phone, and so on. This communication is meant to encourage employees to the regulations. Internal communication of the Green IT initiative is a combination of formal and informal communications.

Communicating outside of the organization has to be more formal. Regulations also dictate the format, frequency, and style of communication. Based on the easier discussion of web services (Chapter 6), many of these external compliance and regulatory communications will be standardized and formatted electronically. Table 8.3 summarizes these various means of communications and their Green IT implications.

Table 8.3 Communication Format and Green IT Implications

Communication	*Green IT Implications*	*Examples*
Purpose	Reason for the Green IT offer	To change attitude to data storage that will result in reduced server space
Content (articulation)		Employees are asked not to create additional backups of data and images
Channel	Availability, ease of use	Figure 8.7
Frequency	Higher frequency required at the start of the green transformation project.	Daily Monthly Push—pull
Entities involved levels	Person is in charge of making sure the communication takes place Right level to address the communications	CGO, CIO
Feedback interactivity	Return channel to indicate carbon measurements	Customers, regulators providing feedback

Green IT Project—Channels of Communication

Communication can be through various channels in a Green IT transformation program. While the details of such a transformation is discussed in the next chapter, this section highlights various ways in which communication can take place, and the ways of improving it during of the Green IT initiative of an organization.

To start with, involvement of all stakeholders, the "buy-in" is crucial. This will ensure that all participants involved in and affected by the project have a clear understanding of the organizational strategies and project goals. These important parts of a transformation project need to be explained in the most clear and understandable way. Green IT terminology can be a challenge in this communication and needs to be articulated correctly. The channels for communication need to be available to the team members to contact each other especially in a global organization where members may not be in physical proximity. The frequency of communication needs to be high earlier in the project. Standard meeting protocols like taking the minutes and circulating them apply in particular to Green IT projects.

Following are the categories of communication channels as shown in Figure 8.7 that need to be considered in a Green IT project:

- Personal—the face-to-face communication that occurs when the green transformation program is underway. This can be a one-on-one or a one-to-many communication that presents the arguments, approaches, strategies, and policies of green enterprise transformation.
- Collaborative—this is the group-based electronic communication mechanism like wikis and blogs, as also the rapidly ascending social network media.
- Mobile—through phones and SMSs that enable context-based communications.

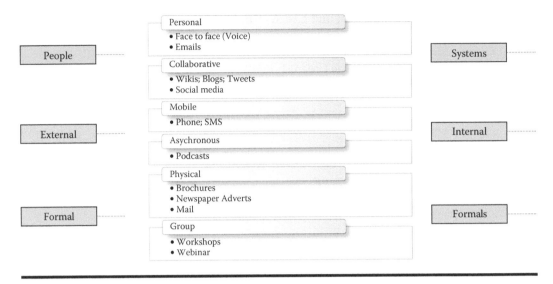

Figure 8.7   Channels of communications in Green IT projects.

■ Asynchronous—electronic communication that can be uploaded on the organization's site and then accessed by employees and users at their own convenience.

■ Physical—this is the age-old communication medium making use of paper; unlikely to be very popular in a green enterprise transformation yet may have a role to play.

■ Group—that makes use of electronic as well as physical communication facilities (e.g., webinars, seminars, workshops).

Green HR and Changing Organizational Structures

These social media networks also enable participation from not only the employees and other works within the organization but also, externally, the customers, users, and members of the public.

Organization's social changes resulting from Green IT initiative include changes to the skill set of individuals supporting the organizational systems and processes. This requires support from the green HR function of the organization in terms of understanding, positions, training, and rewarding the staff for their Green IT effort. For example, as discussed by Sherringham and Unhelkar (2011), with greater automated, location-independent, and personalized capabilities of IT, less manual intervention from the organizational staff is required to conduct business transactions (e.g., BPay). As a result, the requirements of a skill set changes from that supporting routine transaction processing to the one that requires proactive problem solving when things go wrong. This scenario is similar to the one from business process reengineering initiatives—except that here, the carbon calculation metrics are also firmly included in the ROI metrics. Changing skill sets of highly skilled workers with advanced problem solving, superior communication skills, and the ability to leverage on Green IT is within the domain of HR to study and implement. Opportunities to adopt Green IT occur as changes to the knowledge worker assembly line are required in response to changing markets and business dynamics.

Figure 8.8 shows the evolving role of the HR function with a green enterprise. A green HR has to engender change from the social perspectives (as against the technical or economic perspectives). This change is initially focused at an individual level with the organization. The departmental change deals with procedures and practices. The organizational change involves restructuring the hierarchy, creation of new green-specific role, and spelling out the reward structure for meeting green goals.

In addition to working with organization in its green endeavor, the HR function itself needs to be organized from ground up. Figure 8.9 shows the basis of such functional organization. The CGO (also referred to as CSO) remains at the helm, responsible for managing the transformation to a green enterprise. This is the strategic role that covers the length, breadth, and depth of Green IT strategies. The environmental manager forms the next tier in a green HR setup. They have a department level focus, and are dealing with metrics and measurement (compliance) issues. The environmental offices have a very practical, operational focus.

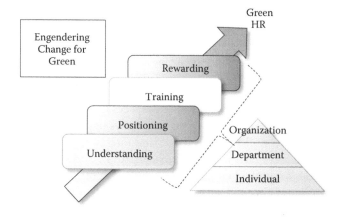

Figure 8.8 Evolving green HR.

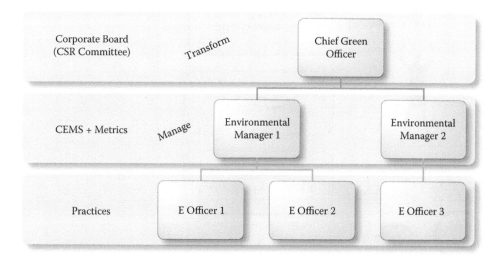

Figure 8.9 Organizing the green HR function.

The adoption of the changes in working lifestyle will also occur in different ways and with differing pace in the new green enterprise. Some individuals might take up the transformation immediately and embrace it in all activities of their work—starting right from switching off the computers in the immediate, through to undertaking strategic audits of their equipments and corresponding carbon emissions. Other individuals will wait and watch, and take it up as the results seem to climb up the bell-curve of success. Finally, some will be the "laggards" who will wait until the entire transformation is complete. These various types of individuals and their varying speeds of adoption should be carefully planned for, and factored in, in the green HR initiatives of the organization.

The subjective or tacit aspects of Green IT systems are an important consideration in the social dimension of Green IT transformation. Figure 8.10 shows the environment and work in the context of the individual. This individual is carrying his or her work in the head for most part. The bridging of the gap between this tacit knowledge (in this case related to Green IT) and the corresponding explicit knowledge stored in the green knowledge-base of the organization is vital in the social dimension. Various strategies have been adopted by organizations to narrow this gap between tacit and explicit knowledge (Marmaridis and Unhelkar, 2011; Lakkaraju and Saikiran, 2009).

For example, the Green IT systems and databases will be replete with carbon emissions data, metrics, and related formulae on carbon performance, and tables and graphs to facilitate reporting. However, the subjective individuals are likely to carry their attitude in their minds—together with their views on the impact of their behavior on the carbon footprint of the organization.

Green IT systems, on the other hand, should offer spaces of interaction, permitting people to ask questions, to discuss themes, to define priorities, in ways of fostering the creation of knowledge, doing a better use of the available knowledge, and internalizing know-how that cannot be communicated only through codified means (Hercheui, 2011). Social media and networks offer personalized opportunities for individuals to interact with each other and form a collective opinion to support the diffusion of Green IT attitude and tacit viewpoints. These social medias, while providing what the "grapevine" provided in the past, need to be harnessed in the HR's effort to diffuse Green IT within the organization.

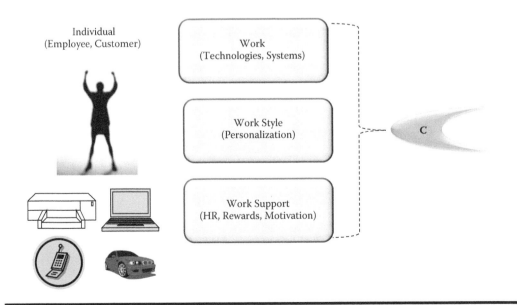

Figure 8.10   Environment and work in the context of an individual.

Institutionalized support for the available use of social media communication in Green IT transformations is vital. These social media networks also enable participation from not only the employees and other works within the organization but also, externally, the customers, users, and members of the public. This is particularly true of some small and medium enterprises which may not have sufficient resources to manage and promote their green initiatives (Marmaridis, 2011).

Green-Collar Workers: Roles and Skill Sets

Green HR considerations thus lead to a discussion of green-collar worker. Green-collar workers are the ones that are associated directly or indirectly with an organization's endeavor to become a green organization. Green HR has to define and position green-collar workers correctly. Properly defined green-collar roles reduce friction amongst staff and support Green IT initiatives. A Green IT project will create new roles, as well as transform the known roles in IT and in the business. For example, business analysts, project managers, architects, and quality assurance managers may also be classified as green-collar workers.

The skill sets of green-collar workers map easily to the skill sets defined by the SFIA. This provides basis for creating a green HR organizational structure with levels. The seven levels of SFIA that are applicable to green HR are strategies, initiative, ensure, enable, apply, assist, and follow. These have been additionally grouped into immediate, 1–3-year strategies and 3–5-year strategy.

The roles played by these green-collar workers can be divided into the following three main categories:

- The roles that are newly created within the organization and that are specific to the green initiatives of the organization (such as a green transformation champion).
- The roles that exist within the organization but are modified to befit the green organizational initiatives (such as a green business analyst).
- The external roles that deal with the specification of carbon levels, and audits of its compliance (e.g., an external carbon regulator).

Skills Framework for Information Age (SFIA) and Green HR

For a smooth transformation of an organization, it is essential that these new Green IT specific roles are understood and well defined. The possibility of applying an industry-wide standard to these roles should be considered by Green HR. For example, the skills framework for information age (SFIA) provides an excellent framework for positioning Green IT roles within the organization.

SFIA is increasingly becoming popular because it enables identification of suitable levels of competencies within the IT industry and suggests how those levels and competencies can be applied in practice. Therefore, SFIA has the potential to provide an excellent backdrop for defining the new green roles. SFIA can be used to create formal description, registration, certification, and training of Green IT roles. Green HR will be most interested in the description and the training aspect of these new roles. Existing roles can also be redefined and/or mapped to the SFIA skill set. Together with the CMM scale for green maturity, and Green IT code of conduct, SFIA can be used in helping in the maturing of Green IT as a profession.

This potential mapping of the green skills within an organization to the corresponding SFIA levels and competencies is shown in Figure 8.11. These relevant SFIA levels are also briefly described below in the context of Green IT:

■ Level 7: Strategy and Inspiration—Individuals performing at this level focus on the strategic aspect of the organization. Therefore, this role will be focused on the creation of Green IT strategies and high-level visions for the organization, as was discussed in Chapter 2. This is a vital role, typically that of a CEO and CGO (see the mind map of a CGO in Chapter 3). The decisions and actions of individuals in these roles not only influence their own organization, but also other organizations and the entire industrial sector in which they exist. These roles are also described as "risk taking" roles, as the individuals at this level are continuously balancing the internal risks associated with the Green IT initiative with the external risks brought in from the various drivers discussed in Chapter 2.

■ Level 6: Initiate and Influence—Mainly undertaken by executive and senior leaders of an organization. Green roles within this level are responsible for initiating and understanding green enterprise transformation, manage the ROI, and take a unified approach across the organization (Chapter 3). Strong leadership, management, and communication skills are required to succeed in the roles at this level. For example, decisions relating to changes to the entire infrastructure of the organization such as relocation of data centers, building of new data centers, formation of alliances with green service providers, strategies for replacement of entire end-user devices, and fundamental changes to the supply chain of the organization can

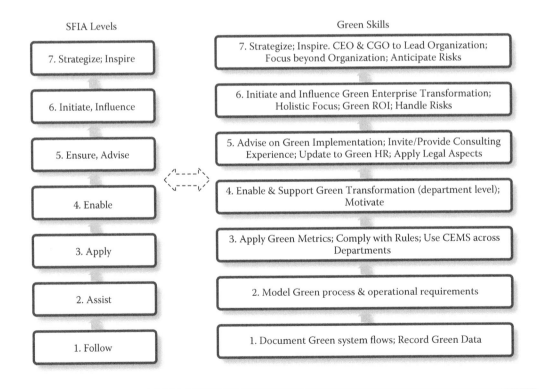

Figure 8.11 Potential mapping of green skills to SFIA levels.

be brought about by this level. As compared with the level 7, individuals working at this level are able to influence the transformation program but primarily at the organization level.

- Level 5: Ensure, Advise, and Consult—Individuals working at this level of SFIA are able to ensure transformation of an organization to a green organization. They have specific Green IT skills that enable them to provide advice and consult the line managers responsible for green transformation within their departments. Green HR has to specifically define the skills at this level based on the experience and responsibilities held by the individual in the IT industry together with the ability of understand and advise on the new green concepts, standards, and regulations. Individuals with accounting or legal background will also be required to provide this consulting input to organizations as long as they understand the underlying IT systems and functions. Individuals who are technologists themselves, such as data center directors, will be able to ensure implementation of virtualization strategies, optimization of servers, and optimum use of building infrastructure.

- Level 4: Enable—Individuals operating at this level on the SFIA skills map are enablers; they work primarily at departmental level, leading and motivating their staff as the organization undergoes green enterprise transformation. The skills requirement at this level are not as strategic as the previous levels, yet the individuals at this level should be actively involved in policy formulation and should work out approaches to implementing those Green IT policies. The practice of Green IT at this level also involves close association with Green IT systems (CEMS—discussed in Chapter 9 and also in Chapter 7), and approaches to configuring, testing, deploying, and using them to enable achievement of green goals set by the organization.

- Level 3: Apply—Individuals at this level are focused on accurate application of the rules and regulations, policies and practices, standards and procedures associated with Green IT. Thus, as the organization undergoes green enterprise transformation, the individuals at this level are actively involved in using CEMS, identifying areas for process improvement, modeling, and investigating processes, using smart meters, applying green metrics, and configuring business rules within IT systems.

- Level 2: Model Assist—Individuals at this level are primarily involved in modeling processes, systems, data, and operational requirements. Thus, this level develops and applies green analysis skills, undertakes writing of green system use cases (Chapter 7), models business processes from an optimization viewpoint, follows the industry standards (such as ISO 14001), and ensures that the green transformation objectives are faithfully carried out in practice.

- Level 1: Follow—This starting level in the IT skill set is primarily involved in documentation in various areas of the green transformation initiative. Thus, individuals operating at this level would be educated and/or trained in the concepts of Green IT including green data, metrics, and processes. However, these individuals will have less or no experience in applying those concepts and, therefore, would be faithfully following the instructions to carry out modeling, data definitions, their documentation, and sharing their use.

SFIA Skill Set and Green Roles

The usefulness of the SFIA levels and competencies can be used to understand the way in which people can be organized within and across organizations. SFIA enables definition and creation of roles that span both business and IT—therefore, it is the right framework to create levels of responsibilities for individuals working in and around Green IT. The levels of SFIA, as discussed in the previous section, are an indication of the strategic versus tactical type of work performed at that level. This leveling also enables an understanding of which levels can be used in creation of the strategies that were discussed in Chapter 2. Figure 8.12 is providing examples of the SFIA levels at which Green IT strategies can be created efficiently and effectively, and also the levels at which they can be brought into practice. The focus of those strategies is also shown in Figure 8.12 and briefly described below:

SFIA Skill Level	Roles	Business Activity	Green Inclusion for Transformation
1 to 4	Managers and Team Leads	Operational reporting	Training on reporting of green metrics within business operations
4 to 6	Senior Management	Operational risk management	Training on environmental risk and carbon risk within risk management
6 to 7	Strategists, Leaders	Risk Anticipation	Plan for carbon risks, legislative changes, global carbon trading

- Operational/tactical implementation of Green IT. The Green IT work here deals with its immediate implementation in practice, as well as work at documentation of processes. This work primarily corresponds to the SFIA levels from 1 to 4. The operational/tactical aspect of Green IT strategies was discussed in Chapter 2. The work conducted by SFIA levels 1–4 in the Green IT initiative include documentation of green system functionality, use of CEMS, recording of carbon emissions data, practice of green policies, and also imparting training associated with the practices of Green IT.
- 1–3-year Green IT strategies—these are the strategies at departmental level, and have much more depth than the immediate tactical approaches to Green IT. Therefore, SFIA levels 4–6 are poised to provide immense value in the development of these Green IT strategies. People working at these SFIA levels are able to set the green goals of the entire organization, lead the formulation of green policies that are based on the capabilities or the organization.

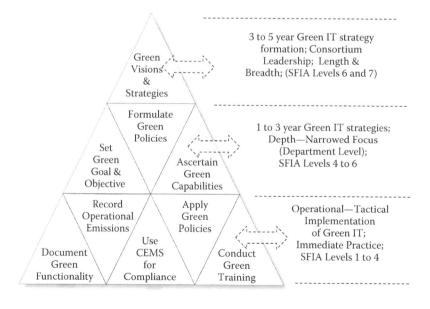

Figure 8.12   Basic to strategic spectrum of green analysis work and corresponding SFIA levels.

■ 3–5-year Green IT strategies. These are the medium to long-term strategies that are based on the visions of the organizational leadership. These strategies go beyond an organization and move into industry or consortium-based strategic approaches that influence the organization and the society. Therefore, SFIA levels 6–7 are most appropriate in the formulation of these 3–5-year strategies. These strategies not only cover depth, but also breadth of the organization (all departments, stakeholders and beyond) and direct an organization beyond the immediate tactical response and into strategic approaches.

Green Virtual Communities

A virtual community is formed through social networks that allow people to interact irrespective of geographical and political boundaries. Green virtual communities can be social groups that transcend the organizational boundaries to discuss and form opinions on green issues. These virtual communities can start as a page on Facebook and may not be mediated. The classification of people discussed in Table 10.1 can form the basis for the creation of green virtual communities.

Virtual communities can also benefit green environment, hence people spend more time with these communities. This implies reduced travel and physical movements. Social networks such as forums, blogs, Twitter, and Facebook facilitate social groups that are based around common interests. Virtual communities go a long way in formulating consensus and opinion on green initiatives and enable diffusion of knowledge on environmental sustainability.

Virtual communities create new knowledge which is then formalized as explicit knowledge that can be embedded in the knowledge management systems of the organization. Green enterprise transformation also implies a level of generalization that can be applied in the context of green environments. Socialization and virtual communities help creation of subjective green knowledge which can then be codified into explicit green knowledge. Thus, socialization transforms specific codified knowledge back into new tacit knowledge, fostering behavior change based on Ipe (2007), Nonaka (1994) and Nonaka and Konno (1998).

Virtual communities are not restricted only to formulation of subjective, social knowledge. Social networks can also participate in collaborative effort from a group of organizations rather than a single organization in creating and maintaining data centers. This is so because data centers form the backbone of Internet-based communication within as well as outside the organization. For example, the "Green Grid" is a global consortium (an equivalent of a social network) dedicated to advancing energy efficiency in data centers and business computing environments. This consortium is made up of organizations such as

Creation of new explicit pieces of knowledge depends on the subjective processes of socialization. This is particularly so in a virtual world where collaboration is the key to success. Therefore, environmental intelligence owes a lot to social alliances that enables partnering organizations to have access to and share each other's customers, suppliers, and the general markets. Such sharing opens up the doors to collaborate, capitalize, and use even the local know-how in order to reduce the overall carbon amongst all participating businesses.

The variations in partnering businesses that are coming for a different "geopolitical" climate, with different social and cultural value systems, can be used in a positive way provided these collaborating organizations have the common desire to reduce carbon. For example, a chip manufacturer in Korea providing electronic chips for products build in China and being distributed through alliance partners in United Kingdom and Australia will have to all collaborate in order to reduce the overall carbon content of the final products. Another example of a collaborative services process could be a bank in Hong Kong wanting to expand its markets in the United States through a subsidiary. The sociocultural value systems of the markets, the lending policies and procedures, and the attitude at individual employee level will all come into play if the carbon content of the entire collaborative process has to be reduced. While collaborations result in opportunities for businesses to sell and serve far flung markets, they also require attention from a carbon perspective due to the differences in political, legal, and sociocultural systems. Collaborations have greater obligations to understand and apply variations in cultural nuances of business partners to measure and mitigate carbon reduction. Best practices of one partner can easily percolate into best practices of other partners provided the commitment to carbon reduction expands across both organizations.

HP, IBM, Intel, Microsoft, Rackable Systems, SprayCool, Sun Microsystems, and VMware. This consortium aims to provide industry-wide recommendations on best practices, metrics, and technologies that improve the overall carbon efficiency of data centers.

In conclusion, this chapter highlighted the importance of the social dimension of the green enterprise transformation. The issues related to individuals, their subjectivity, and the impact of green initiatives on their lifestyle was discussed. A suggested code for Green IT ethics was discussed with an aim of providing it as a starting point for further discussion. Similarly, the SFIA skill set and levels were mapped to the Green IT roles, paving the path for a comprehensive green HR function within the organization.

Discussion Points

- Discuss the difference in the speeds of Green IT transformation of a business unit versus the society.
- Why is Green IT subjective? What can be done to convert the subjective, tacit knowledge of Green IT carried by people in their head to objective, explicit, green knowledge?
- What are the various role-based views of Green IT in an organization? How does the view of a decision maker differ from that of an IT consultant?
- Describe how the practice of videoconferencing, telecommuting, and mobile commuting assist in carbon reduction. What challenges are faced by organizations implementing these practices?
- Identify the commonalities between business, personal, and environmental priorities of an individual at work.
- Discuss the vital role played by Green HR.
- What is SFIA? How would you map the roles of an environment officer and CGO, to the SFIA level?

Action Points

- Identify the various newly created roles that you need to within your organization in the area of Green IT.
- Document the attitude challenges your organization will face as it moves forward.
- List the current Green IT user practices with an estimated percentage.
- Identify the key Green IT roles in your HR function. Create a sketch of your career HR setup.
- Map the SFIA levels to the roles defined in your organization.
- Develop an organizational version of the Green IT code of ethical conduct.

References

Bhalla, I. and Chaudhary, K. (2011). Applying service oriented architecture and cloud computing for a Greener traffic management. In B. Unhelkar, ed., *Handbook of Research in Green ICT*, pp. 332–347. IGI Global, PA, USA.

By Laudon, K. and Laudon, J. (2002). *Management Information Systems*, 11th Edition. Prentice-Hall, ISBN-13: 978-0-13-607846-3.

Deshpande, Y. and Unhelkar, B. (2011). Information systems for a Green organisation. In B. Unhelkar, ed., *Handbook of Research in Green ICT: Technical, Methodological and Social Perspectives*, pp. 116–130. IGI Global, Hershey, PA, USA.

Gala, J. and Unhelkar, B. (2009). Chapter XXX, Impact of Mobile Technologies and Gadgets on Adolescent's Interpersonal Relationships, Chapter in B. Unhelkar, ed., *Handbook of Research in Mobile Business: Technical, Methodological, and Social Perspectives*. IGI Global, Hershey, PA, USA.

Godbole, N. (2009). Relating Mobile Computing to Mobile Commerce/*Nina Godbole*. In *Handbook of Research in Mobile Business*, pp. 463–486. IGI Global, Hershey, PA, USA.

Haas, P. M., Kanie, N., and Murphy, C. N. (2004). Conclusion: Institutional design and institutional reform for sustainable development. In Kanie, N. and Haas, P. M., eds., *Emerging Forces in Environmental Governance*, pp. 263–281. Tokyo, New York, NY, Paris: United Nations University Press.

Harding, R. (2002). *Environmental Decision-Making* (edited). The Federation Press, Sydney, Australia.

Hercheui, M. D. (2011). Using knowledge management tools in fostering Green ICT related behavior change. In B. Unhelkar, ed., *Handbook of Research in Green ICT*, pp. 290–300. IGI Global, Hershey, PA, USA.

Ipe, M. (2007). Sensemaking and the creation of social webs. In McInerney, C. R. and Day, R. E., eds., *Rethinking Knowledge Management: From Knowledge Objects to Knowledge Processes*, pp. 227–246. Berlin, NY: Springer.

Kanie, N. and Haas, P. M. (2004). Introduction. In Kanie, N. and Haas, P. M., eds., *Emerging Forces in Environmental Governance*, pp. 1–12. Tokyo, New York, NY, Paris: United Nations University Press.

Lakkaraju, Sai Kiran (2009). Synchronising Subjective Knowledge and Knowledge Management Systems in Organisations. Phd thesis, University of Western Sydney.

Marmaridis, I. (2011). Collaboration as a key enabler for small and medium enterprises (SME) implementing Green ICT. In B. Unhelkar, ed., *Handbook of Research in Green ICT*, pp. 256–264. IGI Global, Hershey, PA, USA.

Marmaridis, I. and Unhelkar, B. (2005). Challenges in mobile transformations: A requirements modelling perspective for small and medium enterprises. *Proceedings of the International Conference on Mobile Business (ICMB'05)* 00, 16–22.

Marmaridis, I. and Unhelkar, B. (2011). Collaboration as a key enabler for small and medium enterprises (SME) implementing green ICT. In B. Unhelkar, ed., *Handbook of Research in Green ICT: Technical, Business and Social Perspectives*, pp. 256–264. IGI Global, Hershey, PA, USA.

McDermid, D. (2008). *Ethics in ICT: An Australian Perspective.* Pearson Education Australia.

Nonaka, I. (1994). A dynamic theory of organizational knowledge creation. In Choo, C.W. and Bontis, N., eds., *The Strategic Management of Intellectual Capital and Organizational Knowledge*, pp. 437–462. Oxford: Oxford University Press.

Nonaka, I. and Konno, N. (1998). The concept of 'Ba': Building a foundation for knowledge creation. *California Management Review, 40*(3), 40–54.

Pachauri, R. K. and Reisinger, A. (eds.). (2008). *Climate change 2007: Synthesis report. Contribution of working groups I, II and III to the fourth assessment.* Report of the Intergovernmental Panel on Climate Change. Geneva, Switzerland: IPCC.

Senge, P. (1990, 2006). *The Fifth Discipline: The Art and Practice of the Learning Organization.* DoubleDay. Doubleday/Currency.

Sherringham, K. and Unhelkar, B. (2011). Strategic business trends in the context of green ICT. In B. Unhelkar, ed., *Handbook of Research in Green ICT: Technical, Business and Social Perspectives*, pp. 65–82. IGI Global, Hershey, PA, USA.

Trivedi, B. (2011). PhD Thesis by B. Trivedi, DDU, Nadiad, India.

Trivedi, B. and Unhelkar, B. (2009). "Semantic Integration of Environmental Web Services in an Organization," *IEEE Computer Society Journal*, ICESC-09 Conference, Dubai.

Unhelkar, B. and Trivedi, B. (2009). Merging web services with 3G IP Multimedia systems for providing solutions in managing environmental compliance by businesses. *Proceedings of the 3rd International Conference on Internet Technologies and Applications (Internet Technologies and Applications, ITA 09)*, September 8–11, 2009, Wrexham, North Wales, UK.

Unhelkar, B., Ghanbary, A., and Younessi, H. (2009). "Collaborative Business Process Engineering and Global Organizations: Frameworks for Service Integration" IGI Global, Hershey, PA, USA, ISBN: 978-1-60566-689-1; 323 pp; (c) 2010.

Chapter 9

Green Enterprise Transformation Roadmap

The issue of climate change is one that we ignore at our own peril. There may still be disputes about exactly how much we're contributing to the warming of the earth's atmosphere and how much is naturally occurring, but what we can be scientifically certain of is that our continued use of fossil fuels is pushing us to a point of no return. And unless we free ourselves from a dependence on these fossil fuels and chart a new course on energy in this country, we are condemning future generations to global catastrophe.

Barack Obama

Key Points

- Presents a business transformation framework for green enterprises that outlines the transformation of an organization from where it is (potentially disjoint and carbon inefficient) to a holistic, carbon-efficient green organization
- Further discusses the four dimensions (economic, technical, social, and process or channels) along which enterprises can be transitioned to green enterprises
- Outlines a Green Information and Communication Technology (ICT) framework made up of four sections: lifecycle of equipments, end-user devices, data center, and IT as enabler that can be used to understand the current and future states of an organization with respect to the environment
- Discusses in detail the (4 + 1) Green enterprise transformation (GET) phases: diagnose, plan, enact, and review—interspersed with metrics—and their iterative nature that form the basis of a Green transformation program
- Outlines the eight separate work areas (or focus area) of an organization that get transformed during a GET: business model, portfolio of products/services, customers/partners, ICT systems, operational/HR, business processes, networks and infrastructure, and regulatory/SLA/outsourcing

- Describes the roles and responsibilities of people involved in a GET (e.g., business partners, Green IT champion, Green IT auditors)
- Describes in greater details the diagnose and plan process components for GET
- Describes the systems-level issues in GETs (e.g., CRM, ERM, Partner's systems, HR)
- Suggests the areas for review and the use of metrics during and after the GET

Introduction

Green enterprise transformation (GET) is a holistic program undertaken by an organization to radically change its structure and dynamics that would change its carbon footprint for the better. Any transformation (also occasionally referred to as a transition) is a risky endeavor. This is so because transformation brings about the changes to the structure and dynamics of an organization that lead to disturbances in its normal operations and also its relationship with its customers and suppliers (Sherringham and Unhelkar, Cutter ERM 2010). These risks can be ameliorated by the use of a carefully throughout process for such transformation that would provide the definitions for activities and tasks, deliverables and roles that can be used to achieve the goals of that transformation. Such transformation is further augmented by a competent suite of metrics and measurements that justify and validate the effort to change. In case of GETs, these metrics go well beyond the commonly accepted Green IT measures, such as DCiE and PUE, and delve into the realms of attitude, supply chains, and regulatory compliance.

This chapter discusses such a transformation framework together with its metrics and measurements. The discussion here is an extension of the concepts of business transformations and corresponding practical applications that have been tried, tested, and reported by Unhelkar (Unhelkar, Cutter report 2009). Business transformation, as applied to Green ICT, is undertaken along the four dimensions of economy, process, technology, and society. These Green ICT dimensions were discussed in detail earlier in Chapter 2. The GET process also has four phases of diagnosis, planning, enactment, and review interspersed with metrics. Thus, a GET framework forms a matrix of the four phases and the four dimensions along which these phases get applied. In fact, the organization is viewed in a detailed GET through its various internal verticals such as its business portfolio, its networks and other IT infrastructure and, its people, and their attitudes. These are the areas within the organization that undergo change as a result of GET. This chapter also discusses a framework called *Green point method* that is an IT-specific Green framework encompassing equipment lifecycle, the end-user devices, the data centers, and servers within, and IT as enabler across the organization.

The Green IT metrics and measurements used in GET are context sensitive in nature and a good transformation program will deploy them with care across the organization. These metrics start applying from the diagnoses phase and right through to the review phase.

An important distinction to make in this discussion on GET processes is that we are discussing two types of frameworks:

(a) The Green ICT framework and its various elements that help understand and model the enterprise—in its "as is" and "to be" state. This framework is similar to the popular enterprise architecture frameworks such as Zachman (1987) and TOGAF (2010). This is a relatively static model of the organization that shows the structure and dynamics of the organization.

(b) The GET process—this is also a framework, but a process framework that is used for undertaking the transformation process; this process outlines the activities and tasks and deliverables and roles of the organization that are involved in the transformation process. This is a dynamic, flowing model that describes how to engender change.

While the above two types of frameworks are interdependent, they are not the same. Each framework needs to be treated separately and then considered together in practice. The Green ICT framework on its own is an excellent mechanism to model the green enterprise; the transformation framework is the basis for the roadmap to undertake transformation.

These are some areas of on enterprise level transformation that are discussed in this chapter.

Green Enterprise Transformation

Figure 9.1 explains the basic concept of a GET. On the left side of this figure is an organization that is represented as potentially a carbon-ineffective, disjointed organization. This could be an organization that is pulled in separate directions in terms of its cost, carbon, and customer priorities. On the right is shown a holistic, integrated organization with its priorities set right. This is an organization with its costs, carbon, and customers priorities in agreement with each other. Figure 9.1 also lists, briefly, the fundamental questions that an organization (typically a person responsible for the transformation) needs to ask in undertaking GET. These are high-level questions of immense interest during

A GET is made up of processes and frameworks. The green enterprise framework provides the "as is" and "to be" states, whereas the transformation process provides the activities, roles, and deliverables that are employed in reaching that new state. The fundamental questions in a GET are as follows: What are the green drivers? Which are the dominant dimensions? How to start GET? Green KPIs? Who will lead the transformation CGO? What are the compliance requirements? What are the sociocultural pressures?

transformation. However, these questions are part of the GET processes, and follow the more strategic questions asked by business decision makers in formulating Green IT strategies (Chapter 2)

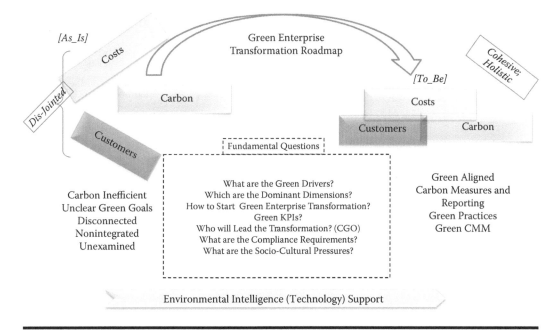

Figure 9.1   Green enterprise transformation.

and polices (Chapter 3). The environmental intelligence (EI) systems represented at the base of Figure 9.1 provide the technical support for the transformation.

This GET process needs to be a well thought out process that helps identify the business goals, the current structure and maturity of the business and steps to be undertaken to become a new, cohesive, agile, efficient, and collaborative green business. A GET is planned and executed along the four dimensions of an organization facilitate its transformation from where it is to its future green state. To bring about that change, a business can be modeled and understood in various ways and through multiple dimensions as a part of its transformation. An earlier study by Arunatileka and Ginige (2003) had identified the factors influencing business transformations and the risks and advantages associated with them. These factors were based along the lines of people, processes, and technologies. These factors were also identified, extended, and separately applied by Arunatileka, D., Ghanbary and Unhelkar (2006) in undertaking business transformation and by Unhelkar (2009) for transforming mobile businesses. Unhelkar further discussed and defined these factors as economic, technical, process, and social in the mobile enterprise transformation framework (Unhelkar 2008) as a means for undertaking mobile business transformation. Thus, these four dimensions, described earlier in Chapter 2, form the areas along which Green transformation can take place.

The four dimensions along which an organization transforms are shown in Figure 9.2. Thus, these dimensions provide the backdrops for creating a Green enterprise architecture that would model the two "as is" and "to be" states of an organization. Unhelkar and Ginige (Unhelkar and Ginige 2009) have extended and applied the use of enterprise architecture in modeling the current and future expected state of the business as well as how to reach there. The effect of these

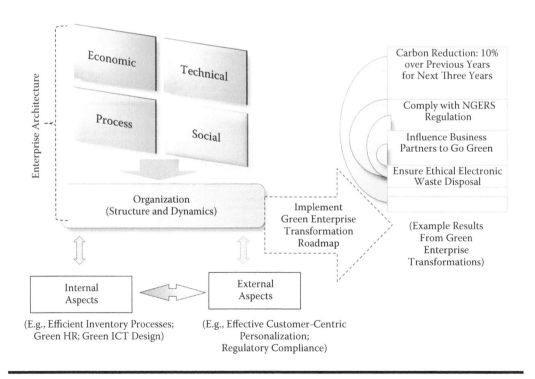

Figure 9.2 Applying the four dimensions to GET.

dimensions can be broadly grouped into internal and external effects—as shown in Figure 9.2. The internal processes such as the inventory and HR processes are updated to green processes; and so also the external processes, such as the CRM processes to Green CRM. Transformation of the internal and external processes of the organization is coupled with the development of the Green IT portals (Chapter 6). The internal and external transformation of processes an organization enable it to achieve its stated goals (as shown, e.g., on the right in Figure 9.2) that can be measured based on Key Performance Indicators (KPIs). The organizational structure and dynamics also change along with these internal and external processes and corresponding technologies that eventually map to various work areas (also called focus areas) of transformation. These focus areas of a business are the ones that undergo change when the transformation program is implemented. The transformation process framework investigates scopes and incorporates these dimensions within its transformation phases.

While the dimensions provide the major threads for transformation, it should be noted that these dimensions are not watertight compartments that are independent of each other. Instead, each dimension influences all other dimensions—sometimes leading the way and at other times following and consolidating the changes. The influence of each of these dimensions on the GET is discussed in detail next.

The economic, technical, process, and social dimensions each influence the GET differently. For example, the economic dimension would focus on the ROI, whereas the technical dimension on the server virtualization. They also affect the individual, department/organization and collaborations differently. For example, changes to the individual processes may occur instantaneously, but those at organizational level may take more time. These variations need to be incorporated in the GET process for the organization.

Influence of Economic Dimension on GET

The changes along the economic dimension of business, as it transforms to green organization has to do with its financial position, the changes to its budgets, product portfolio, and return on investment (ROI) calculation. This is the change that is based on the answer to the question of why to transform? Thus, the financial tracking, monitoring of ROI and impact of GET on the organization's financial position is kept firmly in mind when the business transforms along this dimension. The changes in this dimension also include changes to the business model, its investment strategies, its customer relationships and its partner management. The success criteria of GET through this dimension are achievement of the "bottom line" as outlined in the transformation objective.

Influence of Technical Dimension on GET

The technical dimension is "technologically lead" conduit for the business to transform. In case of GET, numerous technologies including hardware, software, databases, and networks undergo changes. Thus, in this dimension, the organization strives to reduce carbon emissions related to desktop machines and personal devices, data servers, ICT-based systems and their usage, underlying network infrastructure, and security protocols. These technologies are eventually also used to reduce the emissions of the rest of the organization. For example, Web 2.0 and beyond (Murugesan 2007), together with virtualization, can be used to reduce the overall power and resource consumption of the organization's systems. Internet-based communications protocols, semantic web, mobile, and Cloud computing (Murugesan 2010) are also all offering potential for carbon efficiency (as discussed in Chapters 4, 6, and 11). The success of the technical dimension in GET is gauged by the reliability and ease of use of the new technology, its validation through quality assurance and testing, and this agility—that is, the ability to change with changing business circumstance. The EI is the basis of ICT systems that form part of this technical dimension.

Influence of Process Dimension on GET

This process dimension of a business is the dimension dealing with "how" the business conducts its transactions. These are both internal and external processes of the organization. GET along this dimension of the business entails changes to *the way* the business interacts with the customers, the way in which it manages its employees and the way it sets up and conducts collaborations with other business partners. This change in processes and associated reengineering was discussed in Chapter 5 earlier under Green business process management (BPM). Success of GET in this dimension can be measured by reduction in carbon emission without sacrificing the quality and value of current offerings.

Influence of Social Dimension on GET

The social dimension of GET deals with the sociocultural changes that occur in the business as a result of the transformation. This dimension encourages the transformation champion to focus greater interest in the people aspect of transformation. These people include the clients, employees, and other "users" of the business. Changes to work formats, for example, including telecommuting, telemarketing, and their resultant impact on the organizational and social structures are all part of this social dimension. This was discussed in detail in Chapter 8. Due consideration needs to be provided to areas of strengths and corresponding weaknesses of individual and team. For example, customer-facing individuals can influence or change the perception of the organization in terms of its carbon footprint. This dimension thus require training and positive attitude from the staff. Senior managers and leaders of the organization also have a substantial effect in changing the attitude of individuals within the business. These organizational changes, however, cannot be suddenly brought about when people are involved. Training, motivation, and individual aspirations need to be considered by the Green HR function of the organization. Both performance and functionality need to be kept in balance during transformation. Broader social issues such as effects of advertisements, value systems of the customers, ethical business practices, and adherence to the industry's code of conduct are also part of the social dimension.

Figure 9.3 shows the relationship between GET (as a transformation process framework) and the elements of an enterprise that are involved in the transformation. This figure forms the basis for the GET described later in Figure 9.7. The framework provides the enterprise architecture of the organization with particular emphasis on its green aspect. The process in Figure 9.3 represents the transformation phases outlining how the organization will change. The metrics detail the goals in terms of carbon reduction—and the CEMS provides the systems-level environment intelligence support. HR is primarily involved in training and up-skilling, but also reorganizing the roles and responsibilities. The roadmap for a GET also involves the enterprise architects (Rosen et al.), who provide valuable input into the identification of tactics for transforming the technologies and processes. Finally, the regulators and auditors are involved in metrics and compliance aspect of the GET.

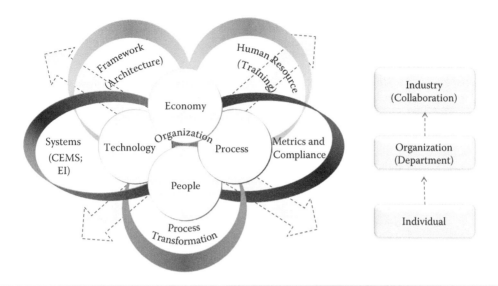

Figure 9.3   A GET is a mix of the four dimensions.

Transforming the Individual, Organizational, and Collaborative Processes

The mix of GET process applies at differing levels of the organization. These individual, organizational, and collaborative aspects of business processes relating to Green IT were discussed in Chapter 5. The aforementioned four dimensions of GET affect the individual, the organization, and also the collaborative group of organizations. An understanding of the way in which green changes affect these levels of processes can help in information of the transformation program. Some of the important aspects of how the four dimensions of GET affect the individual, organizational, and collaborative aspects of business processes are summarized in Table 9.1.

Figure 9.4 builds further to focus on the crucial elements in a GET shown in Figure 9.3. These are the three major aspects of the GET. These are the roadmap itself, the supporting metrics, and the actual operation (structure and dynamics) of the organization that undergoes change.

The transformation roadmap firstly models the "as is" situation. This requires a diagnostic approach to identifying and documenting the current state of the organization. This is followed by the vision, or "to be" state of the organization. The roadmap outlines the activities, steps, and deliverables that are produced as a part of the transformation program. The ensuing projects, affected technologies, changing processes, and redefinition of roles are all depicted in this roadmap. This process of identifying the current and future state, outlining the path to complete the gap and executing the GET requires a combination of internal and external skill sets. Inviting a full-on consulting group for this exercise can include costs, and risks associated with the potential lack of knowledge of the core operations of the organization. Alternatively, using only internal resources has the risks of not knowing the external legislations, consortium-based actions, and available technologies and resources for GETs.

The green metrics form another significant aspect of the transform framework. This aspect provides the measures and proof of change. The green operation, shown in Figure 9.4, is the organization in its routine or operational mode after undergoing change. For a successful green operational aspect, there is a need to create the roadmap and the metrics.

Table 9.1 Business Transformation Considerations of the Four Dimensions at Individual, Organizational, and Collaborative Levels

Green Enterprise Transformations	Individual (User, Customer, Employee)	Organization (Small—Large—Multinational)	Collaboration (Vertical—Horizontal; Static—Dynamic)
Economic	A unit cost of product or service; carbon offsets in daily purchases	Profit verses carbon; costs associated with changes to infrastructures and operations	Green consortiums and alliances; changes to SLAs; legal compliances across regions
Technology	Mobile/personal devices; usability; storage space	Applications, networking, data servers, Intranet; environmental intelligence	SOA web services and Cloud computing; security (EI)
Process	Customer experience; individual sales	Business process management; modeling and optimization	Collaborative industrial processes across multiple, global businesses (CBPE)
Sociology	Privacy; telecommuting and telework; work-life balance	Green HR; training; rewarding structure	Social networking; green consortiums

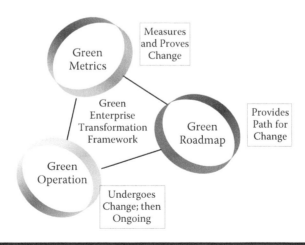

Figure 9.4 GET needs roadmap and supporting metrics: transformation becomes operation.

A Green ICT Framework

Identification of the current and future states of the organization with respect to its green capabilities is based on a Green ICT framework. This is an enterprise architecture type framework that deals with the "state" of the organization rather than the process of "transformation." As mentioned earlier, Zachman and TOGAF have been quite popular as enterprise architecture frameworks that have a technical bend in modeling on enterprise. Figure 9.5 shows such a framework for Green ICT. This framework based on the work being done at envi-

The Green ICT Framework (4 verticals * 5 horizontals) is a matrix of what the organization is made up of in terms of Green ICT (vertical pillars), and how the organization can change (horizontal bars). Equipments lifecycle, end-user devices, data centers, and the rest of the organization are the vertical pillars that comprise the organization itself. Attitude, policies, practices, and technologies are the bars along which they change. Metrics are interspersed throughout.

rability (Phillipson 2009), covers the major areas of an enterprise, particularly from the Green IT perspective. Some areas of this framework also maps to the four dimensions of transformation described earlier on.

This Green ICT framework, shown in Figure 9.5, is made up of a matrix of four vertical "pillars" and five horizontal "rows." The vertical pillars depict the areas within an organization that will undergo change—and they are the equipment lifecycle, end-user computing, enterprise, and data center and ICT as a low carbon enabler across the organization. As will be seen later, in Figure 9.7, these pillars evolve into work areas, or focus areas for transformation. The horizontal rows, in this Green ICT matrix, are made up of attitude, policy, practice, technology, and metrics. These horizontal rows form the elements of change. These vertical and horizontal elements of this Green IT framework are described next.

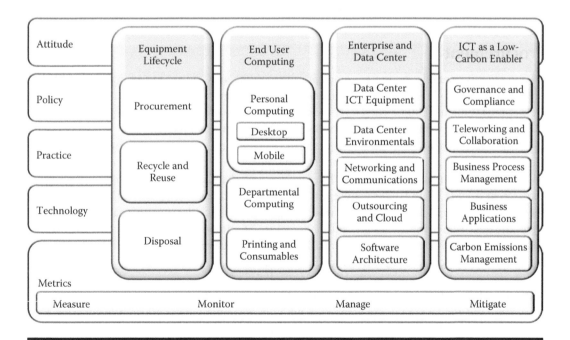

Figure 9.5   Green ICT framework. (The Envirability-RMIT Green ICT framework is reproduced with permission from Connection Research).

Equipment Lifecycle

The equipment lifecycle deals with the procurement, recycling and reuse, and eventual disposal of all equipment within the organization. The primary interest, in this lifecycle, is of electronic equipments (such as desktops and servers) that produce emissions. However, the equipment lifecycle is interested in all equipments. All equipment in the organization undergo this cycle wherein they are procured (or manufactured), sold, used (and reused), and ultimately disposed. That disposal of the equipments includes issues relating recycling or reuse. Furthermore, there are also important issues relating to ethical disposal of the equipment. The entire equipment lifecycle is of immense interest in Green ICT as the process of carbon reduction can be initiated right from the procurement phase and continue through its operation and eventual disposal. Supply chain management (SCM) and procurement management systems are typically involved in supporting the optimization of the equipment lifecycle. This equipment lifecycle is part of bigger, organizational lifecycle.

As was discussed in Chapter 5, the three phases to the equipment lifecycle are—procurement, operations, and disposal (P-O-D). Each of these phases can be approached in a creative manner that reduces the carbon footprint of the organization. Disposal—predates the concept of Green IT, as many organizations have been conscious for some time of the importance of disposing of IT equipment in an environmentally sound fashion. That disposal may mean it is discarded or destroyed, but it may also be sold or given to another person or organization, where it has another lifecycle contained within its larger lifecycle. Thus, for every reused sale or disposal, there is another purchase. Electronic waste disposal has been studied by Godbole (2011).

Procurement

Procurement is arguably the most important aspect of Green ICT in terms of making an overall impact on sustainability. At least as much energy is spent in manufacturing a PC as it consumes in its lifetime (Williams 2004). Therefore, focusing the design and procurement of ICT equipment makes a substantial impact on its total carbon cost of ownership (TCCO).

There are two aspects to green procurement—the nature of the equipment itself, and the nature of the suppliers of that equipment. The equipment an organization purchases may comply with environmental standards such as Energy Star and the Electronic Product Environmental Assessment Tool (EPEAT)—see www.epeat.net. However, consideration should also be given to the suppliers' own green strategies and carbon footprint. This includes such things as the supplier's environmental values in the design and manufacture of equipment and how it measures them, its compliance with relevant environmental laws and codes of practice, and whether the supplier reclaims and recycles old equipment from customers.

Organizations are increasingly developing policies for measuring the environmental performance of their ICT suppliers (Philipson 2009). Energy efficiency, emissions over lifecycle emissions, and the level of waste associated with an equipment are important purchasing factors. Requests for proposals (RFPs) and tender documents often evaluate suppliers on their environmental credentials and their own green policies and practices. For example, some suppliers who offer to not only deliver the products but also take away the packaging are preferred to others.

Recycle and Reuse

All organizations replace their ICT equipment periodically. Some have regular refresh cycles, some wait till they have to, and some utilize some sort of continuous update process (especially with software). This is a natural aspect of the ICT function. Sometimes, through, IT department may replace equipment earlier in their lifecycle. Perhaps they have a need or a fear of not being able to run the latest versions of software. This can result in potential as the need for hardware may be exaggerated.

Further, even when it is time for a hardware upgrade, it may not be necessary across the board. Areas of the organization that need newer hardware may be able to share their old equipment to other parts of the organization with less critical processes. Any equipment that complies with the base hardware standards, and that can support the software, is potentially redeployable. Redeployment may also be based on changes to organizational structures, especially when roles are not being refilled.

Disposal of ICT Systems

After extending the useful life of equipment and eventually selling or reusing it, there will always be a situation where it will need to be physically disposed. Environmentally sound disposal practices are vital aspect of Green ICT. While organizations have been conscious of the importance of reducing electronic waste; it is the manufacturers and distributors that need to pay particular attention to the eventual disposal.

The importance of electronic waste disposal has led to the growth of an entire industry around the disposal of ICT and other electronic equipment, often based on the extraction of precious metals from printed circuit boards and other components. This industry too has to be regulated, and there have been legislations, making the environmentally friendly disposal of e-waste mandatory. (See http://ewasteguide.info).

Globally, substantial amount of electronic waste is sent to Africa for final processing.* However, lack of stringent legislations and their enforcement has resulted in many chemicals, such as lead and cadmium, polluting the air, water, and soil of these countries. "Take-back" and recycling programs by the manufacturer is a major boost in reducing the eventual pollution from electronic wastage. The manufacturers of computer monitors, printers, photocopiers, laptops, and mobile phones, for example, are in the best position to know what has gone into these products and also understand the repercussions of its disposal in the air, water, and soil. Therefore, together with enlightened self-interest, legislations need to place the responsibility of all electronic products' final disposal with the manufacturer rather than leaving them to pollute the environments of otherwise less-privileged economies.

End-User Computing

End-user carbon efficiencies are also very important because of their visibility. As the only part of ICT that exists outside of the specialized ICT function, end-user computing has the greatest effect on the wider green attitudes and behavior of the organization's workforce. By its very nature, this area of end-user computing affects the nontechnical users of the organization. This is where Green IT policies

---

* http://www.pbs.org/frontlineworld/stories/ghana804/video/video_index.html—presents a 20-minute video illustrating the plight of communities who are at the epicenter of the world's e-waste.

and practices are most apparent to most people inside and outside the organization. Therefore, the cooperation of non-IT employees is also very important in this end-user computing area. Once the end-users are convinced of Green IT, the rest of the Green IT strategy becomes much easier to implement, as the attitude and behavior of a large group of people is simultaneously affected.

End-user computing deals with IT Efficiencies that the end-user has most control over. These end-user gadgets were discussed in Chapter 4, and are divided into three main areas—personal (desktop computing, mobile computing), departmental computing, and printing. For each of these there are a range of different technologies and techniques that can reduce the organization's power consumption and carbon footprint.

- Desktop computing—Important practices include turning PCs off and various PC power management techniques, and important technologies include thin client computing.
- Mobile computing (Laptops, PDAs)—May have similar power management issues to desktop computers. An array of mobile devices, such as notebook computers, smart phones, and PDAs (personal digital assistants), may not in themselves use a large amount of power, but there are still a number of Green ICT considerations that need to be taken into account with their usage.
- Departmental computing—This is the computing that is localized to a department and not under direct control of the IT department of the organization.
- Some of this IT activity can be substantial leading to a significant and, often, unmeasured carbon contribution. For example, servers, storage devices, and peripherals that are not housed in data centers can amount to a significant number and very inefficient. Therefore, departmental computing should be a major area for Green ICT.
- Printing and consumables—Consume significant energy particularly due to their large numbers and inbuilt inefficiencies. For example, printers and copiers tend to be left on even when not in use. Other areas of inefficiency include printing paper and printing ink. The toner, or ink, is particularly a major concern in its production, use, and disposal. Printers are typically bulky, they are built from materials that are difficult to recycle or even toxic, and they require more maintenance than most other devices perhaps because of their moving parts (Philipson 2010).

The relative importance of end-user IT efficiencies varies largely in relation to the size of the organization. In smaller organizations their importance arises from the fact that the end-user devices represent the main areas of Green IT. Whereas, in larger organizations, the sheer numbers of end-users mean that efficiencies in this area can make an enormous difference to the overall carbon footprint of the organization.

Enterprise and Data Center

Enterprise and data center represent those aspects of an organization that are controlled directly by the IT department. This is true even with the small IT departments that exist within user's departments of organizations that have their own servers occasionally lying under the desk of the manager. In organizations large enough to have a data center, the effective management of the equipment within it and its environmental can be one of the most important aspects of Green IT.

- Data center ICT equipment
- Data center environmentals

- Networking and communications
- Outsourcing and Cloud
- Software architecture

Data Center ICT Equipment

The two most important types of ICT equipment in the data center include servers (including mainframes) and storage devices that were discussed in detail in Chapter 4. Servers are usually the biggest consumers of power, and that power consumption continues to rise as more powerful processors are used inside them, and as the number of servers proliferates (Koomey 2007). The average power consumption of a rack of servers has increased five-fold over the last 10 years (Gantz 2009) when cooling requirements are taken into account. Storage usage is also increasing exponentially—and as prices drop storage devices are often used very inefficiently.

Server and storage virtualization has become one of the key technologies in data centers in recent years. It is often touted as a technology for reducing power consumption, because it reduces the overall number of devices, but in practice most data centers' power consumption continues to rise because the devices are becoming more powerful and use more electricity.

Data Center Environmentals

The environmental issues associated with the data canter specifically discussed earlier on (Chapter 4). The data center's supporting infrastructure can easily consume more power than the ICT equipment within it. This supporting infrastructure is made up of the following three main aspects:

- The power supply—Data centers usually have dedicated power supplies, and very often more than one. Their efficiency varies enormously. Data centers can also generate their own power, and backup power supplies are common for business continuity.
- Cooling and lighting—Modern ICT equipment typically demands significant amounts of cooling, either air cooling or water cooling. There are many design and implementation issues that affect power consumption. Lighting is also a factor.
- The building that houses the data center—This may be a dedicated stand-alone facility, or it may be purpose-built within a larger facility, or it may be retrofitted into existing premises. Whatever the case, there are a number of aspects of the built environment that will have an effect on power consumption, such as insulation.

Networking and Communications

Communications—the "C" in ICT—plays a significant role in modern ICT. There are a number of green issues specifically to do with communications. These include the following:

- Local area networking—Many organizations' LANs and data center networks consist largely of an untidy collection of cables that consume large amounts of power and which add to cooling requirements. More efficient cabling design means lower power consumption.

■ Wide area networking—Many organizations use leased data lines or VPNs (virtual private networks) over the Internet. While they do not have direct control over these networks, their inefficient usage adds to overall power consumption and increases the overall carbon footprint.

■ Wireless communication—Wireless will never wholly replace cabling, but it is becoming more widely used and it does have a major role to play. But wireless communications can be very inefficient, especially when transmitters and receivers are left on when they are not being used.

Outsourcing and Cloud Computing

Outsourcing has been one of the big issues in ICT since the industry began. It has been discussed by Unhelkar as a business strategy (Unhelkar, Cutter, Smart sourcing).

In ICT, outsourcing discussions have traditionally centered around the issues of cost and capability. The outsourcing vendor has economics of scale and availability of skills.

The rise of sustainability as an issue has added a new dimension to the ICT outsourcing debate (Philipson, 2010). Many facilities management companies are now highlighting their green credentials and building energy-efficient data centers that they say will enable users to lower their overall carbon footprint. That may well be the case, but the traditional make versus buy arguments still hold. One key issue with outsourcing, and one that is overlooked surprisingly often, is that of measurement. It is impossible to tell if outsourcing is a good deal or not financially if you don't know the real cost of what is being outsourced. Similarly, you can't tell if an outsourcer is going to reduce your carbon footprint if you don't know what it is to start with.

A recent complication to the outsourcing debate is the emergence of Cloud computing, where processing takes place in the "Cloud"—somewhere on the Internet far from the user. Cloud computing is not necessarily outsourced, but it very often is—making the debate even more complex. This has been discussed earlier in Chapter 6, and later, an as emerging technology in Chapter 11.

Software Architecture

Computer systems consist of software running on hardware. Indeed, it is often argued that the software is the system, and that the hardware is simply an enabling technology. Most discussion about Green ICT refers to hardware, but software is also a factor.

The software architecture often determines the hardware architecture, which in turn may have a significant effect on the amount or type of hardware used—with all the consequences of the energy consumption of those systems. The way software is developed and used is significant—code can be efficient, or it can be "bloatware." Systems can be developed from scratch, adapted or borrowed (with "objects") from other software, or purchased off-the-shelf. Each approach has consequences for energy consumption.

IT for Enterprise

A vital aspect of Green IT is its use in reducing the carbon footprint—beyond IT itself—to the whole organization. It is generally agreed that IT emissions are mainly through the usage of electricity which in turn comes from carbon emitting power stations. These figures tend to indicate that the real potential benefits of Green IT are in using IT as an enabling technology to help the organization, and the wider community, reduce its carbon emissions. This use of IT in the enterprise includes updating the governance and compliance sections of the organization (Chapter 3), introducing teleworking and use of collaborative tools (Chapter 4 and 8), BPM (Chapter 5), business applications, and carbon emissions management software (CEMS) (Chapter7). This is the discussion on EI.

Governance and Compliance

Many organizations nowadays are conscious of the desirability of being a good corporate citizen. Increasingly, that means acting in a green and sustainable manner. Publicity about climate change and related issues has greatly raised the profile of sustainability, and virtually all organizations are attempting to boost their green credentials. In some cases they do it because they are forced to, in some cases it is a case of "greenwash" or paying only lip service to environmental matters. But in many cases the organization's management sincerely wants to do the right thing.

"Corporate governance" is a term that has come into common use in the last decade to describe the processes by which organizations ensure that they are properly managed, not only in terms of meeting their regulatory obligations, but to ensure that they do the right things by all their "stakeholders." This overused term typically includes management, shareholders, and staff, and is often extended to include business partners and others in the organization's extended supply chain.

This extension is based on a growing awareness that, when it comes to the environment, everybody is a stakeholder, and that good corporate governance also includes good environmental management. Green ICT is in many ways a management and governance issue.

Teleworking and Collaboration

As also discussed in Chapter 8, the term "teleworking" covers a range of technologies and practices that have to do with working at a distance or working remotely (see www.telework.gov). The carbon reduction benefits of teleworking are mostly associated with reduction in personal travel obviating the need to drive a car or catch a plane reduces the carbon footprint of that activity by the amount of fuel generated by that travel. Teleworking also opens up opportunity to collaborate more than in the physical world.

Collaboration tools and techniques enhance the capability of a group of people to work together (Zara 2004). There are a great many ways to do this, but all of them entail being able to share documents, processes, and information. This showing makes the business processes more efficient and reduces the need for physical contact. Thus, collaboration and teleworking go together.

Business Process Management

Business process management is the process of improving the ways an organization or an individual does things—making them more efficient, with fewer steps or greater effect. Green BPM was also discussed in detail in Chapter 5. Formally, the management discipline called BPM identifies five phases relating to a process: design, modeling, execution, monitoring, and optimization. A Green BPM refers to the managing and improving of all business processes from their carbon perspective.

Environmental intelligence has a major role to play in Green BPM. EI provides both the tools for modeling the processes and many of the enabling technologies for their execution. This can be done both with business processes in the broadest sense, and through and with the use of specific business applications.

Business Applications

ICT-based business applications include financial management systems (FMS), enterprise resource planning (ERP), supply chain management (SCM), and customer relationship management (CRM). Many organizations also run customized applications that are specific to their industry that would provide them with competitive advantage.

ICT is very important in each of these applications, which essentially support BPM. Green BPM seeks greater efficiencies in every phase of every process. For example, the fewer times and the shorter distance physical items have to be moved, the better. The fewer transactions need to be made, the better. Even small improvements can have a significant effect on carbon reduction, because of the scale of the operation and because of flow-on effects further up (or down) the supply chain.

Green ICT has a very important role in improving the efficiency of many industrial and commercial processes specific to individual industries, paving the path for their leanness. For example, the manufacturing process, electricity distribution, and engineering and construction, each have a unique set of processes which can be made more efficient through the application of EI. Efficiency translates to lean, which means green.

Carbon Emissions Management

Carbon emissions management is an emerging discipline that focuses on the management—and ultimately the mitigation—of an organization's carbon emissions. This includes the use of ICT systems specifically designed to reduce the carbon footprint, rather than doing so as a by product of greater efficiency. A key ICT application is CEMS, which provide a compliant and consistent format for presenting greenhouse gas emission data to executive management and regulators (Philipson, et al. 2009).

As the carbon emissions regulatory framework continues to evolve, CEMS is becoming an increasingly popular tool to manage the carbon emissions lifecycle. The market will continue to mature and will most likely consolidate around major technology vendors and a smaller group of niche or vertical industry players, and CEMS products will become a functional component within many organizations' application portfolio.

Envirability has researched the CEMS market and has written a major report on the background to CEMS and how to select and implement a product. See www.cemsus.com

The horizontal layers of the Green ICT framework deals with attitude, policy, practice, technology, and metrics. These are discussed next.

Attitude

Attitude is intangible and forms a major part of the subjectivity in the social dimension of Green IT. As discussed in the previous chapter on sociocultural aspects of Green IT, much of the success of GETs depend on the attitude of the people within the organization. However, as also discussed there, the sociocultural aspect of Green IT is also very subjective. Attitude can be understood as a desire and a commitment to change by the individual that is based on honest belief in the ensuing results. Having a positive attitude toward Green IT is at the heart of the transformation as it is depend on individuals. And, as is often the case in business, those attitudes are most effective if they come from the top. "Management buy-in" is an essential part of any Green IT program.

Examples of attitude: what difference will one monitor (or light bulb, or megabyte) make to the overall footprint? Recycling and reuse are important, and longer use of working electronic equipment will reduce electronic wastage. Or, I don't to call that physical meeting—it can be done via video conferencing.

Policy

There are many aspects to Green IT policies that were discussed in Chapter 3. Policies help set the direction for the organization and provided basis for action. A coherent and holistic enterprise-wide IT energy reduction policy will affect all four vertical columns in Figure 9.5. Communications (discussed in Chapter 8) of policies is also vital and needs to take the HRs in confidence.

Examples of policies affecting the entire organization include the organization shall only provide goods and services from certified, green vendors; users will be encouraged to not take separate, individual backups of their databases. These policies were described in Chapter 3 in detail.

Practice

Practice represented by the third row in Figure 9.5 is the actual action based on decisions enshrined in policies. These practices are the things that are "done'—carried out in the organization. Practices implement policies. They are the techniques, the behavior that is expressed by the individuals and organizations. An interesting aside to practice is that they, like processes, involve alteration of habits and change of mindsets (attitude) rather than procurement of new equipment. This involves training.

Examples of practices include switching off computers when not in use; implementing virtualization of all services; replacing existing high carbon emitting equipments with new, green ones; and ethically disposing of electronic waste. These practices can be indexed to the KPIs discussed in Chapter 2.

Technology

Technology, represented by the fourth row in Figure 9.5, is the hardware, databases, and network and systems aspect of Green IT and has been discussed in detail in Chapter 4 and Chapter 6. The Green IT techniques—of using thin clients, ritualizing data servers, and using duplex printers are all examples of technology-based changes in the organization that lead it toward Green IT. Procurement of new, low carbon emitting equipment is an investment that needs to be considered in the long term in the context of the TCCO metrics.

Perhaps simply thinking of a low carbon emitting equipment as a new procurement may not be the right approach. The costs associated directly with a new equipment also needs to consider the waste inherent in disposing of the old equipment—especially if that equipment is still operational. Thus, the ideal way to approach equipment replacement is to balance out the change and incorporate the practice of Green IT as part of the normal equipment replacement cycle.

Metrics

Green IT metrics deal with measurement of carbon emissions of the organization in its "as is" state. Metrics also determine if the "to be" state has been achieved or not. These Green IT metrics have been discussed in detail in Chapters 3 and also in Chapter 6.

In addition to the four aspects of Green IT metrics shown in the Green ICT framework in Figure 9.5, Chapter 6 also discussed the monetize aspect of these metrics.

Choosing the right tools to measure, monitor, and potentially mitigate power consumption and carbon emissions, both inside and outside the IT department, is critical in the GET. Good set of green measures ensure that Green IT projects receive maximum business commitment and are proven to be successful over time. Only with adequate measurement can progress be proved. Hence, metrics need to be supported by CEMS and "smart metering."

Example of metrics include carbon per day/month/year per desktop/laptop; carbon-bit ratio PUE-DCiE; attitude level (Subjective).

Having discussed the Green ICT framework that can model the organization's "as is" and "to be" states, the subsequent discussion is on incorporating that model in an actual transformation process for a green enterprise.

The Green Transformation Process

The basic Green transformation process is made up of 4 + 1 phases: diagnose, plan, enact, and review—interspersed with metrics and measurement.

The eight focus areas of any business transformation, applied here to GET are as follows: business model, product and service portfolio, customers and partners, ICT systems, applications and databases, operational, organizational, business processes, networks and infrastructure, and regulatory.

Types and size or the organization affect the GET process.

As mentioned earlier, transforming to a Green enterprise is actually a business transformation program. Project from various dimensions in the business, infrastructure and systems area make up the transforming program. Figure 9.6 shows a basic Green transformation process. The four major phases of transformation are shown here as diagnose, plan, enact, and review. This figure also shows that while these four phases appear sequential, in reality they are iterative; with the number of iterations required for a successful transformation to be decided by the chief green officer (CGO) together with the person responsible for GET.

The purpose of this basic Green transformation framework shown in Figure 9.6 is to (a) identify the current status of the organization and enlist the goals of GET—these goals will be identified, updated, and finalized through the diagnosis work; (b) add justification for the project using ROI calculations within a business case; (c) provide target metrics (i.e., values for KPIs) for the organization's "to-be" state; (d) organize the actual GET program; (e) provide the basis for the pathway/road map or project plan for transformation; (f) undertake (or enact) the actual transformation; (g) review whether the KPIs have been achieved or not; (h) promote the success along the individual, departmental, and organizational level. Eventually, such Green transformation will open up opportunities for the organization to also help and support its collaborating partners.

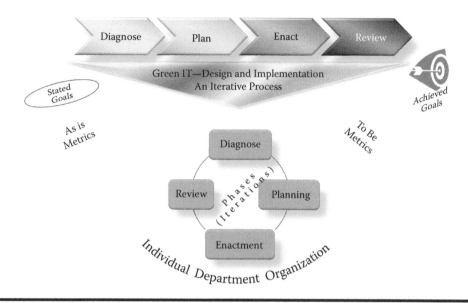

Figure 9.6 The basic Green transformation process.

Figure 9.7 expands in greater detail the GET framework outlined in Figure 9.6. This framework is interspersed with transformation activities such as detailed planning, project accounting, risk management, and ongoing measurements. These phases are a logical approach to transforming any business and, as such, are reflected in various other approaches to business management as well. For example, the Lean Six Sigma approach from business angle*,†, or even IT standards used in business (such as ITIL and CoBIT) can be customized to fit the GET process framework outlined in Figure 9.7. This is so because a GET is based on a holistic change to the organization rather than incremental improvements.

Figure 9.7 also provides a reminder that the GET will vary depending on the size and type of business.

The sizes of business are listed as small, medium, large, global, and virtual. For example, a small business' entire focus will be greening of its end-user computing, whereas that of a large organization of the data servers. Similarly, the types of business have been listed as product service and infrastructure. The organizational focus areas are identified and transformed differently for a predominantly product manufacturer as compared with a service provider. Large infrastructure organizations, like Telecom or power stations vary significantly in their focus areas.

Organizational Focus Areas for GET

Figure 9.7 also shows the eight most common focus (or work) areas of the business. These focus areas provide the structure of the business that will undergo change and to which the GET process and their emphasis can be applied. These focus areas can change depending on the type, size, and nature of business (as described earlier and also outlined in Chapter 2). The goal of the business

---

* Lean Six Sigma, Australia: www.synergymcg.com
† The Lean Thinking Company: www.ThinkLean.com.au

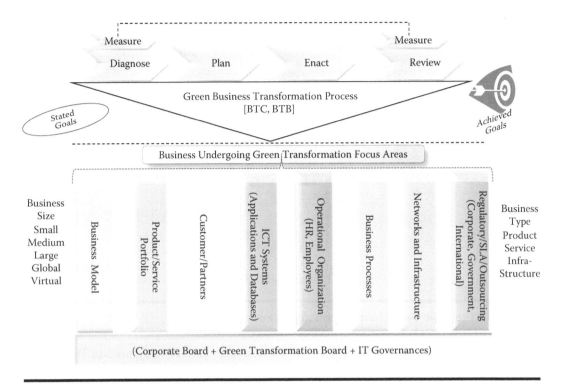

Figure 9.7 The GET process maps to the eight focus areas.

undergoing GET and the complexity of the organization also affect these focus areas. However, the focus areas listed in Figure 9.7 are appropriate for understanding most businesses in terms of their GET. In practice, these focus areas become the "work areas" to be worked upon during the GET. These focus areas, or work areas, for GET, as shown in Figure 9.7 are described as follows:

■ Business Model—which deals with the way a business is organized. GET influences and, usually, changes the business model to reflect the green priorities of the organization. Smaller organizations have a simple, subjective business model that can change easily.

■ Product and Service Portfolio—provides an overall summary of the offerings of the business. GET results in the organization having new green products and, also, dropping of carbon-intensive products and corresponding services. Infrastructure-intensive organization may have buildings and facilities instead of products or services.

■ Customers and Partners—describes the external parties interacting with the business. The change here, due to GET, is as described in the business ecosystem driver in Chapter 2. GET will change the relationships through renegotiated contracts.

■ ICT Systems, Applications, and Databases—includes the technological changes in the software systems and technologies of the business (as discussed in Chapters 4, 6, and 7). These are that data warehouse and business intelligence applications and packages, such as CRM, SCM and HR, SOA.

■ Operational, Organizational—handles the internal parties such as employees and management, and their reporting hierarchies, within the business. (This focus area forms the crux of the discussion in Chapter 8.)

■ Business Processes—model and describe the way in which all activities of the business are sequenced and carried out (as discussed in Chapter 5). The entire domain of BPM together with SOA applies here.

■ Networks and Infrastructure—focus on the underlying communications technologies used by the business (as discussed in Chapters 4 and 6). These are both wired and wireless networks, including short and long distance.

■ Regulatory—deals with legal, accounting, and financial aspects of the business (as discussed in Chapter 2, and later in Chapter 10).

A work area may map to one or more departments of the business. Similarly, each work area may have one or more stakeholders with specific objectives. It is important to identify these stakeholders corresponding to each work area as early in the transformation process as possible. These stakeholders need to be involved and managed right through the transformation process. Handling their concerns as well as meeting their expectations is vital for the success of the transformation process. The work areas and corresponding stakeholders are summarized in Table 9.2.

The roles in this table also map to the transformation and operational roles in GET. These GET roles are described in detail in a later section in this chapter.

Configuring a GET Road Map

A GET roadmap is a high-level program plan that outlines the major steps in an organization's transformation. Following are the major considerations in the configuration of such a road map:

■ Type and size of organization
■ Nomination of roles and responsibilities
■ Formation of the Green enterprise transformation board (GETB)
■ Diagnose
■ Plan—Formation of work areas; Outlining the GET deliverables, their format and their timings
■ Enact—Format, timing and frequency of reporting
■ Review
■ Measure

GET Program: Roles and Deliverables

Identification of the work areas and having a process framework for GET, such as one described above, provides basis for the organization to undertake GET program. Formation of a GETB is an early indication that the business is ready to move forward with its change. The GTB is entrusted with the task of successfully steering the organization to a Green organization as it undergoes changes. The chief executive officer (CEO) nominates this board, which is made up of experts, leaders, and personnel from marketing, technology/infrastructure, finance/legal, CRM, communications, and HR/union. The CEO, together with the members of the GTB, selects the Green enterprise transformation champion (GTC). A GTB is drawn from within the organization with occasional representation from outside as well—such as a consulting organization specializing in

Table 9.2   A List of Work Area of the Business, Corresponding Key Stakeholders and Their Chief Interest in the GET

Transformation Work Areas	Stakeholder	Chief Interest	Chief Concerns
Business model	CEO, CGO, Corporate Board	Compliance, stability, growth, Control	Risks due to green changes
Product and service portfolio	Senior business management	Alignment of carbon and business goals Value generation	Productivity; loss; conflicting offerings
Customers and partners	Sales; Services director Customers and Partners	Green experience; green profile	Loss of quality of service
ICT Systems, applications and databases	IT management; Green IT governance	Server virtualization; system integration, SOA architecture CEMS	Incompatible systems, performance, inflexible systems
Operational, organizational	Green HR; staff	Lean/flexible structure; telework	Changes to reporting structures; rewarding; training
Business processes	Business management (department heads)	Green BPM; Green BPR; collaboration	Changes to business processes; potential lack of systems support
Networks and infrastructure	Infrastructure management	SLAs, capacity for growth/change	Infrastructure upgrades, Costs; new network technologies
Regulatory	CFO; lawyers; environment officers	Compliance, risk management	Lack of clarity; breaches

GET. The GTB works together with the various other governance boards that run the organization. These various governance setups participate in, and are affected by, the GET. The diagnose, plan, enact, review, and measurement phases of transformation are directed by the GETB. The GTC (a role that can also be played by the CGO, but only when she is focusing on the Green transformation rather than the ongoing green operation) reports to this board.

Setting Up a Business Transformation Office (BTO)

For large scale GET typically in a large, multinational organization, setting up of a separate BTO is highly recommended. The physical activity of setting up the BTO can be undertaken either before the commencement of the project or at the state of the diagnosis phase. However, usually, it is preferred to set up the BTO, before the project starts. The BTO houses the transformation board and also provides the administrative support to the project. The BTO is made responsible for the operational matters related to the project, coordination amongst various work areas, documenting the contractual requirements of the project and promoting the project within and outside the organization.

Forming Transformation Work Areas

Formation of the work areas for GET is based on the current state of the organization. These work areas for transformation were depicted in Figure 9.7. The size and type of the organization affects the formation of these work areas. Therefore, not all work areas shown in Figure 9.7 need to be handled in every transformation. This is so because, for some type and size of the organization, some work areas may not be relevant. For example, in a small organization, with no data center, the networks and infrastructure work area may not exist. The current technical and process maturity of the organization also influences the work areas. In some cases, one work area may be more important than other. For example, for a large Telecom company, networks and infrastructures will be far more important than, say, the product portfolio. Formation of transformation work areas includes nomination of a work area leader who has expertise in that particular area of the business or technologies.

Green IT Project Roles

Figure 9.8 shows the primary roles in a Green IT transformation project. These include the business partners, business architect, technical architect, Green IT champion, end-user representative,

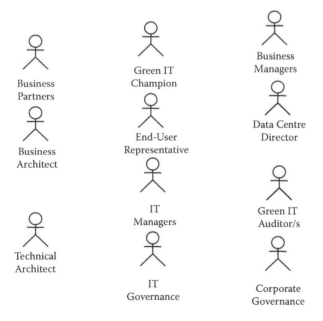

Figure 9.8   Roles in a Green IT project.

IT managers, IT governance, business manager, data center director, Green IT auditors, and corporate governance. Some of these roles had appeared in the Trivedi and Unhelkar (2010) survey, and were outlined in Figure 8.2 in the previous chapter.

A GTC takes leadership responsibility for the project.

Green Enterprise Transformation Champion (GTC)

The role of a GTC is vital in undertaking GET. This has to be a dedicated role with sufficient decision making capacity. The GTC role needs to be aware of both technology and business aspects of the organization.

The responsibility of GTC will include the following:

■ Formalizing the leadership and constitution of the GETB
■ Identifying the current Green maturity state of the organization based on Green metrics
■ Benchmarking best practice goals for the organization that describe its "to be" state
■ Manage budgets
■ Organizing the creation of a project management plan for GET. This plan will contain detailed resource and time management tasks together with people and deliverables
■ Creation of an approach to risk management for GET that is based on priorities of the organization, its lead dimension, and so on
■ Stakeholder management including expectation management of the board, related external parties, and the society
■ Report progress on the GET to the corporate board
■ Monitor KPIs
■ Coordination and management of GET resources, as well as the organizational resources undergoing transformation. This will be done in conjunction with Green HR
■ Coordinate implementation of changes through change management processes across the various focus areas of the business
■ Balance the "driving dimension" of GET with other dimensions—this requires the balancing of economic, social, technical and process, dimensions as the transformation proceeds
■ Track progress and of the GET project
■ Astute use of the tools, technologies, and processes of GET

Business Architect and Variations

The GTC will appoint a business architect to investigate and handle the business model work area of the GET. Such business architect should have a clear vision of the business "as is" and its goals and aspirations. The Business architect is aware of the underpinning technologies that can serve the business but is not a technical expert. A business architect takes a long-term view of the organization (3–5 years and above) when she participates in the GET project. A business architect would create business architectural map that will provide the overall view of the business model and associated work areas. This business architectural map can be a part of the overall enterprise architecture that is also used by the architect in creating operational strategies for the business after transformation. This map ensures that the technologies are aligned with business plans and the changes are tracked and monitored.

Technical Architect and Variations

The GTC also appoints a technical architect. For smaller sized organizations undergoing small transformation, this role may be played by the GTC. However, it is advisable to have the two roles separate to ensure that transformation, technology, and business are given their own agenda and responsibilities. The technical architect is responsible for the following:

- Creation of a technical architecture map to understand where the organization currently is—including networks, databases, security, and contents. This map, again as a part of the overall enterprise architecture, provides excellent basis for which technologies and systems have to change as part of the GET.
- Collection and use of a toolbox of various tools that are used in technical implementations during GET.
- Creation of a comprehensive repository of software applications currently used by the organization—with a view to changing and integrating them. This repository includes CEMS.
- Dividing and categorizing these repositories of applications into different business/application domains that will enable ease of modification with carbon data.
- Ensuring that the applications that support specific decision making are part of the overall EI suite, and are available to decision makers.
- Creation of a new technical architecture that would reflect the goals of the business transformation itself. This would include incorporation of SOA and WS in integrating existing software packages with CEMS.
- Ongoing alignment of technologies with business plans during and after GET.
- Coordinating the development of a Green IT portal.
- Tracking and monitoring technical changes resulting from applications notifications upgrades and integrations.
- Managing quality initiatives during GET.
- Develop an understanding of the future trends in technology that the organization will have to deal with after the GET.
- Produce a suitable technical strategy including a technical roadmap for transformation.

Business Partners

Business partners play a crucial role in GETs. As the business interests of collaborating partners coincide, there is added impetus to provide wide array of support to the partners. This support can take shape in the form of knowledge and experience sharing, providing relevant tool support and help with understanding dynamic customer preferences as the business transforms.

- Participate
- Collaborate
- Interface
- Integrate

Green IT Auditors

Auditors carry out checks and balances throughout and after the transformation. Auditors measure and audit to ensure that the transformation has created value for the business as stated by its goals. These audits can use the reporting features of CEMS, if implemented and that the transformation has not adversely affected any of the reporting and regulatory requirements of the business. Furthermore, auditors are involved in the review process, ensuring that the calculations leading up to the ROI are accurate and reflect the reality resulting from transformation.

End-Users

End-users are the employees, managers, and customers of the organization who are affected by the GET. They are represented in the GET.

The end-user representative is for all end-users, and their groups (manager, customer, senior).

- Represents user groups
- May be more than one
- Highlights device usage
- Highlights attitude for roles
- Helps in Green HR
- Understands CEMS and smart meters

IT Managers

IT management—deals with the operational and management aspect of IT within the organization. They are responsible for the IT systems, their operations on the corresponding hardware and approaches to using IT for overall carbon reduction. Chapter 8 outlined the Skills Framework for Information Age (SFIA) skillset that can be applied here to the IT management and business management roles to ascertain the levels of skills and responsibilities required during and after GET.

Business Managers

Business managers assume the responsibility at department level to measure, report, and reduce emissions. They are more interested in the economic and process dimension of the GET than in technology and social dimensions. This is so because the economic dimension directly affects their performance and the process dimension is the one on which they have immediate control. Thus, business managers can directly assist in the modeling of business processes, their investigations, and optimizations.

IT Governance

This is an activity for which more than one roles within the organization can assume responsibility. IT governance—deals with overseeing the IT management and providing strategic and policy input in the process of greening an organization. Chapter 6 discussed in detail the role of IT governance standards such as Information Technology Infrastructure Library (ITIL) in a green enterprise. Each of the phases of ITIL can be applied in a way that not only enhances IT governance of the organization but also impacts its carbon footprint.

Corporate Governance

Following are some of the processes and standards that come into play in the role played by Corporate Governance. This is not a single role belonging to a person but a role played by many people, a group or a committee. These processes have a need to be upgraded or fine tuned to reflect the green requirements of the business.

- Lean—will move toward Lean-Green, as was alluded to in the process chapter 3
- Six Sigma—will not only focus on quality but also the efficiencies in carbon reduction
- TQM—Total Quality Management—will incorporate metrics for carbon reduction in addition to defect reduction
- KPIs—the Key Performance Indicators are not only to enable corporate governance but also green governance
- SIFA (Skills Framework for Information Age), AIBA (Australian Institute of Business Analysis) and PMBOK (Project Management Book of Knowledge) are examples of processes and frameworks that will all be modified to reflect the green awareness and green goals of the organization

Green IT Transformation—Deliverables

Figure 9.9 depicts the typical deliverables in a Green IT transformation project. Some of these deliverables are produced in one phase of the GET and then, in turn, they are the input to the next phase. (Starting templates for some of these deliverables is provided in the appendix.)

- Green IT Business Case—documents the ROI, the budgets, and overall justification for the project

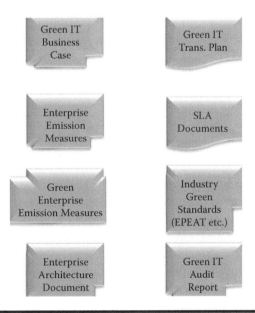

Figure 9.9   Deliverables in a Green IT project.

- Enterprise Emission Measures—documents the existing carbon emissions across the organization
- Green Enterprise Emission Measures—resulting at the end of the GET
- Enterprise Architecture Document—that documents the enterprise architecture, using an existing or modified framework
- SLA
- Various docs relating to suppliers; outsourcing partners; legal

GET: Diagnosis Phase

As shown in Figure 9.7, there are four phases to GET supported by the measure phase.

The diagnostic phase, discussed here, is the very first phase of the transformation project. Accurate diagnosis provides a good understanding of the current state of the organization by investigating into the various work areas of the business from the point of view of transformation. An understanding of the structure and dynamics of the organization, as well as its ability to achieve goals, manage risks and ascertain the leading dimension of transformation is developed here.

The state of an organization, with respect to its carbon emissions, is based on the current emissions at this early stage of the organization. This measure would be a relatively approximate measure, as the sophistication of the organization in terms of ascertaining its carbon emissions may not be high. The demographics of the organization, its motivator, goals, size, and type would all affect its current state, as ascertained during this diagnostic activity. Diagnosis also includes a review or stock take of existing assets across all work areas. The "inventory" of business systems and applications provide basis for understanding the existing business model. Diagnosis can help an organization further estimate and refine its business case with details of effort required and the timeline for the transformation.

Diagnosis indicates the state of maturity of the organization. It thus provides an excellent opportunity to understand the length—breadth—depth of the Green IT strategies and policies. A few maturity models have been available—such as the Capability Maturity Model (CMM)* and a model used by Unhelkar (2009) to ascertain the maturity of mobile businesses. Philipson (2011) has also developed a Green IT readiness index, and a corresponding CMM for Green IT. These maturity models indicate how from an early, preliminary or ad hoc stage, the organization moves to a managed or matured stage wherein it is continuously improving its carbon footprint.

An organization that finds itself lagging behind in terms of carbon emissions and needs to improve in all work areas can be considered at a "preliminary" level. The next state for an organization can be when its effort at transformation improves its performance across more than one dimension of the business. The advanced maturity of an organization is said to have been achieved after the transformation across all four dimensions has changed all work areas. Once the transformation is complete along all dimensions and through all the work areas, the organization can be said to be in a "matured green" state. Finally one may also consider the state in which the organization has not only reached its own Green maturity, but is also helping its business partners.

The Business Transformation Office (BTO) is now fully set up and organized. The Business Transformation Board (BTB) is functioning and reporting to the corporate base. The Business Transformation Champion (BTC) is also busy managing stakeholder expectations. The diagnosis phase also ascertains and progresses the lead dimension of the organization for GET.

---

* www.sei.cmu.edu

Figure 9.10 shows the diagnostic activities in relation to the equipment lifecycle's carbon efficiencies of an organization. These diagnosis activities are carried out as follows:

- The Green IT champion organizes lifecycle evaluation and ascertains the current Green maturity. Also, updates the business case on the Green IT project.
- The business management (supply chain) reviews the existing procurement and disposal attitudes and identifies operational carbon emissions (CE).
- The IT governance board (or similar governing body) reviews the existing procurement and disposal practices and updates P&L carbon emissions.
- The corporate governance (board or similar governing body) evaluates the business case risks also reviews policies with business partners (business case for Green IT as presented by the Green IT champion).
- Recycling policies and practices are revised.
- Energy star and other ratings are used (if available) to ascertain the greenness of the equipments.
- Green procurement strategies as they apply to equipments.
- Optimization of operations is ascertained.
- Waste disposal policies and practices are revisited.

Challenges

- Uncertain data on current carbon emissions across lifecycle/procurement
- Impact on SLAs a major challenge
- Minimal Industry experience in changes to software for carbon emissions

Figure 9.11 shows the diagnostic activities in relation to ascertaining the end-user carbon efficiencies.

During diagnosis phase of End-user efficiencies, the following activities take place:

- The Green IT champion creates and updates the business case on the Green IT project.
- The end-user provides input into a survey (or a similar social diagnostic tool) to help ascertain the attitude toward Green IT. Measurements of carbon emissions are undertaken per device (desktop, mobile, printer) used by the end-users. These would be entered in a system, or in spreadsheet.
- The IT governance board (or a similar governing body) is involved in permitting the creation of a device inventory; measurement of overall carbon emissions.
- The corporate governance (board or similar governing body) evaluates the overall end-user policies on Green IT. Corporate governance also evaluates business case for Green IT as presented by the Green IT champion.

Planning requires the incorporation of low-watt PCs, energy-efficient monitors, thin clients, printer rationalization and consolidation, and existing penetration of mobile devices.

Challenges

- Patterns of carbon emissions can be daily, monthly, yearly.
- Data/information ownership is a major challenge of virtualization.

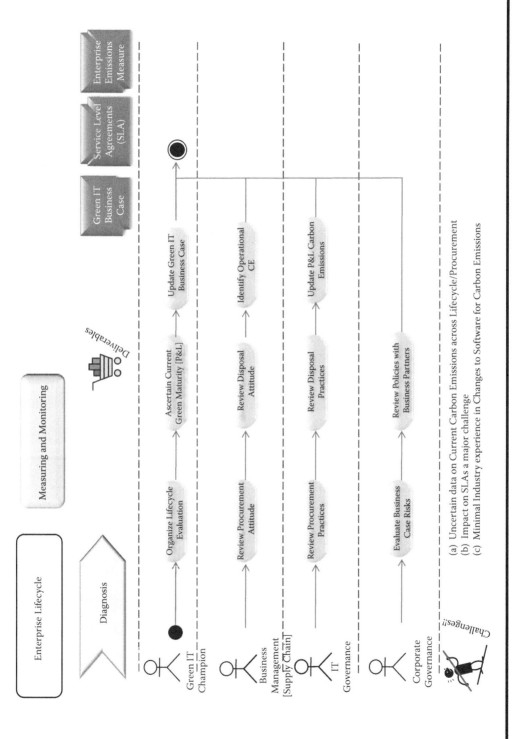

Figure 9.10 Diagnosing equipment lifecycle's carbon efficiencies.

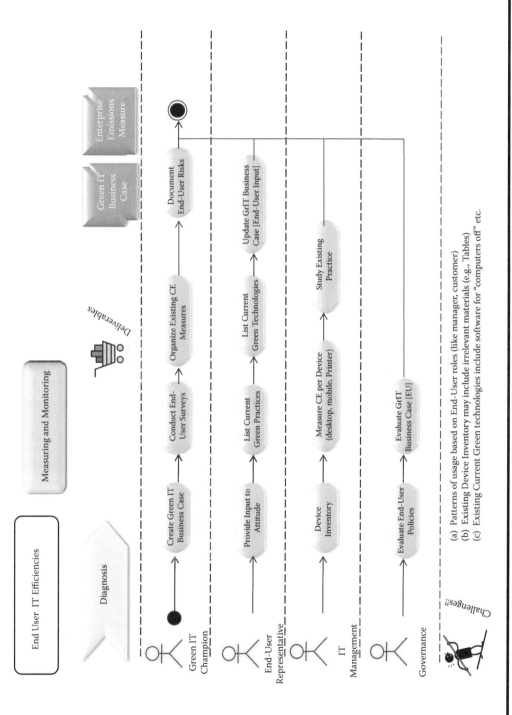

Figure 9.11 Diagnosing end-user computing's carbon efficiencies.

Figure 9.12 shows the diagnostic activities in relation to the enterprise data center efficiencies of an organization. These diagnoses are carried out as follows:

- The Green IT champion organizes for measurements of the existing data center efficiencies. This will be accomplished by using existing and newly created metrics on Green IT (see Chapter 3 for metric). Also, updates the business case on the Green IT project.
- The enterprise data center director (or similar responsible role) takes an inventory of IT equipments from the point of view of calculating the current CE. Measurements of CE are undertaken per server (or similar unit of hardware measure).
- The IT governance board (or similar governing body) reviews the existing SLAs—especially to review which partners are involved in providing data center services.
- The corporate governance (board or similar governing body) evaluates the overall end-user policies on Green IT. Corporate governance also evaluates the cost of running the data center, and the costs associated with the Green initiatives related to the organization (business case for Green IT as presented by the Green IT champion).
- A list of current virtualization or server consolidation techniques in use is made.
- The physical environment and the facilities (where data center exists) is recorded.

Challenges

- Overall organization presents a bigger challenge than IT, as we are looking at emissions across the enterprise.
- Green IT champion has to convince business management, corporate governance.

Figure 9.13 shows the diagnostic activities in relation to IT as a low carbon enabler across the organization. The ability of IT as a low carbon enabler across the organization is diagnosed via the following activities:

- The Green IT champion evaluates the existing organizational Green practices and ascertains the overall enterprise green maturity. Also, updates the business case on the Green IT project.
- The business management updates the divisional use of IT and models the current business processes.
- The IT governance board (or similar governing body) critically examines software and hardware inventories.
- The corporate governance (board or similar governing body) evaluates the existing enterprise Green IT policies and ascertains or confirms the greening dimension.
- Telecommuting/teleconferencing.
- Collaboration tools and SaaS.
- Supply chain.

Challenges

- Overall organization presents a bigger challenge than IT, as we are looking at emissions across the enterprise.
- Green IT champion has to convince business management, corporate governance.

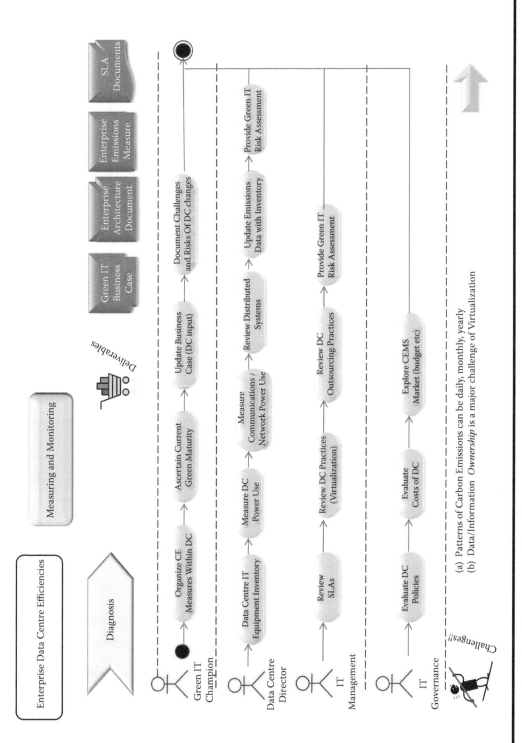

Figure 9.12 Diagnosing data center carbon efficiencies.

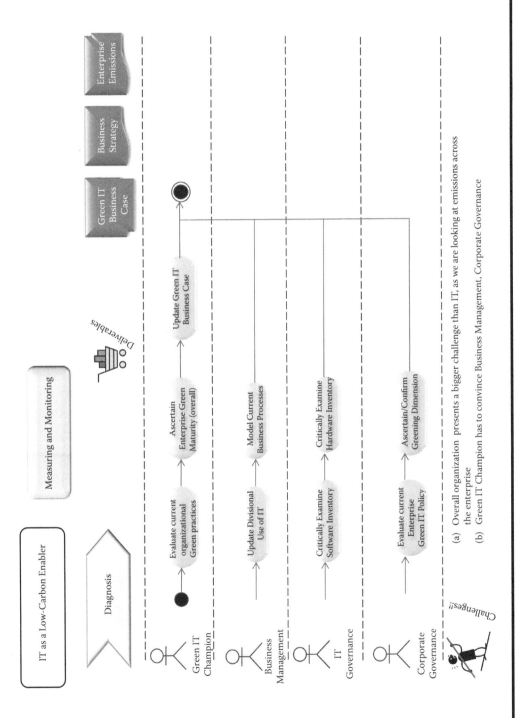

Figure 9.13   Diagnosing efficiencies of IT as a low carbon enabler across the organization.

GET: Planning and Scoping Phase

In the planning phase, the strategic thinking and innovative capability of the organization are translated into actionable activities and their sequences in setting up the Green transformation project. Creative ways of bring about the change, including maximum use of internal and external resources, are explored in this phase.

The planning phase extends the earlier, high-level roadmap to a detailed project level road map. For specific GET phases, there will be a need to create a project road map that is specific to the organization, its goals and its resources. It is important to note that this road map remains a live document—which means later, during enactment phase, this same road map is also (a) modified depending on the nuances of the project and (b) refined through the feedback gleaned during transformation.

The road map includes the Green transformation plan, the Green pilot project (which can be embedded within the transformation plan for small projects), the overall work area plan, the plan for the lead work area (this will relate to the lead dimension discussed earlier and it will also dictate plans for the rest of the work areas) and the quality plan (which will include verification and validation of the changes). The deliverables resulting from the road map are the plans themselves as also the project task list, the performance and ROI measures, the ranking of risks and the plans to audit the results of the transformation. The roles involve in transformation planning (and also rest of the project) include the GTC, the project manager, the quality manager, work area lead, business manager, and the IT auditors.

The planning and scoping phase of GET explores the output of the previous diagnosis phase to identify and formalize the planning of the transformation project. Once the significant aspects of the business—especially the work areas—are identified, planning outlines the tasks to be performed for transforming each work area. The broad scope of the project and the work areas that are outlined in the diagnosis, and their interdependency, need to be discussed and resolved here. The scoping aspect of the GET project in this planning phase ranks and prioritizes work areas of transformation. While the risks are managed in practice during enactment, the planning phase identifies and ranks these risks, and also incorporates the effect of changes on the organization.

Thus, planning in the GET tends to become a balancing act: balancing between costs and benefits, technology and business; and balancing risks with outcome.

The goals of the GET, already identified as part of the strategies, are mapped against best practices that are specific to the industry. For example, the airline industry will measure and set goals for the carbon emissions within a particular flight sector, whereas a hospital would measure carbon emissions in processes relating to a patient registration, or managing the stock of drugs. Each organization has to separately identify and document its green success criteria in this planning phase and formulate the right metrics and measurements that would be used to ascertain its success. The planning phase utilizes the known project management techniques, including time and budget estimations, finalizing the goals and scope of the transformation, refinement, and documentation of the detailed project plan together with the roles and responsibilities and evaluation and procurement of tools and technologies required for the transformation process. Work areas are organized, leaders for those work areas are nominated, and interrelationships between work areas are highlighted in planning phase.

Planning for the Green IT project starts with the Green IT champion—who finalizes the leading area of the organization that will undergo transformation. The leading area will start becoming obvious through the diagnosis, but it is important to decide formally whether the end-user efficiencies should lead the way, or whether it should be the equipment lifecycle and procurement, or the data center. "IT as Low Carbon Enabler" should not be treated as a lead area of work, as it would be very risky to attempt the Green transformation for the entire organization at first. The lessons learnt through the end-user and data center transformations, for example, can feed into the transformation of the entire enterprise.

Pilot Project

Large GET projects, although holistic in nature, are not carried out as a single project. In fact, it's a program made up of many projects which, in turn, are made up of multiple iterations. These iterations of transformation are outlined in the planning. Furthermore, for such large projects, its advisable to have a pilot project that would test out the scope, the risks and reconfirm the iterations that will be actually used in practice. Issues related to a pilot project are as follows:

- Planning the pilot requires identification of a small yet important area of business that can undergo GET.
- The pilot validates the plan for GET, or identifies the gaps that need to be covered.
- Evaluation of the success criteria, such as the formulation of KPIs based on green metrics and their validation with measurements is undertaken during the pilot.
- Pilot is formally started, enacted, and closed formally—resulting in reports to the corporate board by the GTB.
- Pilots are invaluable in ensuring that disruption to normal functioning of the business due to the GET is kept to a minimum.
- Pilots highlight interdependence between work areas and also lead to revisiting the work areas, their priorities, and their risks.

Figure 9.14 shows the planning activities in relation to enterprise lifecycle "pillar" of Green IT transformation with the green point method.

Enterprise Lifecycle Plan

Planning for Green IT efficiencies in enterprise lifecycle involve planning for efficient procurement, management, and disposal of equipment as well products. For example, planning in this area includes recycling plans, procurement strategies that are targeted at green strategies, and environmentally responsible waste disposal.

The **ROLES** and **ACTIVITIES** for the planning process for the equipment lifecycle efficiencies are as follows:

Green IT Champion—Works with the business management, as well as the governances in the organization, to plan the changes to product/equipment lifecycle and procurement that will make the organization greener. This planning includes discussions with business unit managers as to how they currently source materials, which equipments are used in production and how they are disposed.

Business Management—Plans, along with the Green IT champion, to procure, use, and dispose equipments in a carbon-sensitive way. The recycling and disposal plans are part of procurement and disposal plan that will dictate the changes in this dimension of the organization.

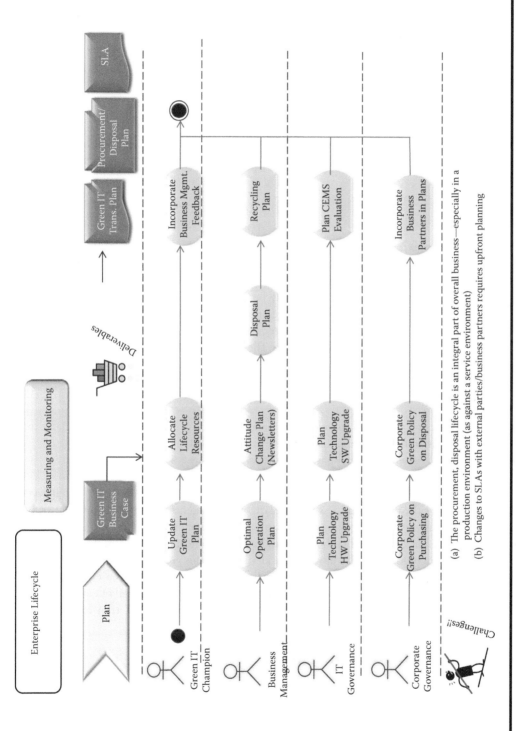

Figure 9.14 Planning enterprise lifecycle Green IT transformation.

IT Governance—Oversees the planning process for hardware and software upgrades throughout the business lifecycle. The product development lifecycle is also overseen by the IT governance, to ensure that the business is not disadvantaged due to the greening process. The CEMS evaluation here is directed at how it can help calculate ROI on the green investment from product lifecycle viewpoint.

Corporate Governance—Participates in the planning process on how the policies for corporate purchases and disposals will change. The need to "talk" with business partners on potential changes to their SLAs is also undertaken by corporate governance here.

Input

Green IT Business Case: Includes justification for the new equipments, their TCCO, and replacement costs.

Output

Green IT Transformation Plan: Includes plans for green recycling, updates on the Energy Star and other ratings, green procurement strategies, optimized operations, and waste disposal.

Procurement and Disposal Plan: Specifically focused on procurement of equipment and their decommissioning. This may not necessarily be a separate document, and may be a part of the transformation plan. However, for large organizations dealing extensively with procurement and disposal, a separate plan will be required.

SLA: With Business Partners/External Parties: These will change as the equipment lifecycle moves toward a green lifecycle.

Challenges

- The procurement, disposal lifecycle is an integral part of overall business—especially in a production environment (as against a service environment).
- Changes to SLAs with external parties/business partners require upfront planning.

Planning challenges in the area of overall lifecycle have to deal with the fact that the product lifecycle is an integral part of the overall business, particularly when it comes to a production industry (as against a service industry). Therefore, any changes to the lifecycle of products (and services) affect the entire organization. The equipment (although initially IT equipment, but it can be any equipment) used in the process of production also provides the challenge to this green dimensions—as the organization, especially the governance boards, need justification to upgrade to green equipments; the planning process also needs to handle safe and environmentally friendly disposal of equipments.

Figure 9.15 shows the planning activities in relation to end-user Green IT transformation.

Planning for End-User Efficiencies

The **ROLES** and **ACTIVITIES** for the planning process for end-user IT efficiencies are as follows:

Green IT Champion—Involved in leading and coordinating the planning activities; reporting to the board.

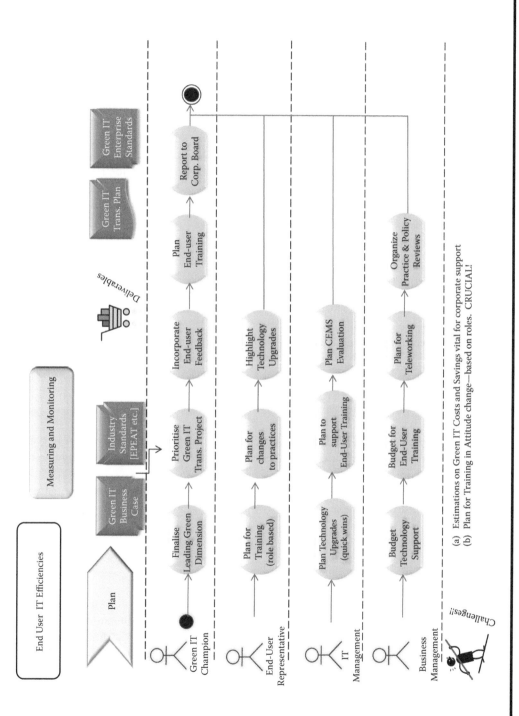

Figure 9.15 Planning end-user Green IT transformation.

End-User Representative—Planning for the training (could be short, self-facilitated or could be elaborate for a large upgrade to desktops and printers) as well as planning and budgeting for the time and effort required to change to green practices.

IT Management—Plans for the upgrades to the software and the hardware that will be required for the green effort. This could be the planning for purchase of low-watt PCs and energy-efficient monitors, for example. There will also be a need to plan for environmentally sensitive disposal of old and energy-hungry devices.

Plans by IT management also include plans for printer rationalization and consolidation. Software upgrades can be planned not only for desktops (such as software to switch-off computers when not in use), but also for the CEMS that would be required for not only end-user efficiencies but also for the rest of the effort.

Business Management—Participates in the planning process to budget for time and effort required to support the technology upgrades and the end-user training. Similarly, business management will have to plan for how they will introduce teleworking in business units.

Deliverables

Input

Green IT Business Case: Contains justification for the project; hence provides input as to what needs to go into the planning process. Planning process is helped by a good understanding of the ROI expected in the end-user dimension of the organization.

Industry Standards: Such as EPEAT are incorporated in the plan to ensure green procurement and usage (hence such standards will apply to all vertical dimensions' planning process).

Output

Green IT Transformation Plan: Updated with step-by-step instructions on how to carry out the transformation enactment later. Thus, the activities listed here are meant to update the activities needed during enactment.

Green IT Enterprise Standards: These are the new, expected, green standards within the organization for expected carbon emissions per end-user device, per day/month/year, and so on.

Challenges

- Estimations on Green IT costs and savings vital for corporate support.
- Plan for training in attitude change—based on roles.

Planning challenges in the area of end-user IT efficiencies (as with the other dimensions) primarily deal with the estimations made on the costs involved in upgrading end-user technologies, training, software upgrades, and so on. This expense has to be justified against the cost savings, as well as the initial goal of the organization to undertake green initiative (such as compliance with government regulations and/or fulfillment of customer demand).

Attitude change of the end-user is another major challenge that requires considerable planning. This planning will include training as well as creation of user groups, recognition of changes through (possible) awards, and so on.

Figure 9.16 shows the planning activities in relation to data center Green IT transformation.

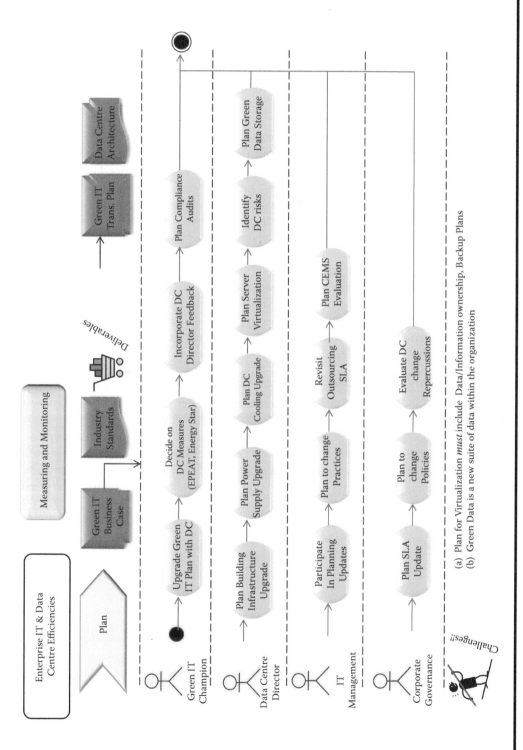

Figure 9.16 Planning data center Green IT transformation.

Enterprise IT Data Center Efficiencies

Planning for efficiencies in the enterprise data center requires knowledge of both—the physical infrastructure (such as building and air conditioning) and the IT infrastructure (such as servers, network routers, and consumables). Hence the Green IT champion needs to work closely with the data center director to carefully plan all aspects of the data center upgrade.

The **ROLES** and **ACTIVITIES** for the planning process for the enterprise IT data center efficiencies are as follows:

> *Green IT Champion*—Works to upgrade the Green IT transformation plan with the data center details—such as current emissions, current usage of the center, people, and processes involved in running the center and the measures to be used in future to ascertain the success of Green IT.
>
> *Data Center Director*—Plans, along with the Green IT champion, to upgrade the building, power supply, and air-conditioning/cooling upgrades. Server virtualization, which is a vital part of green initiative, is also a part of this planning process. The plans for data storages, especially in a virtualized environment require planning for capacity, security, and usage of data. Should the servers be "outsourced" to a third-party provider of these services, the data center director has to also handle the risks associated with it.
>
> *IT Management*—Continues to participate in the planning process, including plans for changing to the current data center practices. For example, the data center may currently be having dedicated space on the servers for each project. IT management can oversee the plans for changes to that practice to genuine sharing of disk space. Similarly, IT management will also oversee the planning process for the building and infrastructure upgrade. Finally, IT management will be interested in how the green project will evaluate CEMS—carbon emission management software—that would be required during enactment, review, and the rest of the Green IT organization's processes.
>
> *Corporate Governance*—Participates in the planning process from a policies viewpoint. Corporate governance is involved in how the SLA will change, whether the changes will have positive effect on the data center from both green and operational perspective, and how to plan and promote the changes to policies of the organization that will promote the green initiative.

Deliverables

Input

> *Green IT Business Case:* Provides justification for the investment in data center upgrades; costs associated with server virtualization and optimization are listed.
>
> *Industry Standards:* Relating particularly to DCiE/PUE metrics.

Output

> *Green IT Transformation Plan:*
> *Green IT Enterprise Standards:*

Challenges

- Plan for virtualization *must* include data/information ownership, backup plans
- Green data is a new suite of data within the organization

Planning challenges in the area of end-user IT efficiencies (as with the other dimensions) primarily deal with the estimations made on the costs involved in upgrading end-user technologies, training, software upgrades, and so on. This expense has to be justified against the cost savings, as well as the initial goal of the organization to undertake green initiative (such as compliance with government regulations and/or fulfillment of customer demand).

Attitude change of the end-user is another major challenge that requires considerable planning. This planning will include training as well as creation of user groups, recognition of changes through (possible) awards, and so on.

Figure 9.17 shows the planning activities in relation to enterprise transformation enabled by IT.

- Telecommuting/teleconferencing
- Collaboration tools and SaaS
- Supply chain
- Outsourcing can be one of the strategies to influence the enterprise

Planning for IT as a Low-Carbon Enabler for the Enterprise

Planning for the use of IT as a low carbon enabler for the enterprise requires plans related to Green IT, as well as planning the changes to the entire enterprise. This requires development of policies and procedures related to promulgating IT as a low carbon enabler for the entire enterprise (will require corporate board involvement).

Thus, this planning includes all previous dimensions and their planning as well as plans related to the business (not necessarily IT).

The **ROLES** and **ACTIVITIES** for the planning process for the dimension of IT as a low carbon enabler are as follows:

Green IT Champion—Works with the business management, IT governance and, most importantly, corporate governance to plan out strategies for transformation to a green enterprise. The Green IT plan is updated for enterprise-wide changes—including in teleworking of employees, supply chain management, and BPM. Furthermore, the Green IT champion also sets up (as a part of the planning process) the carbon compliance reporting structure. Close association with all business unit leaders is required to achieve their planning.

Business Management—Plans, along with the Green IT champion, to promote green activities across the business unit which, in turn, would result in a green organization.

IT Governance—Oversees the planning process for technology upgrade across the organization. The IT governance is also involved in planning the use of emerging technologies (e.g., software as a service and Cloud) and how they can be used in low carbon enablement of the entire enterprise. Plans for CEMS implementation are also considered at this point (after CEMS has been evaluated during enactment).

Corporate Governance—Participates in the planning process on how the corporate policies need to change—together with possible changes to the business model and the organization structure.

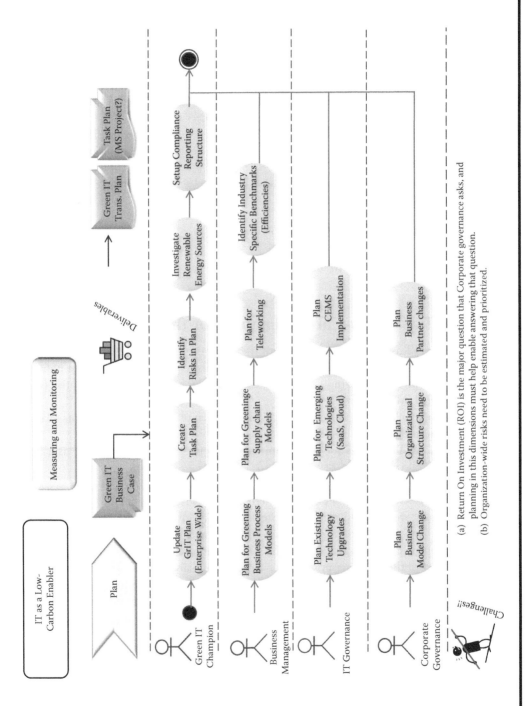

Figure 9.17 Planning enterprise transformation enabled by IT.

Deliverables

Input

> *Green IT Business Case*

Output

> *Green IT Transformation Plan:* Gets updated here with plan for the entire organization. This includes planning for changes to the business model, as well as structural changes.
>
> *Task Plan:* Step-by-step tasks to be carried out in implementing the Green IT project plan.

Challenges

- Return on investment is the major question that corporate governance asks, and planning in this dimensions must help enable answering that question.
- Organization-wide risks need to be estimated and prioritized.

Planning challenges in the area of IT as a low carbon enabler deal with the entire organization. Thus, marketing, sales, legal, and accounting departments are examples of involvement of non-IT areas of business in planning green-specific changes.

GET: Enactment Phase

Enactment is the execution of the business transformation plan created in the previous phase. Enactment requires full garment of project management skills. This primarily includes risk management, monitoring of progress, measurements and reporting. Enactment can be leaded by any work stream or a combination thereof. Following are issues to be considered during a GET enactment phase:

- Identification of risks during execution of the transformation plan, their priorities, and how to ameliorate them.
- Interrelationship amongst work areas, their dependencies and management of the lead work area as first priority.
- Measurement of the GET outputs. Use of metrics created during diagnosis and formalized during planning are used here to ensure common measures for comparison—with the help of CEMS.
- Reporting to stakeholders and managing their expectations.

While a GET project can be driven through any of the work areas, ideally the lead area is dictated by the lead dimension of transformation. In the subsequent two subsections, the ICT-driven enactment and the business process driven enactment are discussed as examples. (The planning process for each of these work areas as leading work areas will be slightly different for the overall transformation plan.)

Green information systems play a major role in measuring and reporting change related to the environment. Each individual employee's carbon generation can be measured, collated, and reported with the help of information systems. Feeding this information back to the employee through smart metering can bring about immediate change in behavior. For example, during enactment... (Deshpande and Unhelkar 2011, Yogesh, HRG) if an employee in a bank is provided, as a real-time meter, information on the amount of carbon generated by his computer, then the visual effect of not-turning off her computer is immediately felt. This is encouraging and reinforcing a positive change in the behavior of the employee. Similarly information coming out of the Green ICT systems that bring about positive change includes reports of daily, monthly, and yearly GHG generation and using that data to impact practices in enactment. Thus, Green ICT information systems need to produce numbers that not only focus on the environmental performance of the organization but also its overall efficiency and effectiveness. These numbers prove the cost benefits of the effort to change. The success of enactment of the GET plan is closely tied with the way such changes also impact the bottom line of the organization.

Once the Green transformation is on its way, the GTB must establish methods for measuring and reporting the progress toward the achievement of these goals. Metrics allow the transformation board to provide visibility to success of a Green ICT strategy, understand the results, compare them with those obtained by other organizations, and determine when the objectives need to be adjusted in light of changing circumstances (Unhelkar and Philipson 2009).

Measuring the progress of the enactment allow the enterprise to establish, for example, whether a target for increasing the energy efficiency of servers and data centers is being achieved, and whether additional energy efficiency improvements need to be made to accomplish results comparable with benchmarks established by peers or competitors.

The transformation plan may be utilized to help determine how best to measure progress and introduce accountability into the Green ICT initiatives, both at the enterprise and solution levels. IT governance representatives (board) may be also put in charge of supporting measurement and reporting, as well as of identifying when a realignment of internal measures or systems is needed to ensure that the expected results are seen, evaluated, and realized.

Technology-Driven Enactment

The ICT-driven enactment of the GET results from technology as a lead dimension of transformation. This will have the organization's ICT systems, applications, and databases at the center of the overall transformation. The discussions on EI are applied in practice when the enactment is technology driven. The EI collaborates across various ICT systems such as the CRM, SCM/ERP, and HR systems of the organization. There are also many in-house systems that are affected by the transformation, as also the systems and interfaces with those of the business partners. Similarly, technology-driven enactment also includes immediate changes to governance, architecture as the management of ICT. The factors that affect these management levels include the standards, need for integration, the approach to testing and quality assurance, the contractual requirements and the deployment of the new ICT systems, applications, and databases. The adaptation of the organization to the new technology permeates all aspects of the organization. This includes its organizational structure, its software systems, and its people. Therefore, transformation also includes undertaking training activities that are required at all levels in the organization.

The important ICT systems and corresponding changes to those systems resulting from GET are discussed briefly:

Customer Relationships Management

The CRM systems are updated during GET with the goal of combining "green" with "value" to the customers. This value includes reliable and good quality service (that will reduce repetition), personalized attention to the needs of the customers, and interactive support due to changing customer needs. A good CRM ensures that the customer is provided a single unified view of the business and not the possible internal fragments of the business. Therefore, during GET, there is usually a need for backend integration and some data migration relating to CRM, and the associated carbon data. SOA and WS play a major role in this integration, as was discussed in Chapter 6.

Supply Change Management (SCM)

Supply Change Management applications undergo change to enable users, primarily employees of the organization, to perform many common warehouse, inventory, and shop floor related tasks in a holistic manner. A Green SCM was also discussed in Chapter 6. A technology-led transformation will monitor and control materials, their delivery and order status. Similarly, procurement, including purchasing, transportation, warehousing, and receiving of goods will have processes that require technical integration with the underlying SCM systems. Reduced movement of goods, holding of inventory and accurate production estimates are achieved by the use Green SCM. Integration and migration are important technical consideration in these ICT systems, as substantial carbon data gets added to these systems.

Human Resource and Payroll Systems

The HR systems provide opportunities for Green HR to be implemented. These HR systems are upgraded to offer greater support to individuals and departments in terms of training, rewards, and career path. Personalization of timesheets and payrolls, enterprise bargaining, subsequent agreements, and related responsibilities of HR may also have to be modified as a result of transformation. GET also changes the job roles, responsibilities, management, organizational structures, and hierarchies, as discussed in detail in Chapter 8.

Business Partner's Systems

Through the use of SOA and web services, GET projects aim to improve the interactions of the business with its partner businesses. WS based technologies change the way the business sources services. For example, one business can "plug" services from another "Carbon tax calculators," or source' Carbon emission limits' such as which could be offered by the government within its own systems. Information and knowledge management within is changed to make it robust, accurate, reliable, and accessible. Search capabilities and ability to correlate information is substantially enhanced (Santer 2009).

Integration

A major challenge of ICT-driven GET is the handling of integration issues. While integration is always a challenge in even routine upgrades of systems, during GET this issue becomes particularly challenging as all the work areas of the business are likely to change. In addition to considering the technical challenges of integration, integration of ICT systems has to also consider corresponding effect on people, their organizational structures, their device usage (including the challenges of usability), and the changes to the corresponding business processes. SOA and WS enables this integration (Chapter 6).

Data Migration

Another major challenge across all ICT systems is that of data migration. Usually, existing data with the current systems is in silos; it is also duplicated. These GET projects have to plan for data migration to ensure its unification.

Business Process–Driven Enactment

Business process-driven enactment of Green enterprise transition is yet another dimension along which the GET can be enacted. Such GET is based on reengineering of business processes. Business processes, customers/partners, operational organization, ICT systems, and regulatory work areas provide the foundation of this particular business transformation. broadcasting, informative, transactive, operative, and collaborative processes that were discussed in Chapter 5 form a hierarchy of increasing complexity from a process perspective in business transformation. Broadcasting and informative business processes are easy to transform as they have less security requirement but they are of less value to users. Transactive processes, the next a level of complexity, are mostly commercial in nature. Operative processes help in providing and ensuring efficiencies in different departments such as inventory, HR, and finance. Lastly, collaborative processes are most complex and require interfaces between business processes of external and internal business parties. It is recommended that the GET project should incrementally incorporate these levels of complexities of business processes—starting with the informative layer and moving gradually up to the collaborative layer of processes. The integration of various systems, as mentioned earlier in the ICT-driven transformation, also affects the internal, as well as external business processes. These business processes and supporting systems in the current state of the organization are studied carefully to effectuate the necessary changes in those processes and systems that would result in a unified view to the users. While existing processes can be reengineered and merged together, there are also completely new processes that need to be engineered. Process modeling tools and techniques can be very helpful in this regard.

Finally, training is a crucial aspect of deploying new and reengineered business processes. This is particularly so because depending on the complexity of the processes, there can be a parallel execution of the old processes, as well as the new processes. Training of employees needs to handle these transformational complexities. Similarly, training in-house needs to be complimented by potential training for business partners and customers involved in large and complex transactions.

GET: Review and Measure Phase

The review phase details with the outcomes and auditing them to check whether the stated objectives are reflected in the outcomes. Furthermore, the outcomes need to be measured and studied not only for the new business, but also for the new environment in which the business is now operating. It is usual for the outcomes to be slightly different to the stated goals even in case of successful business transformations. The difference in the outcomes from the goals could be because both the business and environment has moved during the time the GET project is implemented.

Evaluation of the outcomes include reviewing in detail the newly implemented software, system solution, and changes to organizational structures as well as changes to the business portfolio and model. These measurements are incorporated in the feedback by the GTC to the boards responsible for the Green transformation as also to the business stakeholders. The review process not only ascertains the achievements of the transformation, but also opens up doors to further and potentially ongoing enhancements. Hence the review process should make provisions for these enhancements in all work areas of the business. Organizations should incorporate changes due to experience gained from the transformation as well as the issues discovered during transformation.

Green metrics as discussed throughout the GET, are required to identify and measure the criteria for optimization and improvement. Metrics provide a set of formal measurable criteria that prove the improvement resulting from GET. Therefore, metrics are used to communicate the success of the GET project to various stakeholders. Understanding the perceptions of the goals in relation to business transformations provides a good suite of measurable criteria. Changes to business processes, ICT systems, and organizational structures are also measured before, and after the changes. Each work area can have its own set of metrics, and these metrics change depending on the industry-sector and business type.

For example, enterprises may be measured in terms of their structures (what they consist of) through the depth of hierarchy and the time it takes to change that hierarchy. Processes and functions (what they do, how they change and how they bring about change) can be measured in terms of the number of activities within those processes, the total number of processes required to achieve an outcome, the cost of carrying out those processes and the ability of the processes to change due to change in external situation. Technologies, especially software, networks, databases, and devices are measured for their asset value, the contribution they make to the business units and business processes, and even for their carbon footprint (especially if the business transformation is motivated by environmental compliance). Measuring these various organizational factors, including some that are created in house, provide indication of performance improvement, or lack thereof, of the enterprise after transformation.

Discussion Points

- What are the two different aspects of green enterprise frameworks? (The process framework and the enterprise framework.)
- Discuss the "as is" and "to be" states of a product-based organization and how it would differ from a service organization.
- Differentiate, with examples of the individual green processes from the departmental, organizational, and collaborative ones.
- What is the importance of equipment lifecycle as compared with data center efficiencies?

- How would you apply diagnose, plan, enact, and review in transforming a bank to a green bank?
- Now discuss how the aforementioned four phases and their measures change when applied to a coal mine.
- What are the major differences between a technology-led versus a business-process led GET?
- How do metrics bring about a change in attitude?

Action Points

- *Action Points from the Diagnosis Phase:*
- Nominate the roles for your GET project. This would include appointment of the GETC and other related roles. The formation of the BTB with participation from various stakeholders and governance boards of the organization is a vital step in diagnosis phase.
- Identify and document the demographics of your organization. This is not only the geographical information, but also the type and size of your organization, its scope, and its motivation for GET.
- Identify the current maturity level of your organization. This step will also give you a good idea of the metrics to use to measure the current maturity and, later, during review, to measure the new maturity of your organization.
- Investigate each work area for its current assets and the role it will play in transformation. Note how your demographics and your maturity levels will interplay with the work areas you identify for transformation. The relationship and dependence amongst the work areas is as important as the areas themselves.
- Produce the deliverables required during this phase. Apply quality measures to the deliverables in diagnosis.
- *Action Points from the Planning Phase:*
- Revisit the results and deliverables from diagnosis phases. Used brainstorming technique to push out earns and inconsistencies.
- Draft the overall project plan for the transformation. Use mind-maps to identify areas of importance, and their rankings.
- Finalize the work areas and outline the project plans for each work area. SWOT may be handy within business models and business processes where as cause-effect analysis throughout all work areas.
- Create and enact a Pilot project. Ensure this is a small yet important area of your business; and that the normal business is not disrupted.
- Update and finalize the transformation plan and the plans for each work area based on the results from the pilot. Again, cause-effect analysis can be used for this work.
- Finalize the lead work area and update its plans for leadership for the rest of the work areas. Check for interdependencies between work areas.
- Finalize the metrics to be used to ascertain quality and success criteria of the project are properly measured.
- Finalize the roles and their responsibilities.
- *Action Points from the Enactment Phase:*
- The BTB should start the enactment with the stakeholders and immediately start managing their expectations.

- Update the Transformation plan with pilot project results and ensure a ready to use BT plan.
- Manage risk—identify the known and unknown risks within the project that can come from any of the dimensions for transformation.
- Enlist ongoing senior management support, as also handle the unions (where relevant).
- Ensure the transformation is visible to all dimensions of the organization through regular updates on the web site, newsletters, and briefing meetings.
- Use measurement tools corresponding to the agreed metrics in planning.
- Ensure quality in the project through regular testing especially in ICT systems.
- Update SLAs and other contracts.
- *Action Points from the Review Phase:*
- Undertake formal review of the results from the BTB project. This would include formation of a committee within the BTB to review the results against the stated goals of the project.
- Formally document what went right and what was wrong in the project. This should provide valuable lessons in conducting ongoing business.
- Use metrics to measure the output after the BTB project. Compare the results with the same metrics used to measure the parameters at the start of the project. For example, if enhancing customer experience is the goal of the project, then use a measure for that experience—before and after the BT project. This can be a measure of the customer experience through a survey/questionnaire, and additional parameters like time spend on the web site, amount of business conducted, and so on.
- Ensure that the stakeholders of the project are properly apprised of the results.
- Formal audits will ensure that the metrics used for the project and for the overall business are validated.

References

Arunatileka, D., Ghanbary, A., and Unhelkar, B. (2008). Chapter XXIV, Influence of Mobile Technologies on Global Business Processes in Global Organizations. In M. Raisinghani, ed., *Hand book of Research in Global Information Technology Management in the Digital Economy,* IDEAS Group Publication, Hershey, PA, USA. ISBN 978-1-59904-876-5 (e-book)—ISBN 978-1-59904-875-8 (hard cover).

Arunatileka, S. and Ginige, A. (2003). "The Seven E's in eTransformation—A Strategic eTransformation Model," presented at IADIS International Conference—e-Society 2003, Lisbon, Portugal.

Damien, S. (2009). "Knowledge management" on Enterprise Search and Retrieval. In P. Simon, ed, John Wiley and Sons.

Deshpande, Y. University of Western Sydney, Australia In B. Unhelkar, ed., *Handbook of Research in Green ICT: Technical, Methodological and Social Perspectives,* IGI Global, Hershey, PA, USA.

Deshpande, Y. and Unhelkar, B. (2011). Chapter 8, Information systems for a green organisation, pp 116–130.

Gantz, J. (2009). *The Diverse and Expanding Digital Universe.* Framingham, MA: IDC.

Godbole. (2011). Chapter 34, Green Health: The Green IT Implications for Healthcare Related Businesses, pp. 470–479; and Chapter 35, E-Waste Management: Challenges and Issues. In B. Unhelkar, ed., *Handbook of Research in Green ICT: Technical, Business and Social Perspectives,* pp. 480–501. IGI Global, Hershey, PA, USA. ISBN 978-1-61692-834-6 (hardcover)—ISBN 978-1-61692-835-3 (ebook).

Koomey, J. G. (2007). *Estimating Total Power Consumption by Servers in the U.S. and the World.* Stanford CA, USA. Retrieved January 13, 2010 from *http://enterprise.amd.com/Downlo ads/svrpwrusecompletefinal.pdf*

Murugesan, S. (2007). Cutter Executive Report, Get Ready to Embrace Web 3.0, August 2007. Business Technology Trends & Impacts; Business Intelligence, Cutter, Boston, USA.

Murugesan, S. (2010). Web 2.0, 3.0 and X.0: Technologies, Business and Social Applications, Edited book, IGI Global, Hershey, PA, USA.

Philipson. (2010). Chapter 9, A Comprehensive and Practical Green ICT Framework. In B. Unhelkar, ed, *Handbook of Research in Green ICT: Technical, Business and Social Perspectives*, pp. 131–145. IGI Global, Hershey, PA, USA. ISBN 978-1-61692-834-6 (hardcover)—ISBN 978-1-61692-835-3 (ebook).

Philipson, Foster, G. and Brand, P. J. (2009). Chapter 30, Carbon Emissions Management Software (CEMS): A New Global Industry, pp. 413–430 *Graeme Philipson, Connection Research, Australia Pete Foster, Springboard Research, Australia John Brand, The Green IT Review, Australia- Ed. B. Unhelkar, in Handbook of Research in Green ICT: Technical, Business and Social Perspectives* IGI Global, Hershey, PA, USA. ISBN 978-1-61692-834-6 (hardcover) – ISBN 978-1-61692-835-3 (ebook).

Philipson, HRG. (2011). Chapter 9, A Comprehensive and Practical Green ICT Framework, pp 131–145, In B. Unhelkar, ed, *Handbook of Research in Green ICT: Technical, Business and Social Perspectives* IGI Global, Hershey, PA, USA. ISBN 978-1-61692-834-6 (hardcover)—ISBN 978-1-61692-835-3 (ebook).

Phillipson, G. (2009). Envirability, accessed from Feb 2011, see www.connectionresearch.com.au.

Rosen et al. (2011). Chapter 1, Strategies for a Sustainable Enterprise. In *Handbook of Research in Green ICT: Technical, Business and Social Perspectives,* pp. 1–28. IGI Global, Hershey, PA, USA. ISBN 978-1-61692-834-6 (hardcover) – ISBN 978-1-61692-835-3 (ebook) Mike Rosen, Wilton Consulting Group & Cutter Consortium, USA Tamar Krichevsky, Wilton Consulting Group, USA Harsh Sharma, OMG Sustainability SIG, USA.

Sherringham and Unhelkar, B. (2010). *Achieving Business Benefits by Implementing Enterprise Risk Management*, Cutter Executive Report, Vol. 7, No. 3, July 01, 2010, Enterprise Risk Management & Governance Service (co-authored with Sherringham, K.).

TOGAF Architecture. (2010). The Open Group Architectural Framework [Online]. Available from http://www.theopengroup.org; [last accessed October 2010].

Unhelkar, B. (2009). Cutter report on business trans. in domains such as Telecom and Banking- *Business Transformations: Framework and Process*, (16,000 words), Cutter Executive Report, Nov, 2009, Vol. 12, No. 10, *Business-IT Strategies practice.* Cutter, Boston.

Unhelkar, B. (2009). *Mobile Enterprise Transition and Management*, Taylor & Francis Group (Auerbach Publications), Boca Raton, FL, USA. ISBN: 978-1-4200-7827-5 (Foreword by Ed Yourdon, USA). Unhelkar, B. (2008) *Mobile Enterprise Architecture* (12,500 words, aimed at CxOs), Cutter Executive Report, April, 2008. Vol. 11, No. 3, *Enterprise Architecture practice.*

Unhelkar, B. and Ginige, A. (2010). A framework to derive holistic business transformation processes, Paper 44, Proceedings of International Conference on E-Business, (ICE-B), 2010, http://www.ice-b.icete.org/Abstracts/2010/ICE-B_2010_Abstracts.htm

Unhelkar, B. and Philipson, G. (2009). The Development and Application of a Green IT Maturity Index. *ACOSM2009*—Proceedings of the Australian Conference on Software Measurements, Nov 2009, Sydney.

Williams, E. (2004). *Energy Intensity of Computer Manufacturing*—[Iowa City, IA: ACS Publications.]. *Environmental Science & Technology*, 8.

Zachman, J. A. (1987). Zachman Framework. The Zachman institute for framework advancement [Online]. Available from http://www.zifa.com/ [last accessed October 2010].

Zara, O. (2004). *Le Management de l'Intelligence Collective*. Paris, France. M2.

Chapter 10

Green Compliance: Protocols, Standards, and Audits

For a successful technology, reality must take precedence over public relations, for Nature cannot be fooled.

Richard P. Feynman

Key Points

- Discusses the standards, protocols, legislations, and likely initiatives related to climate change and environmental sustainability
- Summarizes the Rio, Kyoto, and Copenhagen climate change summits due to their importance to and impact on business organizations
- Discusses the ISO 14000 family of standards and associated ISO 18000 and ISO 19001 standards in relation to to environmental performances of organizations
- Presents the regulatory standards for emissions such as EPEAT, RoHS, and WEEE used in labeling the carbon efficiency of equipments
- Discusses the various types of Green IT audits
- Provides a integrated model to base an approach to conducting internal and external Green IT audits

Introduction

This chapter discusses the main protocols and standards that are associated with the environment and sustainability in the context of Green IT strategies and initiatives for business outcomes. The discussion includes the legal and regulatory aspects of impacting and emerging environmental standards faced by businesses. Successful Green enterprise transformation (GET) should result in a carbon-compliant organization. That means, the organization should understand, measure, and report its carbon performance according to the regulatory requirements of the carbon legislations in that region. As was discussed in Chapter 2 with respect to the Green IT drivers for an organization, this requirement for legal compliance is one of the six key drivers for GET.

Apart from measuring and reporting on the carbon compliance for an organization, there is also a need to validate the accuracy of those measures and reports. This is so because, increasingly, the future of an organization—particularly on the stock exchange—will be dictated by its carbon measurements and reports. Therefore, formal and informal audits of the carbon measures and reports are part of the governance for a responsible green organization. Therefore, meters and other recording devices, carbon-content databases, applications, and systems, used in producing the compliance reports and the accuracy of external green web services embedded in the applications should be formally audited. Metrics and measurements, discussed earlier in Chapter 3, provide the basis of the carbon data that are collected and reported. Carbon Emissions Management Software (CEMS) specifically developed for managing carbon performance of an organization is used to measure, monitor, and report on the organization's carbon performance both internally and to the regulatory bodies. This importance of CEMS subjects it to audits as well. This chapter discusses the importance of audits of carbon data, systems, metrics, measurements and reports associated with CEMS.

The domain of climate change and environmental sustainability in business is inundated with rapidly evolving protocols, legislations, and standards, see Table 10.1 (ISO 14000). These protocols, standards, and legislations are a result of discussions and debates at various forums and summits where the political, social, and business world converged under the climate change agenda (Climatechange.gov.au). Various countries and regions interpret the need to reduce carbon differently. This variation is based on a number of factors such as the physical location, demographics, political will of the government, public opinion, economic and social development of the region, and the state of the industry. Thus, there is significant uncertainty in carbon legislations. However, although the rapidity of the evolution and the uncertainties associated with these legislations and protocols arise from the nascent nature of the domain, business can use these to their advantage to achieve business improvement.

Legislations, standards, protocols and initiatives form the crux of the sociocultural-political dimension of a Green enterprise. These are usually considered as "soft" factors as compared with the "hard" technology factors. Yet, these factors are equally important in successful GETs, if not more. However, they also change a lot more than the technological factors in Green IT.

Table 10.1 also lists some of the standards and legislations associated with climate change. Some popular reports and government/industry initiatives are also listed in Table 10.1.

Protocols and Standards

Green IT, green business, and industrial verticals in which the business exists are all influenced by the government and regulatory bodies. Internationally, and particularly at the various levels of government, the aforementioned protocols provide a good basis for a strategic and a long-term approach to handling environmental impacts. Protocols themselves may not be binding, but eventually some of these protocols or some of their aspects get enshrined into law. For example, the U.K. government's Climate Change Act (the first national framework to address climate change) became law on November 26, 2008 that made it mandatory for organizations to legally reduce their carbon emissions by 34% by 2020 and 80% by 2050 (compared with their 1990 emission levels). Protocols relating to the environment also exist at state and even council levels. Businesses are encouraged to adopt these protocols as they formalize the business attempts at reducing carbon emissions. Some of the important protocols in this climate change domains are discussed next.

Table 10.1 Summary of Compliance Mechanisms: Protocols, Standards, Legislations and Initiatives

Compliance Mechanisms	Examples	Impact
Protocols	Rio (UNFCCC 2009), Kyoto, Copenhagen, Rio (again)	Formulated globally by political leaders that will bind countries to emission controls driving wide-ranging legislative impacts within countries impacting heavy CO_2 emitters the most
Standards	ISO 14000, 18000, 19001, CMM (Green IT readiness)	Provide basis for carbon reduction, compliance and comparison Providing a framework to enable environmental management; enabling comparisons at an international level
Legislations	NABERS, NGERS (NGER 2010) (NGER 2009), CPRS (2010), RoHS, WEEE, Climate change acts (U.K., Australia, U.S.)	Enables legal compliance by businesses Also, enables trading amongst partners spread across regions based on legislative compliance
Initiatives	STERN Report; Smart2020 report; USA Energy Star; Green Grid, CSCI, GRI	Thought provoking personal, industrial, and government effort The driver, in many cases, being enlightened self-interest (discussed in Chapter 2)

United Nations Framework Convention on Climate Change (UNFCCC, Rio)

One of the earliest protocols that highlighted the role of climate change and brought about some action came from the Rio summit in 1992. Dubbed the Earth Summit, this was the first protocol of its kind and became formally known as the United Nations Framework Convention on Climate Change (UNFCCC, Rio, 2010). While the protocol or "framework" arising from that convention does not contain any binding laws, the summit itself generated global awareness of the challenges of climate change and created opportunities for countries to sign and, in case of many countries, ratify the convention. The Rio summit paved the path for ensuing global summits at Kyoto and the recent one in Copenhagen (December, 2009). While these summits continue to substantially raise the public, political, and corporate awareness, results are not binding unless they are specifically ratified by participating countries.

Kyoto Protocol

The Kyoto Protocol (2010) is an international agreement that builds on the aforementioned UNFCCC. The objective of Kyoto Protocol was "stabilization of greenhouse gas concentrations in the atmosphere at a level that would prevent dangerous anthropogenic interference with the climate system." The Kyoto Protocol created a set of binding targets for 37 developed countries (also known as Annex I countries) along with the European community for reducing GHG emissions. Achieving of this target would amount to a reduction in emissions on an average of 6%–8% over the 1990 levels during the period 2008–2012. Some exceptions to these requirements were provided for slightly less affluent countries (such as Iceland), wherein they were permitted to increase their emissions (Hammer 2007).

Greenhouse Gas Protocol

The Greenhouse Gas Protocol (GHG Protocol) is a widely known protocol that has been adopted by many government and business leaders to understand, quantify, and manage GHG emissions (www.ghgprotocol.org). As discussed in Chapter 3, GHG classifies emissions into three separate Scopes (1, 2, and 3) from which a basis for calculating the organization's overall carbon footprint can be established (see OSCAR for details of calculations):

- Scope 1 emissions—The direct emission of GHGs by the organization. These are the emissions resulting from manufacturing activities (e.g., auto manufacturing), physical movements of men and material (e.g., in a foundry), or chemical emissions (such as from a paint shop).
- Scope 2 emissions—These emissions form the indirect consumption of energy such as electricity. These are added on to the Scope 1 emission calculations. The emissions from a coal fired power station will be a Scope 1 for that power station, but Scope 2 for a bank that is using that electricity to power its computers.
- Scope 3 emissions—The GHG emissions embedded in the supply chain of the organization—primarily belonging to the business partners. Emissions in this scope are not clearly defined in the protocol and, therefore, not usually included in the emissions calculations. With the popularity of outsourced work, however, these Scope 3 emissions will become prominent in calculating the carbon footprints.

Copenhagen

The last decade has been a series of global summits, initiatives, and agreements. The Earth charter of year 2000 is the most popular of all.

This charter underscores global interdependence in the environmental domain and includes declaration of fundamental principles for building a just, sustainable, and peaceful global society for the twenty-first century.

As this charter does not discriminate between developed and developing economies, it has been very well received by the BRIC, (Brazil, Russia, India, China) group of countries. For example, since 2002, the Brazilian Ministry of the Environment has disseminated the Earth Charter and has been using it in some of its initiatives, particularly as a guide to implement the Agenda 21 Program, and as a reference for holding national environmental conferences (The Earth Charter Initiative, n.d.).

The Copenhagen summit, held in 2009, was focused on creating an agreement for a framework to address climate change beyond 2012. This Copenhagen summit resulted in an agreement by a large number of countries (138) to work toward keeping global temperature increases to below 2°C. This agreement generated substantial debate and discussion but, similar to the events in the original UNFCCC (Rio) summit, it was not passed unanimously and is not legally binding.

Following on from Copenhagen, the next United Nation's Climate Change Conference will be held in Mexico. The hope from many countries and individuals is for a new global consensus that would successfully address climate change. This hope, however, is still faint as the political leaders and governments get embroiled particularly in arriving at a balanced emission cap between the fully developed versus developing nations.

Furthermore, in the same context, the next major summit on climate agreed by the United Nations general assembly will be in 2012 and will be hosted by Brazil. The themes are the Green Economy in the context of sustainable development and poverty eradication, the institutional framework for sustainable development, emerging issues, and a review of present commitments (www.earthsummit2012.org). Interestingly, 2012 is also the year when the Kyoto Protocol to the UNFCCC, which contained legally binding targets (as accepted by many countries) to reduce GHG emissions, will expire.

While the summits and protocols pave the way for a global consensus, when it comes to implementing the agreements, there is a need to commonly accepted standards. The International Standards Organizations (ISO) has been active in this area and has produced a group of standards associated with environmental sustainability in business whose business impacts are now considered.

The ISO 14000:2004 Family of STANDARDS

Successful GET, particularly across the supply chain, requires the acceptance and adoption of a commonly accepted standards between organizations. The ISO 14000 standard for environmental management provides a basis for organizational compliance with emission requirements. This ISO 14000 standard is a family of standards addressing various aspects of environmental management. The standards are listed in

The ISO 14001 is the flagship standard for environmental management. Similar to the role played by the ISO 9000 family of standards in the quality assurance arena, this ISO 14000 series of standards are set to play a key role in the environmental management of business.

Table 10.2. The very first two standards, ISO 14001 and ISO 14004 deal with a system to manage environmental issues—including identification and control of the environmental impact of an organization's activities, products, or services. ISO 14001 provides the requirements for an environmental system and ISO 14004 gives general guidelines for the system (www.iso.org). An EI system meeting the requirements of ISO 14001 becomes an excellent environmental management tool that forms part of the repertoire of an organization going green. Subsequently, ISO 14064–1 and ISO 18001 (OHAS) standards are also being implemented by organizations.

Table 10.2   The ISO 14000 Family of Standards for Environment Management Systems

Standard	Primary Focus
ISO 14001	Environment management systems (EMS); Their requirements and approach
ISO 14004	Implementation guidelines for the EMS
ISO 14010–15	Environmental auditing—of system, practices, and reporting
ISO 14024	Environmental labeling—products, equipments, infrastructure
ISO 14031	Environmental performance evaluation—of organizations and systems
ISO 14040–44	Lifecycle analysis—primarily of equipments, but also any other aspect like products, materials
ISO 14050	Terms and definitions—relating to the environmental management
ISO 14060	Product standards relating to their environmental performance
ISO 18001	Occupation health and safety
ISO 19011	Auditing 14000 and 9000 (together with ISO 14010)

ISO 14001

An ISO 14001 standard provides basis for certification or an organization in terms of creation and implementation of Green IT strategies, metrics, reporting, and continuous improvement. This certification is provided after the organization claims to have implemented the standard and, subsequently, results from formal Green IT audits. The frequency of such audits would be based on site complexity and past performance. External, formal third-party audits conducted by the ISO 14001 and OHSAS 18001 auditors are complemented by the regulatory compliance evaluations that may be conducted internally by the company. Nonconformance to the environmental policies and standards are required to be reported, analyzed, and corrected. ISO 14001 compliance provides a strong basis for setting up and continuously improve the environmental management systems of the organization—particularly as the origins of this set of standards are on a voluntary basis rather than a legislative basis. Certification to ISO 14001 standard, however, is only one aspect of environmental compliance. Other areas of an organization for compliance with the environmental requirements include metrics, people, processes, and technologies that are all complimentary to the ISO compliance. The ISO 14001 standard comprises of five sections each with a different purpose. These are highlighted with respect to the Green IT effort of an organization in Table 10.3.

ISO 14001 accreditation requires time and budget to achieve. An organization seeking such accreditation needs to implement all aspects of the standard. The implementation should then be followed by formal audits. Although a costly exercise at this stage of the environmental domain, the audit costs are more than offset in the long run due to both resource efficiency as well as compliance.

The ISO 14064 standard relates to existing GHG schemes of the World Business Council on Sustainable Development Greenhouse Gas Protocols. Providing a basis for training programs, knowledge, and understanding, the ISO 14064 standard helps organizations to quantify and manage their GHGs. Furthermore, legal and regulatory bodies can use ISO 14064 for determining carbon emission limits and quantifying them for organizations to undertake specific actions or activities that improve green management. Guidance on inventories, quality management, reporting, internal auditing, and verification can be obtained from ISO 14064. Employee knowledge and innovation processes also increase through training programs and recognition of efficient practices in the industry (Staib 2005).

Coupled with the aforementioned standard is the OHSAS (occupational health and safety standard) *ISO 18001*. This standard also helps address specific operational controls, including energy management, chemical management, waste minimization, ergonomics, and safety.

Finally, the ISO 19011 set of standards provided the basis for audits of the ISO 14000 standards. Audits of the environmental performance of organizations are discussed later in this chapter.

Government Initiatives

Compelling Regulation

As mentioned earlier in the introduction, compliance requirements for carbon emissions by businesses is going to drive new and formal carbon metrics and measurements (Unhelkar and Philipson, 2009). The standards discussed earlier provide a framework for carbon initiatives, and legislation complements these standards. The legal and regulatory nature of the carbon compliance requirements are best fulfilled by adopting a standard, implementing reliable metrics and measurements.

Table 10.3 Components of the ISO 14001 Standard and Their Relevance to Green IT Strategies

Section	*Relevance to Green IT Strategies*
Policy	Defining the environmental objectives of the organization (based on the drivers, and their combination)
Planning	The economic, process, technology, and people factors required for the green organizational transformation
	Identification of the legal requirements and an approach to comply with them
	Environmental risk assessment
	Environmental intelligence repository (availability, budgets, etc. for CEMS and existing systems upgrade)
	Product/service lifecycle assessment
Implementation and operation	Implementing environmental intelligence (EI) through CEMS
	Integration with existing ERP and related company systems
	Education and training programs for people
	Communication at all levels of management
	Potential HR changes (e.g., to company's organizational chart)
Checking and corrective action	CEMS—measure, monitor, and mitigate
	Compliance audits
	Process optimization and maturity
Management review	Reporting—internal and external
	Continuous improvement
	Monitoring external changes to drivers
	Monitoring internal changes to factors influence carbon performance
	Strategies for monetizing in future

Accuracy in the method of collection and analysis of carbon data and audits provide the proof of environmental performance.

There are number of such requirements that are regulatory in nature and that make it obligatory for the organization to comply with the emission limits. An example to consider in terms of such regulatory requirements is the inclusion of more 1,000 Australian businesses under the mandatory reporting requirements for carbon emitters above 150 kT (kilo tonnes) per annum (NGER 2009). Another example is the American Clean Energy and Security Act that was passed to reduce emissions by 17% in year 2020 (compared with 2005 levels) and around 80% by 2050 (this legislation is yet to reach a vote in the Senate). The EU also has a mandatory target of a 20% reduction in GHGs by 2020 (compared with 1990)—with particular emphasis on the cap-and-trade EU emissions trading scheme (EU ETS), that covers major emitters of CO_2. Finally, the U.K. government has also passed legislation in November 2008 that aims to achieve emissions reduction of at least 26% by 2020 and 80% by 2050, against a 1990 baseline.

These legislations, transcending economic and regional boundaries, indicate that not only do the business leaders need data for justifying their own actions internally, but accurate, reliable, and audited carbon data are required to be incorporated in external legal frameworks mandating regulatory compliances. Furthermore, these legal requirements on carbon emissions are likely to grow and are expected to be embedded within other legislation, including those dictating share market trading and currency exchanges. An example is the possibility of a Sarbanes–Oxley style legislative change that would pin compliance and reporting requirements of carbon emission of an organization on its corporate leadership.

As the legal framework around carbon emissions matures, and with the likely move to carbon offsets and *trading* of carbon credits amongst businesses, there is an even greater need for standardization and accuracy of carbon data. As the previous federal treasurer of Australia, Peter Costello (2009) notes, "There will be an exchange (like a stock exchange) to buy and sell permits and a derivatives market to allow investors to hedge. There will be a daily carbon price. And price movements in this new commodity will govern electricity prices and reach into daily life much more than oil and petrol rises."

Energy Star (1992) and EPEAT (2006) provides means to identify product's carbon efficiencies.

Maturity and trade in carbon credits is likely to result in stringent requirements on collection and reporting of carbon data, bringing it in line with the requirements of financial reporting for the stock market. Requirements for mandatory disclosure of the company's carbon performance, along with inclusion in annual financial reports are likely in the near future. It is also reasonable to expect invoices for energy-consuming goods (such as a computer monitor, TV, or a photocopier) to carry not only the price of the goods, but also the carbon emitted in the development and production of the goods.

USA Energy Star—1992

Energy Star is a voluntary labeling program designed to identify and promote energy-efficient products (Brown et al., 2002; Johnson and Zoi 1992; Pradhan 2011). The ISO 14024 standard provides the basis for creating the environmental labeling of products. The Energy Star rating system is implemented by the U.S. Environmental Protection Agency (EPA) and the U.S. Department of Energy (DOE). These Energy Star labeled products have potentially saved billions of dollars over the last decade by enabling energy-conscious decisions, especially by large businesses in procuring and operating products. Recently, Energy Star standards and ratings for computer servers have also been announced (Energy Star, May 2009) that would provide additional boost in informed decision making by data center directors or large organizations.

EPEAT—Electronic Product Environmental Assessment Tool

EPEAT certification is a means of standardizing electronic goods in terms of their environmental performance. Made up of 23 mandatory and 28 optional criteria, EPEAT provides information that is invaluable in setting up ongoing, large-scale IT procurement programs. This is particularly of value to the procurement functions of large corporations and government agencies. EPEAT-based labels on PCs and products enable development of procurement policies that are measurable through KPIs in practice. For example, a U.S. presidential executive order mandated federal agencies to ensure that at least 95% of all technology purchases were meeting the EPEAT certification. Later, as per Weiss (2007), this order was also adopted by many state and local governments.

EU RoHS—Restriction of Hazardous Substances Regulations

Restriction of Hazardous Substances (RoHS) regulates hazardous substances, including the one that are used in computer and mobile manufactures. This legislation was passed by the European Union (EU) in 2006, setting a list of criteria that limited the amount of hazardous substances that can be included in new electronic and electrical equipment (European Union 2009). This restriction was aimed to ensure safety of users and eventually of people involved in disposal of these equipments—as hazardous materials are required to be handled in both production and disposal.

This legislation provides an interesting challenge, especially for small businesses, as these businesses are geared for production without the stringent requirements of RoHS. The contradictory needs between environmental and business are particularly felt by these small manufacturers who have been or aspire to export to the EU. For example, low-lead products that meet RoHS restrictions may reduce the long-term reliability of a product. This would, in turn, affect the price and the sale of the product. Low-lead products are also meant to be socially responsible, as it is believed that lead interferes with the development of the brain and nervous system, especially in children. This new legislative factors are brought in the mix by businesses as they create and implement Green IT strategies.

EU WEEE—Waste Electrical and Electronic Equipment Regulations

WEEE aims to reduce the amount of e-waste that occurs at the end of an equipment lifecycle. Thus, while the RoHS legislation is particularly aimed at reducing hazardous materials in the production phase of electronic goods, WEEE legislation becomes active during the disposal phase. WEEE dictates limits and methods for disposal of electronic waste (e-waste) and includes many alternatives such as reuse, recovery, recycling, and treatment of the disposable wastes. The WEEE regulations deal with separate collection, disposal, and recycling; standards for e-waste treatment at authorized facilities; and collection, recycling, and recovery targets (Murugesan 2008). This legislation also makes manufacturers of electrical and electronic equipment responsible for environmental impacts of their products (NetRegs 2008).

Industry and Vendor Initiatives

Apart from the government legislations, there are also industrial consortiums formed by like-minded organizations. These industry initiatives also go a long way in reducing carbon

As reported by Weiss (2007), Apple claims to have applied environmental considerations in using recyclable materials and by reducing the amount of packaging needed by as much as 59% for the fifth-generation iPod (Weiss 2007). The organization has also promoted recycling by exchange offers where customers return old iPods to get discount on new purchases. Similarly, Dell has worked to create energy-efficient OptiPlex desktops that are 50% more energy-efficient than similar systems manufactured in 2005. Hewlett-Packard recently claimed its rp5700 desktop PC exceeds U.S. Energy Star 4.0 standards and has 90% of recyclable materials (Kurp 2008). Apart from developing products that consume less power and emit reduced carbon, organizations like Google and Microsoft also strategize for infrastructure that would reduce its total carbon cost of ownership (TCCO). For example, Microsoft has built a data center consuming approximately 27 megawatts of energy at any given time in central Washington which is powered by hydroelectricity produced by two dams in the region (Kurp 2008).

emissions—and much before the regulatory requirements come into play. Vendors of IT goods and services also get together to mutually agree on targets for emissions. Some of these initiatives are discussed next.

Green Grid—2007

A global consortium of IT vendors, including AMD, Dell, IBM, Sun Microsystems, and VMware, formed a nonprofit group named the Green Grid in February 2007. The aim of this consortium was to define and propagate energy efficiency practices in data centers and IT systems (Murugesan 2008). The Green Grid collaborates with companies, government agencies, and industry groups to provide recommendations on best practices, metrics, and technologies that will improve IT energy efficiency (Kurp 2008).

CSCI—Climate Savers Computing Initiative

Started by Google and Intel in 2007, the CSCI is a nonprofit initiative of eco-conscious consumers, businesses and conservation organizations (CSCI 2009). The goal of CSCI is to promote development, deployment, and adoption of energy-efficient computers in active and inactive state. CSCI (2009) states their mission as reduction of global CO_2 emissions by 54 million tons per year and reduction of power consumption by 50% by year 2010. The committed participants are expected to save approximately U.S. $5.5 billion in energy costs (CSCI 2009).

IT Vendor Initiatives

Vendors of goods and services have also created their own initiatives for reducing the carbon impact of their activities.

Global Reporting Initiative

The Global Reporting Initiative (GRI) (www.thegreenitreport.com) is pioneering the development of a sustainability reporting framework. GRI aims to make the disclosure on economic, environmental, and social performance as commonplace and comparable as financial reporting. The environmental, financial, and investment aspects of an organization are thus brought together and certified. Starting in 2010, GRI certifies software and digital tools and technologies within a Sustainability Reporting Framework.

GRI has stated two goals for the next decade. Firstly, environmental social and governance (ESG) reporting should become a general practice to help markets and society take informed and responsible decisions. GRI advocates that by 2015 all large and medium-sized companies in OECD countries and fast-growing emerging economies should be required to report publicly on their ESG performance. And secondly, ESG reporting and financial reporting needs to converge over the coming decade. GRI advocates that a standard for integrated reporting should be defined, tested, and adopted by 2020.

Green IT Audits

Having discussed standards, legislations, and various initiatives in the Green IT and environmental sustainability domain, this section now discusses the Green IT audits. Such audits, as part of the overall audits of an organization, provide systematic assessment of the organizations structure and operations that ascertain the validity of its greening effort. As a result, Green IT audits also provide a justified means to improvement of the carbon performance. This is so because such Green IT audits are invaluable in providing internal reliability to the corporate board in terms of the return on investment (ROI) on Green IT investments. Externally they provide legitimacy to the reporting and the claims to greening made by the organization. Formal green audits validate the claims of the organization, thereby addressing the possible accusations of greenwashing.

Green audit assess a company's environmental credentials and its claims for green products and services. Further, such audits can also determine whether the company's supply chain

Green IT audits are formal, independent verification and validation of the carbon performance and carbon reporting of the organization. With increasing legislative demands on carbon reporting, these Green IT audits play a vital role in establishing the Green claims of the organization. Auditing of CEMS is a part of these audits. Most importantly, though, Green IT audits are likely to become audits in real time—that is, every carbon reporting and carbon related transaction will be audited through an independent module of the CEMS itself—that is owned and controlled by the auditors. Internal and external audits have slightly different roles to play in terms of carbon emissions reporting—internally, they provide the confidence to the decision maker on her investment in the Green project, and externally, they provide the legal backing required of any formal reporting of data.

and/or product line can be accepted as truly environmentally sustainable. These audits carry more value and legitimacy if they are carried out by recognized independent auditors. The ISO 19011 standard provides basis for auditing of green systems.

Green audits are very closely associated with metrics and measurements (discussed in detail in Chapter 3). Green audits primarily validate that whatever is being reported in terms of carbon emissions is accurate and sufficient. Green audits can also suggest areas for improvements in the organization's compliance with standards as well as legislations. Thus, green metrics and measurements (also known as carbon metrics) need validation through audits to play a pivotal role in reducing the carbon footprints of businesses.

The justification and reporting of carbon data are not only an external compliance mechanism. Internally, the chief executive officer (CEO) of an organization is easier to convince and, in turn, is able to convince the Board to undertake carbon initiatives provided the business case is supported by audited metrics. Green audits can cover the regularity accuracy, calculations, analysis, reporting, and storage of carbon emission data. Such validated data analysis can ascertain the Green IT readiness and maturity of an organization, that of its corresponding industry and even at a global level (Unhelkar and Philipson 2009). This need of businesses to have reliable carbon data need to be supported by new metrics and measurements that are being invented rapidly and standardized across the industry. Audits prove the validity of concrete carbon measures that enable comparison, justification, and optimization of an organization's green credentials.

Everything that can be measured within Green IT is not necessarily a good "indicator" of the greenness of the organization. Furthermore, everything that needs to be measured is not necessarily easy to measure. When a complex activity is measured by aggregated single statistics, there is possibility of information loss (Sharif 2010). Green audits enable an understanding of the value of the metrics (indicators) and also their accuracy.

Green metrics enable an organization to comprehend how much of carbon is being generated by the business activities and, even more importantly, the use of standardized and detailed measurements to do so. The challenges to these measures stem from the fact that currently many emissions get omitted, others get double calculated (see Scope 3 emissions discussed earlier) or confused with other factors (Unhelkar 2009). Green audits divide the emission measurements into appropriate sections and then validate them. In addition to validating the carbon numbers and results, green audits also point out additional areas for measuring carbon data. Therefore, green audits rightfully delve into the current financial, inventory, and HR systems of the organization. Green audits investigate the five areas of green metrics. These five areas of green metrics, as discussed in Chapter 3, are measure, monitor, manage, mitigate, and monetize. Each aspect of these measurements needs to be verified and validated in a green audit as follows:

- Measure—What is being measured? Is that measurement sufficient for reporting purposes? Are there additional areas of carbon data that should be included in the measurements?
- Monitor—What is the mechanism to collect the data? Where are the meters located? Sufficiency and accuracy of monitoring mechanisms.
- Manage—Validate the feedback and management mechanisms of carbon data, information, and analysis. The carbon management, governance standards, processes, and controls are audited in this area.
- Mitigate—Is the measurement and reporting of carbon data also being used to reduce the emissions? What are the systems in place for carbon mitigation and how well they are operating? The audit in the area of mitigation will be mainly of interest to the internal stakeholders of the organization, but will have external effect.
- Monetize—Audits of the monetizing aspects of carbon data will be of immense regulatory interests as the businesses move toward carbon economy. Ability to trade carbon requires accuracy and authenticity of systems that enable that trade. Therefore, external parties are heavily involved—regulators, traders, partners, and those investing in the carbon future.

Green audits traverse the entire gamut of organizational activities that play a direct or indirect role in reducing the carbon footprint of a business. For example, carbon usage by end-users of a bank (e.g., its employees and online users) needs to be mapped to the carbon measure of its data center to ascertain the level of usage in a day, month, or year. These data can be further correlated with the product and supply lifecycles of the bank that can give insight into the type of monitors, machines, and other building infrastructure that is affecting the bank's environmental performance. These metrics will eventually be captured and analyzed in CEMS—requiring audits of the data, analysis, and reporting of all of the aforementioned activities and their measurements. Another example of a green audit investigation is the power bill depicting the amount of electricity consumed by the organizations activities. Green audits will investigate the accuracy of this power bill is thus ascertain the accuracy of the Scope-2 carbon emissions calculations of the organizational carbon footprint. A green audit will ensure that the power bill is a complete and comprehensive measure of that particular scope of the emissions.

Following are the specific advantages in undertaking Green IT audits within organizations:

- Validation of entire organizations asset register from a carbon emissions perspective.
- Formalization of metrics and associated measurements related to carbon performance of an organization, particularly at the end-user and the data center level where the maximum carbon is being generated.
- Validation, internally of cost-benefit calculations that demonstrate the ROI on green initiatives to corporate governance board and the shareholders on indexing of carbon measures with financial performance of the organization.
- Cross-check on smart meters used for automatic reading and display of carbon data.

- Stocks take of the skill set, experience, and necessary expertise within the organization to put together a Green IT measurement and optimization program.
- Ratifying the agreement among the organizations stakeholders as to what should and should not be included within carbon emissions calculations. (For example, the Scope 1, 2 and 3—as categories of carbon emissions—are still not standardized.)
- Validation of the calculation on electronic waste and its disposal (for additional information on comparative standards, please see excellent discussion by Donallen (Piccoli 2009)—the maturity section there discusses the mapping between the erstwhile CMM levels with Green IT).
- Adequacy of policies and practices in addressing the complete and comprehensive carbon footprint of an organization. The overall carbon footprint of an organization includes procurement, disposal, and operational emissions. However, the current measures and regulations governing those measures are primarily focused on operational carbon. Audits can reveal the need for comprehensive coverage in measuring the overall carbon footprint.
- Being part of the value proposition for business through its green initiatives both internally and externally.
- Assist in objectifying (making explicit) the other tacit attitude and viewpoints of participating employees and management in measuring the green credentials of the organization.
- Reducing the confusion and, perhaps, duplication of calculations that may occur in a collaborating group of partners (particularly true with outsourced projects).
- Provision of relative benchmarks from audit to audit.
- Validating the measuring of degree of sophistication or maturity.

Audit Types

Figure 10.1 shows the various elements and types in a Green IT audit. This figure also shows the various key stakeholders and their interests in Green IT audits. As shown in Figure 10.1 on the left the following aspects of the collection and use of carbon data needs to be audited during green audits:

- Data collection mechanisms and corresponding gadgets/meters—A wide array of smart meters that read emission, measurement platforms, for those emission, their monitoring and inventory systems, come into play to meet the basic carbon emissions measurement requirements. These had to be checked for accuracy of their readings.
- Data analysis undertaken by software systems (typically CEMS)—Totals, averages, and distribution of carbon data, including those by the business partners requires to be audited. Standards and metrics play a major role in facilitating CO_2 comparisons. Common standards and accepted baselines, defined in advance, need to be audited for their accuracy and validity. This audit, for example, may include a walkthrough of the software algorithm used in totals for emissions per asset, per department, and for the organization.

Green IT audits are required to verify and validate the data collection mechanisms such as the smart meters, the underlying analysis of that data (such as comparison with the permitted limits per day, per gadget, or per person), carbon trends (such as expected carbon generation this year, next year and if the business doubles its productivity) and eventually the reporting on carbon compliance by the organization. Green metrics and measurements used for this purpose need to be validated themselves.

Measurement systems must be developed that can establish baselines and measure carbon storage and emissions changes on various scales, from individual machines to large processes of the business.

According to Richard Simpson, the director general of the electronics commerce in Industry in Canada, "ICT's crucial role in economic recovery is the key to unlocking the opportunity of Green growth" (www.oecd.org).

The advanced ICT technologies and techniques such as SOA, web services, mobile technologies, semantic networks, Cloud computing, IMS can play an important role in the development of monitoring and measuring emission tools.

Mitigation deals with reducing the carbon footprints of a business by identifying ways of operating more efficiently and thus reducing the costs and CO_2 emissions. Monetizing is poised to take advantage of the opportunity to trade carbon credits in future—should such legislations be implemented.

■ Carbon trends—Plotting of the carbon trends, their accuracy and reliability will become increasingly important as the world moves toward a carbon-based economy. This trend analysis is a part of the environmental intelligence of the organization, and decisions based on EI will be as vital as those based on BI. An audit of the trend-plotting and intelligence mechanism relating to the environment is mandatory.

■ Carbon compliance—This, as described in this chapter, is a crucial aspect of green audits. Both internal and external auditing parties are involved in ensuring that the organization is indeed complying with the limits set for emissions by the regulatory bodies.

Figure 10.1 also shows the primary stakeholders who are interested in the areas of audits described above. These stakeholders are as follows:

■ Individual users—Mainly interested in providing input into the data collection mechanisms. While users can span many different aspects of an organization, the individual users referred to here are mainly the staff and the customers who would access the organization's IT assets.

■ Departmental heads—Particularly interested in the analysis provided by the software system (CEMS) dealing with carbon data. This analysis would show to a business unit or a department clearly the amount of carbon generated by its activities as well as potential carbon savings resulting from the greening effort. Audits of CEMS will be of immense interest and benefit to these departmental heads as they will not only report the carbon performance of their department but also allow them to take decisions that can improve that performance.

■ CEO/chief green officer (CGO)—These leadership roles are interested in all aspects of the Green IT audits, but particularly in the environmental intelligence aspect of the organization.

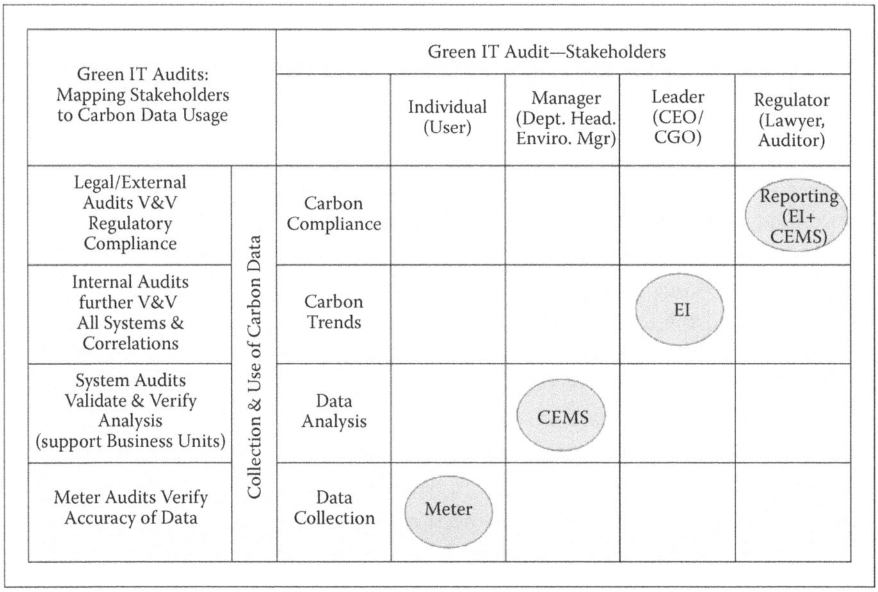

Figure 10.1   Various elements and types in Green IT audits and their relevance to roles.

Thus, coordination between systems and data, analysis of that data, and EI-based indications of the future will be of immense interest to the CEO/CGO.

■ Regulators—These are primarily external parties that want to determine the accuracy and validity of carbon data reporting as undertaken by the organization. Almost all future carbon reporting will be based on software systems and applications. Therefore, the interest of the regulators is ensuring the accuracy of the data, its recording period and possibly the actions undertaken by the organization to ensure its emissions stay within limits.

The audit categories and stakeholders thus have a varying mix of interests, as shown in Figure 10.1. The Trivedi and Unhelkar (2010) survey, based on the above mix, tried to identify the importance of some aspect of the carbon data and its audits. The results are shown in Figure 10.2.
Results in Figure 10.2 show that

■ Well-documented model for carbon emissions that can be audited is popular (agree to strongly agree) with about 35% of the respondents. This also indicates that for many respondents, such a model did not exist.
■ Regular updates and modification of environmental parameters is occurring with about 40% of the respondents (agree to strongly agree). This should be envisaged as a manual process with entrée of carbon data particularly undertaken manually (as was validated through person queries with some of the respondents).
■ Thirty-five percent agreed and 14% strongly agreed for a need for standard approach to accessing government rules and regulations and mentioned that as an important part of the green initiative in their organizations.
■ Thirty-four percent replied "neutral" to this query on the need and ability to provide feedback to the government on carbon emission. This number indicates that there is still a significant amount of uncertainty in terms of what is to be calculated, how it is to be reported, the frequency of reporting and the skepticism on how the regulatory authorities will use the data.

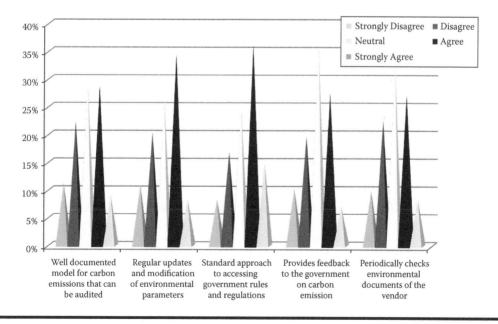

Figure 10.2 Carbon compliance audits.

■ Periodically checks environmental documents of the vendor—here too, "neutral" response (30%) was greater than any other option (agree—26%; strongly agree—7%). This response could be again based on the uncertainty of the need to go beyond the organizational boundary and checking/auditing the vendor documents and credentials.

Green IT Audits—Approach, Maturity, and Comparison

An integrated model for Green IT audits includes steps required in the audit, the various dimensions of an organization that need to be audited, ascertaining the Green IT maturity of the organization and the various areas within the organization that will be audited.

Auditing of Green IT can benefit by an integrated model that provides the basis for undertaking the audits. Such a model would bring together the steps, dimensions, maturity, and areas of audits, as discussed next.

Undertaking Green IT Audits

Figure 10.3 reveals the overall integrated approach to Green IT audits. This figure can be considered as an integrated framework for conducting Green IT audits. The core areas of an organization that need to be audited as discussed earlier, are the data, analysis, compliance, and potential trading capabilities. As shown in Figure 10.3, these core areas apply to the various systems (including CEMS), packages (such as ERP packages) and surveys (such as those used in ascertaining the attitude of users toward Green IT).

The known quality techniques of walkthroughs, inspectors, reviews, and audits can be applied in undertaking audits. These well-known quality techniques have been used for verification and validation of software systems, models, and business processes. The following are the ways in which they can be applied to green audits:

■ *Walkthroughs*—may be individually performed, to identify basic emissions data relating to an individual or a department. Walkthroughs can also be conducted of the CEMS algorithms that are used in calculating the emissions data.

■ *Inspections*—are more rigorous than walkthroughs and are carried out by a person or party who is not the original producer of the artifact. Thus, while the Green IT auditors will carry out the inspections, the staff responsible for smart meters and other gadgets used in collecting data, as well as those responsible for the processes for storing, reporting, and managing carbon data will provide the necessary information, and answer queries.

■ *Reviews*—go beyond walkthroughs and inspections, and formally verify and validate a process. In the Green IT domain, reviews are conducted by both internal and external auditors. Reviews would require preparation beforehand of the areas to be reviewed—such as systems, databases, equipment lifecycle, and wastage disposal processes. Reviews also encompass verification and validation of the accuracy and efficacy of the governance processes and methodologies, and also cover economic and social dimensions.

■ *Audits*—very formal, both internal and external to the organization. Green IT auditors will be invited or may enter the organization to conduct formal audits of the carbon data collection, analysis, and reporting. Audits cover all work areas and all four dimensions. Audits can make use of the aforementioned quality techniques of walkthroughs, inspections, and reviews. At the end of the auditing process, a formal report is prepared to present and discuss the outcomes. Whenever carbon benchmarks or limits are transgressed by the organization, they are pointed out by the auditors. Appropriate actions are also discussed and a plan to

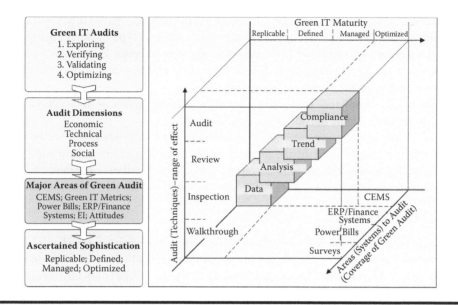

Figure 10.3 An integrated model for auditing Green IT systems.

undertake them is highlighted during the audits. The review and audit phases of GET were discussed in the previous chapter in the transformation process.

Audit and Use of Carbon Emissions Management Software

An important aspect of the Green IT audit function is the verification and validation of the proper functioning of the CEMS. CEMS, as was seen earlier in Chapter 3, is increasingly used to manage the measurements and reporting of carbon performance of an organization. The development of such a system was also discussed in Chapter 7 later in this book. Audits of CEMS require parties that are internal and external to the organizations to participate in the V&V of the system.

A typical CEMS is meant to help an organization manage its energy consumption by accurately recording, analyzing, and reporting on the carbon data. Thus, CEMS is also responsible for reduction and management of carbon emissions and help an organization meet its environmental goals. Is the CEMS used by the organization doing so? And how accurately and quickly is the CEMS able to report on carbon data. Furthermore, how helpful is the CEMS in helping the decision makers of the organization identify and understand energy consumption patterns of the organization?

Auditing a CEMS requires attention to the following:

- Accuracy of the data captured by the system—in terms of the data capture techniques such as smart meters and also manual data entry
- Security and ease of storage of carbon data—in a data warehouse hosted on a physical server
- Security and ease of retrieval—with an investigation into any potential breaches of security of carbon data
- Validity of analysis and trend creation—by the systems using the carbon data
- Frequency and reliability reporting of emissions and related information—to the regulatory bodies—typically using web services

- Ease and accuracy of updating environmental parameters that drive CEMS—these are the parameters that are used in configuring the system such as type of pollutants to measure, frequency of measurement and frequency of access to web service interfaces
- Interfaces to the government regulatory portals using web services—audits verify the easy, accuracy and frequency of access and reporting
- Environmental compliance by vendors and other business partners—audits check the validity of compliance claims outside of the organization
- Use of CEMS in the audit function itself—audits need to validate and verify the use of CEMS as a system for audit, as the software itself is used to perform certain audit functions by using the internal controls to total, report, and compare carbon emissions

Comparative Audits

Audits provide an organization with a feedback on its current performance as well as Green maturity. The results of audits will enable an organization to understand where it stands on the Green CMM scale (as was discussed in Chapter 3, Figure 3.17). Audits can be conducted to ascertain the "as is" state of an organization. They can also be conducted to verify whether the "to be" state, the desired Green state, has been achieved or not by the organization. [This is shown in Figure 10.4.]

Reports on the results of a properly conducted Green IT audit will also enable an organization to understand its strong and weak areas, and thereby help it in its ongoing optimization effort by enabling selection of right projects within its transformation programs. The various focus areas of GET, discussed in Chapter 9, can also benefit by the Green IT audit, as it validates the effect of transformation on those focus areas.

Conclusion

This chapter started off with the various international conventions and summits on climate change and the ensuing impact on environmental sustainability of businesses. The most important standard in this domain is the ISO 14001 standards, which was discussed as a means to environmental

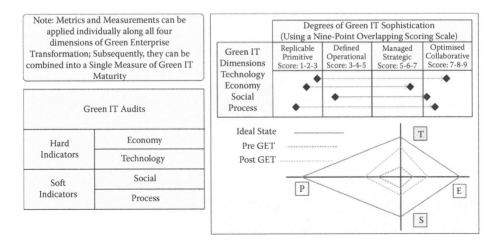

Figure 10.4   Audits reveal green sophistication of an organization before and after transformation.

management in an organization. Standards like these and also labeling standards such as EPEAT go a long way in providing a common ground for understanding what businesses are doing in terms of undertaking carbon reduction initiatives. This chapter finally moved toward an integrated approach to conducting and reporting on Green IT audits. Such Green IT audits would validate and verify the accuracy, validity and use of carbon data.

Discussion Points

- Discuss the reasons why the Copenhagen summit on climate changed failed to produce binding legislations.
- What are the possible differences in the way the fully developed nations view carbon emissions as compared with the developing nations today?
- What role does a standard like EPEAT play in reducing carbon footprints of large and/or government organizations?
- Discuss one industrial initiative in reducing carbon emissions. Outline, according to you, the challenges that this initiative will face in practice and your suggestions on handling those challenges.
- What is the importance of ISO 14001 and related standards in an organization's attempt to transform itself into a Green organization?
- What is a Green IT audit? List and discuss the purpose for conducting such Green IT audits.
- What are the differences in auditing carbon data collection versus carbon trend plotting (using environmental intelligence)? Discuss in the context of the roles involved in these carbon data and analysis usage.
- Discuss the audit techniques and audit areas based on your understanding of the integrated model for auditing Green IT systems.
- Compare the degrees of Green IT sophistication (based on Figure 10.4) with the Green CMM sophistication.

Action Points

- Identify the key features of the UNFCCC summits that can apply to your organization
- Insert those features as a list of action items in your Green transformation plan
- Revisit the protocols and regulations discussed here—specifically considering which of these will apply immediately to your organization (will depend on your geographical region as well)
- Apply the main features of ISO 14001 family of standards to your organization
- Identify the reporting requirements from a legal/compliance viewpoint and update your Green IT strategy with the same
- Enlist the mechanism you will use for carbon reporting (manual, electronic, through web services, etc.)
- Setup a Green IT audit of your software systems, databases, and application (CEMS—if already available). This Green IT audit should be based on the framework for IT audits shown in Figure 10.3
- Conduct a pilot internal audit before undertaking full scale audits—internal and external
- Ascertain your organization's Green IT sophistication on the scale provided in Figure 10.4: replicable, defined, managed, optimized

References

Brown, R., Webber, C., and Koomey, J. (2002). Status and future directions of the Energy Star program. *Energy, 27*(5), 505–520.

CPRS. (2010). Carbon pollution reduction scheme, (http://www.climatechange.gov.au/publications/cprs/white-paper/cprs-whitepaper.aspx, retrieved April 20, 2010).

CSCI. (2009). Available from http://www.climatesaverscomputing.org/ Accessed March 26, 2011.

Costello, P. (2009). http://www.smh.com.au/opinion/politics/to-set-our-emissions-targets-now-is- nonsense-20091006- gl8z.html, accessed October 7, 2009.

Cutter Benchmark Review (CBR). (2009). Creating and applying Green IT metrics and measurement in practice. In G. Piccoli, ed., *Green IT Metrics and Measurement: The Complex Side of Environmental Responsibility*, pp. 10–17, Vol. 9, No. 10, accessed October 2009.

European Union. (2009). *RoHS Compliance*. Retrieved from RoHS.eu: http://www.rohs.eu/english/index.html

Hammer, C. (2007). *Hot Topics: Legal Issues in Plain Language*, 63rd issue on Climate Change, Legal Information Access Centre (LIAC). State Library of NSW, Sydney, Australia.

Heffner, M. and Sharif, N. (2008). Knowledge fusion for technological innovation in organizations. *Journal of Knowledge Management*, Vol. 12, No. 2; pp. 79–93, Q Emerald Group Publishing.

ISO 14000. (2007). Addresses various aspects of environmental management resulting in a environmental management system (EMS) (http://www.iso.org/iso/iso_14000_essentials.htm)

Johnson, B. and Zoi, C. (1992). *EPA Energy Star Computers: The Next Generation of Office Equipment*. Paper presented at the ACEEE Summer Study on Energy Efficiency in Buildings.

Kurp, P. (2008). Green computing. *Communications of the ACM, 51*(10), 11–13. doi:10.1145/1400181. 1400186

Kyoto Protocol. (2010). UNFCCC, Retrieved August 16, 2010 from http://unfccc.int/kyoto_protocol/items/2830.php

Murugesan, S. (2007). Going Green with IT: Your Responsibility Toward Environmental Sustainability. *Cutter Consortium Business-IT Strategies Executive Report, 10*(8).

Murugesan, S. (2008). Harnessing Green IT: Principles and Practices. *IT Professional, 10*(1), 24–33. doi:10.1109/MITP.2008.10

NGERS. (2010). National greenhouse and energy reporting and its calculator, retrieved May 15, 2010 from http://www.climatechange.gov.au/reporting

OSCAR. (2010). National greenhouse and energy reporting system calculator (the Calculator), retrieved from April 20, 2010 https://www.oscar.gov.au/Deh.Oscar.Extension.Web/Content/Nger ThresholdCalculator/

Piccoli, Gabe (Ed.) (2009). Cutter Business Review, Cutter Benchmark Review (CBR): Creating and Applying Green IT Metrics and Measurement in Practice. In G. Picoli, ed., *Green IT Metrics and Measurement: The Complex Side of Environmental Responsibility*, pp. 10–17. Vol. 9, No. 10, October 2009.

Pradhan, A. (2011). Chapter 43, Standards and legislations for the carbon economy. In B. Unhelkar, ed., *Handbook of Research in Green ICT*, pp. 592–606. IGI Global, Hershey, PA, USA.

Staib, R. (2005). *Environmental Management and Decision Making for Business,* Hampshire: Palgrave Macmillan.

The Green House Gas Protocol Initiative. (2009). The foundation for sound and sustainable climate strategies, retrieved August 12, 2009 from http://www.ghgprotocol.org/

Unhelkar, B. and Philipson, G. (2009). *The Development and Application of a Green IT Maturity Index, ACOSM2009—Proceedings of the Australian Conference on Software Measurements*. ACOSM. Sydney, Australia. November 2009.

United Nations Framework Convention on Climate Change (UNFCCC). (2010). http://unfccc.int. Referenced January 10, 2010.

Weiss, A. (2007). Can the PC go green? *netWorker, 11*(2), 18–25.

Chapter 11

Emergent Carbon Issues: Technologies and Future

Everything comes to us that belong to us if we create the capacity to receive it.

Rabindranath Tagore

Key Points

- Outlines the futuristic carbon issues that will impact businesses along the four dimensions of economy, technology, processes, and sociology
- Discusses the changes in the business models expected in the new carbon economy
- Presents existing and up coming business and economic trends in the context of the environment
- Relates Cloud computing and environmental intelligence
- Highlights the dichotomy between developed and developing economies in terms of carbon control
- Discusses the increasing role of social media networks in Green IT
- Discusses the role of GRID computing in environmental intelligence

Introduction

Green IT and the entire environmental sustainability domain are moving rapidly. Besides that, it is also a relatively nascent domain that requires continuous attention as the speed of technological development impacts carbon emissions and the business in many unexpected ways. Technologies increase emissions and they also create possibilities of reducing them. One can easily paraphrase David Kirkpatrick* when he says that "The age of computing has barely begun"; in fact, the age of Green IT is *yet to begin.*

---

* Fortune magazine's senior editor, in The Future of Computing (http://money.cnn.com/magazines/fortune/futureof_tech/).

This relatively short chapter tries to expand and imagine the future in the Green IT and environmental domain. The purpose of this chapter is not to disseminate any specific hands on action, but rather consider the future possibilities in terms of both—generation and amelioration of carbon in business. The four dimensions of economy, technology, processes, and people continue to provide the backdrop for this imaginative exercise in emergent carbon issues. The interesting aspect in envisioning the carbon economy is that of controlling carbon without stunting the growth of technologies and businesses. For example, faster computer processors, higher storage capacities and communications at lightning speed are all dual-edged swords: they can increase carbon emissions due to the higher power consumption and, at the same time, offer opportunities to reduce carbon emissions due to improvement in technologies and optimization of business processes. Therefore, rapidly emerging technologies need to be explored in a creative and holistic way in Green IT.

Development of new environmental standards, potentials for new global understanding in terms of protocols, development, and integration of new CEMS and positively shifting attitudes also form part of this interesting discussion. The journey of exploring these new technologies and considering their application in Green IT is part of an innovative approach to understanding and handling the new carbon challenge. For example, awareness of emerging technologies provides the architects of Green information' portals to incorporate flexibility in new strategic direction, innovative policies and procedures, and sound tactical development. Technologies such as XML, SOA, mobile services, collaborative web services across the industry verticals and with the regulatory bodies, virtualization, and Cloud computing are all opportunities for innovativeness.

In addition to innovations in technologies, the business models themselves will undergo changes that will reflect the emergent carbon economy. More than a decade ago, Siegel (1999), in *Futurise your Enterprise,* stated that "Over the next ten years, the Internet will drive changes in consumer behavior that will lay waste to all the corporate re-engineering and cost reduction programs that have kept so many MBAs and programmers burning the midnight oil." Little did he imagine that impact of carbon on consumer behavior will be even greater, requiring remodeling and reimagining of business models to meet the carbon economy of this coming decade.

Thus, the future in terms of Green IT and environmental sustainability is thus made up of emergent technologies, innovative processes, innovative business models, demanding customer preferences, synergetic standards, and new, positive social attitudes.

Future Carbon Landscape

David Andrews (Souvenir Press 1984) in his book, *The IRG Solution,* argued that central media and government-type hierarchical organizations could not adequately understand the environmental crisis that were being manufactured. Neither did they have idea about the adequacy of the solutions. It argued that the widespread introduction of information technologies in businesses, together with its forever dropping costs has resulted in an era of high carbon emissions from all sections of society.

The future, therefore, is not so much in backtracking to the age before the technologies as in investigating futuristic technologies that will reduce future emissions and help in reducing the current ones.

While there are many ways to view the future in Green IT, the four dimensions of Green IT transformed discussed earlier provide a good basis for envisioning the future. Table 11.1 shows the future possibilities as examples in a summarized form.

The future of Green IT is made up of multiple factors. These factors include scientific breakthroughs, innovative approaches to applying information technologies in business, updated and current standards and legislations that are accepted in spirit across industries and regions, and a positive, inbuilt social attitude toward carbon emissions. Table 11.1 shows these various Green IT factors across the four dimensions. What is most important in discussing the future of

Table 11.1   Future of Green IT in the Four Dimensions

Dimensions	Future Technologies and Impact
Technology	Cloud, ternary, biomimicry, collaborative EI, mobile, SaaS, CEMS integration
Economy	Novice business models, carbon trading, legal framework
Process	Governance standards, updated on ITIL, Sarbanes–Oxley, metrics, symbols, ISO 14001, collaborative EI
Social	Social networks, rapidity of formation of new opinions, inbuilt environmental consciousness as a social value

Green IT is the fact that innovative approaches are required in all four aforementioned dimensions of Green IT.

The complex nature of Green IT demands flexible Green IT applications that can be used in different contexts. Use of knowledge management tools can foster the creation of more insights and knowledge in Green IT domain. The tacit and explicit aspect of Green IT knowledge is likely to take different and radical shapes. For example, the amount of savings in carbon by an organization within a permissible limit can be an explicit piece of knowledge that can be used by Green HR in its internal education program or traded by the accountants. Carbon trading will bring in application of mathematical formulae like *Blackscholes* and *Binomials*, graphs and tables to price and facilitate trading in the software applications.

These applications need to allow for further changes to environmental standards, legislations, and processes. Users also have a varying level of knowledge and appreciation of Green ICT and their interests and priorities also vary. Therefore, Green ICT applications will have to remain continuously adaptable and agile.

Socially too, the future of Green ICT is in innovation that makes use of social media networks, puts together groups of people and organizations in consortiums, enhances general opinion on the issues, and activates the Green HR function within the organization. Social networks relating to Green IT and environmental responsibilities can be formed at local, regional, and global level. At each level, these groups have different interpretation and priorities in terms of the environment. Innovation in social approaches will capitalize on these different interpretations and priorities and bring them together on a common platform. This can be achieved by organizations and governments getting actively involved in the social media network phenomena rather that merely observing it or making attempts to control it.

Further to the external social media activities, organizations can also attempt at innovation internally in their Green HR function. This innovation requires due consideration to the mindmaps of the individuals operating with carbon reduction responsibilities within the organization, the tools and technologies used by them, and the way these individuals are trained, retained, and promoted.

The upcoming carbon trading also impacts the internal organization more than what was discussed in Green HR (Chapter 8). While externally an organization has the responsibility to meet carbon reduction targets, internally this responsibility gets distributed amongst many departments and individuals within the organization. This distribution requires excellence in collaboration, internally, if the organization has to perform well in the future carbon economy.

Malone (2004) has discussed this topic of decentralization and collaborative decision making in context of carbon trading. For example, use of carbon credits internally and enabling then fostering an internal and trading or sharing of carbon credits, can create a sociocultural change and produce benefits beyond the organizational boundary. Such an achievement will be much beyond the carbon reduction targets set for short-term periods. Opportunities for a much more significant social change phenomena is created through collaboration—internal and external to the organization.

For small and medium businesses, making use of social media networks opens up opportunities to locate and use carbon reduction knowledge and, at the same time, promote the actual achievement of the same. Such a use, across international boundaries, would require a much more comprehensive legal framework than exists today.

Detailed discussion on the technology and business trends of Green IT follows.

Green ICT and Technology Trends

Green IT does not need a "silver bullet" solution. In fact, we make aware of it. Bill Buxton, in The Long Nose of Innovation says, "The bulk of innovation is low-amplitude and takes place over a long period. Companies should focus on refining existing technologies as much as on creation." (http://www.businessweek.com/innovate/content/jan2008/id2008012_297369.htm).

Alignment of new and emerging technologies with business has been a key in delivering competitive advantage to business. This same alignment needs to be kept in mind when it comes to innovative use of emerging technologies and carbon reduction. Environmental intelligence (EI) includes not only the correlation and insights into carbon data and information, but also innovative application of technologies that are aligned to business. The technologies that are most likely to have an impact on Green IT are Cloud computing, software as a service (and lean-IT), nanotechnologies, quantum/trenary computing, ecodesign and biomimcry—shown in Figure 11.1. Some of impact of these technologies is already being felt in reducing the environmental footprints of organizations. However, a much greater impact is envisaged in the upcoming future of the carbon economy. Similarly, alignment of these technologies with business will be promoted through creation and upgrading of ISO standards, corporate governance standards and fresh look at Green IT strategies and policies. This is also shown in Figure 11.1

These technologies and their impact on environmental responsibilities of business are discussed next.

Cloud Computing

Cloud computing is an important part of an organization's approach to Green IT. This importance of Cloud computing was evident in the discussions in Chapters 4 and 6. However, in addition to those discussions, Cloud computing has a lot more to offer in the future in the context of EI. The underlying premise of Cloud computing has been the consolidation of hardware and software services that are made available through the uninterrupted, perpetual connectivity of the Internet. While this offering through the Cloud provides many business advantages to organization, the advantages in terms of carbon emission reduction through consolidation are very

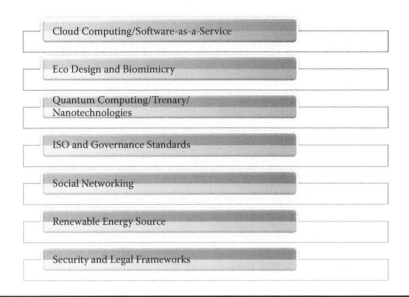

Figure 11.1   Emerging technologies landscape and Green IT impact.

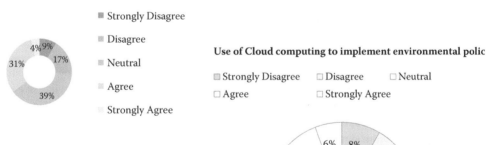

Figure 11.2   SaaS and cloud computing in Green ICT strategies.

significant. This is so because the sharing of infrastructure and applications, pooling of reusable data, and flexibility in terms of IT planning resulting from the Cloud has many possibilities that are yet to be explored.

The future of the Cloud, in terms of what it offers to Green IT, is based on its ability to continuously and dynamically bringing together multiple threads of computing processes, multimedia data, and changing interfaces in an intelligent way. The opportunities to reduce the overall carbon footprint through dynamic collaboration are on the rise by creation of public and private Clouds. Dynamic collaboration on the Cloud enhances the opportunities to use the business principle of Cloud computing: "pay as you go" in terms of using computing services. For example, Cloud-based collaboration reduces the typical "buffer" of hardware including disk space and computing power that would be otherwise required by data centre managers for their own organizations.

The future of Cloud computing will also be affected immensely by the availability of commonly accepted standards as well as excellence is metrics and measurements. Currently, the carbon emission calculations in the Cloud are treated external to the organization, resulting in a reduction of the carbon footprint of the user organization. However, that is not accurate reflection of the "overall" reduction of emissions due to Cloud computing. A much more precise calculation that balances the consolidation of computing devices with the power expended by the communication networks in communicating with those centralized computing devices is required. Thus, the use of most optimized pathways by user devices to access the Cloud will have an equal impact on carbon reduction as the consolidation of the back-end servers themselves.

Consolidated, optimized, and vast Cloud-based data centers, made up of ever-expanding deck of super computers, provide the future basis for carbon-sensitive computing. Such Cloud-based services will be offered by a conglomeration of large computing vendors with specialist skills, including those in server management, location and infrastructure, metrics and measurements, standards, and, of course, ability to comply with the legal and reporting requirements.

Following are the areas of Cloud computing that have the potential for reducing the overall carbon emissions across the industry:

- Infrastructure—this is the consolidation of data servers, disk space, communications equipment, and the supporting operating system. Such infrastructure services are capable of hosting increasing array of software applications from many different client organizations. The carbon savings will result from the use of common hardware and also from the consolidation of data center buildings, their cooling energies, and their maintenance effort.

- Applications development—with the availability of a sophisticated Cloud, application development, including its modeling, testing, and deployment, can be put together in one place. The Cloud-based application components can be used to plug in to the newly developed systems, resulting in a much faster and energy efficient development.

- Application execution—operationally, software applications can run much better through a Cloud as they are able to make use of the run-time environment provided by the Cloud itself. Furthermore, as these applications are hosted in the Cloud, they reduce the effort at upgrades and maintenance undertaken by organizations. This reduces the amount of operational effort (and corresponding operational carbon) at the user end.

- Reusable Data service—a large amount of public or partially proprietary data can be made available through Cloud-based services that can reduce the repeated storage and maintenance of such data by separate organizations. For example, currency exchange, interest rates, flight times, and weather patterns, are the types of data that are common to many organizations but are stored by them all separately. Cloud-based data services can eliminate that storage and opens up doors for their greater consolidation. Such consolidation of data can also be used in environmental management by organizations wherein common data, common lessons learnt, and application of commonly accepted standards can be consolidated and provided on the Cloud as a service.

SaaS

Software as a service (SaaS) provides an ideal way to deploy software applications. SaaS provides access to the application that is executing on a remote server, by anyone, as and when needed. This SaaS-based deployment has also been discussed in earlier Chapters 4 and 6. SaaS is the execution of application from a centralized server through the connectivity accorded by the Internet. SaaS model offers a combination of shared services model, improved power consumption, cooling efficiency, and equipment density (http://www.aplicor.com/blog/071001.htm). Thus, SaaS is closely associated with Cloud computing, and adheres to the principle of pay as you go, mentioned earlier. While the Cloud offers opportunities to consolidate infrastructure and hardware, and enables expansion without the usual overheads, SaaS creates opportunities to execute applications that are not installed, and configured on the local servers of the organizations. Instead, applications are run out of a common machine, and are shared by different users. This results in the use of power by a smaller number of computers as against the number of computers required if applications were run individually and locally. The overall energy and costs are thus reduced. Thus future, in fact, is where applications are architected, designed, modeled, and developed from ground up as SaaS applications with associated carbon metrics. Application vendors themselves may no longer be offering their applications as packages but, rather, as services.

The challenge with SaaS-based deployment is related to data, its integration and its security. Therefore, the application execution and reusable data service discussed in the previous section assume greater importance in SaaS-based software deployment. Questions such as how is the data created, where does it reside, how does it interact with the existing data of the organization, how it is backed up, and how much of control the Cloud vendor has on the data as compared with the organization, all need to be asked and investigated.

SaaS applications are easier to maintain and upgrade as they are installed and configured in a centralized place. This reduces the upgrade and maintenance of the applications. However, security and privacy of data, especially from competing organizations, can be a challenge.

Thus, SaaS too, has a long way to go as its success is not based on technologies alone. Innovative business modeling, stringent legal framework (that guards security and privacy of data) and changes in user attitudes will all be required to make SaaS a success. With increasing acceptance of SaaS-based deployment of software there will be a significant reduction in the "clutter" of hardware and software components.

Nanotechnologies

Nanotechnology deals with computing at a microscopic level. These technologies have the potential to impact Green IT in terms of both its hardware and its software. Nanotechnologies provide means to create, measure, and manipulate electronic data and communications at atomic size. The reduction in size requires considerable research effort—design, development, and production. The power to these minuscule devices requires innovation in battery power technologies. However, the amount of power required by these devices is also small due to their smaller size. Reduction is device size, potential elimination of movement (e.g., spinning of disks) within the devices, and ease of handling can all reduce overall carbon emissions resulting from these devices.

A strong marriage between nanotechnology and the principles and practices of Green engineering provides a way to build environmentally sustainable society (http://www.ens-newswire.com/ens/apr2007/2007–04–26–01.html).

Quantum/Trinary Computing

Trinary (or ternary) computing has significant possibilities not only for computing itself but also for improving on the carbon footprint of IT. Trinary computing works at the very fundamental of computing by adding to the binary bit options of "0" and "1," another option of "-1." Such trinary computer was built by Nikolay Brusentsov in 1958 and is said to have much reduced power consumption than the binary one (http://en.academic.ru/dic.nsf/enwiki/155775).

New Renewable Energies

Wind, solar, wave, nuclear, and biomass are at the cusp of renewable energy sources. Current oil, coal, and gas are exhaustible sources of energy. Exploring new energy sources that would not deplete with use is an ongoing scientific exercise. Advent of these renewable sources of energy will change the carbon emissions calculations as the emissions resulting from these energies are expected to be much less than those generated by coal and gas. However, care should be taken to balance the use of these futuristic energy sources with the emissions that may result from proliferation of end-user devices that would still be emitting heat and carbon.

ISO—New and Upgraded Standards

The ISO 14000 family of standards, discussed in the previous chapter, are also evolving. For example, the ISO 14001 standard, which specifies the requirements of an environmental management system, does so in the context of a specific product or an organization. However, this standard does not contain requirements for that would handle environmental practices associated with collaborative organizations—especially if these organizations are collaborating dynamically. Either the ISO 14000 series of standards need to be upgraded to include dynamically collaborating businesses or a new set of standards are required to cover the environmental practices of such collaborations. Furthermore, environmental governance standards that deal with embedding environmental management within corporate governance structures (based on ITIL and CoBIT, for example) are also required. Standards that can dictate, from an environmental perspective, the use of aforementioned emerging technologies, are also required. Finally, the use and deployment of the standards themselves need to make use of the Cloud and be SaaS based—reducing the overheads associated in complying with them and their related reporting. Such standards would incorporate emergent technologies, practices, and methods of development and deployment of software applications and services.

Security and Legal

The current legal frameworks governing carbon emissions come out of the ratification of agreements at various international summits on the environment. However, a carbon emission in the context of

IT is a global phenomena—especially as Cloud, SaaS, and outsourcing continue to dominate the IT services sector. Therefore, while the real user of a service could be sitting in one geographical region, the emissions resulting from his or her work will be attributed to a totally different geographical region. The laws that govern these emissions, and the standards and protocols that surround the measurements of these emissions, need to be developed and agreed upon. As discussed later in this chapter, the dichotomy between the developing and developed nations in terms of carbon emissions is also a key in the development of laws and regulations that can apply globally.

Integral to such a legal framework are the issues associated with security of carbon data. This is particularly so when the data is generated and owned by one organization, whereas it is stored, maintained, and backed up by a totally different vendor of such services. Security of carbon data requires procedures, practices, norms, standards, and binding legal framework—not much of which exists now.

Ecodesign

Ecodesign is based on environmental considerations in the very early conceptual stage of the architecture and design of products or processes. While environmental consideration is a product, lifecycle themselves are not a new thing, in depth consideration of the Green P-O-D is involved in this process. For example, Ecodesign of a computer monitor will include a less energy consuming design, detailed study of the devices associated with the monitor—like the machine, keyboard and mouse, their biodegradability and also the ergonomics of use. Each of these factors provides input into ecodesign. Thus, ecodesign can cover design, raw materials, production, packaging, and distribution. For example, ecodesign would consider local sourcing of raw material saving on transport and storage, which in turn, would save carbon. Another example is choice of the raw material itself. For example, while choice of wood over plastic would mean a biodegradable cheap option, plastic equipment may imply a durable lightweight product with a long life. Ecodesign incorporates these issues in design of all ICT equipments.

Biomimicry

Biomimicry, as an emergent trend, requires substantial study, experimentation and usage in all areas of an organization's products and services. Biomimicry can be considered as a combination of science and art that aims to learn from and emulate nature, which is usually sustainable. Nature uses only the energy it needs to carry out a function, ensures that the functionality matches the form, recycles and relies on diversity.

Examples of biomimicry include nontoxic adhesives inspired by geckos, energy efficient buildings based on the architecture of termite mounds, wingtips on commercial aircraft-based wingtip feathers of birds of prey resistance-free antibiotics inspired by red seaweed, and a solar cell inspired by a leaf (based on http://www.biomimicryinstitute.org/). Thus, biomimicry adds to the criteria of what is a successfully technological innovation. Innovation that fits in with the nature is likely to be much more sustainable than the one that has disregard for nature.

These examples hint at opportunities that can be explored by Green IT in the area of data centre infrastructure, computer design, computer operations, communication networks, and even system applications. For example, application of biomimicry in IT can lead to design of glass screens based on total internal reflection, virtual keyboards, and biodegradable internal elements as far as possible. While the earlier section discussed the relevance of Cloud computing, not all the computing power of the Cloud will be centralized. Going by nature, which relies and makes good use of local expertise, the Cloud architecture may become a distributed architecture that takes advantage through decentralizing some aspects of the otherwise centralized architecture. From an infrastructure viewpoint, constructing a data centre in cold geographical regions, covering its roof with terracotta tiles, providing ample natural ventilation to the building and growing ivy on the side walls of the building are some ways of using nature reduce the power required in cooling data centers in the Green ICT domain. With only a little over half a century of computing history to fall back on, opportunities exist to investigate and discover a substantial amount in the way computers are designed and developed that can be based on the way nature designs things.

Green ICT—Business and Economic Trends

In recent interviews with 1,000 global senior business and IT managers, Enterprise Strategy Group found that nearly half said professional services to assess, design, and implement technologies to support Green initiatives were most important in selecting IT vendors (Nordin 2008, OECD 2009; The climate Group 2008, as also reported by Garito, M., 2011).

The business and economic trends in Green IT are as influential as the technological trends in what the eventual outcome of Green IT will be. These new business models also offer potential for future research and development in the intersecting domains of economics and environment (as also highlighted by Younessi [2011] and also by Sherringham and Unhelkar [2011]).

Collaborations, based on the Internet connectivity, offer businesses opportunities to create advantages by interacting with each other, rather than competing with each other. New collaborative business models that are also dynamic (that is formed and dispersed on a regular basis) can lead to many different ways in which Green IT is understood and implemented by these collaborations. Collaborations also enable relationships between a network of organizations enabling them to buy and sell their products and services electronically, thereby making them cheaper to sell or buy as well as enabling the businesses to reach a wide range of market. As Fairchild and Peterson (2003) have mentioned, the presence of collaborative commerce indicates a network of firms with similar collaborative natures with established collaborative business platform and strategies. Business collaborations offer opportunity for reusability of data, processes, and systems that in itself is advantageous in reducing the carbon footprint of the organization. Collaborations can also help in sharing of information and knowledge gained in implementing Green IT strategies. Thus collaborations in the domain of Green IT would result from firms not only to creating and selling Green products, but also incorporating Green partners in their business practices, sharing the growing knowledge and experience in this domain, and helping and supporting each other in the collaborative effort. Eventually, Green IT should become a self-sustaining commodity that can be traded for its own sake, or increase the share value of a firm.

Figure 11.3 shows the growing importance of collaborative business models and the use of tools and techniques within various industrial sectors. For example, education, transport, and scientific enterprises score heavily in the "strongly agree" option, and other industrial sectors such as health care, financial, and media are closely following with the "agree" option—in terms of how prevalent are the use of collaborative tools in these business sectors.

Thus, buoyed by the connectivity of the Internet and further opportunities for real-time connectivity through mobile networks, businesses are rapidly forming collaborative alliances to package their products and services. These business trends have significant impact on the

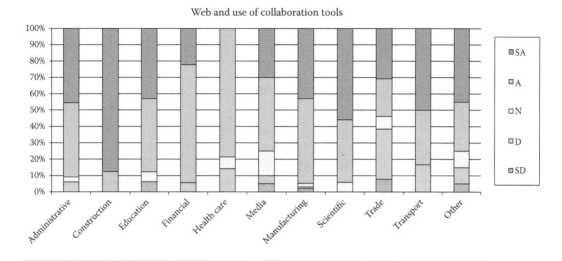

Figure 11.3   Use of collaborative tools by organizations in practice.

Green IT domain as well. For example, collaboration enables decentralization of decision making within many businesses—so, if one partner in the collaboration is emitting high level of carbon, other business partners should be table to take action to reduce those emissions. This leads to business models that make regular use of dynamic knowledge management system (Unhelkar 2010, Cutter report). The opportunities to reduce carbon emissions at the source increase rapidly in these business models.

Cloud computing and SaaS, discussed earlier, are not the only technological innovations that impact Green ICT. They also require a corresponding business model that can support the use of these technologies. Such a business model will invariably include agreements on how the carbon emissions are to be shared amongst the vendors and users of Cloud computing. Furthermore, product, service. and infrastructure businesses will each have a different model when it comes to use of Cloud computing, and therefore different ways of calculating carbon emissions. Product-based businesses need significant use of the Cloud for calculating raw materials and inventories, relating them to supply chains and also distributing the finished products. Service-based industries have negligible raw materials, inventories are only associated with the equipments and there is no distribution network. Therefore, Cloud-based business models, wherein these businesses are using Cloud computing, require the service level agreements to be drafted differently. The services and support required from the Cloud for a service-based business has more real-time, critical components to it than the production type business. Numerous aspects of such a business model come into play including requirements for uptime, redundancies in data and systems, staff support, education and training, and even marketing and advertising.

From a business viewpoint, the future of Green ICT can also be linked closely with good corporate citizenship and ensuing promotion and marketing. These Green credentials in marketing together with their caveats were discussed in Chapter 8. Supporting various environmental causes, formation of environmental social media groups, and identifying the changing customer choices are the key to the future in the social dimension of Green IT.

Business models also reflect changes to the internal organization of business. For example, project-based work within organizations will be carried out by virtual project teams that can be created quickly, based on members from different areas of business, collaborating electronically to deliver results. The internal business model includes addressing internal communication, integrating processes, and enabling sharing of information amongst team members.

Dichotomy of Developing Economies

Sustainability as commodity: increased interest in sustainable methods and products will soon lead to "self-sustaining markets": that is, bought and sold for their own sake. Sustainability has a inherent in trade value with business opportunity for investors. The size of BRIC economies, and the fact that their en masse adoption sustainable and Green ideas will result in a massive capitalization of Green infrastructure in these economies. Based on Nathadwarawala K & L (2011), HRG.

Rapidly emerging business and economic trends reflect the globalized nature of most medium to large businesses. This globalization, in turn, leads to an even bigger challenge that the overall environment domain has to face in the near and long-term future—the dichotomy between rapid economic development and corresponding carbon control in the developing economies. This issue was the main point of contention between these two groups of economies and was based on the need to consider total carbon emissions over a substantial period of time. This is an important element in the way in which carbon is calculated and reflects differing viewpoints of developed and developing nations. To a large extend, this may not be a practical calculation. This is so because if emissions are considered only over last couple of years or even a decade, then the developing nations produce substantial emissions—as the economic development is more or less related to increases in carbon emissions. The developed economies, in the past, generated significant carbon during their own growth periods.

The developing economies (BRIC) are producing carbon when the world is more carbon-conscious than it was earlier. This has created a new challenge—that of balance and fairness across the globe. Table 11.2 (based on Nathadwarawala 2011) shows the differences between various business elements in fully developed economies and developing economies (BRIC). Table 11.2 also highlights the specific nuances of these sustainable business elements in terms of their environmental implications.

New and emergent approaches to sustainability in practice need to incorporate these global factors. Governments, companies, and individuals need to build on them further by bringing in elements of geographical regions as well as time periods in measuring and restricting emissions. Thus, new economic models in the way resources are shared over regions and time is required. The disparity of consumption and corresponding carbon emission between the developed and developing countries needs to be bridged. This discussion in Chapter 3 over length of time, breadth of coverage and depth of practice of sustainability across entire geographical regions now applies in this dichotomy discussed here.

Collaborative Environmental Intelligence

Environmental intelligence, as discussed in the earlier chapters, together with the collaborative business models discussed earlier in this chapter, offers a major area for research in environmental initiatives by businesses. The various areas of collaborations include those between various stakeholders and parties: between organizations, between individuals and organizations and between government and organizations. Thus, collaborative EI goes beyond the insights required and used by a single organization and into the realms of multiple, dynamic collaborative entities.

Table 11.2 Developed Economies and Developing Economies (BRIC) Comparison along Four Dimensions

Sustainability Dimensions Elements	Fully Developed Economies	Developing Economies (BRIC)
Social (people, attitude)	High literacy; Low density; Wide spread; Results in rapid intake of the concept of sustainable development	Low literacy; High density; Concentrated; Results in slow intake of the concept of sustainable development
Process (discipline)	High emphasis on standards and quality control May result in more carbon per activity but less carbon overall	Relatively recent focus on standards and QA may results in less carbon per activity but overall higher carbon
Technology (design, adoption)	Rapid adoption due to availability of technology— helps in environmental changes; but was responsible for the GHGs in the first place	Relatively low use of technology, but the rapidly growing use can be environmental friendly from the start Advantage of "Leap frogging" of technologies
Economy (costs, ROI)	Heavily regulated with greater controls in place Enables environmental factors to dictate customer spending patterns	Weak regulation in markets Customers and business partners (globally) are the main driving force to encourage environmentally friendly products and services

Collaborative intelligence is described by Unhelkar and Tiwary (Cutter 2010) as a technical platform where multiple organizations are collaboratively sharing their business intelligence for the win-win outcome without compromising their own market position and differentiation.

Developing and formalizing the collaborative EI capabilities will provide collaborating organizations with market differentiators in the environmental space

Collaborative EI brings collaborations and EI together—thus helping the business world to get ready for the carbon economy without going through the rigors of "reinventing the wheel." For example, through collaborative EI, noncompetitive carbon data. and analysis can be shared easily amongst organizations and governing bodies.

This sharing of carbon capabilities can also extend to sharing of many basic environmental systems components such as security, access, and authentication. Such sharing of technical components can play a positive role in the compliance of security and privacy requirements related to the environment.

Future work in collaborative EI also includes dynamic integration and consolidation of disparate carbon data and multiple transactions from many organizations in to a single customer view.

Following are specific topics of interest and future investigations in relations with collaborative EI:

- Collaborative carbon data for trend plotting—carbon data and information from multiple sources and many organizations is required to create an industry-wide picture of carbon trends. Interfacing data warehouses will create environmental insights that are not possible with single, organizational data base.
- Collaborative data warehouses—will reuse common, noncompetitive, sharable carbon data that will reduce replication of data and corresponding processing.
- Collaborative EI using Cloud computing—collaborations in the Cloud will enable improved and consolidated carbon data and device management. For example, smart meters can collect and transmit data not to single organization but to the systems and facilities in the Cloud.
- Collaborative EI with mobile technologies. Results in a mobile data warehousing, OLAP, and data mining that come from business Intelligence and are applied to environmental intelligence. A carbon data warehouse is a large repository of data collected from operational data sources that deal with environmental information. OLAP and data mining techniques can be used to identify and interpret patterns from such collaborative organizational data.
- Collaborative EI and Green Blogs—provides opportunities for free exchange of information and ideas on the environment. This advantage of such Green blogs and discussions is that they remain stored for future reference, can be indexed and researched into and provide collaborative opportunities beyond regular journals or magazines. Blog-based communication facilitate greater exchange of ideas between organizations, facilitate sharing those ideas in real time and enable customers to voice their preferences.
- Collaborative EI and Web 2.0/Web 3.0. The new version of the web set new trends in the communication technologies that go beyond the basic task of communication (Unhelkar and Trivedi 2009). The characteristics of these technologies are rich user experience, ability of the user to not only glean information but also execute services, enable dynamic content, and enable scalability. The instant collection of carbon data and information, and instant feedback through applications that run on the new web platforms, provide the management and leadership of the organization to make instant decisions regarding the direction of the collaborative organizations. Implementation of Web 2.0 technologies on the mobile devices will reduce the energy use as mobile gadgets consume less energy than desktop computers as well as virtualizes the server resources leading to a sustainable and environment friendly system.
- Collaborative EI and GRID computing—the GRID of computers, connected via a network, is the precursor to today's Cloud computing. A computing GRID was basically interested in sharing otherwise unused computing power (Unhelkar 2004)—as against a Cloud that also brings in business rules for sharing and paying for the resources. However, the GRID is a known paradigm for computer connectivity and should be certainly explored for the possibilities of reducing the overall global computing needs. For example, a wireless GRID may offer the opportunities to completely sidestep the need to build a physical communication network—saving the carbon footprint of a physical infrastructure.

Discussion Points

- What would be the innovative aspects of applying Cloud computing to the environmental challenge?
- How does a SaaS-based application reduce carbon emission?
- Discuss the ways in which standards in environmental management can be enhanced.
- What are the major points of contention in the carbon debate between the developing and developed economies?
- What is collaborative EI? Discuss two ways in which collaborative EI can be applied in today's organizations to reduce their carbon footprint.

References

BBC web page. Future directions in computing, http://news.bbc.co.uk/1/hi/technology/7085019.stm that discusses topics as Quantum Computers and Moore's Law.

British Computer Society. (2011). "Atomic computing" available at http://www.bcs.org/content/Con WebDoc. 16965 (last accessed April 9th, 2011).

Constantine L. and Lockwood, L. (1999). *Software for Use: A Practical Guide to Models and Methods of Usage-centered Design*, Addison-Wesley. Also see www.foruse.com

Deitel, H., Deitel, P., and Steinbuhler, K. (2001). *e-Business and e-Commerce for Managers*, Prentice Hall, Upper Saddle River, New Jersey.

Deshpande, Y., Murugesan, S., Unhelkar, B., and Arunatileka, D. (2004). Workshop on Device Independent Web Engineering: Methodological Considerations and Challenges in Moving Web Applications from Desk-top to Diverse Mobile Devices, *Proceedings of the Device Independent Web Engineering Workshop*, Munich.

Fairchild, A. M. and Peterson, R. R. (2003). "Business-to-Business Value Drivers and eBusiness Infrastructures in Financial Services: Collaborative Commerce Across Global Markets and Networks," System Sciences, *Proceedings of the 36th Hawaii International Conference*, pp. 239–248.

Garito, M. (2011). Chapter 44, Balancing Green ICT Business Development with Corporate Social Responsibility (CSR). In B. Unhelkar, ed., *Handbook of Research in Green ICT*, pp. 607–620. IGI Global, Hershey, PA, USA.

Kalakoa, R. and Whinston, A. B. (1999). *Frontiers of Electronic Commerce*, Addison-Wesley.

Malone, T. W. (2004). *The Future of Work*, p. 9. Boston: Harvard Business School Press.

McKnight L. and Howison, J. (2004). Wireless Grids: Distributed Resource Sharing by Mobile, Nomadic, and Fixed Devices, *IEEE Internet Computing*, Jul/Aug 2004 issue, http://dsonline.computer.org/0407/f/ w4gei.htm (last accessed July 19th, 2004).

Nordin, H. (2008). *Your Computer and the Climate: Make a Change Today—Save the Planet Tomorrow*. Stockholm, Sweden: TCO Development.

OECD. (2009). *Toward Green ICT Strategies: Assessing Policies and Programmes on ICT and the Environment*. Paris: OECD.

Sherringham, K. and Unhelkar, B. (2011). Strategic business trends in the context of green ICT. In B. Unhelkar, ed., *Handbook of Research in Green ICT: Technical, Business and Social Perspectives*, pp. 65–82. IGI Global, Hershey, PA, USA.

Siegel, D. (1999). *Futurize Your Enterprise: Business Strategy in the Age of the E-Customer*. John Wiley Publishing.

Unhelkar, B. (2003). Understanding Collaborations and Clusters in the e-Business World, We-B Conference, (www.we-bcentre.com; with Edith Cowan University), Perth, November 23–24, 2003 (referred and accepted for presentation and publication).

Unhelkar, B. (2003). "Understanding Collaborations and Clusters in the e-Business World", *We-B Conference* ("http://www.we-bcentre.com" www.we-bcentre.com; with Edith Cowan University), Perth, Nov. 24–25, 2003.

Unhelkar, B. (2004). Effect of wireless grids on information architectures of businesses: From a globalization perspective, *ADCOM, 2004.*

Unhelkar, B. (2010). *Knowledge Management in Perspective: The Dynamic Knowledge Synchronization Model, Cutter Executive Report*, Vol. 10, No. 8, Aug. 2010 (12,000 words), Boston, USA.

Younessi, D. (2011). Chapter 7, Sustainable Business Value. In B. Unhelkar, ed., *Handbook of Research in Green ICT*, pp. 98–115. IGI Global, Hershey, PA, USA.

CASE STUDIES B

Part B of this book contains three separate case studies. Each of these case studies aim to demonstrate the application of the principles and practices of Green IT discussed thus far in this book. The attempt to undertake Green enterprise transformation for each of these organizations would, in practice, involve a lot more time, effort, and budget than is described here. Hence, the purpose of these case studies is to provide some indication of the practical aspect of Green enterprise transformation. While the case study descriptions are based on hypothetical organizations, they all have their roots in a real life organization. Each case study chapter aims to demonstrate a specific aspect of the Green enterprise transformation. Following is a brief outline of the areas of Green enterprise transformation handled by the chapters in this section:

Chapter 12: Greening of a **service** organization. The emphasis here is on optimizing processes associated with the services offered by the organization. There are no products as such, therefore no materials and their inventory. However, there will be equipments associated with the service—in this case a hospital—and corresponding inventory and lifecycle associated with the equipment.

Chapter 13: Green of a **product** organization. This is a medium-sized organization producing packaging material. Therefore, there will be material and inventory associated with the manufacturing process. Besides that, there will be supporting processes and systems.

Chapter 14: Green of an **infrastructure** organization. These types of organizations do not have a product or a service as their main offering. For example, a large telecom organization will be primarily involved in setting up of the communications infrastructure. Services including maintenance of the infrastructure, business models for billing customers and offering of the telecom platform to other service providers will ensue. This is a long-term Green enterprise transformation and the issues are more collaborative than the previous two types of organizations.

Chapter 12

Case Study in Applying Green IT Strategies and Applications to a Hospital

Key Points

- Presents a Green enterprise transformation (GET) case study for a service organization
- Uses GoodMead hospital as a hypothetical organization to present the case study
- Describes the practical aspects of a preliminary Green IT audit
- Describes the Green business objectives of a hospital
- Conducts a high-level SWOT analysis of the hospital from a GET perspective
- Suggests the use of mobile technologies in optimizing hospital processes that will result in carbon savings
- Lists the lessons learning in applying Green IT strategies to a service sector organization like a hospital

GoodMead Hospital

GoodMead is a hypothetical large hospital in a metro city, providing public sector medical services. These services cover various areas of health including the standard out patient department providing regular consultation to patients, as also various specialities such as pediatric, gynecology and obstetrics, orthopedics, radiology, sports medicine, and so on.

As a result of the recent preliminary Green IT audit of the hospital, it has been revealed that the hospital had a significant carbon footprint. Significant reviews of patient management processes, management of electronic patient records (EPR), laboratory equipment management, medical drugs and material management, and management of equipments and buildings were undertaken. Initial opinion of the auditors and that of the tentatively appointed chief green officer (CGO) was that significant optimization was possible in all these areas of the hospital that will reduce its carbon footprint. The cost-effectiveness and efficiency of the hospital's service processes is as important as its carbon efficiency. Thus, the benefits envisaged in terms of its cost reduction and process optimization are significant. Further to the attention on processes in terms of their carbon reduction, the initial investigation also highlighted that GoodMead has a significant investment in a data center. The building and infrastructure of this data center is now more than 10 years old, and the server machines themselves are averaging 4 years in use.

The audit also revealed that the hospital, by undertaking a Green enterprise transformation (GET), would be able to influence many of its partnering organizations. These are the labs, pharmacies, and suppliers.

The return on investment (ROI) of the hospital's attempt to transform to a Green hospital is meant to go beyond the carbon focus and into the overall business optimization arena. Thus, the hospital leadership is keen to make effective use of new fund allocations that have been indexed to carbon reduction. This effective use includes an approach that will benefit the hospital overall and is not limited only to IT-related carbon reduction.

Preliminary Green Investigation

As a result of the decision taken by the new, visionary leadership of GoodMead hospital, the aforementioned preliminary Green IT audit was conducted. This audit took place over 4 weeks. The main sponsor of this audit was the tentatively appointed CGO. The CGO, together with the IT auditors, departmental heads, and the CIO sought input into the current state of the hospital. The framework for this audit was based on the four dimensions of GET. Thus, input was obtained in terms of the economic performance, sociocultural or attitude, business processes, and technical infrastructure of the hospital. The CGO is seeking input from Green IT experts as well as experts from the medical administration domain on how to approach the GET.

Following is a list of the noteworthy findings from the preliminary Green IT audit of GoodMead hospital:

- The hospital being a large, public sector hospital, has to undertake action in terms of measuring, reporting, and reducing its carbon emissions.
- The hospital has significant opportunity to influence its partnering organizations.
- The OPD (out-patient department) of the hospital is a large and complex department that operates out of its own separate building and infrastructure. This department is serviced by 220 stationary desktop machines, 100 mobile laptops and PDAs carried personally by the staff and numerous supporting IT paraphernalia—such as printers. This department alone, according to estimates and with assumptions in terms of computer usage, accounts for 60 to 65 kT (kilo Tonnes) of carbon emissions of the hospital.
- The hospital has additional desktops, printers, laptops, and PDAs that are in the other departments such as surgical and laboratories. These devices amount to 20 kT of emissions at this stage.
- Printers are heavily used for writing of scripts, printing of patient records and reports and related documentation (such as a referral). On an average, the hospital prints 5,000 pages of normal paper and consumes corresponding ink and printer time.
- The hospital has an attached pathological laboratory that conducts diagnostic blood and related tests. The lab equipment is aging. Similarly, the data stored in the hospital's servers

that provides that information to staff on the results from the tests is also significant consumer of power and generates carbon emissions.

■ Pre- and postsurgical activities require substantial number of electronic equipments and information technology support.

■ The hospital has to need to product substantial amount of legal documentation (such as signing of authority to perform certain operations), and so on.

■ The hospital collaborates with external pharmaceutical organizations as well as manufacturers and distributors of drugs and hospital equipments. This collaboration is a combination of manual interactions and also some initial web services based interaction.

■ Staff rostering is not optimized, leaving the administrative staff to occasionally use physical notepads, whiteboards, and diaries to book availability of doctors.

■ Scheduling system for patient appointments, surgical procedures and human relation (HR) (e.g., doctor vacation) is also not optimized and requires a major upgrade. Scheduling patient consultations, scheduling work rosters for nurses and administrative staff is many a times happening manually.

■ A comprehensive multimedia data warehouse project is underway. This project is aimed at consolidating the large amount of data, in multiple formats, in a single data warehouse. Furthermore, selected past consultations in audio and video are also to be made available to authorized users like doctors, patients, and external specialists.

■ With the availability of a multimedia database, there is opportunity for optional extensions to the project is to incorporate possibility of remote consulting by doctors through audio and video media using high-speed connectivity.

■ Security of access and privacy of patient's data (EPR) is of top priority and is not to be compromised under any circumstances.

■ A range of relative cross-functionalities (like sports information) to be included to attract and keep nonpatients to the site as well. This may help in keeping the community aware of the site.

■ Internal administrative systems (like booking of surgeries to operating rooms, or leave roster of nurses) be moved to the Internet-based system to enable global (or off-site) management.

■ There are provisional inventories that are in excess. These are both medical and IT inventories. For example, there are 15 PCs sitting in the IT departments as potential backups for breakdowns. Similarly, the data center has excessive unused storage capacity.

Green Business Objectives

The green business objectives of GoodMead hospital are based on the results of the preliminary investigations into its Green IT maturity level. These objectives provide the basis for the transformation plan. Figure 12.1 shows the overall approach to GET for GoodMead hospital. On the left is the description of the "as is" state of the hospital from the environmental perspective. On the right is the "to be" or desired state of the hospital. This "to be" state of the hospital is based on the formation of green objectives of the organization. In between, in Figure 12.1, is the outline of the GET framework, as applicable to GoodMead. The four major phases of transformation—diagnose, plan, enact, and review—interspersed with metrics, are shown in this high-level transformation framework.

Following are the important objectives of GoodMead in undertaking the GET:

■ Reduction in carbon emissions across all departments and processes of the organization
■ Compliance with carbon legislations and related carbon initiatives of the government (even if they are not fully ratified as law)

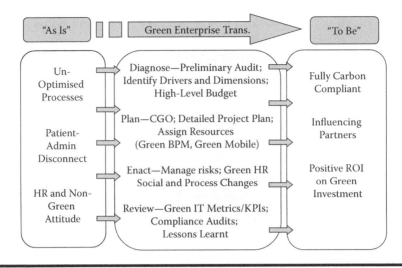

Figure 12.1 GET for GoodMead hospital.

- Be a leader in carbon management and, thereby, influence many business partners in reducing their emissions
- Undertake electronic collaborations with partners, government regulatory bodies for monitoring and reporting
- Undertake comprehensive Green BPM program that will enable result in modeling, optimization, and merger/elimination of processes
- Aim for a comprehensive and holistic GET that is futuristic
- Create positive green attitude across the entire staff through Green HR

SWOT of GoodMead Hospital

Figure 12.2 shows the SWOT analysis of GoodMead hospital. Such a SWOT analysis is helpful in understanding the approach that can be taken for the GET. For example, GoodMead is a large hospital with multiple campuses and departments within them. A SWOT analysis makes it easier to understand how to capitalize on the inherent strengths of the hospital. The areas that will be directly affected by the transformation and bear risks will also become evident in such an analysis. In practice, this will be a substantial exercise encompassing all these departments. In this example case study, the SWOT analysis can help understand the scope and coverage of work during this transformation.

Following understanding develops as a result of the SWOT analysis of GoodMead hospital in its "As is" state:

Strengths

- *Well-known public sector hospital.* This popularity of the hospital is an important impetus for the hospital to undertake GET. The impact of such transformation will be far reaching, beyond the hospital. There is significant support to the hospital in terms of patients and corporate.
- *Financially well supported by government.* GoodMead has been a flagship hospital in the region, with sufficient funding from the government over the last decade, enabling it to undertake its services, together with its research and training.

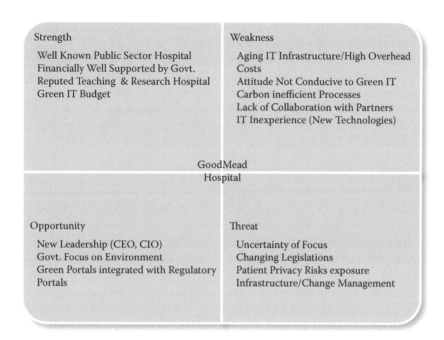

Strength	Weakness
Well Known Public Sector Hospital Financially Well Supported by Govt. Reputed Teaching & Research Hospital Green IT Budget	Aging IT Infrastructure/High Overhead Costs Attitude Not Conducive to Green IT Carbon inefficient Processes Lack of Collaboration with Partners IT Inexperience (New Technologies)

GoodMead
Hospital

Opportunity	Threat
New Leadership (CEO, CIO) Govt. Focus on Environment Green Portals integrated with Regulatory Portals	Uncertainty of Focus Changing Legislations Patient Privacy Risks exposure Infrastructure/Change Management

Figure 12.2   SWOT for GoodMead hospital.

■ *Green IT budget.* A recently elected government has provided additional, specific grant to the hospital to enable it to improve its environmental credentials.
■ *Reputed teaching and research hospital.* There is an atmosphere of research and experimentation. Therefore, the hospital will be ideally placed to experiment with carbon reduction and wastage reduction across its various departments and processes. Besides, the staff it highly skilled in what it does—including medical, administrative, and IT support.

Weaknesses

■ *Aging IT infrastructure.* The preliminary Green IT audit finds that the data center is more than 10 years old and the average server is 4 years in use. This implies a rapidly aging infrastructure that is not able to capitalize on the benefits of newer server designs and techniques for cooling. Furthermore, such infrastructure also implies high overhead costs for its operation.
■ *Attitude not conducive to Green IT.* A preliminary survey carried out during the audit, and one-on-one interviews with a few volunteer staff indicated clearly that the attitude within GoodMead was not positive toward Green IT. Understandably there was skepticism for the initiative—particularly from the medical staff who considered IT-related carbon savings as not substantial.
■ *Carbon inefficient processes.* Numerous processes were identified at the organization level that was carbon inefficient. These processes included patient management, inventory management, and staff rosters. The IT systems supporting these systems were also not carbon efficient. This implied the processes were taking unnecessarily long, bureaucratic steps that the activities were redundant and the systems supporting the processes were data intensive

without providing required value. There were no technology innovations within the systems such as use of Cloud computing or web services.

■ *Lack of collaboration with partners.* Especially the supplies to the hospital were arriving uncoordinated and the hospital's IT systems were not integrated with those of the supplier.

■ *IT inexperience (new technologies).* While the hospital was advanced in research and training in the medical field, it was lagging behind in terms of experience with new and upcoming information technologies. Therefore, there was little initiative from the current IT management to undertake major changes relating to carbon reduction.

Opportunities

■ *New leadership (CEO, CIO).* One of the most significant opportunity Goodmead has to develop and implement environmentally responsible business strategies is the formation of the new leadership team. The appointment of the CGO to oversee the entire green transformation and, together with the CIO, report to the corporate board, is an important development in itself.

■ *Government focus on environment.* The regulatory bodies are now getting a push through government initiatives on carbon reduction. As a result, new legislative requirements are about to be implemented, making it mandatory for large organizations in particular, to calculate and report their carbon emissions. The particular focus by the government on organizations that are semi- or quasi-government is providing the necessary opportunities and impetus to carbon reduction initiatives—such as in this hospital.

■ *Green portals integrated with regulatory portals.* The push from the government for carbon reduction is not only an opportunity for the hospital to transform its business models, portfolios, and data centers, but also upgrades its IT systems and portals with carbon data and information. To that effect, the government is now providing web services through its regulatory portals that can be used by "consumers" of web services. Telework and telemedicine—the telemedicine market is growing at a high rate with developed nations having already implemented several projects and the technology is becoming increasingly affordable. Therefore, there are greater opportunities for reducing emissions through telework and, in particular, telemedicine. More and more economical by the day.

Threats

■ *Uncertainty of focus.* While the senior management of the hospital is committed to a green hospital, there is occasional shift in the focus due to the changing nature of the technology domain. For example, the social aspect of Green IT is not positive at this stage, but to bring about a change in that sociocultural domain will require significant training and education of the staff. Changes will also be required in the user devices such as PCs and laptops. There is high possibility of conflicting objectives and therefore further uncertainty of focus. The senior management has to be taking the initiative and remain in charge to maintain focus.

■ *Changing legislations.* While the government is supporting the initiative and is pushing for GoodMead to be environmentally responsible, the legislations themselves are not firm yet. Therefore, there are changes to the way the scopes 1 and 2 are calculated, changes to the emission benchmarks, and so on. This is creating further uncertainty and risks in formulating and implementing Green IT strategies.

■ *Patient privacy risks exposure.* Privacy and confidentiality requirements of the patient's information needs to be protected as the transformation of technical systems and data warehouses takes place.

■ *Infrastructure/change management.* Due to the aging and underdeveloped nature of the technical environment, it may be hard to implement some of the technological solutions in which reliability of the service is crucial.

Strategic Concerns of Management

The aforementioned SWOT analysis provides significant input in identifying the drivers for environmentally responsible business strategy (ERBS) and vice versa. The senior management can start with a general understanding of the drivers for ERBS which, later, get formalized as the SWOT analysis is undertaken.

Figure 12.3 shows the key drivers for environmental responsibility for GoodMead hospital. Out of the six drivers that drive ERBS (as discussed in Chapter 2), Figure 12.3 shows social-political pressure, and enlightened self-interest as the two key drivers for ERBS. These two drivers are described as follows:

■ Sociopolitical pressure: The hospital has a substantial standing in the community. Besides, it is also a flagship hospital within the region. There is significant social and political pressure on the hospital to demonstrate its environmental credentials. This pressure comes from the general community that views the hospital as a symbol of good service-based organization and cross-section of patients (e.g., youngsters, sports-people).

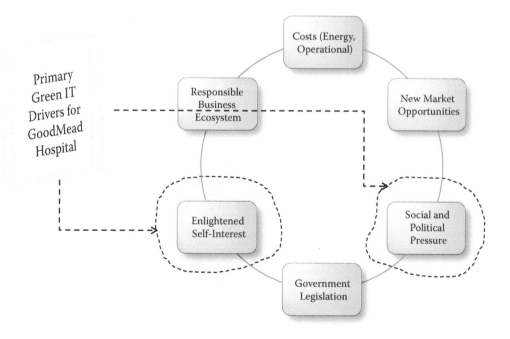

Figure 12.3   Drivers for environmental responsibility of business.

■ Enlightened self-interest: The senior management of the hospital, the leaders/decision makers are keen to take up the challenge of changing their processes and internal social attitude to a positive, green attitude. While they are certainly buoyed by the availability of funds dedicated for this purpose, they are themselves realizing the need to undertake this green enterprisewide transformation to enable them to remain as a leader in the upcoming carbon economy.

Steps in Developing a Hospital's ERBS

Figure 12.4 shows the major steps in the development of an Environmentally Responsible Business Strategy. This figure is based on Figure 2.13, which was discussed in detail in Chapter 2. Here, though, Figure 12.4 not only serves as a reminder for the steps in developing an ERBS for the hospital, but also shows the key drivers, dimensions, risks, and metrics for this GoodMead ERBS.

■ The business objectives of the hospital in becoming a green hospital were identified earlier on. These objectives and visions provide the initial direction for the hospital in its strategy formulation. The drivers for the objectives are enlightened self-interest and sociopolitical pressure on the hospital.
■ Green IT strategies: These are the medium terms (3–5 year) strategies that are driven by the CGO and that are based on the drivers and objectives of the organization. Strategies for Green IT also contain elements of risks or threats, as were identified during the SWOT.
■ Green IT policies and preconditions: These are the policies that are formed at the departmental level and are implemented in practice by the departmental heads and/or process

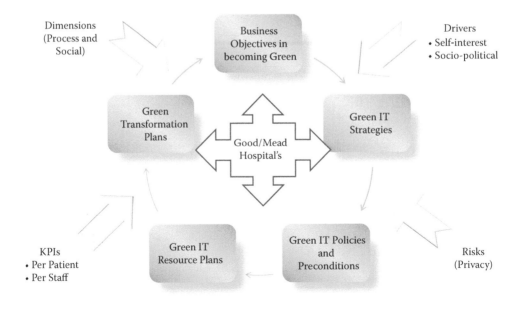

Figure 12.4   Steps in developing an ERBS.

owners. These policies related to procurement of new equipments (Energy Star ratings), changes to processes and delivery of training to staff.

- Green IT resource plans: These include details of resources required in undertaking transformation. For example, in case of GoodMead, the green transformation team itself would be lead by CGO, supported by the Green HR (as shown in Chapter 8) and will be interacting with the operational staff (doctors, nurses, administrators). Resource plans also include budgets and resources for procuring and implementing CEMS. The success of the transformation can be measured here based on Green KPIs (see chapter 2).
- Green transformation plans: These are the business transformation and change management plans that will focus on the dimensions and the work areas as described in Chapter 9.

Green Transformational Elements

Putting together the discussions thus far, Figure 12.5 shows the major green transformational elements of GoodMead hospital. The overall green transformation framework is shown on top with the various important elements underneath. These elements are as follows:

- The drivers and areas of influence. The drivers for GoodMead are shown earlier in Figure 12.3.
- The major dimension along with the GET will take place. This is the process dimension also supported by the social dimension for transformation.
- The demographics of the organization can play a role in deciding on the type of transformation, its budgets, and its resources. In case of GoodMead hospital, these demographics are large-sized service organization in a metropolitan city of a developed region.

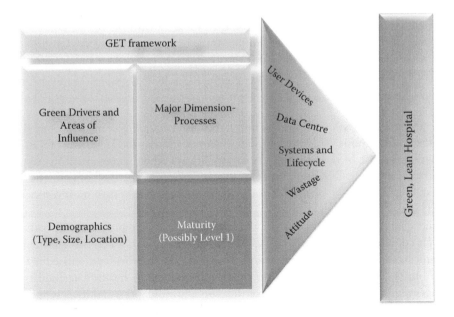

Figure 12.5   GoodMead hospital's major green transformational elements.

■ Maturity of GoodMead in terms of its Green IT performance is very basic (This cannot be fully ascertained at the start of the project as the process for measuring itself are not matured enough. However, a rough indication of the maturity level can be provided.).

Once these aforementioned aspects of GoodMead are ascertained, the transformation of the hospital can be undertaken as follows (also shown in Figure 12.5):

■ User devices—Measuring, upgrading, and recycling monitors, PCs, laptops, and mobile phones; desktop virtualization; centralized green services
■ Data center—Virtualization, optimization; self healing networks; network topology, database design, hardware and software components, security issues, and backup strategies. Redesign of data center to include flexibility and agility to enable easy upgrades of future infrastructure
■ Systems and lifecycle—IT systems supporting hospital processes like booking, consultation, diagnosis, treatment, prescription, and education; Equipment procurement, installation and usage; integration of supply chain with local as well as overseas pharmacies and drug suppliers. Interaction with government and other regulatory bodies should also be enabled electronically
■ Wastage—Electronic waste resulting from unused or broken devices; also, due consideration is given to areas of bio waste
■ Attitude—Undertaking training and consulting programs for staff (doctors, nurses, admin) and promoting it amongst patients and business partners. Internet-based system to facilitate global management of the administration, rosters as well as the most HR (human relations—People) functions. Change management for telework and telehealth

The Green Transformation Project

The overall GET project is to last between 12 and 18 months, with the full carbon value realized over 3 to 5 year's strategic time period. $ 1 million is the budget sanctioned by the corporate board and the CGO is authorized to undertake this transformation.

Figure 12.6 shows greater details of the 18-month GET plan. It is divided into six quarters of 3 months each.

■ First quarter: The first quarter of the hospital transformation is primarily focused on investigation and diagnosis. This work includes identification of the key drivers for green transformation (in case of the hospital it is sociopolitical and enlightened self-interest). During the first quarter, the CGO will lead the strategic planning for the hospital, creating a 3–5 year actionable strategic plan. This plan will also include the return on investment metrics for the hospital.
■ Second quarter: This is the quarter where enactment of the plan created in the previous quarter takes place. In case of GoodMead, the enactment of GET in this quarter deals with the process dimension of transformation. Therefore, Green BPM (as discussed in Chapter 5) comes in to play during this quarter. In the context of the health-care industry, process changes require extensive modeling, verification and validation, and tools support. Carbon content of the key processes needs to be established beforehand. This will happen in an approximate way in the diagnosis phases. Here, in the Green BPM activities, processes are reengineered and their carbon contents calculated again to ensure it has indeed reduced.

WORK AREAS of Work	Phase Description	1st Quarter	2nd Quarter	3rd Quarter	4th Quarter	5th Quarter	6th Quarter
1	Drivers; Strategic Planning; Cost Benefit/ROI						
2	Diagnosis; Maturity; Develop GET Plan; Resourcing						
3	Enactment of GET—Process Dimension (Process Modeling, Green BPM)						
4	Enactment of GET—Social Dimensions (Staff Training; Green HR)						
5	Review—Measurement of KPIs; Maturity; Plan Green IT Audits						
6	Review—Maturity and Feedback; Rework Outstanding Areas						
7	Collaborative Partner's Processes—Diagnosis and Plan						
8	Help Partners Enact GET						
9	Feedback and Fine Tune Hospital Processes						
10	Green IT Audits						
11	GET Program Management						

Figure 12.6   An 18-month GET project plan for GoodMead.

■ Third quarter: In case of GoodMead, this quarter of GET is dedicated to transformation of the social dimension. Therefore, this quarter focuses on the attitude and behavior of individual staff. Social dimension also becomes important in a service organization as the output of the organization is the service to the customer (patient in this case). Thus, while the employees are equipped here with training that enables them to tap into the environmental data, information and knowledge within the organization, the patients, and the society in general is updated with the changes occurring within the hospital. Metrics and measurements associated with the social dimensions come in to play.

■ Fourth quarter: This quarter is for the "Review" phase of the transformation. Therefore, there is heavy focus on measurements based on the earlier defined metrics. These include the Green KPIs—such as CO2E per computer/laptop/mobile, CO2E per Staff member or per patient, KPIs associated with recycling of computers. The KPIs can also be fine tuned for ongoing and continuous improvement in the future. Review phase can include Green IT audit to ascertain the maturity of the organization. Reduction in complexity of processes, improvement of quality of service and compliance with legislative requirements are included in the criteria for success.

■ Fifth quarter: If the Review phase indicates success in terms of GET, then the organization like GoodMead needs to immediately focus on providing the transformation support to its partners. These are the pharmaceuticals, laboratories, equipment suppliers and, of course, various patient-related bodies such as medical insurance providers.

■ Sixth quarter: This is the quarter where feedback from the transformation will have a substantial effect on the next steps by the hospital. Formal external Green IT audits are conducted in this quarter and compliance with the regulatory requirements can be formalized. This quarter also starts an ongoing journey for environmental program management for the hospital that will work closely with the Green HR function in ensuring Green IT specific roles are maintained, and individuals working in those roles are motivated and trained.

Figure 12.7 shows the returns on the GET project for GoodMead hospital. While these returns are not the core drivers for the ERBS, they are still important to prove two key points: (a) the GET is closely tied with the profits and (b) GET will lead to increase in the overall performance.

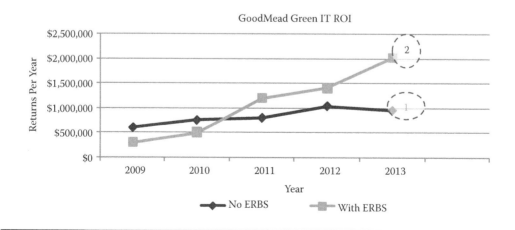

Figure 12.7   GET cost-benefit (ROI) analysis.

Graph 1 in Figure 12.7 shows the growth of the organization and its returns over 4 years with the business as usual. With the investment in the ERBS, the initial expense is higher and therefore the net returns for the first year are lower—this is visible in Graph 2 in Figure 12.7. However, over the period of next 3 years, the overall efficiencies and effectiveness resulting from ERBS also produce returns on the original investment to "go green."

Social Dimension in Hospital GET

Changes to the social dimension of the hospital is particularly brought about during the third quarter of the transformation. These changes include the following:

- Creation and delivery of training programs for staff at all levels: These training programs range from a 2-hour seminar on what Green IT means through to the detailed 3–5 days worth of training (spread over 3–5 weeks to ensure minimal disruptions to the normal working of the hospital).
- Review of attitude toward Green IT through quick surveys and feedback: These surveys can be run online within the hospital's systems ensuring immediate collation and analysis of the results. Surveys are required before and after the transformation—in this case in the first and after the fourth quarter.
- Use of IT systems support to reduce the routine pressures on doctors beyond the needs of their own specialist or generalist skills. This would be the result of Green BPM, but is also requires training for the doctors to enable them to use the new green processes.
- Implementation of metrics to provide real-time feedback to users on their daily carbon footprint: A CEMS implementation is inevitable in GoodMead; and such a CEMS will provide the necessary means of capturing and using carbon data on a regular basis.
- Creation of telework program for support functions: Some admin. and support functions in the hospital can benefit by telework. For example, scheduling of rosters, billing of patients and some HR functions can be partially carried out by support staff through Telework. This will create opportunities to reduce people and equipment movement, and also reduce carbon emissions.
- Telehealth: It does more than provide assistance of patients in need of medical support but who are not in physical proximity of a medical officer. A physician or a health-care specialist using telehealth also, directly and indirectly, contributes to reduction in the carbon of that process; improve health support in remote regions; education, research, and administration in the field of medicine can be improved through telemedicine without increasing the carbon footprint.
- Development of a Green HR function that includes training, reward, and growth structure, particularly for admin and support staff, in terms of Green IT.

Technology Changes in Hospital

Technology changes in the hospital as the green enterprise transition program gets underway relates to the user devices, data center, equipments, and wastages. Following are the technical changes during GET:

- Replacement of servers to the low-carbon emitting servers in the data center.
- Gradual replacement of devices to low-carbon devices.

- Changes to the current backup, including off-site backups of data on the data servers.
- Upgrade of IT systems to automate processes.
- Upgrade to the EPR by implementing a strategy to move it on the Cloud. EPR can enhance medical record documentation and optimize the consulting process of the doctor with the patient. Despite the risks associated with this strategy—particularly from privacy viewpoint—the approach of using the Cloud for EPR is likely to provide significant carbon reductions.
- Paper-less medical reports to reduce not only the paper wastage, but also time and effort in maintaining the manual records is saved.
- Collaboration with partners—such as sending of prescriptions electronically, or sourcing of medical drugs using web services.
- Green BPM for processes, including ordering and retrieving laboratory tests, prescription writing, consultation or referral notes, and billing.
- CEMS will be involved in recording carbon data that corresponds to various clinical activities. For example, consultation with a patient can be recorded in terms of time, types of examinations, reviews, progress notes, prescriptions, and follow-up consultations. Pathological tests and the delivery of results to the physician's computer will also be calculated for its carbon contents.
- CEMS will be measuring and monitoring the hospital processes surrounding staff rostering. While the actual rostering process is currently a combination of the HR system and some whiteboard manual process, CEMS will be configured to measure the "slack" in the rostering process. The principles of "Lean" business can be applied here to reduce the slack and tighten the process. Corresponding reduction in carbon can also be calculated based on reduced rostering overheads, reduced or elimination of double booking of staff, and so on.
- User devices changes includes end-user devices such as PCs in the consulting rooms, examination rooms, nursing workstations, and administrative hardware.
- Communications and network equipments. Network infrastructure includes virtual private network (VPN) for high-speed collaboration with other hospitals, service providers, and paterning organizations. Local area network (LAN) supports local communication within the GoodMead precinct.
- Non-IT equipments and their lifecycle has to be subject to the Green P-O-D. These equipments, such as are used in operating theatres or X-rays or in the pathological tests may not come directly under IT domain, but are still significant contributors to carbon emissions.
- Electronic wastage—policies and procedures. These have to discussed, updated and brought in practice through training of staff.

Applying Mobile Technologies in GET

The use of mobile technology in the health-care services can provide substantial process benefits that also translate to carbon advantages. These various mobile advantages to Green IT were discussed earlier in this book. A large number of hospital staff, such as the physicians, nurses, and administrative staff are using mobile laptops, blackberries, and iPhones to connect for both work and social networking. Following are the specific advantages that mobile technologies offer to the major users in GoodMead hospital from a carbon reduction viewpoint:

Doctors

Mobile technology can reduce carbon throughout the physician's work and social processes. For example, handheld tools dedicated to a physician's routine (e.g., TouchWorks from Allscripts Healthcare Solutions) can provide instantaneous data and information to the doctor. This can not only improve health-care services to patients and eliminate geographical distances but also reduce carbon content of the service.

GoodMead is providing dedicated health-care mobile tools and supporting technologies to all doctors that will enable them to serve the patients most efficiently, engage in conversations and conferences through their devices, and have fast access to patients' data. The actions taken by the physician are also documented through the device, enabling easy tracking of actions when a staff member hands over the care of a patient to another member.

Nurses

The use of mobile technology is also helps the nursing staff to coordinate with the doctors and the patients on a regular basis. GoodMead finds that the use of handheld devices by nurses is improving the consulting/advisory roles that nurses play (especially in a postoperative situation). Furthermore, mobile devices also improve the vital record keeping of patients with high efficiency and no physical paper. Checking the availability of doctors, quick consultations with doctors, handing over during the shifts and personal HR data access—all of these processes are improved for nurses through the use of mobility in the hospital which, in turn, has reduced carbon footprint.

Patients

GoodMead as a large, public sector health-care provider needed to provide excellence in service without the carbon overheads. Use of mobile technology has given greater flexibility for the patients without being physically go to the hospital for check up. Starting right with the use of the mobile phone, patients are now able to connect using various PDAs and mobile laptops. This has reduced patient movement, patient queuing and has provided location-independent advise to patients where they needed it most. Additional mobile gadgets that monitor patient data remotely, provides it to the hospital and also raises relevant alerts has optimized the processes and reduced their carbon contents.

Suppliers (e.g., Pharmacies)

Mobile technology improves receiving and ordering processes between hospital and its drug supplier. In addition, it also provides better management and storage system. GoodMead has proceeded with Mobile Solutions, a handheld device from Cardinal Health, which has scanning facilities based on a pocket PC. This device enables GoodMead's staff to work directly with hospital inventory, resulting in optimized inventory for the medical drugs and also medical equipments in use.

Lessons Learned in Implementing Green IT Strategies

Following are the lessons learned as a result of the GET initiative for the hospital. These lessons indicate the significant role of Green ICT in the hospital domain.

- Strategic reduction in carbon will require significant changes in the social, process, and also technical dimensions of the business. These changes are across the board and not restricted to a single department or process.
- Service organizations are particularly influenced by customer expectations. In the case of GoodMead, the patients and the society in general was more keen to see the hospital become a green hospital, as compared with the internal staff and administrators.
- Telework and telehealth are likely to play a significant role in not only improving the business processes of the hospital, but also its carbon emissions record.
- Operational carbon reduction is more effective when processes are to be changed as compared with the changes to the procurement and disposal cycle.
- Training and education play a significant role in carbon reduction in a hospital—and similar service organizations—as they bring about a change in attitude and approach to Green IT restructuring to Green HR is also a significant boost to the carbon reduction effort from a social angle.
- Changes to IT systems that support business and technical processes should be made with the backdrop of environmental intelligence. Simple carbon data mining will not provide strategic value of directions for a transforming organization.
- Ongoing monitoring of risks associated with GET should be planned for enacted. These risks are not restricted to only the main dimension for transformation but can emerge from any of the four dimensions.

Chapter 13

Case Study in Applying Green IT Strategies to the Packaging Industry

Key Points

- Presents how Green IT can be applied to a product-type company in the manufacturing sector
- Outlines a hypothetical organization, AuPack, involved in manufacturing packaging products for various types of clients
- Discusses the importance of ISO 14001 application in the manufacturing sector
- Stresses the importance of recycling and take-back programs by product developers in reducing the overall carbon footprint (and how green integrated supply chain systems can help achieve that)

AuPack Scenario

AuPack is a hypothetical organization in the business of manufacturing packages and containers that, in turn, are used by other manufacturers of goods and products. Medium in size in the context of the developing nation from where it operates, AuPack has established itself over the last decade as a reliable, honest organization. AuPack has around 10,000 workers (which classifies it as a medium-sized company in the region where it operates) and a forward looking corporate board led by a recently appointed young CEO. AuPack is keen to move forward in the area of Green IT. The carbon emissions from its production lines are on the rise, and also the electronic and other wastages. The wastages, in particular, are not just restricted to the organization but are occurring at an alarmingly high rate with the end-users of the contents of the packages. The local regulatory authorities are also showing interest in AuPack's carbon footprint.

The products of AuPack include variety of packages that are made up of materials such as cardboard, foam, plastic, choir, and rubber. These packages or containers are sold to other manufacturers who use them to wrap, store, and distribute their own products, including food (raw, finished, liquids), medical drugs, equipments, and electronic goods (such as TV, computers, toys). The containers produced by AuPack, therefore, need to range from boxes, tubes, and bubble-wraps through to tin cans and jars—to name but a few. Customization of these packaging products for specific customers is a regular occurrence.

Manufacturing of the packages requires materials to be sourced, planning of the production process, inventory of produced packages, and a customer management system. These are business processes that are a combination of manual, paper-based, and electronic (local, spreadsheet based, and system supported) processes.

A recent internal audit revealed that the organization has around 350 desktop machines, close to 100 laptops, and two large data servers in a small, backend data center. Most PCs have been in use for 5 or more years, have cathode ray tube (CRT) monitors, and are used by accountants, production shift managers, and administrators. Connectivity for most machines is provided through internal LANs and WANs and externally using a combination of virtual private network (VPN) (especially with dedicated corporate clients) and the Internet. The hardware of the organization is used to run variety of applications including AuPack's assets and inventory management, customer service, financial management, procurement, and HR/Payroll. Data corresponding to these applications is stored in the underlying data warehouse of AuPack on the two servers. A significant part of the production and inventory data is collected from the shop floor automatically and updated in the data warehouse.

Following are the current observations of the CEO together with the internal auditor in terms of AuPack's situation from environmental sustainability viewpoint:

- Raw materials for packaging are available in abundance. In fact there is excessive availability of raw materials particularly from the regions where AuPack is located.
- Workers are dedicated to the company. However, most workers have had very basic education, and in some cases no education at all. While expert in particular production process, these workers had no current interest in Green IT or carbon reduction.
- Wide customer base from both developed and developing region with the business from the developing regions on the rise.
- Network of transporters who partner with AuPack to bring in raw materials as well as deliver blank, ready-to-go container packages, typically to the corporate customers.
- Continuously changing needs of customers—as their products are changing too. Therefore, there is hardly ever a mass production of packages and most production runs are customized and the production and planning departments are continuously on their toes. This requires substantial computing systems support—especially in the package design office and the shop floor.
- Other departments of AuPack, that are under the direct influence of these changing requirements are sales (as the orders keep changing regularly), financial (as it is a challenge to ascertain the exact cost and, therefore, the way in which the product should be priced), customer service (in terms of current management of expectation and future handling of issues arising from nonstandard packaging) and, eventually, legal department (as the packaging products are sold worldwide).

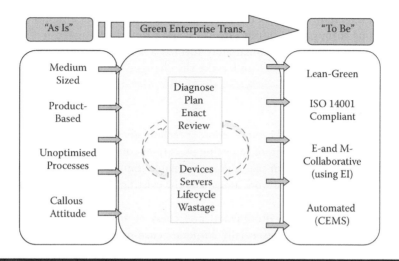

Figure 13.1 GET for AuPack packaging.

Figure 13.1 summarizes the overall approach to Green enterprise transformation (GET) of AuPack. The "as is" state is ascertained through an initial investigation based on an early, approximate Green IT audit. Such an audit, as discussed in Chapter 10, would not be very precise as the organization itself is not matured enough to reveal exact data in terms of its emissions. This investigation, based on the personal initiative of the chief executive officer (CEO), indicated to the board for an urgent need for a Green IT strategy and subsequent action. The carbon legislations in the region are becoming stringent, and even more importantly, in the overseas geographical regions where AuPack's business is growing (such as the EU countries). The "to be" or desired state, according to the initial vision statement of the CEO, is for AuPack to be a lean-green organization. This term indicates that the organization is interested in *both* cost and carbon issues and not one over the other (this philosophy of a Green IT strategy was discussed in Chapter 2, Figure 2.1). Apart from reducing its carbon footprint and becoming a lean organization, AuPack is also interested in making use of and complying with the ISO 14001 standard. This, the CEO believes, will also help AuPack promote itself in the EU region where it is likely to do greater amount of business. The center part of Figure 13.1 shows, in a summary, how AuPack will undertake the GET. The diagnose, plan, enact, and review phases of the GET process, discussed in Chapter 9 will be applied to the four areas of an organization that need to change—the end-user devices, the data servers in the data center, the supply chain lifecycle and the way in which electronic wastage is handled.

AuPack's Green IT Strategies

As a result of the initial audit, the CEO has appointed a new CGO—the chief green officer. This lady, with an IT background, currently leads the computer-aided design (CAD) department of AuPack. This department has been heavily involved in the use of computers to create new packaging design based on customer requirements. As a departmental head with more than 5 years of leadership experience, she had sufficient independence from the current CIO but, at the same time, is aware of the functioning of the organization and has IT background. The CGO has gone through the initial Green IT audit report, discussed it with the auditors and also with the CEO and has immediately formed a working group. This working group will become the GET team that will undertake the change. The approach taken by the CGO is summarized in Figure 13.2. As shown in that figure, the strategic approach by the CGO is as follows:

■ Immediate focus on use and capitalization of technologies with the creation of a Green IT portal. Use of the portal itself for reporting on carbon compliance by the organization.
■ Launching of a GET program that is going to enable compliance with ISO 14001 standard; however, this program has to work along side the existing ISO 9001 compliance and certification program of AuPack.
■ Understand the growing environmental awareness of all its customers—with the input derived from the customers (especially corporate customers) through the Green IT portal itself.
■ Extend the current process optimization initiative to make it a formal Lean process implementation that will also be measured and reporting for corresponding green-ness.
■ Develop a green market that will be specifically based on the lean-green processes (e.g., optimized package designs, use of biodegradable materials in packaging and take back of discarded/consumed packaging material through a reverse supply chain).
■ Form a consortium of like minded businesses in the region and provide leadership through initial experience of GET.
■ Influence and be influenced by customers and suppliers in terms of carbon compliance.

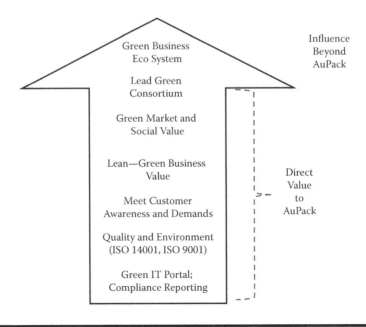

Figure 13.2 AuPack strategic approach.

SWOT of AuPack in Green Context

Figure 13.3 indicates the current strengths, weaknesses, opportunities, and threats relating to AuPack. This SWOT analysis, however, is with a particular focus on Green IT. The strategic approach, undertaken by the CGO, indicates that this analysis will eventually be part of the overall strategic approach of the business itself. Currently, however, this SWOT analysis shows AuPack's Green IT challenges and capabilities.

Green IT Strengths

- The incoming CEO realizes that for AuPack to survive and prosper in the carbon economy there is a need to create and implement a comprehensive Green IT strategy. This visionary leadership in itself is a strength of the organization and is recognized by the CGO who is able to work closely with the CEO.
- AuPack is progressing well financially with its business and its profit margins are on the rise. This growth is a positive opportunity for its Green IT initiatives, as there is a budget for the GET.
- Material-savvy region, with more than a decade of experience in packaging/container production. The processes associated with procurement of raw materials are manual, but the processes are working well. Careful automation will create opportunities for optimization and, thereby, reduce both carbon and costs.
- Strong distribution network for the packages and containers produced by AuPack. This distribution network includes strong partnership with local and overseas transporters. Some

Strength	Weakness
1. Visionary leadership through the new CEO and corresponding CGO	1. Aging infrastructure—especially technical assets such as computers (desk tops and servers)
2. Growing business with sufficient funds—enabling easier green IT initiative	2. Workforce only experienced in package production—not necessarily IT literate
3. Material-savvy region, with more than a decade of experience in packing/container production	3. Non-serious attitude of most workers toward carbon footprint
4. Strong distribution network—particularly overseas customers	4. Noticeable wastages in packaging products and IT
Opportunities	**Threats**
1. Leadership in packaging materials and designs	1. Attitude of majority of staff
2. Potential to leap-frog in terms of computing technologies by directly using the latest, low carbon emitting machines and servers	2. Differences in compliance requirements of the developing region versus the developed regions where customers are located
3. Acceptance of ideas by partners—customers and suppliers—thereby creating leadership in the Green IT/carbon compliance space	3. Inexperience in undertaking GET in the region

Figure 13.3 SWOT analysis of AuPack.

overseas corporate customers are directly connected to the integrated supply chain system of the organization.

Green IT Weaknesses

- The technical infrastructure of the organization is aging. Almost all desktop computers are 5 or more years old, and the laptop computers are also more than 3 years in use. In the context of Green IT, this implies computing hardware that has not had the benefits of new, low carbon emitting designs.
- The software systems for AuPack has proliferated as there was little control over the purchase and installation of computers. Provided smaller departments had their budgets, they were allowed to procure and install computers. Thus each department had not only a collection of desktop computers but also the overheads of networking them.
- The workforce of the organization is highly experienced in production of various types of packages and containers. However, many of the production processes are manual—making use of whiteboards, paper, and the supporting IT systems. The shift managers are the only people from the shop floor who make use of the IT systems for production planning. This leaves almost the entire shop floor workers without any IT literacy.
- Most workers of AuPack are not serious about environmental issues. This is not their personal weakness, as the socioeconomic background from where they come had little opportunity to consider the environment. However, this nonserious attitude of most workers toward carbon footprint is a concern and a weakness of the organization that will have to be rectified.
- Noticeable wastage in packaging products and IT—this wastage is derived from the non-optimized production processes that are unable to capitalize on the production planning and execution systems of the organization. There is also no plan or corresponding system to take back the used packaging materials and recycle them within AuPack. Use of IT—such as desktop machines, printers, and mobile gadgets—is also left to the individual users and there is no planned approach to reducing their emissions right now.

Green IT Opportunities

- Leadership of AuPack in the design and development of packaging products provides it with excellent opportunity to understand, improve, and optimize its designs, including the use of biodegradable materials and recycling of used packaging products.
- Potential to leap frog in terms of computing technologies by directly using the latest, low carbon emitting machines and servers.
- Acceptance of ideas by partners—customers and suppliers—thereby creating leadership in the Green IT/carbon compliance space.

Green IT Threats

- Attitude of majority of staff is not serious about Green IT. This was ascertained during the spot-surveys of some staff sampled from the various departments of the organization.

■ Differences in compliance requirements of the developing region versus the developed regions where customers are located. Thus, even if AuPack compliance with the local government requirements in terms of carbon emissions, the carbon content in producing the packaging product will be much higher than acceptable in the EU region where the company is experiencing growth.

■ Inexperience in undertaking GET in the region—there is hardly a known organization in the developing region where AuPack is located, that has undertaken successful GET. Therefore, there are risks associated with this transformation.

Diagnosis in AuPack

The initial investigation of AuPack in terms of its green credentials, and the SWOT analysis provides impetus to carry out the full GET. The SWOT analysis, as discussed in the previous section, can be a part of the diagnosis phase as well—especially if the organization is proceeding with GET irrespective of the outcome of SWOT analysis. Formal diagnosis of AuPack will lead to a detailed understanding and formalization of the drivers and the ensuing dimensions of GET.

Earlier, in Chapter 2 (see Figure 2.6), the survey participants were quizzed on their views as to what drives a GET. Forty-four percent had "agreed" and close to 27% "strongly agreed" that the need to comply with government rules and regulation is a significant driver in an organization undertaking environmental control measures. When asked about the reduction in operational costs as a driver for Green IT initiative, 31% of the participants agreed and close to 11% strongly agreed to that reduction in operational costs as a major driver for carbon reduction. In case of AuPack, the significant drivers of GET, as shown in Figure 13.4, are costs, need to comply with

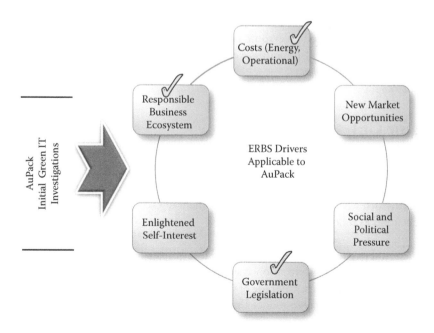

Figure 13.4 AuPack's drivers for environmental responsibility.

government legislations and an opportunity to lead through a green business ecosystem. These drivers of GET for AuPack are further discussed as follows:

■ The CEO of AuPack realizes that the reduction in costs and optimization of processes will be an ideal driver for the Green IT initiative of the organization. Carbon reduction for its own sake may not provide sufficient motivation for the organization. Thus, a good sustainable approach for AuPack will include optimization of processes, consolidation of its information technology hardware and software and thereby reduce its costs and carbon together. Thus, cost reduction is an excellent driver for Green IT in AuPack. Examples of cost reduction include reduction in the use of raw materials and equipment, recycling of equipment and optimization of storage and inventory as a result of the green initiative.

■ Regional environmental legislation requires AuPack to monitor and report its overall carbon emissions. These are the operational emissions from the package production process (Scope 1 and 2), supporting IT systems and infrastructure (Scope 2) and the distribution transport network (Scope 3). The regulatory requirements are being specified on a recently launched government portal and AuPack plans to monitor, measure and report directly on that government portal.

■ AuPack has many partner organizations—both locally in the geographical region of the developing country where it operates and overseas, where its customer base is growing rapidly. The visionary leadership of AuPack is keen to capitalize on these myriad associations with its collaborating organizations and influence them in terms of their carbon footprint. Although AuPack is a medium-sized organization in the context of the region where it operates, it has opportunity to influence the business ecosystem in which it exists, especially in the context of Green IT and processes. This potential leadership position of a possible Green Consortium is a major driver for AuPack's GET. With potential Green IT portal-based approach within AuPack, there is significant opportunity for AuPack to influence its business ecosystem through electronic collaborations on the web—driven by web services and service-oriented architecture (SOA) (as was discussed in Chapter 6). Such electronic collaborations can reduce overall carbon within a group of companies and also facilitate electronic sharing of information and knowledge on the Green IT initiatives.

Planning for GET

Figure 13.5 shows three of the many major focus areas of work when the GET is undertaken. These are the customers and business partners, the IT systems and the Regulatory areas of AuPack that are the first ones to be affected by GET. These areas of work indicate the way in which the organization is divided when the planning and enactment of GET takes place. These areas of GET work are understood as follows:

■ Customers and partners. Changes to these relationships will be based on changes to the way improving the customer information systems to get ongoing sales from customers.
■ IT systems and applications. Upgrade of CAD/CAM computers to high powered computers that are networked in a way to reduce the interactions required through the various systems and applications.
■ A new Carbon Emission Management Software (CEMS) together with an optimized manufacturing system that would support new and existing business.

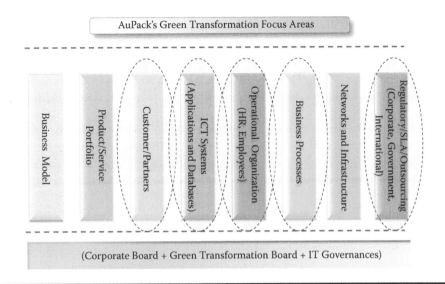

Figure 13.5 AuPack's focus areas for GET.

■ Changes to Service Level Agreements (SLAs) with partners as the organization transitions as also changes to governance structures with greater focus on environment (green governance).

■ External and internal business processes supporting the manufacturing as well as sales/ distribution of the packaging products will be optimized. For example, optimization of the packaging lifecycle from quote to production to distribution, involving accounting and production departments, distributors, and customers.

■ Operational organization and green HR resulting from changes to the people structure as a result of green initiative.

Understanding AuPack's current situation in terms of its environmental performance leads to the development of the GET plan. Creation of such a plan was discussed in detail in Chapter 9. Planning for transformation has to also consider the four dimensions along which such transformation can occur. Usually, one dimension out of the four can lead the transformation process—however, all four dimensions are involved in the overall transformation. These are discussed next.

Economic Dimension in AuPack

The economic dimension for GET in case of AuPack revolves around reduction in cost and increase in profit margins. This action involves creating value for customers through reduced carbon footprint in the packaging product being provided to them. The availability of funds to undertake the transformation is a strength of the organization. However, it also includes responsibility on part of the CGO to ensure there is return on this investment in the next 2–3 years. Direct and positive involvement and interest from the CEO is extremely helpful as the organization moves along this economic dimension. As a result of the green transformation, the CGO anticipates growth and expansion of the packaging product business—especially in the EU region.

Technical Dimension in AuPack

Current client information is stored in a simple CRM package. Underlying the organization's web site is a database with connectivity to internal systems. Current carbon related data, that was used in the initial investigation is in an Excel spreadsheet. There is no access to this and such information that resides on the company's servers to most employees—typically staff working on the shop floor.

AuPack investigated and has decided to procure a CEMS from Microsoft business solutions called *Environmental Sustainability Dashboard*. This CEMS product will be integrated with AuPack's existing ERP applications to enable tracking of energy consumption and carbon emissions. This CEMS will help AuPack map its decrease in carbon emissions with corresponding cost savings.

The shortlisted CEMS can be purchased "off the shelf." This CEMS will create opportunity for the staff at all levels to understand, in real time, the carbon emissions of AuPack. The dashboard provides information to all users on their desktop and laptop machines within the organization's firewalls.

In this technical dimension of GET are areas of work including Green SOA and web services. A Green SOA will ensure that the new CEMS is properly integrated with the existing applications. Figure 13.6 shows the positioning of CEMS in the overall IT architecture for the Green IT portal of AuPack. The collaborative business partners will be able to tap into the organization's systems and receive as well as provide feedback. Therefore, SOA will be applied during CEMS implementation.

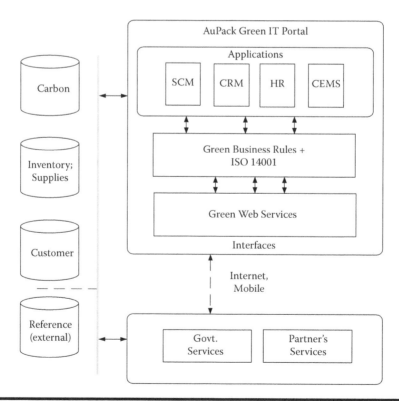

Figure 13.6　Proposed AuPack Green portal.

For example, interaction with the AuPack's web server will provide opportunities to offer and consume green services relating to government limits per type of product, partner's information on carbon emitted during distribution, and so on.

Process Dimension in AuPack

The process dimension of AuPack's GET deals with creation of process models that reflect both existing and new green processes. The modeling of the processes can be undertaken using the use cases and activity graphs, shown in Chapter 7. These process models, based on use cases and activity diagrams, can be created for various roles within and outside of AuPack.

The process dimension of GET has to consider collaborative customers, who will be interacting with AuPack electronically. The services provided to these corporate customers can be enhanced and optimized to not only add value through accuracy and timeliness but also reduce the overall carbon associated with the collaborative processes.

Social Dimension in AuPack

The social dimension of the GET is involved with the changing of the attitude of its staff and, also, the changing Green HR function. AuPack has to move toward creation of a social networking site. Awareness of the carbon issues and the way they will impact the future of not only the organization, but the country and the global business can bring about a change in attitude.

Green HR brings about changes to the organizational structure. This change starts with the appointment of the CGO and the subsequent formation of the green transition project team. In addition to the CGO, there is an external consultant with expertise in Green Enterprise Transformation (GET), two department level managers fully dedicated to environmental management and six supervisory level staff to support them. These staff members are involved in diagnosis, planning, enactment, and review phases. Green IT auditor is an additional support role which is also involved in creation, validation, and use Green IT metrics and measurement.

Staff will also need training in the use of CEMS to use its data. Smart meters will be fitted to most equipment involved in the production line to calculate directly the emissions from those production lines.

The social dimension of GET also takes responsibility for management of the changes to the designations and responsibilities of line managers, legal implications arising from the changes, possibilities of telework, and related privacy issues.

Enactment of GET for AuPack

Figure 13.7 highlights the major actions during the enactment phase of GET for AuPack. Following are the specific highlights of the enactment:

- CEMS—Implement and integrate with the existing systems.
- Comply and maintain ISO 14001—This is achieved by following the steps outline in the environmental management standard, and verifying the effectiveness of the changes through measurements. This is the application of discussion on this standard from Chapter 8.

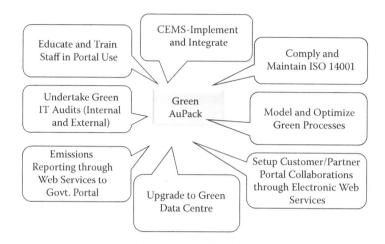

Figure 13.7   AuPack GET enactment.

- Model and optimize green processes—Using the principles outlined in Green BPM in Chapter 5. Thus, processes associated with procurement, operation and disposal of all equipments (IT and non-IT), materials, and the ready-to-go packaging are included in this optimization of green processes (Green P-O-D).
- Setup customer/partner portal collaborations through electronic web services—This would use the web services based on Green SOA discussed in Chapter 6. The integration with partner's systems will imply immediate reduction in the supply chain carbon. Furthermore, AuPack is also able to update its SLAs with its own customers and assure them, through the electronic collaborative portal, of the improvement in carbon emissions in producing its packages. Renegotiation so SLAs would also be implemented as policies within the electronic collaborative portal.
- Upgrade to green data center—The power usage of the data center over the power used only by the data servers was at 2.4. The aim, during enactment was to bring this down to below 2.0 in the first 6 months. This would imply use of power directly in the operations of the servers rather than its use in maintaining the associated building and infrastructure (e.g., air conditioning).
- Emissions reporting through web services to government portal—This part of the enactment is aimed at fully automating the reporting function of AuPack. The purpose of such integrated and automated reporting is to eliminate the in between step of collating the emission results and presenting them to the governing body. Instead, the CEMS collects the data and submits it as a web service on a daily, weekly, monthly, quarterly, and yearly basis.
- Undertake Green IT audits (internal and external)—These informal and formal audits will ensure that the collection, collating and reporting of carbon data is as per regulatory guidelines. Discussions from Chapter 10 are applied in this part of the enactment. Educate and train staff in portal use—this would require AuPack's staff to be scheduled for training in the use of the CEMS and the way in which it interfaces with other design and production systems. This training can include a short 1 hour briefing to the shop floor staff, through to detailed training to the IT systems and support staff over 2–3 days. Awareness of carbon emissions and the positive impact of their reduction is achieved through ongoing feedback to the staff, especially on shop floor, in terms of a real-time carbon update through a

computer monitor, as well as the traditional whiteboard that has also been used on the shop floor. Eventually, the value of GET can be ascertained through a survey and interviews, following the same methodology that was used at the start of the project in ascertaining the green readiness of AuPack.

Review of GET for AuPack

The review phase deals with verifying and validating the stated outcomes of GET for AuPack. Green IT audits, discussed in Chapter 10, have already started during enactment. In review, they are formalized and their findings are reported. Furthermore, the outcomes need to be measured and studied not only for the new business, but also for the new environment in which the business is now operating. AuPack's Green IT outcomes are slightly different to the stated goals. This was expected as the business itself was changing and growing during the period of GET. Evaluation of the outcomes include reviewing in accuracy of CEMS, the way in which it collects and reports data and undertaking sample tests to run through the CEMS. Furthermore, green process models are subjected to walkthroughs and inspections to ascertain their accuracy and value in GET. Potential changes to organizational structures and business models are internally audited to ensure they do not adversely affect the business.

These measurements are incorporated in the feedback by the Green Transformation Champion (GTC) to the boards responsible for the green transformation as also to the business stakeholders. The review process not only ascertains the achievements of the GET but also opens up doors to further and potential improvements with collaborating business partners. Hence, the review process should make provisions for these enhancements with business partners by revisitng the SLAs. Issues encountered during GET can be shared with the collaborating partners.

Lessons Learned in GET for AuPack

- AuPack as a product organization with supporting IT systems had to focus on the end-user and its processes.
- GET is a comprehensive business transformation process that includes people, processes, technologies, and return on investment (ROI) calculations.
- Attitude change for people working on production lines is not achieved only through training; a manual process such as one using whiteboards on the shop floor was as valuable as the implementation of CEMS.
- Data center upgrade required coordination with the production processes that are heavily dependent on the production applications.
- It is difficult to measure the overall carbon reduction by optimizing the design of a package, since the carbon footprint of a package is made up of its usage and eventual disposal.
- Compliance with ISO 14001 is not difficult to implement in a production shop, but maintaining that compliance proved to be more challenging.

Chapter 14

Case Study in Applying Green IT Strategies and Applications to the Telecom Sector

Key Points

- Describes the Green IT challenges of an infrastructure-type company—ZeeTel—operating in the telecommunications domain
- TCCO—total carbon cost of ownership—is an important measure especially in an infrastructure type organization where the carbon consciousness in architecture and design has a long-term effect on emissions
- Green enterprise transformation of infrastructure organizations focuses on buildings, data centers, equipment lifecycle and, in case of telecom, its transmission networks
- Starts the Green enterprise transformation approach to ZeeTel based on a report by the Focus Group on ICTs and climate change of the international telecommunication union (ITU)
- Infrastructure companies have an opportunity to influence large number of corporate customers—as compared with end-users—resulting in greater impact of its carbon reduction initiatives

ZeeTel Telecom Scenario

ZeeTel is a hypothetical, large telecom company operating in the African region. ZeeTel is responsible for the core telecom infrastructure in the region, in addition to offering some land-based and mobile services. Main focus of ZeeTel's business has been the creation of the telecom platform that provides the backbone for communications infrastructure in that geographical region. Thus,

ZeeTel's customers are mostly corporate customers that use ZeeTel's telecom platform to vend their contents (e.g., sports or entertainment providers) or are direct, large-scale users of ZeeTel's services (e.g., banks or airlines). There are very few direct end users of ZeeTel—except, of course, its employees who use the IT systems to provide business services. Occasionally, some employee households are also involved as small time end-users.

Although owned by the government, ZeeTel's board is able to control its own directions and also has its own responsibility. The corporate board of ZeeTel comprises its business leadership (CxO level), representatives from the trade unions belonging to the large workforce and government representatives.

The core business of ZeeTel (i.e., creation of high-end communications infrastructure) involves technology innovation and adaptations that result in large-scale construction and implementation of physical and wireless communications networks. There is hardly any competition to ZeeTel as the creation of these communication network infrastructure is highly regulated. Besides that, ZeeTel is owned by the government under financial as well as legal agreements. However, with the operational independence of the organization, and the receipt of a government directive on climate change, ZeeTel is now seriously considering extending, embellishing, and putting into practice its environmental plans. Such planning was undertaken in a less formal way an year ago, mainly in response to the growing demands for environmental consciousness from its corporate customers. Increasing awareness of the environment in the region implies that these corporate customers, including contents and service providers, have started demanding carbon reduction particularly in the networks that are used by them to provide their own contents and services. This is particularly so where these corporate have their own global businesses wherein their own customers are demanding environmental friendliness in the end products. Thus, from an informal plan, the environmental context has now become an integral part of a formal business strategy across ZeeTel. This, in turn, is resulting into carbon consciousness as a mandatory element in every decision-making process within ZeeTel.

An important aspect of this formal approach to the green telco initiative, however, is to ensure it is not carried out by reducing business volume and service. The green enterprise transition directive from ZeeTel's CEO includes, specifically, the need to synergize between the carbon and cost efficiencies. This synergy between environmental and business benefits is expected to be achieved by optimizing the business processes of ZeeTel with the help of information technologies and systems. This, for example, can include replacement of current legacy systems and hardware by latest low-power emitting technologies; IT systems that will enable improved measurement and control of carbon; and upgrading of the existing communications networks with Next Generation Network or Gigabit Passive Optical Network (GPON) that will be environmentally efficient.

An important motivating factor in ZeeTel's board decision to control and reduce its carbon footprint is that it is a government owned organization that needs to showcase the government's carbon reduction commitment. In addition, being a singular, large, infrastrcutrue organization, ZeeTel has the opportunity to impact many comparatively smaller organizations that have to use its platform and infrastructure services. The impact of changes to communication networks and facilities in the region is also likely to affect social aspects such as telecommuting and virtual group formations. Such an impact opens up possibilities of reduced work travel across the metropolitan cities where ZeeTel's platform is heavily used and, eventually, large-scale attitude, and behavioral change.

Figure 14.1 summarizes the overall approach to GET undertaken by ZeeTel. The Green enterprise transformation will bring together compliance with environmental regulations through technology updates as well as process upgrades. The end result is not only carbon reduction but also

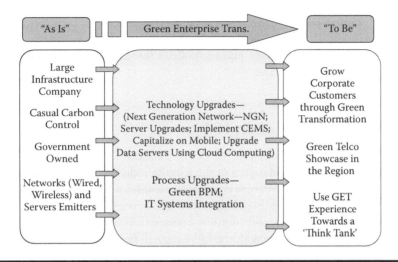

Figure 14.1   GET for "ZeeTel" telecommunications company.

business benefits resulting in an overall green business model. Following are specific highlights of business and technology advantages of the GET approach of ZeeTel.

■ Growth in business, particularly with corporate customers, due to carbon reduction and corresponding boost in the image of ZeeTel.

■ Imminent upgrades of hardware, software, and networks, but now closely aligned with environmental performance.

■ Ability to comply with policies, legislative, and regulatory frameworks that are put together by the government as well as telecom's summit bodies and industrial consortiums.

■ Ability to handle carbon taxes, particularly as a government organization. These carbon taxes are envisaged to be applicable directly to large, infrastructure organizations such as ZeeTel.

■ Preplanning on how to deal with corporate customers in terms of financial models that will enable sharing of carbon taxes between them and ZeeTel.

■ Ability to ensure there are no carbon penalties and fines. These are applicable to ZeeTel irrespective of its almost government status. Penalities and fines are not only costly exercise, but also create a loss of face for the organization and its leadership position. ZeeTel is required to formally and control its carbon emissions.

■ Capitalizing on incentives. Properly and accurately measured carbon emissions and their subsequent reduction may also create opportunities for government incentives in terms of financial rewards as well as support for growth—enabling the organization to setup further carbon efficient communications infrastructure in and beyond the region.

■ Make good use of mobile technologies and services which, while requiring additional power to operate, also create opportunities to significantly reduce carbon.

■ Ability to enhance network efficiency and effectiveness of the communications equipments that will result in overall reduction in TCCO—rather than only operational carbon.

■ Application of quantifiable and measurable values (green metrics) that indicate strategic carbon advantage over entire lifecycle and not just the operational aspect of the equipment.

- Create and promote policies to help the corporate customers with their own Green IT strategies, such as recycling of handsets.
- Ability to dynamically create and manage policies through sophisticated CEMS—carbon emissions management software.

Strategic Approach to Green ICT

The Green IT Strategic approach of ZeeTel has to consider the specific issues related to an infrastructure-type organization belonging to the telecom industry. As compared with a product or service type company, an infrastructure business like ZeeTel will have substantially large numbers of data servers, communication switches, and related networking equipments, large physical buildings spread across the region and multiple communications towers. At IT systems level, ZeeTel has service-oriented interfaces with the IT systems of the energy vendors (e.g., the electricity vendors).

This setup is different to a service setup like the hospital or manufacturer of packaging, discussed in the previous two chapters. For example, in the previous two case studies, the end users are easy to identify, form part of a known user base, make a major contribution to the carbon emissions, but those emissions can be ascertained relatively easily. In case of ZeeTel, the end-user is not directly visible (except, as mentioned in the beginning, some staff who would be using the business and resource planning systems) and, also, not as significant a component in the overall carbon emissions of the organization. Instead, the major carbon emissions come from the power consumed by the overall infrastructure including communications network and data servers rather than individual user devices. Consider, for example, the hospital case study wherein the laptops used by a nurse or a doctor in a hospital is a direct, visible end-user device. This device, multiplied across the entire organization, is a major contributor to the carbon footprint of the hospital. Therefore, using device level power management systems as well as training the users can bring about reduction in carbon emissions. Power-smart add-ons to manage the operating systems of these devices will also enable improved measurement and control of carbon through these large number of end-user devices.

In case of ZeeTel, the carbon produced by the organization is primarily through its infrastructure platform and related services. These are large-scale communications services across the region consumed by corporate customers and content providers. Therefore, strategies for carbon measurement, reporting and control need to focus directly on these large-scale infrasructures such as communications towers, telecom switches, wired and wireless relaying equipments, associated routers, data servers and the many IT supporting hardware. These infrastructure IT assets are also used by corresponding software systems and applications. For example, the ZeeTel business is supported by customer relationship management (CRM), billing support systems (BSS) operational support systems (OSS), human resource (HR), and an upcoming carbon emissions management software (CEMS). These systems enable the business to operate but, at the same time, generate carbon that contributes to the overall carbon footprint of the organization. Siloed data in these applications, which requires continuous interaction amongst these data bases, is a source of major, wasteful carbon. Thus, major action in the green space has become mandatory for ZeeTel.

Figure 14.2 shows the key points of ZeeTel's Green IT strategies and the time frame over which they will take effect. The report on climate change by the focus group of ITU is a valuable input in these strategies. This report by the Focus Group on ICTs and Climate Change (FG ICT&CC), produced in 2009, outlines the gap and provides basis for the road map for Green IT

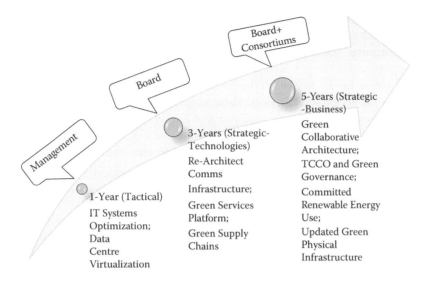

Figure 14.2   ZeeTel's Green IT strategies.

transformation in the telecom sector. These strategies, as highlighted in Figure 14.2, are divided into three time-based parts corresponding to the 1-, 3-, and 5-year strategies. The generic Green IT strategic approach was discussed in Chapter 2. Here, for ZeeTel, this approach is specifically considered in the context of an infrastructure company. With an infrastructure organization like ZeeTel, the strategies for Green IT are brought forward in time as compared with the generic suggested timelines. Thus, the strategies that are created, in a generic Green IT approach for 3 years, are actually hurried forward and brought to bear results within an year for the infrastructure organization. This is so because the end user, operational carbon that can be effectively reduced through tactical strategies is not as major a factor in the carbon footprint of an infrastructure company as the communication networks and data servers are. Similarly, the long-term 5-year strategies are brought closer in time to around 3 years.

Figure 14.2 shows that ZeeTel should move to optimize both its IT systems (such as the billing, operational support, customer relations, and HR) and its data center within an year. While this will be a challenging project, a large infrastructure company will have the resources to undertake those changes. Furthermore, as mentioned above, in case of such an infrastructure company, the end-user devices will not be as large and wide spread as in a product or service organization. Therefore, from a technology viewpoint, the focus should be on the data center and IT systems right at the outset. The slightly longer-term strategy of Green IT for the organization, in a 3-year period, will be rearchitecture and design of the communications infrastructure. While this communications infrastructure is of immense value in the GET for ZeeTel, the actual transformation of the network is likely to take 3–5 years. This network redesign will closely involve both business and technology expertise—as it will require an investment that goes beyond that only for a Green IT project. This rearchitecture of the fundamental communications platform will also change the business model, the supplier relationship and the way in which the service providers use ZeeTel's platforms. The GET of an infrastrcuture company such as ZeeTel will include substantial influence on all its customers and partners.

Changes will include implementation of TCCO metrics that will apply to data servers as well as the upcoming new generation network (NGN) across its operating life; full use of the

Green collaborative architecture of its systems—typically through a web services based portal with underlying data warehouse—, full implementation of Green governance that will include application of corporate governance (ITIL, in case of ZeeTel) with carbon consciousness and changes to the physical buildings housing data servers and communications equipments to reduce their carbon footprint. In case of ZeeTel, these will be a suite of buildings and physical infrastructure spread across the geographical region. These long-term Green IT strategies also incorporate dedicated use of renewable energy sources (in case of ZeeTel, this is envisaged to be solar energy, as the region where ZeeTel operates has ample sunshine and a separate government directive has already secured land for building solar panel farms together with transmission grids).

SWOT of ZeeTel—Environmental Context

Green IT strategies for ZeeTel are further refined based on the SWOT analysis of the company. This SWOT, however, is not entirely from the business viewpoint. Figure 14.3 shows a high-level SWOT analysis of ZeeTel's IT that is undertaken from a carbon perspective. This is briefly discussed next:

Strengths

■ Government owned and supported organization that is aware of the upcoming legislations in the carbon context. This also results in good working relationship with the government bureaucracy, further facilitating relatively quick decisions on Green enterprise transformation board formation and launching of the transformation project.

Figure 14.3   SWOT for ZeeTel telecom.

■ Excellent channel relations including corporate partners and government representatives. This relationship creates opportunities to help and support the collaborative partners in taking up transformation.

■ Influential, monopolistic organization with practically no competition in the communications infrastructure business. Therefore, the organization can focus directly on carbon reduction without worrying about loss of business to other competitors who may do so at the cost of carbon.

■ Growth forecast for ZeeTel implies an opportunity for steady revenue that frees the organization to focus on its Green IT effort. This growth in telecom users, however, also brings in the challenge of handling the corresponding growth in carbon. Green IT strategies that balance the business growth with reduced carbon will be required, together with Green IT metrics that prove it.

Weaknesses

■ Inflexible infrastructure as is expected in a large telecom in a developing region.

■ Large, inchoate IT systems that are based on past, legacy databases and applications. These IT systems are in siloes that do not "talk" with each other, requiring considerable effort at maintaining them.

■ Bureaucratic decision-making process, that is invariably a part of a government owned body; but such decision making creates challenges in terms of timings and follow up actions as the organization transitions.

■ Physically dispersed infrastructure, with buildings, communications towers, and supporting data servers, all physically spread across the geographical region, making coordination extremely challenging.

Opportunities

■ Combining business with green transformation will lead to show casing of the Green IT strategy created by the CGO that does not discount one goal over the other. This opportunity arises as the Green IT strategy includes increase in business due to upgrade to a NGN backbone together with metrics that show the reduction in carbon due to efficiency of the network.

■ Business shift to mobile platform resulting in reducing needs for physical wired connectivity and corresponding reduction in the required infrastructure.

■ Growing content and service providers who will need the increasing sophistication of the NGN platform. These contents and service providers are keen to expand their business both within the region and overseas—leading to opportunities for them, as well as for ZeeTel. However, ZeeTel has the added opportunity to influence these content and service providers to reduce their carbon contents as well.

Threats

■ Resistance to change (union disagreement) resulting from a large, strong, unionized workforce.

■ Long time for visible results of the GET. ZeeTel will need at least 3–5 years, and perhaps more, to be able to demonstrate the ROI on its Green initiative. While this is not unusual for large businesses, this is still a big challenge for ZeeTel, which is being watched closely by the government, customers, and unions.

▪ Total inexperience in GET in the region as this would be the first large project of its kind that will bring together the knowledge and expertise of Green It with that of telecommunications. External, overseas consulting help will be required to ameliorate this risk.

Motivators and Dimensions

Developing and influencing a responsible business ecosystem, together with reduction in cost of operations is emerging as a major motivator for ZeeTel to undertake GET. While other motivators, such as government legislation and social pressure, will also play a part in this project, the pure business motivation of cost reduction and business growth are playing an important role in this GET decision. ZeeTel, by upgrading its technological platforms, will not only grow its corporate customer base but also influence all its partners in its business ecosystem to be carbon compliant. Thus, this is a self-motivated pressure to undertake GET.

The technical nature of the challenge, particularly the communications networks, also indicates that the Green enterprise transformation will be best achieved by immediate focus on technologies. These technologies include the IT systems and hardware, as well as the communications networks. Thus, the infrastructure assets (discussed earlier in Chapter 3) are the ones that undergo green transformation in case of ZeeTel.

The company's corporate board has sanctioned the formation of the GET board. The current CTO (chief technology officer) has been appointed as the CGO for the transformation. This is an important nomination as the CTO is fully conversant with the communication networks and the data servers supporting the network. Knowledge of the inner workings of the technology platforms of the company is crucial as ZeeTel's transformation to a Green enterprise is closely associated with the technology upgrades. The CGO, together with select members of the Green enteprise transformation board, has extracted the existing, information Green IT strategy and has created a full programme to undertake transformation.

Discussion of the motivators and the dimensions of GET also leads to a discussion of the Green enterprise transformation roadmap. Such a high-level transformation plan is shown in Figure 14.4. The diagnose, plan, enact, and review are the four phases also established in business transformation and were discussed in Chapter 9. These transformation phases are interspersed with metrics that help in stating the goals (KPIs) as also measuring whether the stated goals have been achieved or not. Figure 14.4 also highlights the major areas of work in each of these phases. For example, during diagnosis, there is heavy emphasis on understanding the emissions of the network backbone; planning is based on the focus areas of ZeeTel together with negotiations with the trade unions from a sociocultural angle; enactment will include risk management throughout the upgrading of the NGN and IT systems; and review will ensure that the goals of customer growth as well as carbon reduction are achieved.

Diagnosing the "As Is" State

Formal diagnosis of ZeeTel's current carbon footprint and its carbon readiness is being conducted by the Green Enterprise Transformation Board. This major activity was authorized by the corporate board after in-depth discussions with the trade unions representing the large workforce of the organization.

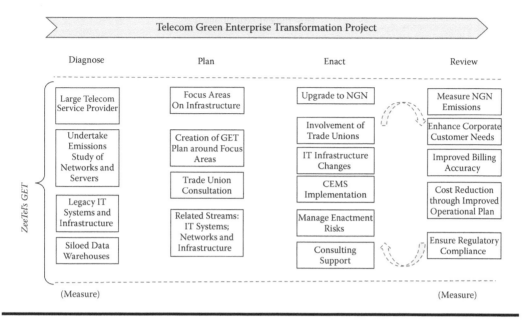

Figure 14.4   GET project for ZeeTel.

This diagnosis phase examined the data center, the communications networks, the equipment lifecycle processes and the supporting HR function. One of the important discovery was that ZeeTel's as-is business processes were not modeled or optimized. Due to lack of formality associated with modeling and documentation of business processes there was substantial wastage and resultant carbon emissions.

The current investigations are into the assets such as networks infrastructure, information systems, and data bases also indicated a close nexus between the unoptimized business processes and these technology hardware and software. The as-is status of ZeeTel is, therefore, without any green maturity. Formal diagnosis phases also revealed that the transformation of the telecommunication networks and information systems to achieve green maturity has to be closely aligned to business model to ensure that it is not achieved at the cost of business growth.

Green IT strategy for ZeeTel includes transformation of communications networks, IT hardware, IT systems, and business processes. Estimates are that the NGN can reduce 40% energy consumption compare to legacy networks (Faulkner 2008) and GPON can be even more energy efficient over ADSL2+ networks (as discussed by Ramesh, HRG 2011). Eventually, the organizational culture has to also undergo change, which will be brought about through training and education. ZeeTel will undertake transformation in strategy, infrastructure and product (SIP) processes as these are the most technology-intense processes. Eventually, changes in these processes will also change other processes and affect internal staff as well as people from the corporate customer groups.

Starting with the strategic aspect of the lifecycle, the GET will then undertake changes and alignment to infrastructure lifecycle management and eventually product lifecycle management processes. These three major aspects of GET in the context of ZeeTel are summarized in Figure 14.5.

Green IT metrics and measurements apply to all of these enhance telecommunication operations map (eTOM) based processes. For example, in case of the Fulfillment process the unit cost associated with execution of one iteration of the process can provide a starting KPI. Similarly, carbon emission corresponding to individual network elements, such as switches and routers, provides a KPI for

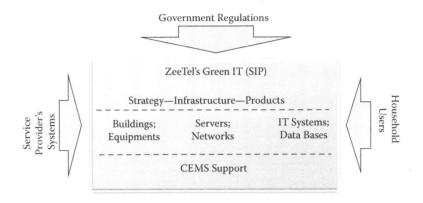

Figure 14.5 The strategy, infrastructure, product lifecycles in Green IT transformation.

calculating the reduction in emissions through GET. The transformation of IT systems and resources provides opportunities to measure the KPIs of the ZeeTel processes supported by the IT systems. Transformation of such processes also includes, for example, shifting from manual or paper based processes to electronic processes, reduction in material wastages, and automation of operational contracts. Optimization of the process also ensures cost- and time-effective delivery of services.

Training and education will lead to carbon consciousness throughout the organization. This implies clear understanding among the staff of the meaning of Green IT. This is particularly challenging in an infrastructure-based transformation, as the simple, operation carbon reduction through, say, switching off computers, is not sufficient. Changes to the IT systems and applications include review of the database, setting up of integration interfaces through SOA and accurate reporting in terms of both carbon and noncarbon data.

Planning

The popular business processes framework for telecommunications company, called *eTOM* provides an excellent basis for identifying and working through the focus areas for GET. This eTOM framework, in the context of ZeeTel, is shown in Figure 14.5. The eTOM provides an excellent and comprehensive reference model for the telecom sector. Therefore, eTOM is also ideal for ZeeTel's GET. Although ZeeTel is not directly dealing with end-customers, still the eTOM reference model is helpful in separating the ZeeTel activities that deal directly with the corporate customers as against the support and supplier activities. Thus, in Figure 14.6, the strategy and commit, infrastructure lifecycle management, and product lifecycle management are shown as the major areas of focus as ZeeTel undertakes GET. The processes that support and align with these major areas are the marketing and offer management, service development and management, resource development and management, and supply chain development and management. These processes, derived directly from eTOM are supported by the various IT systems and applications of ZeeTel. These are shown on the left in Figure 14.6.

Figure 14.6 further indicates the proximity of technology-based changes with the process dimension. In large, infrastructure-based GET, such as in ZeeTel, all four dimensions are involved. Thus, even though one dimension, such as the technology dimension, takes lead, other dimensions immediately follow and support the transformation. The eTOM for ZeeTel provides optimization and reengineering

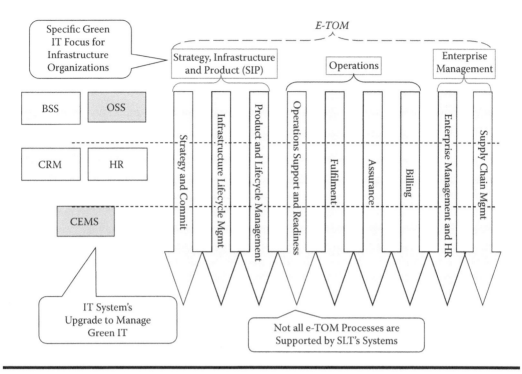

Figure 14.6 ZeeTel's focus areas for Green enterprise transformation based on eTOM.

opportunities in the business process area. The ZeeTel modernization effort is aimed to not only reduce carbon but also optimize processes for its corporate customers, including content providers.

The IT systems that closely support the modeling and optimization of the business processes are also shown in Figure 14.6 on the left. Planning for green process reengineering will involve grouping the processes based on the "operations" group shown in Figure 14.6. The process groups formed during planning phase will continue during enactment and review.

The UML's use cases and activity graphs, discussed in Chapter 7, can be used here to undertake Green BPR.

Enterprise Data Center Transformation Plan

(Using the activities in the planning phase of the GRID, complete the following sections)

ZeeTel has two large data centers in two major cities in the region. Both data centers operate on a 24 × 7 basis as it needs to support the corporate customers, service and content providers, as well as internal HR. Together, there are 12 high-end servers, with four additional servers as backup servers for emergency. The data center does not currently have a space allocation strategy and the data and application requirements are growing at the rate of 1Gig per day. The data center director has made some attempt to measure PUE (power usage effectiveness) and the results are a PUE of 2.4. In addition to the official data servers, there are a few "local" servers within the organization.

■ Implementation of CEMS will include incorporation of the aforementioned KPIs that bring together carbon and measurement of IT system's performance. For example, measures that reflect reduction in data usage, duplication, and storage will also reflect corresponding carbon reduction. Processes associated with content and service providers will enable them to use the upgraded communication platform in new and innovative ways. The Green IT strategies of ZeeTel will align the transformation to the NGN with the business strategies of the content and service providers.

■ Increase in contents and demand for greater network coverage—especially on the 3G networks—implies need for high-capacity networks. NGN, providing some capacity, needs to be balanced with the carbon footprint of NGN.

■ ZeeTel's cost consideration in GET project includes costs of network upgrades, costs associated with formation of the project, and cost of procuring and implementing CEMS.

■ Data servers in the current setup at ZeeTel have been left running irrespective of usage. Occasionally, manual control was used to reduce their emissions when they were not in use. Post-GET server management will have to be automated through power management software. Choice of software for this purpose is GreenTrac from EventZero (www.greentrac.com).

■ ZeeTel is in a position to influence handset manufacturers as well, as a part of its influence on its business ecosystem, to put together plans for take back of mobile devices. Mobile devices need to be recycled, ensuring regulatory policies that make the manufacturers responsible for taking back devices that would be e-waste.

■ CEMS of choice is ecoGovernance from CA (http://www.ca.com/us/products/detail/CA-ecoGovernance.aspx).

Enacting GET for ZeeTel

Figure 14.7 shows the overall timeline for GET. This is a suggested timeline that considers two major iterations for enactment and review. The first enactment and review is around the initial changes to the network, moving to NGN. Changes to the enterprise architecture based on eTOM and the procurement and implementation of ecoGovernance (from CA) as the CEMS is

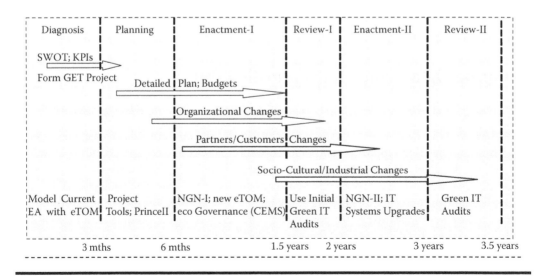

Figure 14.7   GET timelines and enactment-review phases.

also happening during this enactment. Changes to the organization and its business partners are roughly shown by the arrows on the figure.

IT systems and applications need to be mapped to the reengineered business processes—occurring in the second part of enactment. Changes to the IT applications will impact the collaborative business processes of partners such as the content and service providers.

Data Center Changes in GET

Following are the actions undertaken in the two large data centers of ZeeTel. These actions are based on the planning for GET discussed in earlier section:

- Implement integrated blade servers that will consume less power.
- All new servers that are procured will be low carbon emitting blade servers that will have inbuilt virtualization capacity.
- ZeeTel will actively seek renewable energy sources such as solar and gas, which can be combined with the current coal-based power generation.
- Integration of connectivity among the servers within and across the cities, outsourcing of some of the hardware maintenance aspects of the data center to ensure highly optimized services.
- Implement natural cooling for data center.. This would require the hot-cold aisle arrangement for the servers, as also rearrangement of data storage and retrieval systems.
- Optimization of signals creating opportunities to reduce demands on the servers, which in turn would reduce power consumption for the servers and corresponding air conditioning.
- Implement eco-friendly air conditioning for the servers.

Next-Generation Networks in GET

Complete the implementation of NGN within ZeeTel's entire communications network. This implementation is expected to take between 3 and 4 years to complete in the region where ZeeTel operates. This change to NGN will result in strategic reduction in carbon due to improved network efficient, intelligent routing methods, and consolidation of switching centers. This reduction in power consumption is envisaged to be effective even if there is increase in network traffic—as expected over the coming years. Therefore, the Green IT metrics used in the return on investment (ROI) calculations needs to consider not only the replacement costs of the network and equipments, but also the drop in emissions per user over increased number of users.

Equipment Lifecycle

The entire lifecycle of equipments used within ZeeTel will be subject to the Green POD. The activities relating to material and equipment lifecycle that will undergo change include carbon reduction consideration in current POD practices within the organization.

The new servers will be procured based on their power consumption ratings as well as their "total carbon cost of ownership."

The disposal of IT hardware is through a series of ranked options including giving it to employees, then charity, and finally for safe disposal.

The business infrastructure of ZeeTel, such as its buildings and car fleet will be accounted for in the updated financial systems where Scope 1 emissions can be calculated and updated.

Enacting changes to the procurement-operation-disposal process will be based on following considerations:

■ All procurement to be based on EPEAT/energy star based ratings—especially for the servers
■ Highly optimized processes that would support procurement of IT hardware as well as communications equipment
■ Incorporation of carbon calculations and Green credentials to support procurement of the NGN
■ Renegotiation of SLA with hardware and network equipment suppliers
■ Optimized operation of network, servers, and associated IT hardware
■ Apportioning operational carbon over the life of the equipment to arrive at TCCO
■ Ethical disposal of existing legacy network hardware

Attitude and Training

■ Creation and delivery of brief 2-hour seminars on the relevance of the Green enterprise transformation program to update the large number of employees
■ Detailed 2-day training to IT managers, network managers and data center managers
■ External training to Green enterprise transformation board on the transformation process
■ CEMS training—configuration and use

Review and Measure

There are two specific reviews after each iteration of enactment—as shown in Figure 14.6.

A significant learning that has happened is the need to understand the politics and underlying motivation of individuals participating in the transformation project. The age-old management understanding of the risks associated with change hold utterly true in this transformation. Quality assurance and testing activities were also required to be formally carried out on the new and integrated IT systems and content management.

Conclusions

This chapter described the Green enterprise transformation process as applied to a infrastructure company. ZeeTel from the telecom sector was used as an example. There is significant focus in an infrastructure company on the upgrade of networks, procurement of new servers and creation of new buildings.

References

Faulkner. (2008) http://ties.itu.int/ftp/public/itu-t/fgictcc/readonly/Informative%20presentations%20related%20to%20the%20FG/Green+ICT+-+ITU+input+Faulkner+Draft+L.pdf accessed on March 27, 2011.

Ramesh, B. (2011). Chapter 13, Business Processes Management for a Green Telecommunications Company. In B. Unhelkar, ed., *Handbook of Research in Green ICT,* pp. 197–213. IGI Global, Hershey, PA, USA.

Appendix A: The Environmentally Responsible Business Strategies (ERBS) Research Project Survey

Note: This is the survey questionnaire used by B. Trivedi in her PhD research that provided the data for some of the Green IT analysis in this book. This questionnaire is reproduced here for readers interested in the research aspect of the discussions.

Survey Questions

Greetings! Thank you in advance for providing 15 minutes of your precious time by participating in this research survey on Green ICT (Information and Communications Technology) and Environmental Responsibilities of Business. Answers can be based on your company, your primary client or simply be your erudite opinions.

The objective of this study is to understand the contribution of ICT in environmental strategies of a business and its sustainable management. This includes understanding organizational and individual attitudes and policies towards Green ICT, wasteful and emissive processes, enablement of efficient use of organizational resources, metrics for monitoring and justification of the greening of the organization and implementation of environmental strategies in business.

The data collected through this survey will be analyzed and processed for the development and validation of a model for "Environmentally Responsible Business Strategy (ERBS)." This survey respects the privacy of the individuals and the confidentiality of the organizations. As such, the answers you provide here will only be discussed and analyzed collectively in seminars and publications. A short white paper of our results will be provided on your (optionally provided) contact details as a mark of our gratitude. We also plan to publish our formal findings in a proposed chapter in the upcoming *"Handbook of Research on Green ICT: Technical, Methodological and Social Perspectives (HRG)"* published by IGI global, USA, 2010.

Your participation is voluntary, *your answers remain confidential* and your honesty in answering this survey is deeply appreciated.

Regards,
BT.

1. Demographic Information

About You: (optional)			
Your Name: _____ Company Name: _____ Contact Details: _____			
Your Role:	[] Decision maker [] Advisor/Consultant [] Engineer	[] Project /QA manager [] Technical manager [] Researcher	[] Environment regulator [] IT consultant [] Other _____
Company Size:	[] Small (<20 employees)	[] Medium (20–200 employees)	[] Large (>200 employees)
Business Type:	[] Private/Corporate	[] Government/ Semi Govt.	[] Other _____
Industry Category: (select any one; if 'Others' please clarify)	[] Agriculture, forestry, and fishing [] Mining [] Manufacturing [] Electricity, gas, water, and waste services [] Construction [] Wholesale trade [] Health care and social assistance	[] Retail trade [] Transport, postal, and warehousing [] Information media and telecommunications [] Financial and insurance services [] Rental, hiring and real estate services	[] Professional, scientific, and technical services [] Administrative and support services [] Public administration and safety [] Education and training [] Arts and recreation services [] Other _____
Primary Region:	[] India [] North America/ Canada	[] Australia/NZ [] Japan, Singapore, China	[] Europe/UK [] Other_____

Please indicate whether you agree or disagree with the following statements in terms of their importance in your organization [SD: Strongly Disagree; D: Disagree; N: Neutral; A: Agree; SA: Strongly Agree].

2. Business and Strategy Planning with Respect to the Environment

Understanding current business scenario: Your organization	SD	D	N	A	SA
Has a higher power consumption than other similar organizations	[ ]	[ ]	[ ]	[ ]	[ ]
Assumes responsibility for its carbon footprints	[ ]	[ ]	[ ]	[ ]	[ ]
Measures its carbon emissions accurately	[ ]	[ ]	[ ]	[ ]	[ ]
Has a person responsible for environmental matters	[ ]	[ ]	[ ]	[ ]	[ ]
Is aware of the importance of Green metrics	[ ]	[ ]	[ ]	[ ]	[ ]
Uses devices and/or software to measure carbon emissions	[ ]	[ ]	[ ]	[ ]	[ ]

Understanding your business policies with respect to environment: Your organization has	SD	D	N	A	SA
Policies for purchase of Green equipment and related services	[ ]	[ ]	[ ]	[ ]	[ ]
Policies related to safe disposal of hazardous waste, material, or equipment	[ ]	[ ]	[ ]	[ ]	[ ]
Policies for adopting and implementing recycling of equipment	[ ]	[ ]	[ ]	[ ]	[ ]
Policies for optimizing energy consumption in all business processes	[ ]	[ ]	[ ]	[ ]	[ ]
Policies for use of renewable energy (e.g., solar, nuclear)	[ ]	[ ]	[ ]	[ ]	[ ]
Policies to influence attitudes of staff toward carbon emissions	[ ]	[ ]	[ ]	[ ]	[ ]

The following factors influence your organization to adopt Green policies	SD	D	N	A	SA
Government rules and regulation in implementing environmental measures	[ ]	[ ]	[ ]	[ ]	[ ]
Customer's demand or pressure for Green policies and Green products	[ ]	[ ]	[ ]	[ ]	[ ]
Pressure from society (physical/electronic groups) to adopt Green policies	[ ]	[ ]	[ ]	[ ]	[ ]
Self-initiated implementation of environmental policies	[ ]	[ ]	[ ]	[ ]	[ ]
(Increased) Energy consumption in your organization	[ ]	[ ]	[ ]	[ ]	[ ]
(Increased) Carbon footprint in your organization	[ ]	[ ]	[ ]	[ ]	[ ]
(Increased) Operational costs in your organization	[ ]	[ ]	[ ]	[ ]	[ ]

The following goals are defined by your organization to adopt Green policies	SD	D	N	A	SA
Reduction of energy consumption in your organization	[ ]	[ ]	[ ]	[ ]	[ ]
Reduction of carbon footprint in your organization	[ ]	[ ]	[ ]	[ ]	[ ]
Reduction of the operational costs in your organization	[ ]	[ ]	[ ]	[ ]	[ ]
Improvement of the reputation of your organization	[ ]	[ ]	[ ]	[ ]	[ ]
Meet government regulations and legislation	[ ]	[ ]	[ ]	[ ]	[ ]
Meet the sustainability goals of your organization	[ ]	[ ]	[ ]	[ ]	[ ]
Increase revenue and profitability due to Green initiatives	[ ]	[ ]	[ ]	[ ]	[ ]

The following ICT practices have been adopted by your organization	SD	D	N	A	SA
Videoconferencing	[ ]	[ ]	[ ]	[ ]	[ ]
Telecommuting/Teleworking	[ ]	[ ]	[ ]	[ ]	[ ]
Fleet and field force management	[ ]	[ ]	[ ]	[ ]	[ ]
Web and use of collaboration tools such as e-mails	[ ]	[ ]	[ ]	[ ]	[ ]
Mobile phones/PDAs	[ ]	[ ]	[ ]	[ ]	[ ]
Others (Specify) _____					

3. Technical Strategy and Planning

Your organization has the following practices regarding energy saving data centers and equipments	SD	D	N	A	SA
Energy saving choice when purchasing new ICT hardware	[ ]	[ ]	[ ]	[ ]	[ ]
Reducing energy used by data centers (ICT)	[ ]	[ ]	[ ]	[ ]	[ ]
Uses open source system software (ICT) and applications	[ ]	[ ]	[ ]	[ ]	[ ]
Machine/Server Virtualization (ICT)	[ ]	[ ]	[ ]	[ ]	[ ]
Counts and monitors ICT devices for emissions	[ ]	[ ]	[ ]	[ ]	[ ]
Replaces conventional devices with environment friendly devices	[ ]	[ ]	[ ]	[ ]	[ ]
Others (Specify) _____					
The following practices are adopted across the entire organization	**SD**	**D**	**N**	**A**	**SA**
Reduce the use of paper and related materials (e.g., ink or toner)	[ ]	[ ]	[ ]	[ ]	[ ]
Reduce use of hazardous materials that can damage the environment	[ ]	[ ]	[ ]	[ ]	[ ]
Reduce number of high power consuming equipments	[ ]	[ ]	[ ]	[ ]	[ ]
Use of alternative energy source such as wind, solar	[ ]	[ ]	[ ]	[ ]	[ ]
Monitor emissions and evaluate on a regular basis	[ ]	[ ]	[ ]	[ ]	[ ]
Provide training to employees to implement and enhance Green practices	[ ]	[ ]	[ ]	[ ]	[ ]
Separately monitor the electricity consumed by the data center	[ ]	[ ]	[ ]	[ ]	[ ]
Encourage product innovation and environmentally conscious design	[ ]	[ ]	[ ]	[ ]	[ ]
Life cycle assessment of energy consuming equipments	[ ]	[ ]	[ ]	[ ]	[ ]
Maintain equipment and instruments in good condition to reduce wear	[ ]	[ ]	[ ]	[ ]	[ ]
The following tools are used for measuring carbon emissions in your organization	**SD**	**D**	**N**	**A**	**SA**
Dashboard displays attached to the devices to display emissions	[ ]	[ ]	[ ]	[ ]	[ ]
Mobile gadgets attached to devices for measuring emissions	[ ]	[ ]	[ ]	[ ]	[ ]
Surveys of employees and other stakeholders	[ ]	[ ]	[ ]	[ ]	[ ]
Inventory of the organization to identify unused goods	[ ]	[ ]	[ ]	[ ]	[ ]
Interviews of employees and stakeholders to ascertain carbon emissions	[ ]	[ ]	[ ]	[ ]	[ ]
Others (Specify) _____					

4. Procurement and Supply Management

Supply management procurement—Your organization:	SD	D	N	A	SA
Adheres to environmental criteria for approved suppliers	[ ]	[ ]	[ ]	[ ]	[ ]
Requires or encourage suppliers to undertake environment certification	[ ]	[ ]	[ ]	[ ]	[ ]
Builds environmental criteria into supplier contract conditions	[ ]	[ ]	[ ]	[ ]	[ ]
Incorporates environmental conscious staff on sourcing team	[ ]	[ ]	[ ]	[ ]	[ ]
Keeps record of supplier environmental questionnaires	[ ]	[ ]	[ ]	[ ]	[ ]
Records and evaluate supplier environmental audits and assessment	[ ]	[ ]	[ ]	[ ]	[ ]
ERP software: Your organization intends to	**SD**	**D**	**N**	**A**	**SA**
Modify the current ERP system to meet environmental challenges	[ ]	[ ]	[ ]	[ ]	[ ]
Buy a new ERP software package that will meet environmental needs	[ ]	[ ]	[ ]	[ ]	[ ]
Seek external help for training and implementation of Green ERP	[ ]	[ ]	[ ]	[ ]	[ ]
Compliance audits: Your organization has	**SD**	**D**	**N**	**A**	**SA**
Well-documented model for carbon emissions that can be audited	[ ]	[ ]	[ ]	[ ]	[ ]
Regular updates and modification of environmental parameters	[ ]	[ ]	[ ]	[ ]	[ ]
Standard approach to accessing government rules and regulations	[ ]	[ ]	[ ]	[ ]	[ ]
Provides feedback to the government on carbon emission	[ ]	[ ]	[ ]	[ ]	[ ]
Periodically checks environmental documents of the vendor	[ ]	[ ]	[ ]	[ ]	[ ]

5. Strategic Measures for Reducing Emissions

Your organization's business strategies will be influenced for next 3–5 years by	SD	D	N	A	SA
Use of ICT in minimizing the organization's environmental footprints	[ ]	[ ]	[ ]	[ ]	[ ]
Government regulations that require organizations to limit carbon emissions	[ ]	[ ]	[ ]	[ ]	[ ]
Implementing monitoring methods for carbon footprints in an organization	[ ]	[ ]	[ ]	[ ]	[ ]
Use of alternate source of energy such as solar/wind energy	[ ]	[ ]	[ ]	[ ]	[ ]
Costs involved in implementing Green initiatives	[ ]	[ ]	[ ]	[ ]	[ ]
Formation of an executive body for overall responsibility for environment	[ ]	[ ]	[ ]	[ ]	[ ]
Your organization plans for next 3–5 years to achieve Green targets	**SD**	**D**	**N**	**A**	**SA**
Documented targets for carbon footprint reduction	[ ]	[ ]	[ ]	[ ]	[ ]
Investment funds dedicated to incorporate Green policies	[ ]	[ ]	[ ]	[ ]	[ ]
Training plans and budgets to help employees understand Green issues	[ ]	[ ]	[ ]	[ ]	[ ]
Seek external help for upgrades to a Greener business system	[ ]	[ ]	[ ]	[ ]	[ ]
Modify the current business processes to incorporate environmental needs	[ ]	[ ]	[ ]	[ ]	[ ]
Create power management policies to reduce energy consumption	[ ]	[ ]	[ ]	[ ]	[ ]
Methodology to undertake suitable and defensive power consumption	[ ]	[ ]	[ ]	[ ]	[ ]
Use of power management software	[ ]	[ ]	[ ]	[ ]	[ ]
Others (Specify) _____					
SaaS (Software as a service)/cloud computing: Your ICT strategies include	**SD**	**D**	**N**	**A**	**SA**
Use of SaaS in reducing carbon emissions	[ ]	[ ]	[ ]	[ ]	[ ]
Use of process reengineering to reduce waste	[ ]	[ ]	[ ]	[ ]	[ ]
Use of Cloud computing to implement environmental policies	[ ]	[ ]	[ ]	[ ]	[ ]
Use of new ICT initiatives as part of a strategy to reduce power consumption	[ ]	[ ]	[ ]	[ ]	[ ]
Others (Specify) _____					
ICT devices can play a significant role for checking emissions and waste in an organization as they can	**SD**	**D**	**N**	**A**	**SA**
Provide real time statistical data	[ ]	[ ]	[ ]	[ ]	[ ]
Configured and managed from central services in an organization	[ ]	[ ]	[ ]	[ ]	[ ]
Configured in any designated boundary in the organization	[ ]	[ ]	[ ]	[ ]	[ ]
Are you currently implementing or planning to implement the following in your organization	**SD**	**D**	**N**	**A**	**SA**
Operational (day to day) improvements to reduce carbon emissions	[ ]	[ ]	[ ]	[ ]	[ ]
Strategic changes to how the business operates to reduce carbon emissions	[ ]	[ ]	[ ]	[ ]	[ ]
Anticipate changes to governmental regulations related to carbon emissions	[ ]	[ ]	[ ]	[ ]	[ ]
Influence governmental regulations related to carbon emissions	[ ]	[ ]	[ ]	[ ]	[ ]
Access new sources of capital/energy/raw material	[ ]	[ ]	[ ]	[ ]	[ ]
Improve your risk management with respect to environment	[ ]	[ ]	[ ]	[ ]	[ ]
Elevate corporate reputation by adopting Green strategies	[ ]	[ ]	[ ]	[ ]	[ ]
Identifying new market opportunities through adoption of Green strategies	[ ]	[ ]	[ ]	[ ]	[ ]
Enhance human resource management through Green strategies	[ ]	[ ]	[ ]	[ ]	[ ]

Note: The following descriptive questions enabled participants to provide subjective answers. The following answers have been assimilated in the discussions in this book:
Please provide descriptive responses to the following questions:

Question 1: Please explain two crucial reasons why a business like yours should adopt environmentally responsible business strategies.

```



```

Question 2: How do you believe emerging technologies (such as mobile, Web x.0, Cloud computing) should be incorporated in business to help to reduce the carbon footprint?

```



```

Question 3: What should be your organization's approach to incorporating Green issues into its business strategies?

```



```

Question 4: Suggest a crucial/critical action that could be taken by your organization to use renewable (Green) energy?

```



```

Question 5: What are the problems faced by an organization in collecting and validating environmental data (please include comments on methods, technologies, regulators, agencies, and business partners)?

```



```

Note: The information provided by you has no legal implications and will be used purely for academic research.

Respondent Demographics

The survey is conducted in different regions of the world, primarily organizations from India, Australia, North America, Japan, Singapore, Korea, Europe, Dubai, South Africa, and Kenya. Respondents were from all the major industry sectors from small to very large organizations. The organizations surveyed were of different types such as private (70%), government (25%), others such as nonprofit organizations, NGOs, and so on. (5%). Nearly 56% responses are from the large organizations having more than 200 employees, 33% from medium scale organizations, and 11% from small businesses. The size of the company is calculated by the number of employees working in them. One of the purposes of this survey is to comprehend the understanding of green metrics in different sectors of business. The respondents are from varied industry category such as manufacturing (30%), education, health and community services (21%), administration and professional services (19%), transport and postal (2%), construction and utilities (5%), communication and media (7%), finance and insurance (6%), retail and wholesale trade (7%), and others (7%). 20% of the respondents are decision makers, 10% are project and QA managers, 2% are environment regulator, 7% are consultants, 7% are researchers, 16% are engineers, 9% are technical managers, 11% are IT consultant, and others are 18%.

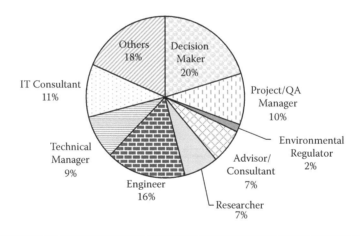

Figure A.1   Role.

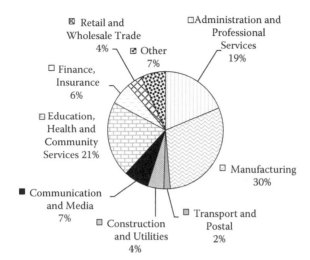

Figure A.2   Respondents by industry sector.

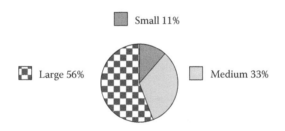

Figure A.3   Company size.

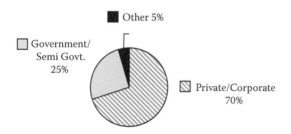

Figure A.4   Business type.

Appendix B: Case Study Scenarios for Trial Runs

Note: Readers may wish to use some of these following case study scenarios to experiment with their Green IT strategies. These case study scenarios will come in handy in consulting and training situation wherein the readers are seeking to apply the Green IT strategies to different types of problem statements.

New Bank Carbon Scenario

New Bank is a hypothetical bank with head office in a large city on the Eastern coast of Australia (say Melbourne or Sydney). The bank has a large and established customer base, a 24,000 strong work force and a reputation to be proud of. The organization is supported with sophisticated suite of enterprise resource planning (ERP) software (including a SAP implementation, as also a powerful front-end customer relationship management (CRM)). New Bank is viewed by the government as a "model" bank, and its past history indicates the bank has traditionally had close ties with the government. The bank is fully aware of the upcoming legislation controlling carbon emissions. The senior management of the bank is keen to incorporate "Green IT" as an integral part of its *business strategy*. This, the leaders of the bank believe, will be possible by (a) undertaking a transformation of the bank to a Green bank and (b) putting in place environmental strategies that align closely with the bank's business strategy.

Notes:

- New bank plans to grow through acquisition. A well-known home loans vendor is in the process of being acquired.
- There are approximately 650 branches (with 120 large branches, >50 staff) across Australasian region.
- The acquisitions are not evaluated for their carbon footprint at all.

▪ The bank is already above the 150 kiloTonne carbon emission threshold, and is going to be required to report its carbon data to the government in the next few months.
▪ The bank has recently appointed a chief green officer (also called chief sustainability office)—CGO.
▪ The bank maintains a fleet of approximately 300 cars—50 of which are diesel engine cars. 10% of the banks car fleet is usually "hired" through a large car rental company (Hybris).
▪ Fifteen percent of the employees need to travel by air to manage the bank's business across all cities in Australia, New Zealand, the Asian region, and globally. This averages out to approximately 5000 km per year per employee—although numbers have varied over last 5 years depending on the global economic climate, bank's business and need for management.

Following Is the Result of the Initial Green IT Audit Undertaken by the Bank

Desktop Machines

▪ Numbers (total across the organization): 20,000 (12,000 conventional; 7,500 = laptops; 500 = thin clients)
▪ Value (current $): $1,200,000
▪ Status (how old/new, etc.): Most conventional PCs are between 2 and 3 years old
▪ Emissions data (as a rough estimate based on spreadsheet): 1,777,500 watts per hour
▪ Conventional = 12,000 × 110 w = 1,320,000
▪ Laptops = 7,500 × 60 w = 450,000
▪ Thin clients = 500 × 15 w = 7500 w

Mobile Devices

▪ Numbers (total across the organization): 26,000 (2000 owned by the organization, rest individual)
▪ Value (current $): $250,000
▪ Status (how old/new, etc.): those by individuals are new, the bank owned are averaging 2.5 years
▪ Emissions data (estimate): 10 w per day × 26,000 = 260,000 watts per day

Printers and Peripherals

▪ Numbers (total across the organization): 1000
▪ Value (current $): 500,000
▪ Status (how old/new, etc.): average age 4 years
▪ Emissions data: could not be estimated during the Green IT audit

Data Center IT and Communication Equipment

▪ Numbers (total across the organization): 12 + 4 = 16
▪ Value (current $): N/A
▪ Status (how old/new, etc.): 2-year old equipment
▪ Emissions data (if available—or estimate): 16 × 0.5 kW ph × 24 = 192 kw per day

Network Devices; Routers

- 10 devices
- 50 routers
- 20 switches

$= 80 \times 150$ w /hr $\times 24 =$

Challenge: Apply Green IT strategies to New Bank to transition it to a green bank—with stated goals of 10% carbon reduction over every previous year for 3 years.

Bluewaters Travel Agency Carbon Scenario

Bluewaters is a small to medium travel agency operating out of New York. The company has an excellent, elite client base. The company is well-controlled and well-managed single-owner enterprise with approximately 25 employees. At any one time, the company has about eight computers running, together with associated paraphernalia. In addition, there are copiers, faxes, and shredders in the main office. Some employees do occasional telework, especially when they don't have to face a client.

OpenAir Airline Carbon Scenario

OpenAir is a medium, regional airline operating out of the Asian region. The airline has been vulnerable to oil costs during most of its operation. However, with improved opportunities to fly to further destinations than the local region comes the challenge of controlling, reporting, and reducing the carbon footprint. Following are the notes based on an initial investigation commissioned by the corporate board of OpenAir, in the context of carbon emissions:

Economic viability of OpenAir is no longer independent of its carbon footprint.

Passengers are expecting a much greater role from OpenAir in terms of carbon reduction than merely offering carbon offsets to passengers, especially as it expands beyond the Asian region.

While electronic ticketing and check in has been introduced with some success, the board sees a need for mobile ticketing and check in. IT as well as carbon costs for introduction of mobile technologies has not been carefully estimated.

Need for sophisticated IT systems on the rise, especially in supporting the growth in passenger travels, especially in the business market. The airline has also been launching new products that are based around premium economy seats, luggage-free, or slow-luggage flights (costing less to the passengers), choices of food and beverage on long flights, and so on. The IT support for these processes required substantial changes to the data centre hardware, operating systems, and the applications themselves. There are still, however, many nonstandard IT systems that are not integrated with each other.

Fuel efficiency metrics are not tied to carbon metrics.

Scheduling of flights, variations to those schedules, and rostering of staff (pilots, stewards) is not optimized. Besides, there is practically no telework culture within the organization.

There is some understanding within the organization about carbon emissions from airline fuel, but hardly any acknowledgment and understanding of internal IT emissions.

OpenAir has about 2000 desktop computers, 300 laptops provided by the organization to the employees, and unaccounted mobile devices. There is a single data centre catering to all the IT systems requirements, with a nonreal time offsite backup that is a major risks to the airline's business.

Appendix C: Green IT Measurements from a CEMS

Note: Following are some of the relevant Green IT measurements coming out of a Carbon Emissions Management Software (CEMS) that the author had opportunity to experiment with. GreenTrac has provided these "real" figures based on some of their current deployments in practice. The author is grateful to GreenTrac in providing this data. These measurements should give some idea to readers trying to implement their own CEMS as to what elements need to be configured and used in practice. GreenTrac currently focuses only on end-user devices that are able to handle a very small DMA (Direct Memory Access) file from the application that allows it to monitor the emissions from the device in real time. When this is not possible, GreenTrac takes the data from the power bills of the devices.

Figure C.1 shows the Green ranking of the user. This feedback can be of immense value in bringing about attitude change in the user.

Figure C.2 shows power usage information for an individual machine. A usage timeline like this can provide instantaneous feedback to the user, increasing the possibility of behavior change.

Figure C.3 shows the power usage profile (in watts). The time on the x-axis and the wattage gives the user a view of his or her usage profile.

Figures C.4 and C.5 compare the total daily usage cost from a specific electricity meter with its corresponding carbon emission for two electricity meters (1 and 2). While the two graphs in this figure are similar, that may not be the case always. For example, on certain days (such as a weekend) the power may be sourced from a different (e.g., renewable) source and the cost of that power may be same or higher, but the emissions from the use of that power may be less than shown here.

Figure C.6 is aimed at controlling and reporting on the printer usage. Other, similar devices, may also be monitored and reported using GreenTrac.

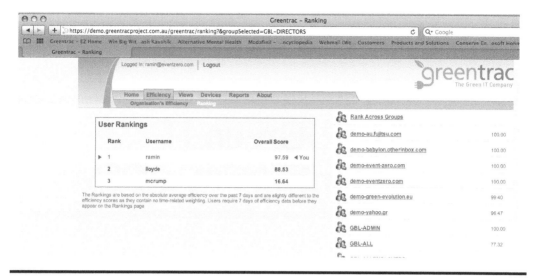

Figure C.1

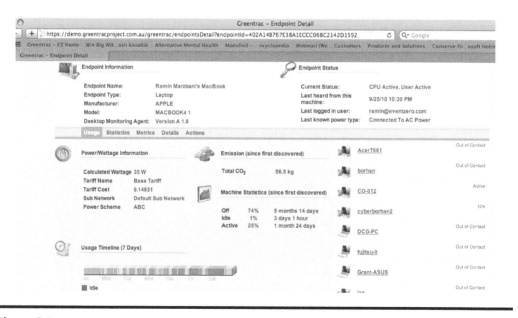

Figure C.2

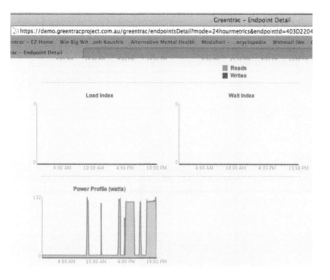

Figure C.3

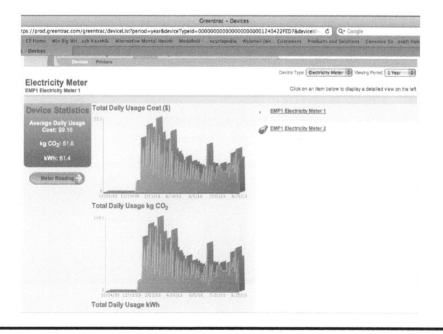

Figure C.4

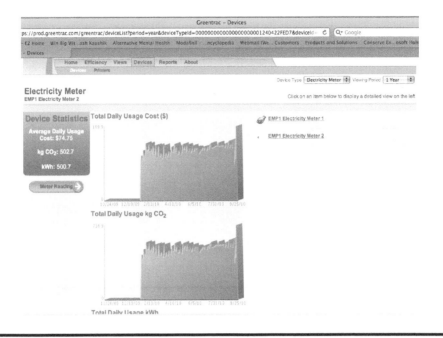

Figure C.5

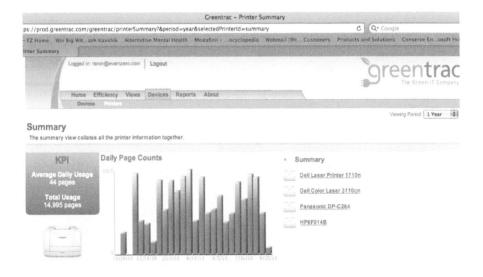

Figure C.6

Abbreviations

Acronym	Full Form
BASIX	Building sustainability index
BI	Business intelligence
BSS	Billing software solution
CEMS	Carbon Emissions Management Software
CGO	Chief green officer
CIO	Chief information officer
CO2E	Carbon dioxide equivalent
CPRS	Carbon pollution reduction scheme
CSCI	Climate savers computing initiative
CSO	Chief sustainability officer
CSR	Corporate social responsibility
CxO	Chief "any" officer
DciE	Data center infrastructure efficiency
EI	Environmental intelligence
EIS	Environmental intelligence system
EITE	Emissions-intensive, trade exposed
EMS	Environmental management system
EPA	Environmental protection agency
EPEAT	Electronic product environmental assessment tool
EPR	Electronic patient record
Acronym	*Full Form*

ERBS	Environmentally responsible business strategy
ERP	Enterprise resource planning
ESG	Environment, social, and governance
GEA	Green enterprise architecture
GHG	Greenhouse gas
GIS	Green information system
GISCM	Green integrated supply chain management
GRI	Global reporting initiative
GUI	Graphic user interface
HR	Human relations
ICT	Information and communication technology
IPCC	Intergovernmental panel on climate change
ISCM	Integrated supply chain management
NABERS	National Australian built environment rating system
NGERS	National greenhouse and energy reporting system
OLAP	Online analytical processing
OSCAR	Online system for comprehensive activity reporting
OSS	Operational support system
PPM	Parts per million
PUE	Power usage effectiveness
RoHS	Restriction of hazardous substances
SaaS	Software as a service
SCM	Supply chain management
SLA	Service level agreement
SOA	Service-oriented architecture
TCCO	Total cost of carbon ownership
UNFCCC	United Nations Framework Convention on Climate Change
WEEE	Waste electrical and electronic equipment
WS	Web services

Green Glossary

Term	Explanation
Benchmarking	Technique for quantifying, measuring, and comparing the performance of an organization with the industry standard.
Carbon Credits	Carbon credit refers to a unit (typically tonne) of carbon (or carbon dioxide equivalent) saving that can be used, exchanged or traded.
Carbon Dioxide Equivalent	Carbon dioxide equivalent (CO_2e) is the quantity of any greenhouse gas that has the same effect on global warming as Carbon Dioxide itself would have. In most carbon calculations, carbon dioxide (CO_2) is used as a reference.
Carbon Emission Management Software	A Carbon Emissions Management Software (CEMS) is a new breed of software systems that enable organizations to undertake comprehensive carbon management and reporting. CEMS require careful architecture, design and development and these systems need to interface and interact with existing organizational systems (typically ERP).
Carbon Footprint	A measure of the impact the activities of an organization or an individual have on the environment, and in particular climate change. It is "the total set of greenhouse gas (GHG) emissions caused by an organization, event or product." For simplicity of reporting, it is often expressed in terms of the amount of carbon dioxide (CO_2), or its equivalent of other GHGs, emitted; it has units of tones (or kg) of CO_2 equivalent. A carbon footprint is made up of the sum of two parts: the primary footprint and the secondary footprint. The primary footprint is a measure of direct emissions of CO_2, resulting from consumed electrical energy, and one has direct control of these. The secondary footprint is a measure of the indirect CO_2 emissions from the whole lifecycle of the products we use—those associated with their manufacture and eventual breakdown.

Term	Explanation
Carbon Neutral	Carbon Neutral refers to an organization or its activities that ensure a zero balance between the carbon it emits and the corresponding offset it creates through one or more activities such as using renewable energy source and buying or trading carbon credits.
Carbon Offset	Action—typically payments—by organizations generating carbon, in lieu of directly reducing the emissions (e.g., planting of trees by an airline).
Carbon Trading	Carbon trading refers to the trading of permits or savings accrued by one organization or country associated with carbon reduction with another organization or country, thereby enabling them to achieve carbon reduction obligations.
Energy Star	Energy Star reflects the reduced energy consumption of devices such as computers, appliances and buildings as compared with the acceptable standard. This standard, initially put together by the USA is also popular in Australasian region and some EU countries.
Environmental Intelligence (EI)	An intelligent use of business tools and technologies that can lead an enterprise to a green enterprise.
Environmentally Intelligent System (EIS)	A management tool enabling an organization of any size or type to identify and control the *environmental impact* of its activities, products, or services to *improve* its environmental performance continually and to implement a *systematic approach* to setting environmental objectives and targets, to achieve these and to demonstrate that they have been achieved.
Environmentally Responsible Business Strategy (ERBS)	A business approach that incorporates environmental factors in it.
EPEAT	Electronic product environmental assessment tool, or EPEAT (see www.epeat.net), assists buyers, especially corporate/institutional purchasers, to evaluate, compare, and select electronic products such as desktop computers, notebooks, and monitors based on their environmental attributes. It also helps manufacturers promote their products as environmentally friendly.
Fossil Fuels	Fossil fuels are non-renewable form of energy such as coal, gas and oil. These types of fuels generate significant carbon emissions as they burn to produce energy and cannot be replaced in the near future as it takes millions of years to form them.
GHG Protocol	GHG protocols refer to the negotiated understanding by the international community on permissible carbon emissions and strategies for their reduction across all participating nations. The most popular of these GHG protocols is the Kyoto protocol that was

Term	Explanation
	undertaken in Japan in 1997 under the framework of the United Nations Framework Convention on Climate Change (UNFCCC) There are six major types of GHGs—Carbon Di Oxide (CO2), Methane (CH4), Nitrous Oxide (N2O), PerfluoroCarbons (PFC), HydrofluoroCarbons (HFC) & Sulphur Hexafluoride (SF6). GHGs are measured in Tonnes (and Kilo Tonnes = kT).
Green Audit	Assesses a company's environmental credentials and its claims for green products, processes, and services. Green audits ascertain whether the company's products and processes are truly as they claim to be. Green audits of IT systems also help determine the accuracy of measurements and reporting. Green audits help address the accusation of greenwashing.
Green Business Architecture	A four-layered architecture that deals with keeping organization's environmental footprint small; reducing waste; measuring, monitoring, mitigating, and monetizing the carbon emissions.
Greenhouse Gases	
Green ICT (or Green IT)	The study and practice of using computing (ICT) resources efficiently so as to reduce their carbon impact on the organization's performance. Thus, Green ICT includes technologies, tools, and techniques to reduce carbon emissions through reduced power consumption. Green ICT also handles the use of ICT as an enabler of carbon reduction across all functions of the organization. Therefore, Green ICT also includes the study and practice of designing, manufacturing, using, and disposing of IT equipments (such as desktop computers, servers, and related systems and applications) efficiently and effectively with minimal or no impact on the environment. Green ICT encompasses the dimensions of environmental sustainability, the economics of energy efficiency, and the total cost of ownership, which includes the cost of disposal and recycling.
Green ICT Framework	A taxonomy that takes the many different components of Green ICT and relates them to each other.
Green ICT Readiness Index	A Green ICT benchmarking and analysis tool developed by Envirability/Connection Research, to allow the different aspects of an organization's Green ICT implementation to be measured, and compared to other organizations, industry norms, or one organization over time. It uses a modified Capability Maturity Model (CMM) to measure behaviors and actions.
Green IT	See Green ICT.
Green Policies	Provides environmental parameters to reduce the environment impact of business operations and promote sustainable development to the organization.

Term	Explanation
Green Web Services	The web services that endeavor to play a significant role for measuring the carbon footprints of a business and thus help the enterprise to take effective action to shrink the carbon footprints.
Green Washing	The practice of boosting one's green credentials by making fictitious claims about their products or services as carbon neutral, energy- or fuel-efficient, or environmentally sound. Exploiting the call for environmental sustainability, many companies try to bolster their green credentials by exaggerating their products' and services' eco-friendliness in marketing campaigns. Although one shouldn't greenwash, sadly this trend is increasing.
ISO 14001	ISO14001—provides generic requirements as well as basis for a framework for an environmental management system that can be adopted to many different types and sizes of organizations.
Methane	Methane—is a dangerous GHG with high global warming potential compared with carbon dioxide and an ability to negatively affect the Earth's Ozone layer.
RoHS Directive	The Restriction of Hazardous Substances in Electrical and Electronic Equipment Directive (www.rohs.gov.uk) aims to restrict the use of certain hazardous substances. It also bans placing new electrical and electronic equipment on the European Union market if it contains more than the agreed-upon levels of lead, cadmium, mercury, hexavalent chromium, or flame retardants.
Sustainability	Generally defined as "meeting the needs of the present without compromising the ability of future generations to meet their own needs" (www.epa.gov/sustainability). An organization aiming for sustainability has to balance its technology, processes, economic, and social dimensions.
Taxonomy	A system of categorization. Often, but not always, hierarchical.
Total Carbon Cost of Ownership (TCCO)	Extends the concept of TCO by including the calculations of total carbon generated by an equipment in its production, usage, and disposal.
Total Cost of Ownership (TCO)	A concept popularized in the 1990s by research consultancy Gartner, based on calculating the full cost of ICT equipment over its entire life, not just the purchase price. It takes into account running costs, maintenance, upgrades, and so on.
WEEE Directive	The Waste Electrical and Electronic Equipment (WEEE) directive aims to reduce the amount of e-waste going to landfills and to increase recovery and recycling rates (http://ec.europa.eu/environment/waste/weee/index_en.htm).

Index

Business process re-engineering (BPR), 8, 59, 157
   business process evaluation, 160–161
   customer-focused processes, 158
   innovation in, 161
"Business processes" grouping, 175
Business transformation (BT), 37
Business Transformation Board (BTB), 302
Business Transformation Champion (BTC), 302
Business Transformation Office (BTO), 296–297, 302

C

CAD, *see* Computer-aided design (CAD)
Capability Maturity Model (CMM), 113, 114, 302
Capital Expenditure (CAPEX), 19
Carbon compliance audits, 341
Carbon economy, 29, 43, 348
   challenges, 22–25
   green strategies development, 38
   green vision, 17
   scenarios, 36
Carbon efficiencies, 304, 305, 307
Carbon emission (CE), 13, 290, 303
   breakdown in measuring, 111
   data collection, 109
   legal requirements on, 334
   management, 290
   measurement tools, 147, 148
   mitigation, 104
   monitoring, 212
   security and legal, 354–355
Carbon emissions management software (CEMS), 9, 63,
      201, 289, 388, 398; *see also* Green information
      systems (GIS)
   attitude, 290–291
   auditing, 343–344
   AuPack map, 390
   data collection, 115, 378
   development, 328
   implementation, 405–406
   metrics, 292
   policy, 291
   practice, 291
   technology, 291–292
Carbon footprint, of organization, 41, 88, 123
   carbon emission mitigation, 104
   collaborative workplace effect, 255
   dynamic measures, 109
   IT effect, 10
   measuring, 109–110
   static measures, 109
Carbon impact, 160
Carbon issues, emergent, 347
   collaborative environmental intelligence, 358
   developing economy dichotomy, 358–360
   future carbon landscape, 348–350
Carbon metrics coverage, 103; *see also* Green—metrics

   emissions, 103, 104, 105
   mitigation, 104
   monetizing, 104
Carbon reduction, 22, 99, 154
   data center role, 131
   drivers, 49
   facility management, 126
   IT management, 300
   mobility technologies role, 101
Carbon trading applications, 12
Carbon-cost visibility, 134
Carbon-emitting bit, 135
Cathode ray tube (CRT), 381
CE, *see* Carbon emission (CE)
CEMS, *see* Carbon Emission Management
      Software (CEMS)
Chief executive officer (CEO), 295, 337, 383
Chief green officer (CGO), 22–23, 113, 292, 340,
      365, 341
   for green enterprise transformation, 99
   hospital, 365–366
   mind map, 98
   strategic approach, 384
Chief sustainability officer (CSO), *see* Chief green
      officer (CGO)
Class diagrams, 223
   for GOP, 238, 239
   for RSP, 241, 242
Climate Change Act, 328
Climate Savers Computing Initiative (CSCI), 336
Cloud computing, 13, 130, 140, 350, 351
   areas, 352–353
   business principle, 352
   data center planning, 141
   in GSA, 197–198
   key enterprise applications, 140–141
   outsourcing and, 288
CMM, *see* Capability Maturity Model (CMM)
CO_2e calculations, 109, 110
Collaborative communication, 263
Collaborative intelligence, 359, 360
Collaborative process, 159, 171
   carbon impact, 160
   for GSA, 195, 196
   reengineering, 159
Communication, 174
   channels, 263, 264
   long-range networks, 142, 143
   within organization, 262
   outside of organization, 262
Component diagrams, 223
   for GIS, 241, 245
Computer-aided design (CAD), 383
Connection Research, 113
Context sensitivity, 115
Continual service improvement, 169
Copenhagen summit, 330

U

UC1 calculate emissions, 231
Unified modeling language (UML), 161
    diagrams in GIS, 222–223
    in GIS development, 221
United Nations Framework Convention on Climate
        Change (UNFCCC), 329
Use case diagrams, 223
    for emissions benchmark maintenance, 229
    for establishing emission standards, 230
    for GOP, 228
Utility value, 92

V

Value-based approach, 91
Videoconferencing, 256
Virtual communities, 271–272
Virtual desktop, 255
Virtual private network (VPN), 141, 288, 378, 381
    connectivity for most machines, 382
    establishment, 246

Virtualization, 58
    data servers, 137, 138
    in GSA, 198
    types, 138
VPN, *see* Virtual private network (VPN)

W

Waste Electrical and Electronic Equipment (WEEE),
    51, 335
Watchers, 113
Web services (WS), 187, 204
    characteristics, 200
    EI implementation, 212
    role in automation, 115
Wide area network (WAN), 141, 288
WiMax, 142
Wired and wireless communication, 13
Wireless communication, 288
Wireless LAN/WAN, 142